Welcome!

CM01670093

$10

$75

FEAST
RADICAL HOSPITALITY IN CONTEMPORARY ART

Stephanie Smith

SMART MUSEUM OF ART
The University of Chicago

FEAST
RADICAL HOSPITALITY IN CONTEMPORARY ART

This publication is produced in conjunction with *Feast: Radical Hospitality in Contemporary Art*
Presented at the Smart Museum of Art, University of Chicago, February 16 – June 10, 2012

The exhibition will travel to:

Blaffer Art Museum, University of Houston, Texas, August 31, 2013 – January 5, 2014

SITE Sante Fe, Sante Fe, New Mexico, February 1 – May 17, 2014

Gund Gallery at Kenyon College, Gambier, Ohio, July 25 – November 30, 2014

Weisman Art Museum, Minneapolis, Minnesota, January 31 – May 10, 2015

Copyright © 2013 The David and Alfred Smart Museum of Art, University of Chicago.
All rights reserved. No part of this book may be reproduced or utilized in any form without permission from the Smart Museum of Art.
Distributed by the University of Chicago Press.

Smart Museum of Art
The University of Chicago
5550 South Greenwood Avenue
Chicago, Illinois 60637
(773) 702-0200
smartmuseum.uchicago.edu

Stephanie Smith with Irina Aristarkhova, Geoff Emberling, Charles Esche, Hannah B Higgins, Carolyn Korsmeyer, Tom Marioni, Red76, David Robbins, Abigail Satinsky, Stephanie Snyder, David Teh, Jacqueline Terrassa, Rirkrit Tiravanija, Jan Verwoert, and Lori Waxman

Feast: Radical Hospitality in Contemporary Art has been made possible by an Emily Hall Tremaine Exhibition Award. Generous major support has also been provided by the Andy Warhol Foundation for the Visual Arts, the Chicago Community Trust, Helen Zell, the Chauncey and Marion Deering McCormick Foundation, the Richard and Mary L. Gray Foundation, the University of Chicago's Arts Council, and Janis Kanter and Tom McCormick. Related programming has been made possible by the Chicago Humanities Festival, the Jane Addams Hull House Museum at the University of Illinois at Chicago, and threewalls, Chicago.

Curator and editor: Stephanie Smith
Copyeditor: Lisa Meyerowitz
Publication manager: Sarah Mendelsohn
Design and Typography: Jason Pickleman, the JNL graphic design
Printing: Everbest

ISBN 978-0-935573-52-7 (pbk.)
1. Dinners and dining in art–Exhibitions.
2. Artists and community–Exhibitions.
I. Smith, Stephanie, 1970–editor of compilation.
II. David and Alfred Smart Museum of Art.
N8217.D67F43 2013
709.05'107477311--dc23
2013001835

PRINTED IN CHINA

OPPOSITE: Lori Waxman (left) and Reneé Sunny Waxman Rakowitz (right) with Felix Gonzalez-Torres's *"Untitled" (Portrait of Ross in L.A.)* at the Smart Museum of Art, 2012

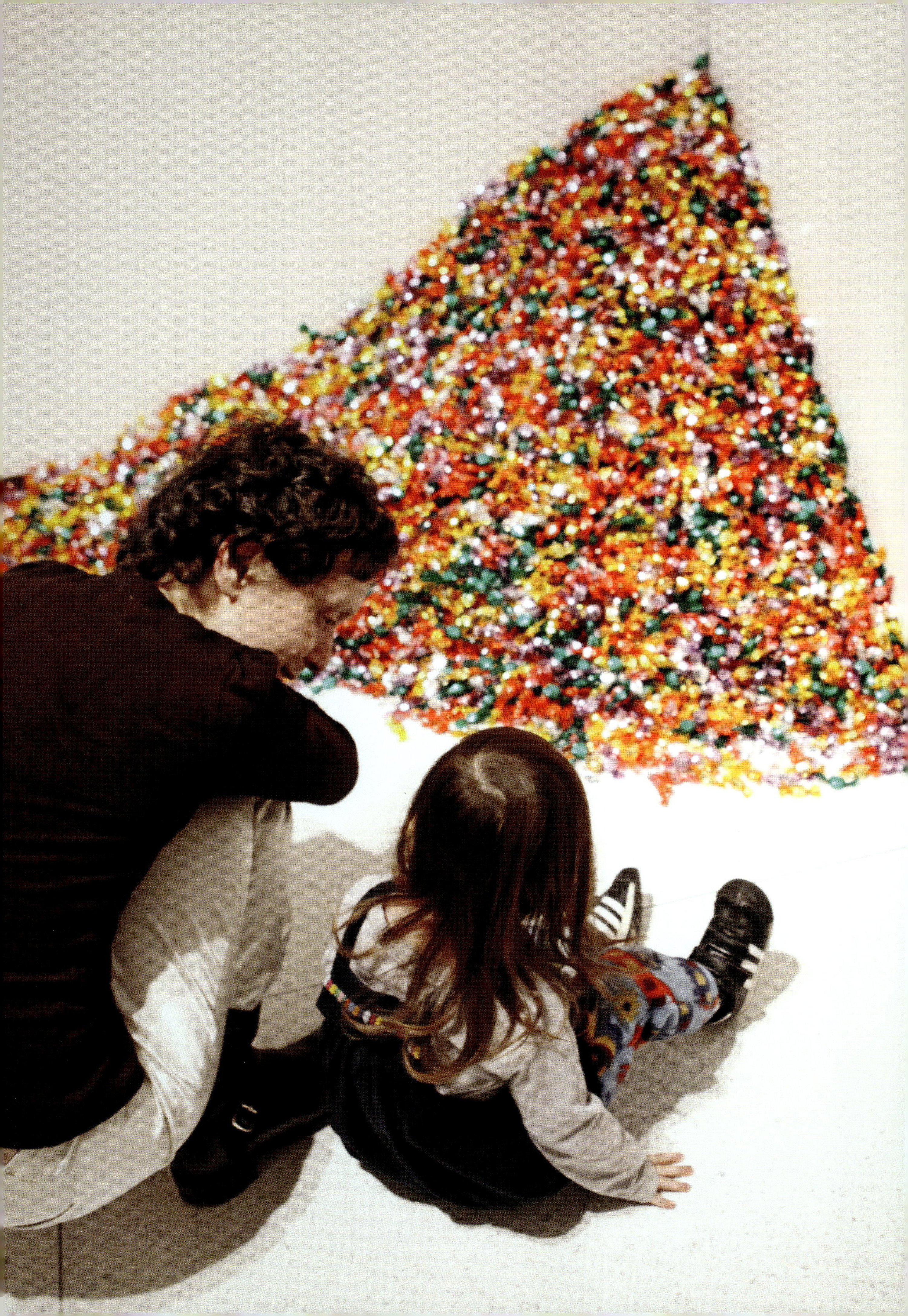

Contents

ESSAYS

Foreword

THE SMART MUSEUM OF ART at the University of Chicago is proud to present this volume, which grew out of the Museum's presentation of *Feast: Radical Hospitality in Contemporary Art*. The exhibition defined an important category of contemporary artistic practice: the artist-orchestrated meal. Through the work of some of the most influential artists of the twentieth century as well as rising stars of our time, *Feast* explored the richly varied meanings that can be sparked when artists reinvent the everyday act of sharing food and drink with others. The exhibition and the programming that accompanied it provided rich new insights while engaging audiences in compelling, often unexpected ways. This publication seeks to capture the energy of the project and the many avenues opened by it. Through its combination of art historical scope and contemporary relevance, experimental format, and connection to topics of wide public interest, the exhibition had a profound effect at the Smart Museum itself, where the focus on issues of hospitality and the ways an art museum in the twenty-first century can and should extend its reach into the city have become ongoing strategic concerns. The vitality of the artist-orchestrated meal was present throughout, prompting interactions between artists and visitors, visitors and staff, staff and artists. Living the spirit of radical hospitality broke down barriers. The delight and camaraderie among participants engendered by Michael Rakowitz's *Enemy Kitchen (Food Truck)* in our courtyard, or Tom Marioni's *The Act of Drinking Beer with Friends Is the Highest Form of Art* in our galleries is hard to describe, and is in many ways even more difficult to achieve in the hushed environment typical of a museum. We are pleased that *Feast* will provide similar opportunities to delight, engage, and inspire reflection by a broad national audience, as it travels to venues around the country. We hope this volume will serve as a provocative and lasting guide to the themes and discussions generated in the course of presenting the exhibition.

This project was the brainchild of Stephanie Smith, the Smart Museum's deputy director and chief curator. For more than a decade at the Smart, she has built a distinguished contemporary art program, organizing stimulating, distinctive exhibitions of unerring timeliness. *Feast* is but the latest and most ambitious example. A curator of rare energy, vision, and effectiveness, Smith has brilliantly orchestrated the development of a complex and important project, successfully enlisting a remarkable range of artists, colleagues, students, and collaborators. We owe her enormous thanks for her multifaceted contributions.

Of course, a project like this could not move beyond an initial concept if it were not for the artists whose creativity and willingness to engage in fertile conversations were not offered so generously. This was particularly relevant in the Smart Museum's context, where collaboration with living artists is a significant priority, an approach that now informs the greatly transformed, expanded presence of artists alongside academics in initiatives across the University of Chicago campus.

For this exhibition, we had the privilege of working closely with artists to re-envision the presentation of iconic works from earlier in their careers, and of supporting the production of a range of new projects. To these artists, and all their many collaborators and co-creators, we offer our profound gratitude; they enrich our lives each day.

Every member of the Smart Museum staff has participated in ways large and small to help realize this project, and they must be thanked for outstanding professionalism and commitment. The core project team included Jessica Moss, associate curator of contemporary art; Angela Steinmetz and Sara Patrello, registrars; Sarah Polachek, events and retail operations manager; Rudy Bernal and Ray Klemchuk, preparators; and Diego Arispe-Bazan, Emily Capper, Sarah Mendelsohn, and Jenn Sichel, University of Chicago student project assistants. Additional student assistance was provided by Chris Aque, Kim Mims, Marisa Nakasone, and Tatiana Natzke. Justin Glasson, our former director of development, and Kate Nardin, manager of development communications, asked critical questions about the exhibition's relevance and impact—helping both to strengthen the project brief and secure funding. Peg Liput, director of finance and administration, and C. J. Lind, associate director of communications, have cheerfully confronted unusually complex challenges in their respective areas. Breck Furnas, who provided interim leadership in the education department, and Michael Christiano, the director of education and interpretation who joined the Museum as the exhibition was about to open, oversaw interpretative programming that likewise went far beyond the norm.

Colleagues across the University and the city have collaborated generously on other elements of the project and related programs. Laura Letinsky, a professor in the Department of Visual Arts and an artist represented in the exhibition, co-taught a course, "Food for Thought" with Stephanie Smith in 2011 and taught it a second time in 2012 in conjunction with the exhibition's presentation in Chicago. We developed a musical program in collaboration with our colleagues at University of Chicago Presents. And we hosted a memorable symposium, *Of Hospitality*, that brought together an array of international artists, students, and scholars, mixing performance and discussion in ways that proved unusually satisfying intellectually and experientially. The symposium also captured the Smart Museum's institutional energy and reflected the remarkable growth in the University of Chicago's commitment to contemporary art. Collaborating partners included the Jane Addams Hull-House Museum at the University of Illinois, Chicago; and the Reva and David Logan Center for the Arts, the Richard and Mary L. Gray Center for Arts and Inquiry, and the Open Practice Committee, all at the University of Chicago; we owe special thanks to Zachary Cahill of OPC for his contributions. The Smart Museum was also pleased to collaborate with the Chicago Humanities Festival and threewalls.

It is a privilege to acknowledge those who have contributed to the beauty and importance of this publication, including all of the artists; contributing authors Irina Aristarkhova, Geoff Emberling, Charles Esche, Hannah B Higgins, Anthony Huberman, Carolyn Korsmeyer, Stephanie Snyder, David Teh, Jan Verwoert, and Lori Waxman; copyeditor Lisa Meyerowitz; and Jason Pickleman of jnl design. Former *Feast* intern Sarah Mendelsohn has joined the Smart's staff and shepherded the final stages of the book's production. We are grateful to our colleagues Claudia Schmuckli, director of the Blaffer Gallery at the University of Houston; Irene Hofmann, Phillips Director and chief of SITE Santa Fe; Natalie Marsh, director of the Gund Gallery at Kenyon College; and Diane Mullin, curator of the Weisman Art Museum for their interest in this project and their determination to bring it to their institutions. They embraced the participatory nature of the project, and will create new opportunities for artists and audiences to interact in mutually satisfying if heretofore unexpected ways.

Last but never least, a project of this ambition would not have been possible without the great generosity of those who have provided financial support. Stephanie Smith received a prestigious Emily Hall Tremaine Exhibition Award, launching *Feast* on its course. The Tremaine Foundation subsequently assisted again, graciously providing additional support to underwrite some of the costs associated with the exhibition's national tour. Generous major support has also been provided by the Andy Warhol Foundation for the Visual Arts, the Chicago Community Trust, Helen Zell, the Chauncey and Marion Deering McCormick Foundation, and the National Endowment for the Arts. Additional support has been provided by the Elizabeth F. Cheney Foundation, the Richard and Mary L. Gray Foundation, the University of Chicago's Arts Council, and Janis Kanter and Tom McCormick. We extend our thanks to all of these individuals and organizations, and to the members of their staffs, who have proven so helpful in so many ways.

In conclusion, it is a privilege to share *Feast: Radical Hospitality in Contemporary Art* with the public. The challenges to convention posed by the variety, experimentation, risk-taking, and convention-breaking provocations inherent in the work of many contemporary artists such as those included here have forced art museums to reconsider the ways in which they present works of art and interact with their audiences. This ongoing consideration has been salutary and energizing, transforming museums and their relationships with artists and audiences. That creative ferment and all the deep thinking that it should, and must, stimulate, is what we hope to have captured in this publication. Please be our guest and enjoy it.

Anthony Hirschel
Dana Feitler Director
Smart Museum of Art
September 2012

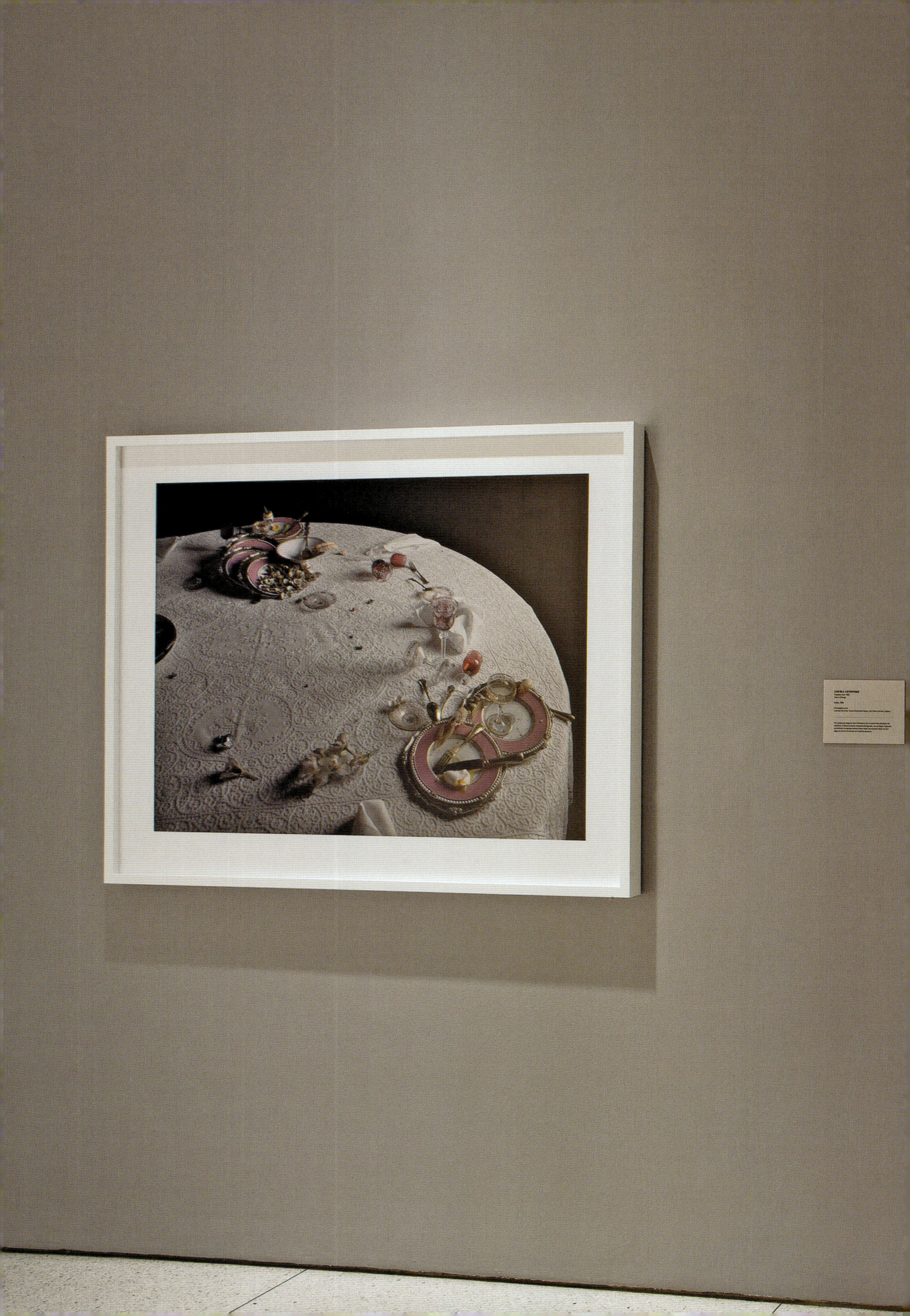

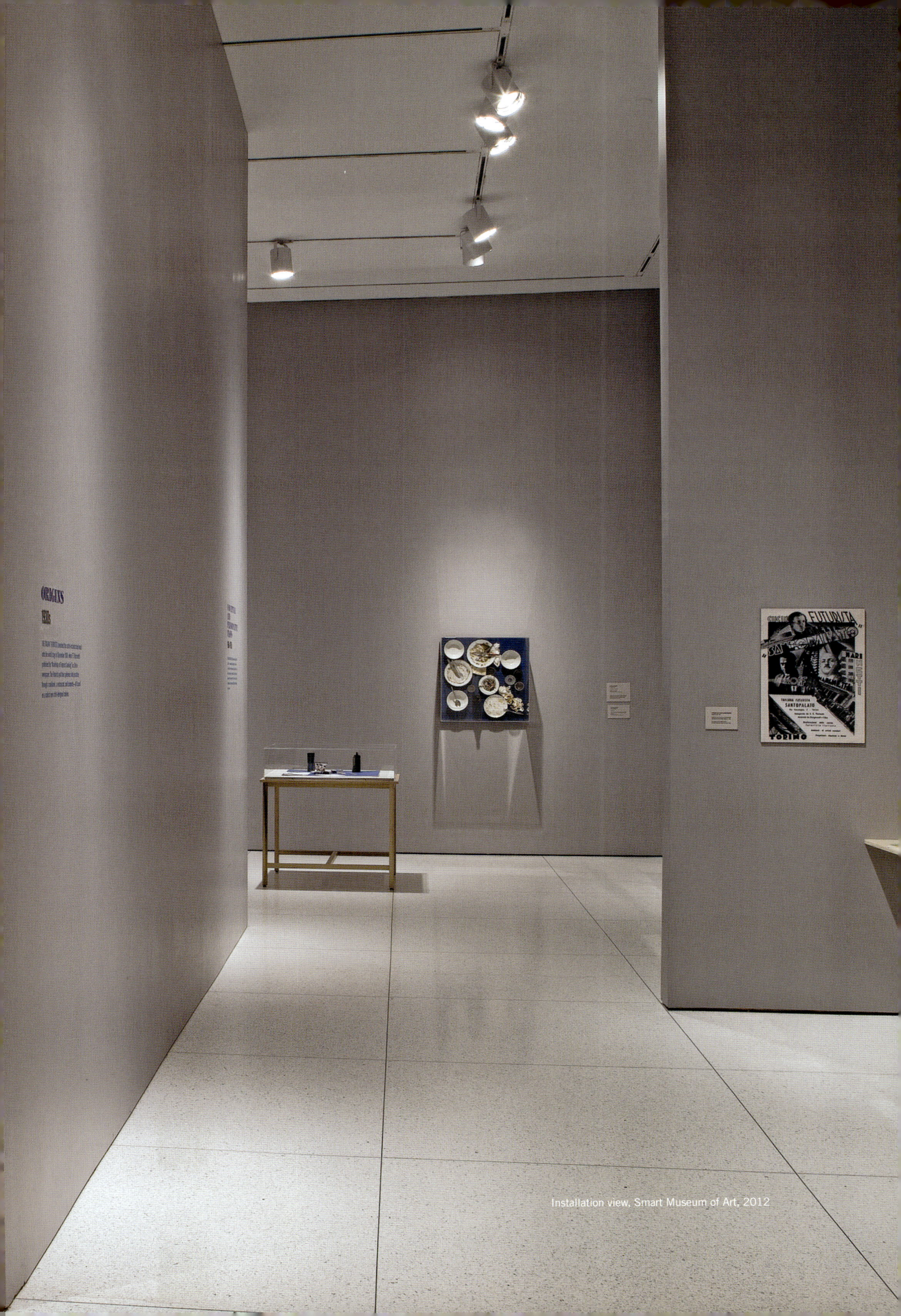

Installation view, Smart Museum of Art, 2012

Introduction: Of Feasts, Hospitality, and Art

Stephanie Smith

> To invite people to dine with us is to make ourselves responsible for their well-being for as long as they are under our roofs.
>
> —Jean Anthelme Brillat-Savarin, 1825[1]

> But perhaps we do not need a generation of young artists converting exhibition spaces into semicasual, make-believe dinner parties, living rooms, cafes, stores, bars, and lounges, etc., to remind us that all aesthetic experience is deeply and always already part of everyday social and political realities.
>
> —Miwon Kwon, 2004[2]

Three Kinds of Welcome

You cross the museum's threshold. A young woman standing near the entrance catches your eye. As you approach, she says hello warmly, picks up an ornate silver tray, and extends its contents toward you: a jar of jam, an array of spoons, napkins, glasses of water. She asks if you'd like a taste. As you pick up a spoon, she smiles and explains that this jam, called *slatko,* comes from a Serbian tradition in which hosts greet guests with a taste of fruit preserves. Her offer combines genuine welcome with a gentle attempt at control: *slatko* is meant both to sweeten the visit and to sweeten the tongue so that guests don't gossip afterwards. Like many rituals of hospitality, in its original context, it simultaneously eased social relations and reinforced normative behavior. But this culturally specific domestic offering has been displaced—transplanted and performed in the museum, where it might mean different things, where it might, in fact, call attention to both the poetics and the problematics of hospitable gestures. You set down the spoon, take a sip of water, and walk into the gallery with the taste of strawberries lingering on your tongue.

You do not cross the museum's threshold. You are, in fact, nowhere near the museum. You stand on a Chicago sidewalk, waiting for a woman wearing a crisp white jacket to extend a laden plate through the window of a food truck. As you bite into savory pie she mentions that she's a US veteran of the Iraq war. Your slice of *kubba mosul* was prepared hours earlier by her companions in the truck—two Iraqi immigrants, one of whom is a chef. As you wipe up a bit of hummus with a fold of bread, you scan the graphics adorning the truck—the imperial logo, the texts in Arabic and English, the unusual flag mounted to the side of the vehicle, the name "Enemy Kitchen." The server explains that the pattern on your paper plate replicates china looted from one of Saddam Hussein's palaces. Perhaps that pattern with its particular history discomforts you: it's a plate that asks questions.[3]

You do not cross the museum's threshold. Or perhaps you did, once, but that was some time in the past. In any case you now cross another threshold, one made of paper or digital screen, as you begin to read the book that accompanies the exhibition *Feast: Radical Hospitality in Contemporary Art.* What lies beyond this beginning?

Feast stems from the recognition that sharing food and drink with others is both a basic human pleasure and an enduring source of aesthetic inspiration. These drives come together within the artist-orchestrated meal, a practice that *Feast* surveys over eighty years, across several cultures, and as manifested through a range of aesthetic approaches. It includes relatively traditional artifacts as well as participatory projects that occur both within the museum and beyond its walls—like Ana Prvacki's jam offering and Michael Rakowitz's food truck described above. *Feast* roots the artist-orchestrated meal in the early twentieth-century European avant-garde, traces its spread via idea-, action-, and performance-based art in the 1960s and 1970s; and considers its present near-ubiquity, entwined with the rise of participatory, socially engaged, and collaborative practices over the past two decades. The "Artists" section of the book documents the art featured in the exhibition, while the "Essays" section considers loosely related topics such as hospitality, feasting, and taste. Together, these components provide ample evidence of the vitality, breadth, and nuance of the artist-orchestrated meal, while opening up lines of inquiry that extend beyond the particular frame of this project.

But not yet. All that will come in later pages. We're still on the threshold, so in the text that follows I want to offer you another kind of welcome: a sketch of the project, and some preliminary proposals about what the recent history and current prevalence of these artist-orchestrated meals might suggest about the roles of hospitality and participation within contemporary art, museums, and society.

Dishes That, While Delectable, Are Not on This Menu

Feast covers a wide but not all-encompassing territory: it does not directly address representations of food, or depictions of meals, or art that uses food as a material to be viewed but not consumed. We might envision those related territories as rows of banquet tables heaped with bounty. On one, for instance, we find beloved literary feasts, from Trimalchio's over-the-top banquet in the ancient Roman *Satyricon* to the Mad Hatter's tea party with Alice in Wonderland. Another brims with cinematic feasts: incidental depictions of royal galas, lavish weddings, bacchanalian revels, and awkward family dinners, plus that whole subgenre of films in which entire plots center on food and meals.

Nearby, several other tables brim with the work of visual artists. One includes an extensive series of paintings that depict food and the meal. This table includes some of the earliest known examples of human creative expression—for surely the animals depicted in so many ancient cave paintings were destined for Paleolithic dinners. Leonardo da Vinci's *Last Supper* (1495–98) offers another touchstone with its depiction of a canonical religious story that pivots on the social, emotional, and ritual associations latent within the meal. There's a table piled high with still life paintings—from seventeenth-century Dutch depictions of exotic foodstuffs and overripe fruit to more recent variants like Wayne Thiebaud's thickly painted cupcakes or Andy Warhol's silkscreened soup cans. Nearby, another table displays works like Dieter Roth's chocolate sculptures that capitalize on food's sensual and organic properties but were not meant to be eaten.[4]

These cultural products relate to *Feast*, for of course any artist-orchestrated meal makes use of the sensory and symbolic associations embedded in foodstuffs and mealtime rituals. But the art in *Feast* is a bit different. It oozes off the table's edges. Since it involves embodied experiences of eating and drinking, this art takes messier forms than the art arrayed on those other tables. It activates senses—touch, smell, and especially taste—that have historically been devalued or simply considered irrelevant to high culture.[5]

And because it involves fleeting actions that often occur in non-art-designated places, it moves through time and space in ways that are not always easy to accommodate within art institutions that have historically prioritized static images, artifacts, and objects.

The Feast Itself

Feast begins with a yellowed newspaper dated December 28, 1930, the moment when the aesthetic provocateurs known as the Italian Futurists launched the artist-orchestrated meal onto the world stage with their "Manifesto of Futurist Cooking."[6] In this brief text, the Futurist impresario F. T. Marinetti laid out a vision for a radical cuisine that could stretch the imagination and nourish a new kind of modern body and spirit—light, fast, experimental. The Futurists put this manifesto into practice in a cookbook, in elaborately theatrical meals that activated all senses and challenged aesthetic and culinary norms, and at the mischievously named Taverna del Santopalato (Restaurant of the Holy Palate). In all of these iterations, the Futurists' work reflected its time and place: marked by casual racism, reflexive machismo, and militant nationalism (for much of his career Marinetti aligned himself with Fascism). The Manifesto was aesthetically of its moment as well, for, like other modernist avant-gardes, the Futurists used cultural gestures as a means to critique an existing social order and propose new modes of being, in part by aggressively upsetting the norms of everyday experience.

In this, the Futurist meal demonstrates how quickly gestures of hospitality can slide into hostility. We might think of this as an inverted form of hospitality in which both guest and host enter into the exchange aware that the host's role is to provoke the guest, and the guest's role is to be (pleasantly?) shocked. Etiquette in this case requires the artist/host to aggressively challenge the guest's sensibilities in ways that ultimately might expand his or her worldview and faculties. This seems a classic avant-garde form of hospitality—part serious and part playful, with the meal providing the mechanism to drive the artists' visions of aesthetic and social progress.[7]

It wasn't until the 1960s and 1970s that such artist-orchestrated meals became a truly robust part of European and American art. During this period, increasing numbers of artists set aside conventional object-making in favor of idea-, process-, and performance-based work. Many also worked outside of traditional art spaces—a movement that critic Lucy Lippard famously defined as "escape attempts."[8] Artists' diverse motivations for these attempts included frustration with existing art world structures as well as curiosity about how new kinds of form and meaning might be generated by intentionally making art for and within "real world" spaces and situations.

In keeping with these art historical arcs, one remarkable feature of this period is the flurry of influential artist-run restaurants and salons founded from 1969 to 1972. Four such projects are featured in *Feast*: Daniel Spoerri's Eat Art gallery and restaurant in Düsseldorf; Allen Ruppersberg's installation-cum-surreal-restaurant *Al's Café* in Los Angeles; the cooperative restaurant FOOD that Gordon Matta-Clark, dancer Carol Gooden, and friends opened in SoHo; and Tom Marioni's still-ongoing, near-weekly gathering *The Act of Drinking Beer with Friends Is the Highest Form of Art*. Each enterprise could be understood as an attempt to escape formal, commercial, and institutional art world structures—in good company, buoyed by food and/or drink, in spaces of the artists' own design and designation.[9]

With these restaurants and salons, the artists and their collaborators foregrounded the task of hosting as art. They served up challenges to both standard and commercial forms of hospitality, as with the famous "Matta Bones" menu offered by FOOD, Ruppersberg's inedible meal-sculptures, Spoerri's use of the debased remains of meals to make art objects, or the playful rules of conduct created by Marioni for his salons. Within these projects, such mildly disruptive gestures would have been part of the expected exchange between host and guest (in this, they faintly echo the Futurists). But these projects also provided a deeper and more traditional form of hospitality. Although open to the public—albeit only rarely in the case of Marioni's salons—they also offered fellow artists the comforts of a gathering among peers. We all need such occasions to assemble with self-selected tribes: to see friends, to strengthen networks, to flirt and gossip and argue, to make plans and spin dreams, and to let loose together over food and drink. A storied tradition of such artistic gatherings has roots in the private salon as well as public spaces like coffee shops, restaurants, and taverns, and has manifested across the twentieth century at dinners and house parties and smoky neighborhood bars. Projects like those featured in *Feast* channeled such impulses into the creation of new works of art. Convivial settings became vehicles for experiments with economic, social, and aesthetic form. They also offered surprisingly classic expressions of hospitality in which the artist-hosts tended to the nuances of the physical setting, attracted interesting guests, and offered enticing things to see and say and eat and drink.[10]

Although the celebrated artist-run restaurants and salons of the 1960s and 1970s were predominantly male-led endeavors, women created many of the most notable meal-based artworks of this period. These, too, could be construed as escape attempts, but rather than reworking public and semipublic formats like the restaurant or salon, much of this art radicalized the form and function of the private domestic meal. These projects were inflected by two other trends of the period: the rethinking of categories like "femininity" and "the domestic" as part of larger arcs of feminism, and the rise of performance as an important genre.[11] In *Ritual Meal* (1969), for instance, Barbara T. Smith transformed a home into the setting for a psychedelic dinner party. Unsuspecting guests became part of a wild performance meant to unlock primal states of consciousness—a project that certainly connects to that disruptive strand of avant-garde hospitality. Bonnie Ora Sherk's classic performance *Public Lunch* (1971) similarly played on contrasts between the raw and the civilized: she calmly ate an elegant meal, alone in a cage at the San Francisco Zoo, while a tiger tore into raw meat in the adjacent cage. Other works connected personal space to more directly political topics: Marina Abramović and Ulay's collaborative performance *Communist Body/Fascist Body* (1979) could be read in this light, and Suzanne Lacy's *International Dinner Party* (1979) explicitly bridged that divide by using international feminist networks to connect thousands of women around the world who participated in near-simultaneous private dinner parties, each held to honor a specific woman.[12]

All of these projects upended conventions around stereotypical roles for women as self-effacing, caretaking hosts. Both Smith's and Lacy's projects derived significant power by deferring the actual work of hosting to others through collaborative co-creation—albeit in very different ways. Lacy's project also built intentionally on her experiences of feminist and aesthetic consciousness-raising within kitchens and around dining tables—a parallel version of the networking that also took place in artist-run salons, restaurants, and bars. In their performances, Abramović and Ulay disengaged from their guests' needs while Sherk dispensed with guests altogether. Such approaches contrast both with the feminized model of hosting and cultural production that Jan Verwoert articulates in his essay in this volume—an often unacknowledged form of hosting comprised of many small, near-invisible acts of tending that make possible the active cultural production of others—and with the artist-run-restaurant/salon model described above.

The flurry of American and European meal-based projects during the 1960s and 1970s subsided for a time, only to emerge in great numbers, new variants, and across a wide geographic territory in the 1990s under such loose and contested labels as "relational aesthetics" and "social practice."[13] These forms of artmaking reflect trends toward Do-It-Yourself modes of making and collaborative practice in contemporary art, and a concomitant search for platforms for aesthetic experience and critical discussion that exist in productive tension with traditional arts institutions. Such practices may include or result in familiar art "products" like painting or video, or they may be fleeting actions connected to specific times and places that are only accessible to others later, via artifacts, documents, relics, and storytelling. But at either end of the process–product continuum, these works both invite and require action and interaction on the part of the person once blithely referred to in texts like this one as "the viewer." And they have become nearly ubiquitous tropes within global contemporary art—even to the point of backlash, as indicated by Miwon Kwon's quote at the beginning of this text.

One key strand of these artist-orchestrated meals has re-engaged the institution as site. Rirkrit Tiravanija's influential meal-based projects from the early 1990s have become semi-mythologized examples of the former, beginning with *untitled 1990 (pad thai)* (1990). In a small project space at Paula Allen Gallery in New York, Tiravanija prepared the then-exotic dish of pad thai, served it up to all comers, and left casually yet precisely arranged remains as an installation. This modest beginning opened into an ongoing series of influential projects in which Tiravanija created frames for varied forms of social interaction, with and without food, in both art and non-art settings. Meanwhile, in 1993, without knowledge of Tiravanija's work, David Robbins began his long-running *Ice Cream Social* project. It includes not only the socials themselves—which serve up specially designed ice cream and cake for audiences both within art- and non-art spaces—but also a novella and TV pilot. Together, these elements reworked the ice cream social into a cipher for contemporary American experience: both genuinely pleasurable and an overdetermined, artificially sweetened moment within a temporary commons. At the opposite scale of intimacy: since 1996, Lee Mingwei has invited a series of strangers to join him for a one-on-one meal in *The Dining Project*, which occurred first within his studio as a graduate student and then over time at museums around the world.[14] And more recently, Sonja Alhäuser's lavish banquet-performances like *Flying Feast* (2012) have introduced Rococo style and a bit of Baroque excess into this institutional strand of practice. Her projects push the pleasurable, excessively sensual, and even grotesque aspects of feasting to the fore. Although driven by different motivations, in each of these projects the artist as host used the meal as a kind of comestible readymade, setting up precise aesthetic mechanisms that gently upturned art world norms. Such projects have since been fully embraced by arts institutions—including, of course, the Smart with *Feast*—with implications that I explore further below.

Meanwhile artists have continued to create meals in other kinds of spaces, sometimes combining aesthetic experimentation and activist aims within intensely re-imagined domestic settings. In *Revolutionary Table* (2007–08), Red76 gathered people for potluck meals in private homes to discuss everyday forms of revolution—and they broadcast those dinner-table debates, live, to the hosts' neighbors. They have updated and extended this premise with a new work for Feast, *Occupy Yr. Home* (2012–ongoing), a series of discussion-dinners in private homes. Although not intended as a work of art, InCUBATE's Sunday Soup microgrant program could also be seen within this context. And in a slightly different vein, the entire ethos of Mildred's Lane—a collaboratively-run experiment in alternative forms of domesticity, artistic pedagogy, and collective living set on several acres of wooded rural Pennsylvania land—uses food and hospitable care as vehicles for transformative experience. In all of these projects, the artists identified a problem that was shared by a wider group, whether a concern about isolation, a dissatisfaction with existing institutions, or a crisis of agency. In response, they use meals both to create an immediate temporary solution for that problem, recognizing that if you're feeling isolated or impotent, a good meal in the company of friends or strangers can do wonders. These projects also offer a way to (potentially, possibly) strengthen participants' collective capacity to act in larger arenas, long after the meal itself.

Other projects have taken such aims out to the streets. In *Pribumi Pribumi* (1998), for instance, the Indonesia-based Dutch artist Mella Jaarsma and a group of colleagues responded to a time of political turmoil and ethnic violence by cooking and serving frog legs to passers-by on the streets of Yogyakarta, using that specific dish to spark conversation and bridge difference during a turbulent moment. Michael Rakowitz began *Enemy Kitchen* (2003–ongoing) as a somewhat parallel response to the jittery combination of aggression and vulnerability that marked the political climate in the United States in the wake of 9/11 and the subsequent invasion of Iraq. In the varied manifestations of this project—including his *Feast* commission, *Enemy Kitchen (Food Truck)* (2012)—Rakowitz has used the act of preparing and serving Iraqi cuisine as a way to unravel the many-faceted ramifications of the US-Iraq conflict. Fallen Fruit's seriously playful *Public Fruit Jams* (2006–ongoing) and *Neighorhood Infusions* (2008–ongoing), as well as many of The National Bitter Melon Council's meal-based projects, pose more general questions about the state of social relations and offer alternate forms of community-building. Another group of projects foregrounds the site-specific combination of place and food. Two commissions for *Feast*—Mary Ellen Carroll's meal at the Chicago Board of Trade, *Open Outcry,* and Theaster Gates's series of *Soul Pavilion* dinners within a once-abandoned home on the South Side of Chicago—offered precisely calibrated combinations of performance, discussion, setting, and meal to curated groups of guests.

While centered in interaction, all of these projects enact the artists' intense focus on aesthetic form—whether through the development of a precise concept, the careful structuring of interactive performance, the use of quasi-branding strategies, or the design and production spaces and accoutrements that intentionally imbue the feast experience with specific qualities. The artist-hosts also capitalize on both the metaphoric content and the embodied, specific tastes of particular drinks and foods: they use intense sensory experience to puncture the smooth surface of everyday life, in tandem with their careful orchestration of the larger frame of each of these meals.

Several other projects have also explored interrelationships between meals and place, but have taken the form of moody, poetic video or photographic images that loosely document specific meals. Ayman Ramadan and Julio Cesar Morales have both staged meals for the video camera in order to explore culturally-charged content—the breaking of the daily fast during the Islamic holy month of Ramadan on the streets of Cairo, and a meal that marked a turning point in California history and US-Mexico relations, respectively. (Both artists have also created participatory, meal-based projects.) Sudsiri Pui-Ock's video *The Dinner* offers a more personal meditation on her experience of isolation and displacement as an immigrant. While studying in the Netherlands, she filmed herself quietly consuming a lavish Thai feast that she set up within the isolation of an otherwise empty Amsterdam studio. And as a kind of a counterpoint to Pui-Ock's use of aesthetic isolation as source material, Laura Letinsky used artistic community as inspiration: she opened her home and hosted a lunch for other artists visiting Chicago for the *Feast* opening, and then reworked and collaged photographic fragments of that hospitable event into a new still life photograph. These works all began with the preparation and consumption of meals, but reintroduce more traditional notions of beauty and craft in their final form. Alhäuser's "recipe drawings" and the Mildred's Lane installation for *Feast* might be considered in this vein, as well. Their center of gravity shifts from process to product—which bring us back to the institution as frame and host.

Escapes and Returns

Why gather examples of this messy art and present them in the form of an exhibition that occurs, in part, within the clean, white space of a museum? Why make an exhibition as opposed to, for instance, simply presenting documentation in this book?

One answer is that, by bringing projects like those in *Feast* inside, the museum is doing nothing more than asserting that social, performative, and participatory forms of art deserve the same degree of museological protection, study, and display as do painting, sculpture, or film. This process is already underway at many museums and seems a natural enough extension given that we're now many decades into action-, process- and idea-based forms of making.[15] At its best, this trend helps audiences connect with important developments in recent culture. It affords museums the opportunities to aerate and energize their work by learning from audiences and artists and fulfilling their missions in fresh ways.

Yet, two central risks loom. One is that in reaching out to embrace these practices, museums create new kinds of conservative orthodoxies that value performative or participatory forms of artmaking at the expense of more static objects and images. "Participation" could come to trump "contemplation," with participatory art cast as a savior for institutions trying to connect with larger and younger audiences through rhetoric that ascribes to such projects' outsized capacity to foster energetic aesthetic, critical, and even political engagement.[16] Simply spending time contemplating a static artwork can be an active, deeply meaningful process that fully engages one's critical faculties—and participatory action (including the consumption of a food and drink within the context of an art project) might be a callow and supremely uncritical experience. That's another part of what Kwon was getting at, I think, in the second epigraph to this text. The other risk is that we might kill the things we love. When brought into the museum, such work may take compelling new forms but they might also be weakened by modes of presentation that feel secondary to the substance of the art. Projects that involve food and drink could also be misunderstood as easy, friendly spectacle or as a mildly elevated form of catering. So even if not killing the work, museum presentations run the risk of diminishing the art or flattening its complexity.

We faced both risks with *Feast*. We took them on intentionally and experimented with solutions, some of which emerged out of the work itself. Documentation of past or distant projects—even those initially conceived as attempts to escape the confines of the museum—can be handled in ways that spark the imagination of gallery audiences—whether through powerful photographs and video, presentations of ephemera, or complex installations. In the best case, such an exhibition can open a relay between the museum and an experience that occurred elsewhere or in the past, while offering something new within the gallery space. This after-the-fact encounter can be rich, even though admittedly never fully able to convey the live complexity of a performance; the depth of a collaborative relationship; the mise-en-scène of a distant site; or the scents, textures, tastes, and interpersonal interactions woven through an artist-orchestrated meal.

Moving beyond more straightforward documentation, most of the projects featured in *Feast* include fully or semi-autonomous elements created by the artists specifically to extend the ideas and experiences of the artist-orchestrated meal into new forms, from Alison Knowles's *Journal of the Identical Lunch*, to Daniel Spoerri's snare pictures, to Laura Letinksy's photographs. In other cases, artists presented experiential projects directly within the gallery so there was no displacement for those who encounter the work during its performative moment. Projects like Ana Prvacki's welcoming offer of jam were designed to be consumed by the museum audience within carefully constructed spatial and experiential protocols. One-time, off-site events like Fallen Fruit's *Neighborhood Infusions* performance took place within the context of the *Feast* symposium, *Of Hospitality*. We experimented with stretching the frame of the exhibition even further beyond the museum's walls by commissioning projects like Mary Ellen Carroll's luncheon at the Chicago Board of Trade, Theaster Gates's *Soul Pavilion* dinners, and Michael Rakowitz's roaming food truck—all of which were conceived as core works within the exhibition even though they occurred outside the museum, and in other parts of the city. Thus, while the commissions, projects, and events related to the exhibition offered real-life, real-time encounters with the kinds of projects documented within the museum, the gallery display in turn provided a broader perspective on the live and public works, offering both historical context and conceptual ballast.

Feast posed one final opportunity and challenge for the museum: can the institution itself be radically hospitable? French theorist Jacques Derrida famously posed the possibility of a radical, universal hospitality that offers unconditional welcome to any guest: "Let us say yes *to who or what turns up*, before any determination, before any anticipation, before any *identification*, whether or not it has to do with a foreigner, an immigrant, an invited guest, or an unexpected visitor, whether or not the new arrival is a citizen of another country, a human, animal, or divine creature, a living or dead thing, male or female."[17] He pointed to the radical potential of hospitable care for others—and especially for the stranger. Derrida was thinking in part about large-scale questions of civic interrelation in the face of immigration and otherness that occurred within a particular late-capitalist context in Europe. But his call to "Say yes to who or what turns up" resonates also with Jean Anthelme Brillat-Savarin's aphorism at the beginning of this text, with its intimate ethic of tending, of taking care. And it throws down a gauntlet for cultural institutions.

We can pick up that gauntlet by asking whether radical hospitality is truly possible within an institutional space. This question prompts other, nested questions. For instance: How might cultural institutions enact hospitality as a creative, ethically grounded, meaningful activity—one that gets beyond the rote pragmatism of the paid greeter who asks "How can I help you" but really means "What can I sell you?" What's at stake when cultural practitioners and/or institutions embrace hospitality as a theoretical framework or a day-to-day activity? What stands to be gained, and what might be lost? What might it mean for the institutional host to say "Yes?" Should we truly be open to any guest, and to all needs and desires? Might it be necessary to say "No" to some guests, in order to more effectively say "Yes" to others?

These are difficult questions that the Smart Museum of Art has broached in this exhibition, and with which we continue to grapple.[18] We strive to enact hospitality as a deep, everyday value, as well as through tactics ranging from big-picture clarity about mission, to small pragmatic changes in the ways we approach our work. The attempt to accommodate this messy art, and to take seriously some of the questions it poses about guests and hosts, thus holds the very real potential for failure but also offers important opportunities for institutional stretch and growth that can serve art and audiences well. Amidst questions and experiments, one thing we're clear about is that the museum must provide a wide range of visitors with a sense of open welcome without creating an expectation that everything across the threshold will be as sweet as the taste of *slatko*. Museums must offer a complicated form of hospitality. They must welcome guests into an encounter with challenging art: safe spaces to experience art of many shades, including those that might be experienced as difficult and even hostile.[19]

Further Thoughts on Why We Might Linger

Let's step back one more time, to look at *Feast* from a greater distance. Why is the history and current practice of the artist-orchestrated meal worth our attention and our care right now?

Let's look at another of the tables adjacent to our feasting-space. This one is laden with packages of Iraqi dates and bags of Cheetos and bottles of small-batch bourbon. Lifestyle magazines and cookbooks are piled in one corner, topped with a mobile phone running the Epicurious app. On a small monitor, *Iron Chef* streams in five languages. Plates of Korean tacos fresh from the food truck and boxes of old-school donuts sit next to exquisite dishes produced by the star chefs of molecular gastronomy. You get the idea: *Feast* intersects with rapid changes in global food culture.

I'm particularly aware of such changes in the United States, for the past decades have seen enormous shifts in food culture. This is due, in part, to recent processes of globalization that make the foods of diverse and distant cultures available at just about any supermarket. At the same time, the country is in the midst of a culinary renaissance, marked by an explosion of interest in urban farming, sustainable agriculture, and eating local; in reclaiming regional cuisines and old-fashioned methods; and in small-scale, high-craft, artisanal techniques. Consider also the rise of chefs like Ferran Adria and Grant Achatz who have developed extraordinarily inventive ways of preparing and presenting food that feel strongly connected to some of the art presented in *Feast*—particularly the elaborate visions proposed by the Italian Futurists in the 1930s. At the opposite end of the socioeconomic spectrum, and as a cause for despair, we remain caught in global spirals of famine and starvation, as well as an epidemic of obesity that not only is the United States *not* controlling but also exporting to developing nations along with our habits of consuming disproportionate amounts of cheap, unhealthy, highly processed foods. Our awareness of these varied trends and the wider conversations that they spark surely play into *Feast*'s resonance.

But those concerns are also, largely, outside the specific frames of interest of these artists. They constitute the backdrop, not the impetus for their work. Consequently, those of us who care about this art right now do so for other reasons. With its messiness and ooze, its life and flux, the best of this art addresses desires and abilities that get to the heart of what it means to be human, in ways both bright and dark. It speaks to the everyday pleasures of the table: conviviality among friends and family, moments of connection with strangers, the comfort of ritual. It speaks to our equally human capacities for hostility, for excess and indulgence, for exclusion, for debauchery and riot and rot. It raises timeless questions of what's at stake when we move through roles of guest and host. And it encourages us to pay critical and open-minded attention to the ways that all host-guest interactions and all meals—not just those orchestrated by artists—are embedded within larger arcs of culture, history, power, economics, and emotion.

Although there are many ways that hospitality unfolds in human life, the experience of being a guest or a host is perhaps most vividly embodied when we are standing at a threshold or seated at table and experiencing whatever unfolds in those particular moments of human connection or distance. (And both communion and alienation are certainly present in *Feast*.) The project thus assesses the artist-orchestrated meal both as a phenomenon with its own weight and interest and as a grounding device to consider hospitality: how it functions within and around these works of art, and when and how hospitality might be construed as radical.

One Kind of Goodbye

To close, let's step away from the banquet hall, the table, the space of the museum.

You're still standing on the edge of a Chicago sidewalk next to Michael Rakowitz's *Enemy Kitchen (Food Truck)*. Sated, you swallow that last bite. You wipe the plate clean, drop it in your bag as a token, nod goodbye to the server, and spritz your hands at a dispenser mounted near her window. You pause and bring your hands to your face to breathe in a pure floral scent that replaces the expected chemical sanitizer, and you bend down to read the engraved text: "Bless your hands." Maybe, because of your family background or your travels or that movie you saw last summer, you know of the Middle Eastern custom in which a host offers departing guests a sprinkle of rosewater. You brush your hands across your head to scent your hair. You walk away musing about what it means to carry this aroma of hospitality along with you. If you've read those words of Brillat-Savarin, you might wonder about the limits and potential of our ability to be good hosts and good guests once we venture beyond that protected space he describes; what happens when there is neither roof nor an invitation to dine? When might it be useful to be a bad host, or a bad guest? Who has the authority to assign such value-laden terms, in any case? You contemplate. You walk on, accompanied by the rose scent as well as the lingering flavors, ideas, and emotions that this experience has set into motion within your mind and body.

Or perhaps not.

But in any case, you're welcome.

---

[1] Jean Anthelme Brillat-Savarin, *The Physiology of Taste: Or, Meditations on Transcendental Gastronomy,* trans. M. F. K. Fisher (New York: Harcourt Brace Jovanovich, 1978, c. 1949), 4.

[2] Miwon Kwon, "The Becoming of a Work of Art: FGT and a Possibility of Renewal, a Chance to Share, a Fragile Truce," in *Félix Gonzalez-Torres*, ed. Julie Ault (Göttingen: Steidl Verlag, 2006), 286.

[3] Here I echo another project by Michael Rakowitz, the artist who created this project, in which he describes Iraqi dates as "fruit that asked questions." See his writings about *Return* (2004–ongoing), accessed January 11, 2013, http://michaelrakowitz.com/projects/return/.

[4] Yet another form worth noting are the extravagant festivals and banquets staged in medieval and Renaissance Europe for the pleasure of aristocratic sponsors and church patrons. Art historian Christina Normore calls such banquets "among the most important art forms of the fourteenth and fifteenth centuries; created by the leading artists and commissioned and appreciated by the most prominent and influential patrons." See Christina Normore, "Feasting the Eye in Valois Burgundy" (PhD diss., University of Chicago, 2008). Artists participated in these events, both by creating edible works of art and by orchestrating the overall mise-en-scène, which often included elaborate, proto-surreal tableaux. One 1430 feast in Burgundy, for instance, reportedly featured a giant pastry "out of which [performers dressed as] a blue sheep with golden horns and a big wild animal leapt, tussling with each other in front of the astounded guests." See Anita Albus, *The Art of Arts: Rediscovering Painting* (New York: Knopf, 2000), 57. In her essay "The Theater of the Dining Table," Charlotte Birnbaum notes that artists like Jacopo Sansovino designed table decorations, including one 1574 banquet in which he adorned the tables with an array of confectionary: animals, Biblical scenes, and even the cutlery were all formed from sugar. She sees such experiences as precursors to both the work of legendary chefs like the nineteenth-century master Marie-Antoine Carême and to twentieth-century artists like F. T. Marinetti and Salvador Dali. See Birnbaum, *Three Banquets for a Queen* (Berlin: Sternberg Press, 2011), 14. Artists thus collaborated with their patrons to entertain and impress feasting guests, but the nature and import of their ephemeral creations are just beginning to be uncovered and assessed by scholars—natural enough since edible objects like Sansovino's sugary sculptures can only be recovered now through the traces they left in eyewitness narratives and other documents of the period. The transitory nature of the artist-orchestrated meal—as opposed to, say, a painting—has surely contributed to it being less well known, even in the case of some of the more contemporary works included in *Feast*. And this ephemerality continues to create challenges for those of us eager to understand and help others to connect with these works after the fact.

[5] See Carolyn Korsmeyer, *Making Sense of Taste: Food and Philosophy* (Ithaca, NY: Cornell University Press, 1999), 1–11, as well as her essay in this volume.

[6] F. T. Marinetti, "The Manifesto of Futurist Cooking," *The Futurist Cookbook,* trans. Suzanne Brill (San Francisco: Bedford Arts, 1989): 30–40; see also p. 34–40 in this volume.

[7] See, for instance, Cecilia Novero on issues such as taste and disgust in *Antidiets of the Avant-Garde, from Futurist Cooking to Eat Art* (Minneapolis: University of Minnesota Press, 2010).

[8] Lucy Lippard, "Escape Attempts," in *Reconsidering The Object of Art* (Cambridge, MA: MIT Press, 1995). This impulse built on the anti-institutional orientation of some modernist predecessors including the Futurists.

[9] There are other examples not included in *Feast*—N. E. Thing Co.'s Eye Scream restaurant in Vancouver, for instance, operated around the same time. Also, both Spoerri's restaurant project and Marioni's salons had some institutional ties. Some of Spoerri's earlier meal-as-art experiments occurred in commercial galleries including his famous "Restaurant Galerie J" intervention, while Marioni's first iteration of *The Act of Drinking Beer with Friends Is the Highest Form of Art* occurred in the Oakland Museum. The ongoing project occasionally returns to museums as it does in *Feast,* but has mostly occurred in the artist's studio or nearby bars.

[10] Think of the fabled Parisian dinners at which Gertrude Stein and Alice B. Toklas hosted cosmopolitan poets and painters, or of the lustrous crowds that ebbed and flowed around bars and restaurants like New York's fabled Max's Kansas City during the 1960s and 1970s. See Gertrude Stein, *The Autobiography of Alice B. Toklas* (New York: Random House, 1993 [1933]).

[11] Judy Chicago's *Dinner Party* (1974–79), which provided the inspiration for Lacy's piece, is not included in *Feast*. Although a classic of the period, it falls outside *Feast*'s parameters because it imagined a meal but did not involve actual consumption. Other classic works such as Martha Rosler's *Semiotics of the Kitchen* (1975) occupy related territory but again fall outside the exhibition's parameters.

[12] Marioni's salon could be thought of within this sphere of activity as well, for his work is also strongly performance-based and reworks a private space. However, in his case the studio with its codings of work and professionalism rather than a strictly domestic arena, and he collaborated with peers like Smith, Sherk, and Abramović.

[13] The most recent history of the art-life blur is still being written (and contested, and rewritten). In the mid- and late-1990s, then-contemporary manifestations of participatory art were characterized by theorist Nicolas Bourriaud as "relational aesthetics," a label that remains in heavy if contentious-to-backlashed use, while more recent strains have been described in terms including "dialogical," "the social turn," and "social practice." See, for instance, Bourriaud, *Relational Aesthetics* (Paris: Presses du Réel, 1998; English trans. 2002); Grant Kester, *Conversation Pieces: Community and Communication in Modern Art* (Berkeley and Los Angeles: University of California Press, 2004); Claire Bishop, "Antagonism and Relational Aesthetics," *October* 110 (Fall 2004): 51–79; and Bishop, "The Social Turn: Collaboration and Its Discontents," *Artforum* (February 2006): 179–85.

[14] For another example of a one-on-one meal-based project, although not included in this exhibition, see Ben Kinmont's *Waffles for an Opening* (1991); accessed January 11, 2013, benkinmont.com/projects/waffles.htm.

[15] These practices have long been favored in biennial-type exhibitions and have been supported by peripatetic organizations like Performa and Creative Time. But to cite just a few examples of recent institutional framings: in terms of performance, Tino Seghal's *This Progress* (2010) at the Guggenheim Museum, *Marina Abramović: The Artist Is Present* (2010) at MoMA, and the Tate Modern's new event/performance space The Tanks; in terms of participatory and social practices, Nato Thompson's work at MassMOCA and with Creative Time, the Walker Art Center's In the Field summer program, and the Hammer Museum's artist residency program. I've also been working on these issues over the past decade at the Smart Museum.

[16] Claire Bishop raised these concerns in the articles cited above, and expands them further in her book *Artificial Hells: Participatory Art and the Politics of Spectatorship* (New York and London: Verso, 2012). Although I disagree with many aspects of Bishop's critique, the temptation to conflate participation with automatically meaningful aesthetic experience and/or serious political and critical engagement is a real and present danger around these practices.

[17] See Jacques Derrida and Anne Dufourmantelle, *Of Hospitality: Anne Dufourmantelle Invites Jacques Derrida to Respond,* trans. Rachel Bowlby (Stanford, CA: Stanford University Press, 2000): 77.

[18] Thanks to Charles Esche, director of the Van Abbemuseum in the Netherlands for first directing me to Derrida's writings on hospitality. I've drawn inspiration from long-standing conversation with Charles about the VanAbbemuseum's commitment to hospitality as an institutional value and creative practice. The Hammer Museum has also inspired me through its recent interest in hospitality and visitor experience.

[19] Matthew Jesse Jackson and Michael Rakowitz drove home this issue during the "Being Bad" panel discussion, which took place at the University of Chicago as part of the "Of Hospitality" symposium hosted by the Smart Museum, May 4–5, 2012. The symposium opened with a dinner and discussion organized in collaboration with chef Tara Lane and the historic Jane Addams Hull-House Museum. A full day of discussions, presentations, performances, and meals explored questions about what it means to practice hospitality within the realm of art and culture: What is at stake when cultural practitioners and/or institutions embrace hospitality as a theoretical framework or a day-to-day activity? What stands to be gained, and what might be lost? Artist presentations, speakers, and participants included Nick Bastis, David Burns, Zachary Cahill, Michael Christiano, Anais Daly, Erika Dudley, Charles Esche, David Giordano, Hannah B Higgins, Anthony Huberman, Matthew Jesse Jackson, Alison Knowles, Laura Letinsky, Ed Marszewski, Eric May, Amy M. Mooney, Ana Prvacki, Michael Rakowitz, Dieter Roelstraete, Abigail Satinsky, Stephanie Smith, Cassandra Troyan, Jan Verwoert, Matias Viegener, Eric Watts, and Austin Young.

Michael Rakowitz's *Enemy Kitchen (Food Truck)* in the Smart Museum of Art courtyard, 2012

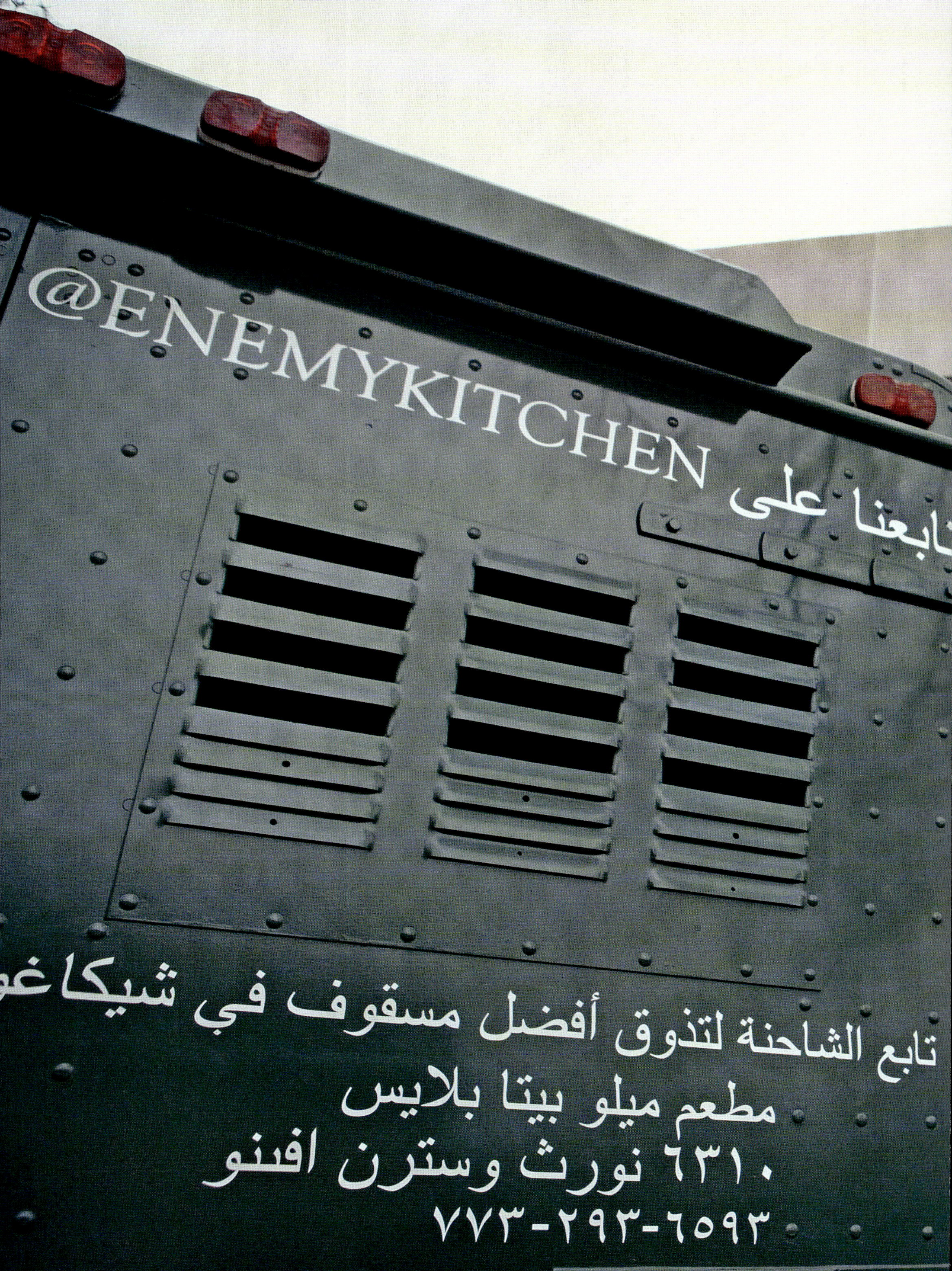

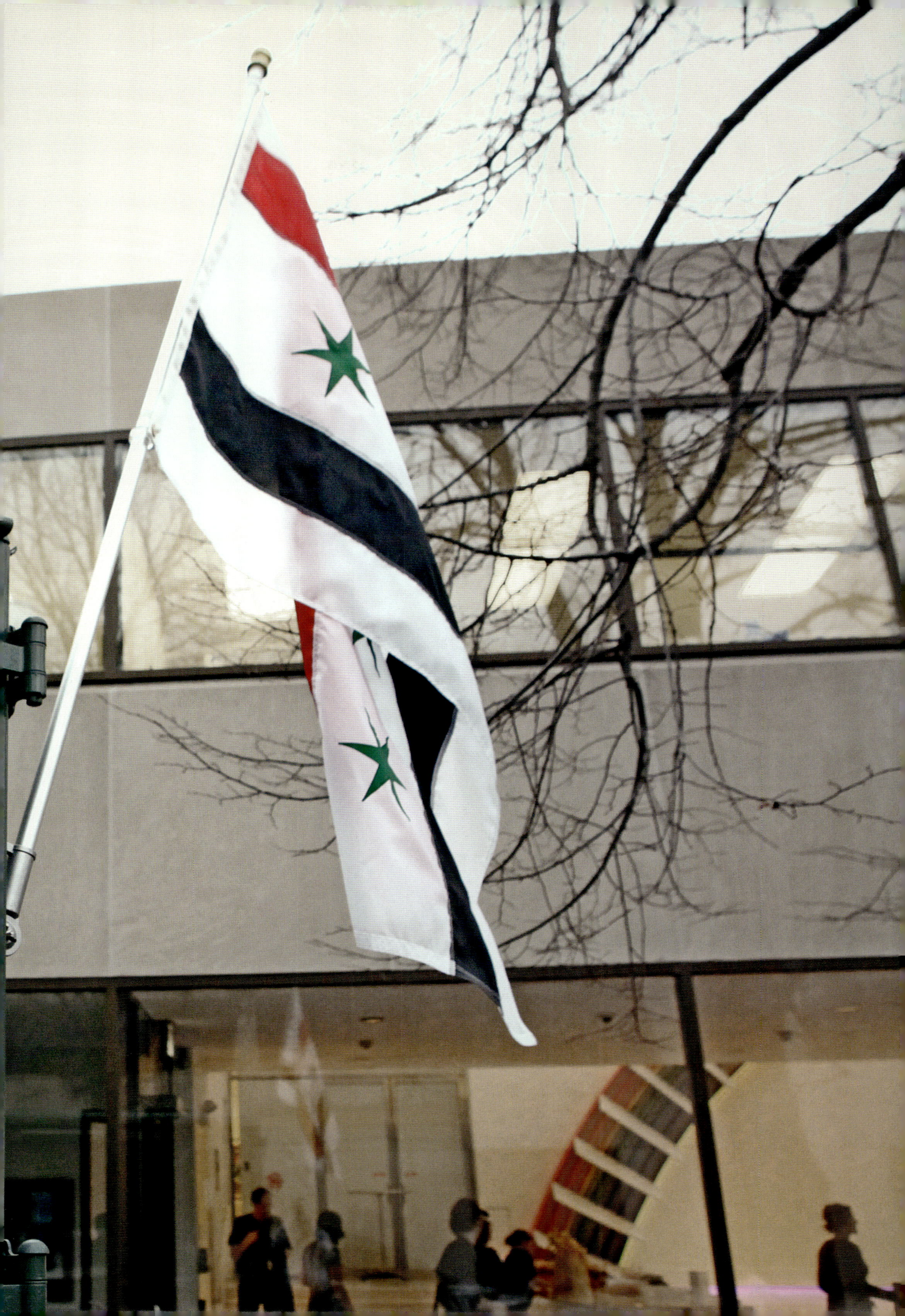

ARTISTS

Feast: Radical Hospitality in Contemporary Art explores the role of the meal in contemporary art. In order to map and to understand this history and its ongoing practices, *Feast* has involved different kinds of writing and documentation. The pages that follow present the artists' projects included in *Feast* through curatorial texts, artists' interviews and writing, and art historical texts, along with reproductions of ephemera, installation views, and a rich array of images depicting behind-the-scenes preparations and performances. Organized in chronological, thematic chapters that mirror the organization of the exhibition and alphabetically by artist, these sections present the full scope of the exhibition.

All curatorial texts were written by Stephanie Smith, with contributions as noted.

All interviews were conducted by a collaborative team of Stephanie Smith; Associate Curator of Contemporary Art Jessica Moss; and interns Emily Capper, Sarah Mendelsohn, and Jennifer Sichel unless otherwise noted. These texts are edited versions of interviews conducted via phone, e-mail, and video during the months prior to *Feast's* opening at the Smart Museum of Art (February 15, 2012).

PROLOGUE AND ORIGINS: 1990s/1930s

Felix Gonzalez-Torres

FELIX GONZALEZ-TORRES CAME OF AGE artistically in the midst of politically active art communities in 1980s New York. In 1987, he joined the collaborative Group Material and worked with fellow members Doug Ashford, Julie Ault, Karen Ramspacher, and Tim Rollins to create vibrant exhibition- and discussion-based projects that explored charged topics, such as the nature of community and the limits of democracy. Gonzalez-Torres's solo approach differed from that group work in its combination of political urgency with poetic sensibility and ingenious economy of form—often manifested through deceptively simple presentations of everyday materials like cellophane-wrapped candy, lightbulbs, and billboards. In 1989, for instance, he commemorated the 1969 Stonewall Rebellion through a nonsequential list of names and dates drawn from historical and current struggles involving gay rights and AIDS, presented as two lines of white text on a simple black background on a billboard near the riot site. His famous paper stack pieces are more open-ended. These blank sheets and prints of both evocative color bands and images—dark waves, a soaring distant bird, a tiny newspaper clipping—are produced in endless supply and displayed on the floor in sculptural stacks whose heights rise and fall as visitors take away copies and new sheets replenish the old.

"Untitled" (Portrait of Ross in L.A.) (1991) is one of a series of sculptures that complicate those strategies of presentation and dispersal through the embodied, sensual act of eating. Gonzales-Torres began this series in 1990 with *"Untitled" (Fortune Cookie Corner)* (1990). Over time, he used other items—from throat lozenges to chocolates and mints—that can be displayed on the floor piled in a corner or stretched into "carpets." Through the specific type and look of the items, the work's parenthetical title, and the stated "ideal weight" of the sculpture installed at the start of each display, Gonzalez-Torres evoked abstract concepts and feelings—revenge, for instance—as well as specific people. *"Untitled" (Portrait of Ross in L.A.)* uses candies wrapped in jewel-toned cellophane, referring in part to the artist's longtime partner, Ross Laycock, at his healthy weight of 175 pounds; in other related sculptures the "ideal weight" drops to a mere 75 pounds. As with the stack pieces, viewers may take and eat a piece of candy that can be endlessly resupplied by museum staff, so that each time the work is displayed, the public participates in its cycle of depletion and replenishment.

Although its inclusion in *Feast* admittedly stretches the idea of the "artist-orchestrated meal," *"Untitled" (Portrait of Ross in L.A.)* is intentionally placed as an introduction to the exhibition. The artist did not overtly create his candy pieces in order to foster conviviality or interaction—although such exchanges may occur around these works. But they distill other essential qualities of feasts as semi-ritualized acts of eating that mingle sensory pleasure, abundance, consumption, and a complicated kind of generosity. And this particular portrait certainly embodies a radical hospitality. It welcomes and seduces with the sensual beauty of its sparkling offering, but for those who fully attend to the embodied gesture of consuming the candy (both literally and metaphorically), the quick hit of sugary pleasure may be cut with darker and more complex flavors: a whiff of cannibalism, a tang of religious sacrament, the poignant and politically charged sadness of this particular loss—and, perhaps, a more lasting sweetness in the hope for renewal.

OPPOSITE: *"Untitled" (Portrait of Ross in L.A.)*, installation view, Smart Museum of Art, 2012

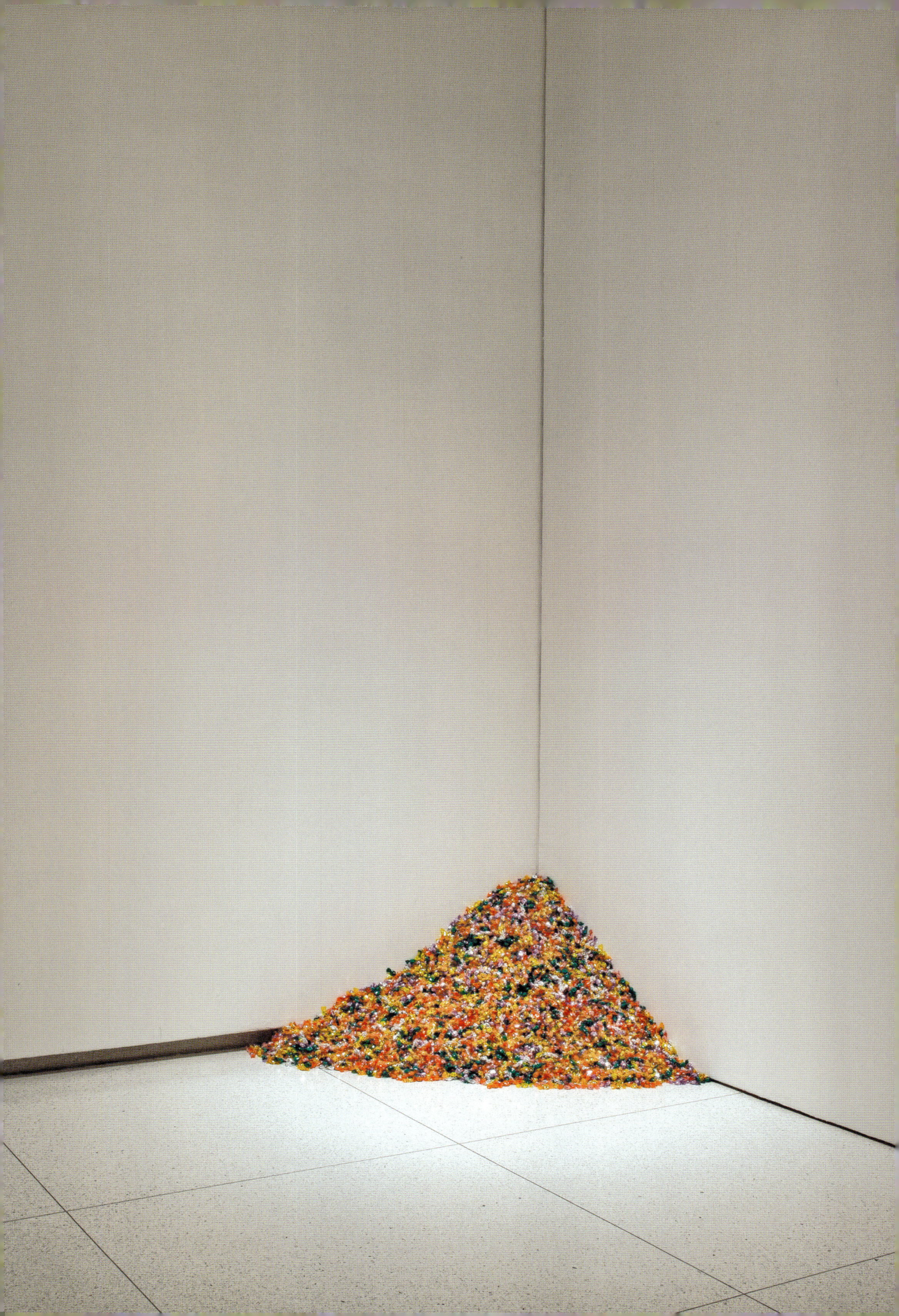

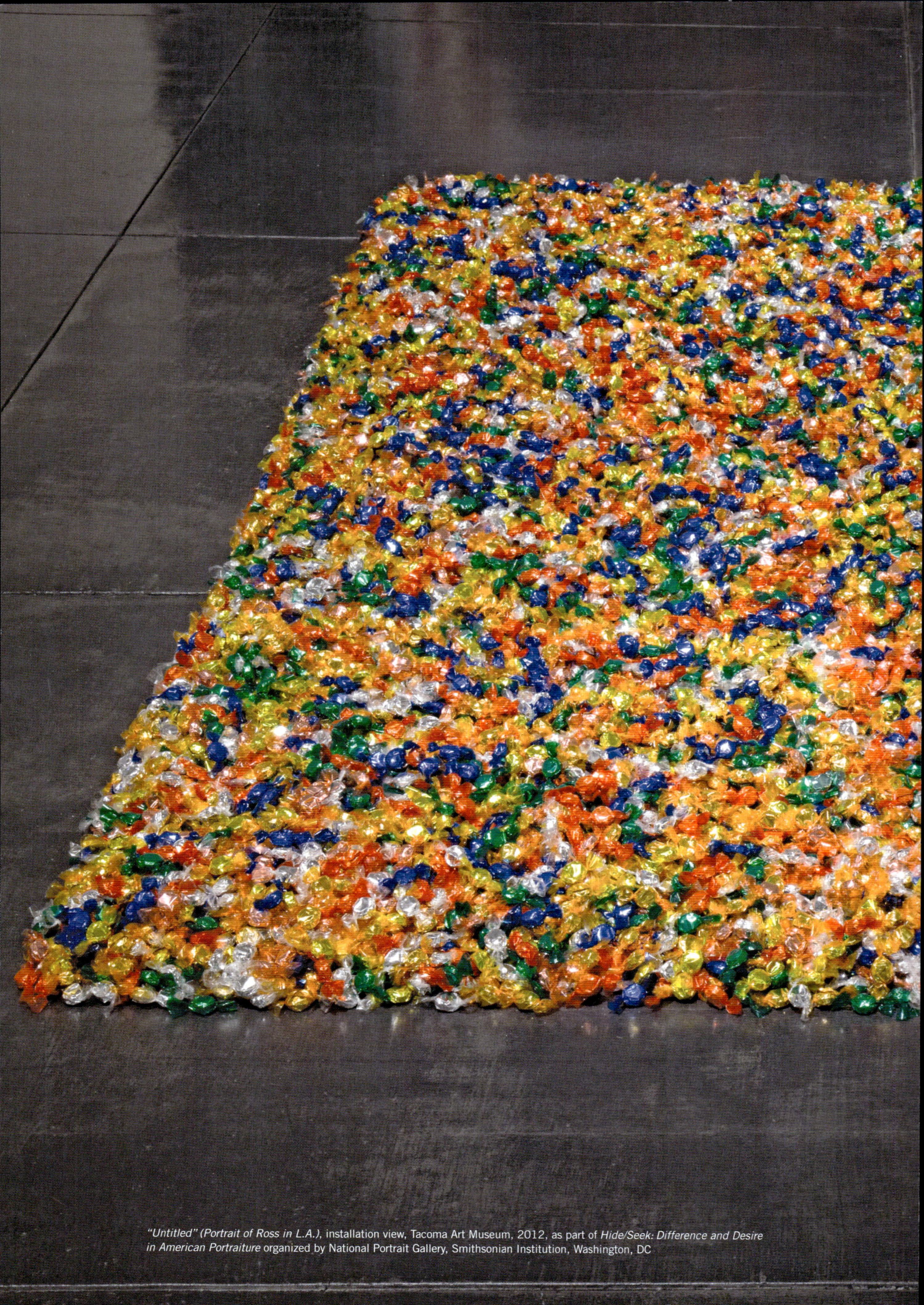

"Untitled" (Portrait of Ross in L.A.), installation view, Tacoma Art Museum, 2012, as part of *Hide/Seek: Difference and Desire in American Portraiture* organized by National Portrait Gallery, Smithsonian Institution, Washington, DC

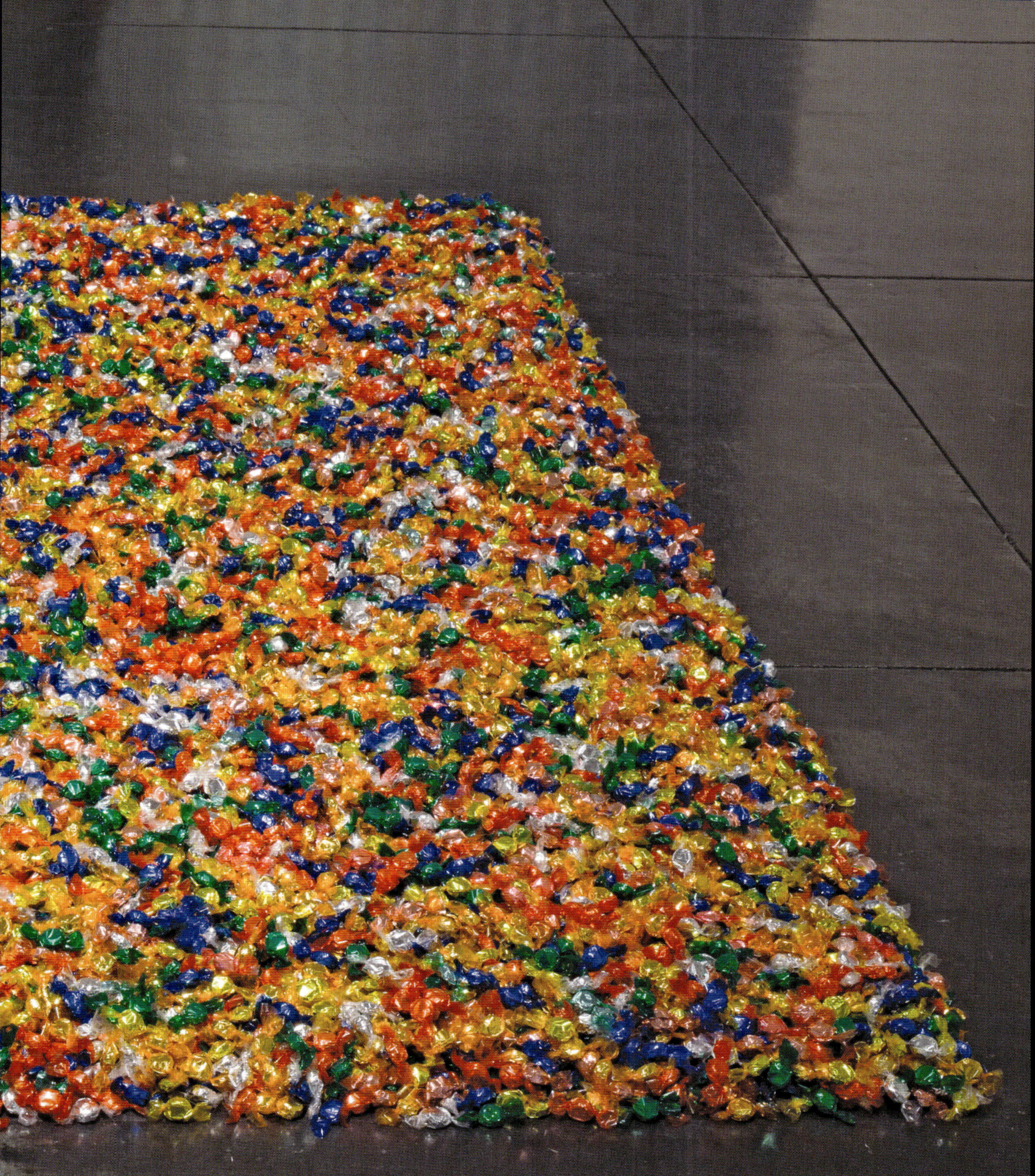

"I suppose I would be satisfied if [the audience] took action sometimes, or if it caused them to be critical, moved, inspired. Or to celebrate difference and the idea of change and renewal, the chance for love. I'd like to propose once more the 'radical' idea that we can make this a better place for everyone."—FELIX GONZALEZ-TORRES

From Milena Kalinovska, *Rhetorical Image* ed. Deirdre Summerbell (Museum of Contemporary Art, 1990).

F. T. Marinetti and the Italian Futurists

THE ARTIST-ORCHESTRATED MEAL burst onto the international scene in the early 1930s through the work of the Italian Futurists. This loose group of aesthetic provocateurs had been developing an aggressively modernistic, militaristic vision for Italian culture since 1909, when founder F. T. Marinetti's influential text, "The Foundation and Manifesto of Futurism," was published in the Paris newspaper *Le Figaro*. That jubilant screed proposed audacious new forms of culture that would jettison tradition—represented by staid museums and libraries—in favor of the dynamism of the machine age and the street. Over time, the group explored a variety of strategies to upend aesthetic norms across many different media—architecture, film, painting, poetry, and sculpture.

The Futurists eventually reimagined traditional cuisine and meals as well, beginning with the 1930 publication of the "Manifesto of Futurist Cooking" in the Turin-based newspaper *Gazetto del Popolo*. In this brief text, Marinetti excoriates pasta, a food that he deplored as an oppressive drag on his nation's gut as well as its competitive spirit. Futurist cuisine, in contrast, would be both nutritious and aesthetically provocative, imbuing mind and body with characteristically modern capacities—lightness, speed, and a willingness to embrace the new and experimental. He proposed radically unconventional yet carefully designed meals, which might include edible sculptures; foods meant to be eaten without silverware; the strategic use of music, poetry, perfume; and even occasional presentations of inedible dishes to diners in order "to increase their curiosity, surprise, and imagination." Marinetti's text received coverage far beyond art communities: the "Manifesto of Futurist Cooking" became that era's version of a viral news story, receiving a mix of serious and bemused responses from the international press and even reaching the *Chicago Tribune* in 1931.

Many of the Futurists' utopian proposals operated abstractly, as speculation and as provocation, but they also put their cuisine into actual practice. They held banquets. The opened the mischievously named Restaurant of the Holy Palate in Milan; its design featured streamlined aluminum curves and its menu offered dishes such as "broth of rose and the sun" and "a rain of cotton candy." They also spread their gospel through the playful *Futurist Cookbook* (1932)—part cookbook, part scrapbook, part polemic—which included the Manifesto, descriptions of actual banquets, and proposals for highly theatrical, wildly inventive, and sometimes even aggressively inedible meals. Through these avant-garde practices, the Futurists broke open the possibility that one might use food and meals not only as subject matter for art (as in the still life genre or depictions of the Last Supper), but as the art itself.

OPPOSITE: Documentation of Futurist banquet, c. 1931–32

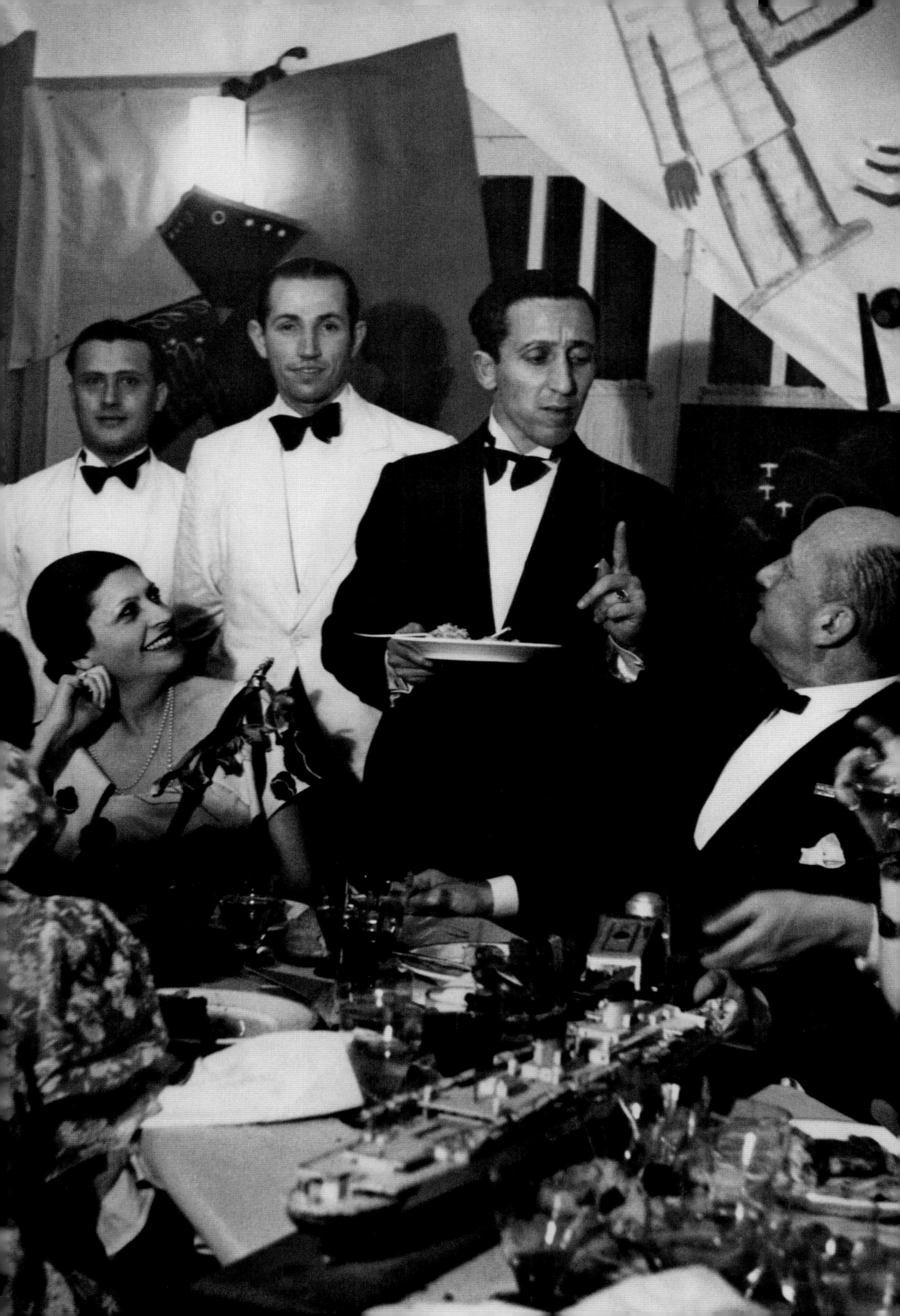

The Manifesto of Futurist Cooking

by F. T. Marinetti

ITALIAN FUTURISM, father of numerous Futurisms and avant-gardisms abroad, will not remain a prisoner of those worldwide victories secured "in twenty years of great artistic and political battles frequently consecrated in blood," as Benito Mussolini put it. Italian Futurism will face unpopularity again with a program for the total renewal of food and cooking.

Of all artistic and literary movements Futurism is the only one whose essence is reckless audacity. Twentieth-century painting and twentieth-century literature are in reality two very moderate and practical Futurisms of the right. Attached to tradition, dependent on each other, they prudently only essay the new.

Against Pasta

Futurism has been defined by the philosophers as "*mysticism in action*," by Benedetto Croce as "*anti-historicism*," by Graça Aranha as "*liberation from aesthetic terror*." We call it "*the renewal of Italian pride*," a formula for "*original synthesis*," "*spiritual hygiene*," "*a method of infallible creation*," "*the geometric splendor of speed*," "*the aesthetics of the machine*."

Against practicality we Futurists therefore disdain the example and admonition of tradition in order to invent at any cost something *new*, which everyone considers.

While recognizing that badly or crudely nourished men have achieved great things in the past, we affirm this truth: men think dream and act according to what they eat and drink.

Let us consult on this matter our lips, tongue, palate, taste buds, glandular secretions, and probe with genius into gastric chemistry.

We Futurists feel that for the male the voluptuousness of love is an abysmal excavator hollowing him out from top to bottom, whereas for the female it works horizontally and fan-wise. The voluptuousness of the palate, however, is for both men and women always an upward movement through the human body. We also feel that we must stop the Italian male from becoming a solid leaden block of blind and opaque density. Instead he should harmonize more and more with the Italian female, a swift spiraling transparency of passion, tenderness, light, will, vitality, heroic constancy. Let us make our Italian bodies agile, ready for the featherweight aluminum trains which will replace the present heavy ones of wood iron steel.

Convinced that in the probable future conflagration those who are most agile, most ready for action, will win, we Futurists have injected agility into world literature with words-in-liberty and simultaneity. We have generated surprises with illogical syntheses and dramas of inanimate objects that have purged the theater of boredom. Having enlarged sculptural possibility with antirealism, having created geometric architectonic splendor without decorativism and made cinematography and photography abstract, we will now establish the way of eating best suited to an ever more high speed, airborne life.

Above all we believe necessary:

a. The abolition of pastasciutta, an absurd Italian gastronomic religion.

It may be that a diet of cod, roast beef, and steamed pudding is beneficial to the English; cold cuts and cheese to the Dutch; and sauerkraut, smoked [salt] pork, and sausage to the Germans, but pasta is not beneficial to the Italians. For example it is completely hostile to the vivacious spirit and passionate, generous, intuitive soul of the Neapolitans. If these people have been heroic fighters, inspired artists, awe-inspiring orators, shrewd lawyers, tenacious farmers it was in spite of their voluminous daily plate of pasta. When they eat it they develop that typical ironic and sentimental skepticism which can often cut short their enthusiasm.

A highly intelligent Neapolitan Professor, Signorelli, writes: "In contrast to bread and rice, pasta is a food which is swallowed, not masticated. Such starchy food should mainly be digested in the mouth

RICORDI DELLA GUERRA

Arrivo a Trieste

Mario Sobrero.

Manifesto della cucina futurista

Il Futurismo italiano, padre di numerosi futurismi e avanguardismi esteri, non rimane prigioniero delle vittorie mondiali ottenute « in venti anni di grandi battaglie artistiche politiche spesso consacrate col sangue » come le chiamò Benito Mussolini. Il Futurismo italiano affronta ancora l'impopolarità con un programma di rinnovamento totale della cucina.

Fra tutti i movimenti artistici letterari è il solo che abbia per essenza l'audacia temeraria. Il novecentismo pittorico e il novecentismo letterario sono in realtà due futurismi di destra moderatissimi e pratici. Attaccati alla tradizione, essi tentano prudentemente il nuovo per trarre dall'una e dall'altro il massimo vantaggio.

Contro la pasta asciutta

Il Futurismo è stato definito dai filosofi « misticismo dell'azione », da Benedetto Croce « antistoricismo », da Graça Aranha « liberazione dal terrore estetico », da noi « orgoglio italiano novatore », formula di « arte-vita originale », « religione della velocità », « massimo sforzo dell'umanità verso la sintesi », « igiene spirituale », « metodo d'immancabile creazione », « splendore geometrico veloce ».

Antipraticamente, quindi, noi futuristi trascuriamo l'esempio e il monito della tradizione per inventare ad ogni costo un nuovo giudicato da tutti pazzesco.

Pur riconoscendo che uomini nutriti male o grossolanamente hanno realizzato cose grandi nel passato, noi affermiamo questa verità: si pensa si sogna e si agisce secondo quel che si beve e si mangia.

Consultiamo in proposito le nostre labbra la nostra lingua, il nostro palato le nostre papille gustative, le nostre secrezioni glandolari ed entriamo genialmente nella chimica gastrica.

Noi futuristi sentiamo che per il maschio la voluttà dell'amore è scavatrice abissale dall'alto al basso, mentre per la femmina è orizzontale a ventaglio. La voluttà del palato è invece per il maschio e per la femmina sempre ascensionale dal basso all'alto del corpo umano. Sentiamo inoltre la necessità di impedire che l'Italiano diventi cubico massiccio impiombato da una compattezza opaca e cieca. Si armonizzi invece sempre più coll'Italiana, snella trasparenza spiralica di passione tenerezza luce volontà slancio tenacia eroica. Prepariamo una agilità di corpi italiani adatti ai leggerissimi treni di alluminio che sostituiranno gli attuali pesanti di ferro legno acciaio.

Convinti che nella probabile conflagrazione futura vincerà il popolo più agile più scattante, noi futuristi dopo avere agilizzato la letteratura mondiale con le parole in libertà e lo stile simultaneo, svuotato il teatro della noia mediante sintesi alogiche a sorpresa e drammi di oggetti inanimati, immensificato la plastica con l'antirealismo, creato lo splendore geometrico architettonico senza decorativismo, la cinematografia e la fotografia astratte, stabiliamo ora il nutrimento adatto ad una vita sempre più aerea e veloce.

Crediamo anzitutto necessaria:

a) L'abolizione della pasta asciutta assurda religione gastronomica italiana.

Forse gioveranno agli inglesi lo stoccafisso il roast-beef e il budino, agli olandesi la carne cotta col formaggio, ai tedeschi il sauer-kraut, il lardone affumicato e il cotechino; ma agli italiani la pasta asciutta non giova. Per esempio, contrasta collo spirito vivace e coll'anima appassionata generosa intuitiva dei napoletani. Questi sono stati combattenti eroici, artisti ispirati, oratori travolgenti, avvocati arguti, agricoltori tenaci a dispetto della voluminosa pasta asciutta quotidiana. Nel mangiarla essi sviluppano il tipico scetticismo ironico e sentimentale che tronca spesso il loro entusiasmo.

Un intelligentissimo professore napoletano il dott. Signorelli scrive: « A differenza del pane e del riso la pasta asciutta è un alimento che si ingozza non si mastica. Questo alimento amidaceo viene in gran parte digerito in bocca dalla saliva e il lavoro di trasformazione è disimpegnato dal pancreas e dal fegato. Ciò porta ad uno squilibrio con disturbi di questi organi. Ne derivano: fiacchezza pessimismo inattività nostalgica e neutralismo ».

Invito alla chimica

La pasta asciutta, nutritivamente inferiore del 40 % alla carne al pesce ai legumi, lega coi suoi grovigli gli italiani di oggi ai lenti telai di Penelope e ai sonnolenti velieri in cerca di vento. Perchè opporre ancora il suo blocco pesante all'immensa rete di onde corte lunghe che il genio italiano ha lanciato sopra oceani e continenti, e ai paesaggi di colore forma rumore che la radiotelevisione fa navigare intorno alla terra? I difensori della pasta asciutta ne portano la palla o il rudero nello stomaco come ergastolani o archeologhi. Ricordatevi poi che l'abolizione della pasta asciutta libererà l'Italia dal costoso grano straniero e favorirà l'industria italiana del riso.

b) L'abolizione del volume e del peso nel modo di concepire e valutare il nutrimento.

c) L'abolizione delle tradizionali miscele per l'esperimento di tutte le nuove miscele apparentemente assurde, secondo il consiglio di Jarro Maincave e altri cuochi futuristi.

d) L'abolizione del quotidianismo mediocrista nei piaceri del palato.

Invitiamo la chimica al dovere di dare presto al corpo le calorie necessarie mediante equivalenti nutritivi gratuiti di Stato, in polvere o pillole, composti albuminoidei, grassi sintetici e vitamine. Si giungerà così ad un reale ribasso del prezzo della vita e dei salari con relativa riduzione delle ore di lavoro. Oggi per duemila Kilowatt occorre soltanto un operaio. Le macchine costituiranno presto un obbediente proletariato di ferro acciaio alluminio al servizio degli uomini quasi totalmente alleggeriti dal lavoro manuale. Questo, essendo ridotto a due o tre ore, permette di perfezionare e nobilitare le altre ore col pensiero le arti e la pregustazione di pranzi perfetti.

In tutti i ceti i pranzi saranno distanziati ma perfetti nel quotidianismo degli equivalenti nutritivi.

Il pranzo perfetto esige:

1° Un'armonia originale della tavola (cristalleria vasellame addobbo) coi sapori e colori delle vivande.

2° L'originalità assoluta delle vivande.

Il « Carneplastico »

Esempio: per preparare il Salmone dell'Alasca ai raggi del sole con salsa Marte si prende un bel salmone dell'Alasca, lo si trancia e passa alla griglia con pepe sale e olio buono finchè è bene dorato. Si aggiungono pomodori tagliati a metà preventivamente cotti sulla griglia con prezzemolo e aglio.

Al momento di servirlo si posano sopra alle trancie dei filetti di acciuga intrecciati a dama. Su ogni trancia una rotellina di limone con capperi. La salsa sarà composta di acciughe tuorli d'uova sode basilico olio d'oliva un bicchierino di liquore italiano Aurum e passata al setaccio. (Formula di Bulgheroni primo cuoco della Penna d'Oca).

Esempio: Per preparare la Beccaccia al Monterosa salsa Venere, prendete una bella beccaccia, pulitela, copritene lo stomaco con delle fette di prosciutto e lardo, mettetela in casseruola con burro sale pepe ginepro, cuocetela in un forno molto caldo per quindici minuti innaffiandola di cognac. Appena tolta dalla casseruola posatela sopra un crostone di pane quadrato inzuppato di Rhum e Cognac e copritela con una pasta sfogliata. Rimettetela poi nel forno finchè la pasta è bene cotta. Servitela con questa salsa: un mezzo bicchiere di marsala e vino bianco, quattro cucchiai di mirtilli della buccia di arancio tagliuzzata, il tutto bollito per 10 minuti. Ponete la salsa nella salsiera e servitela molto calda. (Formula di Bulgheroni primo cuoco della Penna d'Oca).

3° L'invenzione di complessi plastici saporiti, la cui armonia originale di forma e colore nutra gli occhi ed ecciti la fantasia prima di tentare le labbra.

Esempio: Il Carneplastico creato dal pittore futurista Fillìa, interpretazione sintetica dei paesaggi italiani, è composto di una grande polpetta cilindrica di carne di vitello arrostita ripiena di undici qualità diverse di verdure cotte. Questo cilindro disposto verticalmente nel centro del piatto, è incoronato da uno spessore di miele e sostenuto alla base da un anello di salsiccia che poggia su tre sfere dorate di carne di pollo.

« Equatore + Polo Nord »

Esempio: Il complesso plastico mangiabile Equatore + Polo nord *creato dal pittore futurista Enrico Prampolini è composto di un mare equatoriale di tuorli rossi d'uova all'ostrica con pepe sale limone. Nel centro emerge un cono di chiaro d'uovo montato e solidificato pieno di spicchi d'arancio come succose sezioni di sole. La cima del cono sarà tempestata di pezzi di tartufo nero tagliati in forma di aeroplani negri alla conquista dello zenit.*

Questi complessi plastici saporiti colorati profumati e tattili formeranno perfetti pranzi simultanei.

4° L'abolizione della forchetta e del coltello per i complessi plastici che possono dare un piacere tattile prelabiale.

5° L'uso dell'arte dei profumi per favorire la degustazione.

Ogni vivanda deve essere preceduta da un profumo che verrà cancellato dalla tavola mediante ventilatori.

6° L'uso della musica limitato negli intervalli tra vivanda e vivanda perchè non distragga la sensibilità della lingua e del palato e serva ad annientare il sapore goduto ristabilendo una verginità degustativa.

7° L'abolizione dell'eloquenza e della politica a tavola.

8° L'uso dosato della poesia e della musica come ingredienti improvvisi per accendere colla loro intensità sensuale i sapori di una data vivanda.

9° La presentazione rapida tra vivanda e vivanda, sotto le nari e gli occhi dei convitati, di alcune vivande che essi mangeranno e di altre che essi non mangeranno, per favorire la curiosità la sorpresa e la fantasia.

10° La creazione dei bocconi simultanei e cangianti che contengano dieci venti sapori da gustare in pochi attimi. Questi bocconi avranno nella cucina futurista la funzione analogica immensificante che le immagini hanno nella letteratura. Un dato boccone potrà riassumere un'intera zona di vita, lo svolgersi di una passione amorosa o un intero viaggio nell'Estremo Oriente.

Strumenti scientifici in cucina

11° Una dotazione di strumenti scientifici in cucina: ozonizzatori *che diano il profumo dell'ozono a liquidi e a vivande,* lampade per emissione di raggi ultravioletti *(poichè molte sostanze alimentari irradiate con raggi ultravioletti acquistano proprietà attive, diventano più assimilabili, impediscono il rachitismo nei bimbi, ecc.),* elettrolizzatori *per scomporre succhi estratti ecc. in modo da ottenere da un prodotto noto un nuovo prodotto con nuove proprietà,* mulini colloidali *per rendere possibile la polverizzazione di farine frutta secca droghe ecc. ad un elevatissimo grado di dispersione,* apparecchi di distillazione a pressione ordinaria e nel vuoto, autoclavi centrifughe, dializzatori. *L'uso di questi apparecchi dovrà essere scientifico, evitando p. es. l'errore di far cuocere le vivande in pentole a pressione di vapore, il che provoca la distruzione di sostanze attive (vitamine, ecc.) a causa delle alte temperature. Gli indicatori chimici renderanno conto dell'acidità e della basicità degli intingoli e serviranno a correggere eventuali errori: manca il sale, troppo aceto, troppo pepe, troppo dolce.*

F. T. Marinetti.

La prima Quadriennale di Roma sarà inaugurata colla visita dei Reali e con un discorso del Duce

La crisi inglese ha fatto aumentare la produzione libraria e i radioamatori

La commemorazione del Natale Gumano

La rivista dei libri

Paolo Monelli.

Massimo Bontempelli.

Massimo Caputo.

Publicazioni ricevute

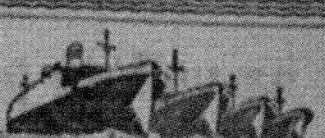

LINEE CELERI DI LUSSO MEDITERRANEO - AMERICHE

NORD AMERICA

CONTE BIANCAMANO

CONTE GRANDE

SUD AMERICA

CONTE ROSSO

CONTE VERDE

AUSTRALIA

M|N REMO

LLOYD SABAUDO

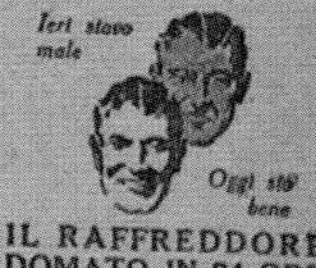

IL RAFFREDDORE DOMATO IN 24 ORE

MAIDA SAK

PER IL RISPARMIO IN CASA

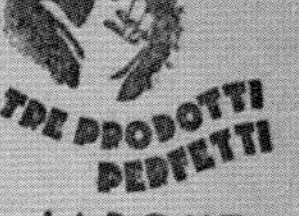

I TRE PRODOTTI PERFETTI

1° SAPONE DELLA BELLEZZA

2° BALSAMO

3° CIPRIA

NIL'S

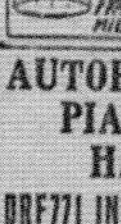

S. PAOLO S. A. ROMA

AUTOPIANI PIANOFORTI HARMONIUMS

PREZZI INFERIORI AL COSTO

F. I. P.

Via Moretta, 55 - Torino

LAP LAP

TRAVASATORE D'OLIO PER BARILI

L. 150

TUMORI BENIGNI MALIGNI

Reproduction of "Manifesto della Cucina Futurista" (Manifesto of Futurist Cooking), as printed in *Gazzetta del Popolo*, Turin, December 28, 1930

by saliva but in this case the task of transformation is carried out by the pancreas and the liver. This leads to an interrupted equilibrium in these organs. From such disturbances derive lassitude, pessimism, nostalgic inactivity and neutralism."

An Invitation to Chemistry

Pastasciutta, 40 percent less nutritious than meat, fish or pulses, ties today's Italians with its tangled threads to Penelope's slow looms and to somnolent old sailing ships in search of wind. Why let its massive heaviness interfere with the immense network of short long waves which Italian genius has thrown across oceans and continents? Why let it block the path of those landscapes of color form sound which circumnavigate the world thanks to radio and television? The defenders of pasta are shackled by its ball and chain like convicted lifers or carry its ruins in their stomachs like archaeologists. And remember too that the abolition of pasta will free Italy from expensive foreign grain and promote the Italian rice industry.

a. The abolition of volume and weight in the conception and evaluation of food.
b. The abolition of traditional mixtures in favor of experimentation with new, apparently absurd mixtures, following the advice of Jarro Maincave and other Futurist cooks.
c. The abolition of everyday mediocrity from the pleasures of the palate.

We invite chemistry immediately to take on the task of providing the body State, in powder or pills, albumoid compounds, synthetic fats, and vitamins. This way we will achieve a real lowering of the cost of living and of salaries, with a relative reduction in working hours. Today only one workman is needed for two kilowatts. Soon machines will constitute an obedient proletariat of iron steel aluminum at the service of men who are almost totally relieved of manual work. With work reduced to two or three hours, the other hours can be perfected and ennobled through study, the arts, and the anticipation of perfect meals.
In all social classes meals will be less frequent but perfect in their daily provision of equivalent nutrients.

The perfect meal requires:

1. Originality and harmony in the table setting (crystal, china, décor) extending to the flavours and colors of the foods.
2. Absolute originality in the food.

"Sculpted meat"

Example: to prepare *Alaskan Salmon in the rays of the sun with Mars sauce*, take a good Alaskan salmon, slice it, and put the slices under the grill with pepper, salt, and high quality oil until golden. Then add halved-tomatoes previously cooked under the grill with parsley and garlic.

Just before serving place on top of the slices some anchovy fillets interlaced in a checkerboard pattern. On every slice a wheel of lemon with capers. The sauce will be composed of anchovies, hard-boiled egg yolks, basil, olive oil and a little glass of Italian Aurum liqueur, all passed through a sieve. (Formula by Bulgheroni, head chef at the Penna d'Oca).

Example: To prepare the *Woodcock Mount Rosa with Venus sauce*, take a good woodcock; clean it; cover its stomach with slices of prosciutto and fat bacon; put it in a casserole with butter, salt, pepper and juniper berries; and cook in a very hot oven for fifteen minutes, basting it with cognac. Remove from the pan and place immediately on a large square slice of bread soaked in rum and cognac, and cover it with puff pastry. Then put it back into the oven until the pastry is well cooked. Serve it with this sauce: half a glass of marsala and white wine, four tablespoons of bilberries and some finely-chopped orange peel, boiled together for ten minutes. Put the sauce in the sauce boat and serve it very hot. (Formula by Bulgheroni, head chef at the Penna d'Oca).

3. The invention of appetizing food sculptures, whose original harmony of form and color feeds the eyes and excites the imagination before it tempts the lips.

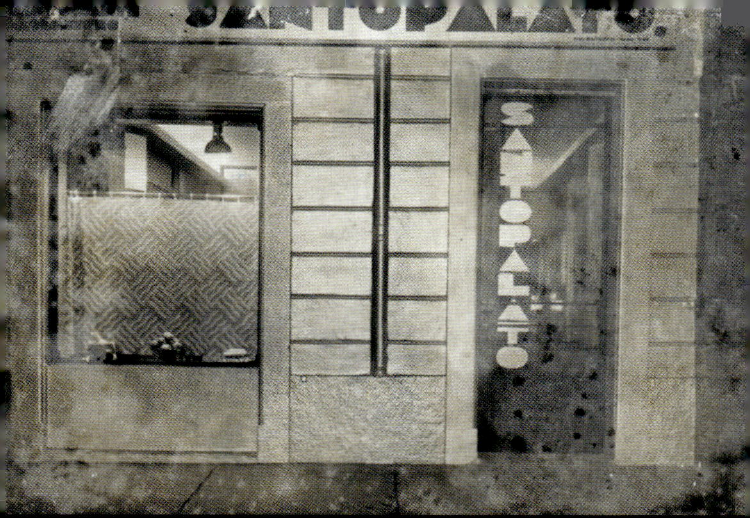

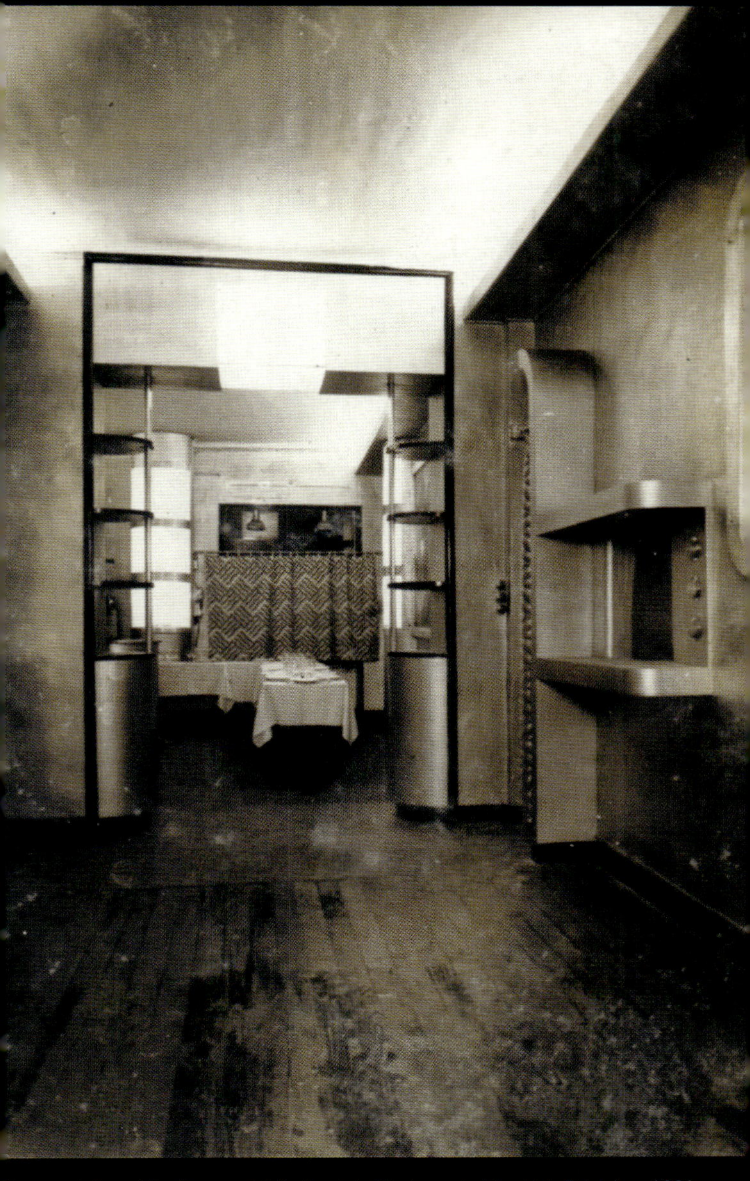

Documentation of the Taverna del Santopalato (Restaurant of the Holy Palate), c. 1931

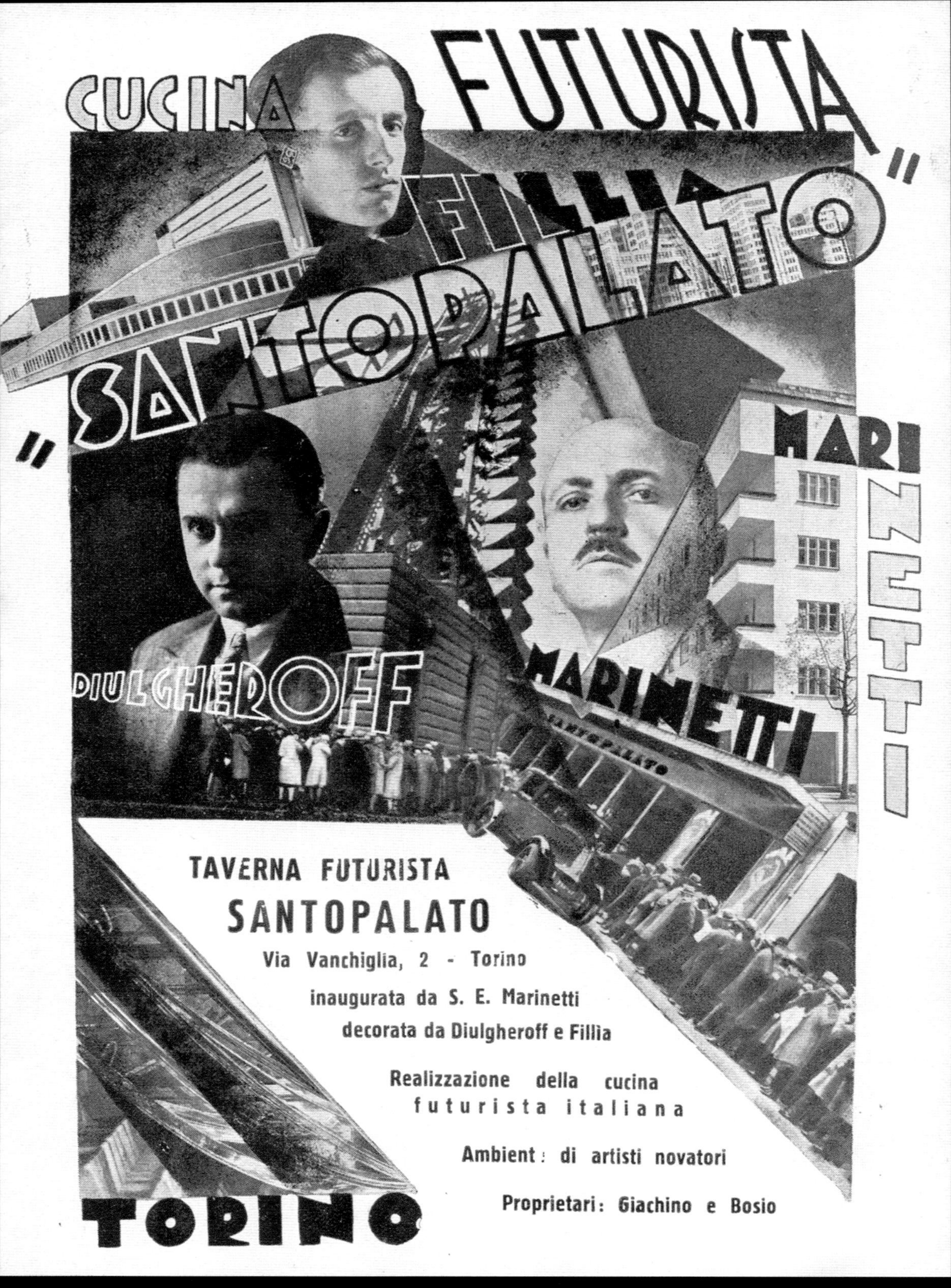

Poster for the Taverna del Santopalato *(Restaurant of the Holy Palate)*, designed by Nikolay Diulgheroff, c. 1932

Example: the *Sculpted meat* created by the Futurist painter Fillìa, a symbolic interpretation of all the varied landscapes of Italy, is composed of a large cylindrical rissole of minced veal stuffed with eleven different kinds of cooked green vegetables and roasted. This cylinder, standing upright in the center of the plate, is crowned by a layer of honey and supported at the base by a ring of sausages resting on three golden spheres of chicken.

Equator + North Pole

Example: The edible food sculpture *Equator + North Pole* created by the Futurist painter Enrico Prampolini is composed of an equatorial sea of poached egg yolks seasoned like oysters with pepper, salt, and lemon. In the center emerges a cone of firmly whipped egg white full of orange segments looking like juicy sections of the sun. The peak of the cone is strewn with pieces of black truffle cut in the form of black aeroplanes conquering the zenith.

These flavorful colorful perfumed and tactile food sculptures will form perfect simultaneous meals.

4. The abolition of the knife and fork for eating food sculptures, which can give prelabial tactile pleasure.
5. The use of the art of perfumes to enhance tasting. Every dish much be preceded by a perfume which will be driven from the table with the help of electric fans.
6. The use of music limited to the intervals between courses so as not to distract the sensitivity of the tongue and palate but to help annul the last taste enjoyed by reestablishing gustatory virginity.
7. The abolition of speech-making and politics at the table.
8. The use in prescribed doses of poetry and music as surprise ingredients to accentuate the flavors of a given dish with their sensual intensity.
9. The rapid presentation, between courses, under the eyes and nostrils of the guests, of some dishes they will eat and others they will not, to increase their curiosity, surprise, and imagination.
10. The creation of simultaneous and changing canapés which contain ten, twenty flavors to be tasted in a few seconds. In Futurist cooking these canapés have by analogy the same amplifying function that images have in literature. A given taste of something can sum up an entire area of life, the history of an amorous passion, or an entire voyage to the Far East.
11. A battery of scientific instruments in the kitchen: *ozonizers* to give liquids and foods the perfume of ozone, *ultra-violet ray lamps* (since many foods when irradiated with ultra-violet rays acquire active properties, become more assimilable, preventing rickets in young children, etc.), *electrolyzers* to decompose juices and extracts, etc. in such away as to obtain from a known product a new product with new properties, *colloidal mills* to pulverize flours, dried fruits, drugs, etc.; *atmospheric and vacuum stills, centrifugal autoclaves, dialyzers*. The use of these appliances will have to be scientific, avoiding the typical error of cooking foods under steam pressure, which provokes the destruction of active substances (vitamins, etc.) because of the high temperatures. *Chemical indicators* will take into account the acidity and alkalinity of the sauces and serve to correct possible errors: too little salt, too much vinegar, too much pepper or too much sugar.

This excerpt was previously published in Filippo Tommaso Marinetti, *The Futurist Cookbook*, trans. Suzanne Brill (San Francisco: Bedford Arts, 1989). Spelling and punctuation have been Americanized. The *Manifesto of Futurist Cooking* was first published in Gazzetta del Popolo in 1930, see p. 35.

mighty roast beef was the Englishman's food

RABBITS IN TWO STYLES

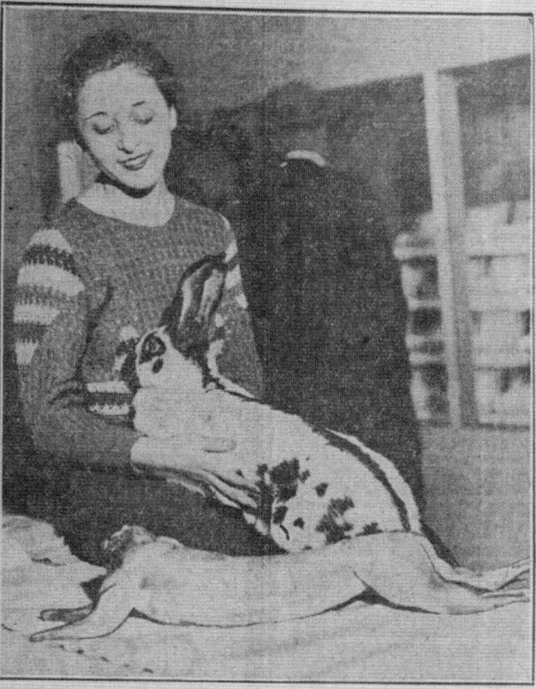

"Dressed" rabbits weigh less and wear less than live rabbits, according to the lesson which Harriet Roth, 5508 Flournoy street, learned from this checkered Flemish giant, the one with the ears, owned by W. Brincka, Chicago rabbit fancier.

THREE MEALS A DAY

From the Tribune Cook Book

By Mary Meade

Inasmuch as we all can't afford to indulge in orange juice for every week day breakfast, we may compromise and substitute other healthful juices, such as grapefruit, kraut, and tomato. While none of these have the same vitamin value as that of oranges, yet their vitamin content has been so protected by the canners who offer them to us that we may drink them with relish and still know they are "good for us."

To many people the whole fruits, particularly grapefruit, oranges, and lemons, are something which must be avoided, because they cause pain in the eating of them. I have seen breakfast guests courageously attack half a grapefruit and wince with every mouthful—not mentioning the faces they made! For such as these, the canned juices should be a boon, as they will not bother a mouth and teeth sensitive to the fruit from which they are derived.

Fruit juices used as an appetizer or cocktail nicely whet a dinner appetite. They may be served alone, or in combination with one another—tomato and sauerkraut juice being the favored "two tone cocktail" so much in vogue. They may be used in a variety of salads, especially those made with a gelatine base. If it's a tart aspic you're after, add a little kraut juice or tomato juice to your gelatine. If it's a fruit salad—frozen or the chilled molded variety—grapefruit, pineapple, or a dash of lemon juice will improve it. The one given below boasts both sauerkraut and lemon juice, which give it a sharp flavor, delicious for an accompaniment in a dinner with a mild meat or baked fish as the entrée.

CABBAGE PIQUANT IN MOLD.

1 package of lime or lemon gelatine
1½ cups of sauerkraut juice
½ cup of water
Juice of ½ lime or lemon
2 tablespoons of vinegar
2 cups of shredded cabbage
½ cup of diced green pepper
½ cup of diced pimiento
Stuffed olives—to taste

Bring the sauerkraut juice and water to the boiling point and pour over the gelatine, stirring until the gelatine is dissolved. When cool, add the lime or lemon juice, vinegar, shredded cabbage, pepper, pimiento, and rings of stuffed olives. Mix well and turn into a mold, or individual molds to set. Turn out on lettuce nets and top with a creamy mayonnaise. Garnish with pimiento squares.

[Copyright: 1931: By The Chicago Tribune.]

Tomorrow's Menu

MORNING
Orange Juice
Griddle Cakes
Maple Sirup
Milk Coffee

NOON
Split Pea Soup
Croutons
Apple, Celery, and Date Salad
Marble Cake
Milk Tea

NIGHT
Mixed Fruit Cocktail
Lamb Chops
Hashed Brown Potatoes
Sliced Tomatoes with Cottage Cheese
Lemon Filled Jelly Roll
Milk Coffee

Sunday's Menu

MORNING
Sauerkraut Juice
Ready to Eat Cereal
French Toast
Bacon
Milk Coffee

NOON
Roast Beef with Yorkshire Pudding
Pan Browned Potatoes
Creamed Onions
Currant Jelly
Avocado and Tomato Salad
Sponge Cake à la Mode
Milk Coffee

NIGHT
Hot Mushroom Sandwiches
Stuffed Olives
Butterscotch Sundae.
Sponge Cake
Milk Hot Chocolate Tea

CANNED GOODS FIND MANY USES ON DAILY MENU

Canned goods need be no barrier to having variety and appetite appeal in many types of dishes for any of the three standard American meals a day, according to the recipes and menus which household experts have devised.

... a salad, soup, or creamed dish. Canned fruits provide an even greater variety in combinations with tapioca, rice, or custard. Frozen desserts may include the products in ices, frozen fruit salads, or Bavarian creams. Pie fillings also suggest another method of using the canned products.

FUTURIST'S IDEA ON FOODS FINDS ITALY CONTRARY

Marinetti's Assault on Spaghetti Fails.

BY DAVID DARRAH.
[Chicago Tribune Press Service.]

ROME, Italy, Dec. 10.—Sig. Marinetti, the Italian futurist, facetiously or otherwise has been trying to reform the art of cooking here and especially to persuade Italians to abolish spaghetti.

His movement appears to have had the contrary effect. Italy is showing a tendency to remain backward in its culinary tastes and even to revert to the old fashioned dishes, which are described in the 13th and 14th centuries and in some of the poems of the 17th.

Florence is particularly faithful to its culinary traditions and in Florence alone does spaghetti lack the favor which it has in all the other Italian cities. Beans, in fact, are to Florentines what spaghetti is to Napolitans and rice to Lombards.

Real Beefsteak Here.

The famous Tuscan oil makes the work of the cook easier in the city of the Medici by giving a wholesome taste to the various kinds of soups, vegetables and meats. Beans with onions and olive oil, tripe, leg of mutton and head of pork are among the dishes that no good Florentine seems to be able to do without, and Florence is the only city in Italy where a real beefsteak can be had, properly cooked and of such dimensions as would furnish food for several people were they not Florentine.

Also, the quantity of beans, savored with onion and floating in oil that a good Florentine can do away with and which he will eat regularly at least every other day, would appear astounding to any other heavy eater.

Everything Cooked in Oil.

In cooking, butter prevails only in the preparation of tripe, leg of veal, and pork head. Every other staple unless the customer of the trattoria specially asks that his viand be prepared in fat of ham, lard, or butter, is cooked in oil. The old tradition prevails in this as in many other respects, and it is as strictly observed by the cabby as by the rich merchant or banker.

Old tradition also prevails in the arrangement, decoration and general atmosphere of the Florentine restaurant where the natives eat. The Florentine will go to a restaurant which advertises "French cooking" only when having foreign guests who may not like the rich though not greasy Florentine meal.

When by himself or with other Florentines he goes to the trattoria. There are several classes of such eating houses, some even garnished with real china plates and silver spoons, forks, and knives. But the majority of trattoria frequented by the Florentines boast rather good solid food than refined paraphernalia.

Generally Underground.

The trattoria itself is generally underground or in the darkest rooms that can be found in the narrow streets of the ancient city. One of these places, a celebrated one, too, started a new decorative fashion some thirty years ago, when advertisements were a novelty in Florence. Its vaulted walls, underground naturally, are all decorated with posters, some of which recall times which only the prewar generation can remember.

But the preference in decoration is given to fresco painting and some of the frescoes are of considerable value. In several instances the frescoes decorating the Florentine trattoria are simply restorations of old frescoes which the 17th century habit of plastering everything over has helped to preserve and which the contemporary liking for primitive art has brought to light again.

There is one restaurant near the Uffizi gallery which occupies part of what was the ancient church of San Pietro Scheraggio: a church which was already antique in the time of Dante. Its walls are frescoed with figures and decorative motives which suggest anything but food.

Church Columns Preserved.

The same place is enriched by some of the most beautiful columns to be found anywhere, all belonging to the ancient church. The capitals are of brick material finely carved in Corinthian style, and every detail is perfectly preserved. They were embedded in a big wall which was built in the late sixteenth century and thus were preserved.

The latest addition to Florentine artistic trattoria is a place called "Beatrice's cave," an underground place where everything is in the style of the 14th century. Walls, linen, cutlery, and waiters give the impression of a tavern of the times of Dante preserved intact to the present day.

It is the fashionable place in Florence these days and its 14th century attired servants serve the typical oil, beans, and onions concoction as well as China tea.

Men Folk, Here's a Chance to … You Can Cook; Try This …

BY WILLIAM K. M'KAY.

Fellow Benedicts, I commend you to a consideration of hash. I would lead you by simple procedure into the production of a family meal which shall make friend wife, howsoever culinarilly clever she be, admit that her old man is not entirely bereft of kitchen capability, and that any time her bridge game or matinee or other late afternoon engagements ensnare her, he can produce a toothsome collation ready for her arrival at the homestead and the coming with her of a guest or two.

Hash too much has been relegated into a low estate—into a concoction of touch and go's and makeshifts—of a combination of leftovers and castoffs, into a what-is-it, what-have-you melange of kitchen discards.

We consider now hash in primis—a delectable compound drawing its components from the best supplies of the markets—not a hodge-podge of relegated meat scraps, cold baked and boiled potatoes and other left-overs of the family table. We talk now of hash in primis—hash made as a dish of its own—not a gooey lot of mascerated refusables.

Corn Beef Hash for Six.

We shall have a corn beef hash—a serving, say, for six. First we shall get our corn beef. We might buy four or five pounds of mostly lean corned brisket, boil it slowly for several hours a day in advance and set it into the refrigerator to cool off for twenty-four hours or so.

That's adding a lot to the work, however. We can avoid all this preliminary effort by getting a pound or two or three of pressed boiled corn beef at the butcher shop. It comes in long loaf-like forms and the butcher will cut off a portion suitable to your needs. Several of the packing companies specialize in this corned beef loaf and it is very tasty, sliced into sandwich form or for our hash.

It Comes in Cans, Too.

Now, if your neighborhood butcher has none of this pressed corn beef loaf, don't worry. At any good delicatessen shop you can get prime corned beef in cans. The cans hold about twelve ounces and are of oblong shape, except they are a little larger at one end than the other. At the larger end there is one of those thumb-and-finger twisting gadgets that enables you to shear off the end of the can and then, by tapping the smaller end with the soft side of your fist, you ease the partly-pyramidal loaf of corned beef into a saucer.

[This entry into minute detail may irritate the skilled and experienced housewife, but please remember, girls, that this is written for mere, unknowing husbands by a mere man, vain of some little rudimentary cooking lore.]

When you buy the corned beef annex also a couple of green peppers, a small jar of pickled pimentos, an onion or two of medium size, and some potatoes.

Cook Needs Inspiration.

Back in the kitchen, wash your hands and clean your nails, roll up your sleeves, tie an apron around your midriff and feel that you're a real chef. One of the essentials of the hash is that its creator feel inspired—that as its preparation joyfully proceeds his pleasant anticipations are aroused, his pride in his performance stimulated and his gustatory yearnings sharpened.

Pull over that high stool which Marie, the colored maid, who is taking her day off, uses when she engages in her culinary rites, lay the cutting board before you on the kitchen table, grab a large, keen edged knife and proceed to dice your corned beef. Cut off a slice one-quarter of an inch thick; draw your knife across the slice up and down and then crosswise until it is separated into one-quarter inch cubes. Continue until you have diced two pounds or so of the beef.

[Of course you at this point are privileged to nibble. You can cut two thin slices of brown bread; lay between them a slice of the corned beef and a thin slice of onion, sprinkle on some salt and pepper, and proceed to munch. A pint of home brew or of high class near beer will add zest.]

Now the Potatoes.

After this little interlude get to work on your potatoes, which, carefully washed, are reposing, immersed, in an aluminum pan. The formula is equal parts of corned beef and potatoes. Scour the potatoes thoroughly in the cold water. Don't peel them. Save those mineral salts which the skins carry. Slice them and dice them, skins and all, into quarter inch cubes.

Meanwhile you have eased the corned beef into that large yellow mixing bowl, and now into the bowl you lift the diced potatoes. Proceed then to slice the green peppers into one-quarter inch squares; yes, let the seeds go in, and ease the cuttings into the mixing bowl. Then chop up a half cupful of onion and toss it in.

You now are ready for the proper blending of a real hash. Get up from your stool and stand by. With opened fingers gently stir the toothsome ingredients; don't press them or crush them, but, letting them slip through your digits, gently mix them thoroughly. Pause now and then to sprinkle in some gray pepper, some whole black peppers, some paprika, and a few cloves. Go light on the salt; there's plenty in the corned beef.

[Here we observe that an important ingredient has been overlooked—the celery. So chop up two or three stalks, a half cupful or so, and add to the bowl; also some of those red pimentos; we'll need them for their colorful effect as well as for their flavor. Mix both into the hash through your open fingers. By this time grateful and aromatic odors are titilating your nostrils. Yes, spread a

I gave them all a new idea

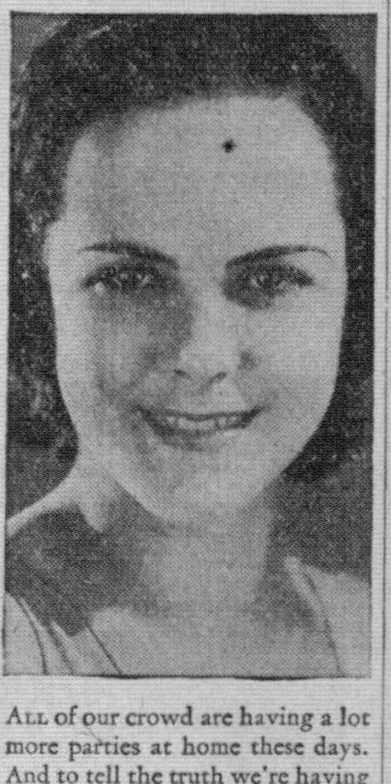

ALL of our crowd are having a lot more parties at home these days. And to tell the truth we're having a lot more fun. Of course, we all try to have our dinners and late suppers a little better than the last one. And believe me, that

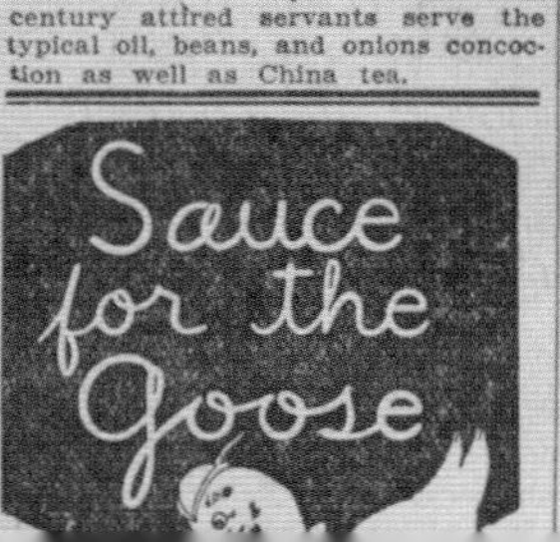

Takes care of itself.

SCHLURRRP!: The Case For and Against Spaghetti

by Hannah B Higgins

SQUAT, AMIABLE, TOOTHLESS, covered head to toe in homespun fabric, Strega Nona is a grandmotherly witch who heals with herbs and spells in the Calabrian hills of Southern Italy. Among the homely implements of her rustic life is an old clay pot that fills itself with spaghetti at her command.[1] This lead character in the popular children's book of the same name by Tomie dePaola, also features an apprentice assistant with the none-too-smart-sounding name, Big Anthony. This dimwitted, lumbering giant mimics the words that fill the pot and (while the boss is away) mumbles the spell. Predictably, after every villager has gobbled two or three plates of the stuff, Big Anthony is unable to slow production.

Oozing across the floor and through the tiny windows and doors of the witch's hut, the spaghetti slops down the road, snakes into town and (ever bigger) threatens, like a curling wave, the town's central piazza. Very nearly burying the villagers, in the end crisis is averted when Strega Nona appears and gently blows three kisses to the disgorging pot, which promptly stops. Big Anthony's penance is to eat it all. On the last page he appears late at night, his tongue distended, his low-slung gut hanging over his beltline, his eyelids draped heavily over bloodshot eyes, obediently forking and slurping his way toward Strega Nona's cottage. Order has been restored, but this gentle (if greedy) giant now exceeds the limits of his already generous girth.

The familiar image of streaming pasta encapsulated in this story reflects not only how spaghetti is slurped, but also how it is manufactured. Hidden from view by a container that holds the dough, endless threads of noodle emerge from a stubby, perforated pipe. In this story, the uncanny quality of spaghetti production is expressed most clearly through the image of Strega Nona's house as an overgrown pasta press, expressing in architectural form the disgorging mouth of the machine. As spaghetti squeezes through the pasta machine, so it proliferates seemingly on its own.

Typical of children's stories the world over, this one affirms established beliefs through overstatement and a tone of timeless truth-telling. *Strega Nona* admonishes against the common vice of gluttony using a string of now familiar symbols emerging from the pasta pot: (1) Pasta is antimodern. It belongs to a world controlled by the mysteries of magic, religion, and village life. (2) Pasta is peasant food. It appeals to the basest culinary instincts and is therefore universally loved. (3) Pasta proliferates. It is particularly prone to expressions of excess.

Timeless though this pasta imagery seems, each element of the familiar view of pasta is, broadly speaking, modern. The notable exception is its association with gluttony. Before the invention of the mechanical pasta press, pasta was made entirely by hand in a laborious process of hand kneading, rolling, and cutting. The Italian word for pasta, *maccheroni* (macaroni in English), may refer to a Neapolitan prince who apparently exclaimed of the pasta with a hole in it "Si buoni ma caroni!" or, "So good, but expensive."[2] *Maccheroni* may also refer to the grand glutton of traditional Commedia dell'Arte, Mascherone.[3] Mascherone = macaroni = gluttony. Already in 1495, Antonio Camelli, a court poet to the Dukes of Milan, decried the link between pasta and obesity as a poor reflection on the elevated social class of the glutton:

> The son of the cow comes to court
> Fat with broth, cheese, and lasagna . . .[4]

With the introduction of proto-industrial processes in about 1600, Southern Italians could access pasta more easily and it became increasingly available to other classes, although it was still a luxury food. Its popularity spread further still after 1800, once thorough drying processes were developed that allowed

OPPOSITE: "Futurist's Idea on Foods Finds Italy Contrary," as printed in *The Chicago Tribune*, December 11, 1931

pasta to be sufficiently dried for long-term storage and shipping.[5] Because of its cheap cost, its class associations shifted from that of a luxury item (hard to make and difficult to store) to an everyday food of the working classes at the same time as it became mechanized. Its status as a staple food in the peasant class therefore dates to this time. Pasta fed the agricultural worker (the peasant in *Strega Nona*) and later, when these workers began to travel for urban jobs, the itinerant laborer.

Where pasta appears in modern art, it affirms these modern associations, while staking claims as to their positive or negative value. This short account looks at spaghetti across the time range associated with this exhibition; in and around Futurism in the early 1930s, Fluxus in the 1960s and 1970s, and in two examples of recent food works. In all cases, spaghetti functions to address the art/life divide in terms of what kind of art community is constituted by food, whom art serves, and what the desired outcome of this relationship is or should be. In doing so, this survey stages the case for and against spaghetti using the evidence of art history.

The Case Against Pasta

Marinetti published his famous "Manifesto of Futurist Cooking" in *Gazzetta del Popolo* in Turin on December 28, 1930.[6] In it, he inveighed against pasta in the familiar terms just described. "Pasta is not beneficial to the Italians . . . Why let its massive heaviness interfere with . . . genius?" In other words, pasta fatigues, interferes with critical thinking, and therefore the industrial and cultural progress so valued by the Futurists. Instead of "traditional mixtures of flavor," Marinetti hailed "a communication to the Roman press from the painter Fillía [which] has set the gastronomes of the capital buzzing, including those journalists particularly attached to the 'Holy Sister Happiness' school of good cooking, to the traditions of the 'spaghetti lover' and to all the other proud insignia of the true epicure."[7]

It gets worse. Pasta's offense approaches the abject, since it "is swallowed, not masticated." Chewing is optional. It can be swallowed whole, essentially inhaled along the length of the tongue, through the esophagus, and into the bowels. Strega Nona, after all, has no teeth. In the words of critic Marco Ramperti, cited in *The Futurist Cookbook*, "The allegorical Italian has always got his avid mouth wide open over a plate of tagliatelle when he isn't dangling dripping strands of vermicelli down his greedy gullet."[8] The long threads of pasta hang both ways. Whether onto the shirt or down the esophagus, the dangling vermicelli evokes a body that has exceeded its natural limits by creating a continuum of strings that link inside and out. Unchewed, these pasta strings resemble too closely the intestines that are their destiny.

To top it off, in the Futurist view, pasta was un-Italian: "Pasta was raised among the Ostragoths," north of the Black Sea in the Late Roman era.[9] Recent scholarly accounts describe pasta in essentially the same terms, as originating in the Baltics in the first millennium BCE and following the amber trade to Rome.[10] Through identification with the invaders of ancient Rome, Marinetti was able to link pasta to the Fascist resistance to foreign influence. To wit, his xenophobic and misogynistic account of these importers/invaders as "gentle little ladies" who "licked their fingers and snouts."

Primitive, grotesque, and foreign-born, Marinetti took offense at the association of pasta and Italy in international circles. The full quotation from the manifesto above would read: "Pasta is not beneficial to the Italians . . . Why let its massive heaviness interfere with the immense network of short long [radio] waves which Italian genius has thrown across oceans?" At the time when the Futurists turned their attention to food, Italy was coming out of a second major wave of migration to the United States. Housed in separate Italian villages when they worked on the American railroads in the 1860s, and, later, in Italian ghettos in American cities, Italian immigrants faced vicious anti-Italian discrimination. The Italian immigrant diet centered on bread and pasta.[11] According to Jane Ziegelman, director of the Tenement Museum in New York, "Food was their cultural touchstone, their way of defying the critics, of tolerating the slurs and all of the other injustices."[12] Perverse as it seems, Marinetti's derision of his countrymen as stupefied by pasta and backwards matches almost exactly the Italian stereotype in America.

Not surprisingly, the Futurist diet favored the aristocrat. The resplendent table would shimmer

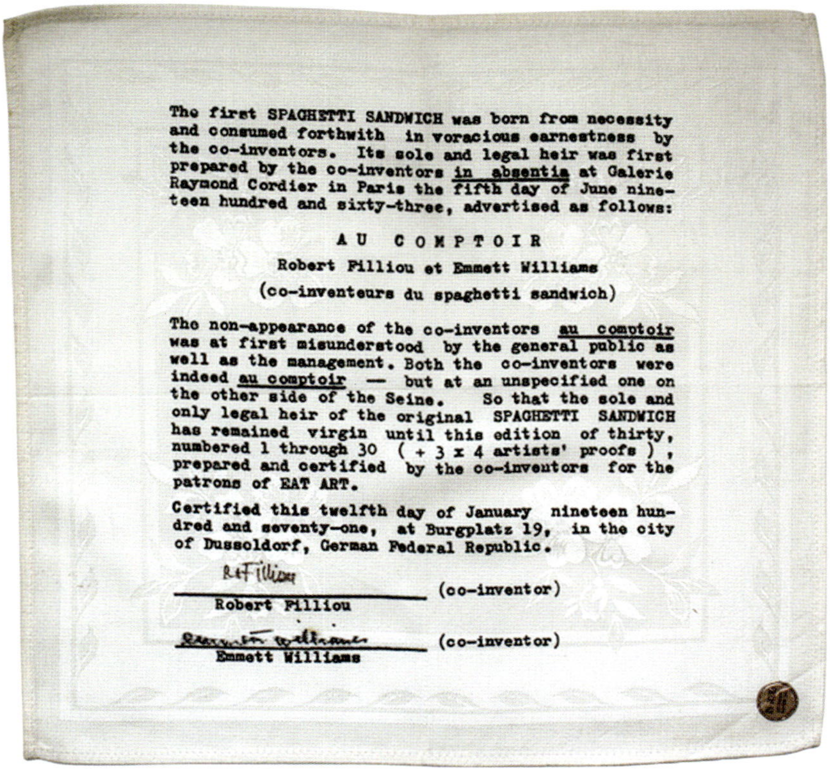
The first SPAGHETTI SANDWICH was born from necessity and consumed forthwith in voracious earnestness by the co-inventors. Its sole and legal heir was first prepared by the co-inventors in absentia at Galerie Raymond Cordier in Paris the fifth day of June nineteen hundred and sixty-three, advertised as follows:

AU COMPTOIR

Robert Filliou et Emmett Williams

(co-inventeurs du spaghetti sandwich)

The non-appearance of the co-inventors au comptoir was at first misunderstood by the general public as well as the management. Both the co-inventors were indeed au comptoir — but at an unspecified one on the other side of the Seine. So that the sole and only legal heir of the original SPAGHETTI SANDWICH has remained virgin until this edition of thirty, numbered 1 through 30 (+ 3 x 4 artists' proofs), prepared and certified by the co-inventors for the patrons of EAT ART.

Certified this twelfth day of January nineteen hundred and seventy-one, at Burgplatz 19, in the city of Dusseldorf, German Federal Republic.

R.Filliou

Robert Filliou (co-inventor)

Emmett Williams (co-inventor)

Napkin signed by Robert Filliou and Emmett Williams, marking the invention of the first *Spaghetti Sandwich*, January 12, 1971

with exotic liquor (Muscat wine, Marsala, Whiskey, Alkermes, and Vermouth), costly and hard to find ingredients (rose petals, caviar, cockscombs, and pineapple), and labor-intensive food (sculpted meat skyscrapers, Chicken Fiat, dried lettuce leaves, and hollow banana peels). If the modern era brought with it the era of cheap pasta (a manufactured food), the futurists aspired to a hand-formed machine aesthetic applied to materially rich ingredients.[13]

In the future, Marinetti claimed, caloric content would be delivered in pills and powders, giving the body "the calories it needs as quickly as possible, utilizing equivalent nutrients (provided free by the state)."[14] From this perspective, the caloric needs of the poor could be handled efficiently, as part of a state system assigned the task of enforcing well-being while substituting the inefficiencies of the home and hearth with technology. The banquet, on the other hand, would provide novel experiences for the mouth and tongue, as well as the fingers, nose, and ears. One example, *aerofood*, combined touch, sound, and scents as substitutions for the nutritive function of food: a waiter would douse the diners with scents from a large spray can, while the diner nibbled a fennel slice, an olive, and a kumquat, alongside which would be set a strip of velvet, silk, and sandpaper glued to cardboard. The tactile object would be used for feeling with one hand, while the other hand ate. Marinetti described it as "a dish I would not recommend for the hungry."[15]

If filling the empty gullet was beside the point in Futurist food works, it can also be noted that the social side of eating, its conviviality, was likewise bracketed from the ideal experience. Instead of a family style pasta plate at the center of a communal table, these banquets would be aesthetically individuating affairs. "We will create meals rich in different qualities," wrote Marinetti, "in which for each person dishes will be designed which take into account sex, character, profession, and sensibility."[16]

The Case For Pasta

Objectionable as it was to Marinetti, pasta's low cost and ready access laid the foundations for Italian food's early association with Bohemian life in the United States. Expanding on the legacy established by Italian restaurants now associated with affordability in places like Little Italy and Grammercy Park in New York, and as canning technology evolved during and after World War II, canned pasta became popular with English, French, and American soldiers. The soldiers brought a taste for this simple version of the food home with them from the war. From humble beginnings cooking at the Plaza Hotel during World War I, Hectar Boiardee opened a restaurant in Cleveland, Ohio, and by 1928 was canning his famous spaghetti under the Americanized name, Chef Boyardee. By the 1960s, canned spaghetti was as American as apple pie: to wit, its predominance in James Rosenquist's images of Americana and Andy Warhol's Heinz spaghetti cans.

And such was the fate of spaghetti, when, in 1963, Fluxus poet Emmett Williams and French poet Robert Filliou introduced to the world a co-invention. *The Spaghetti Sandwich* differs from the Futurist case against spaghetti utterly and is rightly the case *for* it. Clearly embracing the low cost and ease of pasta, *The Spaghetti Sandwich* rebuts each element of Marinetti's pasta class action. The sandwich was first consumed in "voracious earnestness"[17] during its modest origin in 1963:

> I cooked up an enormous batch of the spaghetti sauce for which I am famous, and put it in the refrigerator as a surprise . . . Robert and I decided to sample the sauce. It was very good, even cold. We spread it on bread, and ate it in this fashion several times, and even invited some of our friends to do the same . . . *The Spaghetti Sandwich* was born . . . it was indeed "born from necessity and consumed forthwith."[18]

By this account, low-cost, content, everyday ingredients, and a convivial atmosphere were important.[19] "It was hard enough to feed ourselves," wrote Williams, acknowledging the financial hardship and sense of community found among these artists, "these were happy days."[20]

Food shared is hunger averted. Strega Nona's village, after all, was a mountain village in a region historically prone to poverty, isolation, and famine. For the poor, whether mountain villagers, urban poor, immigrants, or starving artists, apparently gluttonous behavior can as easily be seen as calorie banking. Clearly, the case against pasta is a thinly disguised, upper-class criticism of "poor" taste. Pierre Bourdieu argued along these lines in his assessment of taste:

> It must never be forgotten that the working-class "aesthetic" is a dominated "aesthetic," which is constantly obliged to define itself in terms of the dominant aesthetics. The members of the working class . . . can neither ignore the high-art aesthetic, which denounces their own "aesthetic," nor abandon their socially conditioned inclinations . . .[21]

Tongue firmly in cheek, Filliou likewise assessed the social conditions of both aesthetics: "You can talk about art, music, and poetry all you want, but remember, with The Spaghetti Sandwich you can feed an entire army." This casual quip clearly crosses the class and technological divide so firmly established by Marinetti.

Filliou continues in Cold War terms that theorize a common taste: "And the Astronauts. The Cosmonauts [Soviet astronauts] as well!"[22] With this unpretentious, yet potent, marvel of food diplomacy, Filliou assigns virtue precisely where Marinetti loaded pasta with the germy sauce of polyculture. As if to drive the point home, in 1965 and again in 1971, Filliou and Williams produced a unique multiple (several made, each unique). This *Pink Spaghetti Handshake* was made when the two artists—one French, one American—shook hands with each other through (what else?) an apparent wad of saucy spaghetti (actually paint) between two cloth napkins.

Like *The Spaghetti Sandwich*, food art in the 1960s generally had something of the whiff of easy access about it. Alison Knowles's 1969 performance piece, *The Identical Lunch* (a tuna fish sandwich on whole wheat toast with butter, no mayo and a cup of soup or buttermilk), can be performed for free as when the Museum of Modern Art spent two months giving the lunch away in the winter of 2011. This work, in print and actual form, was displayed at the Smart Museum of Art's *Feast* exhibit. Similarly, Knowles's 1962 performance instructions to "Make a salad" or "Make a soup" instruct the preparer/performer to make the work as a performance piece. By convention, the food is given away. Fluxus banquets of the 1960s and 1970s, whether colored like the rainbow or clear, all black or all white, were only as expensive or as exotic as the dish each artist chose to contribute to the whole.

Finally, Carol Gooden and Gordon Matta-Clark's FOOD restaurant in lower Manhattan (opened 1971) offered local artists a place to work in exchange for food. The kitchen was open and stocked with everyday, as well as exotic ingredients. Even in food art venues marked by the exceptional and outrageous, such as Daniel Spoerri's celebrated restaurant projects of the 1960s and 1970s, exotic fare (insects and game in particular) existed alongside low-cost, good food.[23]

The commitment to shared resources signified in the 1960s by *The Spaghetti Sandwich*, Spoerri's affordable meals, FOOD, and the potluck Fluxus banquets fell by the wayside as the idealism of the 1960s yielded to the pleasure principle 1970s and 1980s. About a decade later, a late or last Flux-pasta work would bemoan the lost cause of spaghetti in fine art. Danish Fluxus artist Eric Anderson published a performance score in 1978 called *Spaghetti al Vento*. In it, the eater weeps. It is performed alone.

> You cook a fine fresh handmade spaghetti in water, salt, and extra virgin olive oil until it is al dente. The cooking is very important. If the spaghetti isn't of excellent quality and cooked exactly al dente, it won't work. You sit in front of an industrial fan with your piatto and take out a single piece of pasta to hold it at mouth level and at the center of the fan. The fan will blow it to form a horizontal line and into your mouth. In addition the fan will make you cry immensely and your tears will become a very delicious and salty sugo to the pasta.[24]

But the story isn't all tragedy. Rirkrit Tiravanija is a Thai-born, culturally hybrid artist who lives in New York City and Chiang Mai, in Northern Thailand. He met Robert Filliou in Canada and has made food works since 1989.[25] Like Filliou and Williams, Tiravanija's commitment to feeding people, to creating access to food, and to the socially binding aspect of food sharing routinely takes him in the direction of the noodle—or more specifically toward an art practice of noodles and dumplings and that great nationalist dish of Thailand: Pad Thai.

Albeit not a noodle dish per se, Rirkrit Tiravanija's *Untitled 2001 (the magnificent seven, spaghetti western)* nevertheless evokes the cross-cultural, class-blending history of spaghetti in its title, as well as in its attitude toward food. The work was installed at the Gallery Civica d'arte moderna e contemporanea, Turin. *Untitled 2001 (the magnificent seven, spaghetti western)* consisted of "a steel floor, 7 propane gas tanks, 800 soup bowls and 800 forks, 7 cook pots, 5 stainless steel hand platters, 2 cutting boards, and 4 concrete walls with openings," all used to make coconut chicken soup. Borrowing the title from John Sturges's film *The Magnificent Seven* (1960), Tiravanija describes the connection between the works. The film depicted:

> a collective of bad guys trying to do good, so I had seven pots of soup for cooking the Tom Ka Gai. So the characters in the film want to help Mexican peasants protecting their village. I am certainly playing with such metaphors and double entendres.[26]

Artist bad guy does good? For sure. Tiravanija's benchmark cooking pieces resist easy commodification by museums and collectors (bad guy), at the same time as they seek to expand the audience for the museum and also to feed the public (doing good). "Hunger," writes curator and Fluxus scholar Thomas Kellein in praise of Tiravanija, "has always been a dominant force, not just today . . ."[27]

By titling the piece "a spaghetti western" (although *The Magnificent Seven* is not one), Tiravanija aligns the piece with the hybrid form of Wild West films produced from the mid-1960s by Italian directors. The term was initially derogatory, but has come into accepted use by fans of this clear expression of a hybridized culture. Speaking of the importance of hybridity to another project, his "Flädlesoup," Tiravanija makes note of another film, this time Jan Schütte's *Drachenfutter* (*Dragon Chow*, 1987). The film tells the modern story of "a Pakistani, an Afghan, and an African working in the kitchen of a German-Chinese restaurant."[28] Each worker secretly flavors the Flädlesoup (a crepe cut up into broth as a pan fried noodle) to their respective taste and the customers love it. It played all day while Tiravanija cooked on the loading dock at the Hamburger Kunstverein in 1993. Any number of other Tiravanija works would suffice to demonstrate that, at least where this artist is concerned, noodles remain poignantly in the acculturating brew of food art.

Closing Arguments

At the other extreme, Martin Riebeek and Inge Riebeek's "Spaghetti with Worms," clip number HO125.05 in their *Stories by Heart* project, returns us to a timeless village, this time in the Netherlands.[29] This video portrait of the small Netherlandish town of Heerhugowaard was composed of residents reading from a favorite book. One reader chose Roald Dahl's 1980 children's book *The Twits*, which is about a dirty, hairy, angry couple (the stereotype of disgruntled hippies comes to mind), who play mean tricks on each other.

The video shows the mouth, nose, and hand of an unshaved, long-haired man forking a heavy load of sauced spaghetti into his mouth: a close-up detail drives home the intentionality of the gesture and intensifies the abject image. Spaghetti hangs out of the mouth and into the gut—its wet, pink, fatty mass wrapped around by unkempt lips. In the video still, the jaw is still open, so we know the threads are in motion toward inside. On closer examination (and as dictated by Roald Dahl's story), some of the spaghetti strings are revealed to be night crawlers. This horrific image made me gag. Like Strega Noni's orally expressive house and Futurism's stereotyped Italian, the spaghetti ties inside to out in a continuous threading between the world and the gut, an image driven home by the slithering worms. In Roald Dahl's words, "Mr. Twit started eating, twisting the long tomato-covered strings around his fork and shoveling them into his mouth. Soon there was tomato sauce all over his hairy chin."[30]

This time, however, instead of quaint villagers from days of yore (or hungry artists from the more recent "days of yore" of the 1960s), the eater, like the twits, has gone to seed, back to nature. Gone is the reassuring arm of the village in the fairy tale's comforting worldview. The conviviality of Italian restaurants and artists' shared plates is also nowhere to be found. Instead, the tale ends with "Mrs. Twit, clapping her hands and stamping her feet and rocking with horrible laughter."[31] Truly horrible. The resemblance between a plate of worms and a plate of spaghetti is, indeed, too close, sometimes abject, and perhaps even fear inducing.

The association linking spaghetti and the world of slithering animals is picked up elsewhere, and also in representational form. In 1999 Vik Muniz produced a Medusa plate that portrays an exact copy of Caravaggio's *Medusa* (1596/97) in marinara sauce.[32] On this plate, the spaghetti has transformed from the merely grotesque (worms) to the horrific (snakes), as the goddess shrieks into the face of the unsuspecting diner. Among the suggestions for how to display it is, by definition, the idea that the Muniz plate should serve as a support for actual pasta. Medusa's image is shown on a shield at the moment of her beheading by Perseus, meaning it is a reflection of her. As blood pours forth from her wound, it would mingle metaphorically with the last spaghetti on the plate, forming an imaginary snake-humanoid, blood-saturated tomato sauce. One imagines the holiday party where the plates were given as gifts: a social atmosphere marked by wine and pasta, friendships, and the easy comforts of the collector's home for whom the plate was made. And then the abject intervenes, or terror or, more likely, joy in the sudden recognition of a well-known masterpiece masquerading under a blanket of pasta.

Judging by the plate and the video and the recent food shared by those lucky enough to attend a meal hosted by Tiravanija, the case for and against pasta is, it seems, very much open.

Hannah B Higgins is Professor and University Scholar in the Department of Art History at the University of Illinois at Chicago.

---

[1] Tomie dePaola, *Strega Nona* (New York: Simon and Schuster, 1975).

[2] Maguelonne Toussaint-Samat, *The History of Food*, trans. Anthea Bell (Cambridge, MA, and Oxford, UK: Blackwell, 1992).

[3] Ibid.

[4] Ibid., 194.

[5] Ibid., 189.

[6] Filippo Tommaso Marinetti, "Manifesto of Futurist Cooking," *Gazzetta del Popolo* (Turin), December 28, 1930, reprinted in *Futurist Cookbook,* trans. Suzanne Brill (San Francisco: Bedford Arts, 1989), 33–40.

[7] Marinetti, "The Holy Palate Restaurant," in Marinetti, *Futurist Cookbook,* 65.

[8] Marco Ramperti, "An Open Letter to F. T. Marinetti," *L'Ambrosiano*, n.d., reprinted in Marinetti, *Futurist Cookbook*, 43.

[9] Marinetti's "Pasta Originated with the Ostrogoths," in Marinetti, *Futurist Cookbook,* contains a long quotation by Silvano, 50.

[10] Pasta was invented in many places, but wasn't cooked at an industrial scale until the invention of the mechanical kneader in early fifteenth-century Naples. Not coincidentally, this is the region where *Strega Nona* takes place. For a list of its appearance at different times, and also its association with the Baltic origins of the Ostrogoths, see Toussaint-Samat, *History of Food,* 187–90.

[11] See Jane Ziegelman, "The Baldizzi Family," in *97 Orchard: An Edible History of Five Immigrant Families in One New York Tenement* (New York: Harper Collins, 2011), 186. During an average month, an Italian laborer living in America could expect to eat: 34.1 pounds of bread, 19.3 pounds of pasta, and .24 pounds of rice, and a scant 2.31 pounds of meat.

[12] Ibid., 193.

[13] Marinetti, "Marinetti will officially open 'The holy palate,'" in Marinetti, *Futurist Cookbook,* 68.

[14] Ibid., 65.

[15] Marinetti, "the aerofood," in Ibid., 84.

[16] Marinetti, "Nourishment by Radio," in Ibid., 67.

[17] Text from the original napkin/certificate, designed by Ann Noël and printed for Emmett Williams and Robert Filliou at Cal-Arts, for the EAT ART show held at Daniel Spoerri's gallery in Düsseldorf. Eat Art Gallery Edition, 1971.

[18] Emmett Williams, *My Life in Flux—And Vice Versa* (London: Thames and Hudson, 1992), 128.

[19] On June 5, 1963, the foodwork was launched in an art context with the artists in absentia at the Galerie Raymond Cordier in Paris—actually they were in a bar on the other side of the Seine.

[20] Ibid.

[21] Pierre Bourdieu, *Distinction: A Social Critique of the Judgment of Taste* (London: Routledge, 1998), 41.

[22] Filliou, quoted in Williams, *My Life in Flux,* 128.

[23] Spoerri opened the Restaurant de la Galerie J in Paris in 1963 and the Restaurant Spoerri in Düsseldorf in 1967, and in 1970 opened the Eat-Art-Gallery upstairs.

[24] Eric Andersen, *Spaghetti al Vento* (Opus 1908), 1978. Text at Archivio Francesco Conz, Verona, Italy.

[25] Thomas Kellein, "Essay," in *Rirkrit Tiravanija: Cook Book* (London: Edition Hansjörg Mayer and Bangkok, Thailand: River Books, 2010), 146.

[26] "Interview with the Artist in His Home in Chiang Mai, Thailand, 22 May 2010," in Ibid., 7.

[27] Ibid., 139.

[28] Ibid., 152.

[29] Martin and Inge Riebeek, "Spaghetti with Worms" (2010), unpaginated film still and recipe card, in *Eat Your Art Out: Food in the Arts* (recipe box catalogue), Harry Ruhé and Jeannette Dekeukeleire, eds., (Amsterdam: Gallery A and artKitchen Gallery, 2010).

[30] Roald Dahl, "The Wormy Spaghetti," in *The Twits* (New York: Puffin, 1980), 16.

[31] Ibid., 17.

[32] The plate was produced as part of an annual Christmas edition for friends of MoMA board members and collectors Peter and Eileen Norton in 1999. I saw this wonderful work in the collection of Nora Halpern and Kerry Brougher, Bethesda, Maryland.

CONCEPTUAL AND PERFORMATIVE FEASTS: 1960s–1970s

Marina Abramović and Ulay

ON NOVEMBER 30, 1979, the performance artists Marina Abramović and Ulay celebrated their shared birthday by creating the performance *Communist Body/Fascist Body*. The piece was part of the long-term collaboration between Abramović and Ulay that began in the mid-1970s. The two artists met in 1975 while Abramović was visiting Amsterdam from her native Serbia (then Yugoslavia) and began working together shortly after. In 1976, Abramović and Ulay purchased a van, where they lived for four years, traveling and performing together throughout Europe. In 1979 they moved into the Amsterdam apartment in which they performed *Communist Body/Fascist Body.* Partners in both art and love, Abramović and Ulay used their own bodies and psyches as primary material for their art. Many of their works took the form of pared-down actions carried to physical and mental extremes. In *Breathing In/Breathing Out* (1977), for instance, they locked lips, breathing in each other's exhalations until the increasingly stale air pushed both to the edge of physical collapse. Simple in structure, their performances were often meant to engage the audience's response on an emotional—even primal—level, while also provoking reflection on classic philosophical problems such as the definition and limits of the self and the body, and the power dynamics inherent to any human relationship. The pair famously ended their collaboration with the performance *The Lovers: The Great Wall Walk* (1988) in which they walked from opposite ends of the Great Wall of China, meeting briefly in the middle as the final moment in their collaborative practice.

Communist Body/Fascist Body took place just before midnight on the artists' birthday, when a small group of friends was invited to their Amsterdam apartment. There, the guests found one small table beautifully set with silver, crystal, German champagne, white bread, and caviar. Another held cheap Russian versions of the same (e.g. toilet paper rather than damask napkins). A third table displayed the artists' birth certificates, each marked with a symbol of national identity: Communist star and Fascist swastika. In the back of the space, Abramović and Ulay lay together on a mattress under a red blanket, apparently asleep.

Communist Body/Fascist Body wove together love and friendship, bodies and politics, guests and hosts. The presence of the quietly sleeping, united couple contrasted with the way the tables foregrounded their separate identities, shaped by all that they had ingested growing up in different—indeed hostile—nations, ideologies, and economies. The juxtaposition also upended the usual interactions between host and guest. The hosts were present—physically—but also absent—asleep (or performing sleep)—and therefore not attending to the host's usual duties in caring for guests. The guests' varied reactions became part of the piece: some were disturbed, others relaxed, but eventually they took responsibility for creating their own party by popping the champagne and consuming the repast. We know about the guests' responses because Abramović and Ulay wove documentation into the fabric of the performance: a friend filmed the evening, they edited that footage together with subsequent audio interviews, and then completed the loop by screening the resulting film for their guests in the very apartment in which the performance occurred.

Although Abramović and Ulay established the original work as a closed circuit, they intended for it to have a life for an audience beyond that initial group of participants. Until now, it has only been shown as a film, but on the occasion of *Feast,* Abramović and Ulay created a new form of presentation. Rather than restaging the event with live performers as they have when re-performing other early work, they designed a new installation in which a sleek tableau recreates the original setting as a way to anchor and vivify the film.

OPPOSITE: *Communist Body/Fascist Body,* installation view, Smart Museum of Art, 2012

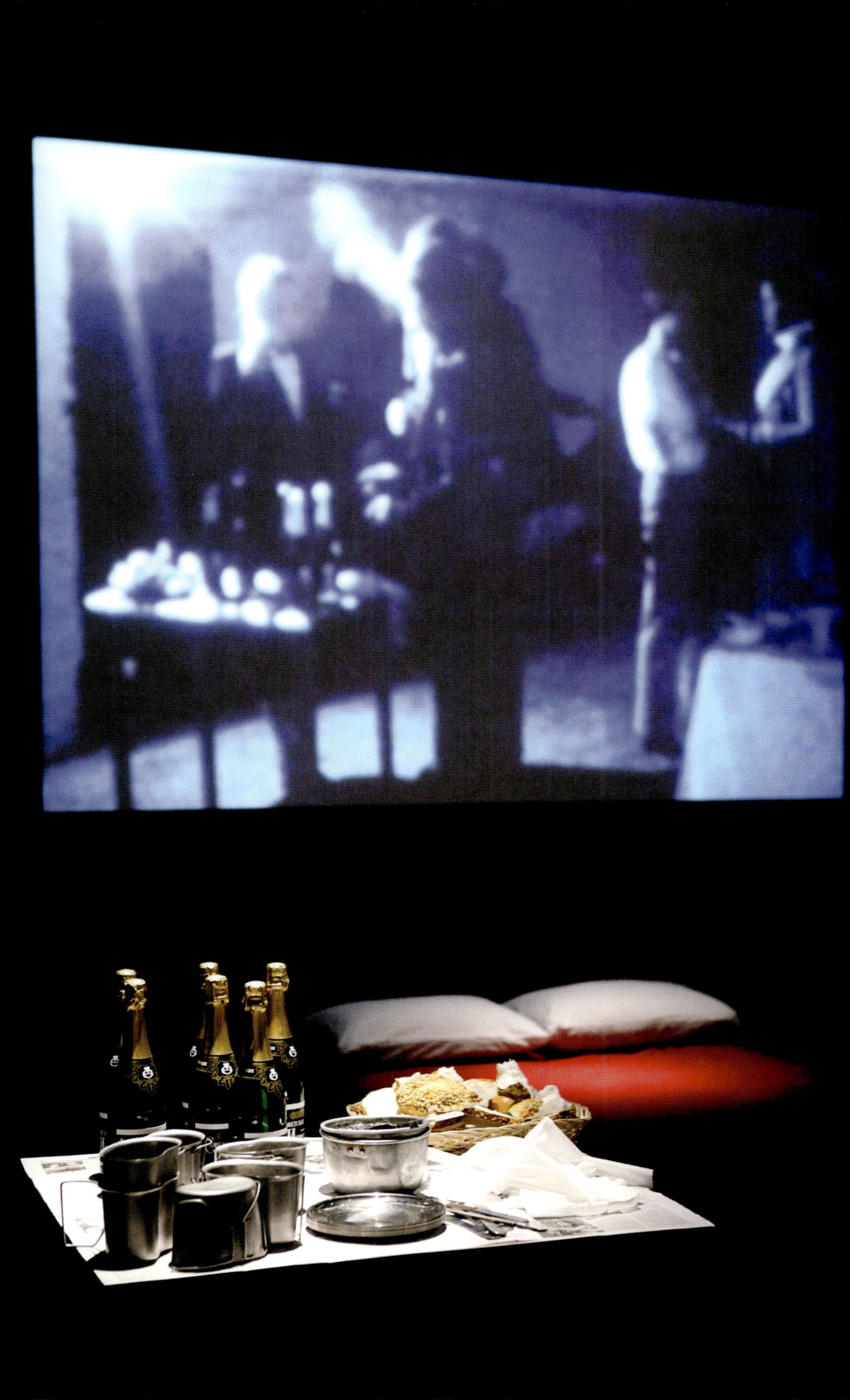

Interview

SMART: Can you please tell us about *Communist Body/Fascist Body*?

MARINA ABRAMOVIĆ: Let's make a long story as short as I can. Ulay and I met on our birthday and we discovered on our meeting that we had the same birthday, which was November 30. When we started working together, we made a tradition that we would make some kind of performance on every birthday.

We have the two birth certificates with two opposite signs of the state. He was born in 1943 in Solingen, Germany—in the middle of the war—and on his certificate is a swastika. I was born in Belgrade, Yugoslavia, in 1946, just after the war, and on my birth certificate is the five-point, red, Communist star. These two certificates can't be more opposite: his presents fascism and mine presents communism. We found this a very interesting basis for an art piece. The piece was set up in the loft, in which we lived. We were living in a very poor state in Holland, just a big, empty space. We invited eleven guests—very close friends—and asked them to come fifteen minutes before midnight. That's all we told them; we didn't even tell them it was our birthday. They arrived and found the following situation: a completely empty loft and the two of us sleeping in a small bed covered by a red blanket. On two tables were different arrangements. On the Ulay table was a beautiful satin cover and linen napkins, and a beautiful silver tray with caviar and bread—white bread, toasted—and then six crystal champagne glasses, and six bottles of the best krug champagne, and six silver spoons and six silver knives ready to be to used. On my side, on the other table, was a *Pravda* newspaper and six bottles of cream Russian champagne, caviar put in metal cups that were very simple and down-to-earth. Then, a third little table on which we placed, very carefully, our two certificates, and there were

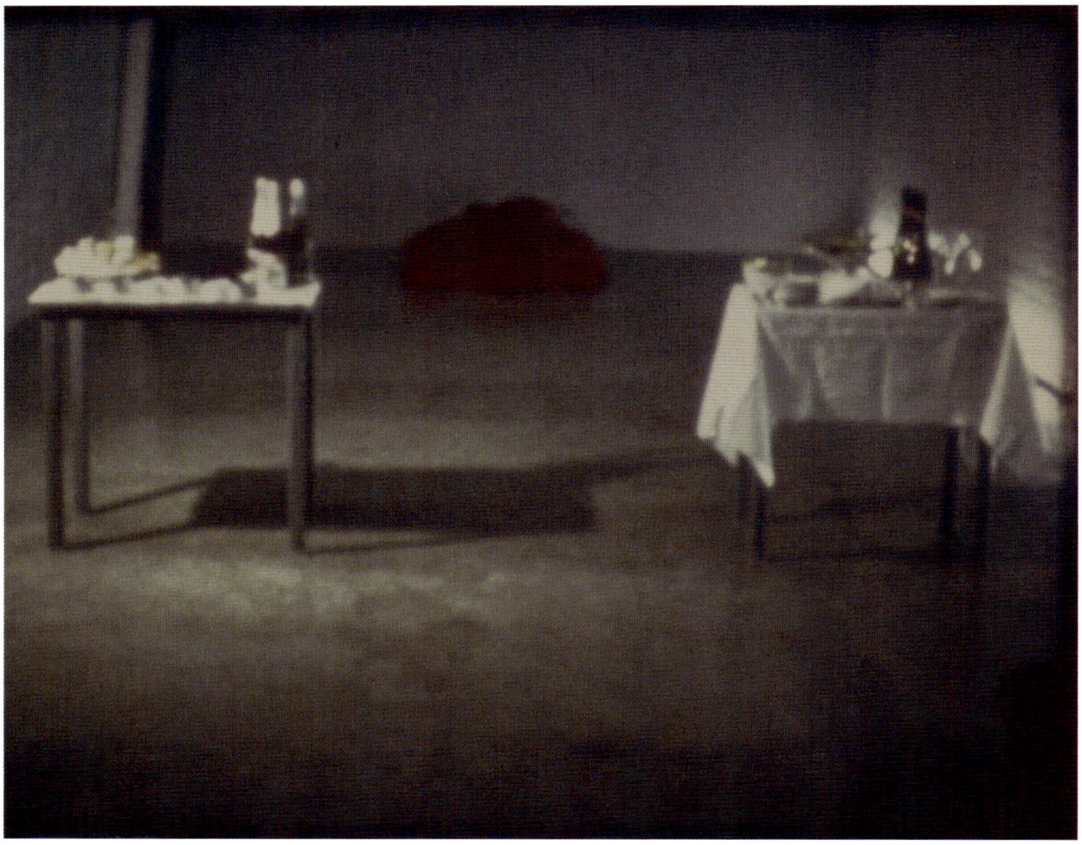

Film still documenting *Communist Body/Fascist Body,* performance at Zoutkeetsgracht 116/118 Amsterdam, November 30, 1979

instructions for guests: you can drink from each of the tables, or eat from one or another or both, and that's it.

When the eleven guests arrived, there was a situation that was very uncomfortable. They came here and they didn't know what to do. We were sleeping and we didn't wake up. After a while they started drinking the Russian champagne and then drinking the champagne from the German side of the table. They stayed for a while, they drank everything, and then one person actually was so tired, she put the little blanket next to us and slept all night. This was that situation. We filmed the whole thing during this process. After three weeks, we revisited these people and asked them what happened and filmed their answers. It was amazing that we got eleven completely different answers. It was similar to *Rashomon*, the Kurosawa movie, when seven different people saw the killing in the forest and then sit around the fire discussing what everybody saw, and everybody saw a little bit, but the story was like seven different stories. We had eleven different stories. This piece stays so much in my memory especially now, looking back. Nine people out of the eleven people are already dead.

SMART: Could you talk about the guests and their responses?

MA: The combination of friends was important. Some friends didn't have something to do with art, but we had the curator of the museum, we had the photographer, the designer. Each person with his or her own profession brought their own reflection to the piece, reflecting their profession, and that was really interesting. Somebody who is busy with industrial design will look more in the architecture of the piece and the way things are placed. There was another friend of ours who's an artist, who sees this as a

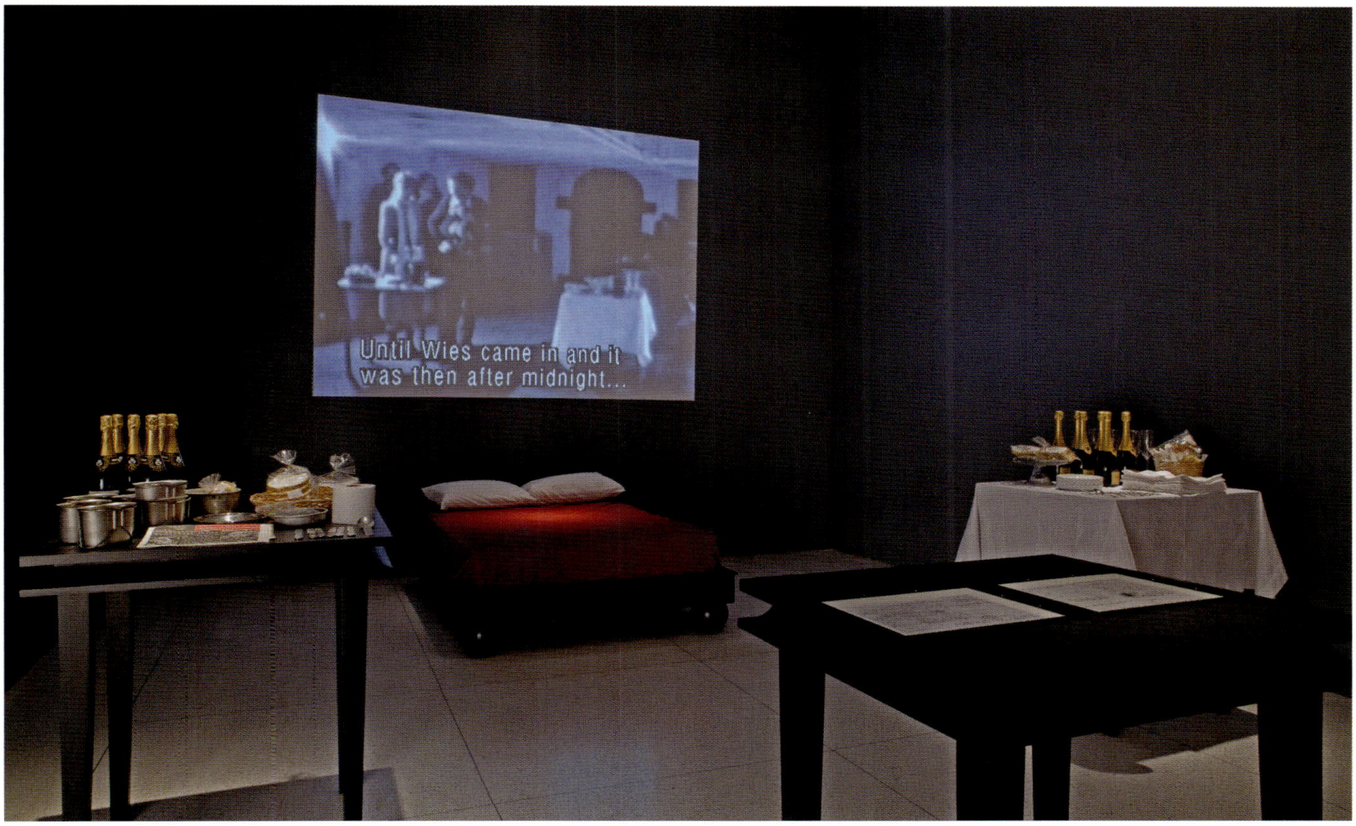

Communist Body/Fascist Body, installation view, Smart Museum of Art, 2012

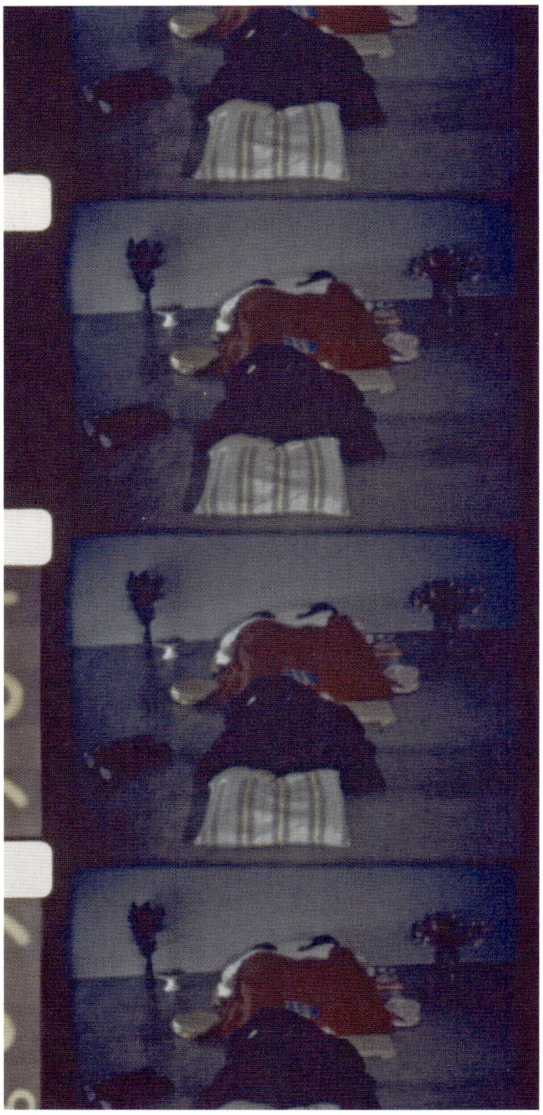

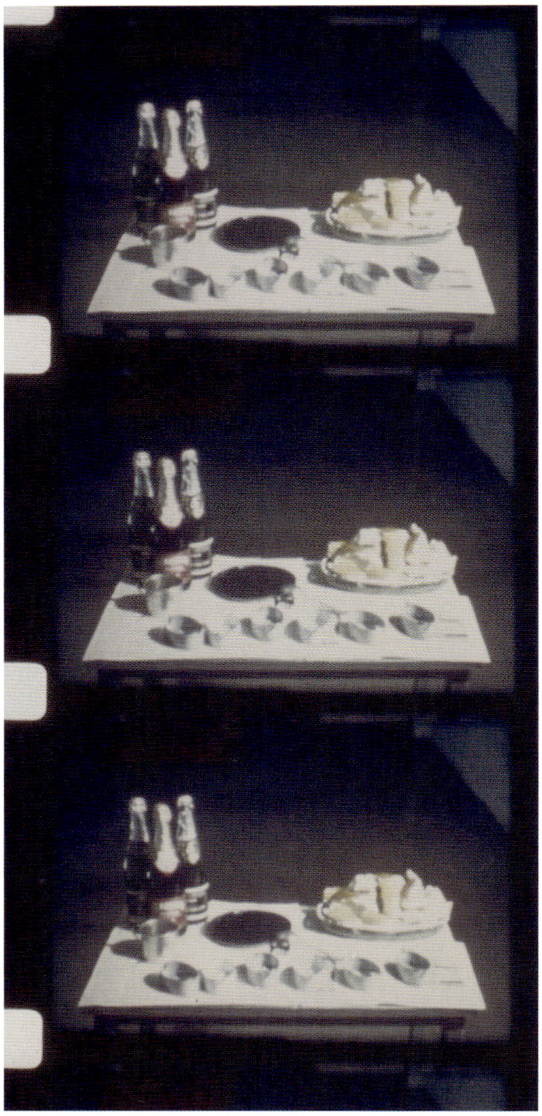

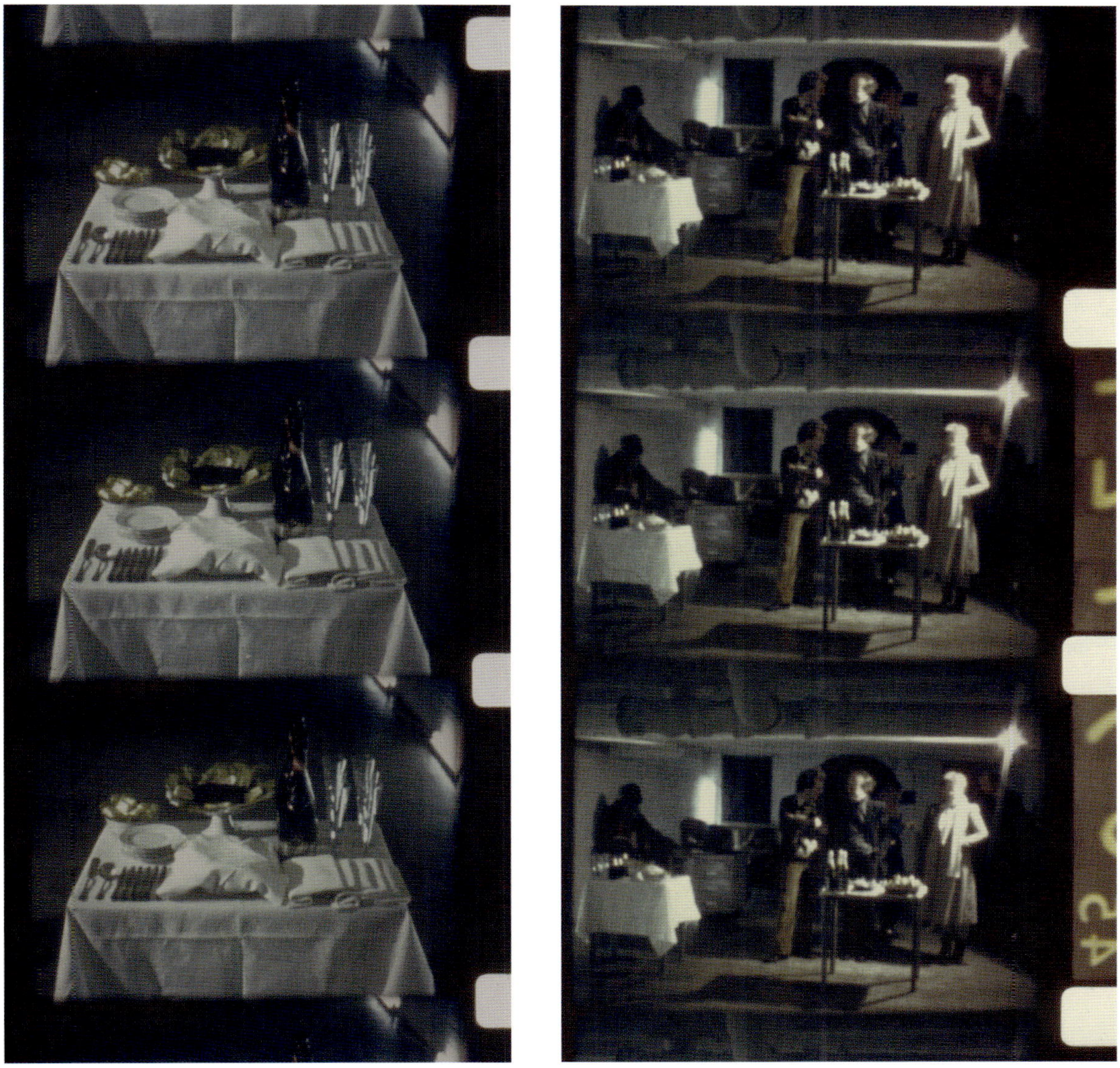

Film stills documenting *Communist Body/Fascist Body* performance at Zoutkeetsgracht 116/118 Amsterdam, November 30, 1979

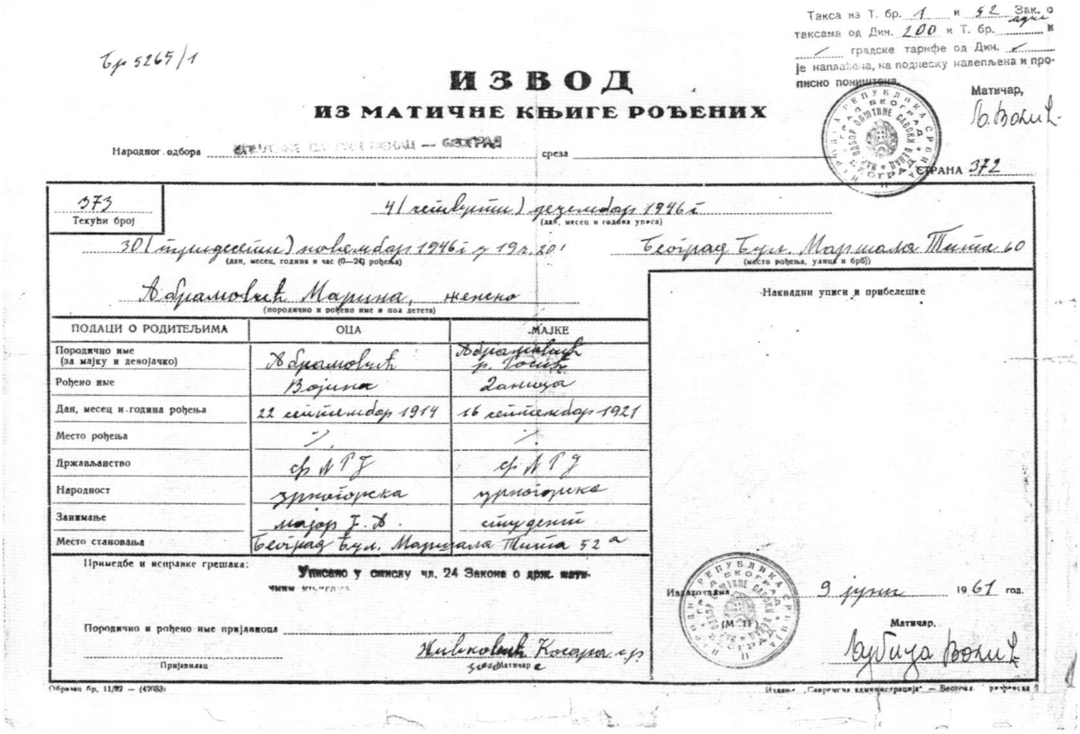

ИЗВОД
ИЗ МАТИЧНЕ КЊИГЕ РОЂЕНИХ

Народног одбора ... — БЕОГРАД среза

Текући број 373

4 (четврти) децембар 1946 г. (дан, месец и година уписа)

30 (тридесети) новембар 1946 г. у 19 ч. 30' (дан, месец, година и час (0—24) рођења)

Београд Бул. Маршала Тита 60 (место рођења, улица и број)

Абрамовић Марина, женско (породично и рођено име и пол детета)

ПОДАЦИ О РОДИТЕЉИМА	ОЦА	МАЈКЕ
Породично име (за мајку и девојачко)	Абрамовић	Абрамовић р. Росић
Рођено име	Војин	Даница
Дан, месец и година рођења	22 септембар 1914	16 септембар 1921
Место рођења		
Држављанство	ФНРЈ	ФНРЈ
Народност	црногорска	црногорка
Занимање	мајор Ј.А.	студент
Место становања	Београд Бул. Маршала Тита 52а	

Примедбе и исправке грешака:

Породично и рођено име пријављиоца

Пријављивац

Матичар

Накнадни уписи и прибелешке

Страна 372

Издато 9 јуни 1961 год.

Матичар

Marina Abramović's birth certificate, issued in the former Yugoslavia, November 30, 1946

kind of Egyptian division of the city of life, and the city of dead, and that one side was dead and one side was life. And another person had problems with his relationships so he was seeing the alienation and loneliness. People actually project their own life onto you, taking elements of what they see, but actually recycling and projecting their own life. We are just the mirror in many ways.

SMART: Could you speak about the role of hospitality in the project, particularly the relationship between guest and host?

MA: I don't think there was any kind of relationship like that because we were not really hosts. We were trying to be remote. We were trying to be like props, like the three tables and the bed. It was true that there were offerings so that people could actually eat and drink from these two tables, but we could not participate. We could not witness it and we could to be part of it in any other way, except acoustically. I could feel their presence, that's all. It was a reverse situation with the food. Lots of artists make work with food being consumed and shared, but in this case it was different.

There were so many contradictions—which was really the purpose of that piece. The display of food was an incredible contradiction, from the perfectly arranged table to the very kind of basic, peasant offering of food.

It was more about having these two artists working together who are born the same day. We met on our birthday, and we had these insane certificates that convey the two opposite beliefs of the governments, which actually strove to keep us apart. Yet we've been fused together. We wanted to show this togetherness because when we sleep and hold each other on this red blanket, somehow we become symbols of togetherness, while the two certificates are really about separation. That was the idea: that we definitely have to sleep and we became the object of reflection of some people who are together and in love. It was an object there for people to

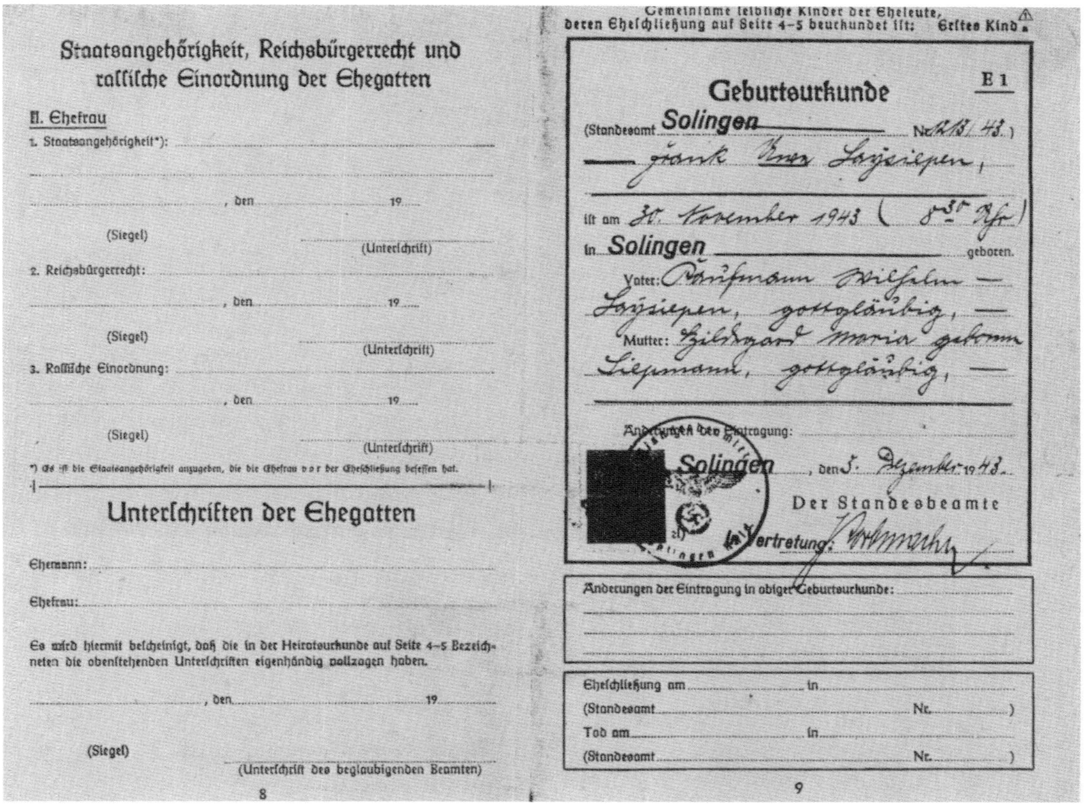

Staatsangehörigkeit, Reichsbürgerrecht und rassische Einordnung der Ehegatten

II. Ehefrau

1. Staatsangehörigkeit*): ....

.........., den .... 19....

(Siegel) (Unterschrift)

2. Reichsbürgerrecht: ....

.........., den .... 19....

(Siegel) (Unterschrift)

3. Rassische Einordnung: ....

.........., den .... 19....

(Siegel) (Unterschrift)

*) Es ist die Staatsangehörigkeit anzugeben, die die Ehefrau vor der Eheschließung besessen hat.

Unterschriften der Ehegatten

Ehemann: ....

Ehefrau: ....

Es wird hiermit bescheinigt, daß die in der Heiratsurkunde auf Seite 4–5 Bezeichneten die obenstehenden Unterschriften eigenhändig vollzogen haben.

.........., den .... 19....

(Siegel) (Unterschrift des beglaubigenden Beamten)

8

Gemeinsame leibliche Kinder der Eheleute, deren Eheschließung auf Seite 4–5 beurkundet ist: Erstes Kind.

Geburtsurkunde E 1

(Standesamt Solingen Nr. [illegible]/43.)

— Frank Uwe Laysiepen, —

ist am 30. November 1943 (8.30 Uhr)

in Solingen geboren.

Vater: Kaufmann Wilhelm — Laysiepen, gottgläubig, —

Mutter: Hildegard Maria geborene Siepmann, gottgläubig, —

Änderungen der Eintragung: ....

[redacted] Solingen, den 5. Dezember 1943.

Der Standesbeamte

In Vertretung: [signature]

Änderungen der Eintragung in obiger Geburtsurkunde: ....

Eheschließung am .... in ....

(Standesamt .... Nr. ....)

Tod am .... in ....

(Standesamt .... Nr. ....)

9

Ulay's birth certificate, issued in Germany, November 30, 1943

reflect. It was about togetherness and being in love.

SMART: You made the process of documentation part of the deep structure of *Communist Body/ Fascist Body*. Could you say more about that?

MA: I think more and more about how to represent a performance once it's done. I sometimes find that just seeing the video documentation is not enough. One of the first presentations I had in that way was *Lips of Thomas*. I made it some years ago, and I created an architectural space with the ice cross, with the cooling system under the podium, which you could not see. As a result, the ice cross was always there, in the museum. It never actually melted. And then the chair, the table, the razor, and on the backside was a projection of the piece itself. The public can react much more strongly when they see something like a model of the space, rather than just seeing the video material. Sometimes you need more than just the video documentation to trigger the mind and reconstruct how the work actually was. That need drives the decision now to actually make this table, and the bed, and the red blanket on which nobody is sleeping. We project the film so the public can access the performance.

SMART: Could you talk about the difference between this kind of re-presentation and the re-performances that were part of your exhibition last year at the Museum of Modern Art, in which you performed one work yourself, but also had live actors recreating some of your earlier performances?

MA: It's a good example. For the piece in MoMA I had three cameras: one camera on me all the time, one other camera on the person sitting opposite of me, and we had a third camera that actually filmed both situations, so there were three points of view. The camera was on all the time, totaling three times 716 hours, which is an enormous amount of material. It took me almost one year of editing, actually non-editing, because we put them in real time next to each other. It's now an installation that was made and built like a diary. It includes three months—March, April, May—and each square of the months presents one day—Monday, Tuesday, Wednesday, whatever—and you see the real people seeing real time. It's not a real experience of performance, but documentation can evoke a lot of emotions if it's done in a certain way. Your approach is very important. I have been busy for a long time with this question of documentation because in the early 1970s there weren't rules on how documentation should be made. The photographer or the filmmaker would just take different shots and then you have to come and look at the material. Mostly it's disastrous. Right now I really like to have control over the documentation, so before I perform, I include it as a part of the project: a very strict, radical way for it to be filmed so that I can use the material in ways that are as close to the performance as possible.

SMART: What instructions did you offer to the cameraperson for *Communist Body/Fascist Body*?

MA: The cameraperson was not just any cameraperson but rather one of the most wonderful and special avant-garde artists: filmmaker Tomislav Gotovac. He was from Croatia and unfortunately died just a few months ago. He was one of the pioneers of the new cinema in ex-Yugoslavia. He was visiting at the time in Amsterdam, which was so lucky. He knew the situation. He knew the rules: that we would never stand up or wake up. He did a great job. But also, we didn't have money, so we're talking about a Super 8 camera and many Super 8 cassettes, no color corrections or any of this, and no sound. This Super 8 material was transferred to video so the quality is not glamorous or high definition like today, but still there is some kind of sentimentality about Super 8 we all have. It's kept the image alive.

SMART: Could you speak about what it means to you to be recreating this piece now?

MA: Now the situation is so different. Ulay and I separated in 1988, walking the Chinese wall. This pressure was very difficult and painful and we didn't see or talk to each other for seven years after that. Then we established contact and it's friendly, but that's all. It's not close. We made a very important body of work together, and it was a big love story too. And right now, Ulay is not well. He's very sick and somehow this piece has taken on additional meaning. In order to reconstruct it right now in this period of our life is very important to me. I've been talking to him about the piece and I don't have any memory of how many bottles we had of champagne, or how many this or that. We also have a huge problem now: he doesn't have his certificate—he doesn't know where it is—so we are trying to look in the books and find a way to reproduce it. We changed so many houses, we traveled so much, we lived in cars. I think it's even a miracle that the documentation I have right now was actually preserved and that we still have it.

De Appel gallery at that time was one of the first galleries in Europe to present performance art. We only showed it as a film then. Later it was shown in several museums and in different festivals, also as a video: people ask and we will show it. But for some time we didn't show it at all; it was not part of my retrospective in MoMA, and not part of my current retrospective at Garage in Moscow. So I feel like taking it out is a great thing to do, and also giving it these new clothes: recreating the objects and figuring it out, giving it space, and seeing how it can function and how the public is going to react. It's very exciting that we now reconstruct this old piece so it can be presented closer to the original.

SMART: How does this piece fit into the broader context of your work?

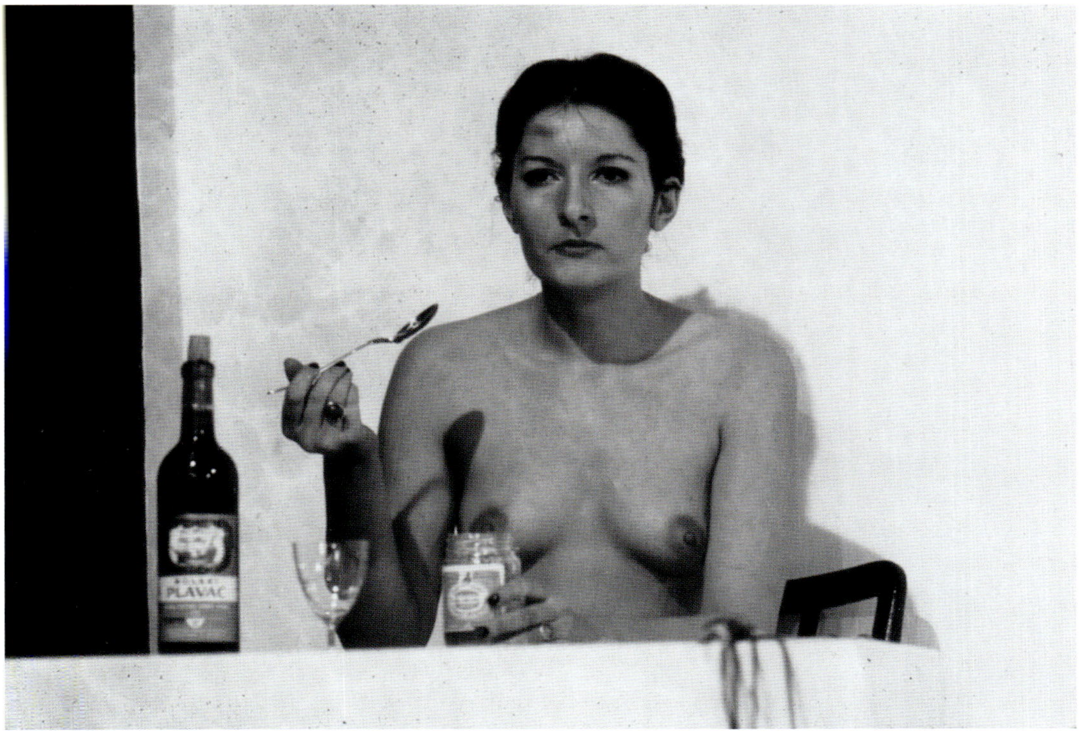

Marina Abramović performing *Lips of Thomas*, Galerie Krinzinger, Innsbruck, 1975

MA: I am not a painter, even if I studied to be a painter for a long time. I really was not interested in having a studio space to create two-dimensional works. When I started working with my body it was a really big realization: that I had become a performance artist. Being a performance artist in the 1970s was very hard, because you can't live from performance art and you have to do other things. I was teaching most of the time to support myself.

If you ask: What is a performance? What is the theater? And what is the difference, between the two—how it all works?—my explanation is I think that performance is when artists create mental and physical space in front of the audience with an exact time and place and you enter into a specific situation, mentally and physically, in front of an audience for the first time, without rehearsing, without playing somebody else. It's a reality-dialogue with the audience and the performance. That is a big difference from the theater. This is what I've been doing for the last forty years or so: being a performance artist and trying to create situations when the performance stopped being an alternative form of art and became mainstream art. In the old days, photography and video were not considered an art form, but now they are. I put all my life into creating space. Performance needed space and dignity, which was denied to it for a long, long time. And I think now it's happening. I'm really happy not only to deal with my own work, but I'm trying also to think about future artists and to create my institute of performing arts. I actually want to preserve the history of performance art for other generations. So that's some idea of the heritage and also the legacy that I'm busy with at this moment.

SMART: How do food and the meal figure into your performance work, beyond *Communist Body/Fascist Body*?

MA: I've used food—a lot! I made a piece called

Onion (1996) in which I'm eating an onion and complaining about my life. I see peeling the onion as peeling the layers and also it's very domestic, I like it. Then in *The Lips of Thomas* (1975), I used honey, I used wine. I also have lots of work with spirit-cooking recipes. I actually create my own recipes for spirit-cooking, which is inedible. I made them as graffiti on the wall using pig blood since it's closest to human blood. One of the spirit-cooking recipes would be: "With a sharp knife, cut deeply into the finger of your left hand. Eat the pain." Or another would be: "In time of doubt, keep small meteorite stone in your mouth." Or my favorite: "Take eleven leaves of fresh green cabbage, mix with thirteen-thousand grams of pure jealousy, cook in iron pot till all the water evaporates and eat it just before attack." Or: "Mix breast milk with sperm milk, drink it on earthquake nights." And so on and so on, I have lots of recipes like this, they are my spirit-cooking recipes in which I deal with food but in very different ways.

SMART: Does thinking about hospitality factor into your practice?

MA: If I think about hospitality it's more in terms of what the public means to me. So many artists say that when they perform they don't see the public. They come into some kind of "zone" or the public is not important to them, they're doing it for themselves, and for me it's very different. Modern dancer Martha Graham once said: "Wherever the dancer dances is holy ground." And I have my own statement. I say, "Wherever the public stands for me is the holy ground." So for me, the public completes the piece. For me, without the public, the performance wouldn't have any sense. I would never perform for myself; it has to be for the public, and in that way I think that performance in the deeper sense is about hospitality. It's that you actually open yourself to the public and show your vulnerability, your contradictions, and be there in the full sense, for them.

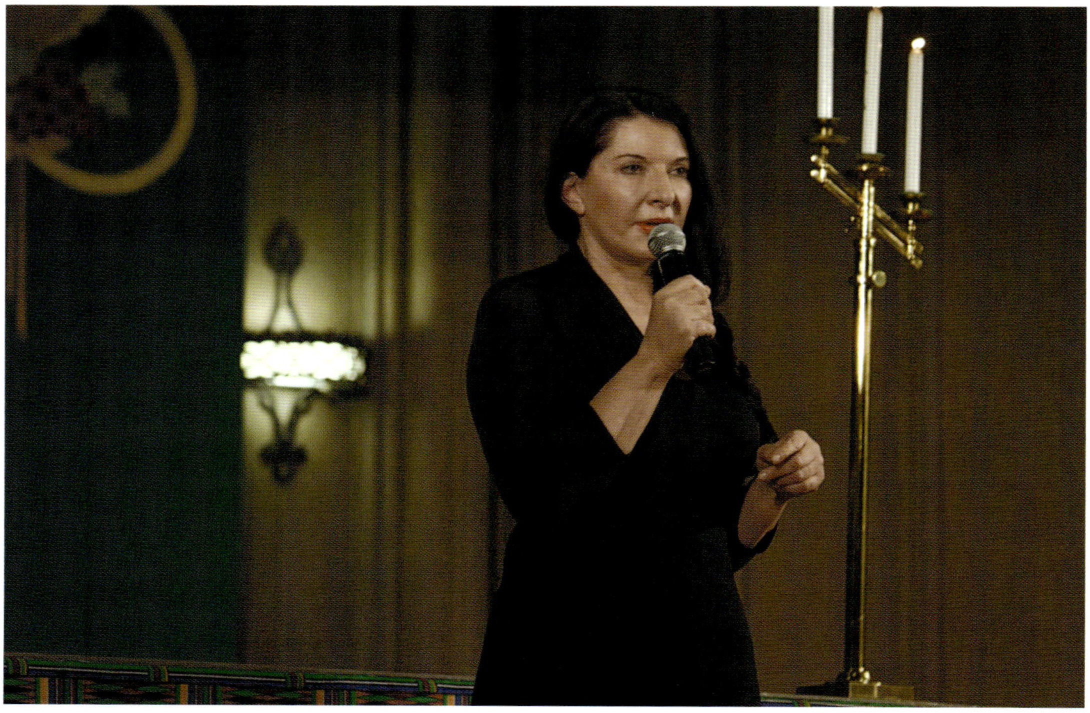

Marina Abramović lectures at the First Methodist Church, presented by the Smart Museum of Art and the Chicago Humanities Festival, February 16, 2012

Communist Body/Fascist Body
by Marina Abramović

In a chosen space. 2 tables placed parallel to each other. One table is set with: a white damask table cloth, damask napkins, porcelain dishes, crystal champagne glasses, silver tableware, German champagne and caviar. The other table is set with: a copy of the newspaper *Pravda*, toilet paper, enamel dishes, enamel cups, aluminum knives and forks, Russian champagne, and caviar. On a third table our birth certificates are displayed:

Marina, born 30 November, 1946 in Belgrade, Yugoslavia.
My certificate bears a government stamp showing the communist star.
Ulay, born 30 November, 1943 in Solingen, Germany.
His certificate bears a government stamp showing the swastika.

10 meters behind the two tables a mattress with a white linen and a red blanket is placed.
11 guests are invited to come 15 minutes before midnight.
Performance.
We sleep on the mattress, covered by a white linen and red blanket.
30 November, 1979, Zoutkeetsgracht 116/118, Amsterdam.

Three weeks later we visited the eleven guests.
With their agreement we recorded their impressions for the film soundtrack.
Three months later we presented the film to the eleven guests at the place where the performance happened.

Communist Body / Fascist Body

Selected excerpts from film transcript

Dorine Mignot

. . . And then exactly the opposite happened of what I had thought would happen: that you were lying in bed, maybe hypnotized, maybe with a sleeping pill. But that wasn't quite clear, actually. So I just sat down at a corner of the table and thought: well, who knows, maybe something else is gonna happen . . . And those two little tables, that too had something of a Last Supper atmosphere. So anything could happen, really.

Then very gradually those other people were coming in, and that was something like a ritual, because you were sleeping over there and nobody really knew how to react. In the beginning nobody dared to come near . . . Then I believe Josien went over to the bed. That seemed a sort of sacrilegious thing to do, to go over there and look if you were really asleep, or perhaps could be woken up. Then it was midnight and your birthday began. Everybody was putting his present somewhere around, because they somehow didn't dare to put them beside your bed . . .

And then people started to investigate things . . . and started to see symbols in everything.

And then we began to eat, when it turned out that you were sound asleep, that you probably wouldn't wake up, that you intended not to, but it seemed a bit strange, a bit awkward, to sit there drinking champagne . . . like: here's to you! Or to ourselves! To the situation!

Hartmut Kowalke

. . . There was a kind of boundary which you couldn't cross at all. And that I found . . . actually I thought that was really a classical picture; somebody makes a thing and you can't understand, you can't come near it . . . But then at one time I also thought that it was a bit ridiculous, because it made me think of a museum, in a very classical way—not the Municipal Museum or something like it, but rather a Madame Tussaud's kind of museum, where people walk past objects, at a distance, and the both of you sort of became wax figures, a kind of cast of yourselves . . .

Elke Osthus

. . . I remember that in the beginning I was only . . . jealous of you, because I was very tired as well and I just wanted to lie down beside you. It all looked very cozy indeed. But I didn't even dare to come near the bed, because there was this weird atmosphere. Until Wies came in and it was already after midnight and the bottles were opened. That was really nice, actually, and also a time when everybody was quite relaxed.

Gijs van Tuyl

So it was a birthday party and you were both having your birthday at the same time. Usually at birthday parties, the people whose birthday it is are at the center of attention . . . they talk to everybody and see to it that everybody is having a good time. But you had turned things upside down by being asleep, by not being present so to speak.

But then I asked myself, if you are absent while sleeping, maybe you are more present than ever, because all of the gestures you make and the words you utter during a conversation, you wonder what it is exactly you are revealing of yourself. And if you're asleep, which means not externalizing anything verbally, maybe then you are present in a much more significant way.

. . . Furthermore, the thing that struck me very much was . . . well, there was an uncertainty with all these people, like: what do we have to do? What don't we have to do? Because for most things there are all sorts of codes. Like how to behave at birthday parties. Yes, you congratulate someone, and then you hand over your present.

But all that was here . . . there was uncertainty about the codes of behavior, which was quite pleasant because I noticed that too, that it wasn't really an aggressive, or alarming kind of uncertainty, but a very relaxed one, one in which at a certain moment people attempted timidly to shift the boundaries . . .

Well, somebody screwed up courage and went over to the tables. And that, I thought, was a sort of change-over, literally a sort of expansion of the boundaries, a trying to get in touch with you directly.

Louwrien Weijers

Your birthday performance—30 November 1979—was a heavy one, I felt. Let's take it to extremes: it was a nightmare.

It was for me like going to a wedding of two people, let's say. A birthday is something which is a happy event. Then, instead of going to the wedding, I went to the funeral of those two people. So I felt very sad in a way when I came in, in a happy mood, and found two people asleep. Being asleep is almost like being dead. So when you didn't wake up I almost felt like I was there looking at you both in the other world beyond this life . . .

There was no center in the atmosphere anymore, because the center was you . . . So these people who were there did not know how to behave. What you saw, and maybe the film will show it, is that the two beautiful tables that were there, were within a few minutes absolutely torn apart like a group of ants had jumped on them.

I didn't know how to react to that. I took a piece of bread with caviar, and I drank champagne, and I liked the champagne. And at one point I thought: well, let's make a party of it. And on the other hand I thought: let me go and look at these two people sleeping. So there were absolutely two extreme emotions clashing all the time.

Until at last there was nothing to fight against anymore and there was acceptance. And it was a little bit . . . a word, more than sad . . . absolutely distressing, I would say.

Antje von Graevenitz

. . . When I came in, I . . . thought it was . . . like a beautiful picture, black, white, red; black hair, white sheet, and scarlet the blanket. And also everything was made ready for the guests. But I still expected it any moment to be blown up.

. . . Actually, that was like a fairy tale, while you were lying there like snow-white and rose-red, or something . . . so completely . . . so gentle, and we over here, we who met up on the other side, that was a bit coldish. And also we were busy talking about art and artists, etc. . . .

And somehow I couldn't really link the two together.

But I could link them together the moment somebody was bold enough to take something from the table and we began to eat. Now we were involved as well. And then we found out . . . yes, also the two tables had to do with your origin. And that was really remarkable, I didn't want . . . though I am German too, in any way to be identified with that exquisite table, and I couldn't imagine that you'd present that . . . this German bourgeois thing. But then I realized that Marina didn't mean to present the Russian food in that way either, really . . . that actually it was just a metaphor.

And . . . for, as I saw Marina's table and liked it at first sight, I really felt the same about it as I had felt about things I'd seen in China. You know, they have a very simple, almost crude form, but still much more elaborate than these champagne glasses. Also, particularly how things had been selected, they were so . . . I believe they were drinking cups from the army, but they had absolutely beautiful proportions.

. . . and of course I noticed that . . . well, contrary to the other birthday performances at which I have been present, this one actually showed complete harmony between the two of you. There weren't two people anymore, who in one way or another stood in opposition to each other, to the room, to the people, and to art also, but there was towards us and between you something very tender . . .

Wies Smals

When everybody had gone away, had been sort of dropping off slowly, then I didn't feel like participating in that; I didn't feel like being sociable in that respect as well and go away as was expected of me. Besides, I was a bit drunk and that's probably the reason why I had the courage to stay without asking permission. So, the moment I really would have had to go home, I took some pillows . . . and I fell asleep immediately and just waited to see how it would all end.

When I woke up the next morning I was sober again, and you were still sound asleep. And then I though it'd be a bit crazy to only have been present . . . and that you hadn't noticed. So I thought that was a double joke! So I left something behind, so you could see that I'd been there, but I sneaked out—which was quite a headache, because all the doors were locked, I had to look for keys . . .

Marina Abramović

When we decided to sleep, we did not think for a moment of using any kind of medicine that could help. We were thinking of just natural sleep. And the performance started actually when the guests came in, we were lying in the bed already. And I was concentrating very much on the idea of falling asleep. But at a certain point many people kept coming and coming. I started to feel their energy. My eyes were closed, but I was completely conscious of the situation and of the kind of vibrations I was getting. And there was less and less the possibility that I would fall asleep. During the whole night, I did not sleep.

But I experienced the whole atmosphere passively. And it was very difficult for me, in the beginning I was very quiet and then the tension started to mount. And I could not participate, but even just hearing the voices and not understanding the language, because most of the people were talking Dutch, I could only imagine what was actually going on.

And then, I knew Wies stayed and she slept with us. And actually I was waiting for the morning.

Ulay

I was awake for fifteen minutes when the guests came. I was very tense, but at the same time during the first fifteen minutes, from fifteen minutes to twelve to midnight, the guests were very disciplined. Probably that fact sent me to sleep. I don't have any further consciousness about what happened.

Alison Knowles

ALISON KNOWLES WAS A KEY PARTICIPANT IN FLUXUS—a loosely affiliated group of international artists who began working together in the early 1960s around a shared interest in chance, indeterminacy, and the everyday. During this period, Knowles experimented with a range of strategies and media including prints, book objects, sound works, and performances—some of which used food as a medium, as in her *Bean Rolls* (1962). Knowles also created Fluxus "events," a type of reduced-means performance in which language elements or everyday actions are bracketed for reflective attention. Several of these involve the preparation and consumption of food. One of the earliest and most famous of her event scores, *#2 Proposition* (1962) consisted simply of the instruction "Make a salad." (A variant from 1964: "Make a soup.") *Feast* features another of Knowles's iconic Fluxus works, *The Identical Lunch* (1969–ongoing).

Throughout the late 1960s, Knowles visited a neighborhood luncheonette at noon and ordered the same meal (the best thing on the menu, she recalls). Prompted by her friend, the composer Philip Corner, Knowles came to think of the lunch as a performance, which she then formalized as a score: "The Identical Lunch: a tuna fish sandwich on wheat toast with lettuce and butter, no mayo, and a large glass of buttermilk or a cup of soup was and is eaten many days of each week at the same place and at about the same time."

As originally conceived, the lunch was eaten often, at the same place and at about the same time, but the score has provoked and guided countless nonidentical performances of the nominally "identical" lunch. Knowles has occasionally documented these performances, with an eye to the way that this simple score unfolds with large and small variations. She gathered stories for an artist's book called *Journal of the Identical Lunch* (1971), while Corner published his narrative about Knowles's piece in his own artist's book, *The Identical Lunch* (1973). And in a series of square yellow silkscreen portraits from 1973, Knowles documented friends and colleagues like Fluxus impresario George Maciunas eating the *Identical Lunch*. An experienced printmaker, Knowles created an intentionally casual feel for these prints that is fully in keeping with the Fluxus spirit—a bit grainy, with image and text slightly askew. Each is captioned with the work's title, the sitter's name, and "Tuna Fish Compliments of Star-Kist Foods, Inc."—a tongue-in-cheek nod to corporate sponsorship and perhaps also a gentle critique of machine-age, identical food systems. (In some later versions, the company's name has been excised.) *Feast* included several manifestations of the project: both of the books, a selection of the silkscreens, and a display of the lunch itself. Though inspired by an installation snapshot from the 1970s, the actual sandwich and buttermilk were necessarily contemporary—made fresh and replaced often. In addition, the Smart Museum's café served Knowles's meal during *Feast* so that visitors could easily perform their own *Identical Lunches*.

As a new extension of Knowles's score, *Feast* also provided the occasion for the world premiere of her *Identical Lunch Symphony* (2012). Knowles drew inspiration for her *Symphony* from the fact that Maciunas had proposed blending the *Identical Lunch* to make a kind of fish soup. Building on his interpretation of her Fluxus score, Knowles created a new performance in which she conducted a group of students, artists, and friends (many of whom were taking *Feast*-connected courses at the University of Chicago and the University of Illinois at Chicago). The performers pulsed their blenders, mixing the components of the lunch and then pouring it into small cups for the audience in a lovingly absurdist homage to Knowles's late friend and colleague, and a perfect evocation of the endless variability inherent in the *Identical Lunch*.

Emily Capper contributed to this text.

OPPOSITE: An earlier installation of *The Identical Lunch* (c. 1970s, exact location and date unknown), the inspiration for Knowles's adaptation for *Feast*

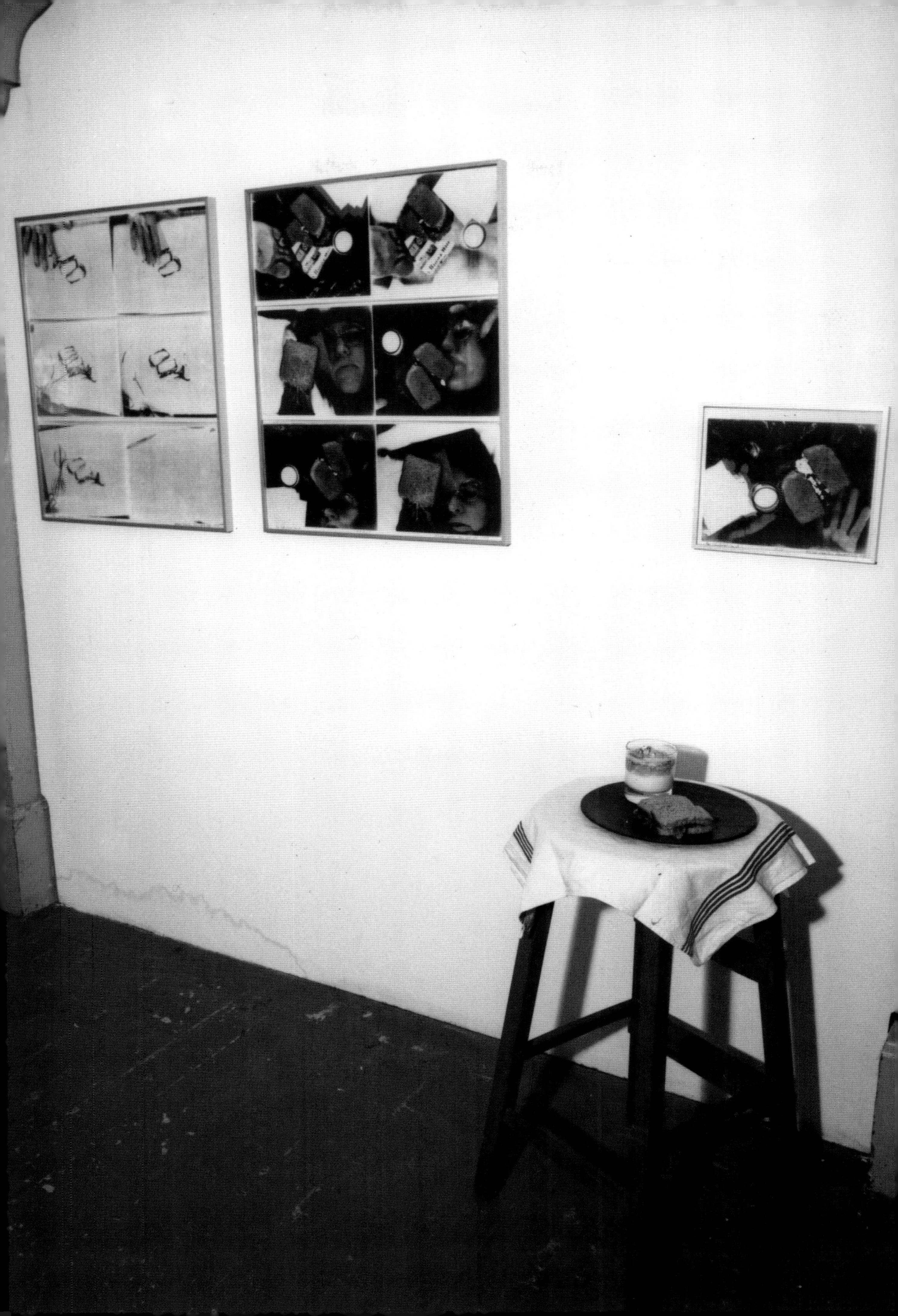

Interview

SMART: Can you describe your path as an artist and sources of inspiration for your work, either in or beyond the context of art?

ALISON KNOWLES: My path as an artist was initiated by my father who directed me to write and illustrate a story for him each day, which he examined when he got back from work. I was seven or eight at the time and Walt Disney was my idol. I did as directed and began making books daily at this age. Fortunately they have all disappeared! My central source of inspiration is the variety and intensity of my daily experience.

SMART: You were an active member of the Fluxus movement, especially through your event scores.

AK: The Fluxus genre stands apart from spectacle postwar culture. It takes an interested look at Dada, and ends up with the street and event scores. In Fluxus, there are no actors; there are just people trying to turn you on to enjoying the simple activities that you do every day. A Fluxus event score is one or two lines. For instance, "Put your shoes on a music stand and discuss them as long as you wish before an audience." There are lots of ways to do these pieces. But I'm not all flexible or loose about what goes on, because I want people to see how really simply things can be done if you concentrate on the idea that that's what you're doing.

SMART: What does it mean to you to be included in a show called *Feast: Radical Hospitality in Contemporary Art*?

AK: It is important for me to be in *Feast* as it acknowledges my obsession with food and what it says about the people who make it and the increasing place of respect it commands in individual lives.

SMART: When did you develop this "obsession with food"?

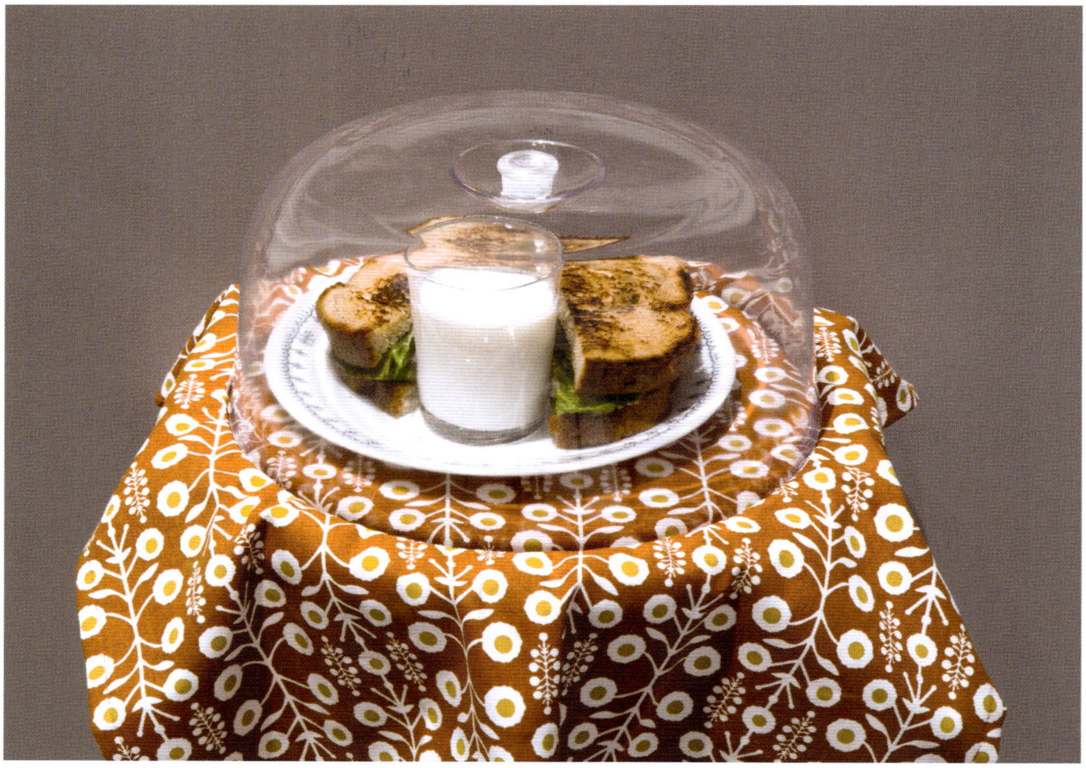

ABOVE AND OPPOSITE: *The Identical Lunch,* installation view, Smart Museum of Art, 2012

AK: I would start with my very early years, which intersected with the war. I was in a family that was not only rationing food, but also short on money. So, when we came to the table, most of the time there was no meat or fish, but we looked forward to one day during that week when there would be either meat or fish. When I said "obsession" I was thinking of the importance of food given the circumstances in our family. My mother, who did the cooking, was from a family that was much more abundant financially and they had guests all the time. Her situation with eating was very different and very elegant. She had learned to bake, which most people don't do anymore. She was able to bake different kinds of cinnamon and molasses cakes, and so within the economy of our family there would be at least once a week, along with meals that were minimal but good, this amazing cinnamon-molasses cake. I can see it in my mind. I would say that we were very pleased to have this double standard—enough money to eat alright, but also my mother, who could do amazing things with pies and cakes. The other thing that snaps into my mind is Sunday night; my father would make fudge. He would make wonderful fudge squares for us.

SMART: Please tell us about *The Identical Lunch*.

AK: *The Identical Lunch* began in Chelsea in the late 1960s. It was very much an initiatory performance in the "food art" genre. But this lunch was actually based—as most of my performances are—in what I'm actually doing during my day. The identical lunch is a tuna fish sandwich on wheat toast with lettuce and butter, no mayo, and a cup of soup or a glass of buttermilk.

I would often go at noon to Riss Food, which was located on 22nd Street and 8th Avenue. It was very close to the Something Else Press, where Dick Higgins was churning

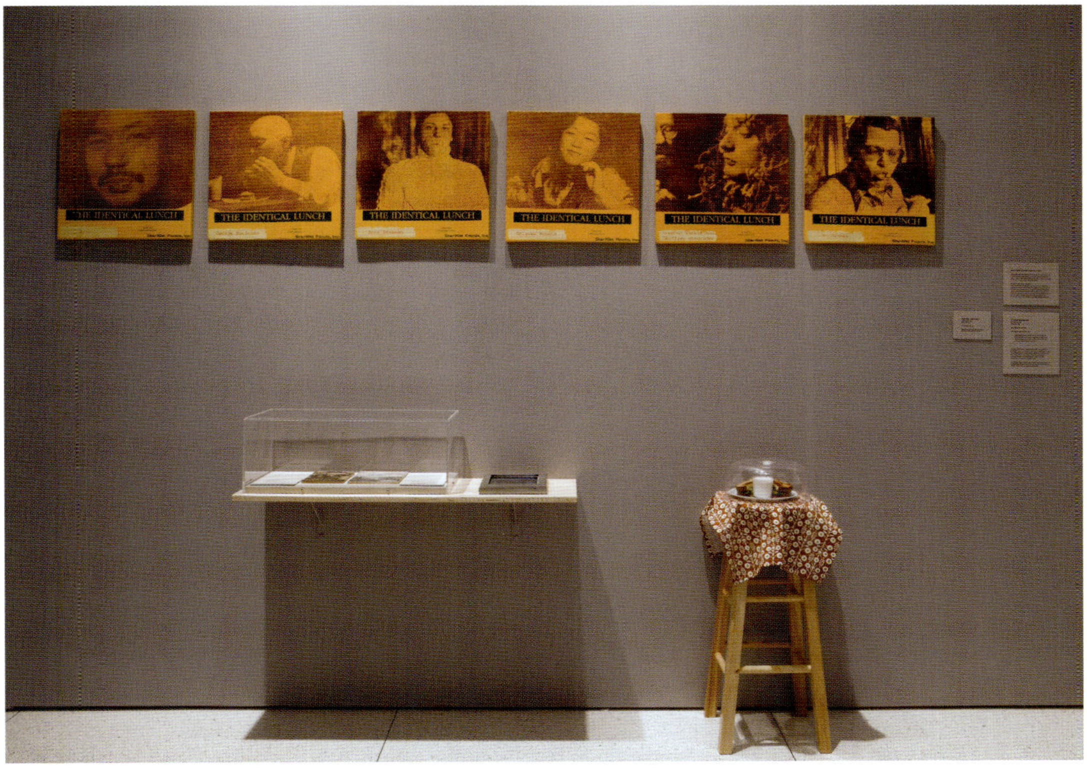

out avant-garde books. I would go with friends, such as Philip Corner or John Giorno, and one day Philip turned to me at lunch and said: "You know, Alison, you always have the same lunch, you have an identical lunch." At that point we realized that I was somehow involved in a performance. I usually had four or five people come and eat the lunch. The respect that I had for that hour and for the people I ate with had to do with the fact that we were doing mutual work as artists and writers. The reactions and the way people ate it and how they felt about it were extremely different. I found it very interesting that Florence and the other waitresses took considerable interest and questioned what I was doing, always having this tuna fish sandwich. For me to say, "It's actually a piece of performance art," made me a completely mysterious object to them.

But the reason I had that lunch in the first place was because it was not a great café. I had tried everything, and ended up with the lunch that was the best thing in that restaurant. That mattered to me. I'm often struck today that people are just feeding their hunger: they'll go into a place and they'll get their burger with cheese and they hardly taste it. They wolf it down and maybe then they have time to do something like look in a window or get a haircut. The idea is that food satisfies hunger, as opposed to being a ritual or an act that is very important in terms of the day and what they're thinking.

SMART: Do you think that the wider culture has changed? Was there more of a sense of ritual around the meal then versus now?

AK: It probably depends more on the people, rather than there being a real change. I find that the people I have known are usually people who would study a menu seriously, instead of just having a steak. And I think it says something about the person eating—that they're aware that this is not a stupid decision. They should be aware of what they're doing and why they're choosing that, and someone next to them is choosing something else. These are important and interesting decisions of the day.

SMART: How has the performance of the event score for *The Identical Lunch* changed in different contexts?

AK: I performed the *Identical Lunch* in Europe—France, Germany, Scandinavia, Copenhagen. I've done the lunch in Japan and Korea. You would think in Germany you could find whole wheat bread. No. The best they could do was a whole wheat baguette. It was a sort of facsimile of the lunch. In Asia, I did not even try. I had pictures to show and then I would enjoy what was regional for them. So what connected it to the *Lunch* was that they could get me a regional tofu soup (or whatever), as my lunch had been regional to me.

SMART: What do you hope people will take away from this presentation of the *Identical Lunch* in *Feast*?

AK: I want them to find their own *Identical Lunch* somewhere. Maybe they love sausage or noodles for lunch—maybe they find a place where they can enact that kind of decision. And maybe not have it every day, but be informed, so if someone said "Why are you going to Harry's café?" they'd say, "Well, because they have the noodles and sausage that I think is the best in Detroit"—just to take charge of their meal. Because when you use the word *feast*, what comes to my mind is the highest level of someone's eating experience, and that people take away from it an experience as special as taking a cold shower on a hot day, or something that is up there in your life experience. And since I want it to be personal, I would like the person who found the sausage and noodle place to honor that in themselves, to be able to tell people about it—so they know it's a lamb sausage and that the noodles are the wide noodles, and have that part of their, if you will, *intellectual* eating experience.

SMART: What sparked your interest in making the new *Identical Lunch Symphony* performance for *Feast*?

AK: The Fluxus artist George Maciunus decided to create his own *Identical Lunch* performance. It seemed to me that if he used

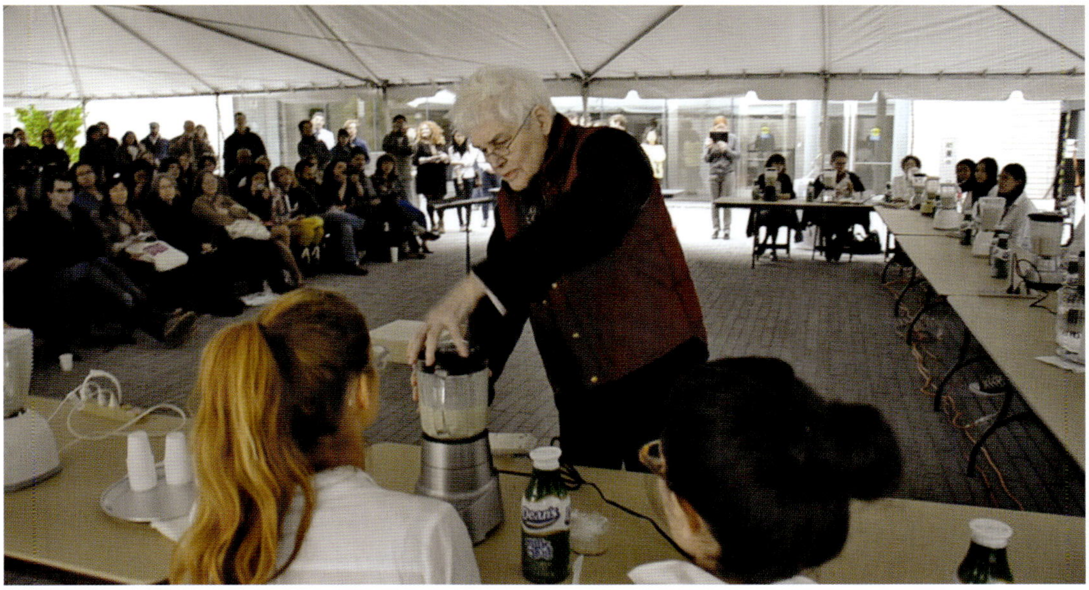

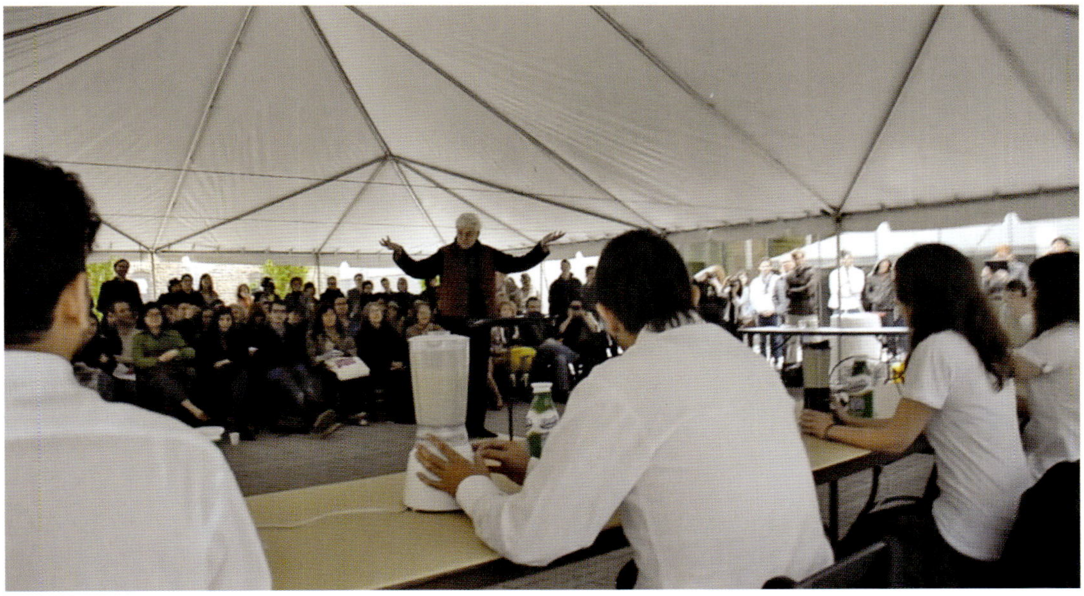

Alison Knowles conducting the *Identical Lunch Symphony* at the *Of Hospitality* symposium, Logan Center for the Arts, University of Chicago, May 5, 2012

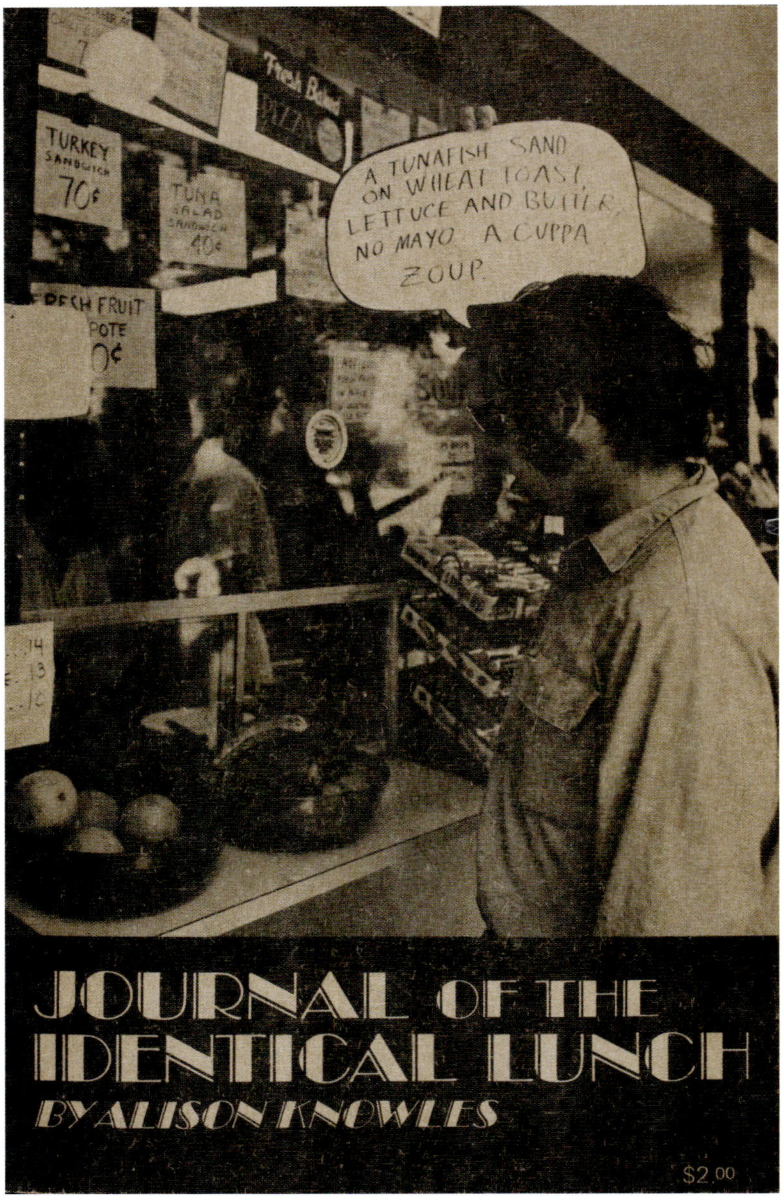

LEFT AND OPPOSITE:
Cover and interior pages from Knowles's, *Journal of the Identical Lunch*, 1971

that exact lunch, he was free to do what he wanted. It was somewhere in a gallery that he arrived with his Waring blender. We blended the lunch and passed it out in little cups, and realized it's a delicious cold fish soup—heavy, fishy, and white. So we'll see if we can pass out tuna fish sandwiches here, where we'll have, I hope, as many as twenty blenders at the same time. I'll be able to conduct the sound—to bring in blender #4, or take #2 down to "low." I think I'll have a lot of fun. I think the way to invite people to perform is to have them bring their own blender, and we will provide everything else.

SMART: Do questions about hospitality figure into your process or thinking?

AK: People slowly learn in their daily lives that good food is not to be taken lightly. For me it is a high pleasure to be invited to a dinner prepared in someone's home. Hospitality is the natural accompaniment of good food. Good people make good food.

JOURNAL OF THE IDENTICAL LUNCH
© 1971 by Alison Knowles

Alison Knowles' own documentations were first published in *The Outsider* Nos. 1–5. New Lunches will include many other people and their own performances.

Photos, outside front and back covers, by David Wing

Photos, inside front and back covers, and pp. 33, 34, by Peter Moore

Nova Broadcast books are edited and published by Jan Herman, and are distributed by IPCO Products, 691 South 31st Street, Richmond, California 94804, USA

JOURNAL OF THE IDENTICAL LUNCH

The Identical Lunch: a tunafish sandwich on wheat toast with lettuce and butter, no mayo and a large glass of buttermilk or a cup of soup was and is eaten many days of each week at the same place and at about the same time.

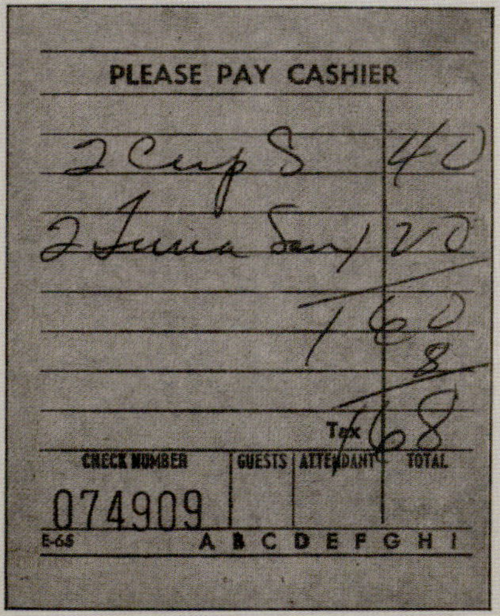

1

PERFORMERS IN N'S DOCUMENTATION

P – Pauline, head waitress at Riss.

C – Counterman in the back section.

L – Greek cashier turned part-time cook.

S – Alternate counterman to C.

B – Regular cashier and bouncer.

M – Lee, alternate countergirl to P.

H – Emmett Williams.

T – John Giorno.

N – Alison Knowles.

D – Tony Andersen.

F – The Dog-woman.

G – Philip Corner.

J – Day replacement for P and M.

A – Susan Hartung

E – Flo, afternoon waitress.

10

N'S PERFORMANCES FROM 1968. PRECEDING THESE DOCUMENTATIONS ARE MANY NOT WRITTEN DOWN

Apr. 2 – N nods, P, "Same?," N nods. .80 + tip

–

Apr. 3 – N sits, nods, P smiles, nods. .80 + tip

–

Apr. 10 – N, "Tunafish on wheat toast, no mayo, lettuce and butter." C says, "Yeah, n' buttermilk." N nods. N has never informed C of his price error. .70 + tip

–

Apr. 17 – N nods, P nods. Tunafish is very watery; it is mid-week. N figures there are large lots made up Thursdays and Mondays of each week. End of the lot tuna has too much mayo and too much celery. .80 + tip.

–

April. 19 – A friend from Denmark is told of this Journal and suggests that he do an entry. This friend, D, performs alone. When he returns from Riss he remarks to N of P's bright manner and efficiency. M is serving when N enters, with C at the far counter. M is short, slovenly and slow with a bored manner. She is never addressed by name by the regulars as is P. M delivers a cold sandwich. N feels M is bored by this lunch research project, whereas P seems relieved and interested to deliver N's identical lunch each day. D also mentioned to N that P touched his hand and smiled directly into his face saying, "Large or small?" when D ordered the buttermilk. P takes

11

DICK HIGGINS' PERFORMANCE **no date**

On March 14, 1969 at 12:40 PM suspect left 238 West 22nd Street in New York City, wearing black italian shoes, black socks, underpants decorated with tiny black and white or black, white, green or blue geometric patterns (arranged alternately in rows), black gaberdeen slacks, a red turtleneck jersey, a brown tweed sports jacket, and a beat-up brown overcoat with a synthetic fur lining. Suspect was 6' 2" and of decidedly stocky build, with blue eyes, brown hair worn somewhat long, bearded but almost without moustache, ectomorphic facial structure, pale complexion and small square silver-rim eye-glasses. Suspect was carrying March 15th, 1969 issue of *The Saturday Review* and March 14th, 1969 "Late City" edition of the NEW YORK POST. Suspect turned left in the street, cut across the street (jaywalking) in front of 262 West 22nd Street towards the facing parking lot, and went left and right around the corner to Riss Foods at 244 Eighth Avenue. Arriving at 12:44. Suspect entered and seated himself in the first section of the two counters, on the ninth of the fifteen seats in this section. Suspect did not have slip of paper to advise him what correct order would be. At 12:45 waitress took order for tuna fish sandwich on whole wheat toast. At 12:46 waitress (wearing red dress, aged roughly 35 to 40 years, about 5' 8" tall, with long brown hair worn high and thick on her head) asked suspect, "Yours is whole wheat toast?" Suspect replied, "Yes, thank you." Sandwich arrived at 12:49. At 12:50 suspect ordered a regular cup of coffee, which arrived at 12:51. In the meantime suspect was eating his sandwich, with no apparent relish. Possibly the acridness of canned tuna fish did not please him, or the cottonseed oil in which the tuna

4

was apparently packed may have disturbed his apparently wiggly stomach. He did, however, note that the sandwich was made on buttered toast, and served with a slice of lettuce. In size it was all too adequate, since this meant there was too much of it to put away. In texture, however, the tuna fish had been altered so that, unlike tuna straight from the can, the usual resemblance to the disected frogs of high school biology classes had disappeared: instead it had been pulped and mashed into something viscous, like melted ice cream. Suspect appeared neither to enjoy nor not to enjoy his coffee. This appeared to be used as a means of downing the tuna. The check had been delivered with the coffee. At 12:52½ suspect completed the consumption of the sandwich and, the waitress being handy, asked should he pay her or up front. She said, "Pay up front, up front please." A glass of water had been served with the sandwich and used as an additional means of washing this down. Some of this water had spilled on the check, and waterlogged it. However, suspect picked this up anyway, ignoring the two business men sitting in the tenth and eleventh chairs of the front section, to his left, who were ordering roast beef sandwiches with green beans, and proceeded to the cashier's register, where he paid the waitress who had served him $0.50 for the sandwich and $0.10 for the coffee, $0.60 total, leaving the restaurant at 12:58. Apparently revived by the fresh air, suspect turned to the right and crossed Eighth Avenue at 23rd Street, turning downtown on the far side of the avenue. There is a delicatessen at 449 Eighth Avenue, whose name remains one of the minor mysteries of our time, since the neon sign above the door says "Delicatessen," the awning says "Fine fruits and groceries" and the cash register slips are entirely unlabelled and noncommital. From the door of this delica-

5

tessen, however, there is an excellent view of Riss Foods' facade, and this was the door that suspect entered. There was one man ahead of suspect in line, waiting for a cold roast beef sandwich to be made up. While waiting, suspect noted that correct time was 1:12, that his watch read 1:01, and that all above times were therefore inaccurate. It now being his turn, suspect ordered two large cans of Schlitz beer, a half pound of roast beef, and a 12-oz. package of Munzenmeier's Genuine Westphalian Pumpernickel Without Crust, all of which cost $2.50. This being duly rung up and bagged, suspect proceeded out the door, took a right, crossed 22nd Street and then Eighth Avenue and continued up the south side of 22nd Street to 238 West 22nd Street, which he entered, arriving in his office at 1:20 (corrected time). Suspect then searched for the lost instruction sheet, which he found and which enlightened him as to why he was suspect: he had forgotten to order a cup of soup.

6

VERNON HINKLE PERFORMANCE **331 W. 20**
New York
June 6, 1969

Note strike-over on date, a 6 over a 2. Was anticipating June 6, but figuring it out from June 2, the day of my arrival in the City, the day of separation from wife. Sense of welcome here on that day, sense of rebirth, perhaps the beginnings of successful re-establishment of relationship with tuna fish sandwich.

Awoke later than usual this morning because of late party last night. (Note strike-over "last" over "the") Started to write "the night before" over "the other night" as indication of more of same.

Talked with Bici about feeding of cats. Tuna fish is bad for them. Creates urethritis. I have urethritis, have had off and on for the past year. Drugs don't work. I am addicted to tuna fish. Wonder if there is a connection. Bici also says that such things can be created by emotional problems. Decide to remove tuna fish from diet for a while. Decide to drink lots of water and flush it out.

Bici tells me of Alison who is collecting documentations of encounters with tuna on wheat toast with lettuce and butter and cup of soup at Riss' between 22nd and 23rd on 8th Ave. Asks if I'd care to join her. I say not today but I'll do it later, because I should be working on rewrites of play. Return to room, see bottle of capsules which I am supposed to take before meals. Fetish about having the meal after taking the capsule. So I take the capsule (for the ailment) and ask Bici if she's gone on her mission yet. She says that she forgot and had lunch at home, toys with idea of having tuna fish after lunch. She doesn't, however, And I proceed on mission thinking that

7

ABOVE AND OPPOSITE: Interior pages from Knowles's *Journal of the Identical Lunch*, 1971

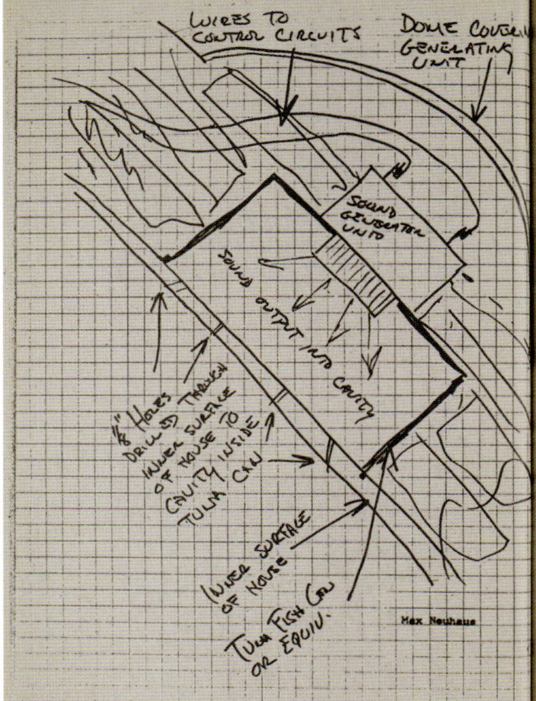

Philip Corner Lunch

There are those who are not immediately enthusiastic. Those who say it's decadent to write this like this. Who say you should be writing about those who have no lunch so what are we (i say) what are we doing with music either new or traditional so let us all give up another generation wait 'till the kulaks are all dead we'll solve the problems of humanity and then start living again. Meanwhile grace has been neglected and what better attention than the fineness of our lives the way it will ever be -- lunches like this kind. The poet says, 'well, it depends on how it is written.'

Dear old friends

It happened to be tunafish on arrival. The child's was cut in four squares -- in the refrig, for later, for someone else. Whole wheat bread, untoasted. Remained uneaten all day.

I did have one meal at the Dragon de Oro within this period.

Breakfast. a cup of tea at 6:30 in the morning (intended)
An hour finishing this proofreading a cup of tea, 7:30 (intending. NOW).

It was hot and humid and I was to meet John for lunch at 12:30. Coming from the garment district with three pounds of turkey feathers, I walked through Chelsea during lunch hour. I was the first to arrive at 12:30. Around 1:30 a group of us invaded the local restaurant to order the same lunch. It was very crowded. I decided I didn't like tuna fish anymore. Spent more time talking than looking. A little after two o'clock I caught the 7th Avenue subway home to pack gear for vacation. My head was already in the country.

D. Hollingworth

At about 12 noon (date?) I walked from my store on 4th st over to John Giorno's loft on the Bowery. We both took some acid and walked back to my place to get my motorcycle and drive up to Grove Press where we met some people to have lunch.

When we got to the restaurant we were instructed to have a specific lunch which consisted of a tunafish sandwich and soup. I told John and some other people what I thought of the lunch, which was I hated it.

After the lunch I drove John home and I continued to drive until I got to the Berkshire Mountains near Great Barrington Mass.

Dear John

I hope I'll see you soon --

love

Michael

Suzanne Lacy

SUZANNE LACY GREW UP IN a working class family in California, studied zoology and psychology, and was trained as a community organizer before turning to art in the early 1970s; during that time she became part of a community of creative women in Los Angeles who were engaged with feminist discourse. By the late 1970s, Lacy had synthesized these interests into a distinctive form: multilayered collaborative artworks, such as *Three Weeks in May* (1977), that addressed specific social issues and particular communities through combinations of performance, community organizing, public display, and media intervention. Writing and teaching are key elements of her practice; her edited volume *Mapping The Terrain: New Genre Public Art* (1995) has become a classic in the field of public and activist art, and she founded the graduate program in social practice at Otis College of Art and Design.

Meals have often been a crucial part of Lacy's art, inspired in part by their use to hone political aims and strengthen bonds among women in both the women's labor movement of the early twentieth century and the feminist community of the 1970s. In *The International Dinner Party* (I.D.P., 1979), for instance, Lacy organized a massive, simultaneous dinner party that involved thousands of people around the world—a scope that seems especially remarkable for an event organized before the Internet age. Using connections within global feminist/activist circles, Lacy and her collaborator Linda Pruess called for women to stage dinners on March 14, 1979 in tribute to a woman from their region and to send telegrams about their meals to the San Francisco Museum of Modern Art (SFMoMA). This structure and the date reflect the project's genesis as a gift to Lacy's mentor Judy Chicago: it coincided with the opening of Chicago's now-iconic feminist installation *The Dinner Party* at SFMoMA. As a performance during the opening, Lacy placed each telegram in a binder and marked the dinner's location on a large map. By the end of the performance she had placed red triangles across five continents: Africa, Asia, Europe, and North and South America. During *Feast*, Lacy presented the large map installation from *The International Dinner Party* for the first time since its original use, along with highlights from a trove of letters, photographs, and other materials that participants sent to her later. For *Feast*, a comprehensive selection of these I.D.P. materials was also scanned into a digital archive to make them more accessible.

Feast also included archival materials from *River Meetings: Lives of Women in the Delta* (1981–82). Lacy created this multilayered project to mobilize support for the Equal Rights Amendment, a constitutional amendment drafted to protect women from discrimination. When the College Art Association held their annual meeting in New Orleans in 1980—at a time when states including Louisiana had not ratified the Equal Rights Amendment—the Women's Caucus for the Arts (WCA) boycotted the conference. Lacy and many collaborators organized *River Meetings*, a performance event on the eve of the WCA conference in which around five hundred women joined in a series of potlucks and a banquet. As part of this event, Lacy and her collaborator Laverne Dunn choreographed a series of smaller meal-based performances that were intended for reproduction and media consumption. She and Dunn cooked camp-style meals in tourist sites, staging photographs to call attention to the boycott agenda. The resulting photographs of a white woman and a black woman sharing staged meals in public made concrete the larger goal of advocating equality for all.

OPPOSITE: *International Dinner Party* (detail), installation view, Smart Museum of Art, 2012

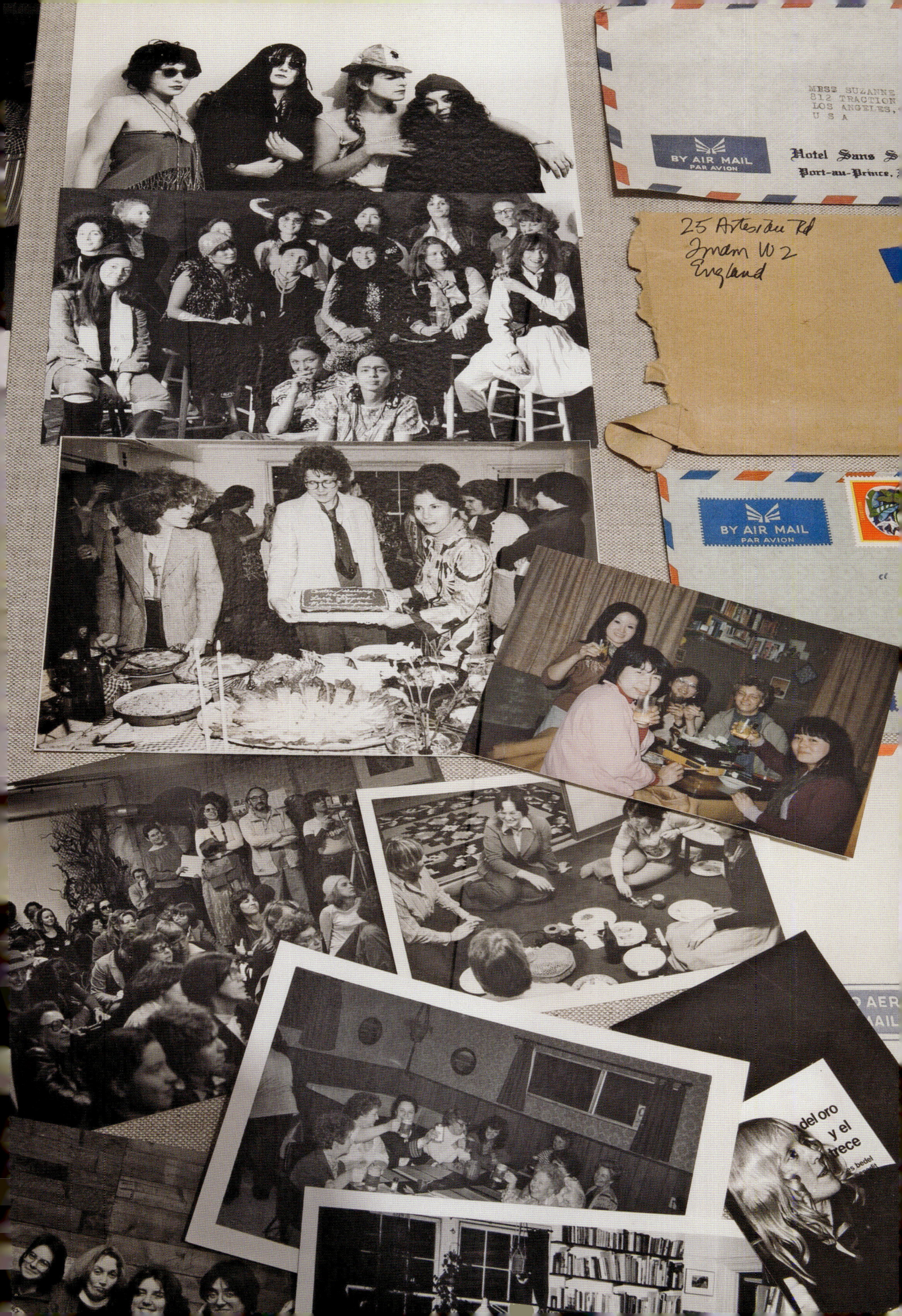

BY AIR MAIL
PAR AVION
Hotel Sans S
Port-au-Prince,
25 Artesian Rd
England
BY AIR MAIL
PAR AVION
del oro
y el
trece

Interview

SMART: Can you tell us about the use of food and meals in your work in the 1970s and 1980s?

SUZANNE LACY: The impetus to use food, in general, and meals, in particular, comes from a couple of places. First, feminism in the 1970s came into being in the context of community between women, often taking place in the kitchen. I remember how doing dishes in the kitchen after social dinners when I was a student in Fresno took on this interesting shift. Earlier I resented doing dishes while the men talked in the living room, but the kitchen and the women doing the dishes became a much more interesting place to be—even THE place to be. Second, there were many examples of dinners in the context of performance and even earlier art history (look at the Futurists or Dieter Roth) that made dinner events/artwork a notion that was easily assimilated into our work.

More complexly, I think, the relationship between consumption of the female body and food; between preparation and serving food and nurturing; between consuming flesh and being flesh, all of these things took on a gendered perspective and became a common trope in women's performance (and performance in general).

It is fair to say I think that being a woman in the context of the feminist movement gave a very particular meaning to those of us working with meals. Think of Barbara T. Smith's black meal, as she emerged from housewife consciousness into the context of the feminist movement that was just beginning (Judy Chicago was in the same scene as Barbara).

After exploring meals/eating/foodstuffs in some of my early performances, I learned about the role of meals in organizing in 1920s labor movements; women specifically called out their organizing strategies as being what we would call today conviviality. I became interested in meals as vehicles for large-scale organizing through art, and in the interaction between people as a form of aesthetic gesture. Food united people, and since I was from a very early stage interested in cultural and social differences, meals provided a way to bring lots of people "to the table," metaphorically speaking. During the 1970s and 1980s, I organized dinners in Watts, Los Angeles, New Orleans, Ithaca, and elsewhere. They were an easy and portable image around which to organize, and I experimented with dimensions of time and impact after the project, etc. The other thing of interest about organizing dinners as performance is the way in which, in the 1970s, they were so clearly and flagrantly associated with women. Cooking and serving and meals were gendered in such a way that not a lot of men artists worked with those metaphors at that time.

I was frustrated about the lack of visual quality to the dinners, although works like *Immigrants and Survivors* (1983) were very powerful in a temporal and emotional way. Eventually I moved toward more formal tableaux. In projects like *Whisper the Waves the Wind* (1983–84) and *Crystal Quilt* (1985–87), I collaborated with groups of older women to stage large-scale public performances in which the women created metaphoric meals over real tables, the food being the conversation. These were much more satisfying visually.

SMART: One of the works exhibited in *Feast*, *River Meetings*, seems especially connected to the meals as an organizing strategy in earlier labor movements. Could you talk about the different ways you used meals in that project?

SL: Yes, *River Meetings* was very much based on early feminist organizing. After all, it was about the lack of our ability, in my lifetime, to pass the Equal Rights Amendment, something feminists had tried to do since it was written in 1923. The project with the Women's Caucus for the Arts (WCA), to turn their entire conference into a boycott event calling attention to the fact that Louisiana hadn't ratified the ERA, was very much in keeping with feminist politics, past and present. When the WCA steering committee for the conference decided to hold their conference in an unratified state, we had to focus on how the attendees would eat and where they would sleep without spending money. In order to not break the boycott, we decided to provide alternative food and lodgings through individual women, who provided homes and catering. The conference became an exercise in Southern hospitality, with WCA members sleeping on the

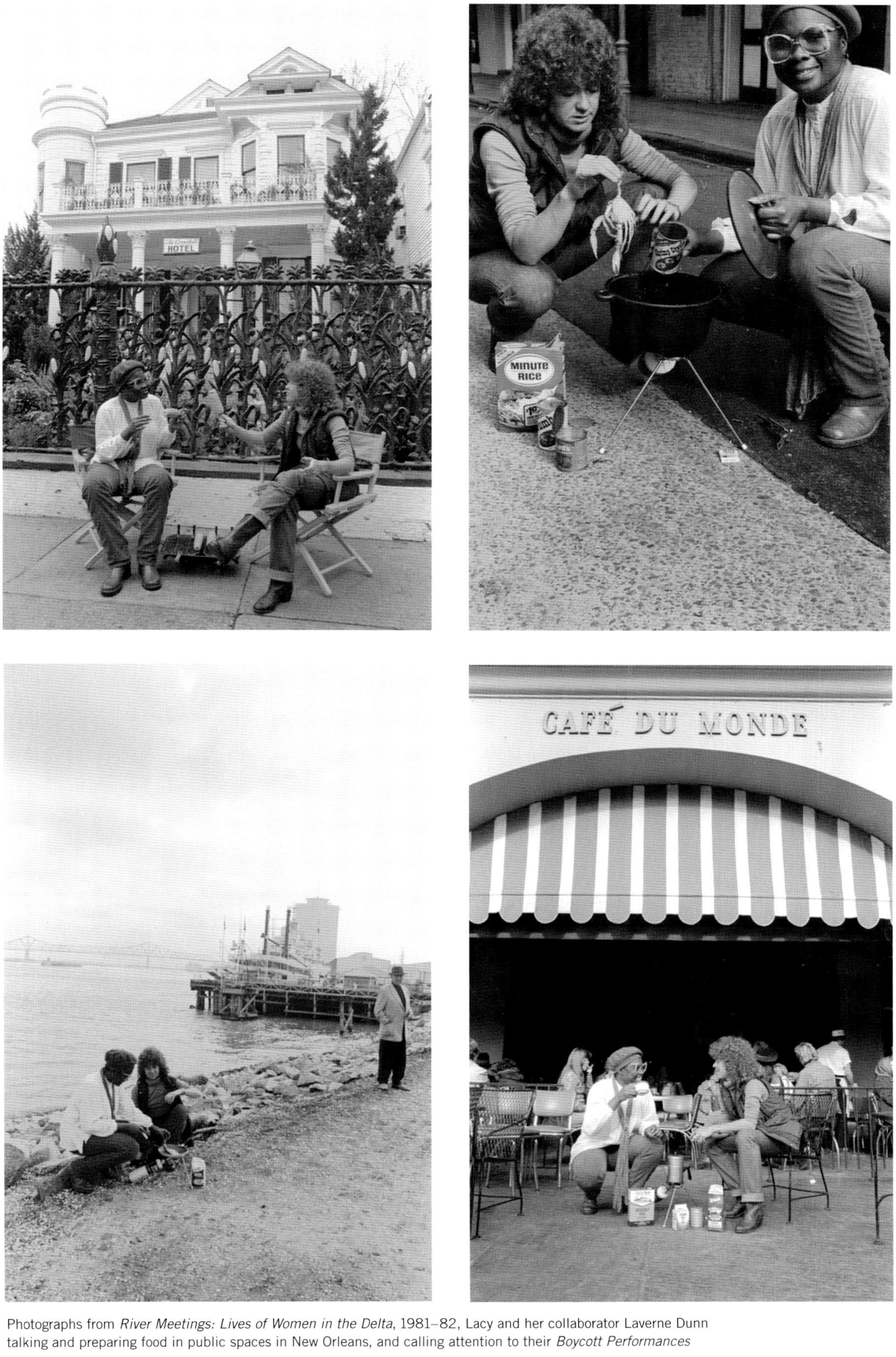

Photographs from *River Meetings: Lives of Women in the Delta*, 1981–82, Lacy and her collaborator Laverne Dunn talking and preparing food in public spaces in New Orleans, and calling attention to their *Boycott Performances*

An International Dinner Party to Celebrate Women's Culture

"Women have never had a Last Supper, but they have had dinner parties—lots and lots of dinner parties where they facilitated and nourished people."

—Judy Chicago

Dear Sisters,

We would like to ask you to participate with us in a worldwide celebration of ourselves! We are asking women in many countries to host dinner parties honoring women important to their own culture. These dinner parties, held simultaneously in March, 1979, will create a network of women-acknowledging-women which will extend around the world.

The occasion is the opening of "The Dinner Party" a celebration of women's history and a work of art of tremendous beauty and scope. For 4½ years artist and writer Judy Chicago, aided by over 250 artists, designers, historians and craftspeople, has been creating this work which pays homage to 39 women who have been major contributors to Western Civilization, and lists 999 others who have left their mark. The Dinner Party is a large triangular table with 39 place settings resting on a porcelain floor, which symbolically tells the story of women throughout Western History. The exhibition opens in March in San Francisco, California, and is scheduled to travel for a year to several other institutions.

Inspired by this work, several California artists want to expand the idea of honoring women from Western History to encompass **living women of all cultures.** We would like to create with you an "International Dinner Party Event," in which women from many cities and countries host **their own** dinner party, paying homage to women in **their area** who have contributed to our lives. The size, format or style of your dinner party is up to you, as well as the women you will honor and how you choose to do so. If each of our dinner parties occurs on the same evening, we will form a continuous 24 hour celebration around the world (because of the time differences).

If you would like to join us, please do the following:

1. Pass this information on to women in other cities and countries so our network can continue to expand. We particularly need to know of women in the Middle and Far East, Africa and South America.
2. Write to us, telling us who you (or your group) are, and we will send you more detailed information about the event.
3. Gather together women in your area to plan your dinner party for March.

We hope to hear from all of you,

Suzanne Lacy
Thea Litsios
Linda Preuss
Audrey Wallace
Susan Brenner
Shannon Hogan
Adrienne Weiss
Sharon Kagan

"International Dinner Party" c/o **Suzanne Lacy. 28 Avenue 27, Venice CA 90291 USA**

The *International Dinner Party* invitation, 1979

couches of local residents and eating food they prepared. Our *River Meetings* banquet on the opening of the conference brought five hundred women together to share food they'd prepared themselves. It was the result of small groups of women eating together, prior to the event, and each pledging to hold their own dinner—a chain letter of dinner parties.

SMART: The presentation of your work in *Feast* centers on the *International Dinner Party*. Could you say a bit about the use of the meal in that work, and about layers of that project (as a tribute, as a participatory artwork, as a performance, as an installation that is being given its first full public presentation since 1979)?

SL: Since the 1970s, I have been very interested in exploring the boundaries of performance. I was part of a formative moment among international artists—we were intuitively and each in our own way, influenced by each other and defining the term for ourselves. *The International Dinner Party* reflects a similar theme in feminist politics—an interest in the global conditions of being female. For me, much of that centered on violence against women, how it was manifest in different places around the world. But I also believed in the possibility of a global women's activism. Women were pretty eagerly seeking each other out—there was the International Tribunal of Crimes Against Women held in Belgium in 1976, for instance. It was much harder to get information from each other then, given the lack of visibility of women in many countries and the paucity of coverage. We were limited technologically of course.

The International Dinner Party was, first, a performative "structure," as I called them. That is, I took a set of lifelike actions and framed them in terms of time, representation, and so on, and made the activities into art. In this case, it was getting more than two thousand women to participate in an event that was both distinctive to each group—self-determined and designed—and yet collective. The instructions were simple: have a dinner with other women (some men came too) to honor a woman in your own community on the same night. Given time changes, it would be a twenty-four-hour celebration. Colonizing global male-directed space with local women's aspirations was a temporary, symbolic intervention. Women sent telegrams from places that I marked on the map that was displayed outside Judy Chicago's first installation of *The Dinner Party*. The performance was a gift to her, a tribute to her accomplishments with that piece.

SMART: What does it mean to you to look back at this work now, after thirty years? And what do you anticipate might come of the call we're going to make, asking people around the world to stage a new round of International Dinner Parties on the anniversary of your original performance? Does this shift in technological possibilities change the nature of the piece?

SL: Yes and no. Communications technology has made broad awareness of the social conditions of women in various parts of the world visible. Bride-burning in India, infibulation or clitorectomy in countries in Africa, or stoning in Iran—this knowledge is available to anyone with a computer. Many things that were so hidden in the 1970s are reported in the media, so not only is the Internet ubiquitous, so are reporters. But the truth is that those issues were known then too, it just took longer and more digging and only a few people might know about a given area. Now, there is a much broader coverage of women's issues globally. With the *International Dinner Party*, it's interesting to consider that this organizing took place pre-Internet. I'd like people to take away the sense of scale of this as an early social practice, and to understand how that sensibility came from a direct set of political imperatives at the time. Much of the work that we associate with early performance today was body-oriented, and of course I did that as well, but this type of project is also an example of performance art, explorations of time, space, relationship, and ritual.

SMART: How would you describe the role of the meal/hospitality in your practice?

SL: Coming from the perspective of public pedagogy and service, and political mobilization, hospitality is always a concern in my work. Not

Mary Beth Edelson
110 Mercer Street
New York, New York 10012
212-226-0832

March 6,1979

Dear Suzanne and Judy

Congradulations to you both!

Wanted to let you know who is coming to the dinned party that Ana Mendieta and I are putting together on March 14 to tie in with your international dinner party.

Our party is to honor Louise Bourgeois .

The guests have been invited- if they are in the mood- to come dressed as either a famous contemporary or herstorical (almost wrote historical whew) women- they of course can come as themselves!

Guest list of accepted invites (Louise made out the list herself)

susan cooper
Michelle Stuart
Barabara Zucker
Hannah Wilke
Judy Barnstein
Anne Sharp
Edit D'Ark
Joyce Kozloff
Barbara Moore
Phyllis Krim
Patrica Hamilton
Poppy Johnson
Marisol

we have been trying to get ahold of Kate Millet, but have not contacted her as yet to invite her. Rumor has it that she might be in Iran.

also Lucy was invited but she will be out there with you.

And of course Louise, Ana and myself.

We will take pictures.

Cheers! and good luck on the various openings and events.

Sunshine,

MBeth
Mary Beth

sent copy to Judy

Letter written by New York-based artist and feminist Mary Beth Edelson, March 6, 1979

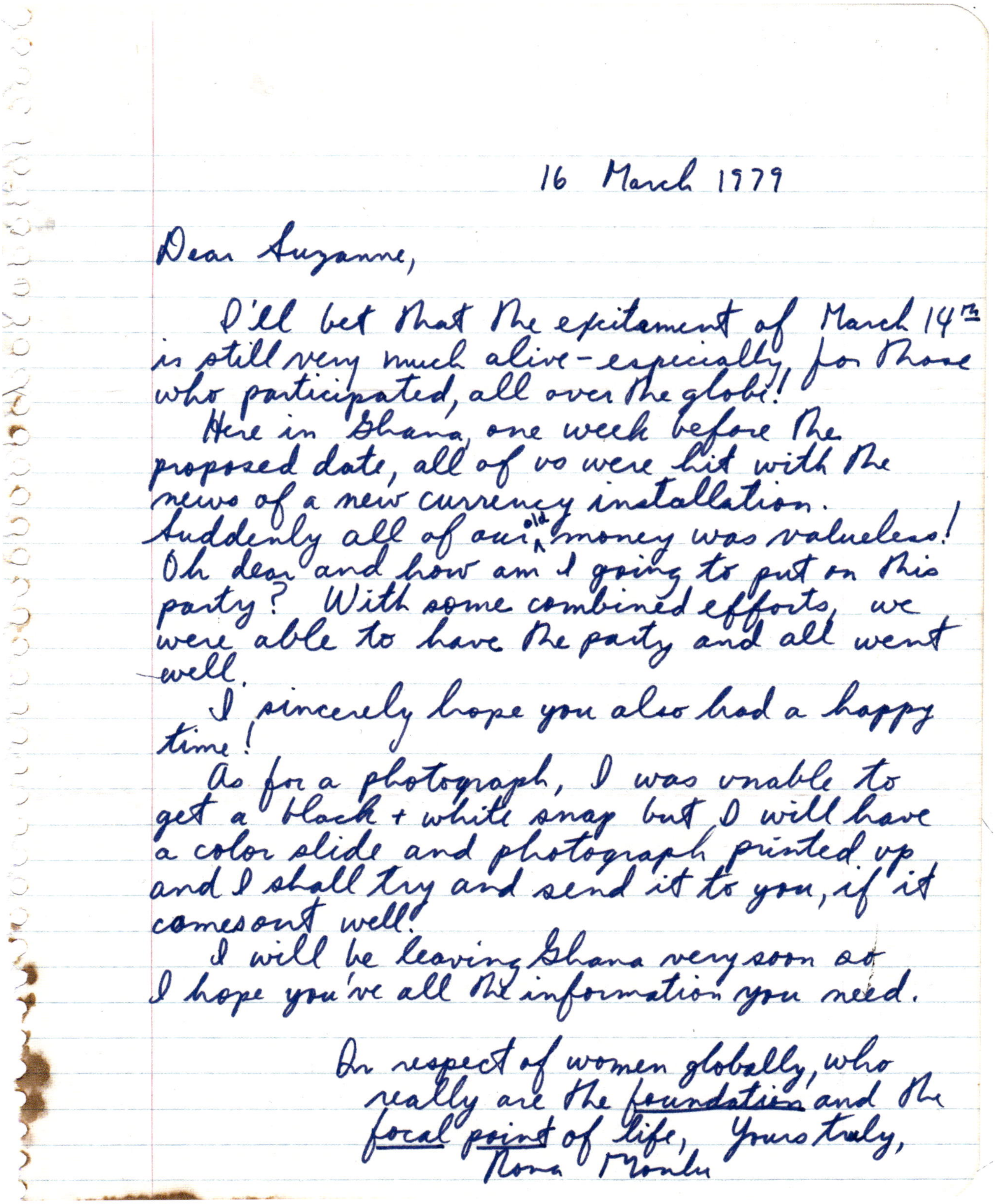
16 March 1979

Dear Suzanne,

I'll bet that the excitement of March 14th is still very much alive—especially for those who participated, all over the globe!

Here in Ghana, one week before the proposed date, all of us were hit with the news of a new currency installation. Suddenly all of our old money was valueless! Oh dear and how am I going to put on this party? With some combined efforts, we were able to have the party and all went well.

I sincerely hope you also had a happy time!

As for a photograph, I was unable to get a black + white snap but I will have a color slide and photograph printed up and I shall try and send it to you, if it comes out well!

I will be leaving Ghana very soon as I hope you've all the information you need.

In respect of women globally, who really are the <u>foundation</u> and the <u>focal point</u> of life, Yours truly,
Nora Moabu

Letter written by Nora Moabu in Ghana, March 16, 1979

so much from the point of view of extending hospitality, but rather, how to make everyone feel comfortable and engaged with what often becomes very large volunteer efforts. How people come to a situation and feel engaged, honored, respected for their part in the whole is always a part of my thinking. Meals per se don't figure into ongoing thinking.

On another front, I am interested in how the body consumes, physically speaking, from eating to being eaten. This is probably more of a strain of animism in my spiritual beliefs. I am close to animals and seek to communicate with them often. I feel keenly my own physical existence and am very connected to my body. I am troubled in a very visceral and particularly embodied way about certain forms of physical violence, like rape or torture. I think these kinds of interests led to *Learn Where the Meat Comes From* (1976) and other more visceral performance and photographic work from the 1970s. I still think about these things; in a recent project in Madrid I did a video where women were filmed from the neck down talking about the direct impacts of violence on parts of their bodies.

SMART: Describe a favorite story about your work.

SL: Not a favorite story particularly, but a story: when I was teaching at the Feminist Studio Workshop in performance, around 1974, I asked students to create a mini-performance they could all perform simultaneously at a long white table—a metaphor of the Last Supper, feminist style. We arrived at the performance site and everyone quietly and methodically began their performances, and at different stages a half hour into the three hour event, things began to get more and more heated. One woman kept shoving oatmeal gruel down the face of a mask of herself (situated in a large bottle). Another smashed chocolate candies with a hammer, one at a time. Each candy was embedded with glass, nails, etc. Another kept pouring herself tequila shots until she was completely drunk, threw off her clothes, and sprayed whipped cream all over herself. It was a cacophony of rage and pain. I was pretty shocked that the notion of food, in and of itself, brought forth so much pain. Needless to say we had a lot of processing to do.

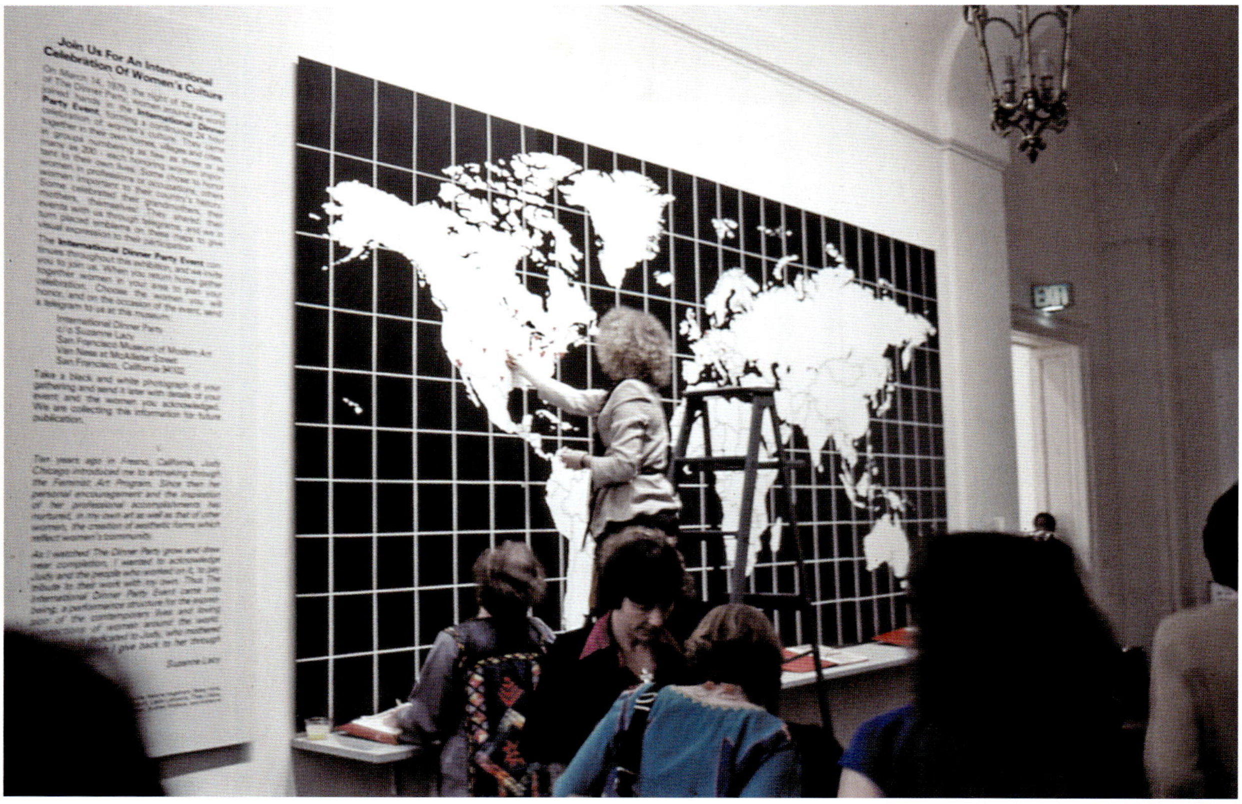

Suzanne Lacy marking locations on the *International Dinner Party* world map, San Francisco Museum of Modern Art, March 14, 1979

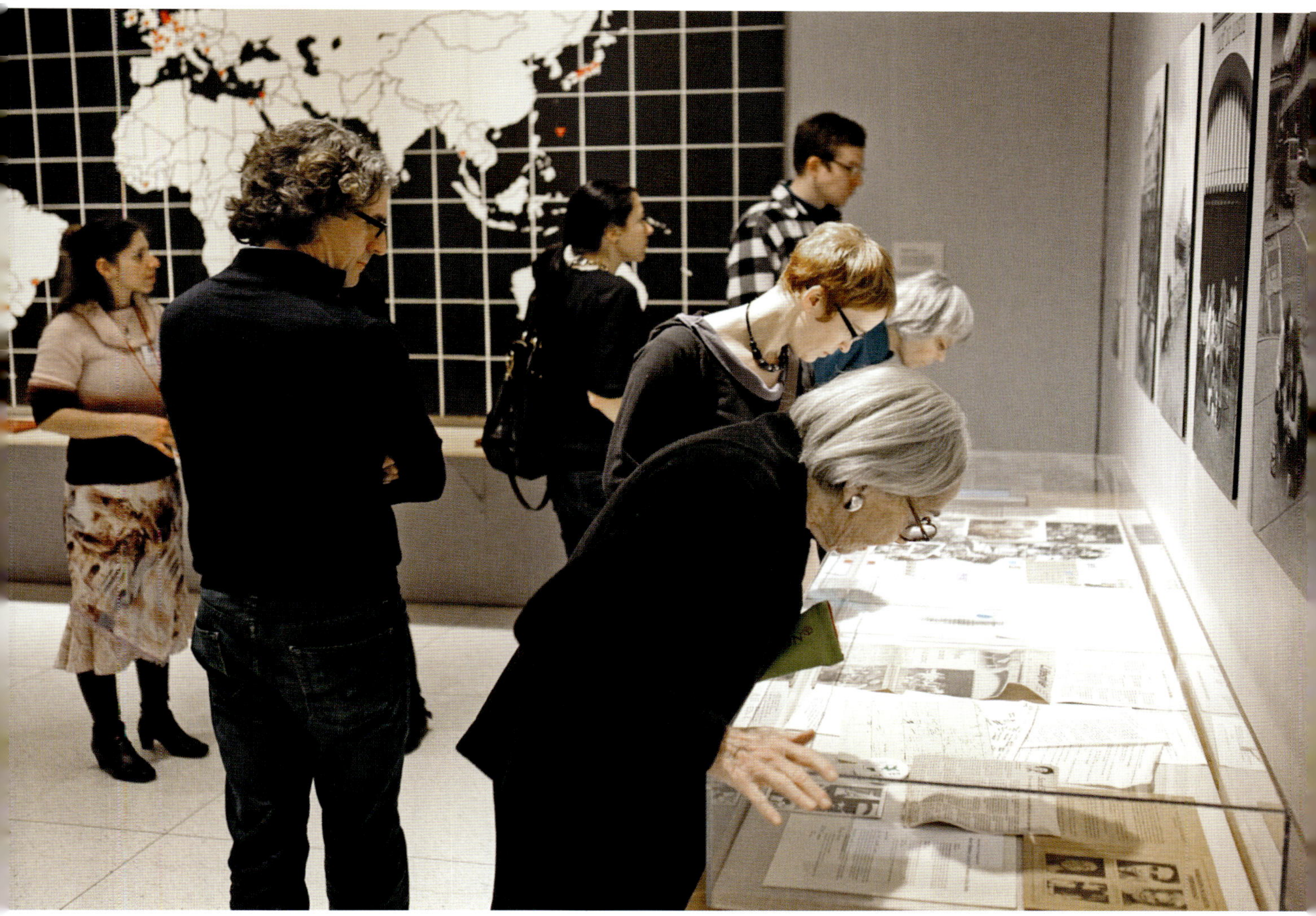

International Dinner Party, installation view,
Smart Museum of Art, 2012

Tom Marioni

SAN FRANCISCO-BASED ARTIST Tom Marioni has been a pivotal figure in the development of conceptual and performance art. His projects since the 1960s have been influenced by his interests in Zen, yoga, and jazz—especially the practice of improvisation within predetermined parameters. In several series of drawings and performances, for instance, he transforms simple, repeatable gestures into works of art that test the body's capacities. In his recent series *Out of Body Free-Hand Circles* (2007–present), each circle is built up through a repeated circling motion with pencil in hand, its diameter determined by the reach of his arm. Marioni also championed early conceptual and performance art as curator at the Richmond Art Center in the late 1960s and at his pioneering artist-run space, the Museum of Conceptual Art (1970–1984). (In both of those roles he presented work by *Feast* artists, including Bonnie Ora Sherk and Barbara T. Smith.)

In 1970, Marioni began a project centered on hospitality: *The Act of Drinking Beer with Friends Is the Highest Form of Art.* He created its first incarnation under the playful pseudonym Allan Fish. For this near-invisible performance for the Oakland Museum, he invited a small group to drink in the exhibition gallery after hours, leaving a scattering of bottles as the only evidence of their presence. These basic elements—beer, friends, a place to drink—remain the core of this now-legendary piece, which Marioni has continued with slight variations for more than forty years. It most commonly takes the form of weekly Wednesday-night salons in the artist's San Francisco studio. He refers to these events as an "artists' club" in which friends and invited guests gather for talk, jazz, and beer (served by guest bartenders; Marioni hosts, but never serves the beer himself). A set of rules (see pp. 95–97) serve as a kind of dryly funny comportment guide: "No collectors except in disguise," for instance. This project has existed with slight variants under other names—Café Wednesday and the Society for Independent Artists—and for a while during the mid-1970s it moved to a bar called Breen's, but Marioni's studio has been its primary home.

Occasionally the project also returns to its roots within museums, as it does for *Feast*. The physical elements of these presentations always include beer, a bar, a refrigerator labeled "FREE BEER," a table and chairs, and jazz music. The installation is always lit with yellow light bulbs—a color that Marioni likens to California sunshine, the intellect, the state of enlightenment, and the amber hue of many beers. The *Feast* installation also incorporates three other works: *Golden Rectangle Beer* (2004): a single-channel video in which the vertical screen becomes an analogue for a glass, filling with beer only to be drained and filled again. *An Aid to Communication* (1999/2012) is a wall-mounted set of beer-filled shelves proportioned—like the beer video—to match the ideal ratio known as the golden mean. Finally, Marioni made a new *Out of Body Free Hand Circle* (2007/2012) and used it as the backdrop for his deadpan stand-up comedy routine during *Feast*'s opening. And during monthly *Free Beer* evenings, all of these elements were activated by guest bartenders and beer drinkers who embrace the spirit of Marioni's art, with the bartenders and the museum staff acting as surrogate hosts on the artist's behalf. Like the circle drawings, the free beer evenings are not reperformances, but rather live incarnations of an ongoing work, in which the guests are invited to step into a space defined by Marioni's parameters—controlled by the artist but also always shaped by chance.

OPPOSITE: Marioni performs stand-up comedy in front of his *Out of Body Free Hand Circle* at the Smart Museum of Art, February 15, 2012

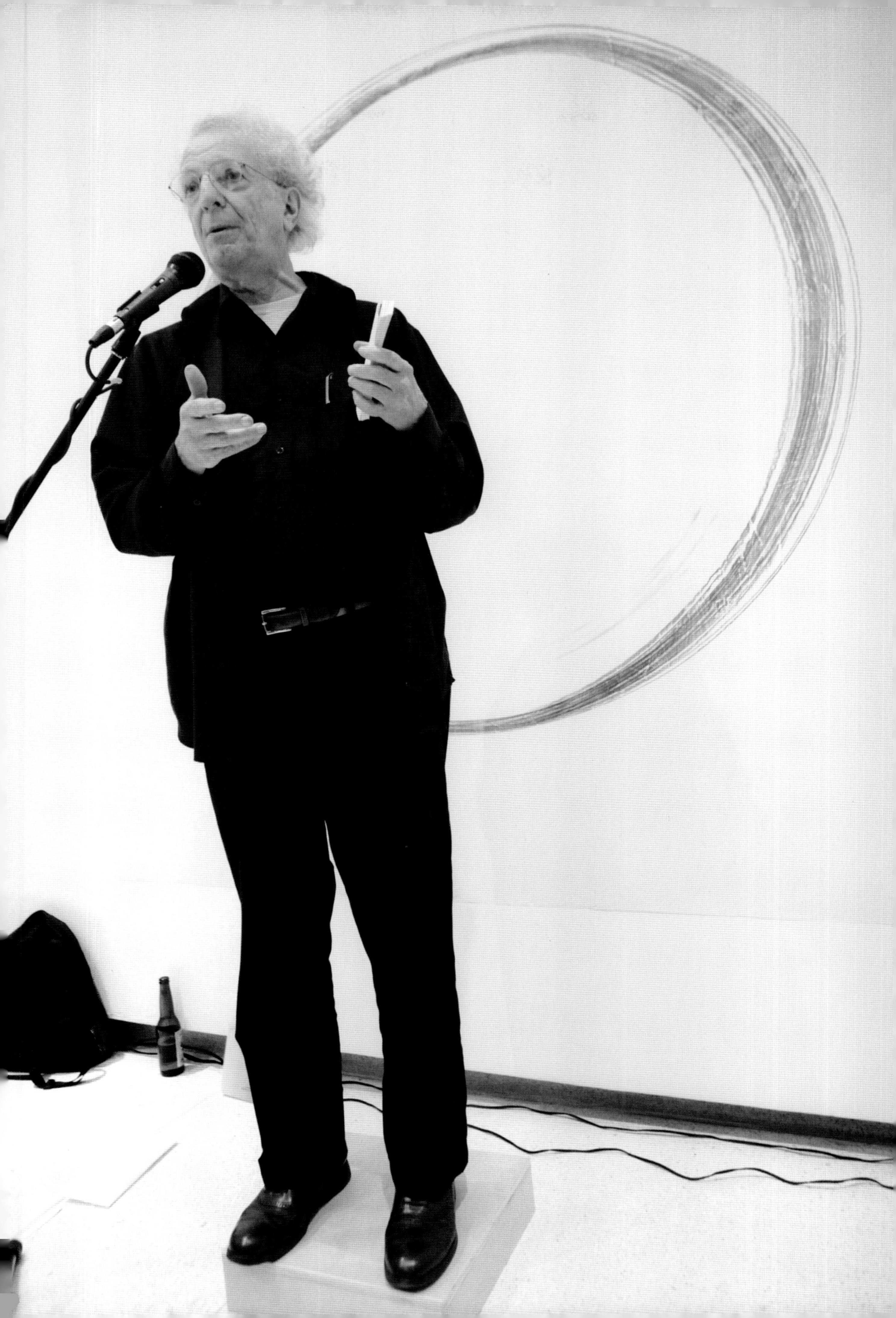

Excerpts from

Beer, Art, and Philosophy: A Memoir

by Tom Marioni

Museum of Conceptual Art, 1970

In 1970, working under the pseudonym Allan Fish, I made an exhibition in the Oakland Museum called *The Act of Drinking Beer with Friends Is the Highest Form of Art*. This was a social artwork. I am the author of this idea. In the '90s the idea of social interaction in an art context became an art movement.

I invited sixteen friends to the museum on a Monday when it was normally closed. Since I didn't want to subject my friends to being performers, the public was not invited. I told the curator, George Neubert, to get the beer and to be there. Everybody showed up, and we drank and had a good time. The debris was left on exhibit as a record of the event. Basically, the show consisted of the evidence of the act. It was an important work for me, because it defined Action rather than Object as art. And drinking beer was one of the things I learned in art school.

Earlier that year, in March, I had started my own museum as an excuse for a party. I was still curator of the Richmond Art Center, but I wanted to do more radical things than I could do at Richmond. I rented a large room at 86 Third Street, south of Market Street in San Francisco. The Museum of Conceptual Art [MOCA] began at the start of a new decade, 1970, and continued until 1984. All the things that happened there in the first few years were actions by sculptors. I even did a show called "Actions by Sculptors for the Home Audience." It was made for KQED-TV, a PBS station, in 1974.

There were very few painters in the Conceptual era; painting was not part of the avant-garde

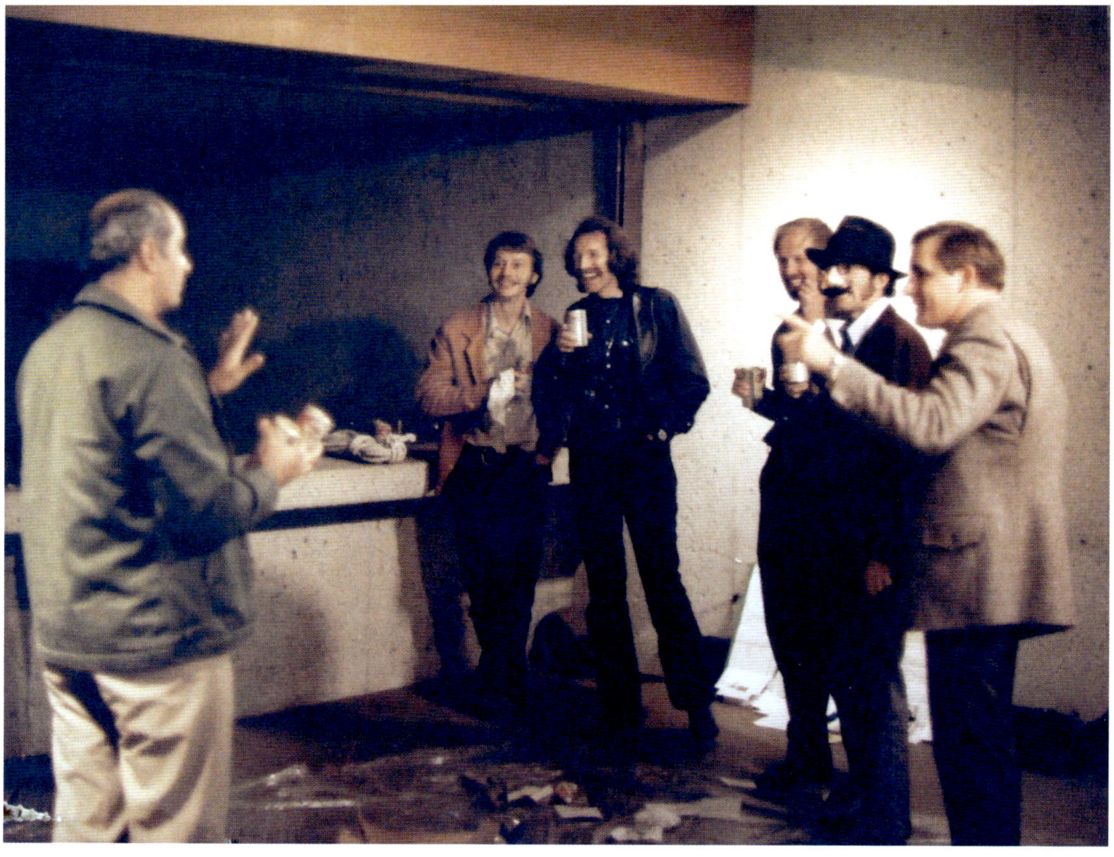

The first iteration of *The Act of Drinking Beer with Friends Is the Highest Form of Art* (by Marioni under the pseudonym Allan Fish), Oakland Museum, 1970

anymore. You evolve from painting to sculpture; that's how I saw it in the '70s. My museum was for action art, actions by sculptors, and site-specific installations . . .

. . . I had lost my job at Richmond in 1971, and by 1973 I was divorced and had moved into my San Francisco studio, which was a tiny room in the back of my Museum of Conceptual Art.

At that time, some critics were starting to write that Performance Art was merging all the arts together into one multimedia happening. They hadn't caught on to the idea that Happenings were over with by the mid-'60s. Performance Art, which as concrete and not decorative or theatrical, replaced Happenings . . .

. . . In '73 there was a show at MOCA called "All Night Sculptures," probably the most interesting show that happened there. It was very serious. Nine artists designed works for all-night viewing: installations that had something to do with nighttime or performances that went on for twelve hours form sunset to sunrise. People could come at any time during the night to see the show . . .

. . . By the end of 1972, I had moved MOCA into a larger space across the street at 75 Third Street. It was a nonprofit organization, and I convinced the building owner to give me the space free because I was providing a service to the community. About a year after I moved in, the San Francisco Redevelopment Agency bought the building, and since their policy was to keep the rent the same as the tenant was paying to the former owner, they continued to give it to me free. The museum stayed in that building for twelve years.

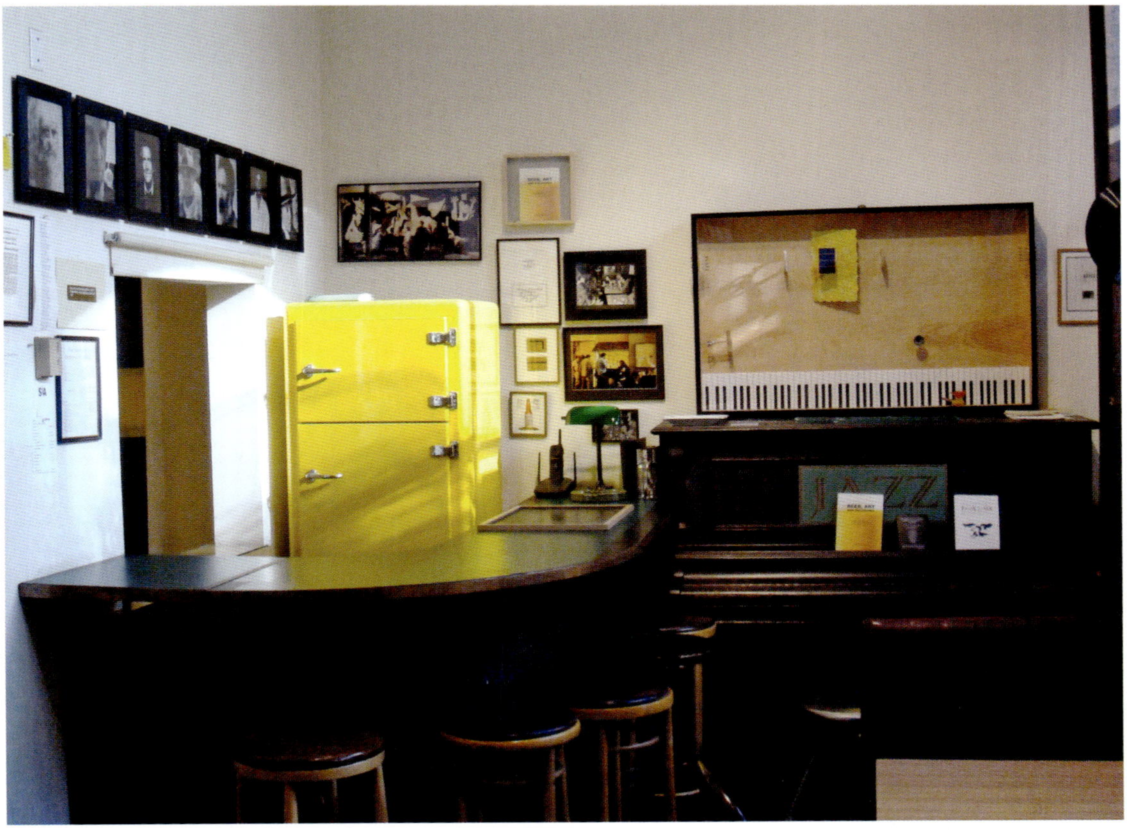

Marioni's studio in San Francisco

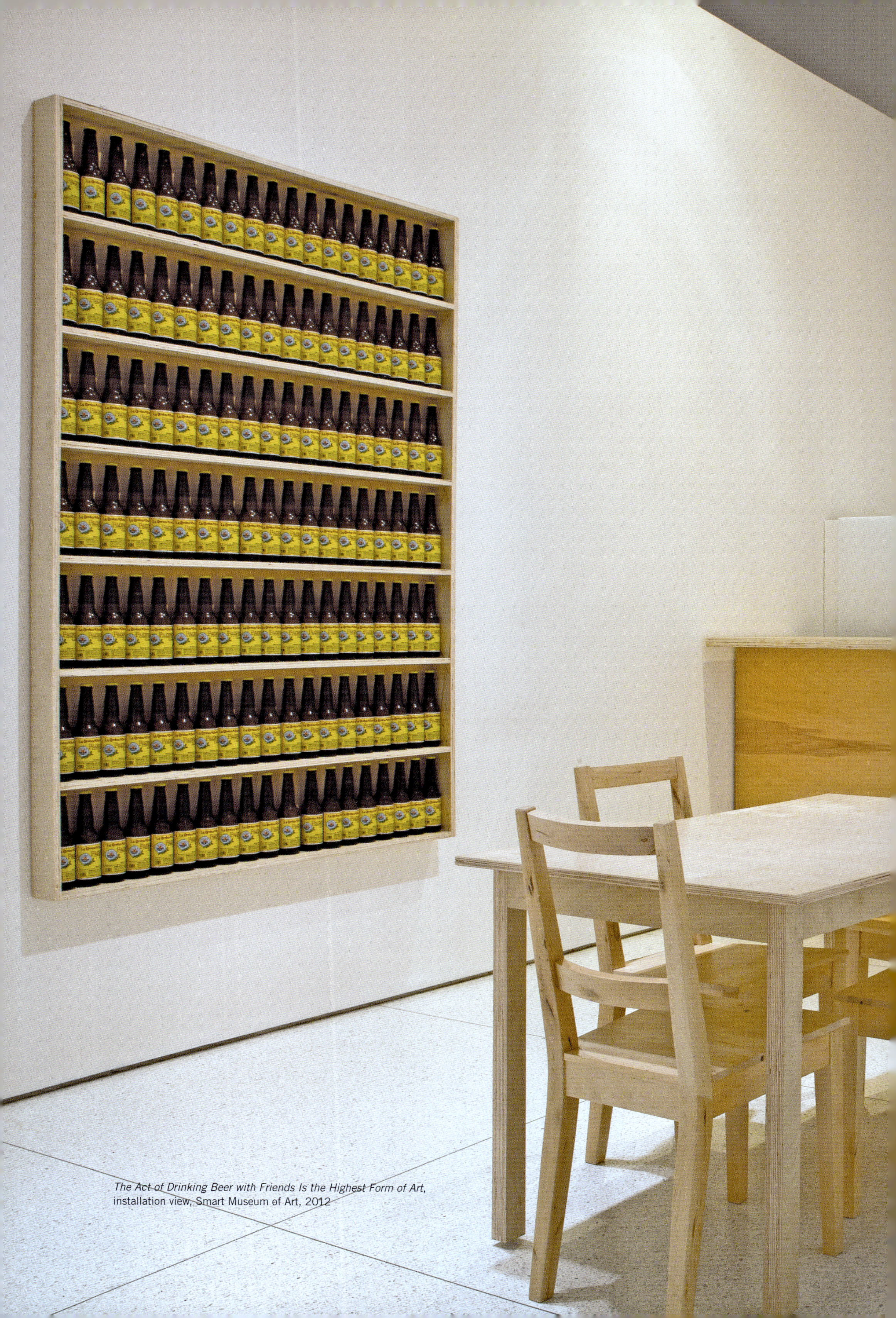

The Act of Drinking Beer with Friends Is the Highest Form of Art, installation view, Smart Museum of Art, 2012

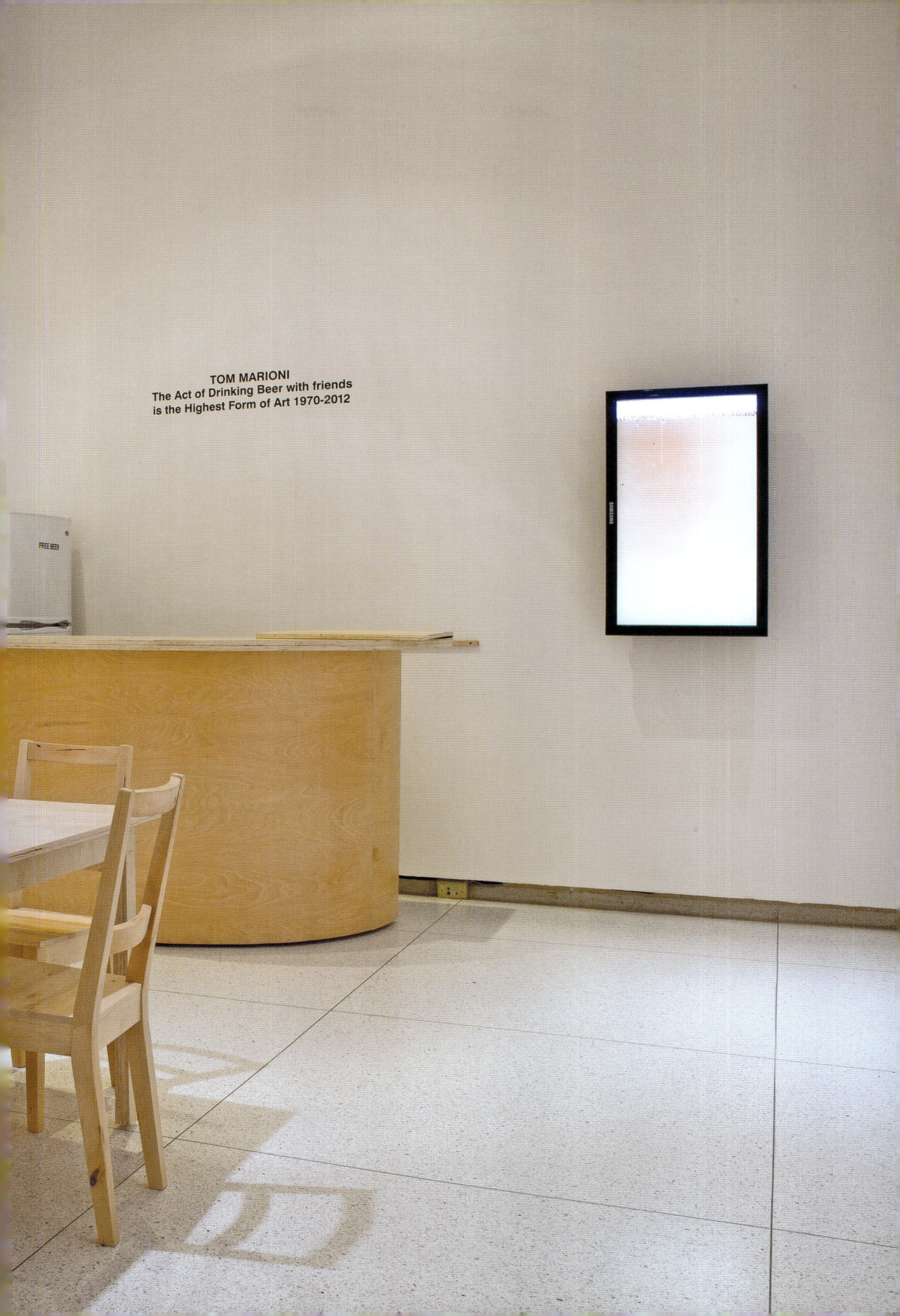
TOM MARIONI
The Act of Drinking Beer with friends
is the Highest Form of Art 1970-2012
FREE BEER
SAMSUNG

The new MOCA was upstairs from Breen's, a historic San Francisco bar and hofbrau-style restaurant with a carved wooden back-bar that had come through the Panama Canal from Germany in the early '20s. I used a booth in front, near the street, as my office. There was a public phone on the wall next to it.

I appealed for museum members and listed the benefits: ten thousand square feet of exhibition space, seven stories of parking next door, a café downstairs, and free beer on Wednesdays while artists' videotapes were shown. I had a refrigerator with the words *Free Beer* on the door. I bought the cheapest beer I could, supermarket beer at eighty nine cents for a six pack of short bottles of Fisher beer.

I defined Conceptual Art as "idea-oriented situations not directed at the production of static objects. . ."

. . . For me, Action Art is social and is about communication . . .

. . . In 1971, I did an endurance piece in an art gallery in San Francisco. It was called *Allan Fish Drinks a Case of Beer*. That piece had its roots in my art school days. Back then, when a guy who said he couldn't afford much said he wanted to buy one of my paintings, I offered to trade the painting for a case of beer. When I gave him the painting he said, "Here's the money for the case of beer," and handed me $5. He even wanted change because a case of beer cost $4.75. This bugged me for years. I had thought that the painting would be worth the experience of getting drunk off a case of beer, because that was an experience you'd remember the rest of your life. But I wanted to barter the painting for the experience, not have money come in between. Of course, in the '50s I didn't know what Conceptual Art was. It wasn't a movement then. But I was starting to think about art as experience. I did go out and buy a case of beer with the money, and I drank it in one day. I was twenty-one at the time.

Thirteen years later when I did the *Allan Fish Drinks a Case of Beer* piece, I tried to drink the whole case, but I only got as far as seventeen bottles. The bottles are a record of the act, seventeen empty Beck's beer bottles upside down in a wooden case that has twenty four slots. I cheated, because two of the bottles were drunk by Howard Fried and Terry Fox, friends who showed up in the afternoon. I signed the bottles I drank and they signed theirs too.

I started at noon and finished at 8pm It turned out that the piece was about creating an art situation that changed as I became more inebriated and that influenced my aesthetic decisions. The piece had the character of jazz, which is a structure for improvisation. I had a refrigerator in the gallery, a comfortable chair, my conga drum, and other things I thought I would need. My hat and my coat were hanging up on the wall. As the show progressed, I arranged the room and made an environment. I ran threads across the room to create a barrier between the public and me. The opening was from 6 to 8, and I was already drunk by the time it began. At the opening I drew some lines on my face. My face looked like a Picasso, or a Futurist painting, like I was moving: three noses going off to the side, an extra eye on my temple, and my mouth made wider. I had a radio, a record player, and a tape recorder going, and I was playing the conga drum. Later I changed the title of the piece to *The Creation of a Situation and Environment while Becoming Increasingly More Intoxicated.*

Another beer piece (1976) took longer to do. I drank a bottle of beer from a different country each day and placed the empty bottles on a long shelf. The work became a world map in beer bottles that I called *From China to Czechoslovakia*. In 1973 in my Museum of Conceptual Art I had a refrigerator filled with free beer and each Wednesday people watched Video Art and drank beer. I put the empty bottles for that whole year on a long shelf . . .

. . . I am fascinated by art that can only be seen if you know it is art. If something that's not painting or sculpture seems interesting and is in an art context it might be a work of invisible art . . .

. . . For a couple of years in 1973 and 1974 every Wednesday afternoon there was free beer in MOCA while artists' videotapes were shown. In '76 I decided to meet people downstairs in Breen's Café, and I sent out cards announcing *Café Society* "twotofour" every Wednesday in the "saloon of MOCA." I got the name from Bob Feldman, a New York publisher. I had just done a one-page photo

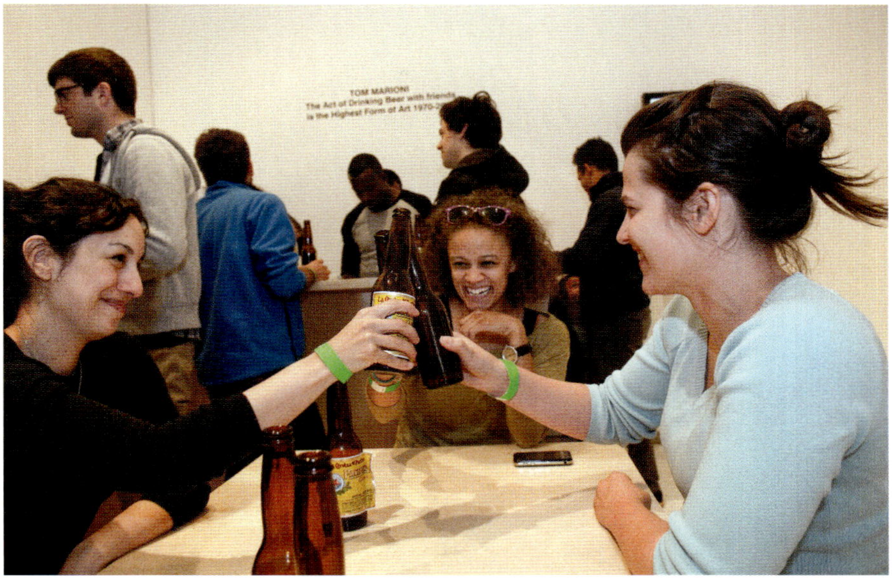

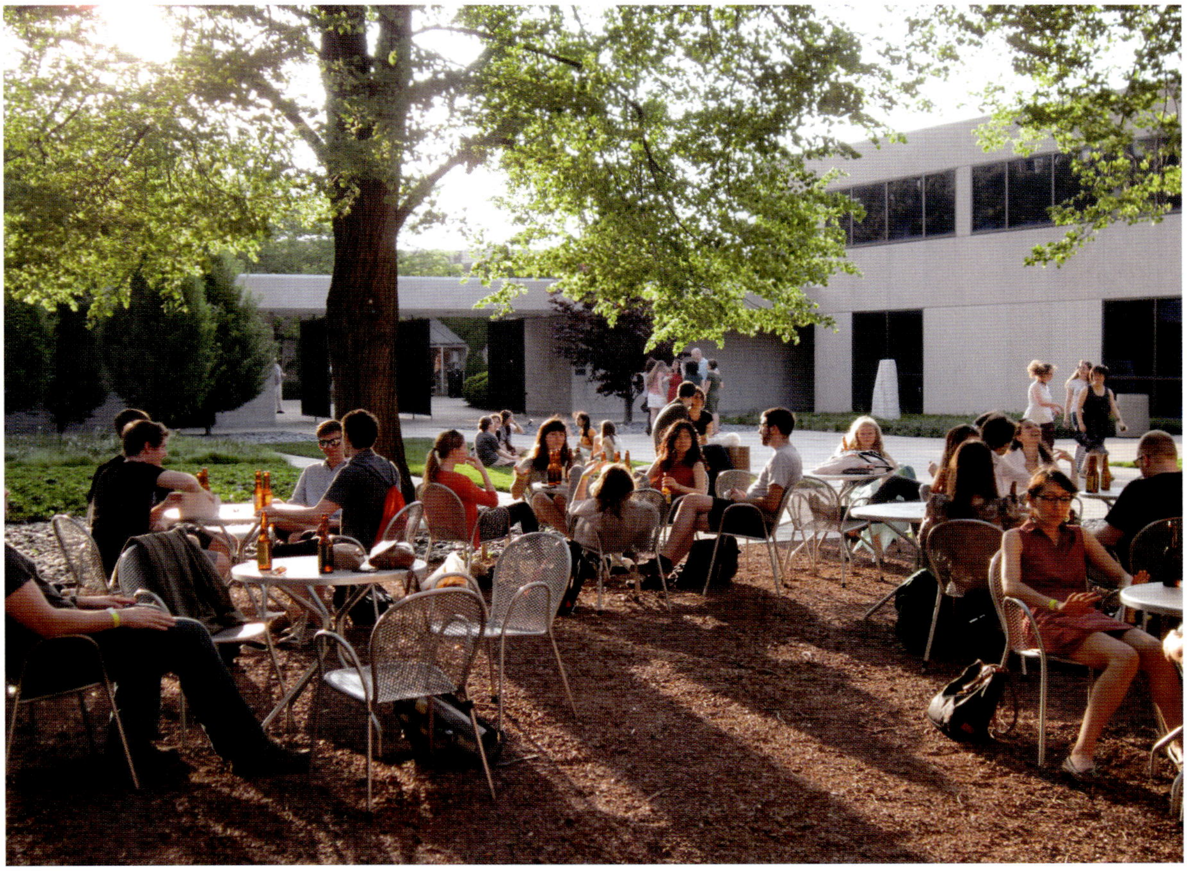

TOP: *The Act of Drinking Beer with Friends Is the Highest Form of Art*, Smart Museum of Art, April 5, 2012

BOTTOM: *The Act of Drinking Beer with Friends Is the Highest Form of Art,* Smart Museum of Art, May 3, 2012

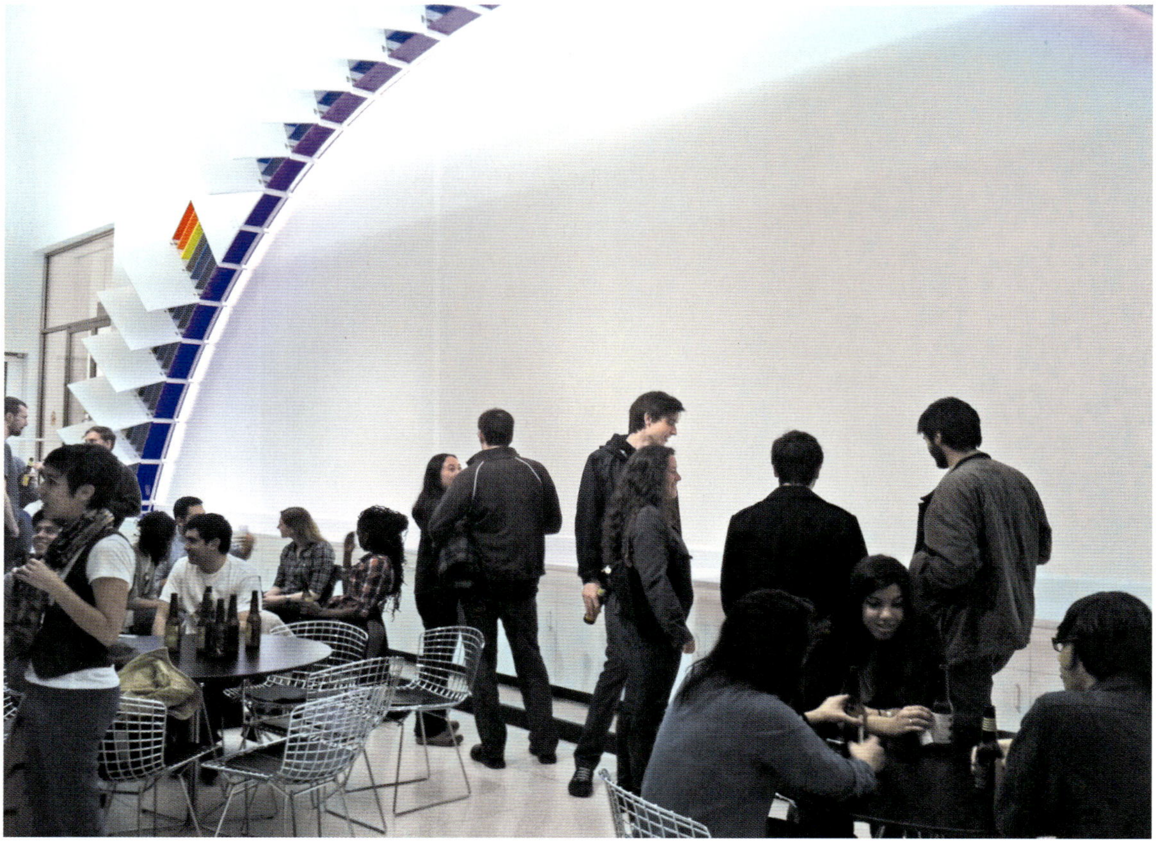

The Act of Drinking Beer with Friends Is the Highest Form of Art,
Smart Museum of Art, March 1, 2012

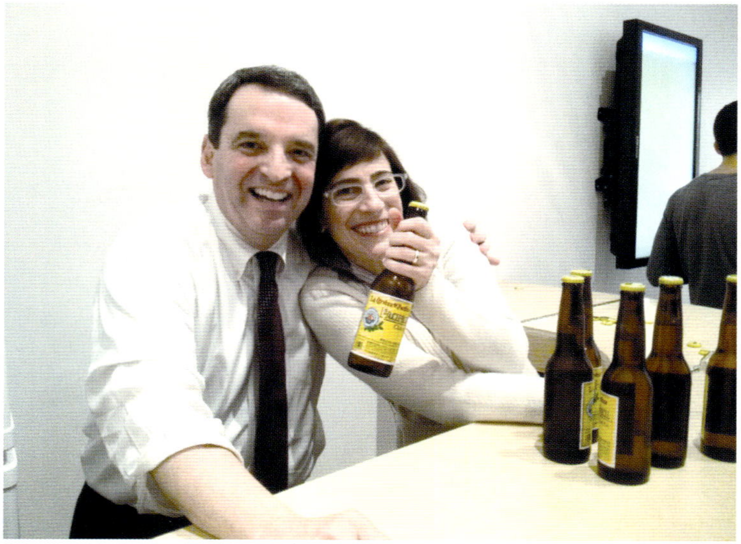

Anthony Hirschel (left) and Madeline Grynsztejn (right) hosting *The Act of Drinking Beer with Friends Is the Highest Form of Art*, Smart Museum of Art, March 1, 2012

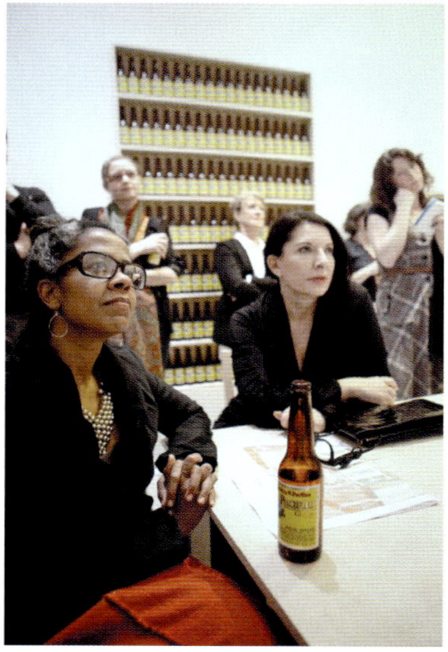

Torkwase Dyson (left) and Marina Abramović attending *The Act of Drinking Beer with Friends Is the Highest Form of Art*, Smart Museum of Art, February 15, 2012

work for *San Francisco Magazine* that said, "There is meaning in life only if you devote yourself to society," and when Feldman saw it he said, "café society."

I went down to Breen's every Wednesday, sat there, and drank a beer. In the afternoon Breen's wasn't busy, and we took over the booths in the front of the bar. Later, the booths were reserved for us. Over the years, the meeting time has gotten later. Now it's in my studio and is from five to eight.

My *Café Society* became a kind of open house for artists, an artists' bar, really. In New York, a lot of artists were living in the same neighborhood, SoHo, which had bars where they hung out. But the only way to get an artists' scene going in San Francisco was to do it in an artificial way, by formalizing it, by inviting people.

This is a social artwork for me, another kind of invisible work. When Breen's closed in '79, I moved to the bar next door, Jerry & Johnny's. In 1980, I printed artists' credit cards and gave one to any artist who asked for it. The artist would show the card to the bartender in order to get free beer. The money for this came from a grant to SITE, Inc., an alternative art space run by a friend of mine, Alan Scarritt. He had closed his space on Mission Street and moved to New York without using up a grant he had received, so he turned over one thousand dollars of it to me. At that point I wasn't receiving NEA grants anymore. I was too elitist for them. I was not an arm of the government with a multicultural board of advisors. They were on to me.

In 1984 I closed MOCA. I lost the building, but also it was the end of an era, and I hadn't done any shows since 1981. Conceptual Art has come back now, but it was dead in the '80s. Art schools were starting to have Conceptual Art departments. It had become an academy. After MOCA officially closed, I changed the name of my meetings to "Academy of MOCA." My meetings were an academy like in the time of Aristotle, basically a bunch of people hanging out, drinking, and having conversations. When I first started the meetings, I was trying to recreate the feel of the Paris café scene in the 1920s where artists and writers met each other. I thought café society meant drunken parties where ideas are born.

I always wanted to be legitimate, to carry on traditions, and at the same time to get away with something. That was why I started a museum in the first place. With my own academy, I was in a position where I didn't have to get a degree from anybody. I was in a position, actually, to give a degree to somebody. Today I give GB (Graduate Bartender) degrees to guest bartenders who sign up three times to tend bar on Wednesdays.

The Academy of MOCA met at Jerry & Johnny's for ten years until the '89 earthquake in San Francisco closed it permanently. I was without a hangout for six months, but temporary Wednesdays continued first in the House of Shields bar a block away and later at the Capp Street Project, an art space where I had an exhibition. Then I got a new studio. There was no bar downstairs, so I built one in my studio.

For two years, 1990–92, until the Berkeley Art Museum at the University of California bought my archives, I called my Wednesday meetings "Archives of MOCA," and after that I switched to calling it "Café Wednesday." As of 2000 it is called the Society of Independent Artists, SIA, which was the name of the organization that organized Duchamp's famous urinal in 1917. Over the years, I have exhibited several social art installations that included bars activated on Wednesdays. My Wednesdays have evolved over the years into a kind of salon. One of the original salons was started by Madame de Rambouillet in eighteenth-century France in order to have discourse that allowed men and women to talk to one another on an equal basis. The concept of the opera was invented in Florence, Italy, by a group of musicians, artists, and writers, a club called the Camerata. Sometimes I tell people I have an Italian social club and I'm the only Italian in it.

Café Wednesday has become by necessity a private club. People bring their own drinks. I had to establish house rules:

People bring their own drinks except first timers who don't know any better.

Two-drink minimum; this means at least two. I don't want people to pop in and have a quick drink, or maybe not even have a drink. I don't want them to come with the idea that they'll look over the situation and then maybe split. I want people to know where they are. One time there was a woman who came as a guest of a guest and then started bringing her lonely friends. They would just sit, like they were watching a play. They wouldn't drink, and they wouldn't talk. Finally, I said to her, "I'm trying to project an air of sophistication here. I'm not running a mission."

No beer in cans except Tecate. I think it is elegant to have glass bottles. Glass is a more noble material than a tin can. Also, people tend to drink directly out of cans, because a can is shaped like a glass. They might not as readily drink out of a bottle. The exception for Tecate is because it is traditionally served with a slice of lemon, and I think this beer actually tastes better out of the can, with the lemon and the metallic taste. Lemon brings out the taste of most things. You can even put a piece of lemon in a Budweiser and it tastes pretty good. And I like the way the lemon looks. Tecate shouldn't be confused with Corona, when it is served with a little wedge of lime. That was a yuppie fad in the '80s.

No drinking from beer bottles except in character. It is not dignified to drink directly out of the bottle. Like the Hennie Youngman joke, "My mother is ninety two years old, never uses glasses. Drinks straight out of the bottle." The exception for character is an acknowledgment of individual style. For instance, a cowboy would drink out of a bottle, never use a glass.

No use of telephone except with consent. That's so people won't take me for granted and think I'm just a public place, a service paid for with a government grant. Those days are gone for good.

No one behind the bar except the bartender.

Bartenders can invite up to three guests. Joyce Umamoto was the permanent bartender for the first five years we met in my studio, and since she "retired" I have had guest bartenders who sign up in advance. The bartenders can invite three guests so they participate by making it partly their own party. That is also a way for me to meet some interesting new people.

Guests do not invite guests without checking with the management. Three obnoxious people can come into a party of twelve and ruin everything. People coming into this scene should be sympathetic to the situation. This is an artists' club. I told one guy who was bugging me not to come back. He didn't know who Sol LeWitt was. If you don't know who Sol LeWitt is, you can't come in.

No theater people except famous movie stars. Theater people are too theatrical. The exception for movie stars is because they are celebrities not theater people.

No art students except those who can pass as professionals. Once a guy showed up in Breen's Bar with his class. There were only enough places for eight or ten people, and he showed up with about ten. They all sat as if they were in class waiting for somebody to teach them. The exception is because sometimes art students are smart and interesting. It could happen.

No smoking, except writers and cigar smokers. The exception for writers is to allow some smokers but limit the number. It has been abused. Anyone can claim to be a writer who can type. The exception for cigar smokers is because cigars are not inhaled and are not intended to be a nicotine delivery system. The experience is about taste and aroma. It enhances a social situation and becomes an aid to communication. Cigarettes use cheaper tobacco and also burn paper, creating an offensive smell. Cigar smoke, like gasoline, can create nostalgia, like memories of childhood sitting in the back seat of your family car gassing up on a trip to Syracuse, New York. The smell of a cigar, for instance, reminds Lydia of her grandfather. The rule prohibiting cigarettes should not be taken as discriminatory against women.

No touching objects or books on shelves.

No art collectors except in disguise. I know the way some artists act around art collectors. I've been guilty myself of kissing up to them, but not enough to actually sell my work. Some collectors get used to artists kissing up to them and take advantage of that. They say they are art collectors as if that were a profession. An art collector is a disguise if he doesn't announce he's an art collector. I don't want my friends to embarrass themselves kissing up in front of others, which is what they should be doing in private.

People should sign the guest book at the bar. The guest book is to keep a record. People like to know who came the week before. Like in a mystery novel, if you want to commit a crime, you could sign in, leave, murder somebody, and be back before closing time.

Hours 5–8, except on special occasions. Like when everyone is having "such a good time." *Leave the bathroom light on.*[1]

. . . Another work of mine owned by the museum also has elements of male, female, and spirit. *Free Beer (The Act of Drinking Beer with Friends Is the Highest Form of Art), 1970–1979*, is an installation that contains my old 1950 Coldspot refrigerator from MOCA with the words *Free Beer* printed on the door and behind it on the wall a shelf unit with 216 empty bottles of Anchor Steam Beer. A yellow lightbulb hangs from the ceiling and illuminates the bottles and the refrigerator. The lightbulb represents the spirit (enlightenment), the refrigerator the female (container, nourishment, womb), and the empty beer bottles the male (phallus).

2001

. . . Living in California, it was impossible for me not to be influenced by Asian culture. Being on the Coast makes it easy to mix European style with Zen philosophy. When you're coasting, you get momentum from the flow of the road under you. I like the simplicity of Zen philosophy and that it doesn't take itself too seriously. And its soul, or spirit, is in nature.

. . . Some artists younger than me complain that "it's all been done before." But someone comes along every once in a while and puts something out there that nobody ever thought of. In the '60s when Carl Andre used bricks as the subject of his art, and Dan Flavin used lighted fluorescent tubes, it seemed that all the materials in life had been claimed. Then an underground Conceptual Art movement was born, and by the early '70s a new field had opened up. By the end of the '70s, after art had become so close to real life that it was invisible to most of the public, painting returned to the marketplace and retreated into safe old styles . . .

. . . At some point, artists and their art became material for the installations of a few curators. As those curators began to think of themselves as artists, they used fine art, folk art, and objects from popular culture as their material, and presented them together, confusing the public about what art is. I don't like to sound pedantic but I believe art is a poetic record of the culture with the power to inspire people to a spiritual awareness. I also think art represents the culture's most excellent examples of visual ideas. You cannot pretend that art and nonart are the same.

Art can become serious again. Even art with wit and art with beauty should have political content, have a subject, make a point, and not be an ornament. Picasso said that when he painted his *Guernica* in 1937 that "painting is not done to decorate apartments; it is an instrument of war . . . against brutality and darkness."

What is art for?

For beauty,
For history,
For decorating apartments,
For people to laugh at,
For imitating nature,
For therapy,
For seeing in a new way,
For an educated audience,
For enlightenment,
For political agendas,
For glorifying the church in the Renaissance,
For glorifying the state under communism,
For glorifying the rich in capitalism,
For recording society in a poetic way.

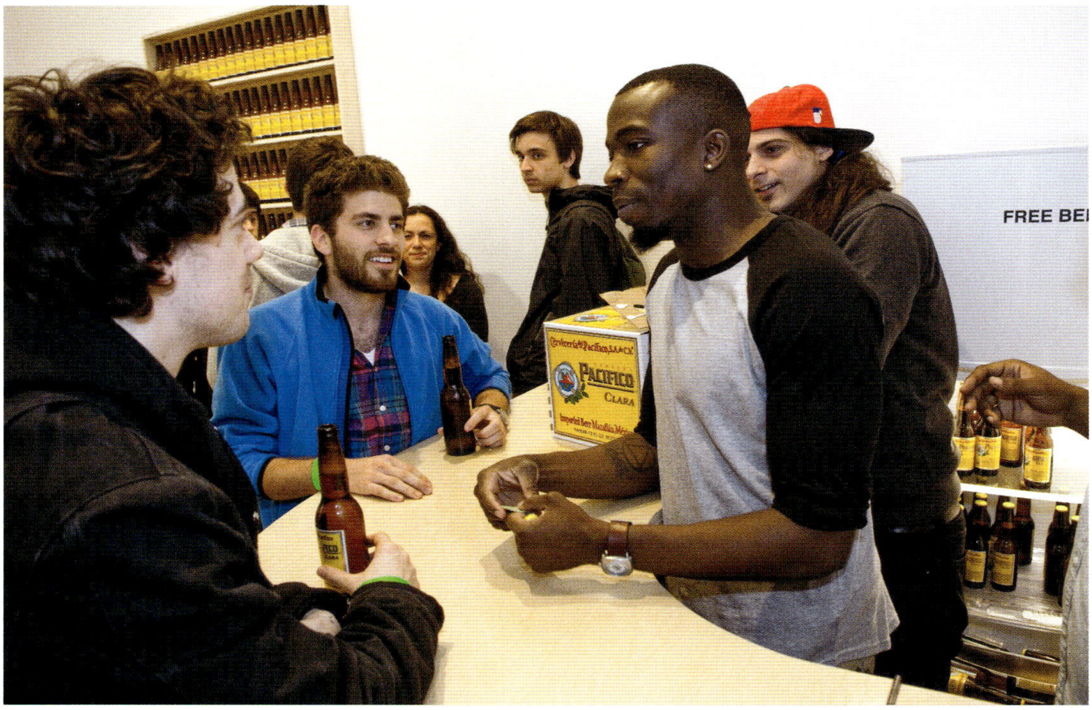

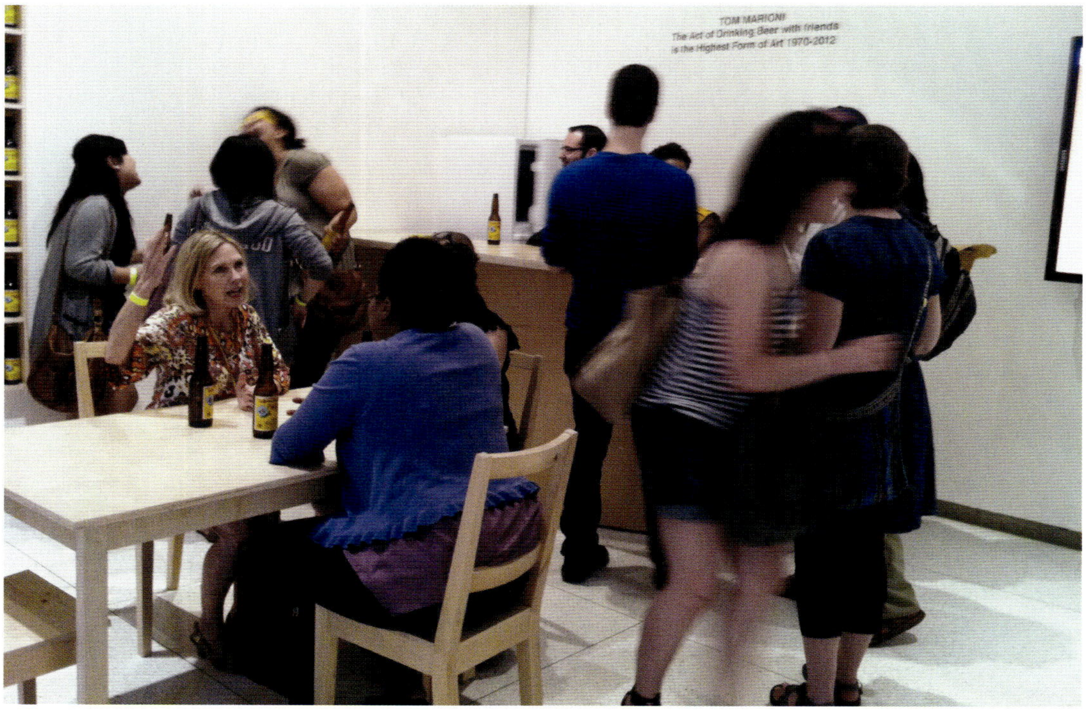

TOP: The hip-hop group BBU guest bartends for *The Act of Drinking Beer with Friends Is the Highest Form of Art*, Smart Museum of Art, April 5, 2012

BOTTOM: *The Act of Drinking Beer with Friends Is the Highest Form of Art*, Smart Museum of Art, May 3, 2012

Epilogue

. . . Sometimes at my Wednesday salon parties there is a moment when only men are present, and it becomes an opportunity to talk about girls without concern for the politically correct terminology. I'm sure women do the same thing when there are no men around. But I created a salon for men and women; an early definition of a salon is a place where men and women can talk on an equal basis. We talk about jazz and art, tell jokes and lies, smoke and drink. The cigar adds to the intoxication in the room. I'm going for a mood.

A French visitor told me that my space was elegant without being bourgeois. The lights are on a rheostat; the floor is hardwood stained dark walnut. The bar is dark and curved so people can see others at the bar; the booths are red and curved to create a second group. The ceiling is thirteen feet high. The bathroom looks like a gallery. Behind my desk is an art library with a blue MOCA neon sign. I have an upright grand piano that gets played sometimes. When a workman was working in my studio he said, "is this going to be a lounge?"

I play music that I recorded on continuous-play tapes so that it seems like a jukebox is always on. The music I play is modern Jazz—by "modern" I mean late '40s bebop through mid '60s hard bop. Once in a while I sneak in some classical music to change the mood for a few minutes, and sometimes I play a tape I made of sounds from Breen's Bar in the '70s. People start to talk more when there is a recorded talking. It sounds like a lot of people are in the room and it picks up a slow party . . .

. . . I don't really have an ending to this book because I have many more years to live. When George Burns was ninety-nine years old he was asked this question: "You smoke nine cigars and have two martinis a day, what does your doctor say about that?" Burns said, "My doctor's dead."

The comedian George Carlin said, "The job of the comedian is to find where the line is drawn, deliberately cross it, and make the audience glad you took them with you."

I would say that's the job of all artists.

These excerpts have been previously published in Tom Marioni, *Beer, Art and Philosophy: A Memoir* (San Francisco: Crown Point Press, 2007), 87–90, 93–94, 99–104, 108–11, 115–22, 182, 199, 203–05, 207–09.

---

[1] Since the publication of *Beer Art and Philosophy: A Memoir*, Marioni has added an important rule #1: "The management reserves the right to refuse service to anyone who doesn't know where they are or what is going on." There is also no longer cigar-smoking.

Gordon Matta-Clark

IN 1971, GORDON MATTA-CLARK and his partner, the dancer Carol Gooden, held a pig roast under the Brooklyn Bridge. After hours of turning a homemade spit, the couple had served hundreds of pork sandwiches to a large group of friends assembled for the event. Gathering in a public space for a spectacle of collective cooking, eating, and shared labor appealed to Matta-Clark's anti-establishment social politics: *Pig Roast* fed and entertained a crowd, and also generated an exciting scene. The event's ethos foreshadows the consideration of urban space, generosity, and commitment that would motivate FOOD—the cooperative restaurant that Matta-Clark and Gooden founded with friends in a SoHo storefront later in 1971. Run and staffed by artists, FOOD became a model for experimental practice and artistic life in lower Manhattan in the 1970s.

During the golden years of operation under Gooden's management, 1971 to 1973, FOOD occupied a middle ground between art project, business, home, intervention, and dinner theater—"a place to meet, discuss and debate... and to redesign, to alter and construct."[1] In addition to the social component, FOOD was an early site for Matta-Clark to experiment with the architectural cutting that he would later pursue more extensively and dramatically elsewhere. The restaurant provided an ideal model for the intersection of disorder, creation and deconstruction fundamental to the way that Matta-Clark worked, and to the nature of his interests in both community and architecture. In a letter to a friend in 1971, Matta-Clark wrote:

> I keep wondering why I am doing this—just what is the purpose of devoting so much energy to a highly demanding activity. It cannot be for business or money alone. There are deeper needs and pleasures at stake. Something more gutsy like a real hang-up with food.[2]

FOOD offered locally sourced, nourishing food at reasonable prices, and a place for artists and friends to gather at a time and in a neighborhood when such places were few and far between. It served as a model for flexible, sympathetic employment for artists: a place where one could work irregular hours, while enjoying the possibility of productive community. Occasionally, FOOD also offered a provocatively themed meal—including one famous "Matta Bones" menu, on which all items were served with unusual animal bones. Even on days when the menu consisted of the standard homemade bread and thick soups, however, FOOD sought to achieve the kind of effervescent energy of a place in which a bone-meal is always a possibility. This energy and ambitiousness is perhaps best documented in the film Matta-Clark made in collaboration with Robert Frank, *A Day in the Life of Food*, which was featured in *Feast*. The film affectionately follows Gooden and other instrumental members through a day of tasks: from an early-morning fish market barter to chopping ingredients for stews, to laughing and drinking with friends, and kneading dough for the next day's bread. *Feast* also included a selection of advertisements printed in the avant-garde magazine *Avalanche* in the early 1970s; these ads would have attracted potential customers while reinforcing FOOD's hybrid status as both a business and a cultural experiment.

Sarah Mendelsohn wrote this text.

---

[1] Gordon Matta-Clark, quoted in *Gordon-Matta Clark: Works and Collected Writings*, ed. Gloria Moure (Barcelona and New York: Ediciones Polígrafa and D.A.P./Distributed Art Publishers, 2006), 13.

[2] Moure, 29. Matta-Clark addressed this letter to St. Lee Junior.

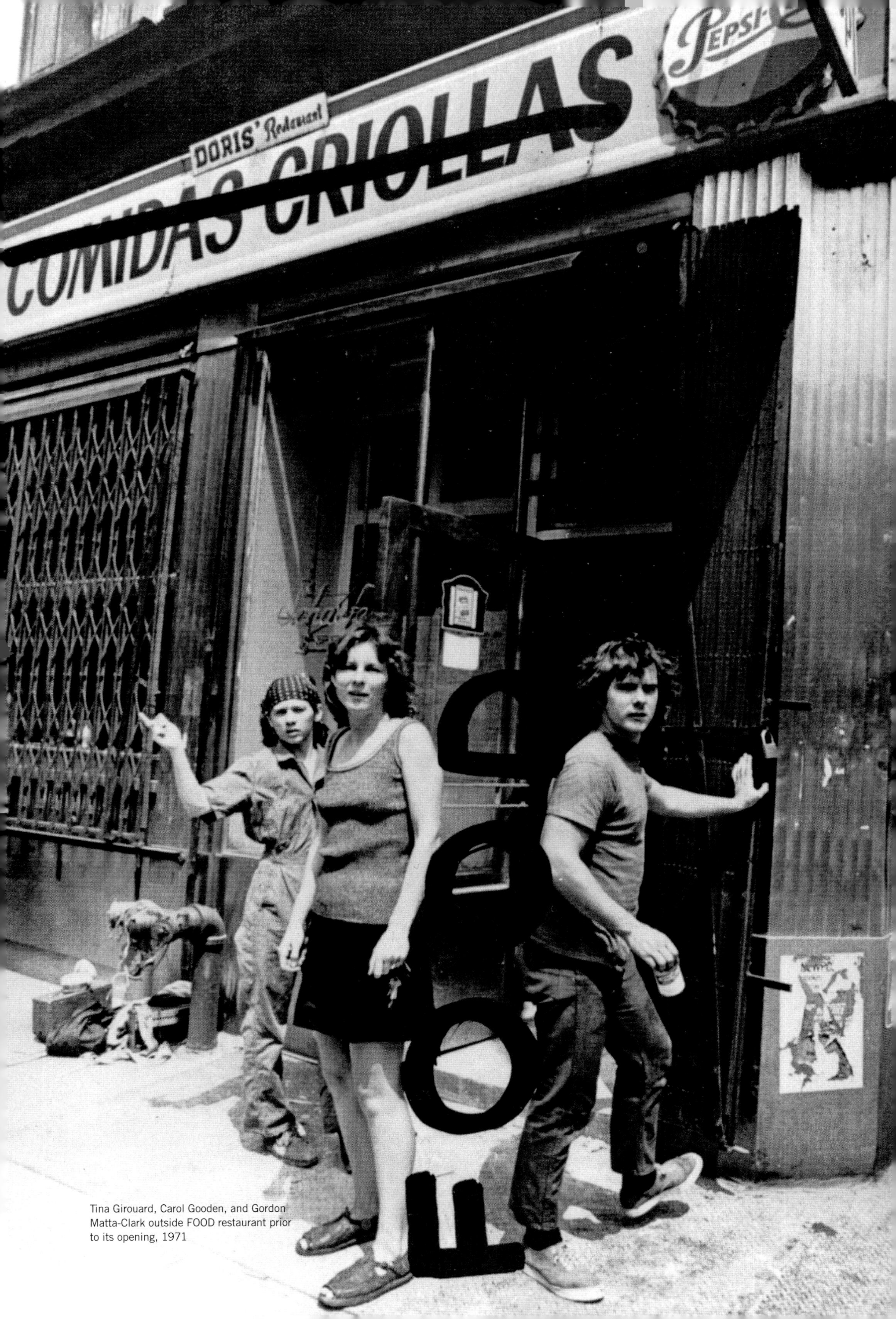

Tina Girouard, Carol Gooden, and Gordon Matta-Clark outside FOOD restaurant prior to its opening, 1971

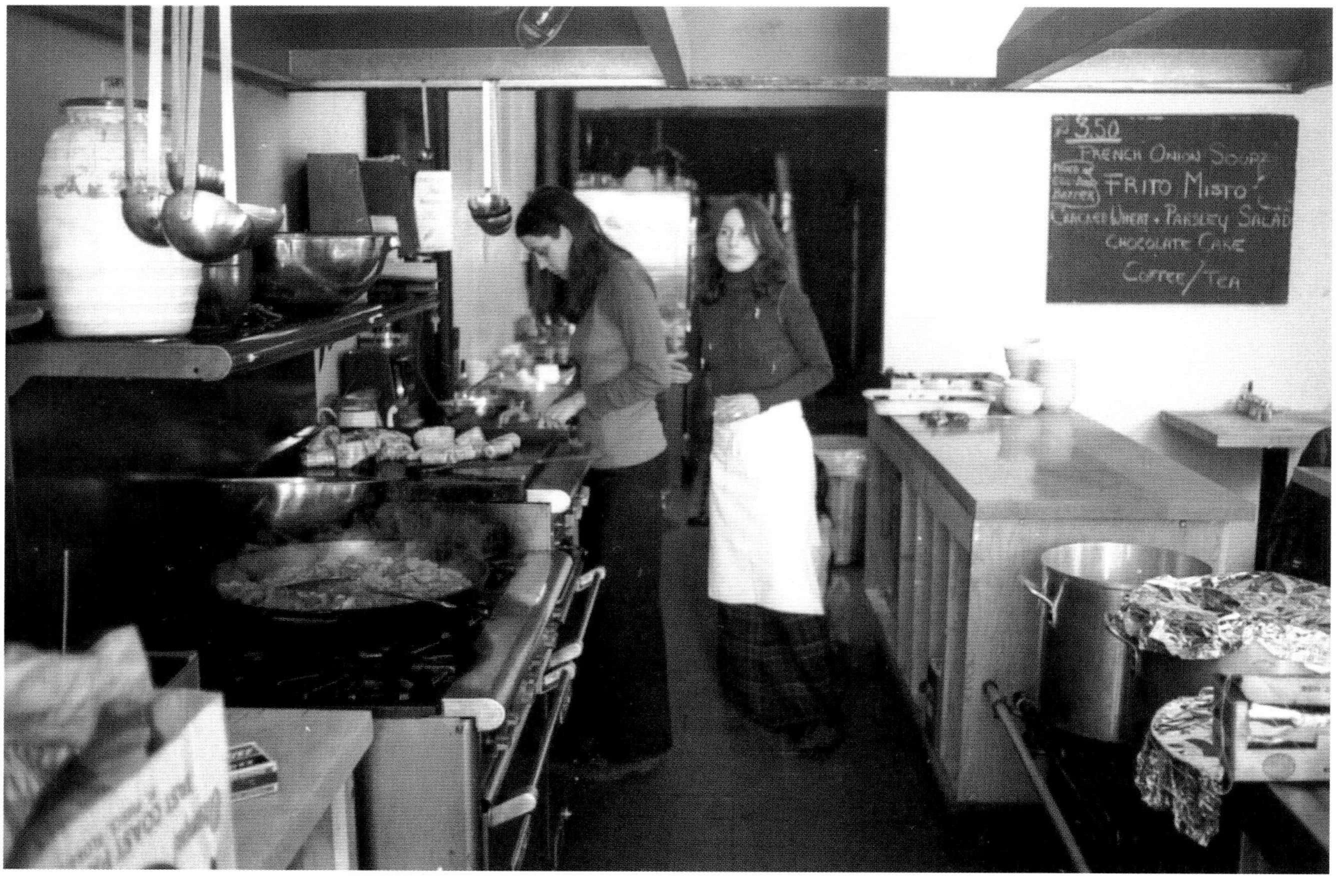

ABOVE AND OPPOSITE: In the kitchen at FOOD, c. 1971 (Carol Gooden above, in apron)

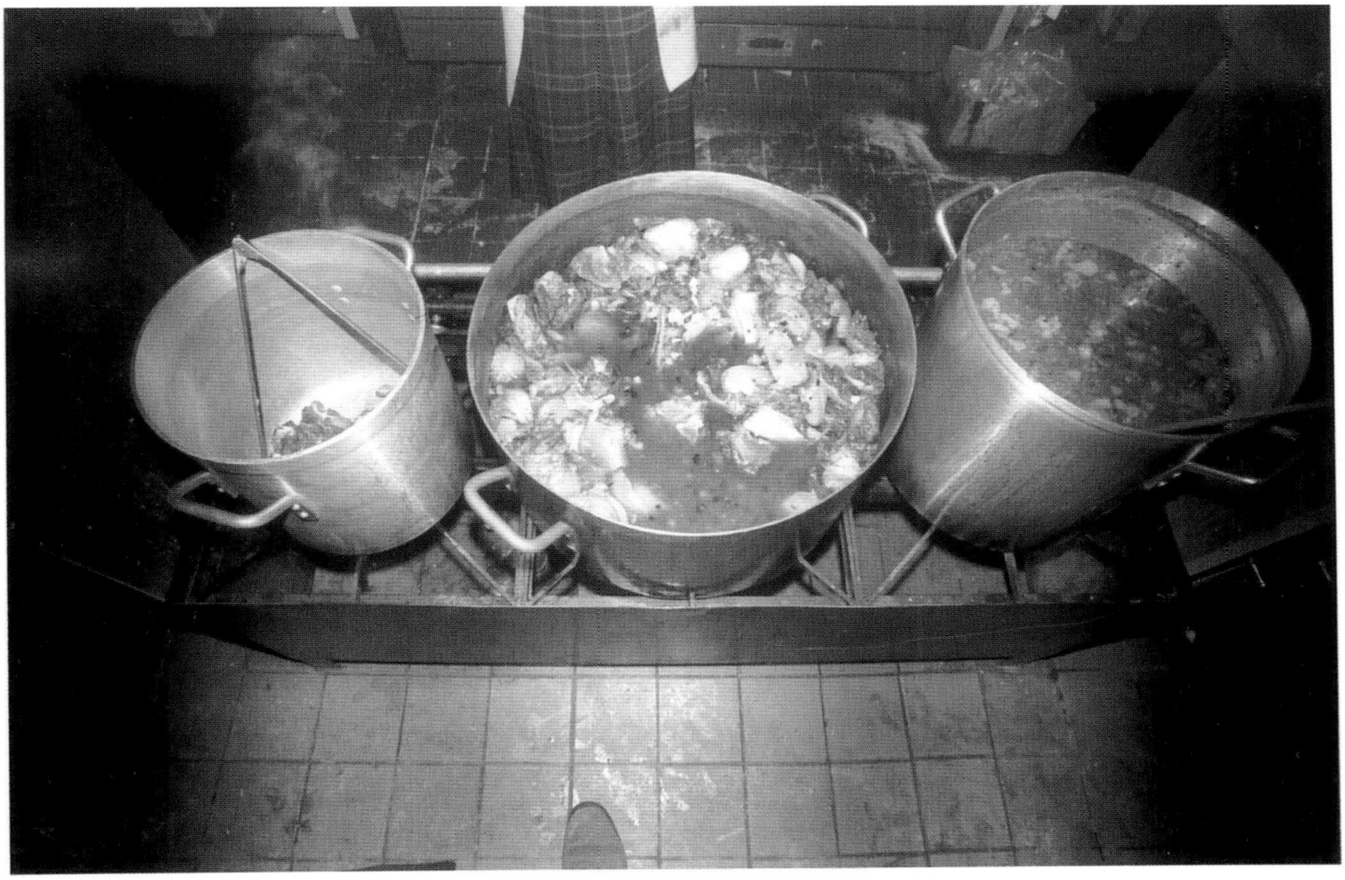

The Banquet Years: FOOD, A SoHo Restaurant

by Lori Waxman

THE FOLLOWING NOTICE appeared in the Fall 1971 issue of the vanguard art magazine *Avalanche*:

> On Saturday, September 25, to mark the unofficial opening of FOOD, an artist-run restaurant at 127 Prince Street, free garlic soup, gumbo, chicken stew, wine, beer, and homemade breads were served to friends, gallery-goers, and passers-by until late in the evening.

So begins the very first published announcement for FOOD, the "restaurant commune"—as it would be dubbed by reviewers for the *New York Times* and *New York* magazine—that in its heyday was a center of life for a diverse group of artists who called Manhattan's then-gritty SoHo their home.[1] Dozens of local sculptors, filmmakers, photographers, musicians, and dancers worked there—variously as cooks, waitresses, or dishwashers—glad to have a paying job flexible enough to allow them time to prepare for an exhibit or skip town for a gig, and still have a job afterwards. Even more of them ate there, partaking not only in fresh, homemade, creative, and affordable dishes—raw mackerel with wasabi sauce, stuffed tongue Creole, and anchovy onion pie, among the more exotic offerings—but also in a community of like-minded familiars who often exhibited together and collaborated on one another's projects.

SoHo circa 1971 was a neighborhood in transition, existing somewhere between its former life as an industrial zone and its new one as the center of the avant-garde art world, which it would become by the middle of the decade. But in the late sixties and early seventies, it was a mostly abandoned space in a city that was itself being increasingly abandoned: white flight to burgeoning suburbs and manufacturing flight to the larger ports of New Jersey were just two of the many factors that led New York City into a deepening cycle of crime and squalor. By 1975 the city was bankrupt, its betrayal by the federal government famously, if somewhat inaccurately, plastered across the front page of the October 30th issue of the *Daily News*: "Ford to City: Drop Dead."

If the city as a whole suffered, however, its woes opened up spaces where alternative cultures could experiment and even thrive. Downtown had long been a zone where artistic transgressions were freely parlayed across canvases, tavern tables, and low-rent studios. The New York School had Eighth Street and The Club; later generations would spread out across the Lower East Side.[2] Since the early sixties, the area south of Houston Street had attracted a steady flow of artists lured by its cheap, sizable, and increasingly deserted loft spaces. A district of light-manufacturing companies, the neighborhood had lost many of its commercial occupants as part of general urban deindustrialization trends, but also as a result of the Lower Manhattan Expressway project, which planned to obliterate the quarter by turning it into a highway corridor. Growing appreciation and concern for the historic architectural fabric of the city, especially for the area's nineteenth-century cast-iron facades, eventually derailed the proposal, but wary manufacturers never returned. Instead, artists moved into more and more of the raw spaces left in their wake, taking occupancy under various legal and extra-legal arrangements. Some received A.I.R. (Artist in Residence) status from the city, but most lived illegally under threat of police raids and evictions.[3] Still others moved into the "fluxhouse" co-operative spaces established by Fluxus artist George Maciunas beginning in 1966.

Throughout the sixties, SoHo, as the area *So*uth of *Ho*uston was unofficially known, remained a raw neighborhood, but one with a growing cultural energy. It was a Do-It-Yourself scene in which artists created their own economy of support, collaboration, and feedback. Extending the tendencies

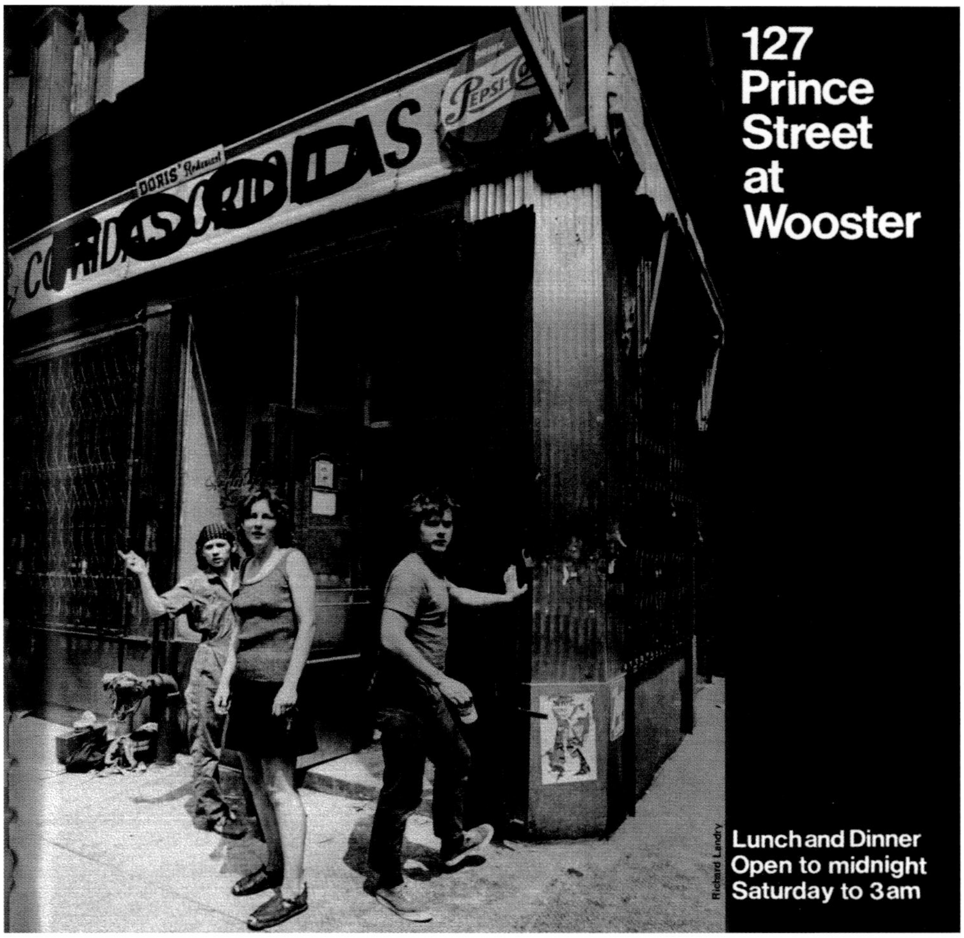

Tina Girouard, Carol Gooden, and Gordon Matta-Clark outside of the space that would be FOOD, printed as an advertisement in *Avalanche*, 1971

of the Assemblage and Happenings generations before them, they eschewed any kind of media specificity, and when they weren't creating works in the streets themselves, they founded spaces in which to experience one another's artistic experiments. Alternative sites abounded: 112 Greene Street Workshop, Holly Solomon's 98 Greene Street loft, Alanna Heiss's Institute for Art and Urban Resources, Inc., Steina and Woody Vasulka's Kitchen, and the Ward-Nasse co-op all opened between 1968 and 1971. SoHo even developed a fledgling market credibility: commercial gallerists Paula Cooper and Ivan Karp set up shop in 1968 and 1969, respectively, to be joined soon thereafter by uptown dealers Leo Castelli and Andre Emmerich. What the neighborhood lacked were not places to show the new kinds of art being made in its plentiful lofts but rather the more basic amenities of urban residential existence—grocery stores, schools, churches, libraries, pharmacies, and restaurants—absences that followed logically enough from the fact that it had never before been a neighborhood where people lived, but rather one where they worked in blue-collar manufacturing jobs. The few restaurants that did exist were luncheonettes that closed their doors at three in the afternoon, plus Fanelli's, a rough Italian bar at the corner of Mercer and Prince, which served terrible food, according to one artist's recollection.[4]

So when Gordon Matta-Clark suggested half-jokingly to Carol Gooden that she should open a restaurant in SoHo, she did. And she asked him to collaborate on it with her. Gooden was a sometimes photographer and dancer with Trisha Brown's nascent company; Matta (as he was then known) was a sculptor who had spurned his Cornell architectural degree to experiment with spatial deconstruction and the alchemical properties of fried photographs. Both were fond of throwing dinner parties, and their lofts were as full of communal gastronomy as were their friends'.[5] Alan Saret, who went to Cornell with Matta and helped found 112 Greene—one of the first artist-run spaces in Soho—held regular Sunday-night banquets at his place on Spring Street. The Louisiana expats who lived at 10 Chatham Square were famous for their Cajun specials. Even the *Brooklyn Bridge Event*, a 1971 outdoor group show organized by Alanna Heiss, concluded with Matta spit-roasting an entire pig over an open fire. Five-hundred pork sandwiches were served—though only after the pig had fallen into the fire the night before, and a group of friends had come down to ensure that it cooked at least most of the way through.[6]

This cohort was not, of course, the first to marry food and art. A long tradition of representing food stretches from Arcimboldo's sixteenth-century portraits of vegetable-headed men, through Chardin's eighteenth-century still-lifes of dead rays and rabbits, to Wayne Thiebaud's twentieth-century cake-like paintings of, well, cake. Vanguard rejection of representation and of traditional materials compelled a diverse array of contemporary artists to work with food in literal and often controversial fashion, as in Dieter Roth's chocolate sculptures and sausage drawings of the mid-sixties; Carolee Schneemann's *Meat Joy* happening (1964), in which nearly nude performers writhed orgiastically with raw chicken, sausage, fish, and each other; Paul McCarthy's abject ketchup-splattered performances, begun in the seventies and continuing through today; or Jana Sterbak's *Vanitas: Flesh Dress for an Albino Anorectic* (1987), sewn from fifty pounds of flank steak.

Closer to the tale at hand is the history of artists' restaurants, commercial establishments that served as regular gathering spots, like the Café Nouvelle-Athènes in Impressionist Paris, La Colombe d'Or in School of Paris Provence, or Max's Kansas City in Warholian New York. On their flipside are those enterprises created by artists who understood eating, drinking, and socializing as aesthetic activities in and of themselves, as did Filippo Marinetti when he opened the Futurist restaurant Penna d'Oco in Milan in 1930; Daniel Spoerri, who set up the first of his various restaurants in 1963 at the Galerie J in Paris, with the intention of using diners' leftovers to create his *tableaux-pièges*; and, more recently, Rirkrit Tiravanija, whose atmospheric Thai cooking—and its remains—have graced many an international exhibition.

The larger category of relational aesthetics, to which Tiravanija's installation-events belong, arguably owes much to the precedent of FOOD, just as FOOD owes something to many of the earlier components of the list above. Nevertheless, for as much as the story of FOOD belongs within this aesthetic-gastronomic narrative, it also has a meaningful place elsewhere, as a unique ingredient of the historical scene that it fed.

The Art and Life of FOOD

Completely taken with the idea of opening a restaurant, Gooden bought out the lease of Comidas Criollas, a Puerto Rican lunch counter at the corner of Prince and Wooster Streets, and in addition to Matta asked her friends sculptor Suzanne Harris and dancer Rachel Lew to participate.[7] Initially, Harris and Lew each agreed to put up one-third of the starter money, but both eventually pulled out financially, leaving Gooden to cover most of the bills with her inheritance. Matta himself had no money, so she paid for them both, and her personal finances would continue to support the restaurant—and many of Matta's increasingly expensive art projects—for the next few years. Tina Girouard, an artist who was part of the 10 Chatham Square crowd, joined in, and the three of them spent the summer of 1971 demolishing the site and building it up from scratch, along with the help of Robert Prado, Richard Landry, Manfred Hecht, and a few other friends.

Matta, the former architecture student, acted as general architect and contractor, drafting everything from the ground up—including designs for pots, dishes, and silverware that were never realized. He crafted the space based on his and Gooden's personal aesthetics rather than on practical ones. As she recalls,

> I wanted wood cabinets because I liked the look and feel of wood. I did not understand how hard they were to clean and that there is a reason for stainless steel cabinets. We wanted tile floors because we liked the look of tile. We did not understand the horrendous noise/echo problem it would cause and the difficulty on people's bodies, working all day on tile floors. We wanted to cook "out in the open" and designed the kitchen that way—hang efficiency! We did not want a noisy, water-consuming, electric-consuming dishwasher, we wanted a person, an artist, one that could use a job.

The gastronomic intentions of the restaurant evolved in a manner as romantic and unconventional as its physical environment, parlaying fresh, often locally-sourced ingredients into creative dishes that changed constantly. "I wanted to change the menu every day," Gooden explains, "because I was tired of going to restaurants and knowing what everything on their menu tasted like; I had already had it many times." But, she adds, "Talk about inefficient!" And though it would have been far easier, and possibly even cheaper, to order foodstuffs from a single supplier, the fresh daily catch was haggled for at four a.m. down at the Fulton Fish Market, and residents of Mad Brook Farm, Vermont, were given free living space in exchange for baking fresh bread nightly. Produce was sourced as locally as possible, but it was scarce, save for the summer season, and eventually the restaurant's regular vegetable supplier insisted on being its sole source.[8] Even the organizational structure of FOOD was idealistic, with a hiring policy that allowed employees to work as many or as few hours as they wished, despite the resulting scheduling difficulties—and tax penalties for irregular employee hours.

Few, if any, of these and the other decisions Gooden, Matta, and Girouard made in setting up and running FOOD made much sense in terms of standard operating procedures. Far from it: the latest restaurant technology called for bringing in precooked frozen dishes, a time- and money-saving procedure learned from the airline industry. Contemporary food trends ranged from corporate branding to chemical processing, standardization, overconsumption, and the rise of junk food and fast food.[9] While the folks at FOOD were certainly in line with some of the most forward-thinking writers and advocates of the time, who were deeply critical of industrialization and agribusiness, they hardly had other restaurants to take as a template. Alice Waters and friends had just started Chez Panisse in Berkeley, California, and the Moosewood Restaurant collective wouldn't open its doors in Ithaca, New York, until two years later. But running a restaurant, at least in the narrow sense of a for-profit business whose product is food service, was never really the point.

On the contrary, *restaurant* might better be understood as a normative model to which FOOD was an alternative, along the lines of Claes Oldenburg's Lower East Side *Store*, where the artist sold messy, expressionistic sculptures of food and clothing for two months in 1961, or the mail-order system George Maciunas set up in the mid-sixties to distribute Fluxus multiples. Such appropriations of recognizable commercial forms would only grow more common in the late seventies and early eighties, when artists associated with COLAB broadcast their own cable television shows and sold multiples at the peripatetic A. More Store.[10] The various vanguard spaces that were FOOD's neighbors, from 98 Greene Street to the Performing Garage to Stefan Eins's 3 Mercer store, can be understood within this framework as well: part D.I.Y., part mimicry, part invention, they were both like and completely unlike the kinds of spaces that existed outside of SoHo. Without them, the experimental work created by SoHo artists would never have been seen; some of it might never have been made. Where else but in the basement of 112 Greene would Matta have had the freedom to dig a massive hole in the foundation and plant a cherry tree in it?[11]

Thanks to Manhattan's indifference, the inhabitants of the island within an island south of

Houston could and did take the opportunity to reinvent what it meant to live in an urban environment—and what it meant to make art. As Suzanne Harris put it, reflecting back on the era, "We didn't need the rest of the world. Rather than attacking a system that was already there, we chose to build a world of our own."[12] The D.I.Y. ethos that suffuses Harris's statement, that built FOOD, and that permeated SoHo more generally, offered a broad, workaday echo of various activist paradigms of the time: the Black Power movement, the Women's movement, and the Gay Liberation movement all provided meaningful examples for rethinking the most basic social and political systems not through rhetoric but through action.[13]

Closer to home, the cultural paradigm of pluralist art proffered its own array of possibilities, rethinking and reworking art into something increasingly unpredictable and uncategorizable, ever closer to life itself. Since the fifties, when John Cage spoke of erasing the gap between art and life, generations of succeeding artists variously heeded his call: FOOD patron and local art star Robert Rauschenberg moved from two-dimensional vertical paintings to horizontal *Combine* junk assemblages to collaborative performative events that involved actions as diverse as roller-skating or shimmying up a rope. Allan Kaprow left behind Expressionist painting to invent Happenings, radical theatrical events that surrounded audience-participants with a bombardment of nonsequential and often quite commonplace activities, from orange juicing to climbing on old tires. Coming out of Judson Dance Theater's exploration of everyday movement, dancers from Trisha Brown's company, to which Carol Gooden belonged, walked down the sides of buildings and across rooftops, sometimes to Cage's music or dressed in Rauschenberg's costumes, exploring everyday space in both ordinary and extraordinary ways. Fluxus artists dispensed with art altogether, scoring the minutiae of daily life—from the making of soup to the polishing of a violin—into absurdist events whose goal was to make one aware of the wondrousness of life, not art. These and other artists, many of whom lived and worked in and around SoHo, experimented radically and often collaboratively, discovering new forms, breaking away from traditional object making, rejecting the confines of the gallery, exhibiting a fervent need to act, to do, to mix, to create. Just as there was no longer any reason to separate sculpture from painting and dance, the boundaries between art and life and anything previously compartmentalized within those two categories dissolved. An artist's life could be art, just as an artist's art could be life.

FOOD thrived within this prevailing impetus to bring art and life ever closer. Conceived as a collaborative enterprise that didn't care much about the enterprise end of things, as a restaurant that would nourish its employees and customers with much more than just food, it fit into no strict categories—neither that of art nor of life—but rather somewhere shifting and in between the two. Despite FOOD's unorthodox layout, menu, hiring policy, and finances, however, its claim to being a real-life business is never challenged. Rather, what is called into question is its status as art.

Gooden recounts that both she and Matta thought of the entire adventure as an art piece. For her it was "a series of live photograph-paintings"; for him, a complete work that could eventually be sold to dealer Leo Castelli. How seriously Matta meant this is debatable; certainly he had expansive—and expanding—notions of what it meant to call something an artwork. Of course, neither Castelli nor any other dealer or collector ever did buy FOOD, but a successful sale does not a work of art make—a lesson long understood by the avant-garde, whose work rarely sold in the era in which it was made, and understood especially by the generation of artists that so recently produced Happenings, wherein there was nothing to buy, only to experience. Nevertheless, art historian Thomas Crow has argued that "it would stretch even the capacious aesthetics of the time to call FOOD a work of art in itself."[14] And in that pronouncement Crow isn't exactly wrong, just perhaps inappropriately stiff. A more generous definition of art might better suit the aesthetics of the time, or even a willingness to dispense with such limitations altogether. Certainly, Matta, Gooden, and the many artists who ate and worked and performed at FOOD seem to have thought so.

FOOD did have direct relationships with more recognizable artworks. It was the subject of one of Matta's first films, the unfinished *A Day in the Life of Food* (1971–73). Shot with the help of Robert Frank, the documentary tracks the round-the-clock life of the restaurant, beginning early in the

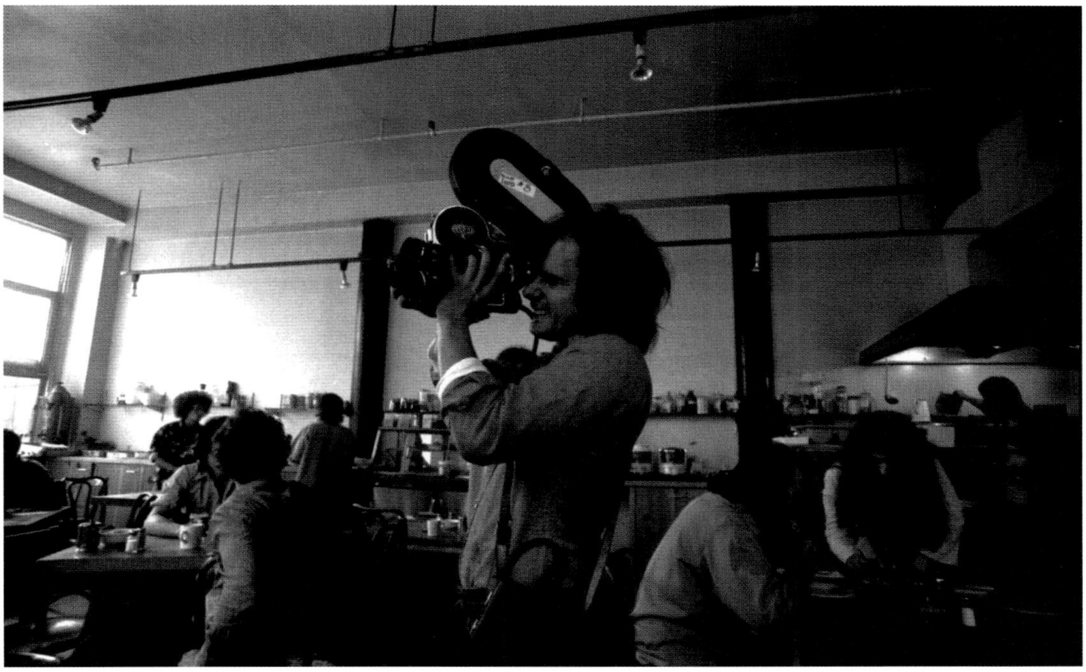

Matta-Clark with camera, shooting for the film
A Day in the Life of Food, c. 1971–73

morning at the Fulton Street Fish Market and finishing even earlier the next morning with the baking of the restaurant's fresh bread—a trajectory that underscores a kind of food-related romanticism that wafted through the restaurant along with the smell of good cooking. Matta also made the first of his "cuttings," his radical means of redefining architectural space by literally cutting it up into pieces, while renovating the restaurant; he later exhibited fragments of the restaurant's original walls and door at 112 Greene alongside his *Bronx Floors* and *Wallspaper*.[15] Bob Kushner, who worked as FOOD's dessert chef and manager from 1972 to 1974—he recalls baking a killer chocolate sour-cream cake and a Syrian coffee cake heavy on the nutmeg—held a fashion show at a nearby loft of clothing stitched from fruit and vegetables, all of which he'd sourced through FOOD and the unused portions of which were later served up at the restaurant.[16]

Kushner's use of foodstuffs in place of traditional art materials echoes one of the more explicitly artistic moments of FOOD, its guest-chef dinners, which Matta originated. Sunday nights were the time for these meals, and while some cooked up straightforward, edible fare—Rauschenberg served homemade chili—others took a more experimental approach, crafting dishes that were often more food for thought than food for eating. One infamous Matta meal, called "Alive," included hard-boiled eggs hollowed out and filled with live brine shrimp. Another, the "Matta Bones" dinner, cost four dollars and featured oxtail soup, marrow bones, stuffed bones, frog legs provençale, and pot roast bones; afterward, Hisachika Takahashi drilled holes through the bones and strung them together, so that diners could wear their leftovers home. On another occasion, Takahashi, who worked as an assistant to Rauschenberg, crafted beautiful paintings out of food plates. Mark di Suvero proposed—but never realized—a sculptor's dinner to be served through the front windows by crane and eaten with screwdrivers, hammers, and chisels.[17] Bob Kushner remembers a red-and-green dinner, where red sauce was served on green pasta and pesto on red pasta, but not who cooked it. Other guest chefs included Michael Goldberg, Donald Judd, Richard Landry, Italo Scanga, Keith Sonnier, Joan Shapiro, and Yvonne Rainer.[18]

The architecture and design of FOOD provide further clues to its larger role as "a work of art in itself." In addition to Matta's aesthetically motivated designs for the restaurant as a whole, including unrealized plans for cooking and serving ware, Girouard recounts how the space was organized as a

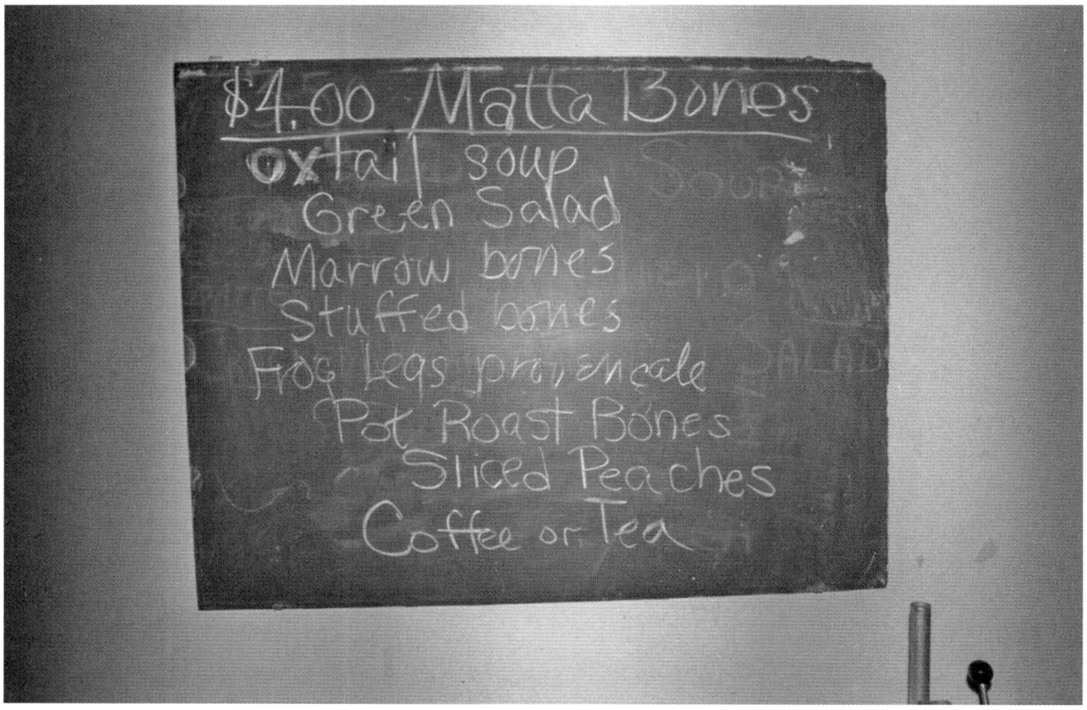

The menu for Matta-Clark's Guest Chef Dinner

kind of stage, from its open kitchen to its long bank of windows, through which one could watch the action from Wooster Street, especially when the restaurant was lit up at night. Open kitchens were not common in American restaurants of the era, which in New York meant upscale food palaces like the Four Seasons, all-you-can-eat steakhouses, English- and Irish-style pubs, fast-food joints, Chinese restaurants, and nostalgic tearooms.[19] FOOD looked elsewhere for inspiration—to Gooden's travel experiences of European eating culture, for one—and the restaurant's open-plan design even allowed dessert-making to be seen from Prince Street, as from the front tables. A rotating roster of chefs—Mabou Mines one night, Philip Glass's ensemble on another, vegetarian dancers on a third—performed at their centrally located stove and prep tables for the surrounding audience of diners. Even the dishwasher was deliberately sited within the space—a moving, breathing, expressive human dishwasher, not a machine.

The broadest reaches of FOOD as a space for creative practice can perhaps be further understood through the context of the Women's Movement. Proclaiming "the personal is the political," feminist artists like Carolee Schneeman and Judy Chicago explored in the late sixties and early seventies how such quotidian aspects of their lives as menses and childbirth could be legitimate subjects for art. The trickle-down of that radical notion meant that all aspects of one's life could be part of the creative process; it doesn't seem too much of a stretch, given the times, to extend that idea to a restaurant run by artists for artists, a place whose original goals, as expressed by Carol Gooden, were not to function as a profitable business but rather to display cooking bravado, to create a sympathetic place for friends to meet and eat, and to provide artists with a flexible working environment. If FOOD still doesn't seem to fit the definition of capital "A" art, why not lose the capital? So Castelli didn't buy it. Happenings, Fluxus, and myriad other kinds of radical artmaking had proved that anything could be art and that the process often mattered more than the end product—regardless of whether or not it sold, or was even saleable.

FOOD'S FAMILY FISCAL FACTS

Investment	$63,000.00
Gross Sales	104,120.72
Total Income	167,120.72
Salaries	37,700.29
Food	37,007.10
Paper Goods	1,647.65
Rent	6,000.00
Telephone	207.70
Con Edison	1,222.45
Office Stuff	514.50
Insurances	1,167.00
Licenses	125.00
Repairs	1,010.24
Legal	1,397.00
Laundry	732.25
Waste	396.50
Advertizing	1,321.64
Dues & Subscriptions	00.00
Trucking	350.37
Miscellaneous	501.27
Book-keeping	2,975.00
Payroll Taxes	3,050.28
Other Taxes	276.80
Sales Taxes	7,288.45
Bank Charges	89.08
Consultant Fees	100.00
Rubber Checks	196.16
Construction & Destruction	28,696.77
Kitchen Equipment & Supplies	33,147.28
Total Expenditure	167,120.72

4½	tons various flours for bread
16,000	oranges squeezed
379	lbs rabbits stewed
1,690	lbs celery chopped
3,050	lbs carrots juiced
1,914	lbs butter
108	lbs tongue
37	bunches dill
2,300	tortillas pressed
4,081	lbs chickens succumbed
708	lbs fish fucked
1,554	lettuce heads
15,660	potential chickens cracked
435	gallons Tilly's organic apple juice
17,760	yards spaghetti steamed
2	acres of mushrooms
5,890	onions peeled
220	bunches parsley sprinkled delicately
17	lbs sassafras, root-powder-leaf, gumboed
16	oz wasabi powder exploded
1,879	lbs pork stuffed
1,480	lbs lamb led astray
4,529	lbs beef bullied
26	lbs poppy seeds
5	cubic feet bay leaves
43	lbs seaweed
2	jars peanut butter
29	boxes brown buckwheat groats
1,111	lbs duck baked
1	cubic foot sage
100	lbs sunflower seeds
442	lbs bell peppers
5,568	loaves of bread baked

41,272	customers
1,083	glasses broken
47	dogs asked to leave
153	chairs broken
15	bottles of champagne disappeared
3	unfulfilled promises by good friends
1	closing order from health department
113	roaches left lying in the back room
0	internal fights
3¾	lbs keys lost
1	truck ruined
2	rebellions:
	The Dishwasher Rebellion of Feb. '72
	The Radio Rebellion of May '72
5	floods by Marco
31	tons of garbage trucked to Gansevoort Pier
243	cubic yds garbage removed by Pasquale Bros.
7	made up Social Security numbers
3	citations granted by City
1,175	notices taped to windows
84%	workers are artists
3,913	shirts, aprons & towels dirtied
1	box toothpicks used
3	items salvaged from restaurant
?	brandied people as opposed to pears
174	days Glaza tied up in front
9	people growled at by him
99	workers
99	cut fingers
7	butterflies used to mend cuts
213	people needed to get it together
	keep it together
3,082	free dinners given

Carol Goodden Tina Girouard Gordon Matta Suzanne Harris Rachel Lew Robert Prado Richard Peck Ann Marshall Douglas Penick Benton Quinn Leilani Schuman Kathe Mahon David Wood Billy Omabehgo Susan Oberhalzer Andrew Bregman Phillip Brenan Richard Taddei Ed Leffingwell Penny Cobbs Ed Harris Barbara Wennersten Mary Overlie John Kalesh Nancy Friedrich Walter Vatter John Parnham Pat Parsons Chuck Phillips Phil Swanson Lew Skinner Maggie Favale Jeff Bingham Mimi Schmidt Rick Wroth Mary Kaye Cheny Lorri Perrone Larry Brighton Carmen Cadorette Jim Cadorette Celia Deardon Kitty Duane Karen Eagan Jeannette Penoyer Chappy Judy Dorav Paul Richter Joan Richter Mr. Peanuts Rusty Gilder Cindy Hoyt Debi Kops Abigail Levy Cas Milt Arthur Murphy Carla Nordstrom Joe Turner Barbara Lloyd Cynthia Hedstrom Michael Goldberg Hisachika Porky Loyal Stimpson Lulu Dower Thom Cathcart Leonardo Negron Lee Brewer Glenda Hydler Dong Mike Kern Michael Koortbojian Susan Endsley Lorelie Brown Karen Balsley Marion Lyjon Phil Swanson Epp Kotkas Mark Knight Kit Parsons Penelope Jeffrey Lew Deborah Hay David Bradshaw Phil Glass Chris McNeur Randal Arabie Keith Sonnier Brad Davis Jed Bark Jo Ann Glass Bill Solomon Wm Sarbello Sylvestre 5 man team de Lorenzo Charles Simmonds Manfred Hecht Rufus Fred Brandes Winston Reolf John Hall Jim Weatherford Arthniel Jim Lewis Dickie Landry Fred Prastine John Gibson Genny' Kapuler Marco Ron Rosezi Helen Conrads Robin Stouber Robert Altman Ray Perrone Carol Zussman Sarah Dane Jay Roseman Brendan Jack Colombo Kate Redicker Melinda Gurevitz Jay Lefke Ruth Brewer Ruth Ackerman Selma Jackie Newlove Raymond Reid Chris Leon Tu Peter Hawkins Peter Barton Bob Rauschenberq

Advertisement for FOOD, in *Avalanche*, 1972

FOOD also published a string of inventive advertisements in *Avalanche*, a magazine owned and edited by friends Liza Béar and Willoughby Sharp. *Avalanche* was dedicated to the radical conceptual art being made not only throughout the world but also very much by the artists who lived and worked around FOOD and 112 Greene.[20] The ads were projects in and of themselves and were likely ad hoc and collaborative. A photo by Richard Landry forms the backdrop for the first ad, which appeared in the Fall 1971 issue: Girouard, Matta, and Gooden stand outside the as-yet-unrenovated restaurant, below the original sign for Comidas Criollas, which, in the photograph, has been casually scrawled over with the word "FOOD." The next ad, published in the Spring 1972 issue, was the creation of Girouard, Gooden, Matta, and editor Liza Béar.[21] "Food's Family Fiscal Facts" detailed not only the restaurant's financial state (in which the total running costs magically equaled total income, to the penny) but also a fantastical accounting of dozens of other kinds of consumption and activity: 379 lbs of rabbits stewed, 4,081 chickens succumbed, 220 bunches of parsley sprinkled delicately, 47 dogs asked to leave, 3 unfulfilled promises by good friends, 2 rebellions, and an unspecified amount of brandied people as opposed to pears. At the bottom of the page, an untitled paragraph of over one-hundred names lists FOOD's big "family."

The first few names in the "family" list are easy to place: Carol Gooden, Tina Girouard, Gordon Matta, Suzanne Harris, and Rachel Lew—the official founders. Here's Robert Prado, a musician with the Philip Glass ensemble, who was one of the first chefs and a maker of superb Cajun gumbos; and Richard Peck, also part of the Glass ensemble, who worked as a dishwasher. Over there some guest-chef names pop up. But soon the list gets hazy and very, very long. Who were all these people, and what was their relationship to FOOD? Incredibly, they all worked at the restaurant,[22] but who exactly did what is to some extent beside the point. The essence of this list is that a whole lot of people were involved in FOOD one way or another, whatever the specifics of their participation, whether it was chopping, cooking, washing, eating, selling, paying, sitting, talking, filming, or picture taking. FOOD would not have existed without all of them. It existed for them: the people who came up with the idea, the ones who put it into play, those who worked daily to keep it functioning, and those who depended on it for social, gastronomic, or financial sustenance—roles that often overlapped.

FOOD's communal nature stemmed from an essentially generous spirit, a noncynical way of being in the world that found expression throughout SoHo at the time. Its nearest neighbors exemplified that essence: 112 Greene Street Workshop operated as a freewheeling creative space, open to the kind of experimentation that could hardly happen elsewhere, in a big, dirty, former rag factory that artist Jeffrey Lew owned and opened up to like-minded artists in 1970. Collectors Holly and Horace Solomon made available their 98 Greene Street loft to "allow artists and poets and performers to *do* their work, and have it be seen. The space was given to them and they could do with it what they wanted." Like the founders of FOOD, Lew, the Solomons, and many of their SoHo neighbors were propelled by a kind of oppositional urgency, a need to make positive, active gestures that would help create the kind of environment they felt was worth living in. The gestures may have been local and ad hoc, but, as Holly Solomon explains, "It was a time of great distress when everything seemed to be falling apart, and for Horace and me opening the space was a political statement. We felt that we couldn't change the world, but that privately we could do something."[23]

But not all communal spirits are created equally. At the same time that FOOD can't be reduced to any one person, it would be disingenuous to ignore the importance of certain individuals. Fundamentally, FOOD was an idea sparked by Gordon Matta and nurtured, financed, and overseen by Carol Gooden. Tina Girouard helped build it and was initially responsible for personnel, remaining active for the first year or so and reappearing now and again to cook up Cajun dishes. Rachel Lew and Suzanne Harris, who were responsible for procurement, pulled out almost immediately—though both spent hours peeling garlic for the opening-day soup. FOOD was conceived as a communal idea, but in the end most of the work fell on the shoulders of a very few people. Matta, according to Gooden, "was the charisma that made it work as well as it did," "the eye of the hurricane," but she ended up responsible for its day-to-day existence.[24] It was a mom-and-pop

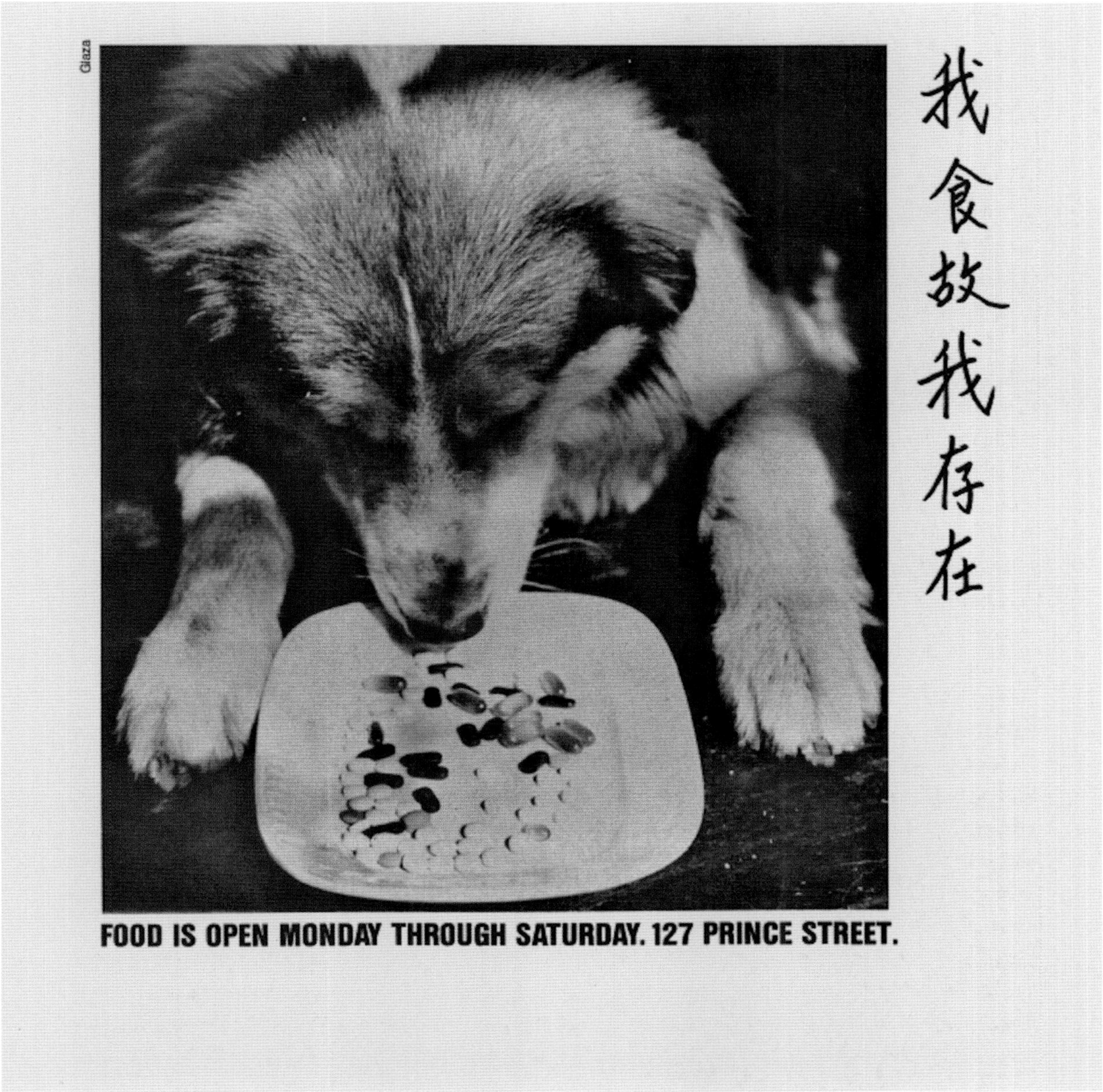

Advertisement for FOOD, in *Avalanche*, 1972

operation, and Gooden was both mom and pop—she got the call if the toilet was blocked or a delivery was late—a banal reality hardly borne out by the small body of literature that treats FOOD.

In part, this oversight can be attributed to FOOD's self-projected image as a collective entity, in which the ads in *Avalanche* played an important role. It follows naturally from the fact that so many different people were, of necessity, involved in the day-to-day activity of running the restaurant. But it is also very much a product of the art world's particular kind of memory, of the need for a celebrated artist like Gordon Matta-Clark (as he is known today) on which to hang an otherwise obscure, hard-to-categorize project like FOOD. The main locale for writings about FOOD are monographs and exhibition catalogues devoted to Matta-Clark, where the restaurant is treated as one among a résumé of ambitious projects completed in his short career.[25] Carol Gooden is the primary source cited within those texts. One exception to this rule is the catalogue for *FOOD: An Exhibition by White Columns, New York*, curated by Catherine Morris in 1999. But even there an entire chapter is devoted to the food art of Matta-Clark. Artworks by the other founders or workers rate little mention, unless they appeared in a group show alongside Matta-Clark's. This is not to deny the importance of Matta-Clark's work nor the fundamental role he played in the inception and spirit of FOOD, but it begs the question: If interest in his work hadn't continued to grow after his early death from cancer in 1978, would any scholarly attention have been given to FOOD at all?

Save for a few crumbs, FOOD would most likely have disappeared along with the memories of many other, less famous individuals who were part of it, Carol Gooden included. A few ads in a defunct avant-garde magazine and a restaurant review or two might constitute its sole remains, and that would be a loss, not just because FOOD stands at a nifty intersection on the food-art continuum, or because it must have been a really cool place to hang out, but because it offers a multipaned window into an era on which it is hard to get a good sightline. Any attempt to understand the culture of early seventies SoHo has to look further afield than the art being shown in its commercial galleries, even further than that being shown in its alternative spaces. FOOD is an exceptionally potent source of information, a key part of the expanded archive that can tell us about what it was like to live, work, breathe, eat, make art, collaborate, and play in SoHo circa 1971.[26]

All Good Things Must Come To an End

FOOD continued to exist in name through the late seventies and possibly even into the early eighties, but only its first two or three years of existence are ever discussed, and with reason. The dates of Matta's film *A Day in the Life of FOOD*, 1971 to 1973, roughly correspond to that period, during which the initial founders and friends remained more or less active participants and the restaurant stayed true to its art-life principles. But by the fall of 1972 Matta had begun to lose interest, if not in the concept of FOOD, then in the actual running of it, coming by only to hang out, rarely attending meetings.[27] Sunday-night guest-chef dinners petered out. Gooden had by this time hired Robert Kushner, a twenty-four-year-old artist newly arrived from Boston, to work as a dessert chef; a few months later he became assistant manager and then acting manager, a position he held through 1973. As Kushner tells it, they were serving at full capacity but still losing money. With the help of some "creative accounting" and a less artistic hiring policy, the restaurant broke even for the first time that year.[28] FOOD began to be just a restaurant. The shop next door was acquired for extra seating. SoHo became an increasingly popular destination for gallery-goers and tourists. The restaurant closed on Sundays, which, perhaps not incidentally, was a day when galleries also shut their doors. In a 1975 *New York Times* article titled "SoHo Grows Up and Grows Rich and Chic," the writer could sniff,

> The artists' collective restaurant at Prince and Wooster, called FOOD, now turns out crispy little salads and crepes instead of ladling out thickened okra broth and mashed eggplant. Few artists eat there because it is less affordable than when it opened three years ago.[29]

Somewhere along the way, Matta and Gooden both dropped out, as did most of their friends. FOOD had become a legitimate business, a triumph by some measure, but not by theirs. As Gooden recalls:

> I did not like cringing when the busboy dropped the tray of glasses, because I knew what that would cost and margins were slim. I did not like being exasperated when the vegetable delivery would not show up. I was irritable going to the fish market at 4 a.m. and fighting for decent fish at decent prices. It had ceased to be an "adventure." I had no time to spend on my photography, was almost too tired to dance with the Trisha Brown Dance Company.

Gooden tried to sell FOOD, but there were no takers. She offered to pass it on to Kushner, with the stipulation that she be able to eat and entertain occasionally, but he was burnt out from his managerial duties and refused—plus, his work had started to sell and he wanted to concentrate on artmaking. She ended up giving it to an English woman named Ruby, a non-artist who had been waitressing at the restaurant and showed some managerial abilities. When Ruby skipped town less than a year later, leaving a few months of unpaid bills and rent in her wake, it was the end of an era that was already on its way out.

Did FOOD become a business because Matta, Girouard, Harris, and finally Gooden left? Or did they leave because it was becoming a business? The answer likely lies somewhere in between. To put it another way, how does an idealistic enterprise survive the departure of the founders who charmed it into being in the first place? Alternately, can such an endeavor survive their continued presence? Speaking of 112 Greene, which eventually became White Columns, New York's oldest artist-run space (and the location for *FOOD: An Exhibition* in 1999), founder Jeffrey Lew recalled, "Something special happened during the first three years, and after we got the grants it didn't happen anymore."[30] Accountability—more often than not assumed due to the acquisition of money, be it from grants or outright profit—invariably alters the dynamics of a spirited adventure, for better or worse. Other factors must also have been felt: many of the original 112 and FOOD artists had begun to show in commercial galleries, and burgeoning art careers took them off to Europe and other places far from SoHo. Priorities, responsibilities, and needs changed. So did the neighborhood, which became increasingly dotted with galleries, restaurants, and shops, including the Spring Street Bar, Kenn & Bob's Broome Street Bar, and the gourmet market Dean & Deluca, to name some of the earliest infusions—all of them still around. Surrounded by so much business, FOOD couldn't continue except as a business. And so it did, for some time, but without the collective energy and intentions of its founders, whose ad in the Fall 1972 issue of *Avalanche* wondrously proclaimed:

LOVE AMONG THE CABBAGES
EAT FOOD 127 PRINCE 260-3730

Rest in peace.

Lori Waxman is a critic and art historian based in Chicago.

This text was previously published as Lori Waxman, "The Banquet Years: FOOD, a SoHo Restaurant," in *Gastronomica: The Journal of Food and Culture* 8, no. 4 (Fall 2008): 24–33.

[1] FOOD was referred to as a "restaurant commune" in Milton Glaser and Jerome Snyder, "The Underground Gourmet: Food, Glorious Food," *New York* (January 3, 1972): 65; and Fred Ferretti, "SoHo Grows Up and Grows Rich and Chic," *New York Times*, October 21, 1975, 184. The title of this essay is borrowed from Roger Shattuck's seminal 1958 book, *The Banquet Years: The Arts in France, 1885–1918: Alfred Jarry, Henri Rousseau, Erik Satie, Guillaume Apollinaire*, which was standard reading material for the FOOD generation, according to Tina Girouard (telephone interview with the author, December 15, 2004). All subsequent references to Girouard are to this interview.

[2] For a firsthand account of the New York School scene, see Irving Sandler, *A Sweeper-Up After Artists: A Memoir* (New York: Thames and Hudson, 2003). The generation of New York artists succeeding FOOD would continue to thrive despite, and arguably because of, the city's socioeconomic difficulties, a phenomenon explored in Marvin J. Taylor, ed., *The Downtown Book: The New York Art Scene 1974–1984* (Princeton: Princeton Architectural Press, 2006).

[3] In the early 1960s, the Artists Tenant Association petitioned Mayor Robert Wagner for permission to live in districts not officially zoned for residential use or in buildings lacking a Certificate of Occupancy. The city agreed to allow a maximum of two artists per such building, which would then be marked "A.I.R" for Artist in Residence. Many of the buildings in SoHo still bear this signage today. See Richard Kostelanetz, *SoHo: The Rise and Fall of an Artists' Colony* (New York and London: Routledge, 2003).

[4] Robert Kushner, who worked at FOOD for two years beginning in 1972, offered this assessment of Fanelli's during an interview with the author, October 15, 2004. Now a SoHo classic, Fanelli's still stands at the corner of Mercer and Prince Streets, and the burgers are actually pretty good, at least in this writer's opinion. All subsequent references to Kushner are to this interview.

[5] As bohemian as these dinner parties must have been, in their attention to the pleasures of food and cookery they correspond to a wider home-cooking trend encouraged by the publication of such books as James Beard's various tomes and Julia Child's *Mastering the Art of French Cooking*, as well as television programs on Greek and Italian cooking. See Waverley Root and Richard de Rochemont, *Eating in America: A History* (New York: William Morrow, 1976), 456.

[6] Girouard, interview.

[7] The story of the genesis of FOOD is told in more or less the same way in most published accounts, the majority of which are drawn from Carol Gooden's recollections. Unless otherwise noted, details about the beginnings of the restaurant are taken from an e-mail Gooden (now McCoy) wrote to the author, December 6, 2004. All subsequent citations to Gooden are to this e-mail as well, unless otherwise noted.

[8] Kushner, interview.

[9] Root and de Rochemont, *Eating in America*, 444–47, 453.

[10] This trend has been dubbed the "mock shop" by Carlo McCormick. For further examples of the phenomenon, see his essay "A Crack in Time" in *The Downtown Book*, 81, 85, as well as a special section on the exhibition website, www.nyu.edu/greyart/exhibits/downtown/mock1.html.

[11] Matta-Clark made a career of radically altering found, neglected architectural spaces, and many of his first such experiments, including the one described here, *Cherry Tree*, 1971, took place in the permissible climate of SoHo. See Thomas Crow, "Gordon Matta-Clark: Survey," in *Gordon Matta-Clark* (London: Phaidon, 2003), 31.

[12] Alan W. Moore, "Collectivities: Protest, Counter-Culture and Political Postmodernism in New York City Artists Organizations 1969–1985" (PhD diss., City University of New York, 2000), 47.

[13] Robert Pincus Witten, "Gordon Matta-Clark: Art in the Interrogative," in *Gordon Matta-Clark: A Retrospective*, ed. Mary Jane Jacob (Chicago: Museum of Contemporary Art, 1985), 14–15.

[14] Crow, "Gordon Matta-Clark: Survey," 44.

[15] Gordon Matta-Clark interviewed in *Gordon Matta-Clark* (Antwerp: International Cultureen Centrum, 1977), 8; Catherine Morris, *FOOD: An Exhibition by White Columns, New York* (Münster: Westfälisches Landesmuseum für Kunst und Kulturgeschichte, 1999), 36.

[16] For more on Kushner's food costumes, see Robert Kushner, "Life in the Produce Aisle," *Art Journal* 54, no. 1, Clothing As Subject (Spring 1995): 62–65; and Robert Kushner, "Food + Clothing," *Gastronomica* 4, no. 1 (Winter 2004): 77–85.

[17] Carol Gooden, quoted in *Gordon Matta-Clark* (Valencia: IVAM Centre Julio Gonzalez, 1992), 370; Alanna Heiss, quoted in Morris, *FOOD: An Exhibition*, 29.

[18] The list of guest chefs is generally hard to confirm; the one I've compiled here, including the Rauschenberg anecdote, derives mainly from Jacob, *Gordon Matta-Clark: A Retrospective*, 38. Nevertheless, though Rauschenberg was a regular at FOOD, Carol Gooden doesn't recall him ever cooking there, nor does she remember Yvonne Rainer participating, but Girouard does; Girouard, interview.

[19] For an overview of the restaurant scene in New York in the late 1960s and early 1970s, see Michael and Ariane Batterberry, *On The Town In New York: From 1776 to the Present* (New York: Charles Scribner's Sons, 1973), 298–313.

[20] See Lisa Le Feuvre, "*Avalanche*," *Art Monthly* 278 (July/August 2004): 7–10.

[21] Morris, *FOOD: An Exhibition*, 33.

[22] Gooden, e-mail to the author, January 9, 2005.

[23] Quoted in *Alternatives in Retrospect: An Historical Overview, 1969–75*, curated by Jacki Apple, with an essay by Mary Delahoyd (New York: New Museum, 1981), 28. This exhibition catalogue provides a good overview of 112 Greene Street Workshop, 98 Greene Street, and related spaces.

[24] Carol Gooden, e-mail to the author, December 11, 2004. Gooden's point is backed up by Kushner and Girouard: Kushner, interview; Girouard, interview.

[25] The Whitney Museum of Modern Art's recent Matta-Clark retrospective devoted some exhibition space to FOOD and inspired a noteworthy article on the restaurant by Randy Kennedy in the Dining and Wine section of the *New York Times*. See Randy Kennedy, "When Meals Played the Muse," *New York Times*, February 21, 2007, accessed online September 21, 2012, www.nytimes.com/2007/02/21/dining/21soho.html?pagewanted=all&_r=0.

[26] Marvin J. Taylor discusses this expanded notion of the archive in "Playing the Field," *The Downtown Book*, 34.

[27] The story of FOOD's transformation and demise is pieced together from the accounts of both Kushner and Gooden; specific attribution is noted only where their stories diverge.

[28] Kushner, interview.

[29] Ferretti, "SoHo Grows Up," 184.

[30] Quoted in Apple, *Alternatives in Retrospect*, 34.

Allen Ruppersberg

AS A YOUNG ARTIST, Allen Ruppersberg made two pioneering participatory works: *Al's Café* (1969, featured in *Feast*) and *Al's Grand Hotel* (1971). Ruppersberg had moved from the Midwest to Los Angeles to study art, and after graduation from the Chouinard Institute he began to make works that responded to his new city. These included photography-based conceptual works as well as mini-tableaux that he made by casually presenting materials like leaves or magazines within small aquariums, which served as readymade containers for displaced bits of the Los Angeles landscape. With their subtle humor and reframing of materials/contexts, these works prefigured some aspects of *Al's Café* and *Al's Grand Hotel*. These much larger and more complex projects were simultaneously installations, participatory artworks, convivial gathering spaces, and temporary pseudo-businesses. Language was key to both projects as well—note the casual Americana of the possessive nickname, in which "Allen Ruppersberg" the artist becomes "Al" the friendly proprietor. This interest in language and wordplay has remained central to the artist's practice. Ruppersberg has often visualized language as a means to explore everyday pop phenomena including advertising, fiction, and music. And while he now generally works within gallery and museum contexts, Ruppersberg's projects often retain participatory elements, for instance in installations of books and posters that can be handled and manipulated by the public.

Ruppersberg's first major installation, *Al's Café*, cast the artist as host within a kind of Do-It-Yourself alternative reality. He transformed a Los Angeles storefront into *Al's Café* by lovingly recreating the feel of an old-school American diner, complete with wood paneling and menus adorned with kitschy nature scenes. (Although the presence of several of his aquarium sculptures might have hinted that all was not as straightforward as the rest of the décor implied.) This process could be thought of as one that created a convincing backdrop for social experience—part simulacrum, part set, part sculptural assemblage/tableau in the tradition of the slightly older Los Angeles-based artist Edward Kienholz. But never inert: *Al's Café* was animated and alive. During its three months of operation, Ruppersberg served as host and short-order sculptor, offering his guests beer, coffee, and an array of surrealistic, small-scale assemblages that were also nominally edible, like the "Patti Melt:" for two dollars, a guest could purchase a "Patti Page photo (or reasonable facsimile) covered with toasted marshmellows." As at any café, these items were sold, not given away: with *Al's Café*, Ruppersberg tested an alternative economy by offering an unmediated way to both highlight his artistic labor and to make money from it.[1]

Al's Café also grew from Ruppersberg's recognition that the members of Los Angeles's then-small art community craved welcoming places to gather, to hang out, and share ideas. Rupperberg satisfied that need as the host of *Al's Café* until the local police shut the project down; he extended it further with *Al's Grand Hotel* a few years later. A quote from a promotional letter that Ruppersberg used to announce the hotel exemplifies both projects' blend of true hospitality with a tongue-in-cheek suggestion that perhaps art is a service industry like any other: "It will be, as Al's Café, in all respects a fully operational hotel . . . everyone is welcome to come, have a drink, and enjoy the luxurious atmosphere whether or not you stay the night . . . I hope everyone is comfortable and can enjoy the piece . . ."[2]

---

[1] See Frédéric Paul, "Interview with Allen Ruppersberg," in *Allen Ruppersberg: Books, Inc.* Exhibition catalogue. (Limoges, France: Le Fonds Régional d'Art Contemporain, 1999).

[2] The *Pacific Standard Time* online archive reproduces Allen Ruppersberg's letter, dated May 2, 1971, and brochure for *Al's Grand Hotel* in full, accessed July 30, 2012, www.getty.edu/pacificstandardtime/explore-the-era/archives/i46/.

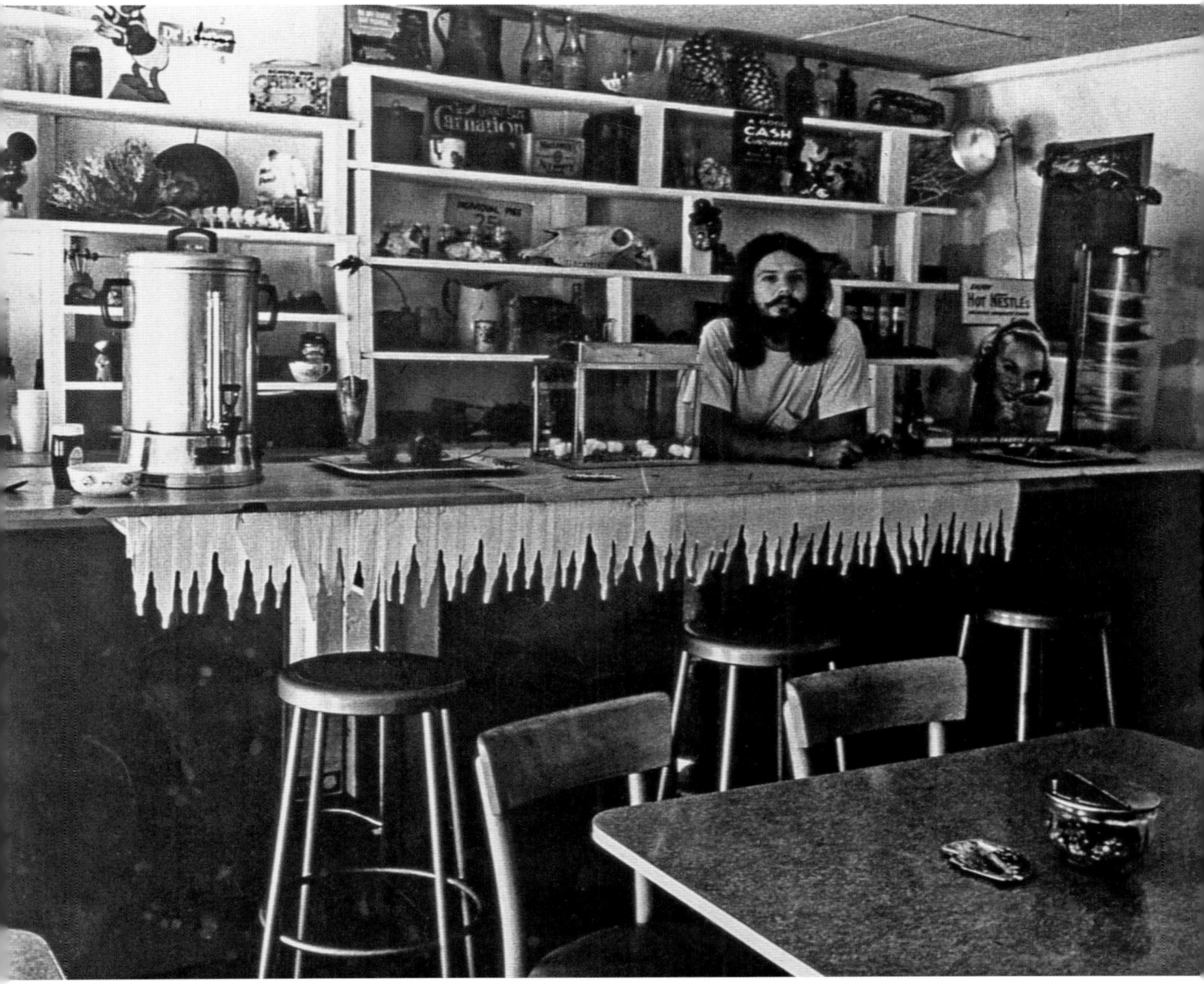

Al's Café, installation view, Los Angeles, 1969

Interview with Constance Lewallen

CONSTANCE LEWALLEN: Al, I'm going to set the stage here. It's 1969, you haven't been out of school very long. Can you tell us briefly what drew you to Los Angeles from your native Cleveland, Ohio?

ALLEN RUPPERSBERG: The beach, girls, rock-and-roll—all of the things that look very exotic when you grow up in Ohio—and a very good art school. I was lucky enough to get into Chouinard Art Institute. The school turned out to be terrific; it became Cal Arts in 1970.

CL: *Al's Café* was one of your early major pieces. It was the dawn of conceptual art, when young artists were rejecting painting and sculpture in favor of performance, the now ubiquitous installation, video, and so on. In a sense *Al's Café* was a kind of alternative site. Could you describe the interior of *Al's Café* and how it functioned?

AR: It was in an old storefront near Chouinard that I could rent pretty cheaply. It wanted it to be a real café. The idea was to set up a situation where anybody was welcome. It happened to be located next to a halfway house, and so there were a lot of people off the street who decided that this was a fun place to be. That was the idea—that anybody could be there. However, the only things that were really edible were beer and coffee.

CL: I'm going to read a quote from someone who wrote that "in direct opposition to what one might have expected from a young conceptual artist at the time, the décor was familiar to the point of strangeness: hyperfamiliar, you might say today."

AR: I ran the whole thing—as the cook, the service manager, the bottle washer. I ran everything behind the counter. There were

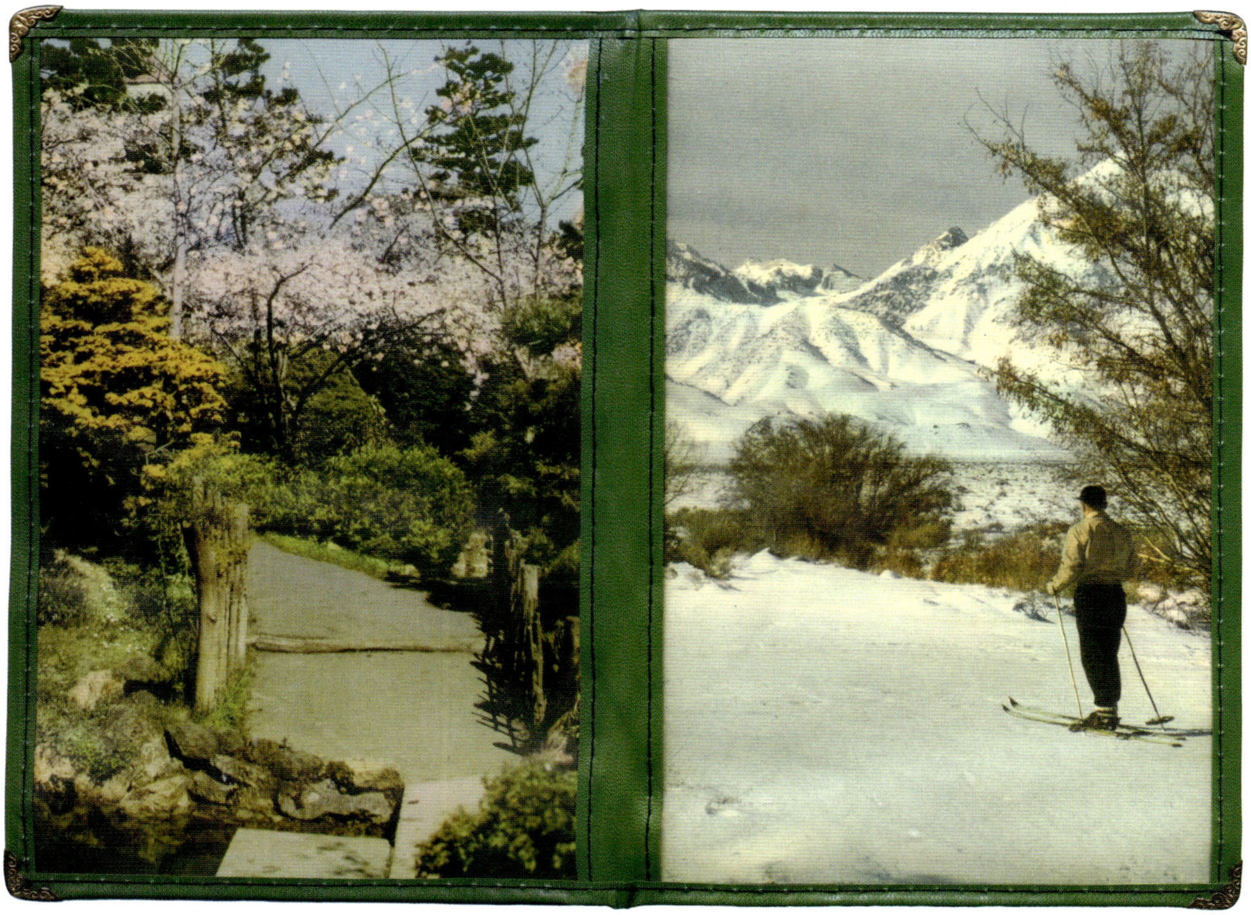

ABOVE AND OPPOSITE: The menu from *Al's Café*

waitresses who, when you came in and you sat down, would give you the menu. It was only publicized through word of mouth, through the small LA art world as it existed at the time.

CL: It predated Gordon Matta-Clark's famous *FOOD*, which was a real restaurant—I should say an installation/performance/restaurant—but you could actually eat food there, unlike at *Al's Café*.

AR: Very good food.

CL: But here you got . . .

AR: Tree-bark and cotton. It's a side dish. The place functioned in two ways. The California assemblage school—including Ed Kienholz, George Herms, Bruce Conner, and so on—was a big influence. But their sculptures were real sculptures, and mine resembled real dishes based on those you would buy in a coffee shop. All the dishes were priced the same as those at Denny's or any local coffee shop. You got a little piece of art for a buck fifty. You could sit around all night and drink beer, and have a good time with your friends—and this was the other aspect of the work. In LA, you didn't really have a place to hang out. The only art bar (and it really wasn't thought of this way) was Barney's Beanery, but that involved a slightly older generation. The café was not only an installation-environment-artwork, but also as a space where you could come and have a beer and sit around.

CL: Do you know how many of the dishes from *Al's Café* are extant?

AR: There is one extant set of all of them. And then there are probably others scattered

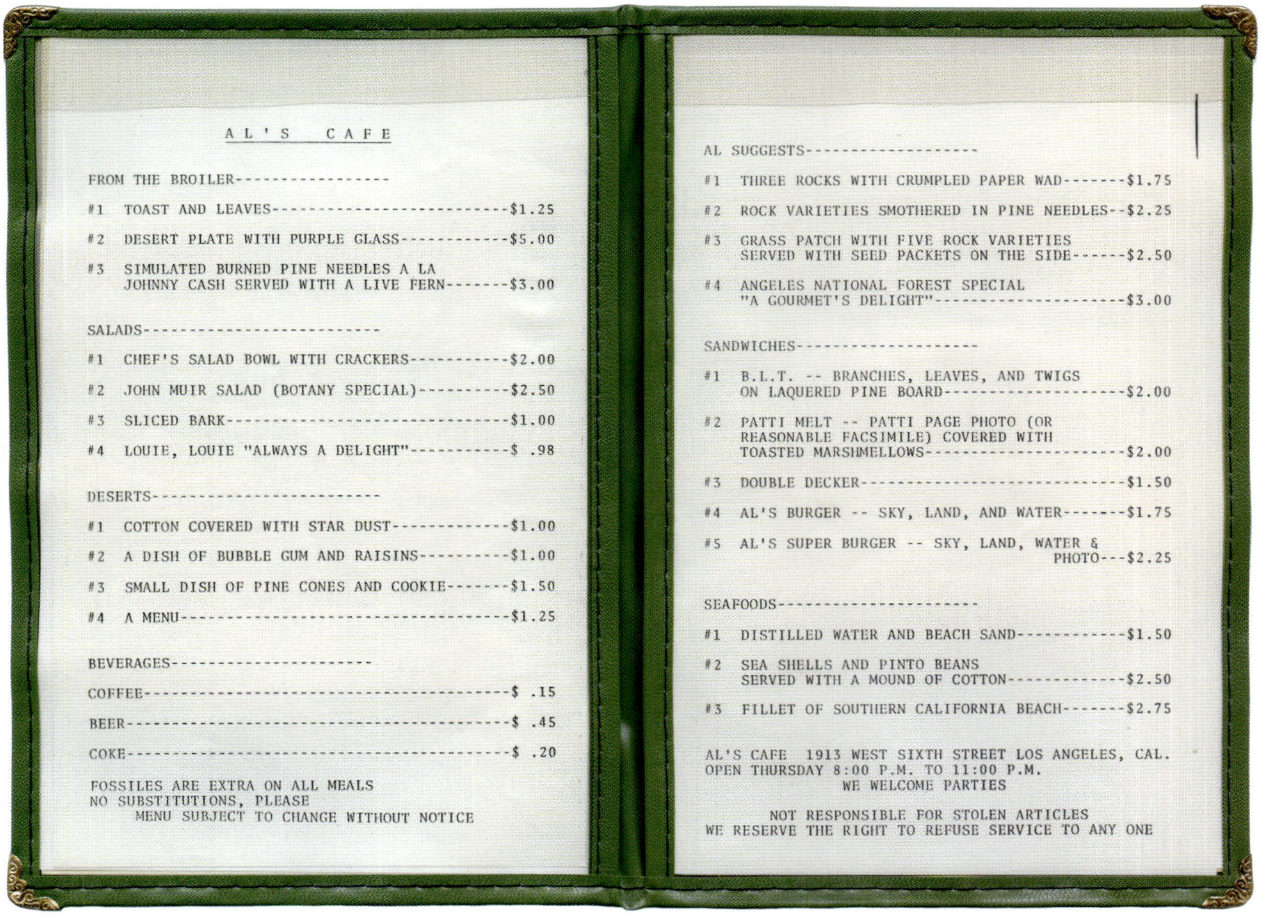

A L ' S   C A F E

FROM THE BROILER-----------------

#1 TOAST AND LEAVES--------------------------$1.25

#2 DESERT PLATE WITH PURPLE GLASS------------$5.00

#3 SIMULATED BURNED PINE NEEDLES A LA JOHNNY CASH SERVED WITH A LIVE FERN-------$3.00

SALADS-------------------------

#1 CHEF'S SALAD BOWL WITH CRACKERS-----------$2.00

#2 JOHN MUIR SALAD (BOTANY SPECIAL)----------$2.50

#3 SLICED BARK-------------------------------$1.00

#4 LOUIE, LOUIE "ALWAYS A DELIGHT"-----------$ .98

DESERTS-------------------------

#1 COTTON COVERED WITH STAR DUST-------------$1.00

#2 A DISH OF BUBBLE GUM AND RAISINS----------$1.00

#3 SMALL DISH OF PINE CONES AND COOKIE-------$1.50

#4 A MENU------------------------------------$1.25

BEVERAGES----------------------

COFFEE---------------------------------------$ .15

BEER---$ .45

COKE---$ .20

FOSSILES ARE EXTRA ON ALL MEALS
NO SUBSTITUTIONS, PLEASE
MENU SUBJECT TO CHANGE WITHOUT NOTICE

AL SUGGESTS-------------------

#1 THREE ROCKS WITH CRUMPLED PAPER WAD-------$1.75

#2 ROCK VARIETIES SMOTHERED IN PINE NEEDLES--$2.25

#3 GRASS PATCH WITH FIVE ROCK VARIETIES SERVED WITH SEED PACKETS ON THE SIDE------$2.50

#4 ANGELES NATIONAL FOREST SPECIAL "A GOURMET'S DELIGHT"---------------------$3.00

SANDWICHES-------------------

#1 B.L.T. -- BRANCHES, LEAVES, AND TWIGS ON LAQUERED PINE BOARD--------------------$2.00

#2 PATTI MELT -- PATTI PAGE PHOTO (OR REASONABLE FACSIMILE) COVERED WITH TOASTED MARSHMELLOWS----------------------$2.00

#3 DOUBLE DECKER-----------------------------$1.50

#4 AL'S BURGER -- SKY, LAND, AND WATER-------$1.75

#5 AL'S SUPER BURGER -- SKY, LAND, WATER & PHOTO---$2.25

SEAFOODS----------------------

#1 DISTILLED WATER AND BEACH SAND-----------$1.50

#2 SEA SHELLS AND PINTO BEANS SERVED WITH A MOUND OF COTTON------------$2.50

#3 FILLET OF SOUTHERN CALIFORNIA BEACH-------$2.75

AL'S CAFE 1913 WEST SIXTH STREET LOS ANGELES, CAL.
OPEN THURSDAY 8:00 P.M. TO 11:00 P.M.
WE WELCOME PARTIES

NOT RESPONSIBLE FOR STOLEN ARTICLES
WE RESERVE THE RIGHT TO REFUSE SERVICE TO ANY ONE

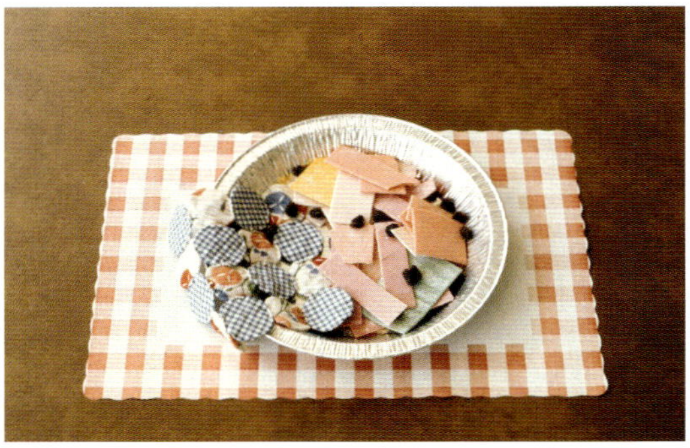

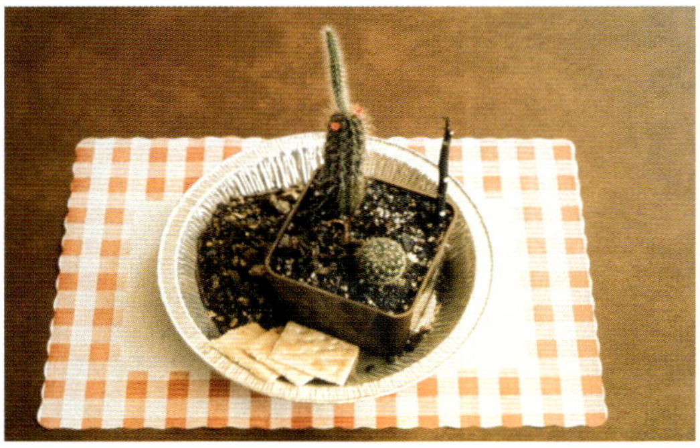

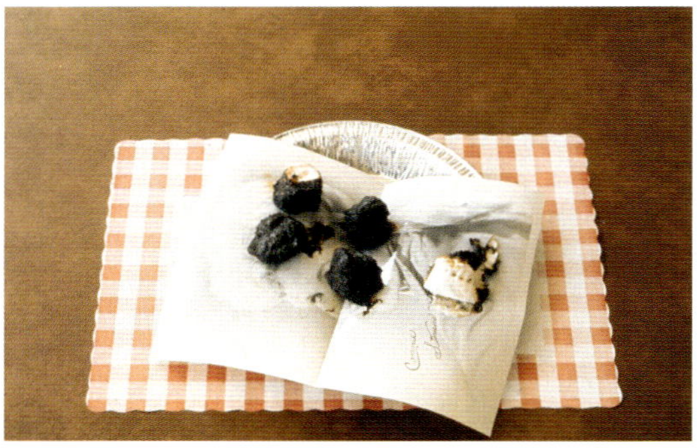

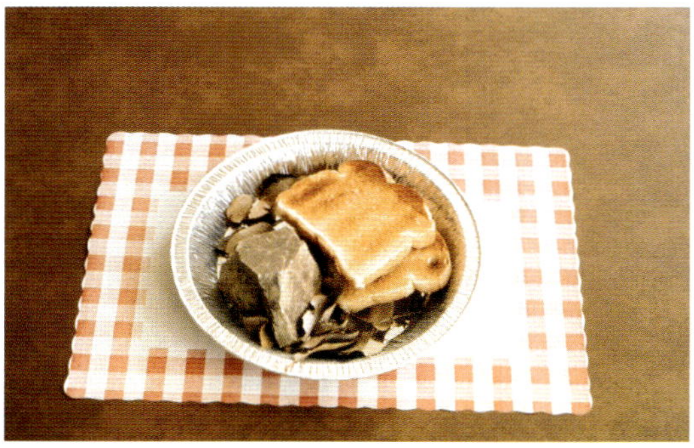

TOP TO BOTTOM: Meals served at *Al's Café*: A Dish of Bubble Gum and Raisins; Chef's Salad Bowl with Crackers; Patti Melt—Patti Page Photo (Or Reasonable Facsimilie) Covered With Toasted Marshmellows; and Toast and Leaves

around somewhere. I don't know. Every once in a while one will pop up. It's ephemera—I mean, it was an artwork, but after a while you get tired of having an object like that on your shelf. You throw it away.

I sold hundreds of them, but I didn't keep any of them myself. I kept some for a while but then the storage bills add up and you think "why do I have boxes of rocks sitting around?"

CL: Did you have a lot of customers?

AR: The place was packed every night. It was only open Thursday nights, 8 to 11 pm. As word spread, it got more and more popular, which was really great, because we were having a good time and I was making more and more dinners. It would take me all week to restock all the necessities. It became a full week's work just to have it open for a few hours. It was also a way for an artist to make some money at the time. When I opened it, I thought of it as a work that would go on for a while, but I had no idea how to finish it or how to close it. Eventually, I couldn't make the dinners fast enough and I began to think—now what happens?

CL: How did it close?

AR: It was in a part of town that was not so nice. It wasn't totally seedy, but was a little on the edges. In those days, everybody who was there was labeled "hippy." There were many people out on the sidewalk, milling around. This caused the powers-that-be to think there was something going on that they didn't know about. I began to see plainclothesmen showing up in the café, thinking that they were invisible of course, when everybody else looked like a stone-cold hippy. Every week there would be more of them. Finally, one night, they said to one of the waitresses, "You're under arrest." At that point the place filled up with cops—they had brought in the squad. They arrested the waitresses and closed the place down because I was selling beer without a license. They looked at the dinners and thought, "This is drug paraphernalia, or this is something that we don't like." That was how we got shut down. Eventually I went to court and it all got thrown out. I thought that's a pretty good ending, and it solved the

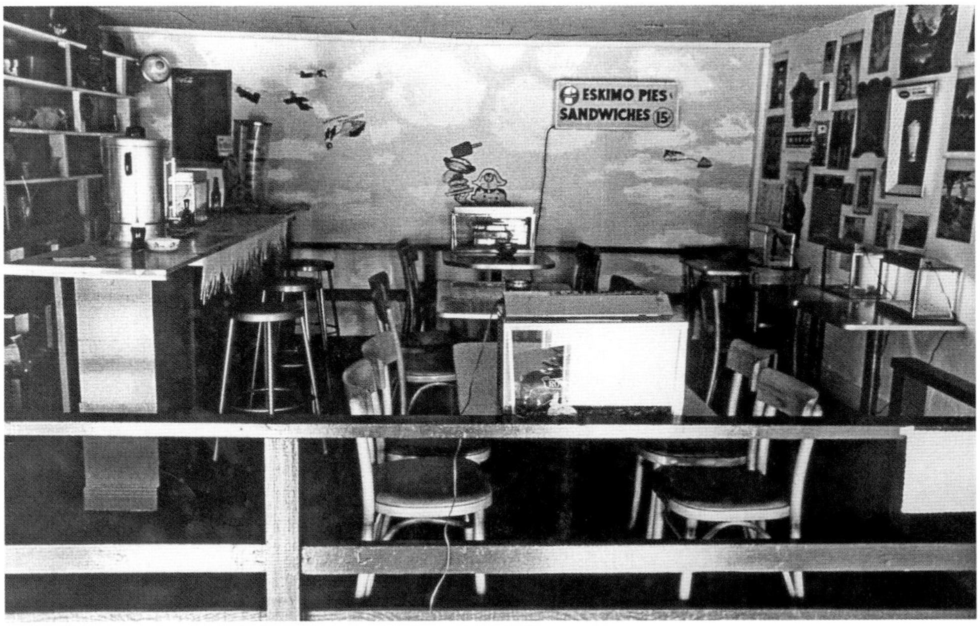

Al's Café,
Los Angeles, 1969

problem of me having to figure out what to do so that I could move on to something else.

CL: I want to ask you about what you knew about other artists who had opened stores of various kinds. We all know about Claes Oldenburg's *Store* of 1961 in which he sold his own artwork as a way to circumvent the gallery system. George Brecht and Robert Filliou, the Fluxus artists, had a store in Southern France. Daniel Spoerri was making his meals and preserving them as wall reliefs. How aware were you of those and if they had any influence on you?

AR: Well, I certainly knew of the Fluxus work. You learned from the generation ahead of you. I didn't know about Oldenburg's *Store*. But when I opened *Al's Café*, I met a lot of those artists. That's when I met Allan Kaprow; that's when I met Bob Rauschenberg. They all came there. People think that Southern California was so isolated, but artists were always coming through.

CL: I should also mention that this idea of the artwork as a social space—or as a meeting space—was something that also flourished in the Bay Area. Especially Tom Marioni's famous *The Act of Drinking Beer with Friends Is the Highest From of Art*, which premiered in 1969 at the Oakland Museum. The show consisted of the debris that was left after the opening. In other words, the opening was the event, and what was left was simply the documentation of the event, and that's what went on view. I know so many younger artists who are interested in this idea of the artist as a host or the artist as a guest. *Relational aesthetics*, a term coined by Nicolas Bourriaud in the 1990s, had to do with the artist sharing, with the artwork as a form of exchange. It's an attitude that seems to have continuing resonance for artists.

AR: Many of the relational aesthetics artists knew of my work.

CL: There was a commemoration of *Al's Café* that took place ten years later, in 1979.

AR: Yes, the main thing that I learned from the commemoration—I called it *Al's Café "Reheated"*—was that you can't repeat things. It seemed like a good idea at the time to have some kind of celebration of *Al's Café*. So I remade some of the dinners (the prices were five times what they had been). Everybody liked it except me. I immediately realized that it was the wrong thing to do. You can't redo these things. They're ephemeral events and belong in their own time and their own place.

This interview took place at the Kadist Art Foundation, San Francisco, September 21, 2011.

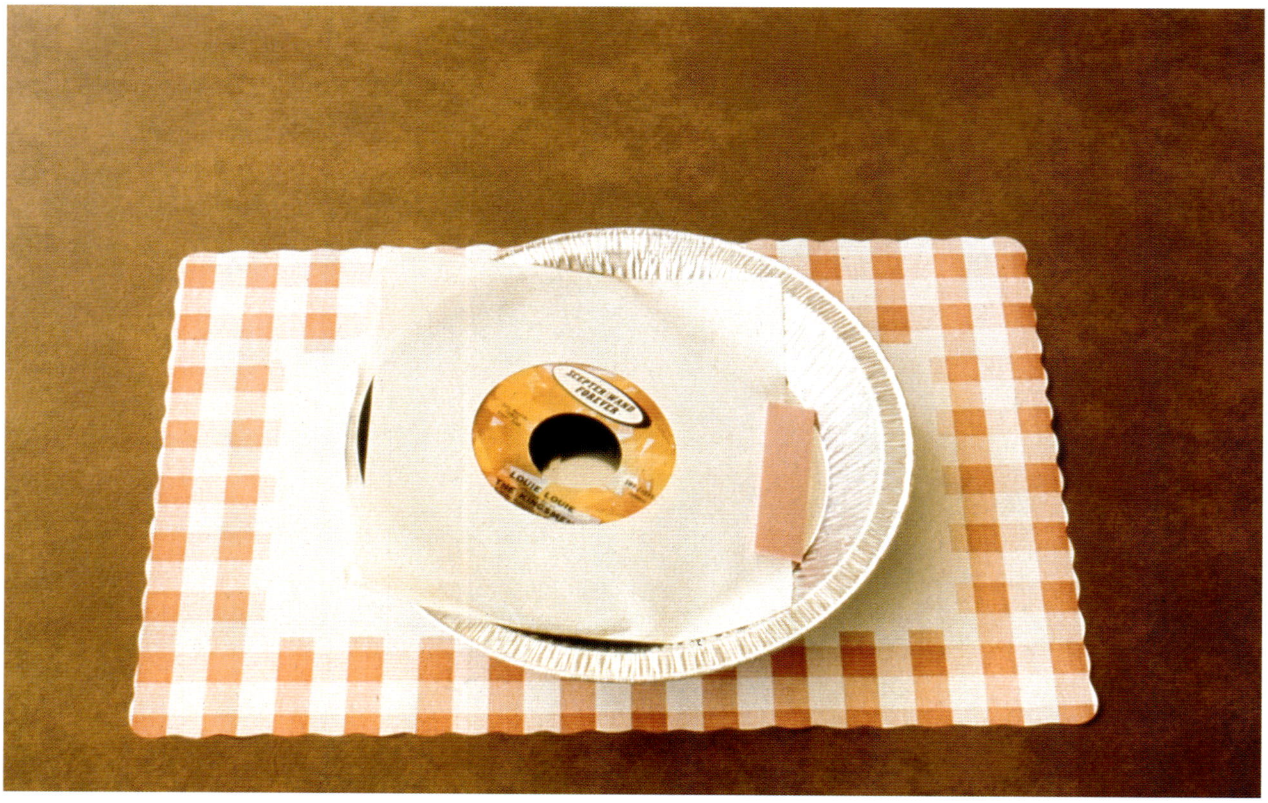

ABOVE AND OPPOSITE: Meals served at *Al's Café*: Louie, Louie "Always a Delight", and Small Dish of Pine Cones and Cookie

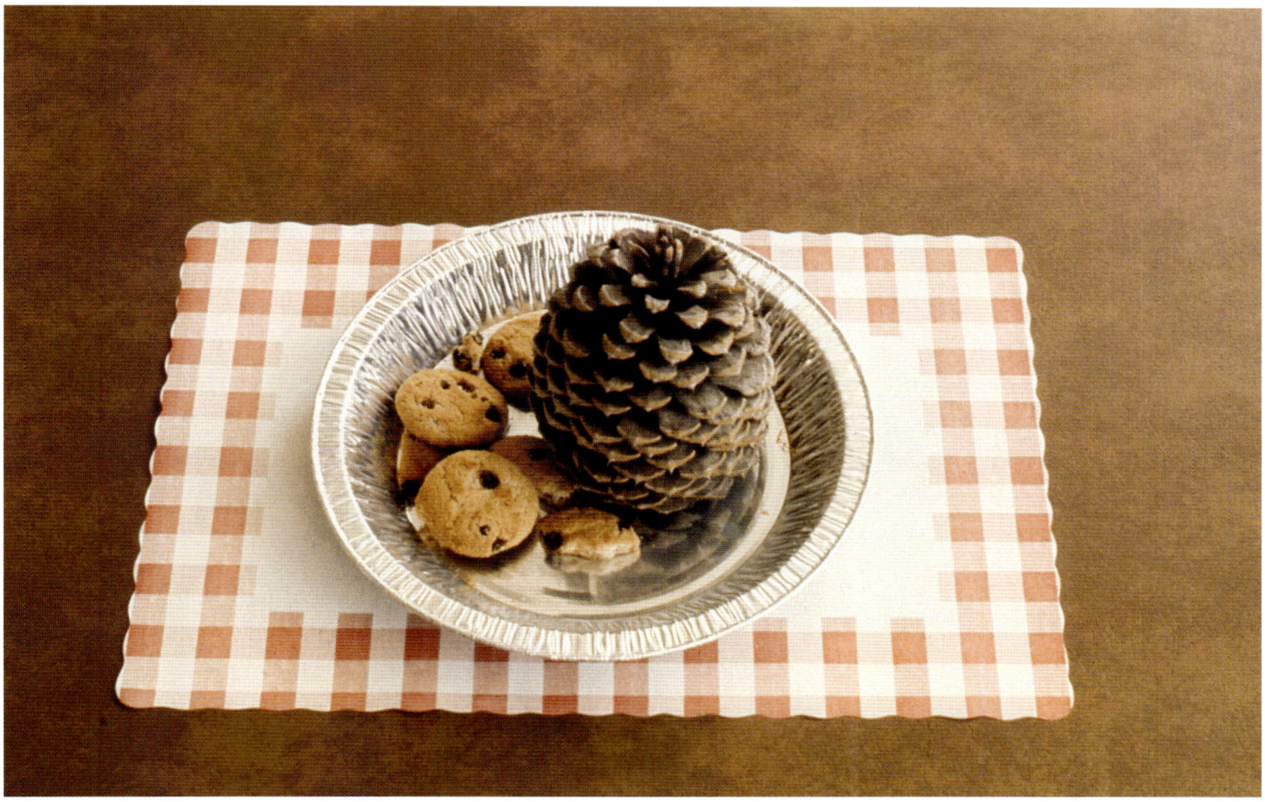

Bonnie Ora Sherk

IN THE EARLY 1970s, Bonnie Ora Sherk created a series of performances in public places: sitting still beside a freeway during its construction, working as a short-order cook in a donut shop, eating lunch in a cage at the San Francisco Zoo. The latter work, *Public Lunch* (1971), was Sherk's contribution to an exhibition of performance art curated for the Richmond Art Center by artist Tom Marioni (who is also included in *Feast*). For this performance, a primly dressed Sherk calmly ate an elegant meal while a tiger devoured raw meat in the next cage. As shown in the documentary photographs and video included in *Feast,* Sherk also paced, made notes, and rested—but kept the act of eating at the center of the piece. This solo meal worked on multiple levels to blur boundaries between human and animal behavior, public and private space, everyday life and spectacle. The piece was pivotal for Sherk. She considers it to be a key precedent for later projects focused on interrelationships, analogies, and communications between diverse species, and on the interconnections between biological, cultural, and technological systems. *Public Lunch* led directly to her study of interspecies communications while living and performing with divese species of animals, and later to her landmark work, *The Farm* (1974–80, also known as *Crossroads Community [the farm]*). In the latter project, she and collaborators transformed a few acres adjacent to, and under, a San Francisco freeway interchange into a small working community farm/garden, environmental education center, and alternative art space that she describes as "a work of life-scale environmental performance sculpture." Such eco-art-education transformation projects continue to be her primary focus through her ongoing project *A Living Library* (*A.L.L.,* for short).

Around the same time as *Public Lunch,* Sherk was exploring an idea she called "cultural costumes:" styles of dress with strong gender, class, and occupational associations that might shape others' perceptions of the wearer, and also might alter the wearer's sense of self. For *Public Lunch* she dressed as "a Woman"—in black dress and heels. This choice was a key part of the performance. *Public Lunch* occurred during a time of intense debate about whether women's roles could or should be limited, and took place in San Francisco—one of the epicenters of 1960s counterculture, and a city where dress was highly coded in expressing ideology. Sherk's choice to combine a typically female ensemble with an often elegant, unflappable persona both amplified and nuanced the contrast between human and animal meals.

For two other site-specific, meal-based performances, Sherk donned attire associated with particular kinds of blue-collar labor. As *The Waitress* (1973), she wore a bouffant hairdo and black and white nylon dress (and even chose to stay in character when called to jury duty in order to further explore reactions to that working class persona and explore the nature of performance art in the courtroom). In the nearly yearlong performance of *The Short Order Cook* (1973–74, shown in *Feast* through documentary photographs), Sherk wore jeans, a t-shirt, an apron and a chef's hat to perform as *The Short Order Cook* while working the graveyard shift at Andy's Donuts in San Francisco's Castro district. Some customers were aware of this performance as a kind of theater, while others obliviously enjoyed a midnight meal. The piece exemplifies the period's commitment to blurring—here nearly erasing—the customary boundaries between art and life.

OPPOSITE: *Public Lunch,* 1971, at the San Francisco Zoo

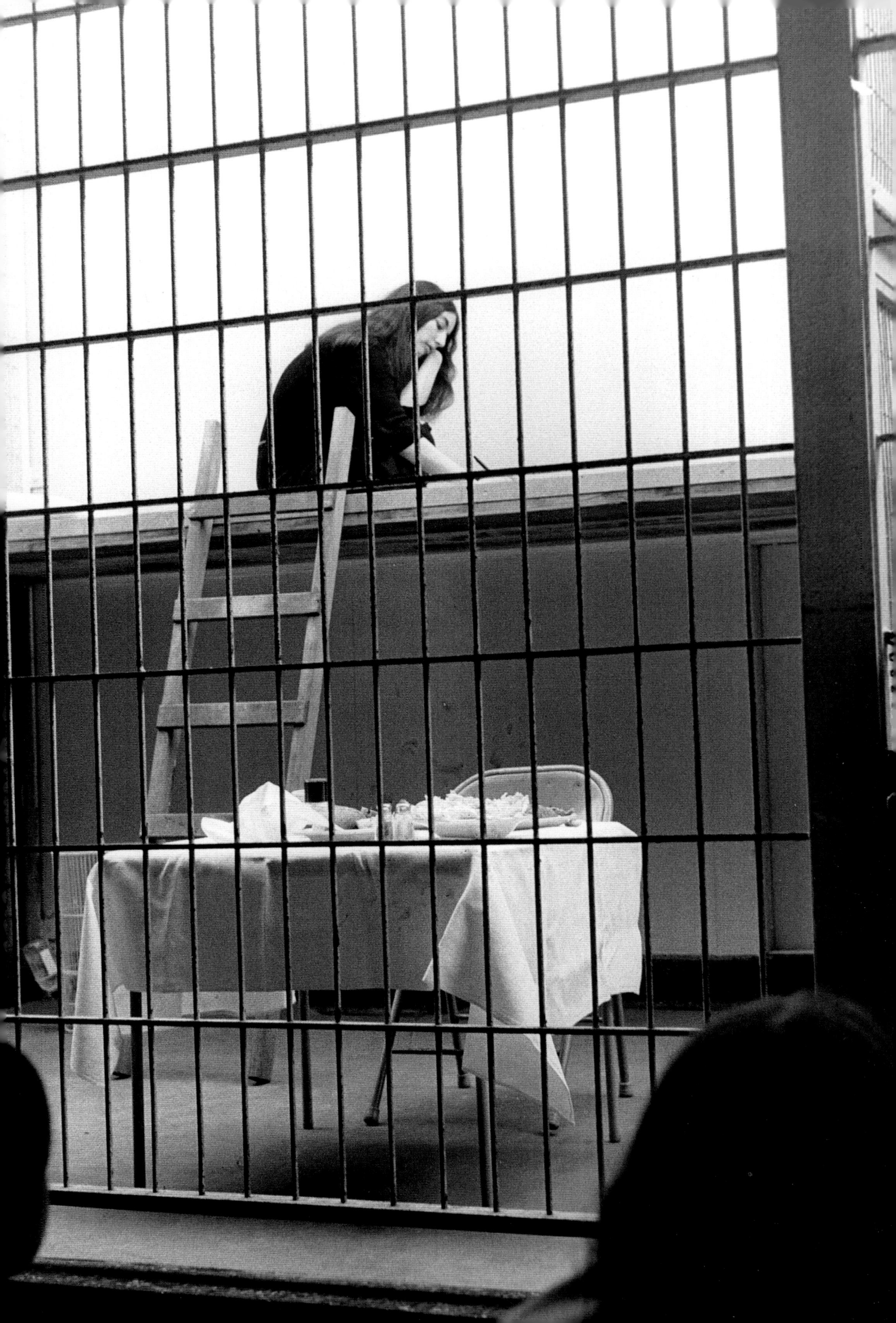

Interview

SMART: Describe your path as an artist and sources of inspiration for your work, either in or beyond the context of art.

BONNIE ORA SHERK: My work has been evolving for more than four decades in performance, installation, public practice, and place-based landscape architecture and planning. In my current work, physical transformations are integrated with communications technologies, hands-on, interdisciplinary and intergenerational curricula, and community programs.

My early work focused on expressing ideas and feelings through performance in a site, either found or created. I thought of myself as an environmental performance sculptor, integrating systemically the expression, performance, or activity within the place. I experimented with many forms of performance: some were open-ended, free flowing, and spontaneous; others were more tightly woven, planned or scripted; some had elements of each.

I was very particular about the place in which the performance would occur. Sometimes I used found environments, such as in the *Sitting Still Series* and *Public Lunch*. Often I created them, such as *Living in the Forest: Demonstrations of Aktin Logic, Balance, Compromise, Devotion, Etc.* (1973).

I understood early on that everything happens in a place, and if the performance and environment are systemically interconnected, then whole experiences are the result. I was very conscious of the physicality of the environment, the look and feel of the place, even if it was an internal environment or state of being.

In my early work, I was exploring the nature of performance and what constituted an audience in its various permutations. I was also looking at ways to transform "dead space." Additionally, I became increasingly involved in understanding and learning about natural systems, including ecology, animal behavior and communication, and interspecies communications. I was led to these areas of exploration as a result of my experiences during *Portable Parks 1–111* (1970) in three urban street environments, and a performance in the lion house of the San Francisco Zoo called *Public Lunch* (1971).

Sitting Still 1 (1970), in which I inserted myself as a seated human figure into a found environment of garbage and water adjacent to a freeway construction site, was actually a watershed piece for me. I thought I was merely showing how a seated human figure can transform the environment facing an "audience" of people in slow-moving cars. But I was actually facing my future: the future site of *The Farm* and the *Islais Creek Watershed*. I learned much later that I was also sitting in water from the Islais Creek that had collected due to the 101 Freeway Interchange being built. For me, this is an extremely profound piece that addresses the deep power and spiritual dimensions of both art and water. My early practice eventually led me to develop an urban farm and art center, beginning in 1974, which incorporated about seven acres of disparate land fragments, including a freeway interchange, into a bucolic new city park, farm, and environmental art and education center replete with farm animals living in *The Raw Egg Animal Theater (TREAT)*. (I was facing this area in *Sitting Still 1*, as described above.) Called *Crossroads Community (The Farm)*, literally in the crossroads of four economically distressed communities, *The Farm* was also one of the first alternative art spaces in the country, and pioneered urban agriculture and watershed management. I also saw *The Farm* as a performance, and similarly regard my current work with communities.

SMART: How has this shaped your ongoing work with your *A Living Library* project?

BOS: Performance in my work has evolved into community programs for hands-on, interdisciplinary learning, which is integrated systemically into an environment, or place, that I also create. I think of all of these works as *Life Frames*. The *Life Frame* literally frames life, so we can see it and experience it more profoundly. As a vehicle and framing device, this idea has consistently evolved with my work. In 1992 I founded *Life Frames, Inc.*,

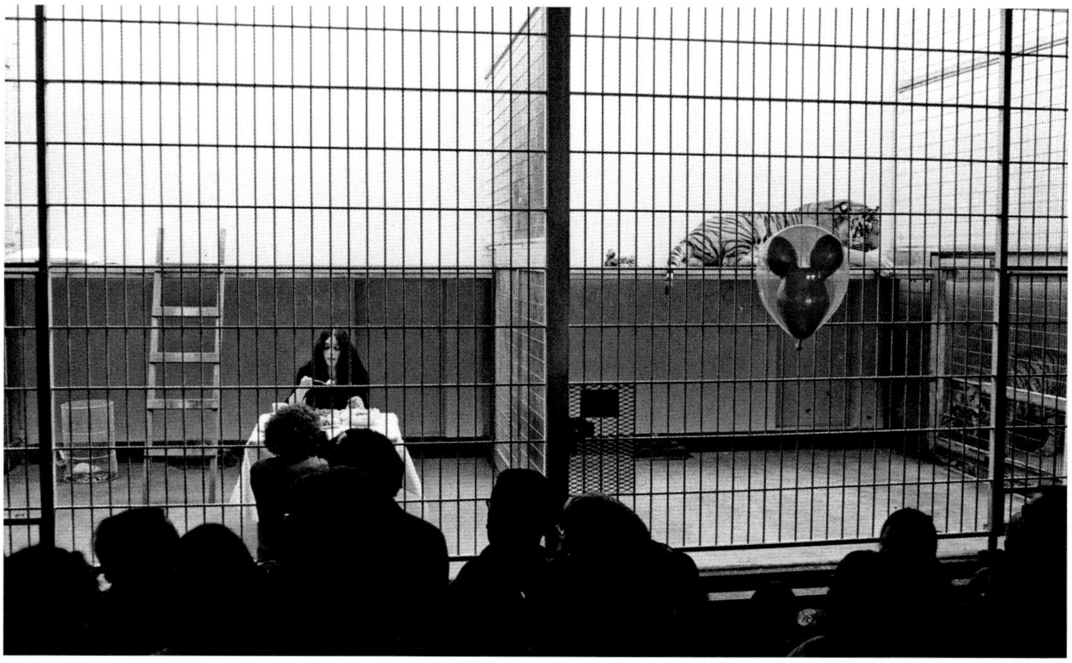

Public Lunch, 1971, at the San Francisco Zoo

a nonprofit that is now focused on sponsoring *A Living Library & Think Parks,* in diverse communities. *A Living Library*, which is still evolving in exceedingly creative ways, integrates biological, cultural, and techno-ogical systems within diverse communities—locally and globally. *A Living Library* (or *A.L.L.*), provides a methodology and strategy for making ecological change in schools and communities, and educating people of all ages about interconnected relationships, systems, and phenomena.

Each *Branch Living Library & Think Park* is place-based and unique, integrating local resources—human, ecological, economic, historic, technological, aesthetic—seen through the lens of time—past, present, future. A goal of mine, and *Life Frames, Inc.*, is to develop *Branch Living Library & Think Parks* in varied locales, and link them digitally, so that we can learn of cultures and ecologies—near and far—and better understand our commonalities and diversities. Currently there are multiple *Branch Living Library & Think Parks* underway in San Francisco and New York City.

SMART: Tell us about *Public Lunch*—its impetus, intention, and production—and how it fits into your broader practice.

BOS: *Public Lunch*, in which I ate a meal in the lion house at the San Francisco Zoo, adjacent to tigers and lions being fed raw meat, was the culmination of the *Sitting Still Series* mentioned above. *Sitting Still* initially began as an exploration of the nature of performance, and demonstrated how a seated human figure could transform the environment by simply being there.

Public Lunch was a seminal piece for me. During the course of the performance, I paced, ate my human meal, climbed up the ladder to the platform above, wrote what I was thinking and feeling (on Waldorf Astoria stationery), lay down, and rested. As I was lying down, gazing through the beautiful skylight above, viewing the clouds and birds flying overhead, the tiger in the adjacent cage, got up on his haunches and peered over at me. I thought, "This tiger is perceiving me; he is looking at me. What is he seeing? What is he thinking? What is he feeling?"

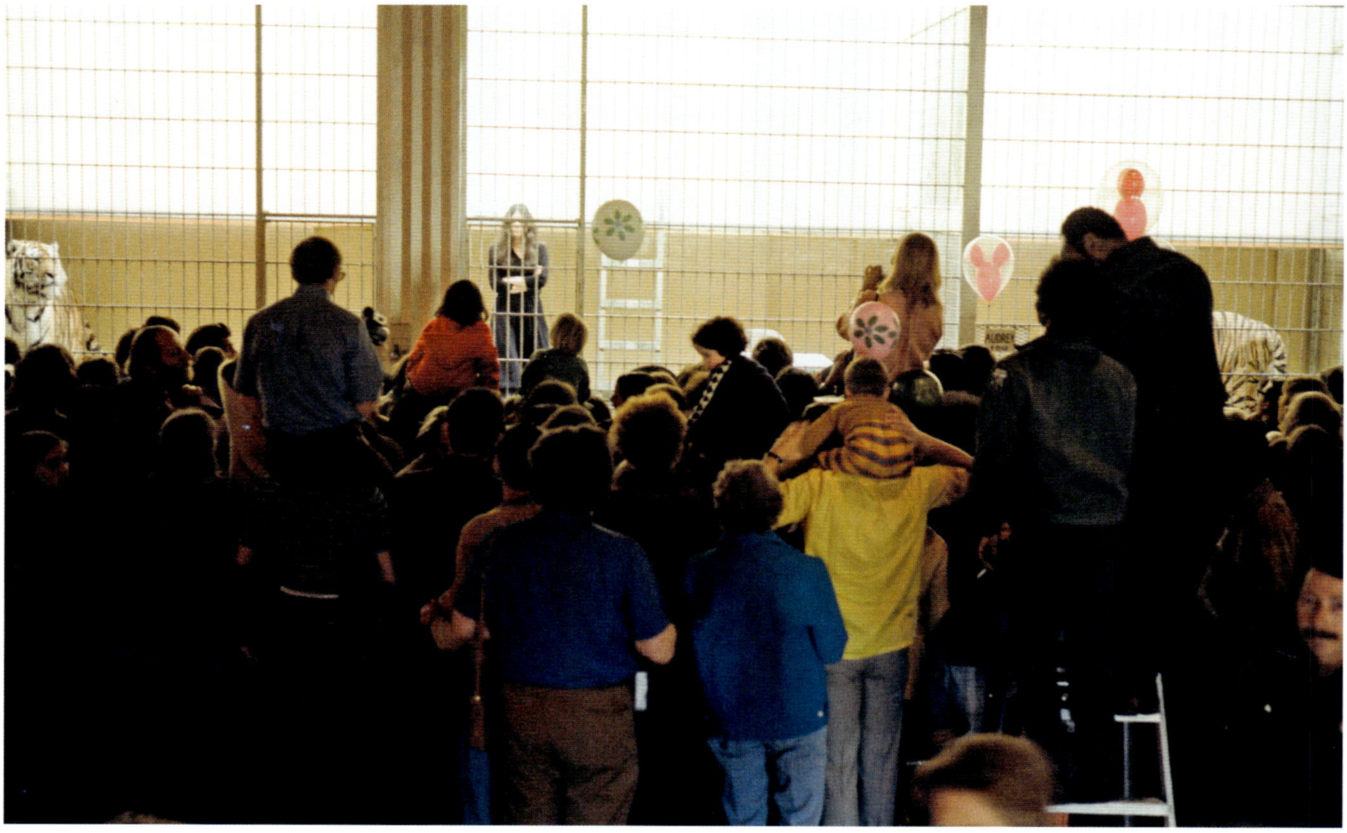

ABOVE AND OPPOSITE: *Public Lunch*, 1971, at the San Francisco Zoo

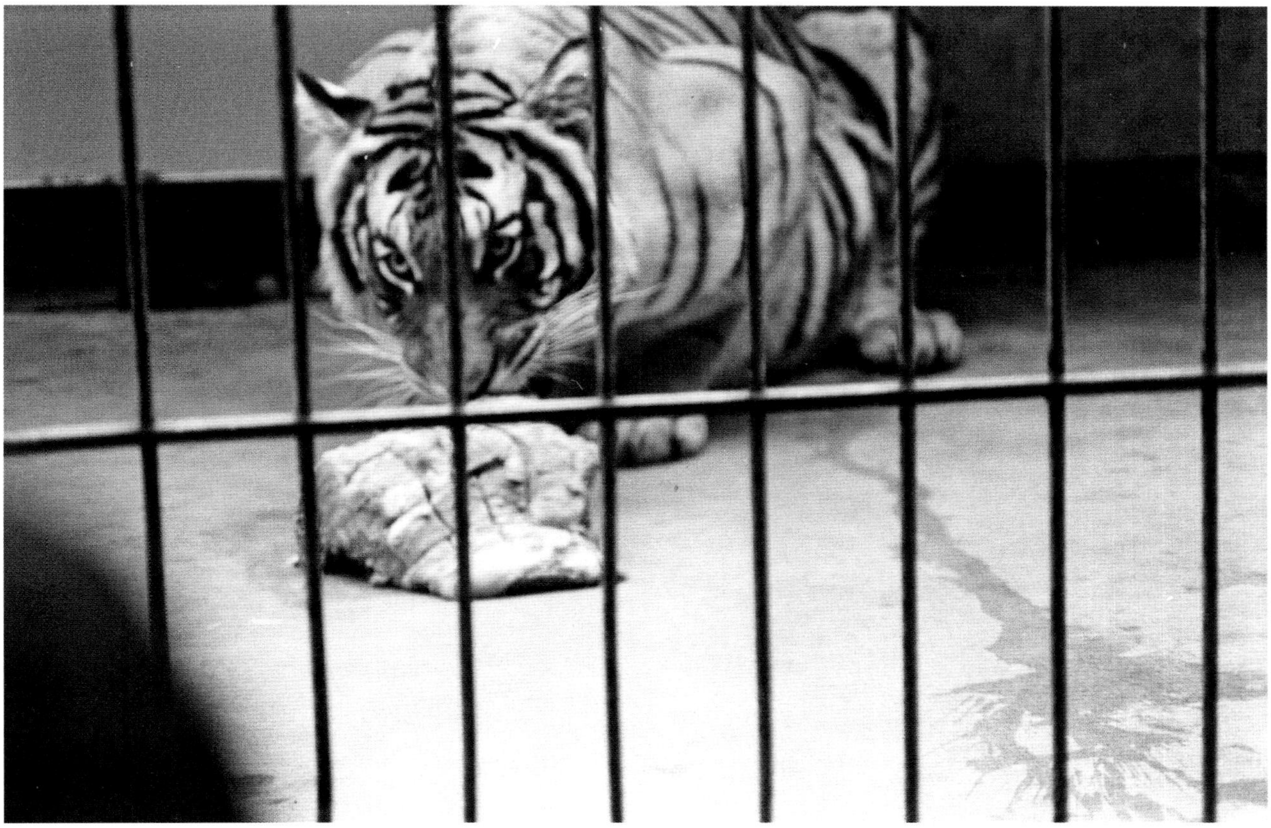

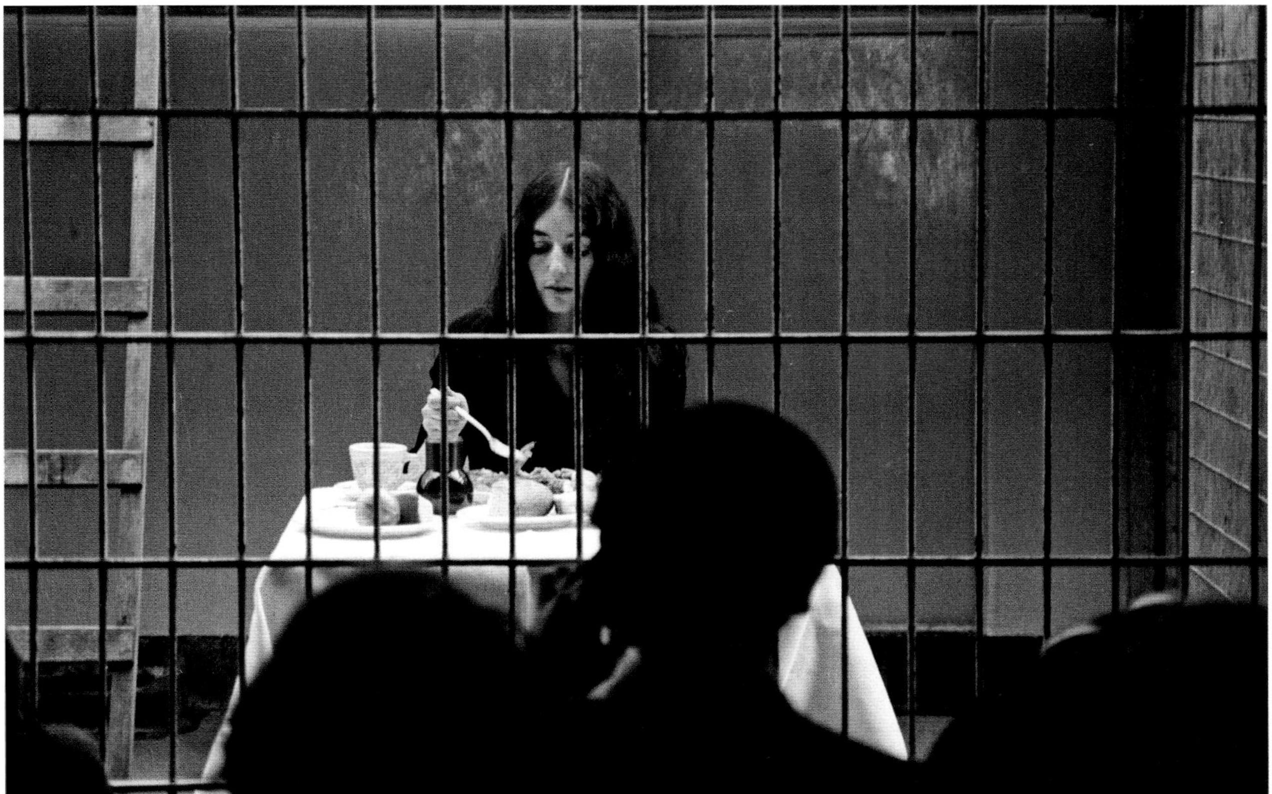

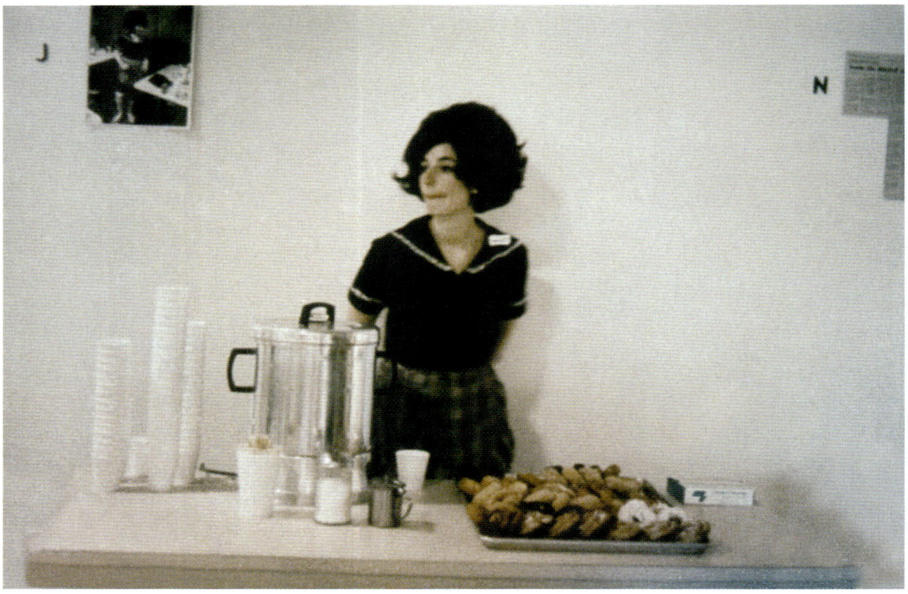

Sherk performs
The Waitress, 1974

This was a profound experience to think about the potential of another creature's intelligence, perception, feeling states, and communications. In the cage with me at the zoo, there was another cage that contained a white rat. I brought that cage and animal within as a way to demonstrate a cage, within a cage, within a cage. Who is in the cage?

As a result of the tiger's actions, I decided to bring the white rat back to my studio. I created a pristine, elegant environment for her. Between two pillars in the space, I built a "rat run," with sod at the bottom and wire mesh on the sides. But I left it open at the top, so the rat could leave if she chose to. She decided to stay, and I named her "Guru Rat." She was the first animal I lived with, and gradually I introduced other species into the environment and studied their behavior and interactions with each other.

At the time, the field of ethology (the study of animal behavior) was new; there was very little literature to read and study. But I learned tremendously by doing and creating experiences. The animals were performers, as was I. But we were also beings in our own right.

This work led me to understand ecology, which at the time was not as much a part of the zeitgeist as it is today. This work eventually led to the creation of *The Farm* and *The Raw Egg Animal Theatre*. I was determined to create a situation where people could learn about and appreciate the natural intelligences of other species. I saw this as a direct analogy to, and metaphor for, issues of racism, sexism, and child abuse.

SMART: The documentary photographs of the performance show a large audience watching you. Did the audience know they were experiencing art?

BOS: Most people came to the zoo at the regular public feeding time of the lions and tigers at 2 pm on a Saturday in February to see the animals being fed. I was one of the animals being fed on that day, and for those spectators it was a surprise. There were also a few people there who came because they knew that there was to be a performance piece that I was presenting, although they did not know what the piece was going to be.

SMART: What made you decide to write about your "private" experience of such a "public" lunch as part of the performance? Do you remember the kinds of things you wrote down?

BOS: Writing is a human activity and I was performing human activities for my performance in *Public Lunch*. I was writing about what I was thinking and feeling about the experience about being there, and what was happening.

I purposely wrote on Waldorf Astoria stationery, as the irony was irresistible, and also because the piece was conceived by my experience at the Waldorf. I stayed there as a guest of Condé Nast, after being named a Woman of the Year by *Mademoiselle* magazine, and was in New York City for their awards ceremony. In the morning, I ordered room service breakfast—a simple poached egg, coffee, and toast. I was struck by the elaborate, formally set table wheeled into my room with so many covered dishes. Extremely elegant but excessive. Soon thereafter, I took a walk in Central Park and went to the zoo, visiting the lion house. The rest is history.

SMART: How would you describe the role of the meal or hospitality in your practice? Do questions about hospitality figure into your process or thinking?

BOS: I have always been interested in communicating ideas or feelings to others, and in creating beautiful places. In some ways, creating art is really a public gift. That, I think, is close to the essence of hospitality, which is being generous, and sharing with others. It also helps if you really love what you do, as that makes the sharing more relaxed, loving, and more "hospitable." I have also used food a lot in my work, as a simple, common element, with multiple symbolic meanings. Food as a material is something accessible to all of us.

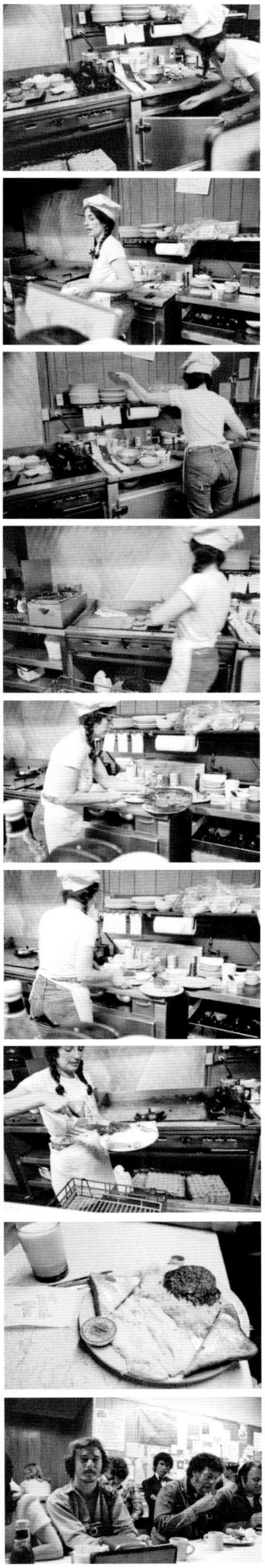

Sherk performs
Short Order Cook,
1973–74, San Francisco

Barbara T. Smith

BARBARA T. SMITH HELPED SHAPE the early development of performance and body art in California, both through her own work and as an active member of Southern California art communities. Along with other graduate students at University of California, Irvine, she cofounded the influential F-Space gallery, which became a hub for experimental projects like cofounder Chris Burden's notorious performance *Shoot* (1971), as well as Smith's *Nude Frieze* (also 1971). Drawing on her studies in art and art history, a deep interest in spirituality and psychology, and her personal experiences as mother, homemaker, and hostess, Smith's classic performances of this period often involved body- and meal-based, ritualized activities and immersive participation on the part of the audience. Performances like *Ritual Meal* (1969); *Celebration of the Holy Squash* (1971); and *Feed Me* (1973), which was created for a group show at artist Tom Marioni's Museum of Conceptual Art; pushed at the boundaries of self and psyche.

Smith launched her performance career with *Ritual Meal* (1969). When commissioned to create a performance in a private home, she designed a work intended to evoke primal states of being—thus undoing norms of etiquette and unleashing behaviors and emotions that might be experienced in an operating room or carnal ritual rather than at the dinner table. Upon arrival and without advance warning, the invited guests were thrown into an intense series of experiences in which they, too, became performers in Smith's art. Attendants directed them to don surgical costumes and apply makeup. Once garbed, guests drank body-fluid-like liquids from test tubes and used medical implements to eat (for example, raw chicken livers which guests could cook in steaming red wine over Bunsen burners). These simultaneously clinical and cannibalistic activities unfolded amidst an aggressively altered environment that included a thrumming psychedelic soundscape. Filmed imagery projected on the home's walls and ceiling further disrupted the domestic space. Smith extended the themes of the meal by projecting slides of great galaxies and films of the sea, open-heart surgery, and nude young people wandering the rough sage-covered hillsides; using the imagery in tandem with the ongoing, morphing performance to set up surreal chains of association around domesticity, wildness, science, sex, ontology, and sustenance.

Feast featured a video created after the performance that evokes the event's delirious sensibility. It pairs a montage of film clips shown at the dinner and documentation of the meal itself. The soundtrack includes fragments of an interview that a journalist conducted with one guest after the event. He describes the extreme emotional impact of *Ritual Meal* and frames it as a Happening, a term coined in the late 1950s by artist Allan Kaprow to describe a new form of collaborative public performance. The guest notes, "When you get involved with any kind of Happening it's usually sort of external, but this was internalized through a very important medium, which is your stomach . . . It was more like a dream than anything that ever happened to me that wasn't a dream."

OPPOSITE: Film stills from *Ritual Meal*, 1969

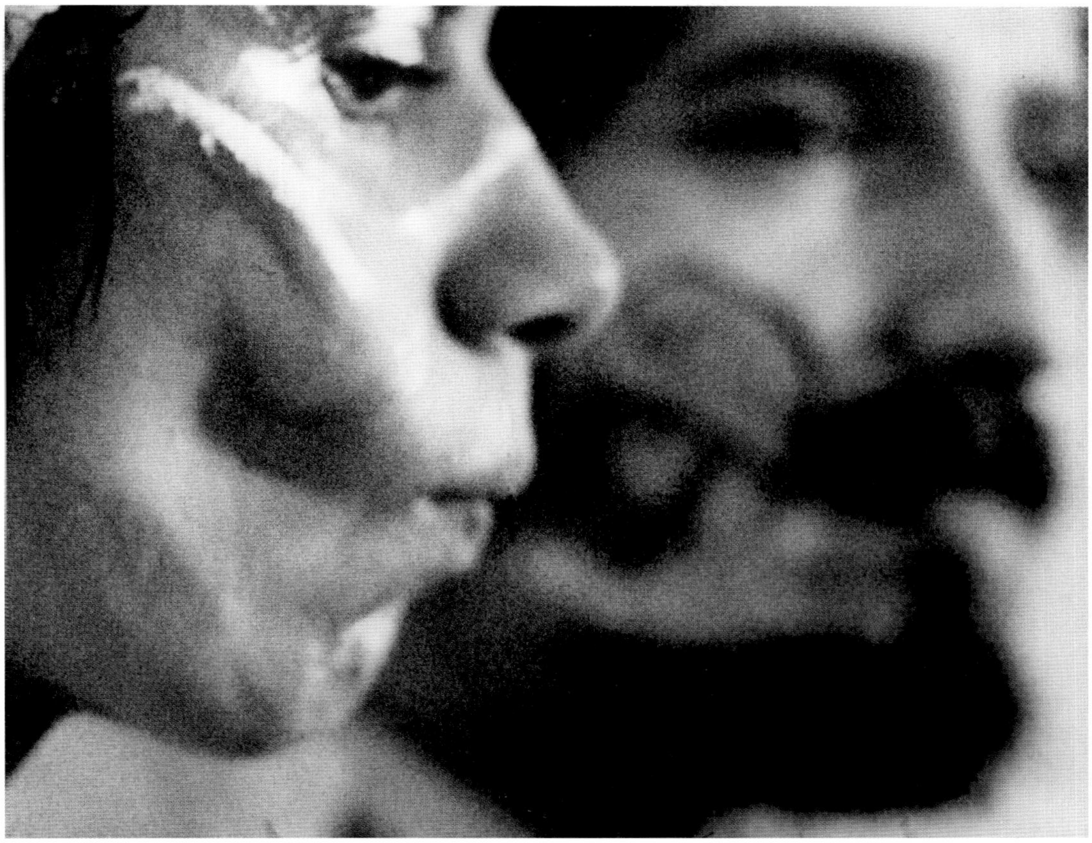

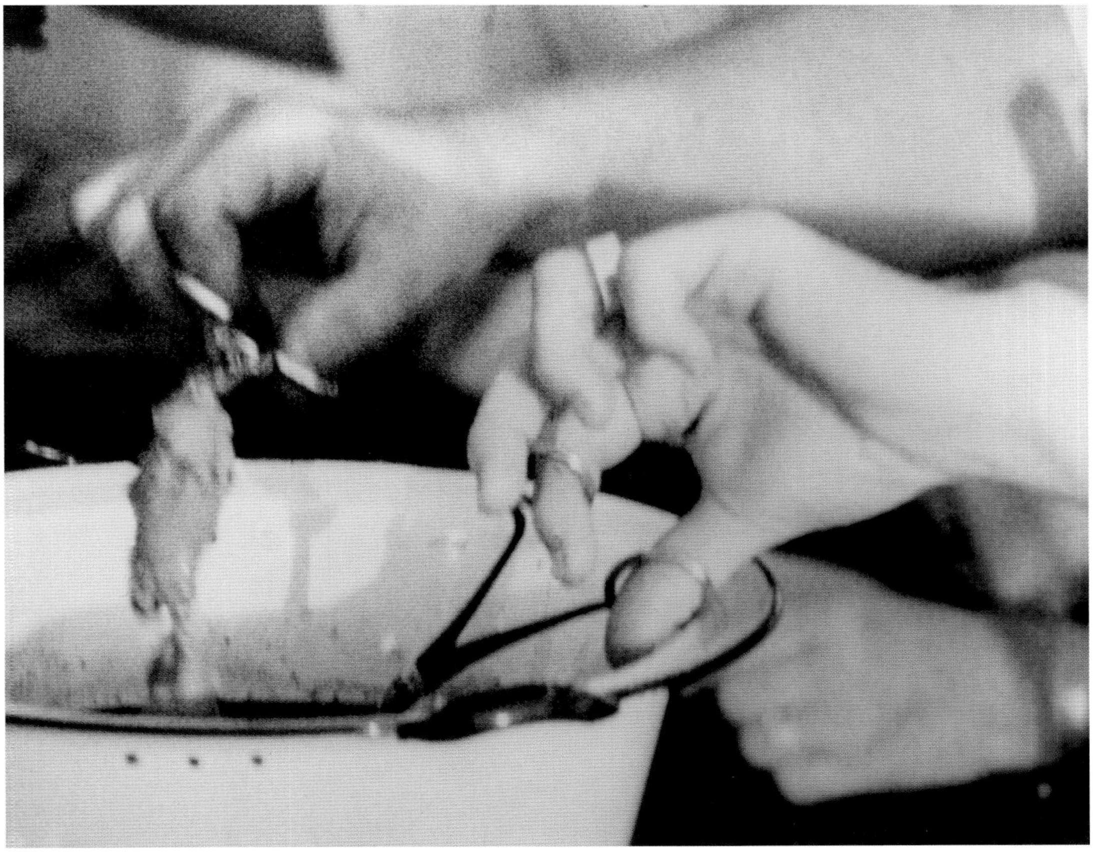

Interview

SMART: Could you describe the performance and the "radical use of food" in *Ritual Meal*? How did the evening begin? How did it unfold? How did you structure the roles of guests/hosts/performer?

BTS: There were sixteen guests. They were kept waiting outside the front door by a male voice repeating "Please wait, please wait" until the last very late couple arrived. This was already unnerving. Immediately upon their arrival, the front door opened and a tall man in a frogman wetsuit beckoned them to enter. He guided them into the living room where a young woman in a filmy, short dress stood on a pedestal. She came to life with a startled "Oh!" and ran out. The waiters appeared wearing tights and surgical masks; they put the guests into white surgical jackets and hats and guided them to their seats in the dining room. A mirror and face makeup waited at each place; the guests had to decide how to use it. Meantime, the minute the door opened, the huge pounding sound of a human heartbeat pervaded the house. Throughout the rest of the evening that sound plus the intense audio composition on a synthesizer accompanied everything.

Six courses of food were served with containers and utensils that referenced surgery. Images of galaxies flooded the ceilings. The walls were filled with slides of body systems and films of the sea as well as clips of the waiters, naked, coming down a path in the scruffy chaparral. If I recall correctly, the courses were: cottage cheese spread evenly on a plate with a small chili pepper in the middle of it that was eaten with the hands, and raw chicken livers served with clamps that guests dipped into enamel bowls of hot wine to cook. There was a whole roast turkey that they had to tear apart with their hands and dip in mounds of white salt. Red and white wine was served in test tubes held with clamps to reference blood or urine. A soup was served with raw eggs broken into the steaming pot. The final course was puréed fruit served in a plasma bottle wheeled around to each guest to suck on.

A flautist began to play as the courses became more benign, and finally a voice instructed them to play a game with the thirty-two white and black balls that were put on the black-clothed table. While the guests could talk to each other, the waiters would never say anything but gibberish, and appeared to serve and clear the courses and to wash their hands. Sometimes the guests were given rubber gloves to wear.

As they played some imagined game, the waiters left the room only to return completely naked and bearing beautiful wreaths of flowers, which they gave to each person as they ushered them into the living room to recover. In this case the gests were the unwitting performers. All were sophisticated in the art world: Steve Paxton, the Leonard Ashers, the Grinsteins, Hal Glicksman and his wife, Ann Ferrier, the Garmires, Malcolm Lubliner, Ed and Avelda Moses, and a couple more whom I can't recall. I had no thought about whether this would be some sort of forced manipulation. I was just compelled and fascinated. My only acknowledgment of the stress the guests were in, was the role reversal at the end allowing the waiters now to be vulnerable and to reward the guests by giving them flowers. Our hosts, Stanley and Elyse, were in the role of guests too and had very little idea of what would happen.

SMART: Why did you ask the guests to wear surgical costumes?

BTS: This was a sacred Mass of sorts and also a surgical operation. If they were in surgical clothes the experience would be more real to them and also erase any class issues. By virtue of the fact that all the participants were put into surgical gowns and caps, and presented right away with the unspoken imperative to put makeup on, they lost their everyday identity and ventured into the piece as voyagers (almost like on a space ship).

SMART: This has become a famous piece. How was it received at the time—both by the guests and within the art community?

BTS: A peculiar thing happened as we were waiting for the piece to start. A woman, Petri

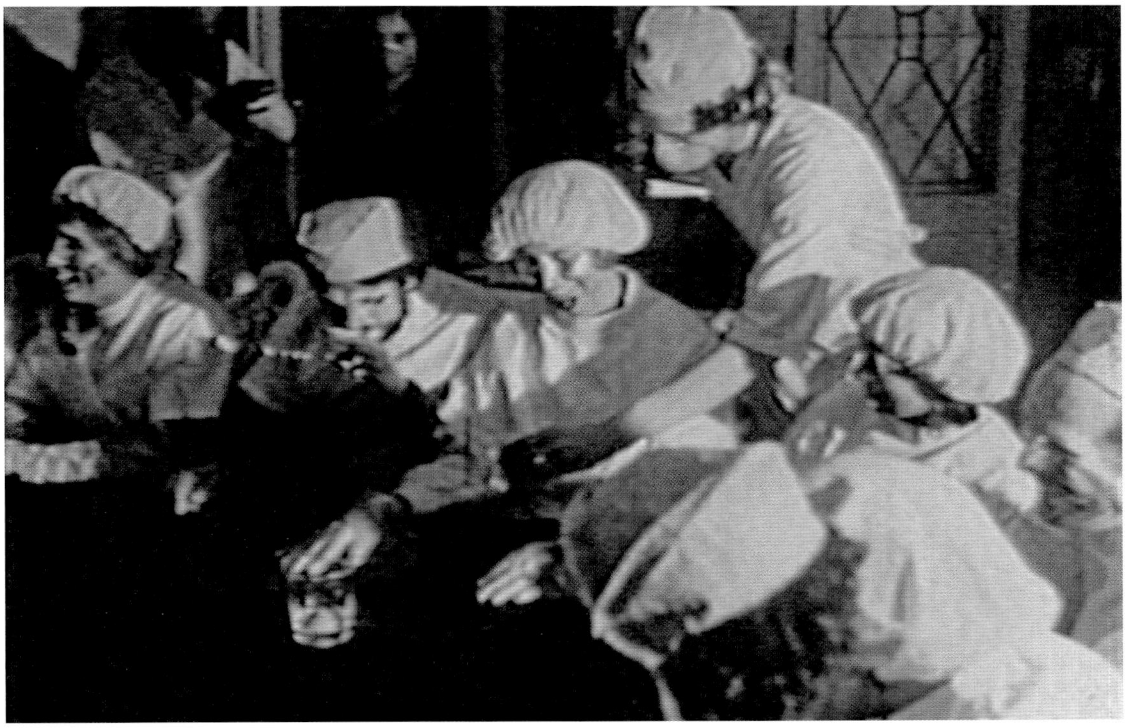

Film still from *Ritual Meal*, 1969

Mason, came in, saying she was from KPFK radio. She asked to interview me or watch. How she got there I will never know. I told her just to stay out of the way and watch. She is the voice you hear in the film. One friend who was a waiter brought a movie camera and on his own, between tasks, filmed what he saw, giving us a record that I did not plan for but now I am glad we have.

Petri interviewed Malcolm Lubliner a couple days later, maybe others, I don't know. We have bit of that on the film. He relates very acutely the outcome of his experience: how he was used to outrageous artworks, but was unable to go to work the next day and felt sort of crazy because of the aftermath. This was a unique experience for him because it went beyond the usual sense experience external to the body; it was internalized through the disturbance of food.

I think that was more or less what everyone felt. For me it was more than just cathartic, I was completely emptied in a way I had never experienced before. There was no art community to respond to the piece. It happened and passed into oblivion except when I was asked about my work later.

SMART: How would you describe the role of the meal in your practice?

BTS: I have used food as a medium in many ways throughout my career. For me, it has to do with the fact that I was born in a woman's body. Automatically my body is the source of not only of life but of food. That reality is so important that without it we would not have survived as a species. It is from this selfless giving that all things are born. My conditioning was to be the cook/housekeeper in a marriage, though I do not consider this indispensible. But having no training in theater or dance, my days as a wife and host of large parties allowed me to shift into planning and producing performed events.

SMART: Do questions about hospitality figure into your process or thinking?

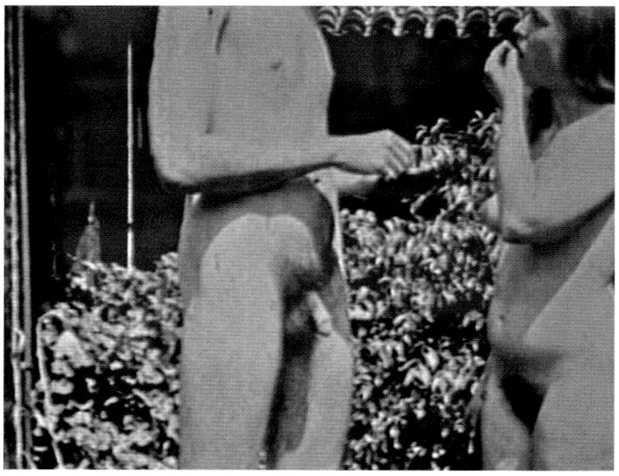

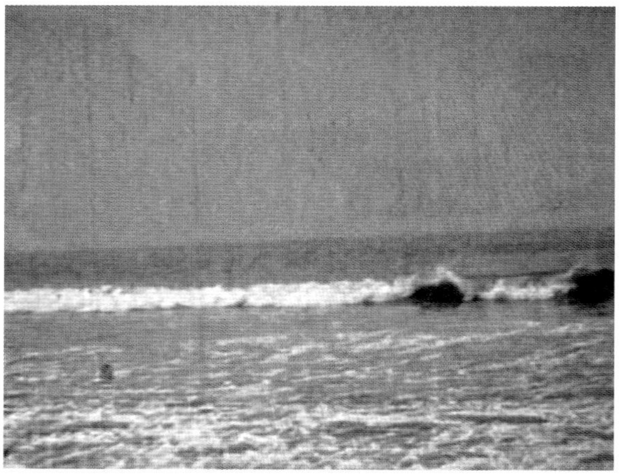

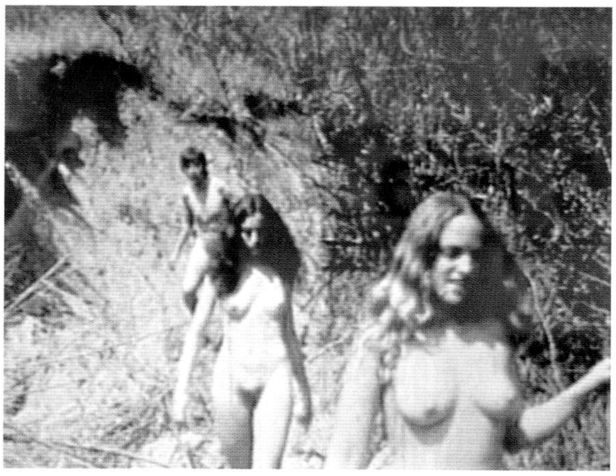

ABOVE AND OPPOSITE: Film stills from *Ritual Meal*, 1969

BTS: Not really in a party-giving sense. The great humor and liberation of the 1960s was that any material whatsoever could be the medium for artmaking: wind, food, water, detritus, etc. Food could be used as paint and as important symbol, as a startling contrary experience and as cosmic exploration (*The Longest Day of Night*, 1973), or ritual ceremony (*The Celebration of the Holy Squash*, 1971).

Only just recently I co-created a meal as a fund raiser for Highways Performance Space called *Chaos Confounded*. An ongoing loop of projected images was the backdrop for the carving of turkeys and the service of the food. We gathered several hundred images of artworks that had food or eating as a focus. The images were quite wonderful, ranging from prehistoric cave paintings through Greek feasts to Mike Kelley as *Banana Man*. This piece was about community and the history of food in art and peace in the midst of chaos. Thus hospitality was an issue.

SMART: Describe a favorite story about your work.

BTS: In 1969 I did a piece in my studio called *Mass Meal*. When the visitors entered the space they were at first blinded by a thousand-watt light. Inside they found various configurations of the space. In one area, hot, cooked roasts of meat hung against Day-Glo 4-by-8-inch plastic foils—all lit again by a thousand-watt light. In another area, there was a corridor at the end of which was a faint target lit by fluorescent light. Piles of foam rubber pieces on the floor and three buckets of red, yellow, or blue paint were situated on a table, an invitation for guests to dip the foam in paint and throw it at the target. A third room was walled in polyethylene film that allowed one to see into a white sanctuarylike space where tiny colored lights glowed beneath white foam covering everything. A strange Mass made of repeated phrases from ethnic music was continuously playing. No one was there to lead or give instructions about what to do. I was hidden in an adjacent office keeping the sound going but I never came out.

Here was a typical case (common in those days) of creating a piece without really considering the consequences. Even if one did

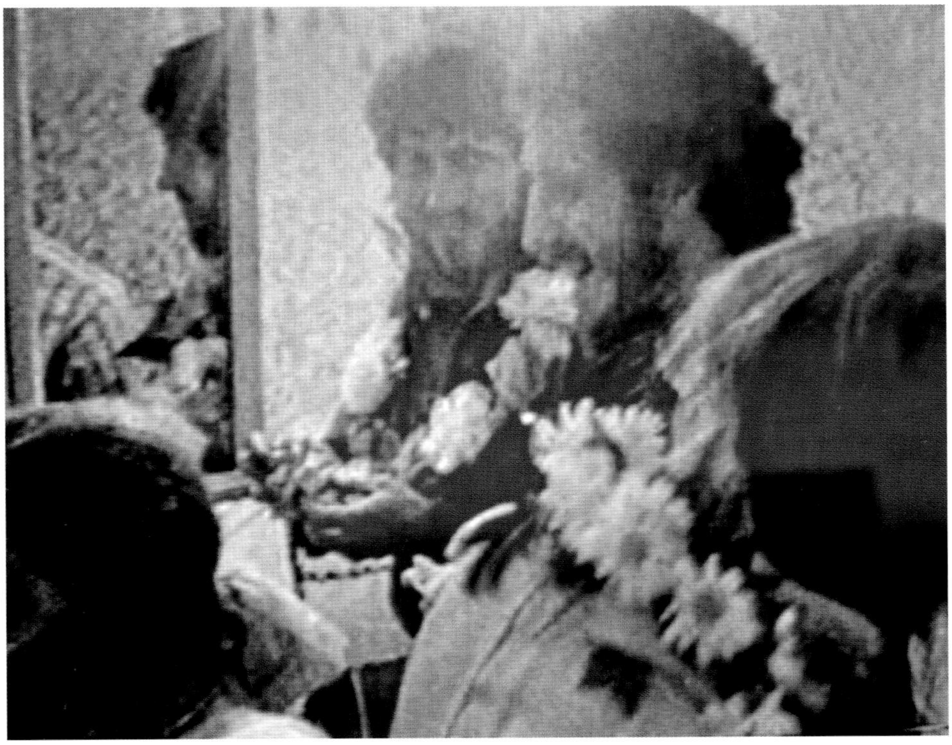

imagine what might happen you might just as easily imagine something else.

So what happened: People began swinging the hanging plastic foils and tearing meat off to eat. Dipping the foam in paint and throwing it. Breaking into the sanctuary room and trampling on the white foam. Grabbing the cups there that had red wine in them, discovering more wine, and sharing it around. Getting hyperexcited and one or two getting naked and wildly dancing. Then, ever more enflamed, beginning to throw the meat dipped in paint at each other. Tearing down the plastic foils and breaking them in pieces, getting ladders out and staging a war from on top of them, creating complete chaos. My studio was completely trashed. The floor and walls were covered with acrylic paint, stomped meat and fat. Later I had to rent a mechanized floor scraper to get the guck off the floor.

By 2 am everyone had left. As I stood in the mayhem, completely dazed, my phone rang. It was one of my friends who had been there, calling in a panic thinking she was going crazy. I had to reassure her that I felt that way too. One artist left angry that I was wasting food, not realizing he could have chosen to take it himself to feed the hungry. Two days later three different friends reported they could not eat meat the next day without gagging. And one friend who had donated the meat, a veterinarian, was furious at me because he thought I had made them act that way. He didn't realize I was as shocked as anyone.

The outcome for me was that in that case I was so identified with my work that it felt like I personally was being violated. It took a few months to get over it. Three psychologist friends explained that this was a case of severe sensory overload and that all the senses were being bombarded at once making it nearly impossible to discriminate alternatives of action. In such a case (as in mob violence), the crowd will follow any suggestion.

SMART: What do you hope people take away from your work?

BTS: A deep, physical response to the materiality of their life. A respect for food and life itself. A sense of humor about how seriously we take things. An inspiration that they, too, can make very free and liberated uses of food. A body bonding with all others.

Daniel Spoerri

DANIEL SPOERRI MADE THE MEAL a central focus of his art, using it to enact a larger interest in chance-based processes and everyday experience. One early manifestation of this interest was his affiliation with the Nouveaux Réalistes—a loose group of European artists who embraced "the real" in order to counteract a perceived ossification of traditional modes of artmaking, particularly painting. The group's manifesto, "The New Realists" (1960), advocated for the

> passionate adventure of the real perceived in itself and not through the prism of conceptual or imaginative transcription . . . Sociology comes to the assistance of consciousness and of chance, whether this be at the level of choice or of the tearing up of posters, of the allure of an object, of the household rubbish or the scraps of the dining-room . . . Man, if he shares in reintegrating himself in reality, identifies it with his own transcendence, which is emotion, feeling and finally, once again, poetry.[1]

Around the time of the manifesto, Spoerri began to experiment with chance and everyday materials as catalysts for art. In his classic artist's book, *An Anecdoted Topography of Chance*, for instance, he drew a map of all of the mundane objects sitting on a blue-painted side table in his hotel room, and then wrote brief meditations on each. He also explored a similar process via sculpture through "snare pictures" or "trap pictures" in which the remains of an activity are affixed to the surface on which they are found. The surface is then turned sideways and hung on the wall to form a kind of readymade painting in which the composition is determined by chance. In the case of the meal-based snare pictures, the surface is a tabletop and "the scraps of the dining room" are glued on, just as they were left after eating. They form a kind of still life, which, however, offers evidence of consumption and convivial interaction rather than aesthetic intention. Spoerri sometimes created snare pictures for specific exhibition situations, as in *31 Variations on a Meal* (1964, initially called *29 Variations on a Meal*), in which meals eaten by artists including Andy Warhol became snare pictures for a show at the Allan Stone Gallery in New York. Others were created in temporary restaurants that Spoerri created within art spaces like the Restaurant de la Galerie J (Paris, 1963) or the Restaurant City Galerie (Cologne, 1965).

Spoerri developed such practices most fully and over time in his Restaurant Spoerri in Düsseldorf, which opened in 1968, and was followed by the Eat Art Gallery upstairs in 1970. These interrelated long-term projects blurred the boundaries between restaurant, gallery, and studio in usefully disorienting ways. They became sites for food- and meal-based experimentation by Spoerri and other artists like Arman and Joseph Beuys, as documented in the exhibition posters included in *Feast*. They also catalyzed both convivial exchange in the moment, and snare pictures like *Tableau piège, 17. Juni 1972* (1972). This work is part of a series created over the course of 1972. Each night, one of the small, square, blue-topped tabletops and the remains it contained were fixed to form a physically tangible, lasting work of art—simultaneously a document of a meal and a new aesthetic object with its own internal logic and connection to larger arcs of art history. Spoerri has continued to produce Eat Art in varied forms, from small sculptures and prints to large thematic banquets; an Eat Art Restaurant, Esslokal, is currently in operation in the Austrian town of Hadersdorf am Kamp.

---

[1] "The New Realists" manifesto was written by critic Pierre Restany and later signed by Yves Klein, Arman, Daniel Spoerri, and Jean Tinguely; in Charles Harrison, and Paul Wood, eds., *Art in Theory: 1900–2000: An Anthology of Changing Ideas* (Oxford, UK: Blackwell Publishing, 2002), 711–12.

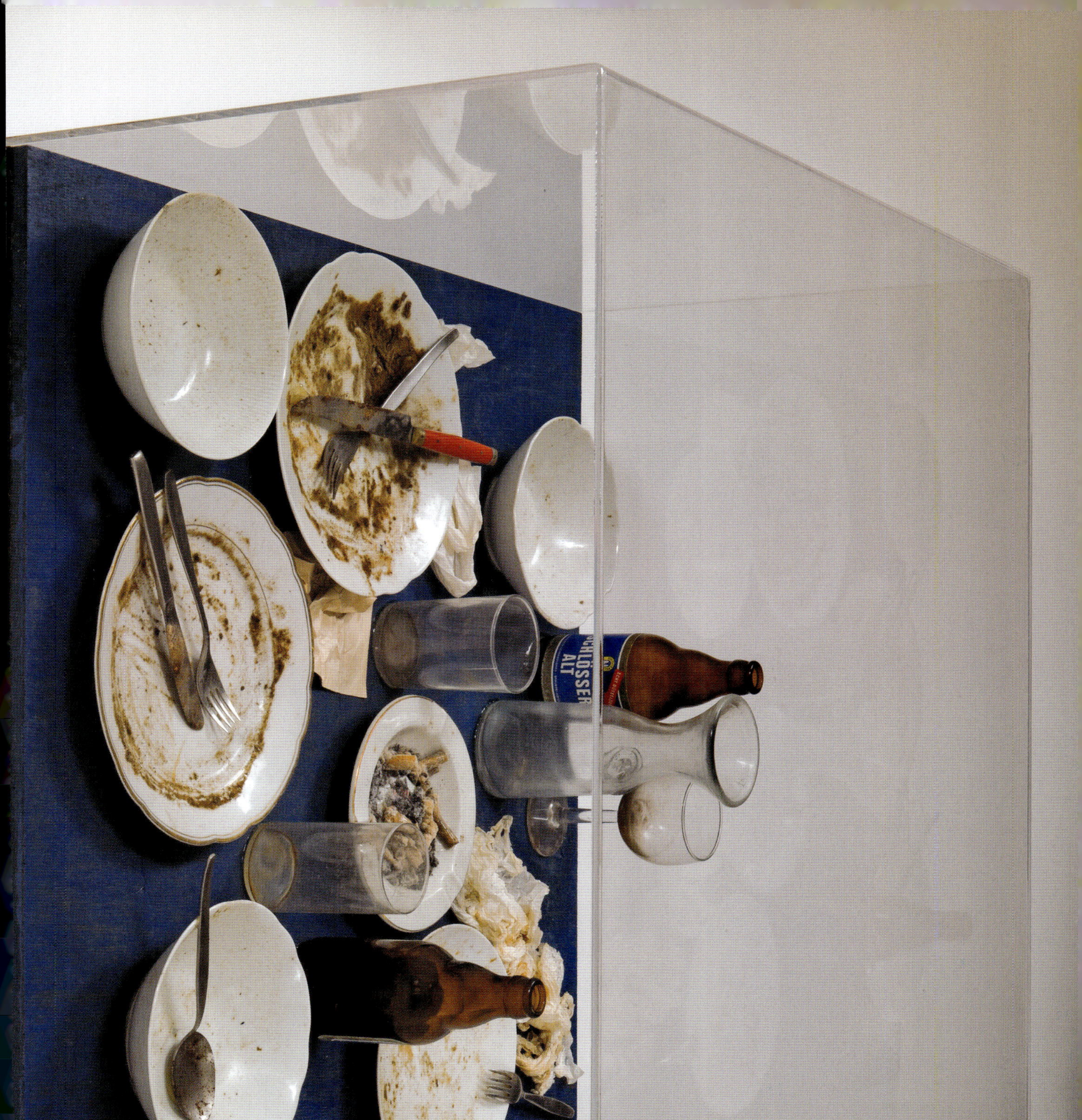

Tableau piège, 17. Juni 1972, 1972, installation view, Smart Museum of Art, 2012

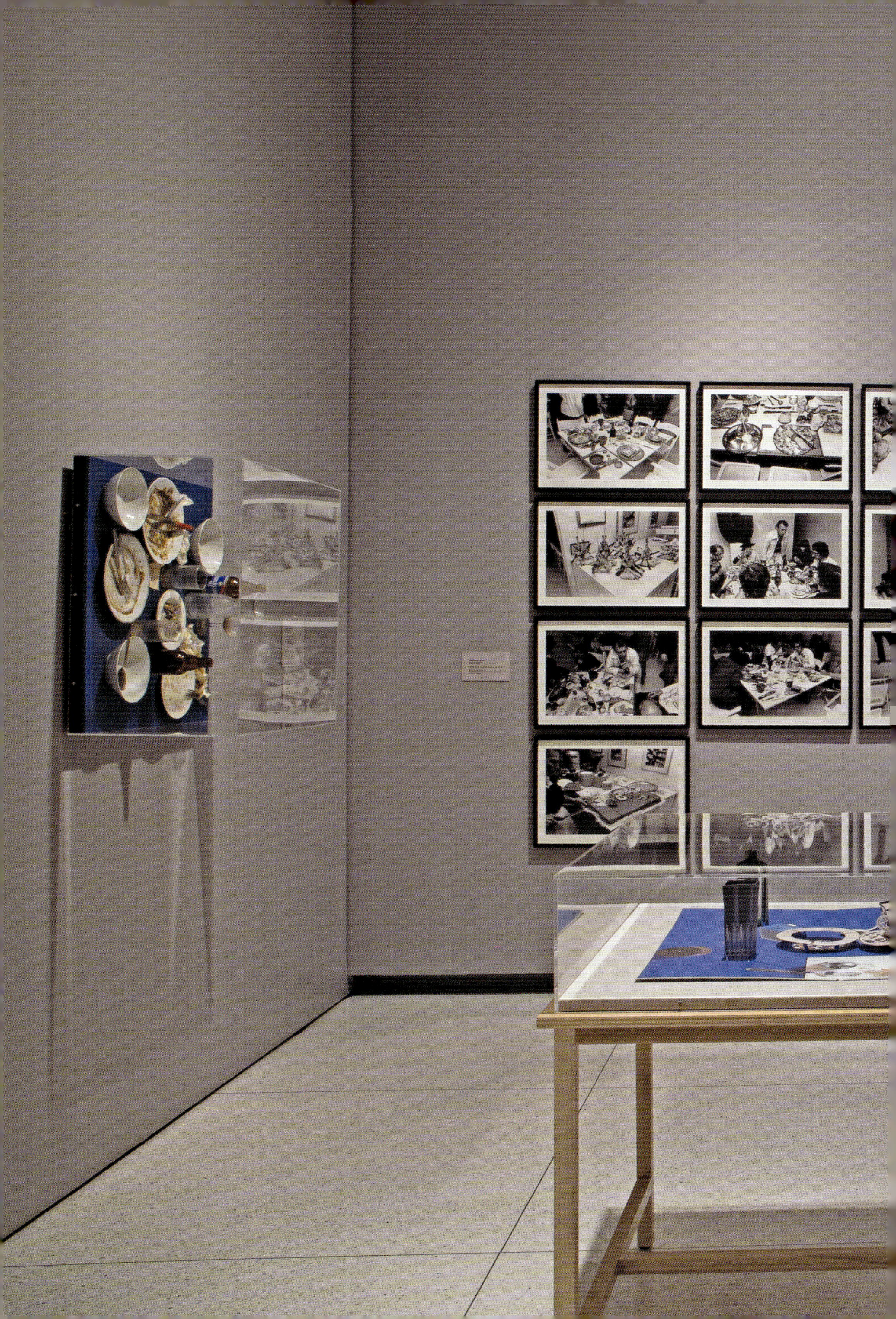

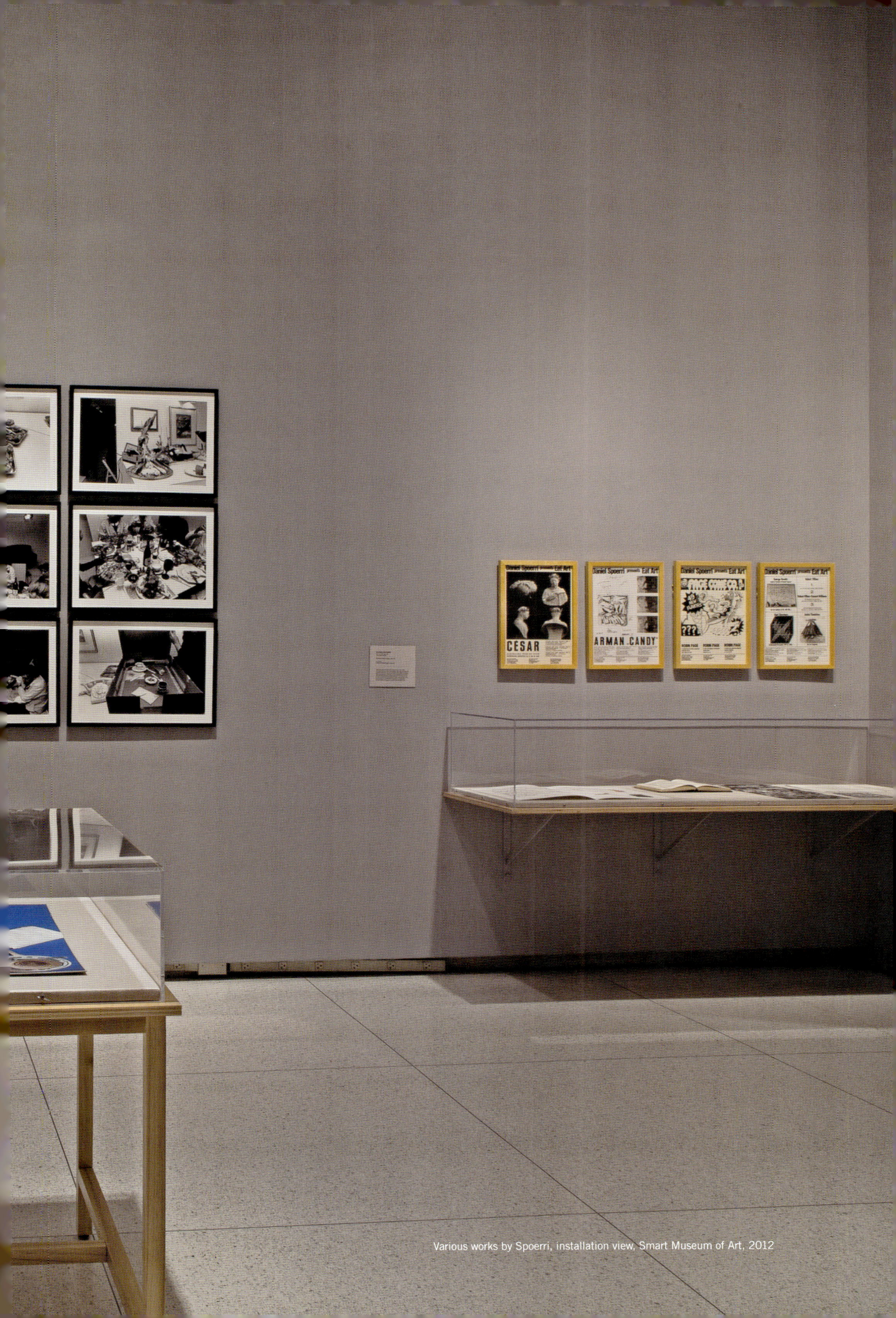

Various works by Spoerri, installation view, Smart Museum of Art, 2012

Hospitality as Witness in the Work of Daniel Spoerri

by Stephanie Snyder

> Art is what makes life more interesting than art.
> —Robert Filliou, 1970[1]

> ROUGHLY NINE YEARS AGO, I bought some groceries and stamped them with the designation "Attention: Artwork!" Then I sold them at their original grocery-store price at the Köpcke Gallery next door. If I had known then where I would be standing today, either I might not have done it at all, or I would have undertaken a ten-year plan much more calmly and purposively—or at least more rationally. A lot had to happen before it became clear to me how important I find this topic which I now call, in a somewhat sloganeering fashion, "Eat Art." Two of the most important instincts are self-preservation and continuation; in plain words, eating and fucking. Others have already commented sufficiently on the topic of sex. I myself was much more interested in my personal problem—how one survives, even whether one survives, and under what conditions. The gesture I made a decade ago when I affixed a random arrangement of things to a table was a gesture of holding fast to the given; a way of adapting oneself to a given situation. I chose a moment that is not thought to be conventionally beautiful because that is how I saw the world—ugly, dirty, and sad, not clean and bright and deceptively orderly. But that was only a gesture; it was not yet the consequence I would eventually draw from it. First I had to know how the table came to be so disordered—I had to go back to the kitchen. I wanted to know how one cooked, what was needed. I wanted to slaughter the hens I would later eat—and thus I became aware that the moment I had frozen on the table was a mere millisecond of an entire cycle of life and death, of decay and rebirth. This vast topic, which I'm calling, with some cockiness, "Eat Art," includes decay as well as the creative act of what is newly emerging. To display life thus, as an artwork, seems to me an entirely worthy life activity.
> —Daniel Spoerri, "Speech for the Henkel Banquet"[2]

Daniel Spoerri's lifelong preoccupation with the biological imperatives, cultural rituals, and economic valuations of human experience—specifically in relationship to survival, belonging, and trauma—has been formed (and re-formed) around a set of underlying existential concerns explored by the artist through an expansive, research-based practice that, to this day, remains deeply skeptical about capitalism's corrupting influence on the human psyche, and on art. Filliou's circuitous declaration (often quoted by Spoerri himself) exemplifies Spoerri's position that art possesses deep ontological significance precisely because it has the power to catalyze a radical awareness of life's *actual* circumstances, to rupture the habitual and recalibrate the senses. For Spoerri, it is life that is valuable; an art devoid of process and transformation is a dead art. French art critic Pierre Restany attempted to harness this concept in his charter manifesto of the Nouveau Réalisme movement in 1960, but founding artists like Spoerri, Jean Tinguely, and Yves Klein were already there. Yet Restany's social

OPPOSITE: Spoerri, in white, standing, at *EAT ART DINNER*, September 28, 1975, *Elaine Ganz Gallery*, San Francisco

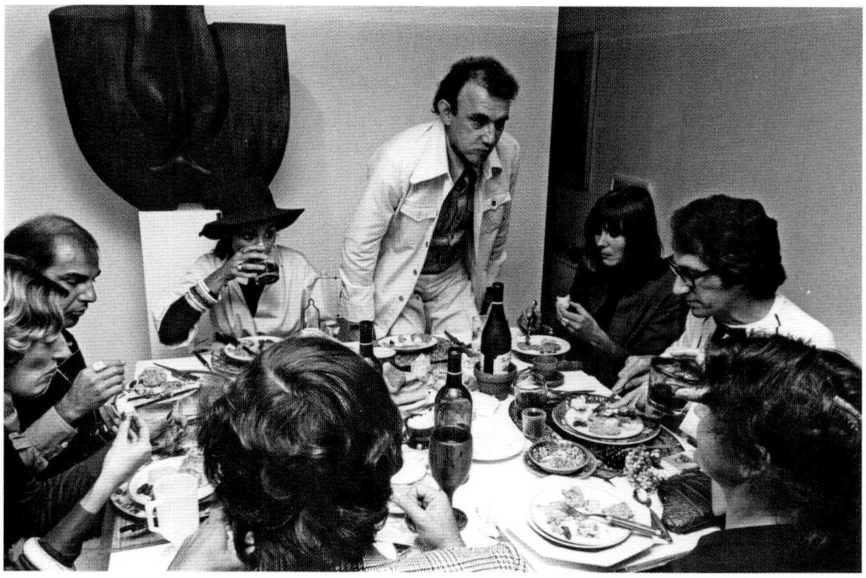

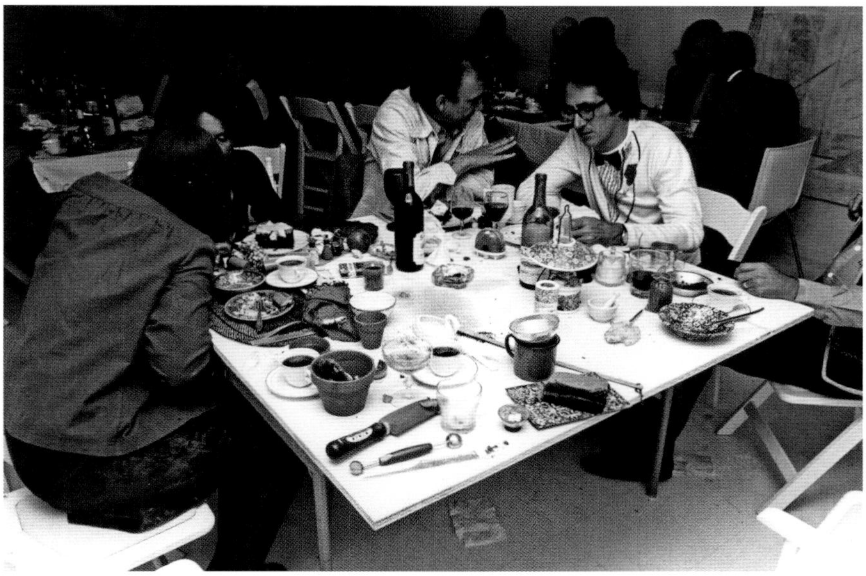

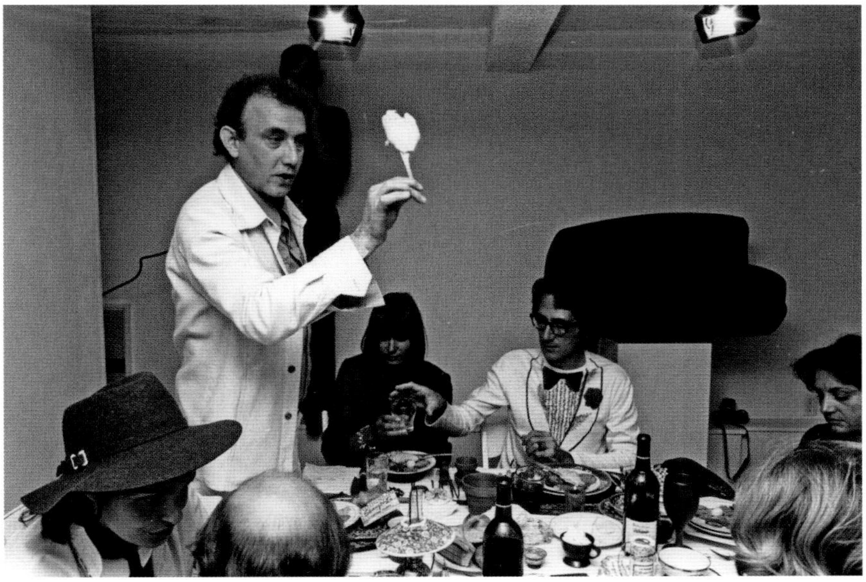

genius brought a vital conviviality to the shared philosophico-spiritual concerns of these pioneering artists. Restany disseminated their mutual belief that it was *art* that held the potential to reanimate life from the destructive forces of politics, war, commerce, and organized religion, and *life* that held the potential to liberate art from bourgeois society.

Throughout the course of Spoerri's sixty-year career, from his first committed endeavors as a poet and dancer in Switzerland and France in the 1950s, the artist has engaged in an adaptational, migratory course of biological and artistic "survival," witnessing life afresh as art (and vice versa), systematically examining systems of cultural value in response to the vulnerability of existence, particularly in relationship to the very foodstuffs necessary for the continuation of the species. For Spoerri, these concerns were violently thrust upon him as a young Jewish refugee during World War II. It was an early, traumatic awareness of death that catalyzed the artist's desire to witness the incidental world around him. Witnessing and arresting life became a means for survival and change, "holding fast to the given, in order to adapt oneself to a given situation."[3] Early on, Spoerri embraced the transfixed moment as a paradoxically fleeting yet eternal part of a fluid life cycle in which no one dimension held value over another. Witnessing, learning, adapting (digesting) became the actions that formed the methodology of his earliest object-based works and, eventually gave birth to the Restaurant Spoerri and Eat Art. As articulated by Spoerri: "It was a question of territory. Because I had lost my territory since childhood, and even during childhood, I never had a territory . . . I swear to you, the first things I glued down were all that, that feeling."[4]

As Spoerri articulates in the passage that begins this essay, an art isolated from the fragile vulnerability of lived experience—from the death at the heart of human exchange—is an art disconnected from its alchemical, transformative origins as a form of psycho-biological reality, like food, and in fact, *as* food. For Spoerri, the cultivation, digestion, and evacuation of food has remained a perennial subject of beauty and horror, the *prima materia* of humanity *as* inhumanity—beauty and suffering crisscrossing like a palindrome. The 1968 film *Resurrection* (filmed by Tony Morgan according to Spoerri's script, with a voice-over by Spoerri) begins with a toilet full of feces and in a disturbing violation of nature, the film follows the protagonist's murky pile back through the body, all the way to the grazing cow that was killed to provide the original steak. Like a visceral, organic palindrome, *Resurrection* shocks the viewer's senses by perverting conventional notions of the body and society's healthful relationship to sustenance. As much as Spoerri has celebrated the conviviality of exquisite food and drink, he has also questioned its ability to nourish the human body, not unlike Piero Manzoni canning his own shit in mockery of capitalist systems of economic and artistic value. From Spoerri's original *tableau piège* (snare picture) works created in his tiny Paris apartment in the late 1950s, and first exhibited in 1961 at the Arturo Schwartz Gallery, Spoerri gave object-permanence to psychic territories—anxious, ritualized spaces that embody the collapse of their own making, while simultaneously speaking to the sociability, fellowship, and sharing of life that constitute their very origins. Spoerri resisted calling his *tableau pièges* works art. Instead, he declared in 1960, that the works were a "provocation," *fixing* (as in, temporarily suspending) life within a given set of circumstances, directing the viewer's perception—phenomenologically—to the inevitability of change and transformation.[5]

Almost constantly on the move at this time, Spoerri came to the United States for the first time in 1964, the year Robert Rauschenberg won the Grand Prize for Painting at the Venice Biennale—a recognized moment in New York's conquest of the international art market. Spoerri remained in New York for about eighteen months, creating two groundbreaking exhibitions that have gone underrecognized for their role in catalyzing subsequent American experiments. The first, held at the Allan Stone Gallery, was entitled *31 Variations on a Meal*. Six years before Gordon Matta-Clark opened FOOD, Spoerri opened a temporary restaurant in the Stone Gallery where he cooked and shared meals with thirty-one guests over a three-day period (the exhibition was originally titled *29 Variations on a Meal* but the project expanded). At a certain, unscripted moment, the eater simply "fixed" their meal by leaving the table and Spoerri then glued every remaining object—leftover food, ashes, dishware,

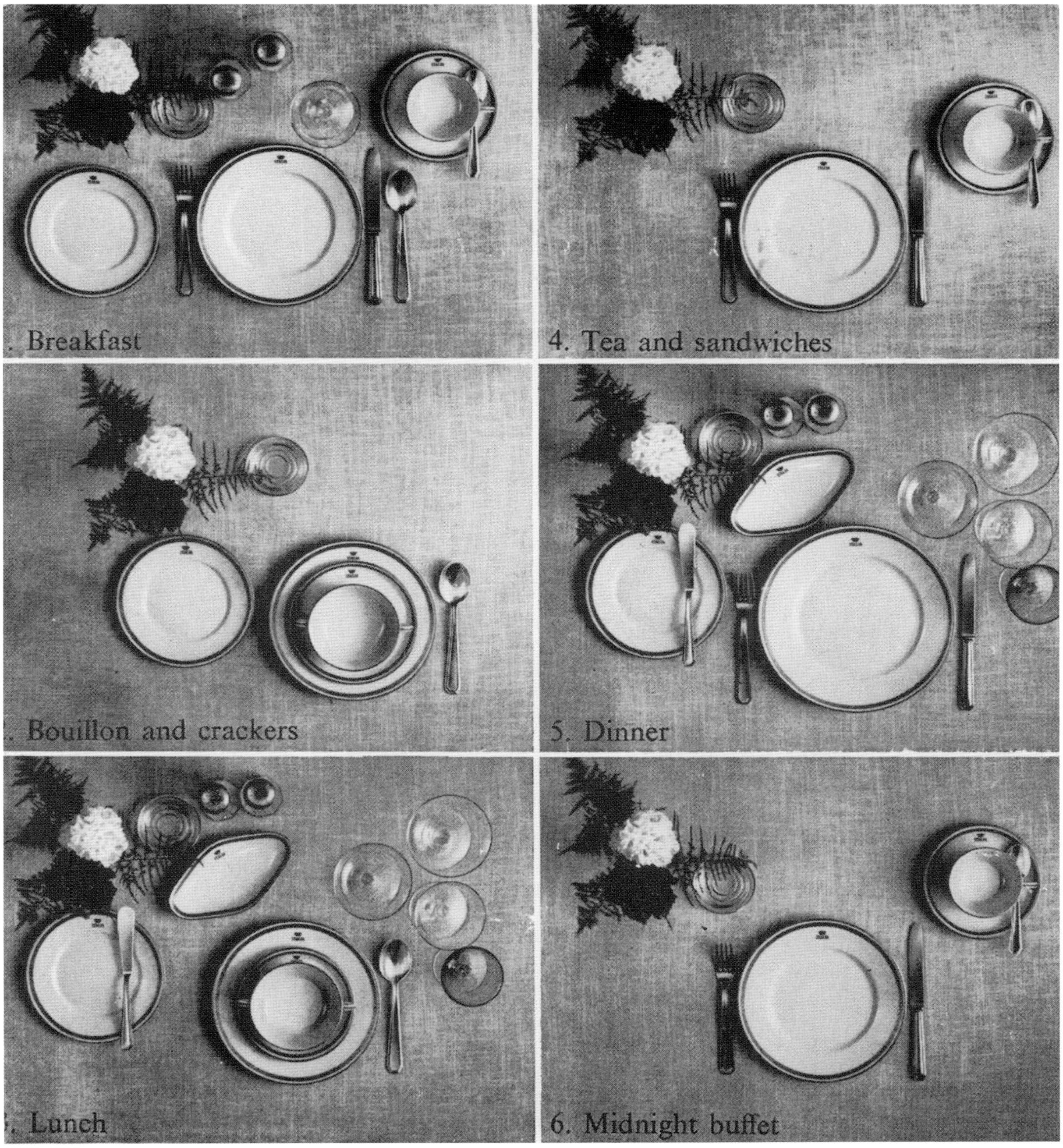

29 Variations on a Meal, exhibition postcard, Allan Stone Gallery, New York, March 1964

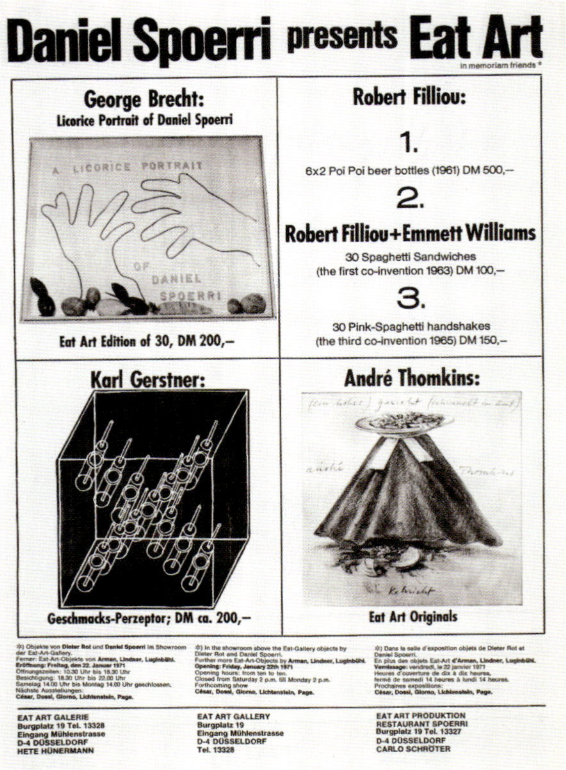

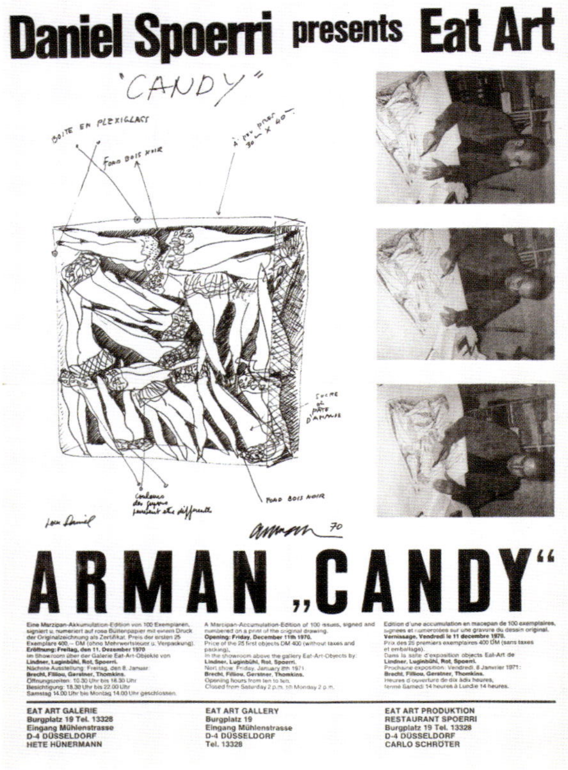

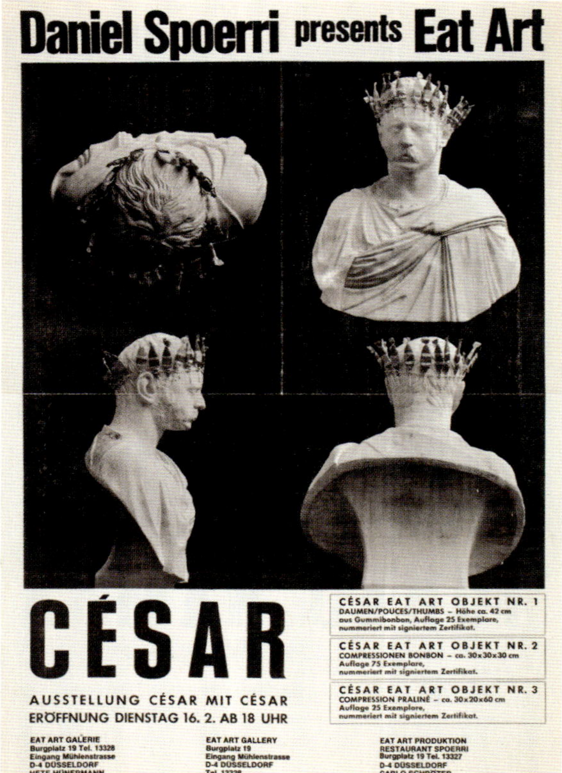

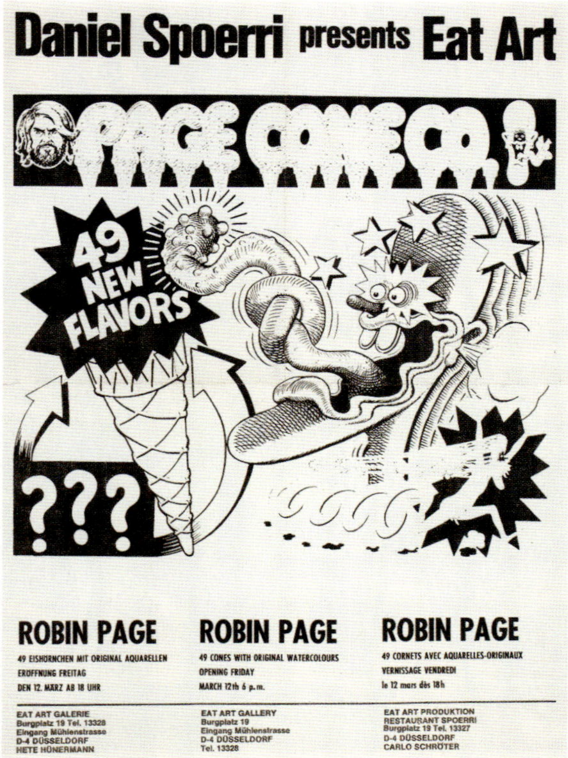

Daniel Spoerri presents Eat Art posters, 1970–72

whatever—on to the surface of the blue wooden board and hung each successive tableau around the walls of the gallery. His various guests included Andy Warhol, Roy Lichtenstein, his friend and mentor Marcel Duchamp, and unsuspecting passersby. Spoerri's second American exhibition took place in 1965 in the artist's room at the Chelsea Hotel, supported by the Greene Gallery. One of Spoerri's few close American colleagues, Allan Kaprow, encouraged the artist to leave the work in situ precisely as it was made and, counter to accepted norms, invite the public into the space. Kaprow wrote a passionate text for the exhibition announcement supporting Spoerri's radically *social* practice:

> Spoerri's philosophical works were made in a hotel room, where he slept, made love, cooked marvelous meals, and defecated. His constructions crowded the space, mingling with the bed, the clothes, the odor of lasagna. One must pick one's way through this intriguing mess. Where does the work of art end and life begin? Here there is no hallucination, only wholeness. I suggested to Spoerri that he invite the public in to see his room, leave the work here, away from the gallery . . . It was in line with his own intentions. I was convinced this work would never appear as meaningfully again. By agreeing, he has contributed to the eventual death of the gallery and the museums. This death will take time, but meanwhile, the world has become endlessly available.[6]

Ultimately, Spoerri found the New York art world of the mid-1960s disappointing, and he returned to Europe. Spoerri states that he left New York because, in general, he was appalled by the American art world's movement away from experimentation and social ideas, toward a rampaging commercialism and social elitism.[7] After several years back in Europe, Spoerri craved further isolation and, in 1968, moved with his girlfriend Kitchka to the Greek island of Symi for eighteen months, where he engaged in a broad spectrum of serious culinary endeavors, wrote copiously about food and culture, and created a body of self-described magical objects from derelict materials.

Spoerri chose to re-enter society by opening Restaurant Spoerri, on June 17, 1968, on a bustling Düsseldorf street corner at 19 Burgplatz. It was the deeply magical and investigatory ethos of life on Symi that Spoerri brought to his new restaurant in Düsseldorf, documented in his gastronomic diary and cultural history *The Mythological Travels*. In keeping with the European tradition of the artist's café, the restaurant, famous for its thick Florentine-style steaks, quickly became a *Locus Solus* for Düsseldorf's adventurous artistic souls, for artist friends such as Arman and André Thomkins who had relocated to Düsseldorf, and for Kunstakademie artists such as Joseph Beuys, who were reshaping and extending art's social potential. In keeping with his longtime investment in the artistic value of lived experience over the establishment of market-driven concerns, Spoerri brought his deep personal relationships, objects, and intellectual interests into the physical space of the restaurant with an exhibitionistic beauty. It began with the exterior of the building. Strange poetic palindromes by André Thomkins adorned the building facade, made to resemble common street signs. Thomkins was one of Spoerri's closest friends and collaborators, and contributed many palindromes in the context of their shared work, such as the infamous "Dogma I am God," part of the title of Spoerri's book *Kosta Theos: Dogma I am God*, which the artist wrote about his remarkable Greek island neighbor Kosta Theos. Across the interior of the small and comfortable bistro, Spoerri papered the walls with fifteen years of his personal correspondence, and hung found objects and tools around the space. Restaurant Spoerri was a serious culinary establishment, but within it the artist created a fluid, exploratory world that more closely resembled his welcoming Paris studio on the Rue de Mouffetard. On Sundays, children were welcomed to the restaurant to engage in cooking projects with the artist. Customers were invited to work in the kitchen to pay for their meals, and Spoerri created a library of cookbooks and culinary histories for customers and friends. In every respect, the restaurant took on the qualities

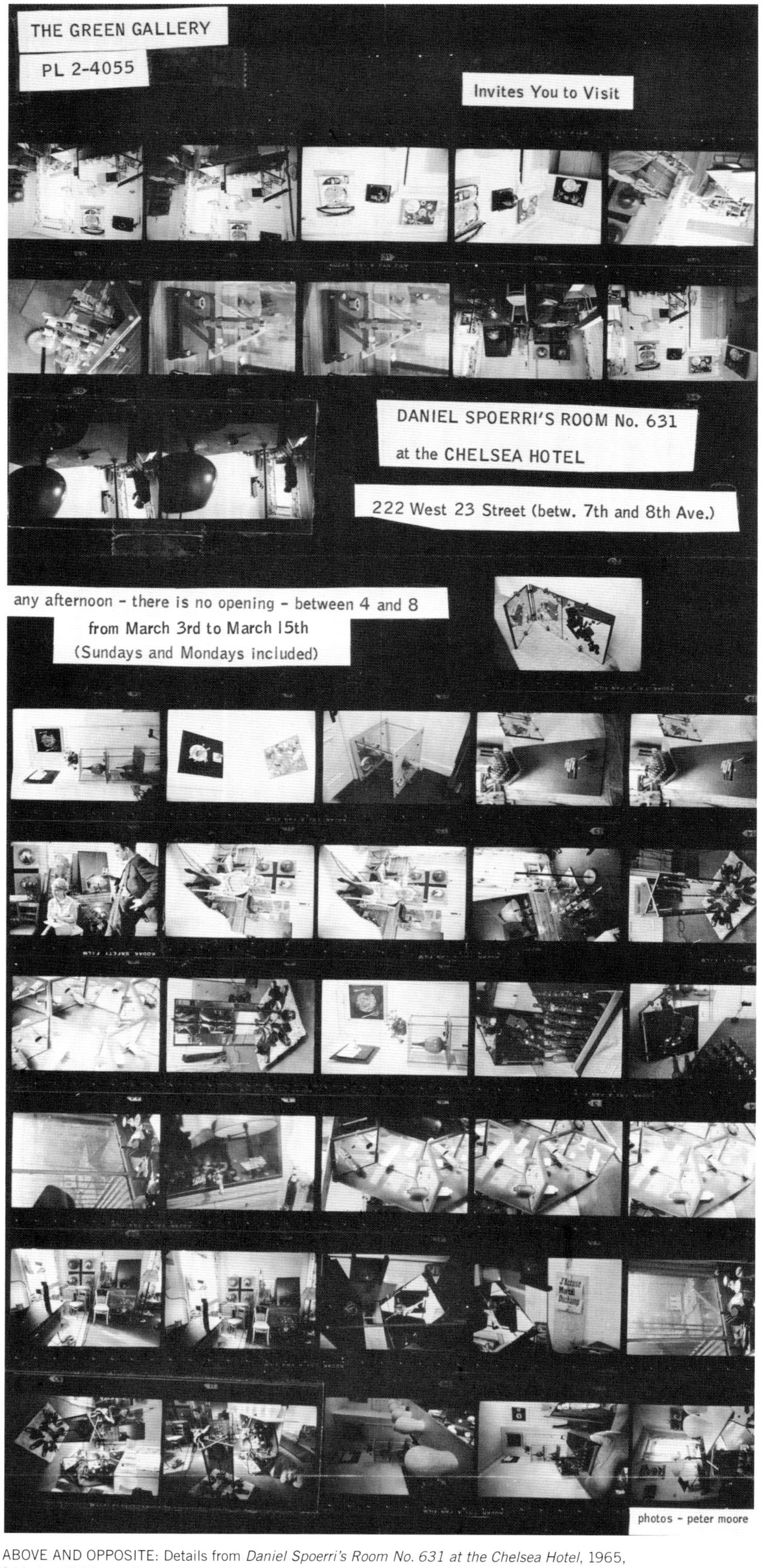

ABOVE AND OPPOSITE: Details from *Daniel Spoerri's Room No. 631 at the Chelsea Hotel*, 1965, folded exhibition mailer and Allan Kaprow's essay

A man in his home and out among his enemies is not the same man. He feels, thinks, asks, even appears different. A cadmium red in one Matisse and the identical color in another, seem to us quite different. Properly so, because the first is surrounded by blue sky, and the second by a sandy beach. A painter hangs his exhibition by paying attention to the composition of the entire gallery and the correct focus of lights. He knows that art works influence each other, that a good painting can be demolished by the presence of bad paintings around it, and vice versa.

But artists have payed only partial attention to how deeply their works reflect and utilize the environment in which they were created. They speak about the light at the seashore appearing in their colors; the profound effect upon their dreams of the filth and reek of urine soaked studio-loft buildings, the pounding of the subway under their feet... Yet, when their works are shown in the neoclassical gallery-box, it is supposed that these qualities of the environment are brought out a fortiori and that the gallery will have no other effect than to focus upon the essentials of the works.

This is patently absurd, utter blindness. Today nine out of ten artists' work is absolutely desiccated by the powerful purity of the gallery and museum atmosphere. Everything whispers "sh, sh, don't touch". If art once was thought to be made from life in order to leave life, now the great bulk of modern creativity is deliberately mixed with life in order to affirm it.

Spoerri's philosophical works were made in a hotel room, where he slept, made love, cooked marvelous meals, and defecated. His constructions crowded the space, mingling with the bed, the clothes, the odor of lasagne. One must pick one's way through this intriguing mess. Where does the work of art end, and life begin? Look into peep holes, turn a mirror and see reflected the curtain, lift the test-tube phallus of a flowered hermaphrodite, contemplate an embalmed meal once eaten, the shoes of lovers facing one another. Here there is no hallucination, only wholeness.

I suggested that Spoerri invite the public to see his room, as it is being lived in, not as a memento or shrine. It was in line with his own intentions. I was convinced that his work would never appear as meaningfully again. By agreeing, he has contributed to the eventual death of the art gallery and museums. This death will take time, but meanwhile, the world has become endlessly available.

Allan Kaprow 2/19/65

of the artist's studio, albeit a convivial one in which guest and host came together to create a radically participatory art form. Spoerri referred to his restaurant as a "laboratory:"[8]

> We made 350 tables that were glued down over a whole year [1972–73] . . . Each day a table was glued. You know the tables that you see from time to time in galleries? It was a whole year. Every day, even when I wasn't there, my associate came and said, 'Excuse me, I have to take the table.' People would say, 'But we haven't finished eating.' 'That doesn't matter, just wait.' And then they would be given another blue table and be told, 'You can now eat whatever you want for free. What would you like?' And every day a table was glued.[9]

The original meal was removed from sight—relegated to digestive memory—and the territory of the original encounter was secured as an object of contemplation whose dishes returned the gaze of the viewer soiled with their own history. Restaurant Spoerri provided the artist with an ideal place to collaborate more subversively with his clients. Unlike the actual Eat Art Gallery that Spoerri opened in 1970 near the restaurant—as celebrated as it has become—the convivial laboratory of the restaurant (which Spoerri had originally intended to name the *Kutteltrog*—the Tripe Trough) created a richer slippage between art and daily life amidst the smells, sounds, and economic exchanges of each meal, in keeping with the rhythms of the city.[10] As mentioned, the restaurant was well known for its excellent steaks (think *Resurrection*), but Spoerri would add outrageous dishes to the daily menu, things such as bear paws, python schnitzels, and lion steaks.[11]

These profane, offensive foods didn't necessarily exist, but the customer didn't know it. Spoerri's symbolic dishes were intended to pollute and excite the senses, to color the customer's perception of strange and immediate improprieties. The dishes presented a hazardous vision of cultural violation and taboo not unlike the cigarette ashes and dried fat encrusted on his earliest *tableaux pièges*. In his 1960 exhibition at Addi Köpcke's gallery, in fact, Spoerri published his own exhibition catalogue consisting of trash baked into loaves of bread.[12] The local baker's guild was so offended that they wrote Spoerri a letter of protest. Food traditions were sacred, they argued. But from Spoerri's perspective, the sanctity of life had been violated so many times over; baking trash into bread was a violation, perhaps, but one in pursuit of life: "Stagnation, fixation, death should provoke change and life, or so I like to believe."[13]

After two successful years operating the restaurant, Spoerri opened the Eat Art Gallery. There, Spoerri hosted a multigenerational array of artists, encouraging them to develop specific food-related projects and performances. Many were old friends and collaborators Spoerri had known since the late 1950s and early 1960s, artists associated with the Nouveau Réalisme movement (Arman, César) and other circles (Joseph Beuys, Ray Johnson, André Thomkins, Ben Vautier). Eat Art exhibitions included food-related performances, exhibitions, and banquets. In one notorious instance, Ben Vautier enclosed himself in a wooden box in the middle of the gallery and staged a twenty-four hour hunger strike. Thomkins created edible palindromes; Beuys sold herring bones wrapped in gauze as multiples. Both literally and conceptually, Eat Art events were staged and performed in relationship to the culinary activity of the restaurant, food-based multiples could be found in either space.[14] And like complementary digestive organs, Restaurant Spoerri and the Eat Art gallery allowed Spoerri and his artist colleagues to explore food's ability to offend taste, stimulate the intellect, and delight the senses. Ten years after his first gallery exhibition at the Arturo Schwartz Gallery, Spoerri had created an independent, self-sustaining territory in which his own experiences of deprivation, migration, and loss could be continually captured and released—an experimental and political home, not just for himself, but for a growing, international community.

Stephanie Snyder is John and Anne Hauberg Curator and Director at the Douglas F. Cooley Memorial Art Gallery, Reed College, Portland, Oregon.

[1] Robert Filliou, Interview, in *Robert Filliou: Génie sans talent*, exh. cat. (Villeneuve d'Ascq: Musée d'Art Moderne Lille Métropole, 2004, back cover.

[2] Daniel Spoerri, "Speech for the Henkel Banquet," in *The Anekdotomania: Collected Writings* (Ostfildern, DE: Hatje Cantz Verlag, 2001), 184–85, unpublished translation by the author. In a margin note accompanying the text, Spoerri states: "This little speech was the introduction to an Eat Art Banquet put on by Gabriele Henkel on October 29, 1970 in the Hösel House, Düsseldorf." The speech is attributed in the *Anekdotomania* as follows: "Typescript, October 23, 1970. Daniel Spoerri Archive, Swiss National Library, Bern." Spoerri wrote these marks in advance of the event, not as a *post facto* reflection.

[3] Ibid.

[4] Daniel Spoerri, quoted in an interview with Giancarlo Politi, *Flash Art*, 23, no. 154 (October, 1990): 117.

[5] Daniel Spoerri, "Trap Pictures," in Kristine Stiles and Peter Howard Selz, eds., *Theories and Documents of Contemporary Art: A Sourcebook of Artists' Writings* (Berkeley: University of California Press, 1995), 310.

[6] Allan Kaprow, text on the exhibition announcement for *Daniel Spoerri's Room No. 631 at the Chelsea Hotel*, New York, Green Gallery, 1965. Reprinted in full on p. 151 of this volume.

[7] Unpublished interview with the author, 2007.

[8] Stiles and Selz, *Theories and Documents of Contemporary Art*, 121.

[9] Ibid.

[10] Renate Buschmann, "Evocations of Pleasure and Disgust: Daniel Spoerri and the Establishment of Eat Art," in *Eating the Universe* (Düsseldorf: Dumont, 2009), 237.

[11] Ibid., 238.

[12] This is the *Grocery Store* exhibition that Spoerri references in the opening passage of this essay. To this day, Spoerri maintains that it is one of his most meaningful exhibitions.

[13] Daniel Spoerri, "Trap Pictures," 1960, in Stiles and Selz, *Theories and Documents of Contemporary Art*, 310.

[14] Although they are referred to as "multiples," Eat Art objects were rarely uniform. The concept of the Eat Art multiple, counter to the consistently produced saleable object of the contemporary art world, was akin to Spoerri's 1959 multiples made under the name MAT Editions (Multiplication d'Art Transformable). MAT Edition objects were transformable, kinetic. They moved and adjusted, increasing, i.e. "multiplying" their symbolic potential—they were "alive." Spoerri sold each edition for the same flat rate (which ultimately lead to the project's economic failure), and created works with the likes of Man Ray, Duchamp, and Tinguely.

SOCIAL AND CRITICAL FEASTS: 1990s–Present

Sonja Alhäuser

SINCE THE LATE 1990s, food has been a primary (but not exclusive) subject and medium for Berlin-based Sonja Alhäuser. Her food-based projects evince a deep attention to craft and beauty and a visual sensibility that draws heavily on art history (especially Baroque sculpture as well as Rococo drawing and painting), while also revealing an earthy delight in humor, the grotesque, bodily cycles, and sensual pleasure. Sculptures like a large-scale, rearing horse formed from chocolate (*Schokoladenpferd*, 1997), or refrigerated vitrines filled with twisting buttery putti (*Das kleine Wilkommen*, 2009) demonstrate her knowledge of traditional sculptural form and her feel for the expressive properties of unusual materials. Such freestanding objects are paralleled by her participatory projects: edible sculptures meant to be destroyed by the nibbling of museum visitors, as well as elegant buffets for events. The latter usually include semi-narrative, figurative tableaux made of edible materials like chocolate, marzipan, and a special type of baker's margarine. These elements often form the backdrop for canapés that are consumed by the audience—who on at least one occasion ate with such voracious destruction that the artist described it as a feeding frenzy.

Alhäuser extended the buffet format to create a catering performance titled *Flying Feast* (2012) for *Feast*'s opening night in Chicago. Alhäuser literally sketched her advance plans for a buffet and performance in a "recipe drawing"—a form the artist has developed to accompany her event-based work. She considers these drawings as "performance plans" that provide structure while allowing for improvisation; she adds and subtracts elements as plans develop so that the drawings provide a subjective yet lasting record of both her creative process and the final ephemeral event. The detailed recipe drawings are made on long sheets of heavy paper and depict preparation and production, with delicate lines filled with rich washes of color. Using this drawing of the *Flying Feast* to aid communication and as a form of documentation, Alhäuser collaborated with University of Chicago students during a week-long residency. One group worked with the artist and Smart Museum staff to sculpt large margarine sculptures as well as tiny marzipan figures and other food to be consumed during the *Flying Feast*. Alhäuser also trained another group to perform as costumed servers.

These preparations resulted in two public manifestations. At the opening night of *Feast* in Chicago, guests were welcomed with a lavish buffet, which the artist described as a "landscape of food open to everyone." She and her student team had arranged rows and piles of finger-foods around margarine sculptures depicting many sources of sustenance—fish and goats as well as mythical figures like Neptune offering up the fruits of the sea in a horn of plenty. In the "flying" portion of the project, her blonde-wigged and silver-garbed performers followed choreographed patterns through the increasingly crowded museum lobby, offering guests canapés on mirrored trays each of which contained its own margarine animal. Each canapé was accompanied by a small drawing, which Alhäuser added as a means to open up questions of originality and art—does the art exist in the canapé, the drawing, the performance, somewhere between? Together, the buffet and performance contributed to a celebratory atmosphere—something specific and beautiful that existed only in public, in company, and in that moment. Further reinforcing this issue of presence, time, and ephemerality, for the rest of the Chicago presentation, the margarine sculptures were moved into a vitrine to form a new sculptural arrangement; they slowly decayed before being discarded at the exhibition's close, leaving the recipe drawing as the only lasting artist-created artifact of Alhäuser's *Flying Feast*.

OPPOSITE: *Flying Feast* performed at the Smart Museum of Art, February 15, 2012

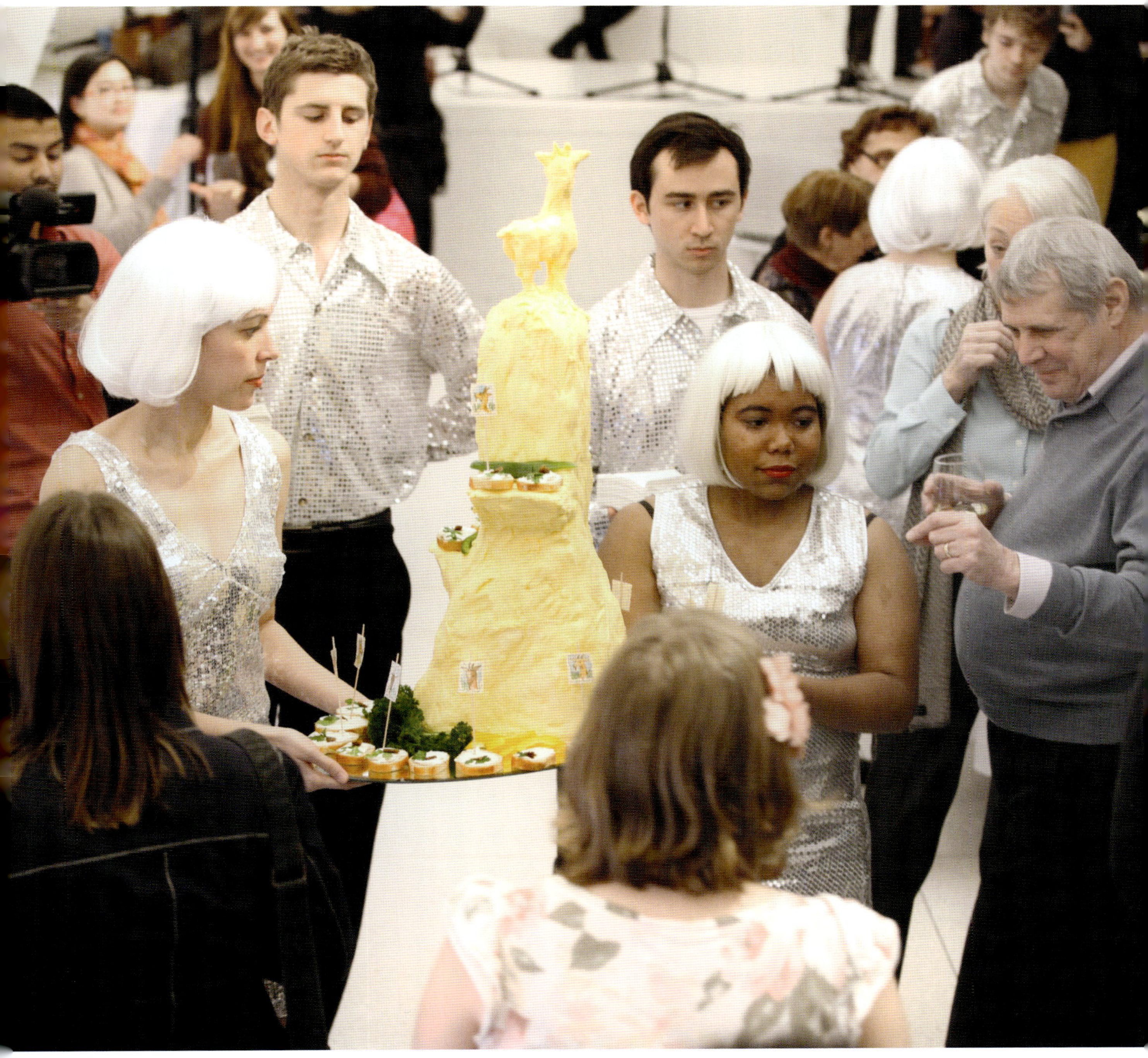

Interview

SMART: Please describe your background. How did you become an artist? How did you begin to work with food as a material, and with performances based on meals?

SONJA ALHÄUSER: During my studies, I started to work with the everyday, including daily activities such as eating. On top of that, I come from a family for whom cooking and the celebration of eating in its many manifestations was an important topic and constituted a good part of the day. I grew up with things constantly being made: cakes, goulash-soups in great quantities, buckets-worth of potato salad. Dairy cows in the village and pigs that would soon be slaughtered all had their fascination. All these things contribute to a sense of community and have a performative aspect—both of which seemed lacking when I started art school. I filled this gap with my first performances. When I showed edible works, the audience's reactions brought this energy back. It is incredibly fascinating what happens when one offers works to be eaten. It is something between joyous orgy, sacrifice, and ritual. Every edible work therefore undergoes different phases and all the visitors to the exhibition are part of the whole.

SMART: What are some of the sources of inspiration for your work, either in or beyond the context of art?

SA: Rather than looking for inspiration, I use the things from my daily life as objects for my artistic work. I am fascinated by daily routines;

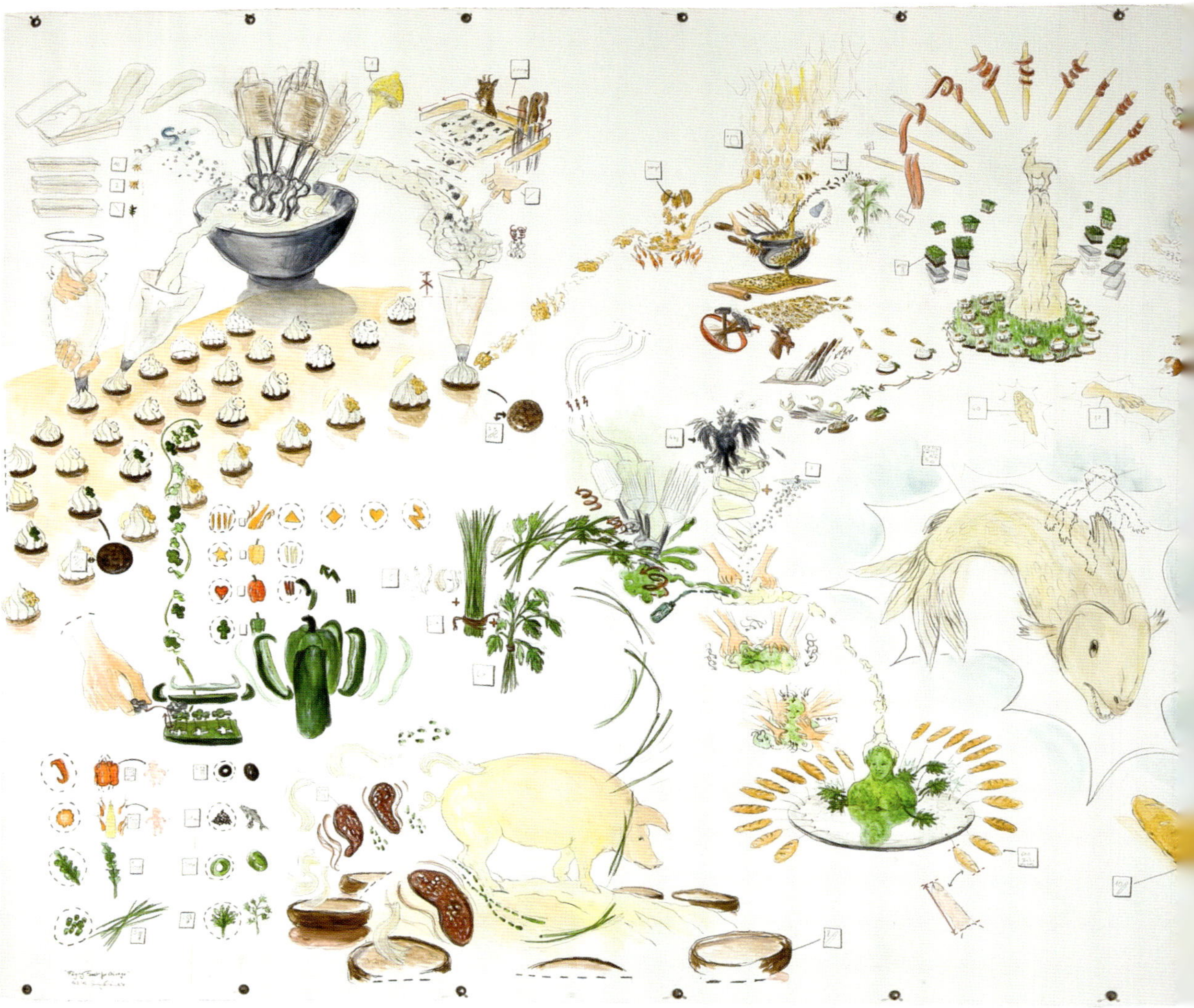

Flying Feast recipe drawing, 2012

I investigate them at first through drawing. The autobiographical has been and remains the engine for my work.

SMART: What aspects of daily life do you find especially inspiring for your art?

SA: Things that stay with you in your head after a long day because they were extraordinary, strange, worrisome, fascinating, or simply beautiful. Events that one would like to share but which would be banal if merely narrated. Drawing turns these events into precious moments, which will take root in their very own way in one's memory. It is also an appreciation of the ephemeral and the short moment.

SMART: Why have you chosen drawing as your medium for these daily investigations? What are those drawings like? Are they similar in style to your "recipe drawings" or do they use a different kind of visual language?

SA: The drawings mostly show operational flows, in the same spirit of the recipe drawings. I choose this kind of sketch because one can look at the events in slow motion and still experience the speed, the fleetingness. In addition to that, all "ingredients" of the drawing gain a new meaning for me. For example: a lemon can suddenly appear very dangerous—squeezing it turns into an explosion—or a queue in the department store turns into a procession.

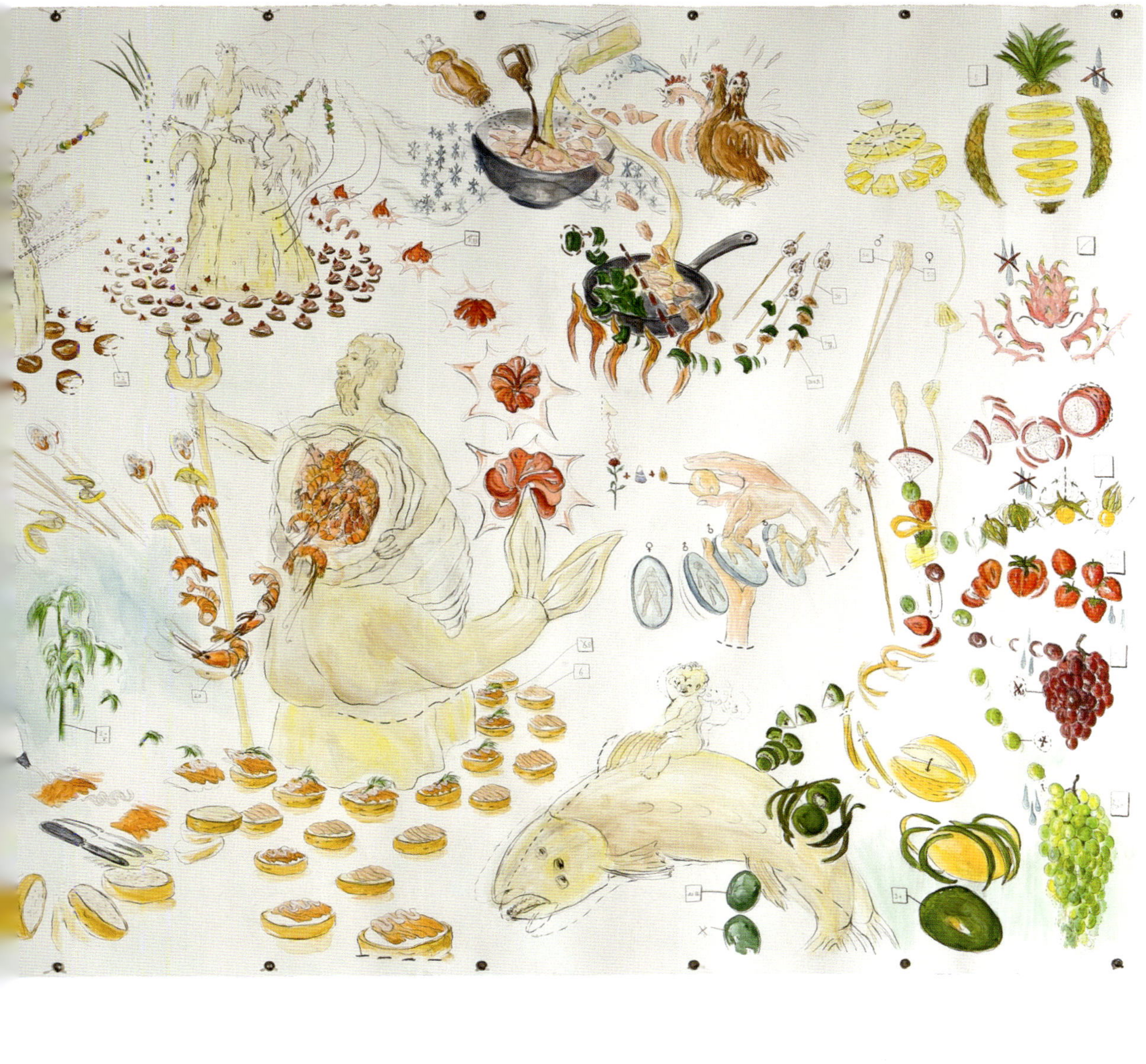

SMART: Please describe your work for the show—its impetus, intention, and production—and how it fits into your broader practice.

SA: My work for this show will be composed of a drawing and a corresponding performance. Together with a team, I am planning to produce a buffet and a series of trays to display appetizers, and that will blend into an edible image. For me, the process of the making is already part of the feast; the bustling preparation belongs to it. The basis for this will be the drawing, which serves as a sketch of the proceedings, a recipe, and a grocery list all at the same time.

These edible stories will be carried through the museum one after the other and are to be eaten. The tray bearers are not, in my view, some sort of submissive service team, but rather have the responsibility to carry the images with solemnity and dignity through the audience.

I see my drawings also as instruction sheets and find it only consequential to couple them with a performance such as this, something I do quite often anyway. What is exciting for me about this show is to see to what extent my drawing will be able to communicate to my team an idea of the unfolding of the performance, and how this will then work out in reality.

SMART: What kind of training do you plan for the tray bearers/performers (who will all be University of Chicago students)?

SA: For a dry run, we will stand in front of the drawing and I will explain the events depicted in it. Then, we will distribute responsibilities, and ideally every performer would choose his or her part of the work. Afterwards, we will train the bearing of the plates in some choreographed form in situ, which will give the performers the necessary security for us to be able to control the flow of events.

SMART: Could you say more about the "edible images" that you plan to create for *Feast*? How do you determine what to cook and serve for the performance? How do you imagine the different parts of the performance will fit together?

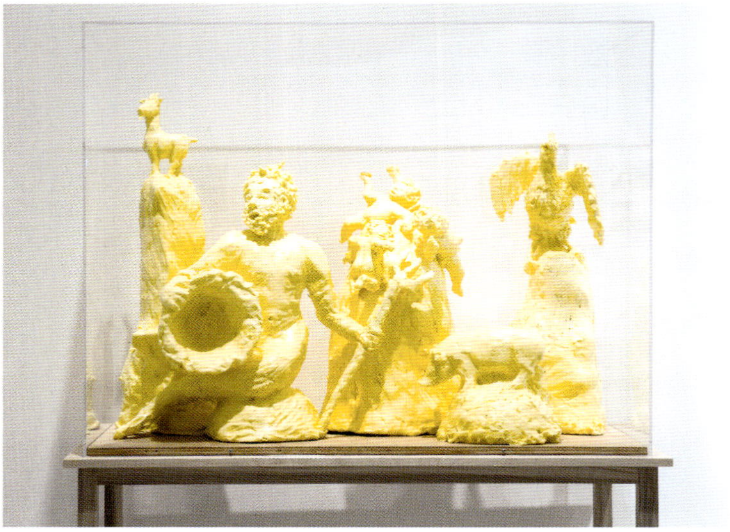

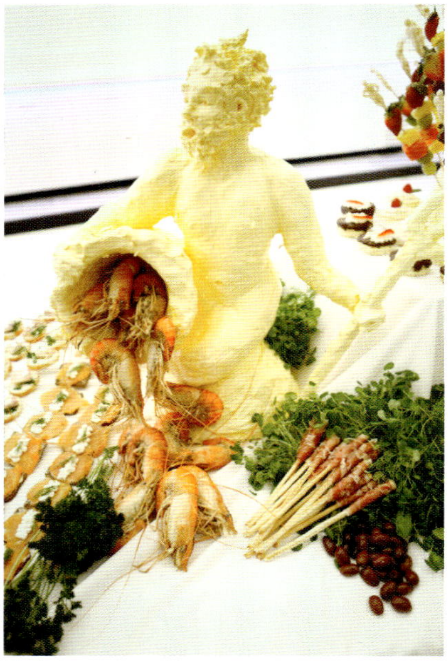

Flying Feast, 2012, margarine sculptures, installation view (ABOVE) and view of banquet table during the performance at the Smart Museum of Art, February 15, 2012 (RIGHT)

SA: The edible works for *Feast* tell stories, which also point back to themselves, i.e. the materials used. It can be best explained with examples: the goat cheese canapés are to be found on a platter on which goats made of butter are climbing a butter mountain, and guests will find little watercolors on skewers that draw attention to the making of the appetizers or relate to a goat's way of life. Mythological excursions will be undertaken, which then will lead to the next work, creating relationships. In my drawing, which is being drawn at the moment, these things are worked through in advance, and all the sculptures should be able to come together in an image later on.

SMART: How did you decide on the title *Flying Feast*?

SA: I've called my piece *Flying Feast*, because the single sculptures aren't arranged in the way of a buffet but are first transported through the crowd of people; they hover, or rather fly. For me, movement becomes important here. The performance is therefore already part of the title, and it's a piece that only becomes accessible through its unfolding.

SMART: After the performance, the drawing will have finished its task of communication and will be an inert object hanging on the wall. Are your drawings still interesting to you after the moment of performance? What do you think they offer to the public at the point when they've become relics rather than tools to be used within the context of performance?

SA: It is not quite like that, as the drawing is not finished until the performance. I go over it once more, things are crossed out that have not actually happened, quantity indications will be adjusted, revisions undertaken. This is very important, because this way one can see afterwards how what has been originally planned diverges from reality—because it never turns out the way one had planned it. That is the exciting part. It is possible that entire sculptures need to be crossed out as they never materialized, but other things need to be added that had not originally been planned. This is why the drawing is also fascinating

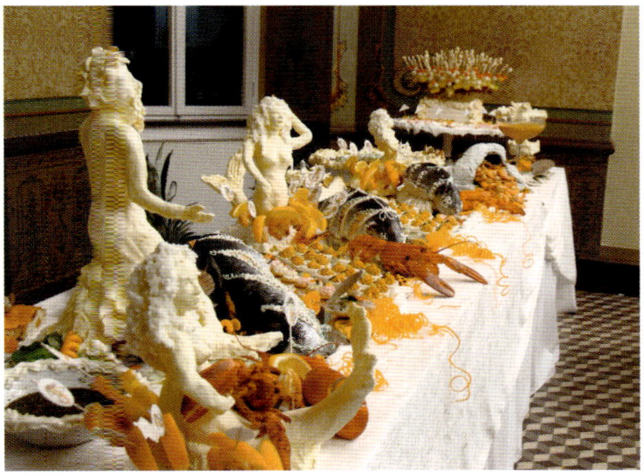

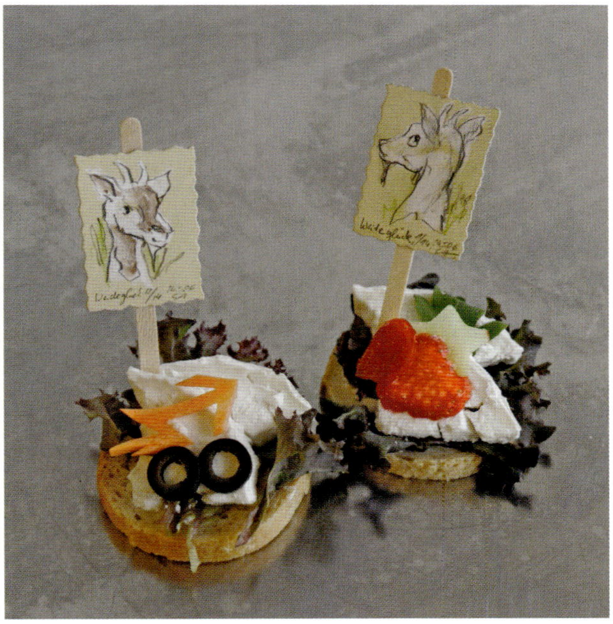

ABOVE: Banquet table from Emsrausch performance, Bonn, 2008

RIGHT: Detail from the series *Banquets for No Reason*, "Guide Waldthausen," Schloss Waldthausen, 2006

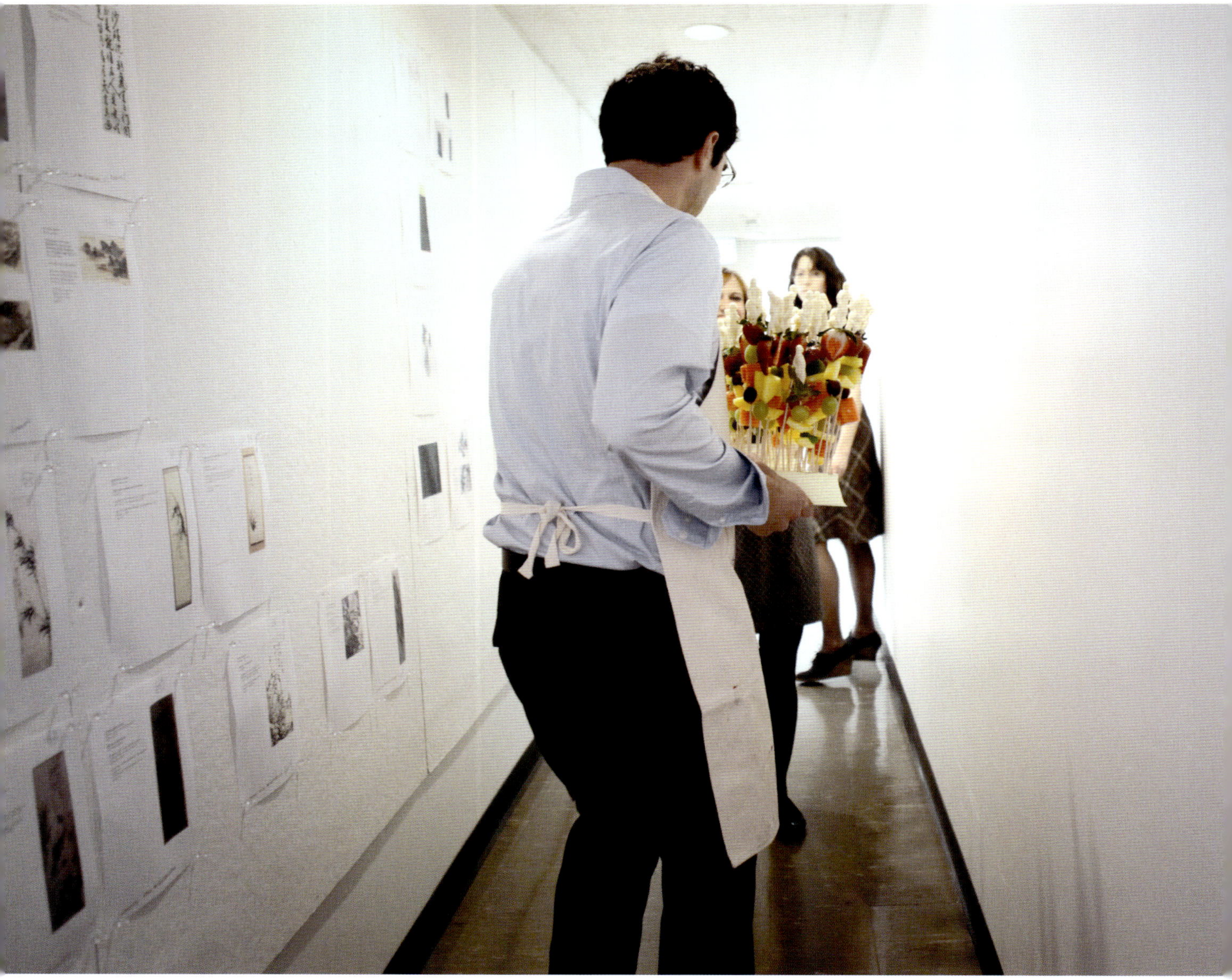

ABOVE: Smart Museum Director of Education and Interpretation Michael Christiano assists with final preparations for the *Flying Feast* performance, Smart Museum of Art, February 15, 2012

OPPOSITE: *Flying Feast*, 2012, performance at Smart Museum of Art, February 15, 2012

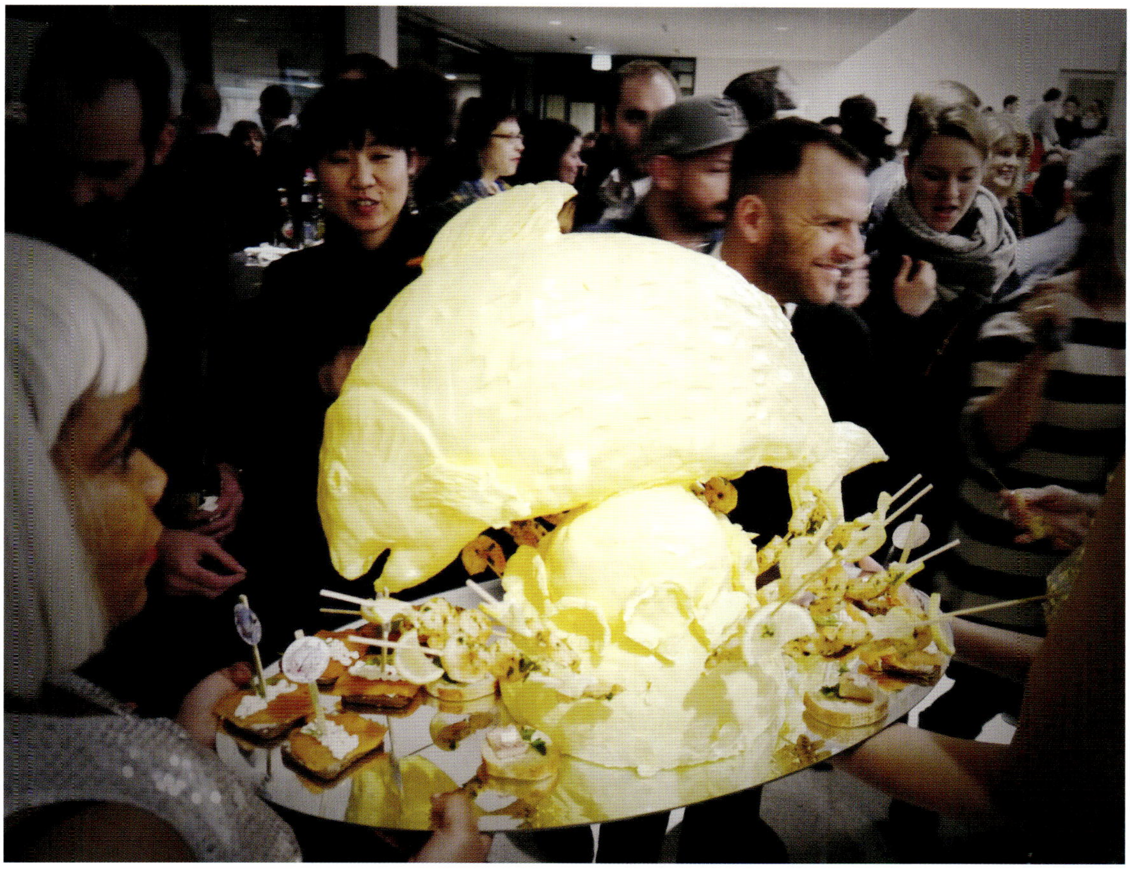

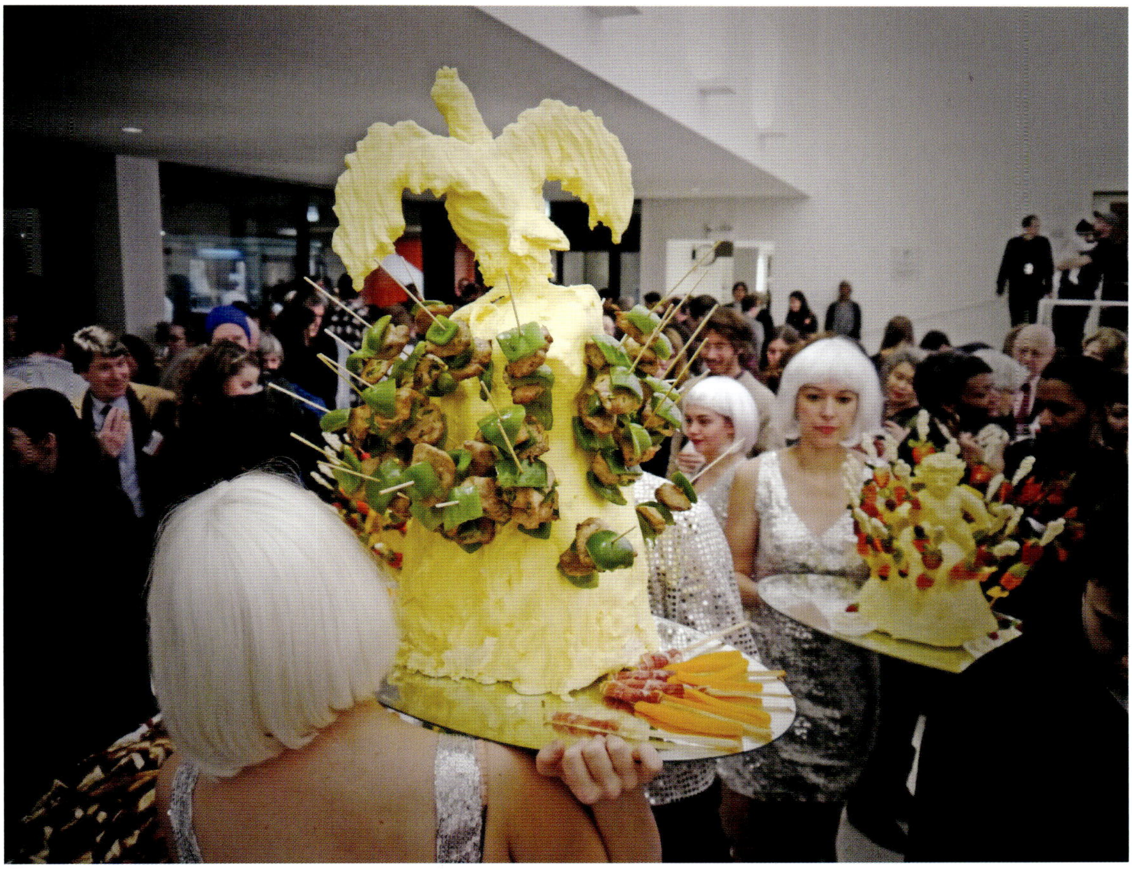

after the performance as I give myself feedback and use the drawing one last time to find a sense of closure for myself. These drawings are also important for future performances, as I can, for example, see my logistical mistakes, and the corrections allow me to remember the events in detail. And it's the same for the audience: the planning of the feast is the basis and the corrections are like a carpet laid on top. The drawing therefore not only contains recipes and instructions, which would be mere relics, but it also tells the story of the eager planning, of the happy success or perhaps of stumbling and of failure in the face of the actuality of performing. For me, these things are always part of the experience: the slight chaos of the actual moment. If one were to recreate a performance in exactly the same order, it would never function the same way.

SMART: How would you describe the role of the meal or hospitality in your practice?

SA: Eating and hospitality are chief ingredients of my works. Not only my performances, but also my drawings are fundamentally convivial

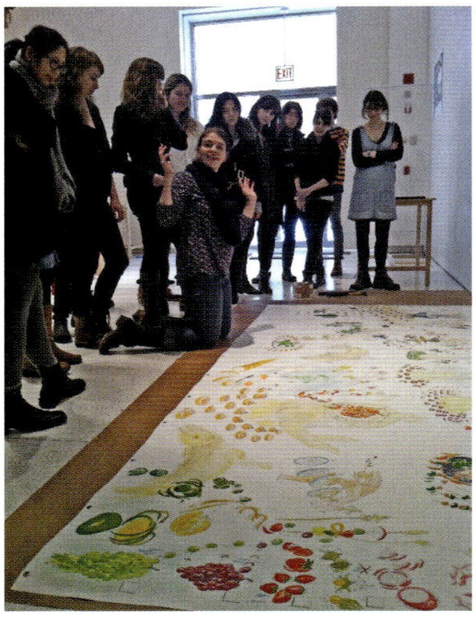

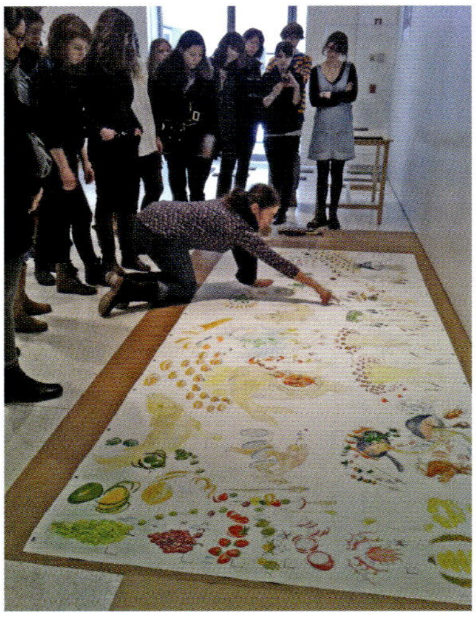

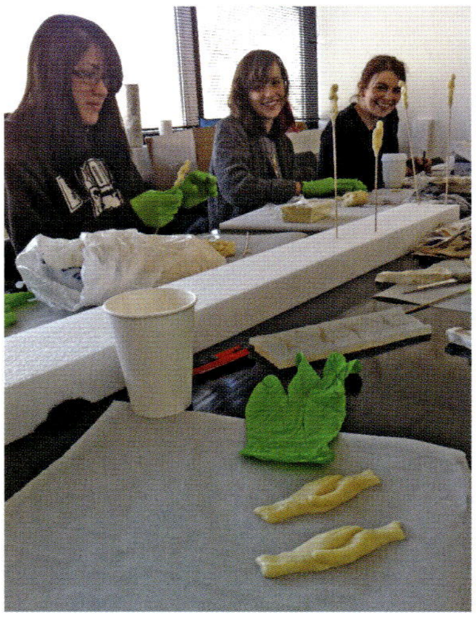

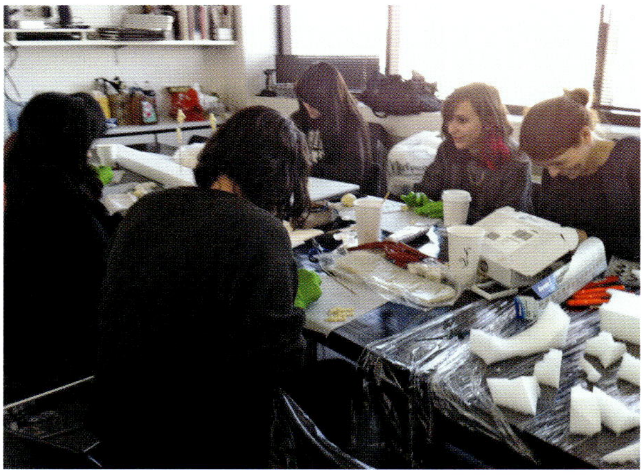

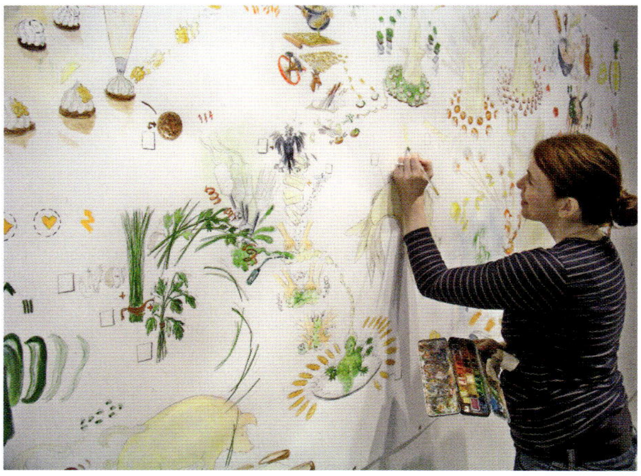

TOP AND BOTTOM LEFT: Alhäuser introducing and developing her project with University of Chicago student assistants, February, 2012

BOTTOM RIGHT: Alhäuser finishing the *Flying Feast* recipe drawing, Smart Museum of Art, February, 2012

invitations. I often use ritual as an element in my works, and it is, in a way, also the basis for a feast or a banquet. Sequences of events are thus created that are being celebrated. The moment of participation in a feast, which includes the sharing of food, creates an unexpected community, from which one can extract oneself only with difficulty. The form of the feast offers me the opportunity to show opulence and vitality, which only gain in significance through their ephemerality—either one was part of it or one has missed it. There is certainly an element of the Baroque here, which celebrates life, as one carries thoughts of transience at the back of one's mind.

I therefore think that it is my artistic challenge to create lively moments and not necessarily lasting objects.

SMART: What does it mean to you to be included in a show called *Feast: Radical Hospitality in Contemporary Art*?

SA: I feel invited to act hospitably as an artist. It calls for action and performance. I understand the theme of artistic hospitality perhaps not only as the provision of a feast for the eyes but for all senses that we are endowed with. I think that when several of one's senses are addressed, one is simply able to gain more from the experience. I find the addition of "radical" in this context very apt, since I appreciate an excessive hospitality, and a feast should have something Dionysian and opulent about it and come across as a big gift for all the guests for it to really earn the title of "feast."

SMART: Could you say more about the Dionysian aspect of your projects? You create very elaborate, almost Baroque displays of food and then they're devoured—sometimes with a kind of violence.

SA: The short of it is: with these kind of ceremonial acts you always have a before and after image, which are usually diametrically opposed and which I find entirely fascinating time and again. The more opulent and lavish the original work is, the more extreme the ecstasy, which turns the whole upside down. I think it is a sort of ritual that is repeated in these performance over and over again, one celebrates the sculptures through their sacrifice and everybody present takes a part of the work home, in their stomachs.

SMART: How does the audience factor into your thinking when you design a performance like this one for *Feast*, which takes place within the context of a museum opening?

SA: The audience in these performances is a direct part of the work. It is fascinating because you can't plan for the reactions of the visitors. To do this performance in a museum, which is a place where touching and grabbing things is usually forbidden, is an exciting intervention for me and contributes to the questioning of those values one was once sure about. Is a butter sculpture or a goat cheese object a "real" work of art, and if so, is one allowed to eat it?

SMART: What do you hope people take away from your work?

SA: I hope that they will take home an experience, which they will remember for a long time or over and over again. It would be good if I were able to create through my work a moment that will linger in the head of the guests as an image with taste and smell.

Alhäuser's responses were given in German, and translated into English by Max Koss, doctoral candidate in art history at the University of Chicago.

Mary Ellen Carroll

MARY ELLEN CARROLL DESCRIBES her practice as "investigating a single, fundamental question: What do we consider a work of art?" A polymath with a strong grounding in math and science who teaches in the architecture program at Rice University, Carroll moves fluidly across a range of disciplines and embraces an equally broad range of research-based projects. She intentionally disavows a signature style, but often uses her initials to "brand" her projects. An MEC artwork might take any number of forms—discussion, film, performance, photography, policy interventions, sculpture, urban planning, and writing—but will always be grounded in her driving interest in relationships among language, subjectivity, and power. The meal has also been a key forum for Carroll's ideas, particularly through *Itinerant Gastronomy* (1996–ongoing), a project in which she and a changing cast of collaborators have created site-specific meals. The first of these occurred on a New York street that Carroll blocked with stolen traffic cones; she served hundreds of oysters to both guests and passersby amidst a loosely curated group of performances by other artists and musicians. Subsequent events have generally been smaller, with invited guests dining in unusual settings: a bridge, a museum construction site, and for *Feast*, a viewing room high above an active trading floor at the Chicago Board of Trade.

A commission for *Feast*, Carroll's *Open Outcry* (2012) was the latest incarnation of *Itinerant Gastronomy*. Like previous iterations, the combination of setting, guests, and menu was designed to spark intense conversation; for *Open Outcry*, she took particular interest in exploring how built seating design might facilitate different kinds of interactions. Carroll enlisted Philip Ording, a mathematician who specializes in knot theory, to consider interrelationships that might be fostered by various seating configurations. She then collaborated with architect Simon Dance on the design of modular table/chair units, and on a specific seating arrangement for this meal. With sous-chef Ron-Jean Gilles, Carroll designed a menu centered on pork belly, corn, and soybeans—tasty, tangible embodiments of the commodities being traded elsewhere in the building. She assembled guests with varied expertise: organic farmers Erika Allen and Jude Becker, chef Homaro Cantu, arts administrator Dionna Griffin-Irons, trader John Pietrzak, philosopher Candace Vogler, economist Glen Wyle, and myself. During the meal, questions written by the artist and others elicited conversation about the intersections of art, finance, food, policy, power, and technology—a discussion heightened by the site, a hub through which global capital moves in abstract forms at nearly unimaginable speeds.

Carroll's primary focus was the event itself, but she hopes it will inspire similar conversations among those who encounter *Open Outcry* as an installation in *Feast*. At the Smart Museum, she integrated the project into the longer history of *Itinerant Gastronomy* through a new installation of documents and artifacts. A transcription from an early *Itinerant Gastronomy* event formed the wallpaper that visually unified the whole presentation. At one level, this simply made dialogue visible. As a mass of text it signified the importance of conversation to *Itinerant Gastronomy* as well as the primacy of language in Carroll's work. But the specific words themselves offered surprisingly vivid documentation of one meal: conveying shifts of mood and pacing through ebbs and flows of dinner chat that ranged from inane to profound. Against this backdrop, a kind of three-dimensional timeline unfolded through evocative artifacts: a battered traffic cone, oyster shells, cutlery, invitations, photographs, and other remnants of early *Itinerant Gastronomy* meals led up to materials related to *Open Outcry* (sketches, models, printed matter, and Michael Isabell's documentary video about the event itself). In Chicago, the *Open Outcry* furniture was also shown, further evoking the specific iteration of *Itinerant Gastronomy* at the Chicago Board of Trade.

OPPOSITE: *Open Outcry* guests watch activity on the trade floor, January 23, 2012

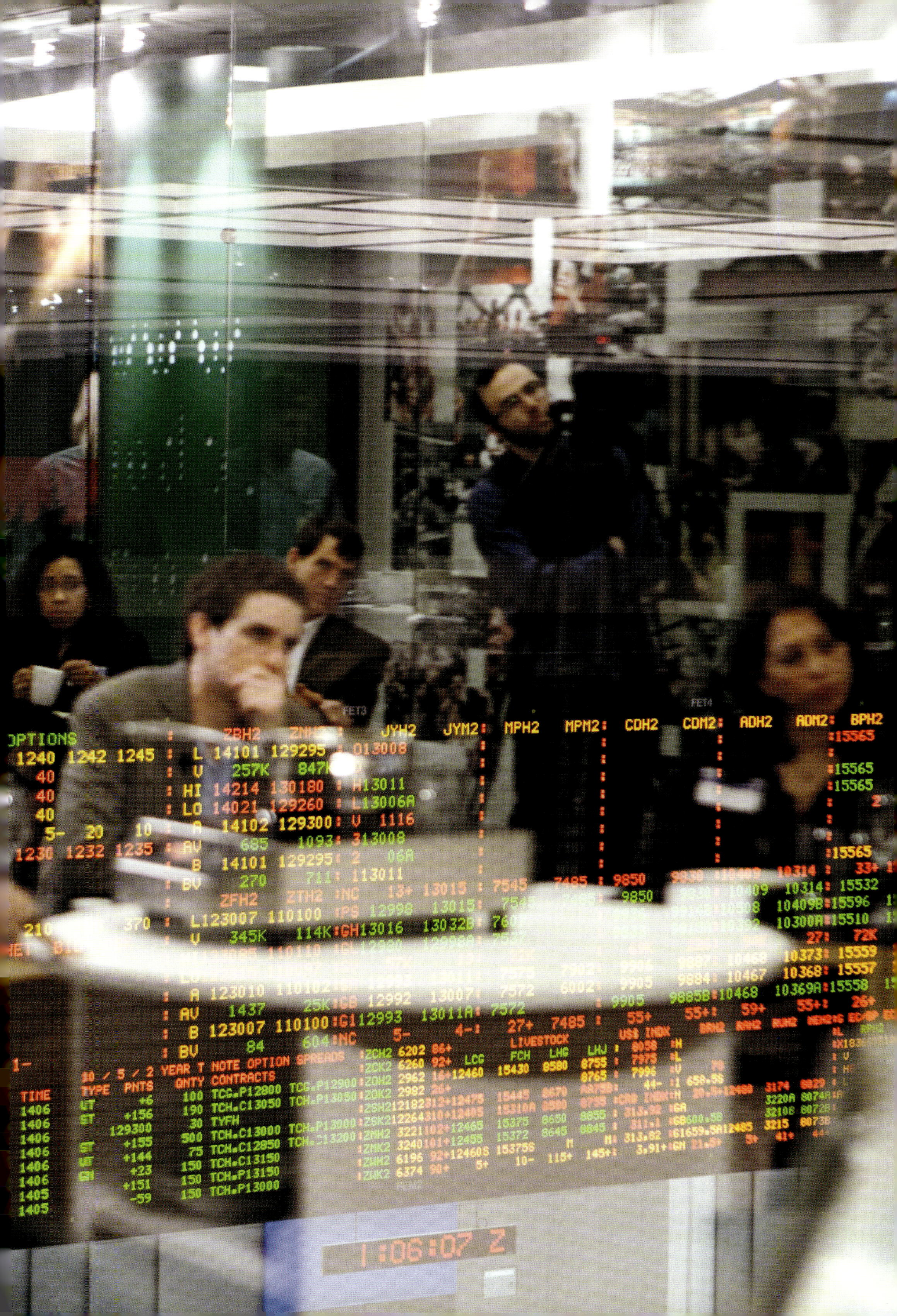
OPTIONS
ZBH2
JYH2
JYM2
MPH2
MPM2
CDH2
CDM2
ADH2
ADM2
BPH2
ZFH2
ZTH2
LIVESTOCK
US$ INDX
10 / 5 / 2 YEAR T NOTE OPTION SPREADS
TIME
TYPE
PNTS
QNTY
CONTRACTS
1:06:07 Z

Interview

SMART: Can you describe your path as an artist and sources of inspiration for your work, either in or beyond the context of art?

MARY ELLEN CARROLL: As an artist, I am influenced by my background and training in science and math. All of my work still begins systematically as a problem or question. Everything is drawn in language. The experimental filmmaker Stan Brakhage was an early influence in my late teens, and when I was sent to an artist colony in Idaho—that changed everything.

A family member had heard me talking about this program in Idaho with the artist June Leaf who was married to Robert Frank. They made the arrangements and a month later I found myself in an intensive printmaking studio and a master's ceramics class. I was always interested in food writing, but this became more intensive and included the food writers M. F. K. Fisher, Elizabeth David, Jean Anthelme Brillat-Savarin, Marie-Antoine Carême, etc., as well as journalists and film writers. I would sleep with Larousse's *Gastronomique* in my bed.

Following the completion of my undergraduate degree, and a stint to learn how to make wine while living in Apulia in the town of Acqua Viva Della Fonti ("the water of life"), in 1983 I set up a microfinance program in the Philippines for the Peace Corps. This included basic infrastructure development for potable water, toilets, and sustainable agricultural practices. While there I experienced the civil war, revolution, a banana republic, the Reagan era from outside the United States, indigenous design, etc., and made many Super 8 films. There was a remarkable art scene in Manila that cut across disciplines and it was all taking place primarily in the center of the city in a restaurant in the red light district of Manila, the Penguin Café. The menu and having the opportunity to cook was always a part of this place and whoever came together—members of the New People's Army, the theater groups, filmmakers, writers, conceptual artists, etc. This was also the start of my interest in self-consciousness and philosophy, namely Nietzsche and Wittgenstein, but also writers like Laura Riding, and the Austrian writers Musil and Bernhard. I was also interested in the development of sustainable architecture and the work of Buckminster Fuller, which led to time in Japan to continue work and research before returning to the US for graduate school at the School of the Art Institute of Chicago.

SMART: Please tell us about the first *Itinerant Gastronomy* event.

MEC: In 1996 I was collaborating with a composer from Berlin, Laurie Schwartz. Laurie had a very popular radio program on Deutschlandfunk that was on the air from 1 am until 4 am in the 1980s and 1990s. She was in New York to conduct interviews for her program and for a performance of her experimental composition for percussion and soprano, *The Shoes*, which was being performed at CBGB's. The composition utilized businessman Pelligrino Artusi's famous self-published treatise, *The Science of Cooking and the Art of Eating Well*. It was a complex piece—performed here by the soprano Ana Clementi, who improvised to a recorded tap dancer who tapped through a list of emotions while she read selected texts from Artusi's tome.

During Laurie's visit, I received a call from a fishmonger I knew at Balducci's who had a cancelled order of oysters and wanted to know if I wanted them. I said yes. Oysters were the perfect food item to start a work of art because the mollusk is so primal and basic. It's something that you either eat or do not eat and this can be a dietary restriction or just a preference. I was reading quite a bit of Martha Nussbaum's work on moral philosophy and choice, and the oyster seemed connected to those ideas.

So I sat down with Laurie and asked if we could reenact *The Shoes* on the street in front of Joanne Hendrick's store Cookbooks on Greenwich Street just above Canal Street. (An important thing about the location of Cookbooks is that the eighteenth-century row house it is in was on the Hudson River before the landfill and there were oyster beds in that part of the river.) The piece would be played through boom boxes that were set up so that it sounded like Mussolini in a football stadium echoing up and down the block. We would serve the oysters and have some simultaneous programming. This included Nancy Linn who took Polaroid portraits of the patrons who were buying their Saturday morning lox at Russ and Daughters. Max Schumann had food paintings at Jefferson Market. Tan Lin wrote poems and read from a table at the uptown Sant Ambroeus. Anthony Coleman improvised jazz on a keyboard to a projected film. Laurie and I discussed what it would be called—I wanted there to be the word gastronome or gastronomy—how the location, people, food (the context) would necessitate it happening in that place, but it would not be fixed location. The relationship to the temporal was paramount to the entire thing. She added the word "itinerant" and that was the start.

I had a Ford pickup truck and decided that we needed to close off the street and bring it all together in front of Cookbooks. I picked up orange construction cones from around the city and we blocked off Greenwich Street between Canal and Spring Street. I hired oyster shuckers who never showed up. And we had about two hundred guests—pre-social networking—including those who just happened to walk by.

SMART: Could you say a bit more about how you see the orchestration of all of these activities connecting back to the idea of the oyster and that primal yes/no choice?

MEC: Conceptually, the consistency in all of my work is about exposing a dialectical process. A successful work of art simply makes the viewer become aware of their own existence. This process is also about the understanding of why something is the way it is and how intuition is really about knowledge. Hence, if I say I like an oyster, as a human being, I am capable of articulating why. The events make it possible to propose choices that are possible and the realization that there are

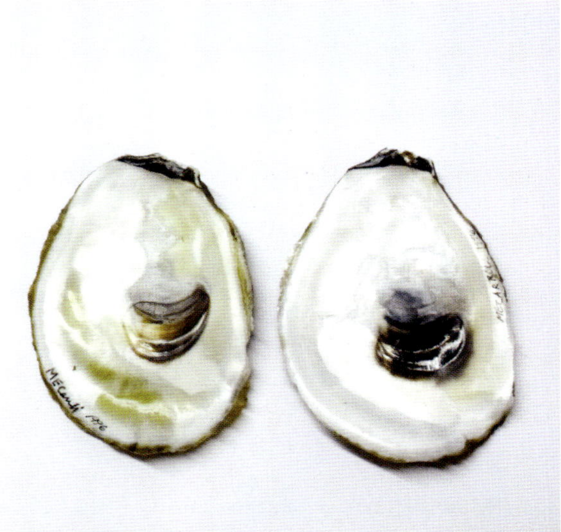

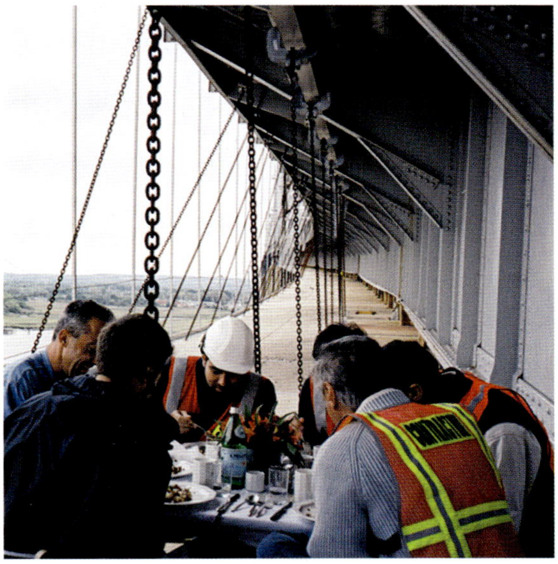

TOP: Oyster shells from the first *Itinerant Gastronomy* event, October 26, 1996

BOTTOM: Guests—all of whom had worked on the Goethals Bridge—experiencing an Itinerant Gastronomy meal by Mary Ellen Carroll with Donna Wingate, *Ploughman's Lunch*, Goethals Bridge, September, 29, 2004

times when we are without choice and that things are just the way that they are. There is a Kafka short story that echoes this sentiment and another by Lydia Davis on the "boring" that I return to frequently in my thinking about the stagings.

SMART: How did the *Itinerant Gastronomy* series evolve?

MEC: The next iteration occurred when an exhibition was cancelled at APEXArt [2002] and they asked artists to program for one day. At the time everyone was DJ-ing or doing readings and it all felt so predictable and lacking pleasure and humor and I thought that it would be good to open a restaurant for one day. There were six meals throughout the day. Reservations were required, from breakfast to late night, dining for four guests, seated at one table. I invited six people to host meals. They were all passionate about food, either as chefs or very good cooks. I also wanted to be able to pay people and make money. There is so much economic disparity in the art world and given my position that food is not art, well it was essential that this actually be an undertaking that was in the black and not the red.

After the first events, I began to think of *Itinerant Gastronomy* improvisationally as a composition, something that could be performed in a variety of ways, but that ultimately the elements of food, location, people, and most importantly the dialogue would always be consistent. The scale can shift from one person to thousands, as it should never become formulaic. The important thing was to document the conversation at the table, which goes back to self-consciousness and existentialism and the autonomy of the work of art. When I speak about the work of art as being autonomous, what I am referring to is how the work of art does not have to be anything other than itself. Food is food, design is design, furniture is furniture, art is art . . .

My long-term technical and media collaborator, Michael Isabell, set up a microphone in the middle of the table and once the initial acknowledgment of its presence took place, it became invisible as the courses started to be served. We had a great group of guests and also some performers who showed up. This included the comedian Demetri Martin who appeared during the

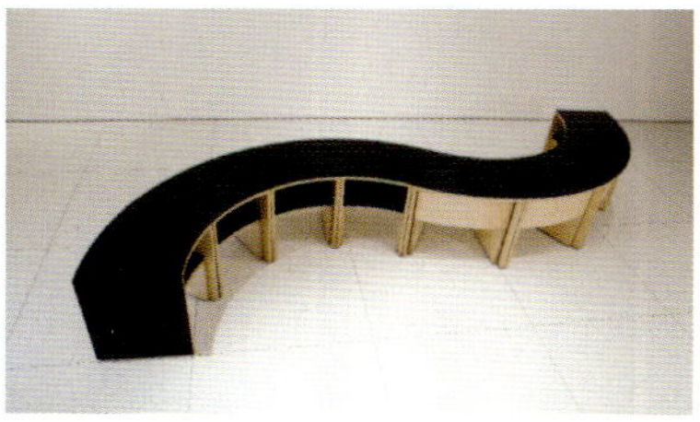

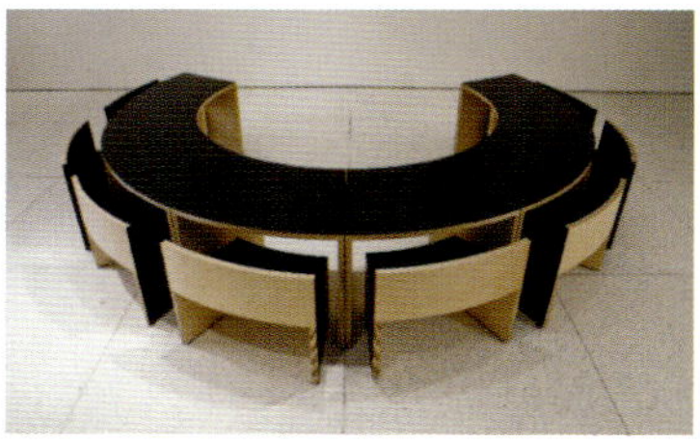

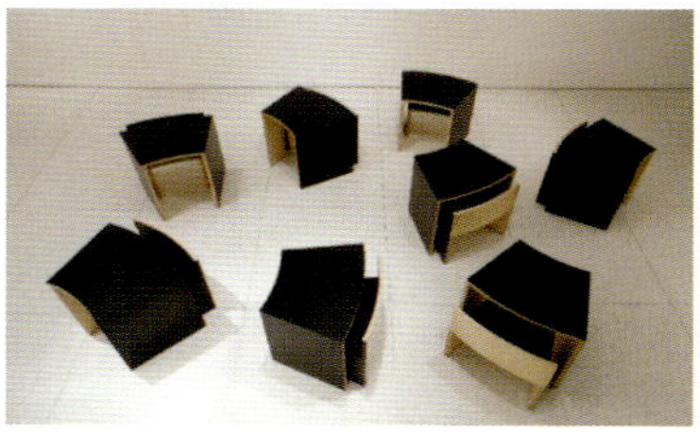

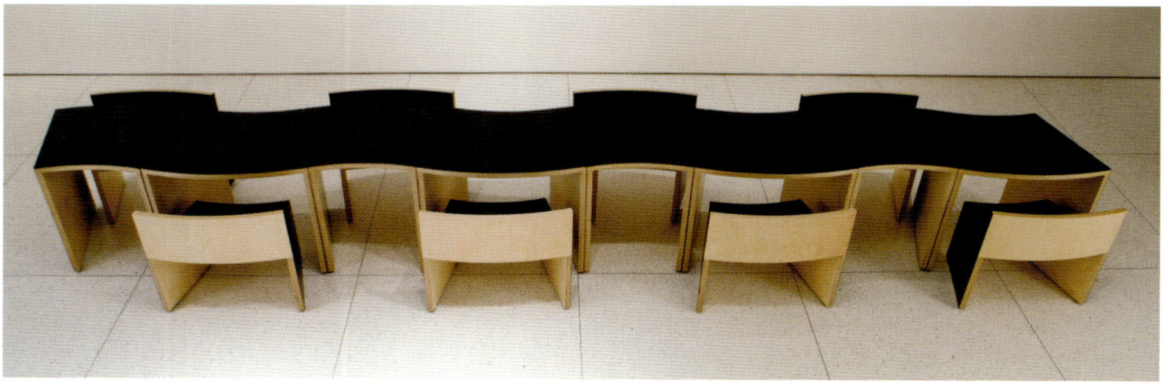

ABOVE: Various configurations of tables created for *Open Outcry* by Carroll and Simon Dance/Simon Dance Design

OPPOSITE: Sketch by mathematician Philip Ording that influenced the design of *Open Outcry* tables, 2011

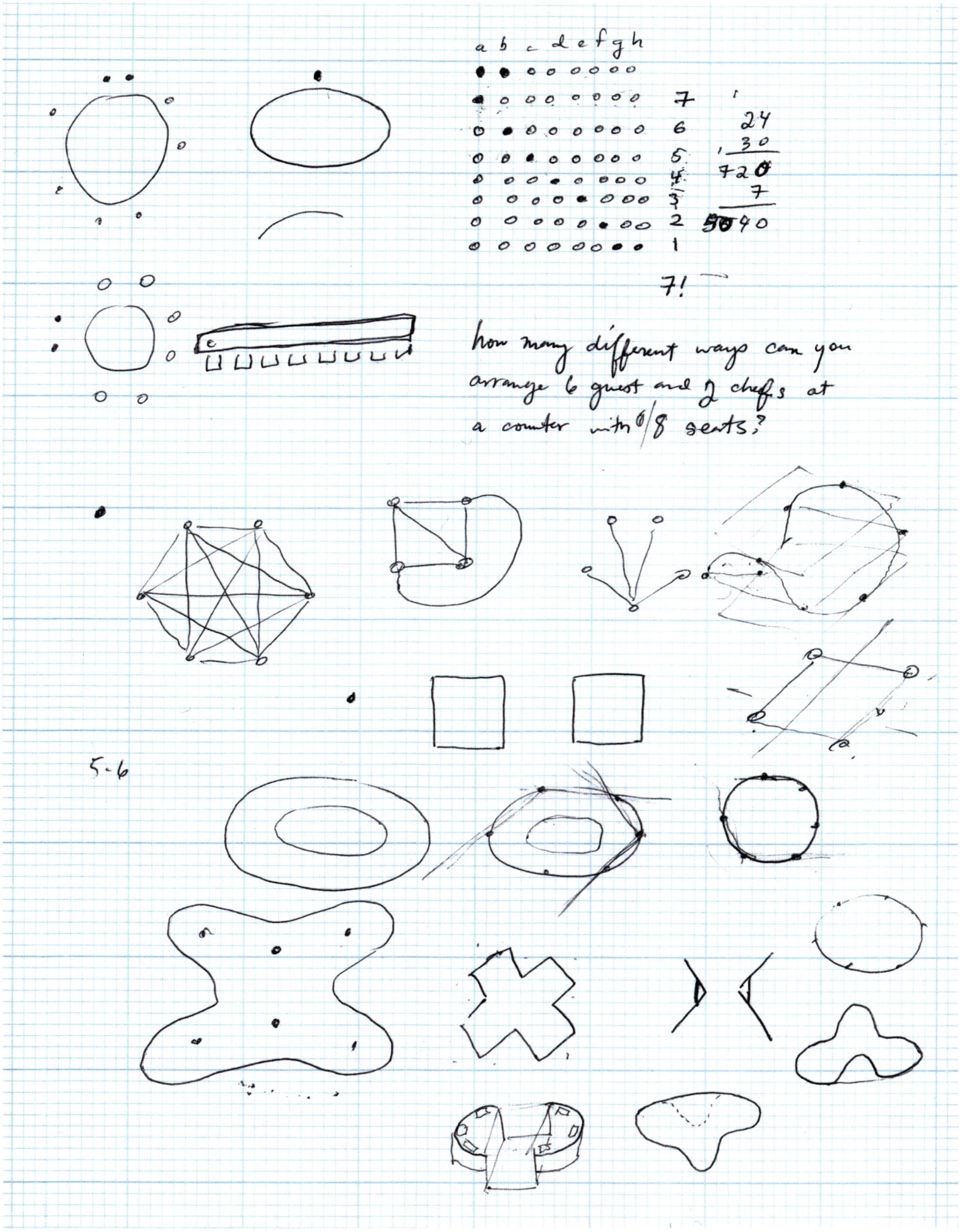
a b c d e f g h
7
6
5
4
3
2
1
24
30
720
7
5040
7!
how many different ways can you arrange 6 guest and 2 chefs at a counter with 6/8 seats?
5-6

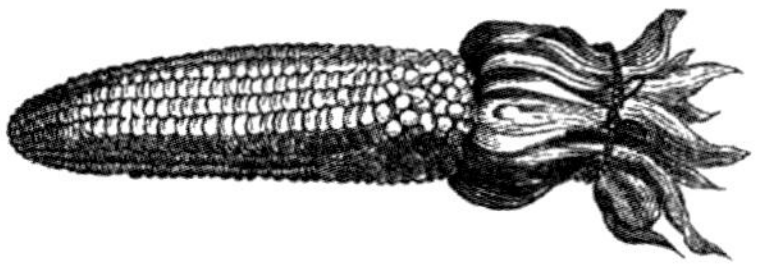

open outcry

Monday, January 23, 2012

Itinerant Gastronomy
at the
Financial Gallery at CME Group
in the Chicago Board of Trade Building

A commission for
FEAST
Radical Hospitality in Contemporary Art
at the Smart Museum of Art at the University of Chicago
February 16–June 10, 2012

Prepared by
Mary Ellen Carroll
with
Ron Jean Gilles

Menu

Sesame Chawan Mushi with Soybeans

Corn Chowder with Jalapeño Oil

Savoy Cabbage with Black Walnuts, Aged Ricotta, Currants
and a Chipotle Dressing

Braised Becker Pork Belly with Kumquat Compote
Polenta and Greens

Raw Chocolate Layered Nutcake
with Espresso Creme

Mary Ellen Carroll and **Open Outcry** gratefully acknowledges:
Becker Farms, James T. Carroll, CookTEC, CME Group, CYB Furniture-Helmut Ehrmann, Simon Dance/SDD-London, Formica Corporation, Ron Giles, Michael Isabell/Eyespy Films, Louis and Company, Laura Madera-Nadal, Seth McCormick, Lindsay, Philips, Takuya Oura/SDO, Larry Smallwood, Stephanie Smith, the staff of the Smart Museum at the University of Chicago, Emily Tillack and the guests for their contributions and participation in **Open Outcry**.

The Sculptural seating arrangement realized in collaboration between Mary Ellen Carroll (MEC, design studios) and Simon Dance (Simon Dance Design) is the first time that the actual seating was considered and designed as a part of Itinerant Gastronomy.

Open Outcry began by Carroll working in conversation with Columbia University mathematician Philip Ording—a specialist in knot theory—who explored the ways that various seating configurations might facilitate different kinds of interaction among guests—and architect Simon Dance of Simon Dance Design, who collaborated to design the modular tables/chairs used in **Open Outcry**. The table/chair is derived from a mathematical system and also reflects the 'pits' where the traders stand and their exchanges take place. The prototype of **Open Outcry** was built by the Master Craftsmen, Helmut Ehrmann of CYB Furniture in Houston, Texas and Formica has generously provided it's unique laminate ColorCare® as the surfacing material.

ABOVE AND OPPOSITE: Menu and conversation prompts for *Open Outcry* luncheon, January 23, 2012

open outcry

THE TOPICS FOR THE COURSES

Communication
Recently, a multimillion-dollar project was completed to connect New York and Chicago through the earth via fiber optic cable in order to shave a few milliseconds off communication times. While such acceleration of transactions offered high-frequency hedge funds enormous opportunity for arbitrage profits between the markets, it seems hard to imagine what real economic benefits such a project affords. Given that we are sitting around the table talking and in front of the trading floor where the Open Outcry system is still in use, this seems naturally to ask, "What are the limits to useful communication speeds that can be valuable to the real economy and how do these relate to the speeds of communication valued by financial markets? And if these are different, what regulation can avoid excessive acceleration?" *(From E. Glen Weyl, Assistant Professor in the Department of Economics and in the College at the University of Chicago where he does research in economics and related fields, including philosophy and the history of economics.)*

Commodity
Rising food prices and demand for food, spurred by the rising middle classes globally and other emerging markets, shows no signs of abating. Since the beginning of the 20th century, we have seen markets created for everything, ranging from butter to the weather. Recently, we have seen the creation of funds and the notion of farmland as an investable asset class. This is disconcerting in some respects: sometimes when an investment idea gets packaged and presented or marketed, it can indicate that the opportunity may have crested. While it is compelling in some ways (land as a finite resource, increasing commodity demands, the potential for commercial development of the land in the future), there are also some concerns, e.g. valuation problems, liquidity constraints, and the issue of who is going to actually run the farms on a daily basis. If precious metals (gold, silver, platinum) were the safe haven for investing and futures markets, albeit inedible ones, what are your thoughts about farmland as a global commodity and the aggregation of an asset that is so labor intensive and involves a commitment that has been equated with the family and the backbone of America. If farmland is now an investable asset class, what else can you imagine or see being brought to market as an investable asset in the future? *(From R. A. Kern, Institutional Investment Consultant)*

Policy
Policy is defined as a course of action that is adopted. This can range from the personal to the corporate, yet is most frequently understood to be a part of government. Food policy has been making headlines with the current back to the farm movement and activism on the part of the First Lady of the United States.

The more general problem of hunger is enmeshed in the set of processes that produce (and consume) agricultural commodities on farms, transform these commodities into food in the marketing sector, and sell the food to consumers to satisfy nutritional as well as aesthetic and social needs. These processes make up the food system. The actual functioning of this system frequently leaves many poor people inadequately fed because of a network of connections that determine their employment and income status, the prices they must pay for food and other goods and services, and their ability to move in search of better opportunities. The same food system, however, offers vehicles for the policy interventions that reach poor people with sustainable improvements in their access to food.

When the price of processed food is far below the prices at Whole Foods isn't there something wrong with the system? A food system that contains many hungry people is a failure in at least one dimension. But is it a failure to produce enough food, to produce the right kinds of food, to generate enough income to buy that food, or to educate families about what foods to eat? *(From Carl H. Gotsch, Food Research Institute, Stanford University)*

Taste
Many practices or disciplines have been compared to art. The art of trade, the art of deal, the art of food, building as art, clothing as art etc. All of these activities and their resultants can be be given aesthetic attention, but are they actually art. Carolyn Korsmeyer in her philosophical work, *Taste* does a great deal to correct the misunderstandings about the sense of taste in order to defend the theoretical significance of food. A question that she answers, but that I am raising to everyone at their/this table is, How ought we to characterize these dissimilarities without at the same losing sight of the important similarities between food or your respective discipline and the arts? If it is not art, then what is it? *(From Carolyn Korsmeyer, Professor of Philosophy, University of Buffalo)*

Intention
G.E M. (Gertrude Elizabeth Margaret) Anscombe (18 March 1919 – 5 January 2001), better known as Elizabeth Anscombe, was a British analytic philosopher. Born in Ireland, she was a student of Ludwig Wittgenstein and became an authority on his work and edited and translated many books drawn from his writings, above all his *Philosophical Investigations*. Her title, *Intention* is known as her greatest work and there is a specific intent as to why you have been invited today to the CME Group's Financial Gallery. One of the most engaging areas of interest in her work has been the question about the difference between intention and prediction. Both are future directed. Both seem to require a belief that a future state of affairs will occur. What would you say for yourself and your individual field would that future will be and how would it be instrumentalized?

Open Outcry gratefully acknowledges: CME Group, CYB Furniture, Formica Corporation, Ron Gilles, Michael Isabell/Eyespy Films, Louis and Company, Laura Madera-Nadal, Takuya Oura/Simon Dance Design and the Smart Museum of Art at the University of Chicago.

Bavarian dinner as a strolling minstrel with his guitar and also came up to the table and did a stand-up routine. We thought it would be amusing to have a comic during the German meal. It was a disaster as the guests did not really understand what was going on, but in reviewing the footage it is actually very funny.

One of the guests at a table was Donna Wingate who worked at the art book distributor DAP. We talked about food and the process and she came to another dinner that I had in my very ship-like apartment and helped me in the kitchen. Following that I invited Donna to collaborate on three *Itinerant* events together that included a meal on the Highline when it was still closed, a breakfast atop the Goethals Bridge for five construction workers, and a meal at the Institute of Contemporary Art in Boston when it was still under construction.

I continued to realize other *Itinerant Gastronomy* events including O.O.W.I.A.H. (Open Only When I Am Here), the restaurant division of *Itinerant Gastronomy*, as well as meals for one and meals where I will take over a restaurant when it is closed, say a lunch counter. It is an open collaboration that is about the context. It's always crucial that the location, guests, and food are all localized and have a reason for coming together in a particular place. Another important aspect of it all is that there is no need for an elaborate setup: one can create with almost nothing and this has often meant that a hot plate and something to prepare the meal and serve the meal on is all that is required. Individuals are always looking for excuses or reasons for not being able to do something, the wrong pot, the stove is not big enough, etc. If I had two sticks to start a fire and a tin can to cook in, it would still work, albeit à la menu.

SMART: Tell us about *Open Outcry*—its impetus, intention, and production—how does it fit into your broader practice?

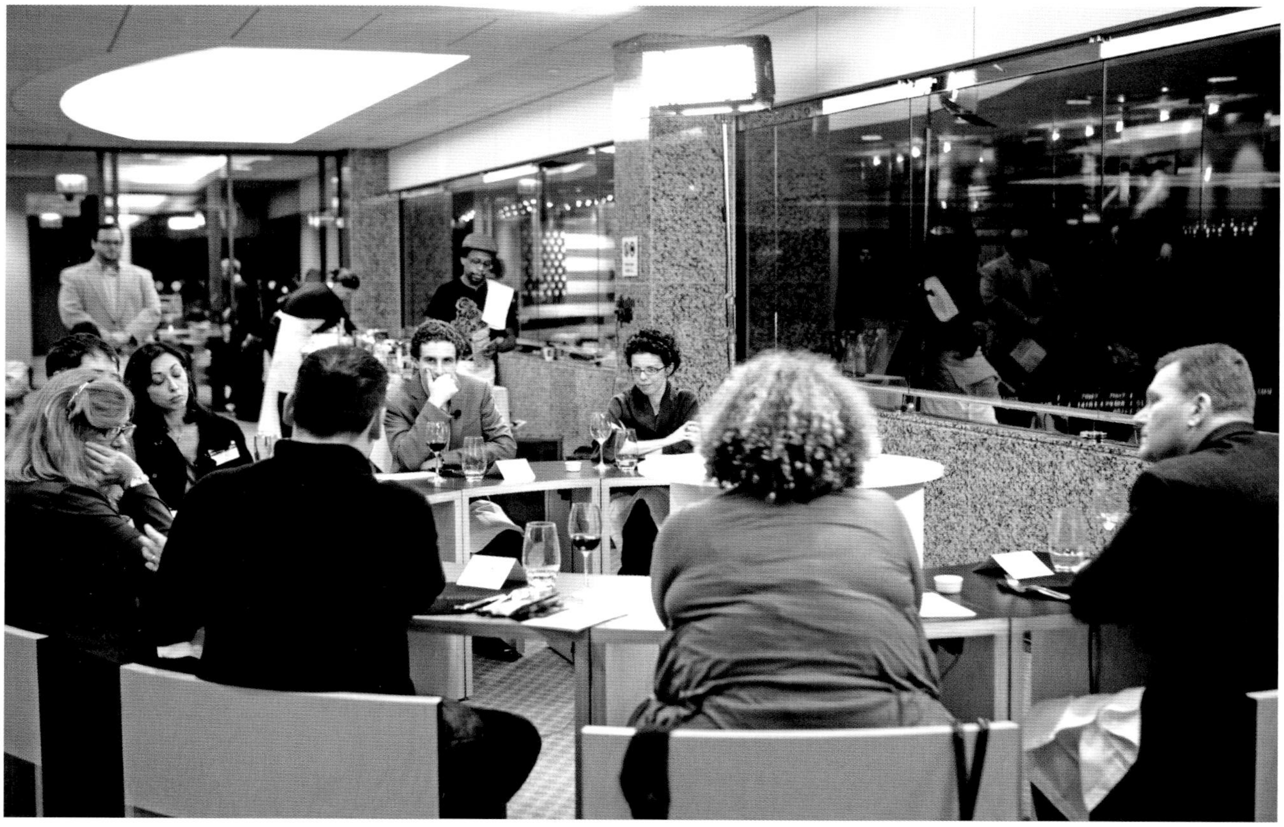

ABOVE AND OPPOSITE: *Open Outcry* at Chicago Board of Trade, CME Group, January 23, 2012

MEC: We are living in the political epoch. Everything is about the political, and policy is the material that can be treated as the readymade. Duchamp utilized the manufactured object; I utilize political structures and policy. *Open Outcry* is tied to the political and economic structure of exchange and commodities and how the pricing and availability of the commodity in the market can be regulated. The CME Group at the Chicago Board of Trade building as a site and location of this process has always been of interest to me—especially given how seemingly archaic it is now. As a process, corporeality and signification come together on the trading floor and in the pits that are physically occupied by the traders. This all started with butter and has evolved to include other commodities and markets including financial instruments as exchange instruments themselves.

For many years I have wanted to stage an *Itinerant Gastronomy* on the trading floor in one of the agricultural pits where the meal would relate to the commodities that are traded. When a piece appeared in the *New York Times* about the *Itinerant Gastronomy* that was held on the Goethals Bridge, then-Mayor Daley contacted me. That focused my thinking about a meal that could be realized at the Mercantile Exchange with politicians and other guests who were involved in food and economic policy. Post–9/11, the production involves more process, but process is always a part of my work and this is diagrammed as a drawing of decision-making and selection.

The meal will take place in the financial gallery above the trading floor while trading is taking place, hence the decision for it to be a lunch. The table is a key element and will be realized in collaboration with Simon Dance of Simon Dance Design and the mathematician Philip Ording, who does work on systems and knots to establish the patterns of interaction. The process is always an expansive proposition. I will be cooking with Ron Gilles, who I collaborated with in the past; Ron shucked two hundred oysters, having never opened a mollusk before.

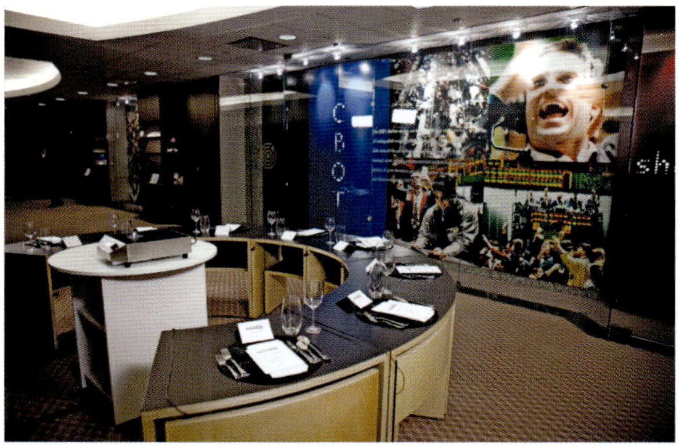

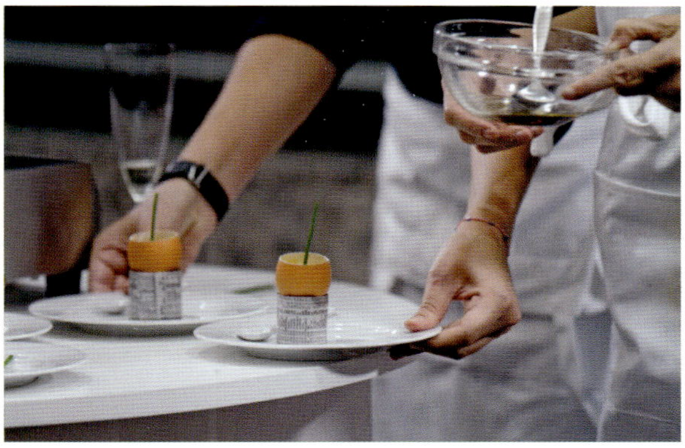

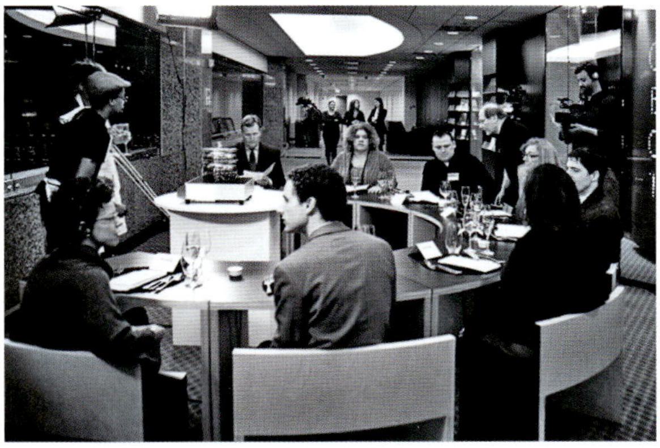

FOLLOWING PAGES: *Itinerant Gastronomy,* 1996–ongoing, installation view, Smart Museum of Art, 2012

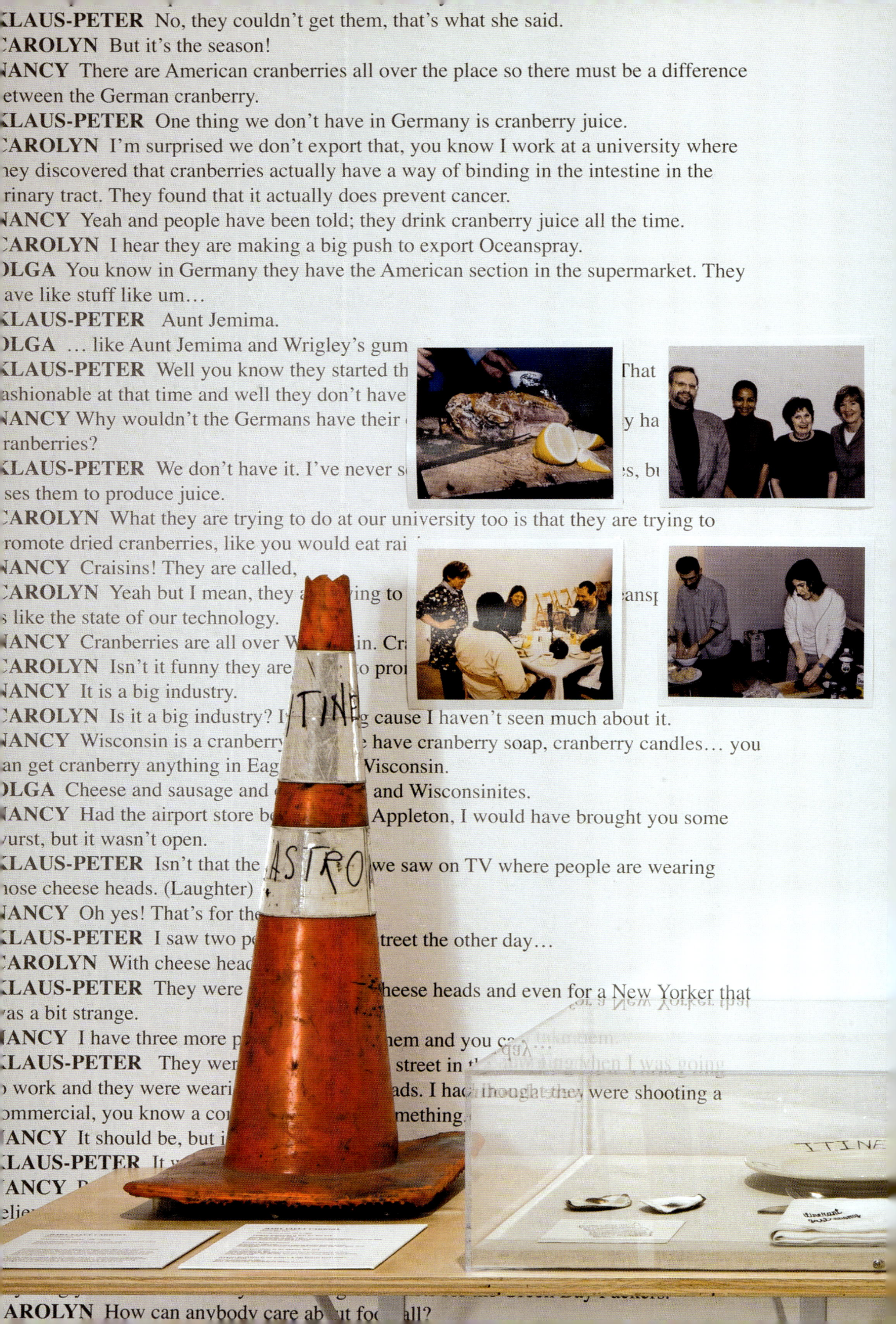
KLAUS-PETER No, they couldn't get them, that's what she said.
CAROLYN But it's the season!
NANCY There are American cranberries all over the place so there must be a difference
etween the German cranberry.
KLAUS-PETER One thing we don't have in Germany is cranberry juice.
CAROLYN I'm surprised we don't export that, you know I work at a university where
ey discovered that cranberries actually have a way of binding in the intestine in the
rinary tract. They found that it actually does prevent cancer.
NANCY Yeah and people have been told; they drink cranberry juice all the time.
CAROLYN I hear they are making a big push to export Oceanspray.
OLGA You know in Germany they have the American section in the supermarket. They
ave like stuff like um…
KLAUS-PETER Aunt Jemima.
OLGA … like Aunt Jemima and Wrigley's gum
KLAUS-PETER Well you know they started th
ashionable at that time and well they don't have
NANCY Why wouldn't the Germans have their
ranberries?
KLAUS-PETER We don't have it. I've never s
ses them to produce juice.
CAROLYN What they are trying to do at our university too is that they are trying to
romote dried cranberries, like you would eat rai
NANCY Craisins! They are called,
CAROLYN Yeah but I mean, they
s like the state of our technology.
NANCY Cranberries are all over W
CAROLYN Isn't it funny they are
NANCY It is a big industry.
CAROLYN Is it a big industry?
cause I haven't seen much about it.
NANCY Wisconsin is a cranberr
have cranberry soap, cranberry candles… you
an get cranberry anything in Eag
Visconsin.
OLGA Cheese and sausage and
and Wisconsinites.
NANCY Had the airport store b
Appleton, I would have brought you some
urst, but it wasn't open.
KLAUS-PETER Isn't that the
we saw on TV where people are wearing
ose cheese heads. (Laughter)
NANCY Oh yes! That's for the
KLAUS-PETER I saw two p
treet the other day…
CAROLYN With cheese head
KLAUS-PETER They were
heese heads and even for a New Yorker that
as a bit strange.
NANCY I have three more p
hem and you c
KLAUS-PETER They wer
street in
work and they were weari
ads. I had thought they were shooting a
ommercial, you know a co
mething
NANCY It should be, but i
KLAUS-PETER
CAROLYN How can anybody care ab
all?
TINE
ASTRO
ITINE

NANCY Foreign tourists from Europe and mostly Italy I think, probably Germany as well. It's in everybody's guide book.

CAROLYN I know what I know. Since I'm not interested in fashion and shopping, how's this anti-Americanism going in Germany?

KLAUS-PETER Well it's an interesting question and I think the topic here is a little over rated. It's not anti-Americanism. It's just that the German Chancellor said during an election campaign that we are not supporting going to war with Iraq.

CAROLYN But it sounds like some of the....

KLAUS-PETER That's not anti-Americanism I would say.

CAROLYN It sounds like a number of the NATO people have more or less changed their minds. I'm not a supporter of the war in Iraq either, and I'm a great supporter of the Palestinian cause, so I want you to know that I'm in

NANCY Why do you think I like her!?

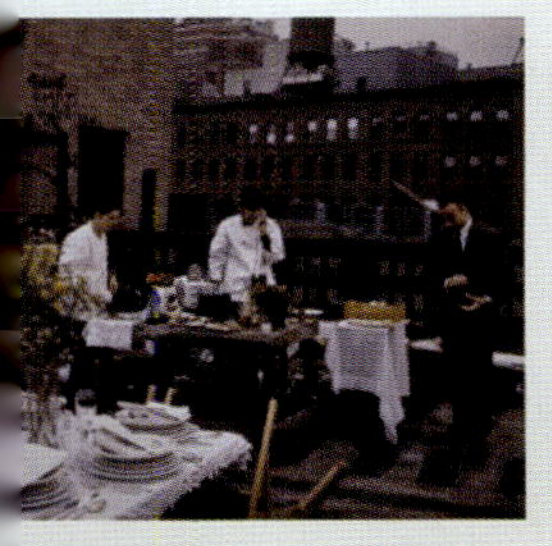

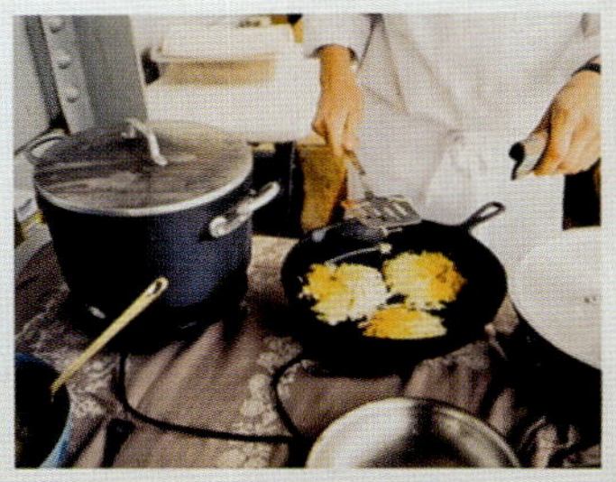

thou in th

g b re su

e's rotoc

ve a are

Tha

rma d w

?

KLAUS-PETER No, they're not. They had a meeti

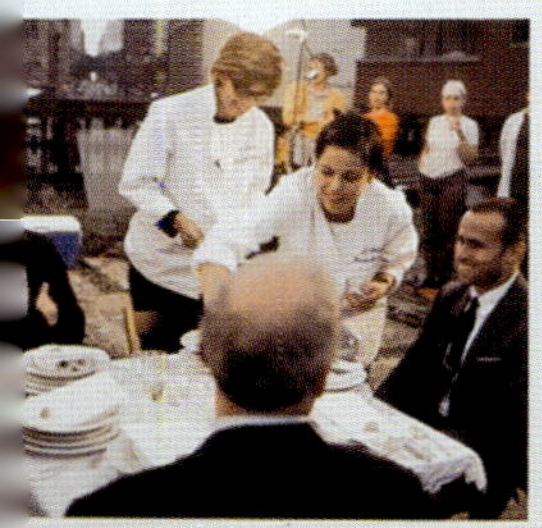

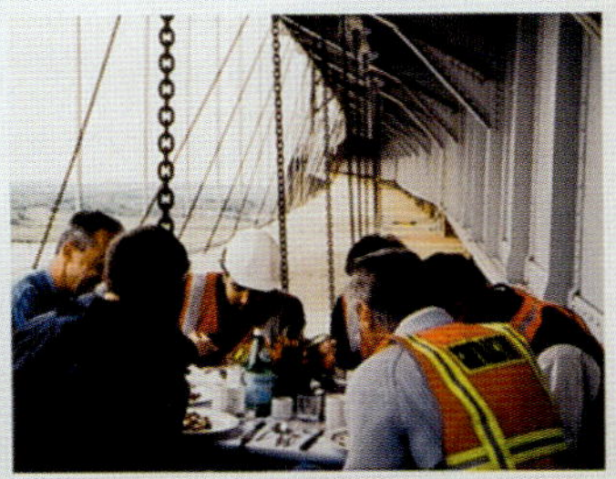

r wl er ha

, yo

Tha s an

the y, he

vill ght

Gern ve a

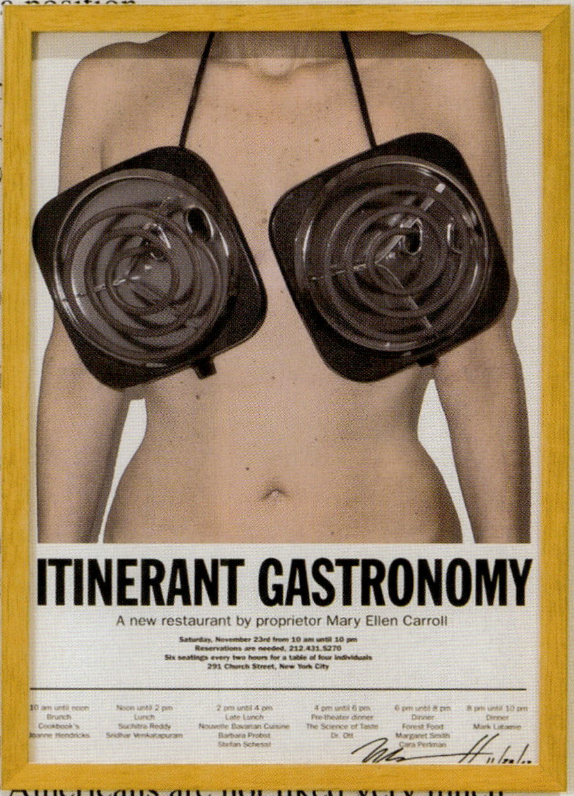

KLAUS-PETER They're talking about air space ri should be. I assume they will use the bases for that, b active participation in the deployment of troops. The Americans are not liked very much in the world.

CAROLYN So, the Germans will not provide any money, troops, support in any way?

KLAUS-PETER That's what he said...

CAROLYN Because I saw I didn't read the article, but I did see something in the New York Times that a number of NATO countries had come around and I, it was in the New York Times yesterday, or the day before.

KLAUS-PETER No, they are not going to support it

NANCY And who are you?

DEMETRI Hi, how are you doing? Sorry to talk to you guys. I'm a comedian and my sides.

le

ped for the an th

NANCY T ey sa nc t co

pass that up

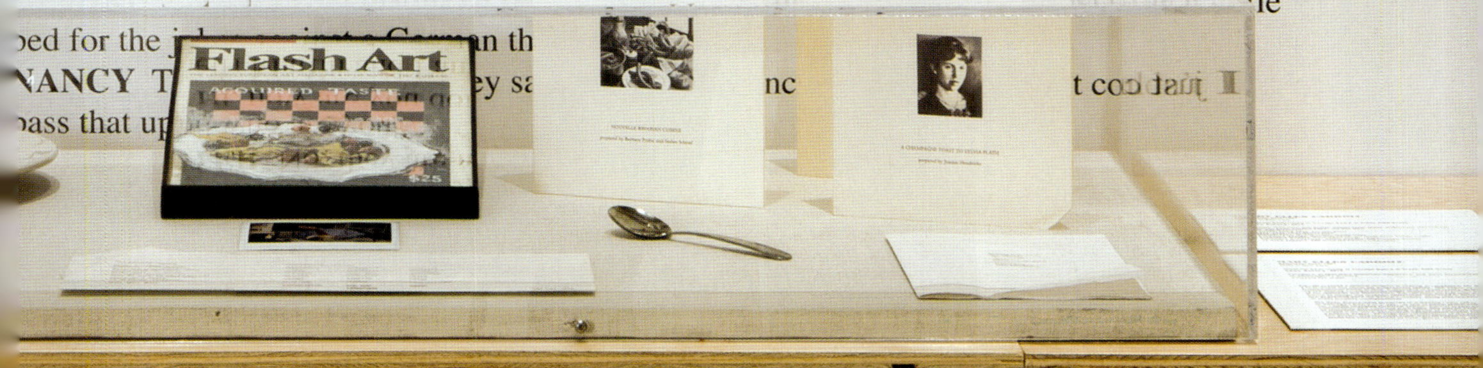

EMETRI I'm Greek, so I gu with my heritage

Fallen Fruit

David Burns, Matias Viegener, and Austin Young

DAVID BURNS, MATIAS VIEGENER, AND AUSTIN YOUNG began collaborating as Fallen Fruit in the mid-2000s, with a series of ongoing projects that focus on what they call "public fruit." The artists use fruit as a lens through which to focus questions about how we occupy urban space; how we define boundaries between public and private; how we might use, neglect, or redirect surplus; and how all of those issues affect how we relate to each other. The artists understand that fruit offers unique properties as subject matter and material: familiar but laden with cultural specificity. And since fruit trees are often found throughout urban neighborhoods, they create readymade opportunities to consider those civic spaces. Fallen Fruit's research results in a range of manifestations including interventions, performances, and collaborative public events, as well as installations, objects, videos, collages, and maps. Recently they have also been commissioned to research and create fruit-themed displays of museum collections, including that of the Los Angeles Museum of Art.

With its long growing season and plentiful fruit trees, Los Angeles has offered an ideal platform for Fallen Fruit's urban interventions. They noticed many fruit trees extending from private land into public space—for instance, an orange tree in a back yard whose branches drop fruit onto an adjacent sidewalk. Such fruit is public property: ripe for gleaning and laden with both actual and metaphoric sustenance. To capitalize on this potential, they mapped public fruit sites in Los Angeles, and have since mapped other cities. They've led performative nighttime expeditions to gather public fruit. And they've organized "fruit jams" that bring people together to collaboratively make jam, without recipes, using fruit that they've grown or gathered.

For *Feast*, Fallen Fruit explored the essence of place through a new iteration of another key public fruit project. In *Neighborhood Infusions* (2008–ongoing), the artists collect fruit in Los Angeles neighborhoods and collaborate with an organic distillery, the GreenBar Collective, to infuse this fruit into vodkas. The project extends the idea of *terroir*—a French winemaking term indicating how soil and climate can infuse grapes and thus shape the character of wine. *Neighborhood Infusions* similarly asks how we ourselves are shaped by the places that we live. When exhibited, the project always includes a display of bottles and a performance in which docents serve small portions of vodka to guests, while encouraging conversation about neighborhoods and taste. For *Feast*, the artists experimented with a different format. To complement a display of bottles at the museum, they staged a participatory performance at the University's Logan Center for the Visual and Performing Arts. To close the symposium "Of Hospitality," the artists introduced their work and then presented a museum-like display of brightly lit vodka bottles arrayed on a thin pedestal. In a celebratory gesture that unsettled usual lines between artist/host and audience/guest, all were invited on stage to drink the vodkas—Atwater Village Calamondin, Edendale Meyer Lemon, Los Angeles Sunshine, and Los Feliz Bitter Orange. Colored wristbands not only marked those of legal age but were also tagged with prompts for discussion about fruit, place, and identity. Through such interventions, Fallen Fruit injects existing structures with a playful dose of social critique and buoyant, messy experience.

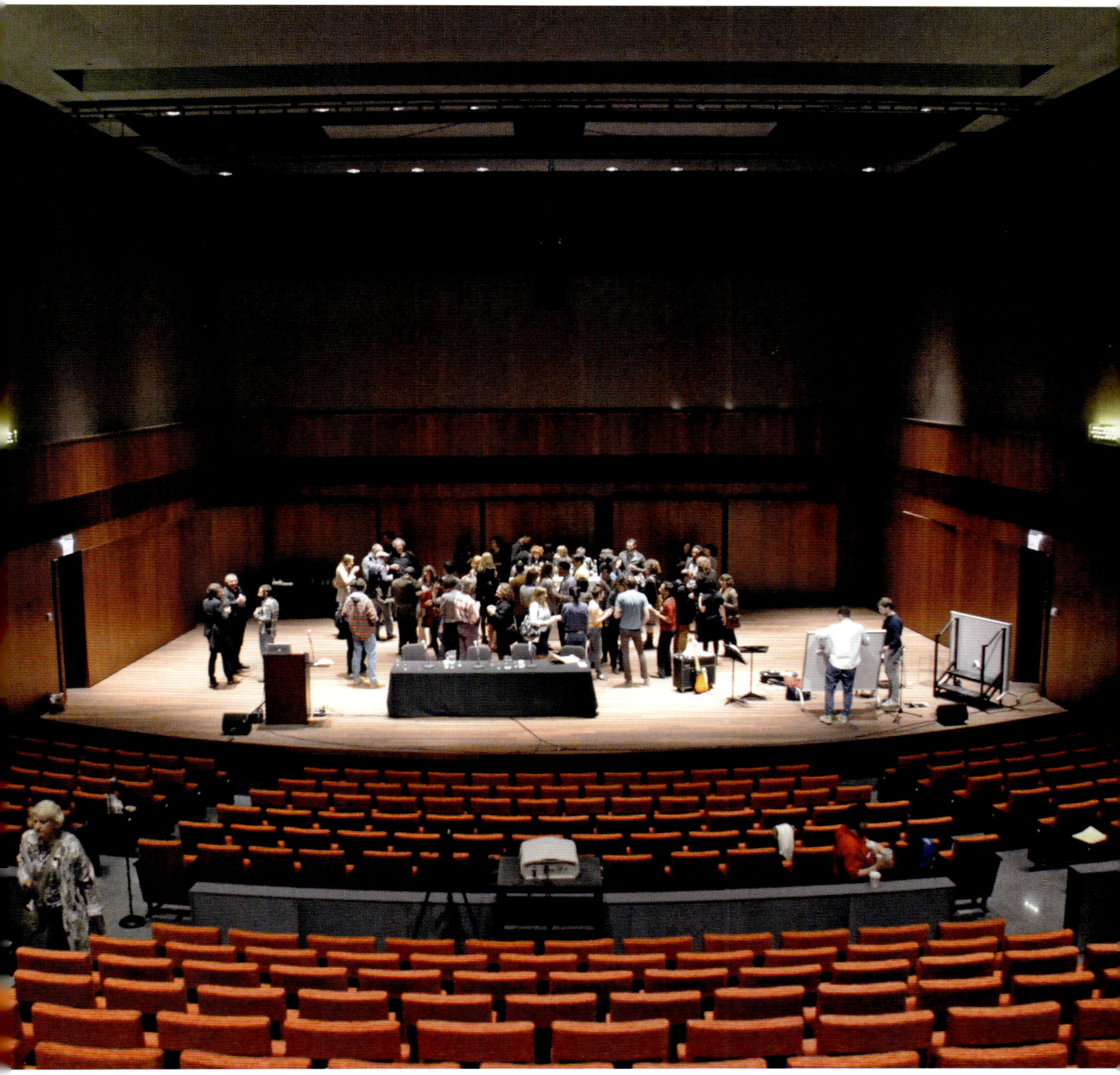

RIGHT: *Neighborhood Infusions* performance during the *Of Hospitality* symposium, Logan Center for the Arts, May 5, 2012

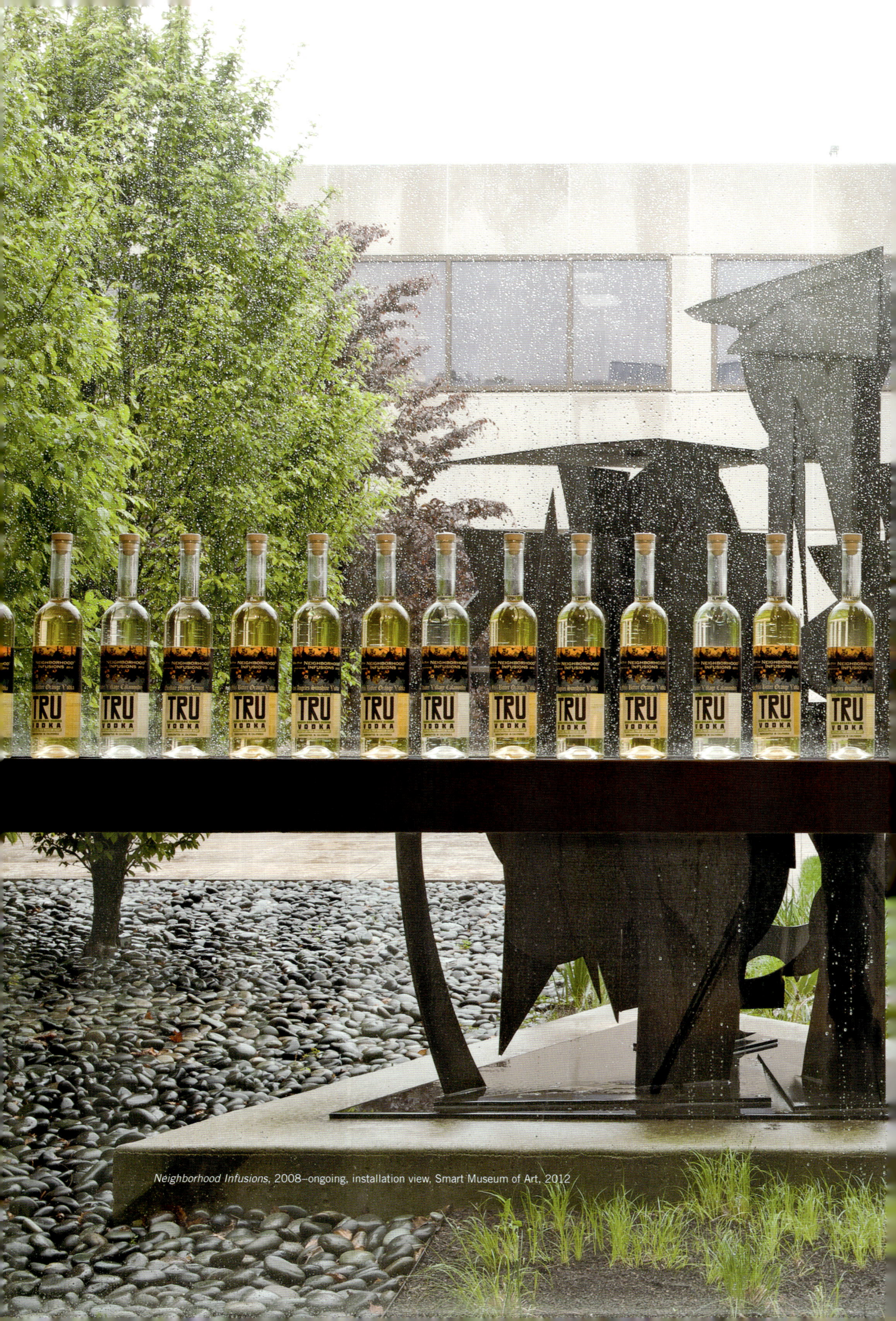

Neighborhood Infusions, 2008–ongoing, installation view, Smart Museum of Art, 2012

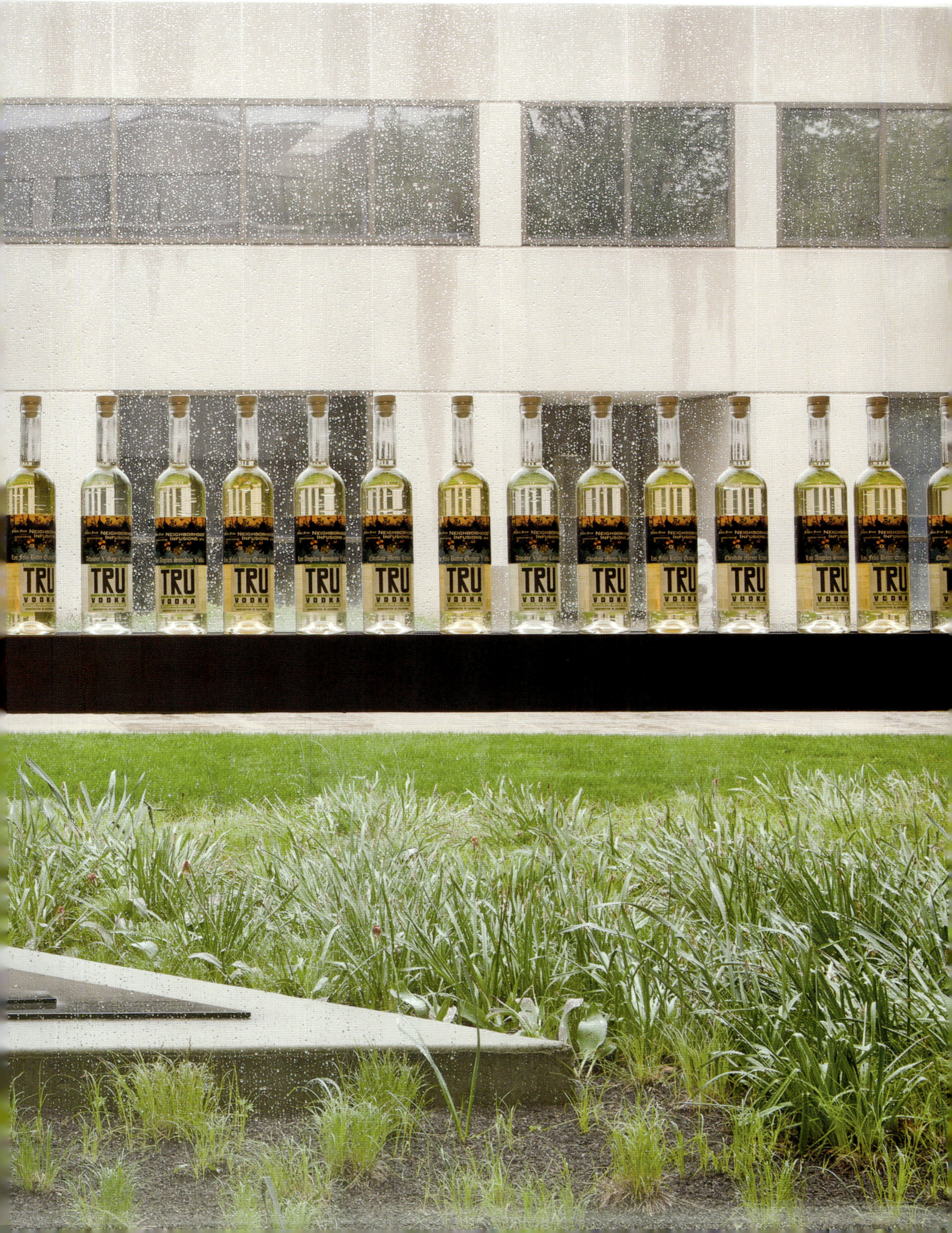
TRU
VODKA

Interview

SMART: Can you describe your paths as artists and sources of inspiration for your work, either in or beyond the context of art?

FALLEN FRUIT: We began our collaboration by looking at urban space and our own neighborhood in Los Angeles and quickly focused on the familiar, overlooked fruit staining the sidewalks and overhanging fences. We decided to call it "public fruit," since it belonged to no one and everyone at the same time; that term pokes at the concept of property, and at whom that concept serves. The object of fruit appears in our work in many forms over time, though none of us had especially worked with it before. David has a background in art installation, video production, and advertising and branding. Matias's background is in writing fiction, writing on art, academic research, and performance art. Austin has a background in photography and video art, and art direction. Fallen Fruit synthesizes our talents in such a way that no single object, text, or image is singly authored. Everything gets cooked together.

Our first collaboration was in 2004 for the *Journal of Aesthetics & Protest*, which issued a call for artist's projects that dealt with a social, political, or urban issue in the form of a proposal rather than a critique. We mapped the public fruit in our neighborhood and wrote a short manifesto. Soon thereafter, we used the map as a guide to take people on evening tours, and a whole other dimension of understanding city neighborhoods opened up. Strangers became friends, homeowners invited us into their yards, and everyone told us stories about fruit, memories, their families, and their neighborhoods. We began to hold *Public Fruit Jams* (2006–ongoing), creating a new temporary public every time we jammed together. Soon the object and symbol of fruit became very attractive to us, and our work concentrated on understanding it both from an objective, political perspective and a more personal and even aesthetic one. We found ways to re-read art or culture and the history of the world, and created new works to present them: wallpapers, installations, and curated archival shows mixing art and everyday objects.

SMART: Tell us about *Neighborhood Infusions*—its impetus, intention, and production—and how it fits into your broader practice.

FF: Like much of our work, *Neighborhood Infusions* is both playful and serious. After working with ideas of place and public fruit, we wanted to see if we could capture the "essence" of a neighborhood in a bottle, the essential flavor or meaning of that place. We picked a dominant or characteristic fruit, bitter oranges in Los Feliz for example, and infused them in vodka to extract their essence. Bottles from different neighborhoods stand on a shelf together and get poured off the gallery wall—as if you could drink the art. We ask people to taste a neighborhood and compare it to their own or another neighborhood. These playful conversations about location and taste give us new ways of thinking about place and the relationship of food to our lives.

SMART: Could you say more about how the performance works? What strategies do you use to open up those conversations? How do they usually function? How does the context shape the kinds of stories that people tell? Is there a Dionysian aspect to this—liquor as an intoxicant that loosens things up? How are these projects weighted differently than those that use jam, etc.?

FF: Originally our goal was to have "docents" serve the bottles off the wall, and it was important that they not be treated anything like bartenders. We wanted to differentiate these bottles from an ordinary bar to signal that they might look like bottles on the wall but they reference something else. The docents had an informal script, which began with asking people where they were from and what kind of things grew in their neighborhood. They also described the flavor essence of the various neighborhoods in the bottles, and this was not scripted—the docents tasted everything and decided for themselves what different neighborhoods taste like (guided of course by the cues in the names, like "Los Feliz Bitter Orange." But of course, the way a plum, or pomegranate, or bitter orange tastes is different to each of us). Docents encouraged people to taste various neighborhoods, compare them, and talk about what their own neighborhood might taste like, which sometimes might be the taste of wet sidewalks, oak trees, or diesel fumes! We hope the conversation broadens out among the group and also broadens into topics like what they expected Hollywood or Venice Beach to taste like.

Several times we could not secure volunteer docents, so we poured the bottles ourselves. We follow the format above but often, knowing the we're the artists, people ask questions about our intentions in the work, and while we don't mind answering, we try to bring the focus back to the idea of neighborhoods and their essence. The Dionysian aspect is inescapable because of the invariable link between fruit, sweetness, and fermentation, which is especially at the core of our relation to the grape and even the apple, through hard cider—which for much of the nineteenth century in the United States was more popular than wine or beer and at the root of Johnny Appleseed's mission.[1] The Dionysian is connected to both delirium but also community festivals, ways of bonding people, making love not war, so in that way sweetness led to delirium, which led to different, intense, and less formal social bonds.

SMART: How would you describe the role of the meal or hospitality in your practice?

FF: We realized early on that the relationship between the guest and the host was central to our project. The first host is the fruit tree, and we are the guests that pick the fruit. Another is the property owner whose tree is in or over public property. Each role carries with it certain obligations, and they often echo back to the obligations between a caregiver and those she or he cares for. Gratitude is one, and cooperation is another. Reciprocity comes into play, especially in the exchange of gifts or food. Compare the term *caregiver* to *caretaker* and you start to see something interesting. Giving and receiving are different from bestowing and taking. Meals are one example,

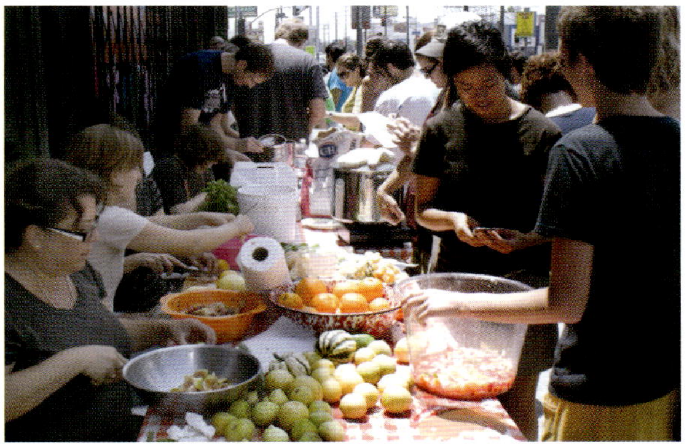

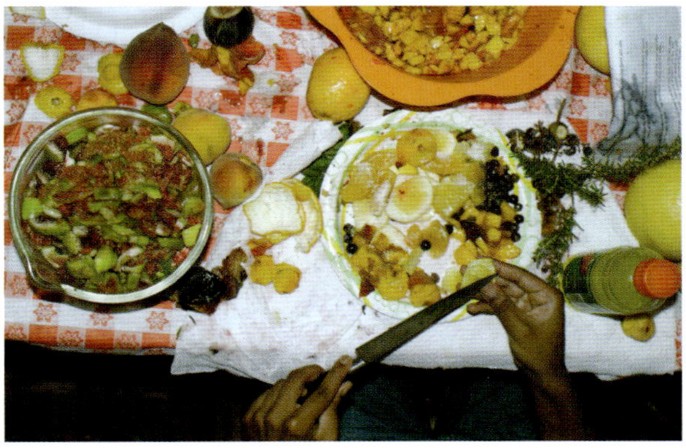

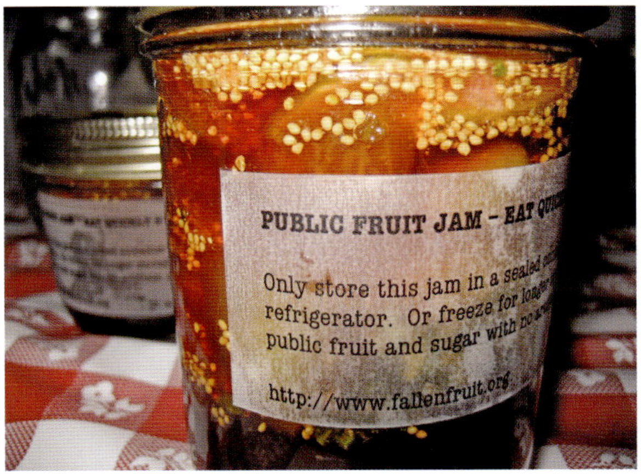

TOP AND MIDDLE: *Public Fruit Jam* at Machine Project, Los Angeles, 2008

BOTTOM: *Public Fruit Jam Jar*, 2006

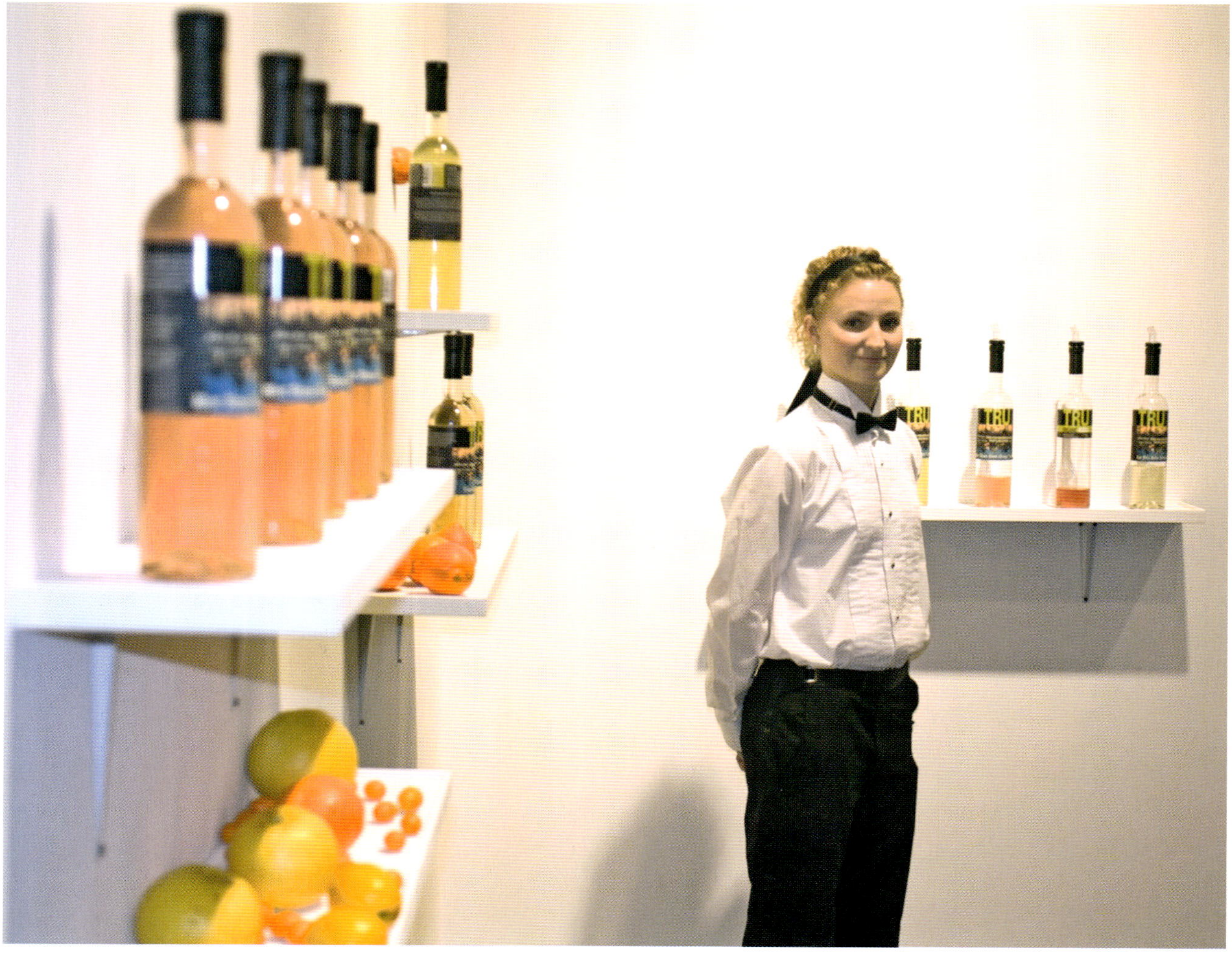

ABOVE AND OPPOSITE: *Neighborhood Infusions*, 2008–ongoing, installation view, Museum of Contemporary Art, San Diego, 2008

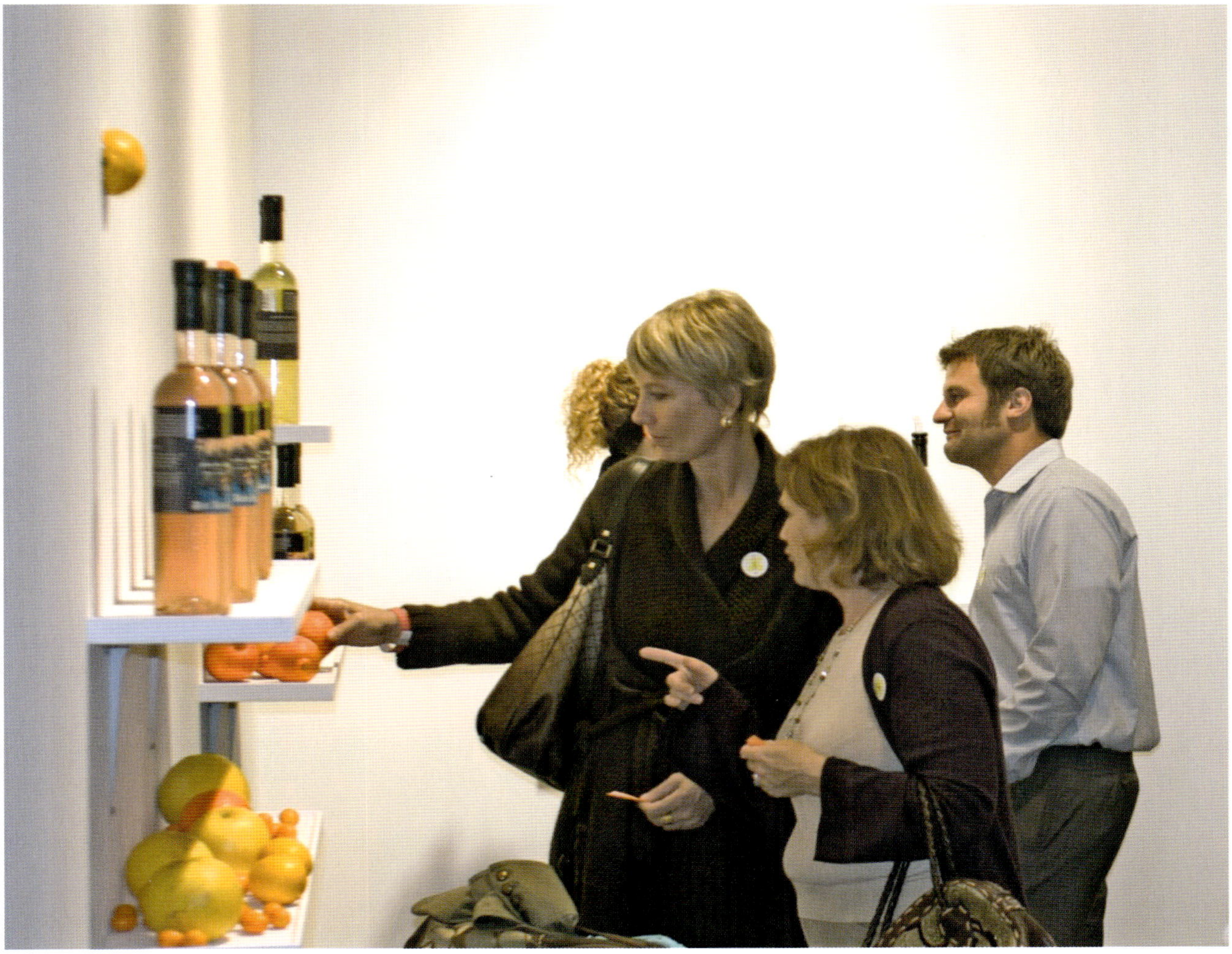

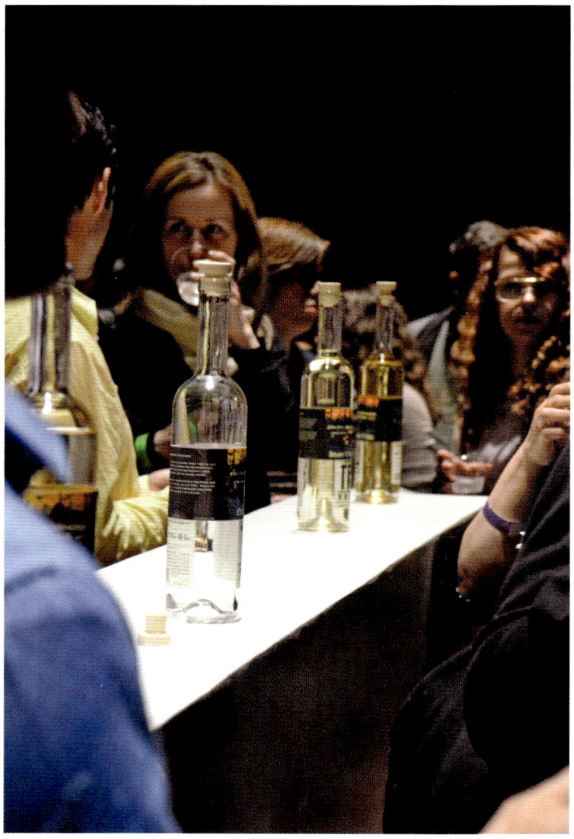

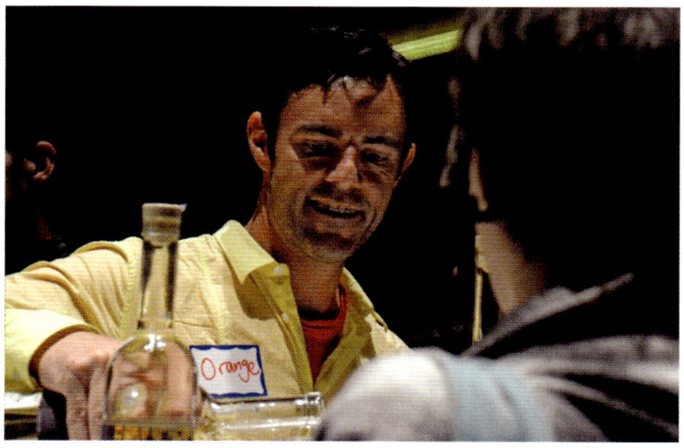

Neighborhood Infusions performance at *Of Hospitality* symposium, Logan Center for the Arts, University of Chicago, May 5, 2012

where guests are expected to receive graciously but also give compliments. Hosts take pleasure in what they do, receive compliments, and get pleasure from them too. The symbol of fruit fuels us in many ways: a symbol of communion, and also a symbol of bounty, as though nature simply gives us fruit without expecting anything in return. There's one thing all fruit has in common: the quality of sweetness, a gentle thing often lacking in everyday life.

The basic relations of guest and host permeate our work. We think a lot about sharing, how something good might not just be owned, given away, or received, but also shared. In exploring urban neighborhoods around the world, we notice how some are stingy and some are generous. We make this assessment based on the amount of public fruit we find. Some neighborhoods share and others hoard.

Our collaboration itself evokes questions of hospitality in a different way. Respect for each other's ideas and labor has a strange relation to food. Whether you labor over an image for ten hours or have a sudden idea (like an apple dropping into your lap), you want your collaborator to at least take a bite and have a taste. Collaboration is not always easy. We extend our concept of collaboration to the audience or participants. In pieces like the *Public Fruit Jam*, they really are collaborators: we're making the work together. The jams are one of our signature creations: it's not us revealing the artwork to a viewer, but all of us bringing both our knowledge and our ingredients to the table. If you bring figs and lavender and we bring lemons to the table, we might make fig-lemon-lavender jam. It's a negotiation and a collaboration. The process is the point, not necessarily the jar of jam. The participatory nature of this work undoes the traditional relationship of artist and viewer. It's not that aesthetics and form don't play into our work, but the participatory is equally important. Our relationship with a host venue is also seen collaboratively. We don't dictate what should happen but arrive at it through a conversation.

SMART: Describe a favorite story about your work.

FF: We regularly collect "fruit stories" when we travel to make work, getting people to tell us a dream, an early memory, or a family story about fruit. Something to show us the speaker's personality or something about the way we think about fruit, positive or negative, factual or imaginary. Many of the things we hear are about childhood, families, lost places or lost fruit trees, and immigration. A man in San Francisco told us about a delicious old apple tree at his family's house. He's the last generation to harvest them, wrap each one in paper, and store them for eating in the cellar. No one younger was interested. Stories like this connect us to a way of life that mostly ended a generation or two ago. Many European immigrants talked about how the family made almond or cherry schnapps for the winter. One girl told us she heard her family talk about bananas and how much they loved them for a long time before she tasted one. When she finally did, she was alone and cut one open and could not believe how disgusting they were, how bitter and tough. A few years later her family asked why she never ate bananas and she said they were too bitter. They laughed and tried to get her to try again. She watched them and realized that the skin was not meant to be eaten, and that actually the banana tasted great.

SMART: What do you hope people take away from your work?

FF: People often see fruit as a symbol of nature, but it's just as much a cultural object, often the result of generations of human selection and hybridization: fruit is a collaboration between us and nature. Fallen Fruit's work plays on fruit as both something very common and something extraordinary or special, even magical: glowing orbs that emerge from trees every year, despite our neglect or ignoring them. There's a sense of wonder and play at the heart of how we approach our material. In one sense, our medium is fruit. We use it as a lens to reimagine the world.

SMART: Could you elaborate on the distinction between public and private fruit? Why do you value public fruit, within the overall category of fruit as a cultural object?

FF: Developing the concept of public fruit was really the linchpin or kernel of our work. We invented the category because it enabled us to talk about two essentially discontinuous paradigms: the public and the private. Fruit is intimate, domestic, ordinary, and personal, while our public life is anonymous, non-specific, and hardly intimate at all. We were interested not just in how urban public space is used, but how people think of us. We were fascinated with the border of private and public property, and the way in which the (legal and conceptual) slipperiness of that border could be examined as a commons. We coined the term *public fruit* as a way to talk about this "new" resource of collectivity. It was a kind of *détournement*, which as McKenzie Wark explains, is the opposite of a quotation. "The key to *détournement* is its challenge to private property," says Wark. "*Détournement* attacks a kind of fetishism, where the products of collective human labor in the cultural realm can become a mere individual's property."[2] Fruit as a cultural object is not just domestic but a radiant example of collective labor, often generations of it. Asking people on our tours to pick the fruit hanging over fences and sidewalks often challenges their ideas of propriety and property, much as putting a bottle of flavored vodka on a gallery wall challenges what they think might be the role of art.

---

[1] For a treatise on that legend, see Michael Pollan, *The Botany of Desire: A Plant's-Eye View of the World* (New York: Random House, 2002).

[2] McKenzie Wark, *The Beach Beneath the Street: The Everyday Life of the Situationist International* (New York: Verso, 2011), 36.

Theaster Gates

THEASTER GATES OFTEN DESCRIBES himself as a potter—a word that conveys a literally down-to-earth sensibility and expert capacity to craft raw material into form. Gates's practice, however, extends far beyond the shaping of clay, to the molding of both the tangible (urban places, old archives) and the immaterial (housing policy, African American culture and history). Dorchester Projects—the metaproject that encompasses Gates's project for *Feast*—blends these materials and categories into a rich brew. This project anchors an international art and urban design practice that includes discussion, meal- and music-based ritual, installation, sculpture, urban planning, and ceramics.[1] In these interrelated activities, Gates creates social sculpture by activating dormant surpluses of care, money, time, expertise, raw materials, and energy. This redirection of economic and creative flows recalls his ease at the potter's wheel, guiding the spinning clay into new forms.

For Dorchester Projects, Gates is transforming several once-vacant buildings in the Grand Crossing neighborhood on Chicago's South Side into a place that cultivates new forms of knowledge exchange, collaborative work, and pleasure. This initiative began to take form in 2006, was officially launched in 2009, and continues to morph. At this writing, one building houses books, ceramics, and a collection of glass slides; another is being transformed to house entire print runs of *JET* and *Ebony* magazines, and a third will soon become the Black Cinema House. All of the buildings are spatially organized to commingle research, work, and play: several contain living areas for Gates or visitors, and each includes open areas for gatherings—always intimately scaled to preserve and respect the domestic nature of the buildings and of the block itself.

For *Feast*, Gates premiered *Soul Pavilion*, the latest addition to Dorchester Projects. He hosted a series of intimate Sunday dinners: ritual meals designed to call out the complex tastes and histories of soul food and to bring people together on this particular block, across lines of race, class, and culture. Building on Gates's premise, chefs Erick Williams and Michael Kornick of Chicago's MK Restaurant and soul food expert Erika Dudley designed the menu. At each dinner, a mix of guests and members of the public chosen by lottery sat elbow to elbow along thin wooden tables. They sampled dishes like the "black sacrament" (chitlins), served on specially designed ceramics that Gates produced in collaboration with Japanese master potter Kouichi Ohara. Sermons by spoken-word artist Orron Kenyatta, neighbor Irma Dixon, and other friends of Dorchester Projects punctuated the meals, alternating with music performed by Yaw Aygeman, Khari Lemuel, Titus Wonsey, and other members of the Black Monks of Mississippi. At each of these occasions, Gates used the history of soul and the rituals of hospitality to bring people together across lines of culture and class—not in order to smooth over difference or difficulty but rather to celebrate the power of a contemporary, hybrid complexity. Intended to evolve into a soul food enterprise on the block, the *Soul Pavilion* may lead to a new South Side soul food initiative, as well as continuing to inform the ongoing events at Dorchester Projects. These rich experiences connected back to the museum in the form of a *Soul Food Starter Kit* (2012), a sculpture made of reclaimed wood, ceramics like those used at the dinners, and a wooden fragment inscribed with Gates's *soul manifesto #2* in graphite.

---

[1] Most recently, Gates founded a nonprofit organization in 2011, the ReBuild Foundation, which runs collaborative building and cultural and economic development projects in under-resourced communities in Chicago, Omaha, and Saint Louis. In another ongoing project, Gates extended his pottery practice in 2009, working with Soul Manufacturing Corporation and local residents in various communities to create new collections of ceramic wares that celebrate traditional African American foods. Soul Manufacturing Corporation currently works with pottery centers and potters in Liling (China), Omaha, Nebraska, and Tokoname (Japan).

OPPOSITE: *Soul Pavilion* dinner at Dorchester Projects, March 11, 2012

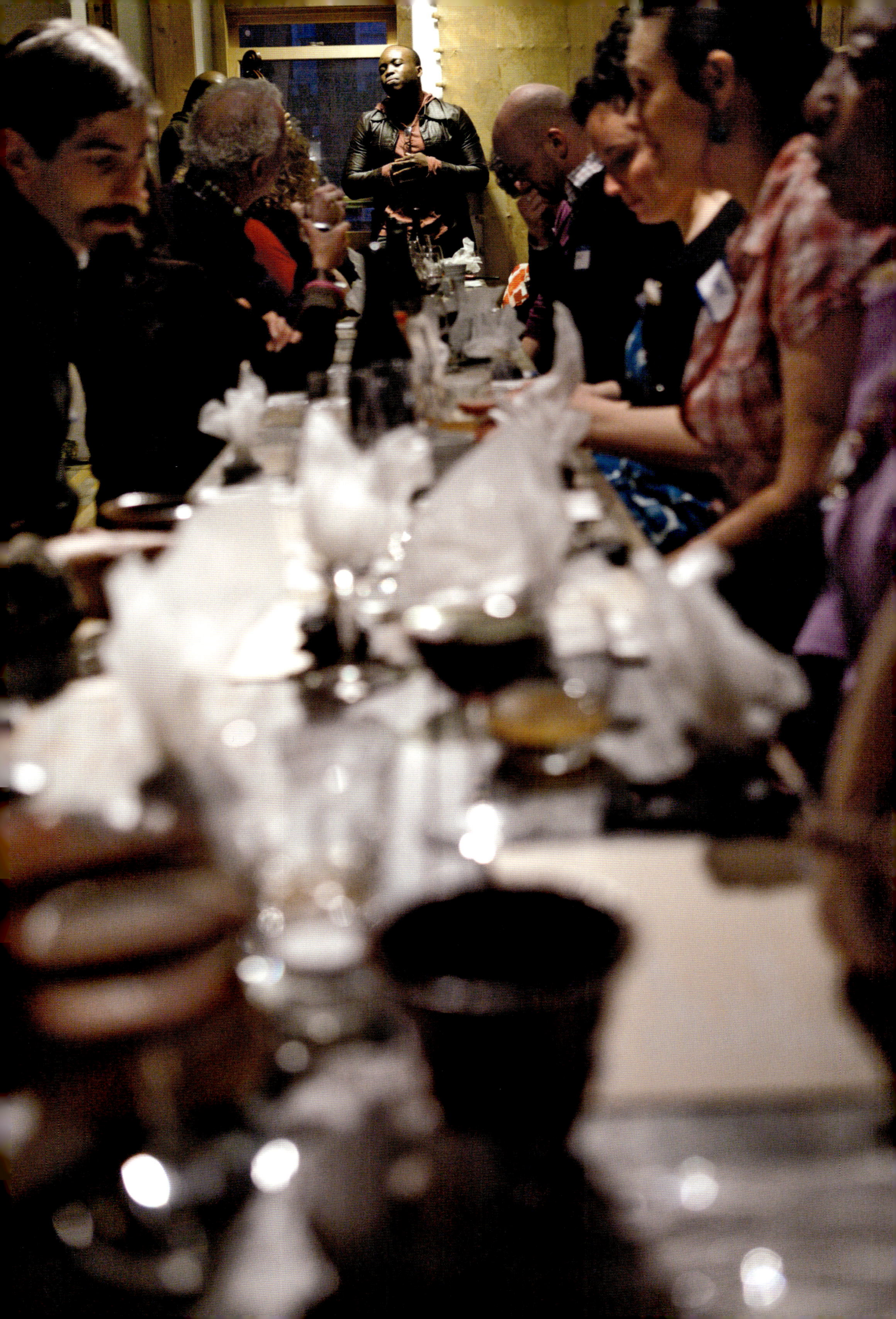

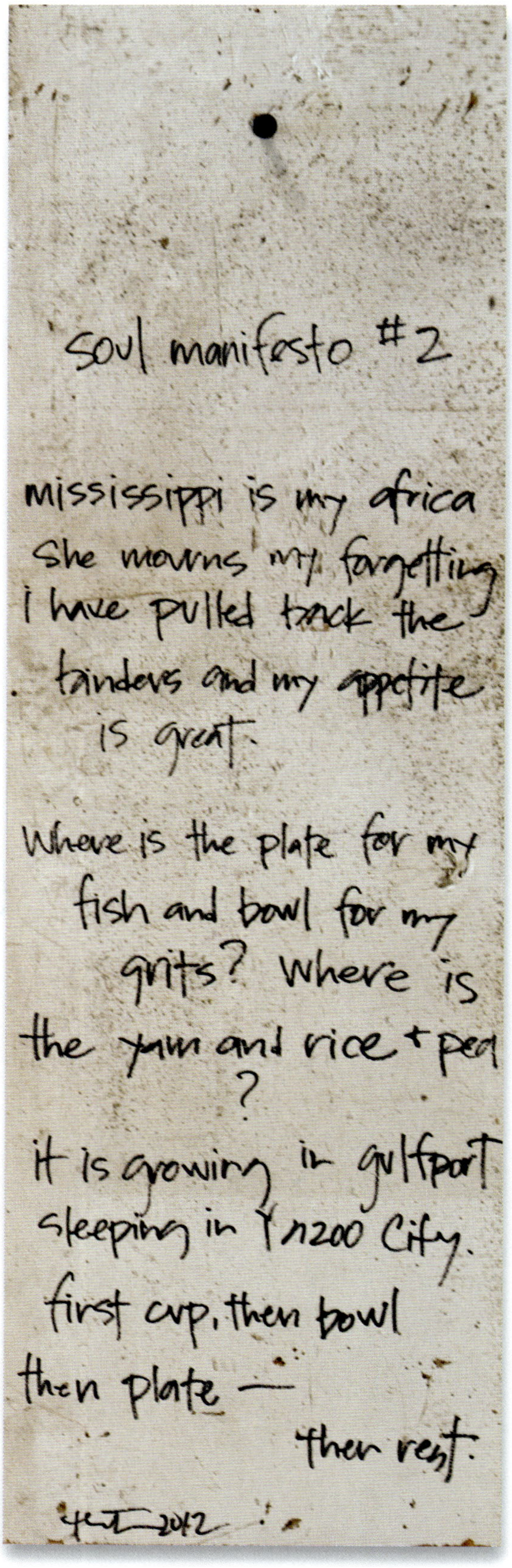

TOP: *Soul Food Starter Kit* (detail), 2012

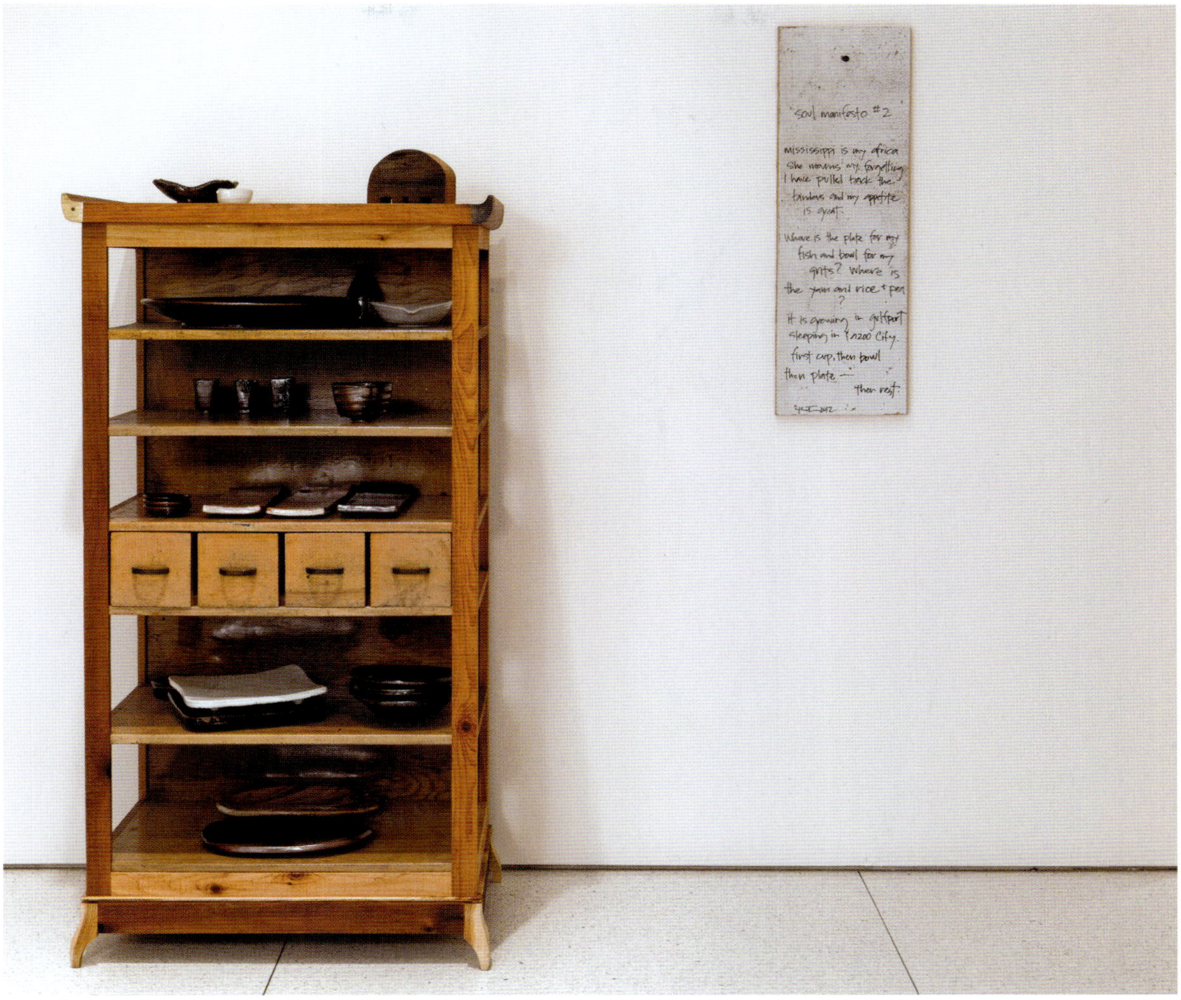

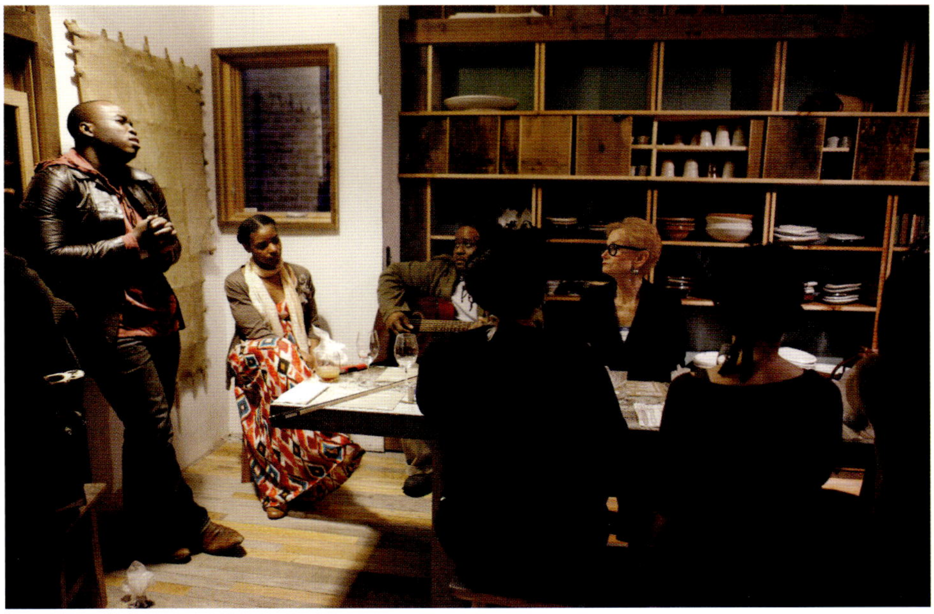

TOP: *Soul Food Starter Kit*, 2012, installation view, Smart Museum of Art, 2012

BOTTOM: Members of the Black Monks of Mississippi perform at *Soul Pavilion* dinner at Dorchester Projects, March 11, 2012

SMART: Can you describe your path as an artist and sources of inspiration for your work, either in or beyond the context of art?

THEASTER GATES: My practice in many ways is still evolving. The black political and religious spheres have a huge impact on my thinking and disposition; they drive why and how I make. The writings of Eldridge Cleaver, Angela Davis, bell hooks, Bobby Seale, and Cornell West were all thrown in the mix over the years. As I began to study urban planning, the world of the spatial-political unfolded: texts by Frantz Fanon, Henri Lefebvre, and Karl Marx became a bigger part of my life. A little later, reflecting on writings of contemporary artists and art historians like Darby English, Adrian Piper, James Porter, and Robert Storr had a huge impact on me. I still remember when Maya Lin won the Vietnam Memorial. Dan Peterman opened his space on the South Side to me as an urban planner and artist when I was just beginning to carve out a larger practice.

Art became a way that I could address both the formal and the guttural.

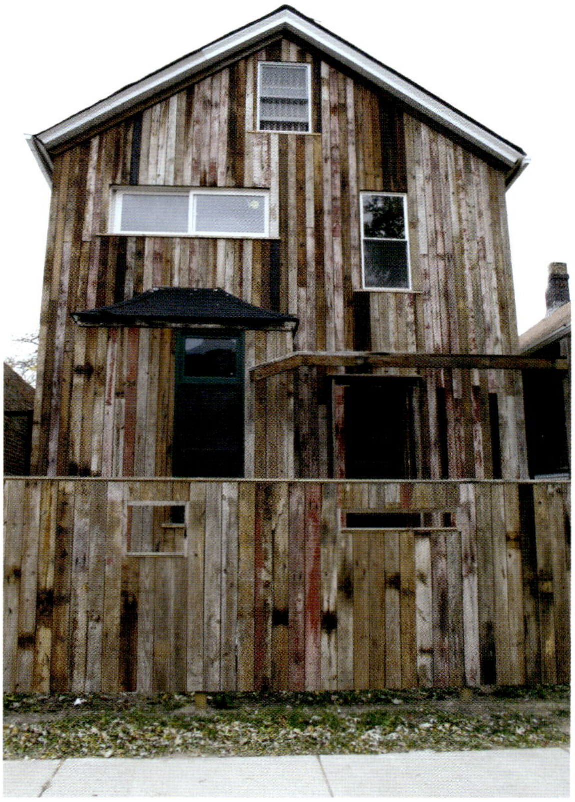

The Dorchester Projects building in which the *Soul Pavilion* dinners for *Feast* were held; the project also includes several other renovated structures

SMART: Tell us about Dorchester Projects—its impetus, intention, and production—and how it fits into your broader practice.

TG: Dorchester Projects was really born out of necessity. I needed a place to stay and make work, then shortly after, the housing market tanked—necessarily so. *Dorchester* was born at the moment when much of the United States was becoming foreclosed. I bought a couple of small buildings on my block. Once there were buildings, programming the spaces was pretty straightforward. I have things that I collected and I wanted to share them. People offered to help—builders, other artists like Matthew Metzger and John Preus, programmers in the city, and folk on the block—and all became invested in the possibility of culture manifesting on the block.

It's only now that words like *intention* are even important, if they are. The word that comes to mind instead is *emergence*. Intention dictates, emergence allows. I have spent much of my time making room for things to happen, creating the conditions whereby great things might happen and new relationships could develop. Most of the time, it works.

With regard to productivity, there were some gaps in the cultural sphere of the city. Folk in some communities were doing an amazing job of mobilizing and organizing, but often, artists of color and folk who lived outside of the city center were left out of the fun, the resources, and the knowledge sharing. Alongside attempting to grow an art practice, I felt it my charge to be a part of the gap-filling, which including space production, place making, and sometimes, financing cultural activity. Over time, it was all just the stuff that needed to happen in a day and slowly the designations of "art" or "not art" went away. I just do what I think I should be doing.

SMART: Tell us about *Soul Pavilion*.

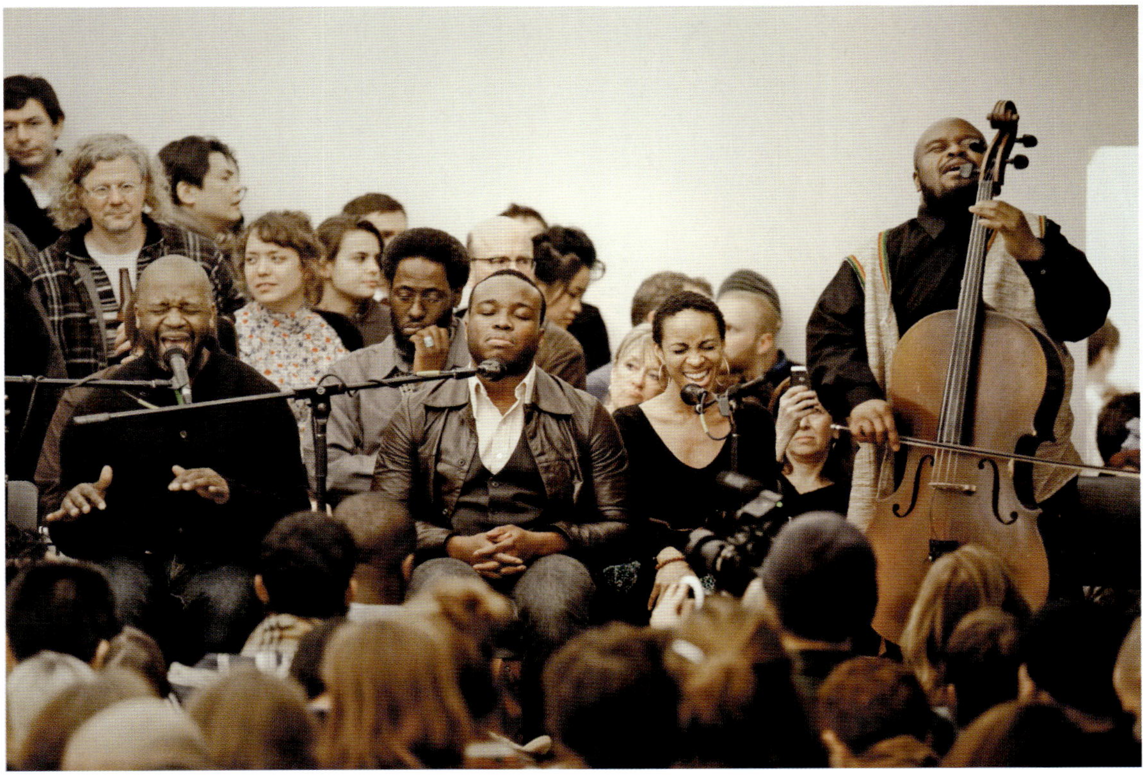

Performance by Theaster Gates (seated left) and the Black Monks of Mississippi, Smart Museum of Art, February 15, 2012

TG: Originally when I conceived of the idea of *Soul Pavilion*, I thought of it as a particular place where ceremonial meals could be served. But over the past year, it has become clear that *Soul Pavilion* is more of an idea. It's the opportunity to make a space where amazing interactions can happen around the foods of black people.

The conversation about food for African Americans in America is a really complicated story, one that is both about our ability to bring foods from other places and also about foods that represent a kind of inferior relationship to a really dark past. So how do you grapple with history via food—especially while also thinking about some of the challenges in African American communities around health and health disparity? In neighborhoods like this on the South Side, access to healthy food is very limited. So how can the *Soul Pavilion* be a space that opens up questions about hospitality and how communities of color are hospitable and how people are hospitable? How do we really reflect on diabetes and high blood pressure in relationship to the things that we eat?

The word *pavilion* is also important. The spaces aren't afraid to be temporary and aren't afraid to incorporate my complex history with the rest of the world. So there will be a lot of Asian influence in the utensils that we use, in the formation of the ceremony, and in the way that portions are presented. I'm really excited to have this kind of mash-up—this collision of cultural ideas—translate into a meal for lots of people.

This project got me really excited to reach out to friends in Japan, China, Korea, and parts of Africa, and ask them about the utensils that they use for the foods of their people. This past year, I'm really honored that I was able to invite three friends from Japan who are production potters and great people who would answer this question with me: "What is soul food ware?"

We reflected on tea ceremony and Shintoism, but also on collard greens and the juice that they produce. How do we make a body of work that really captures the sacredness in food and in sitting down and having a meal together, and also the kind of aesthetic and ritual value in it? In a couple of months we've produced over three thousand ceramic wares that will live as part of this idea of the pavilion until it finally has a permanent home somewhere. The three locations on Dorchester—6916, 6918, and 6901—all function as sites for hosting and eating and entertaining and we'll really use the block as our ritual site instead of one building, and maybe different things will happen in the different buildings.

SMART: Can you talk about the dinners that will be occurring for *Feast* at Dorchester Projects?

TG: The dinners in some way give me an opportunity to leverage ritual and leverage space and to ask hard questions in ways that people don't normally talk about in Chicago, with groups of people who don't normally get together. Not unlike Michael Rakowitz's *Enemy Kitchen,* I imagine, there's a part of the project that is trying to get at sincere conversations between people who maybe live in very different worlds. Ritual becomes this tool that allows for people to feel safe. And ritual combined with dinner does even more. If someone says as part of dinner, "You have to talk about this topic," it gives us all an excuse to be more open, more transparent, more vulnerable than we might be normally. And hopefully people will trust the dinner process enough to allow themselves to be vulnerable.

What is ritual activity? How are rituals born? I'm very excited that as part of the dinner there will also be an opportunity for performance, an opportunity to reflect on beauty.

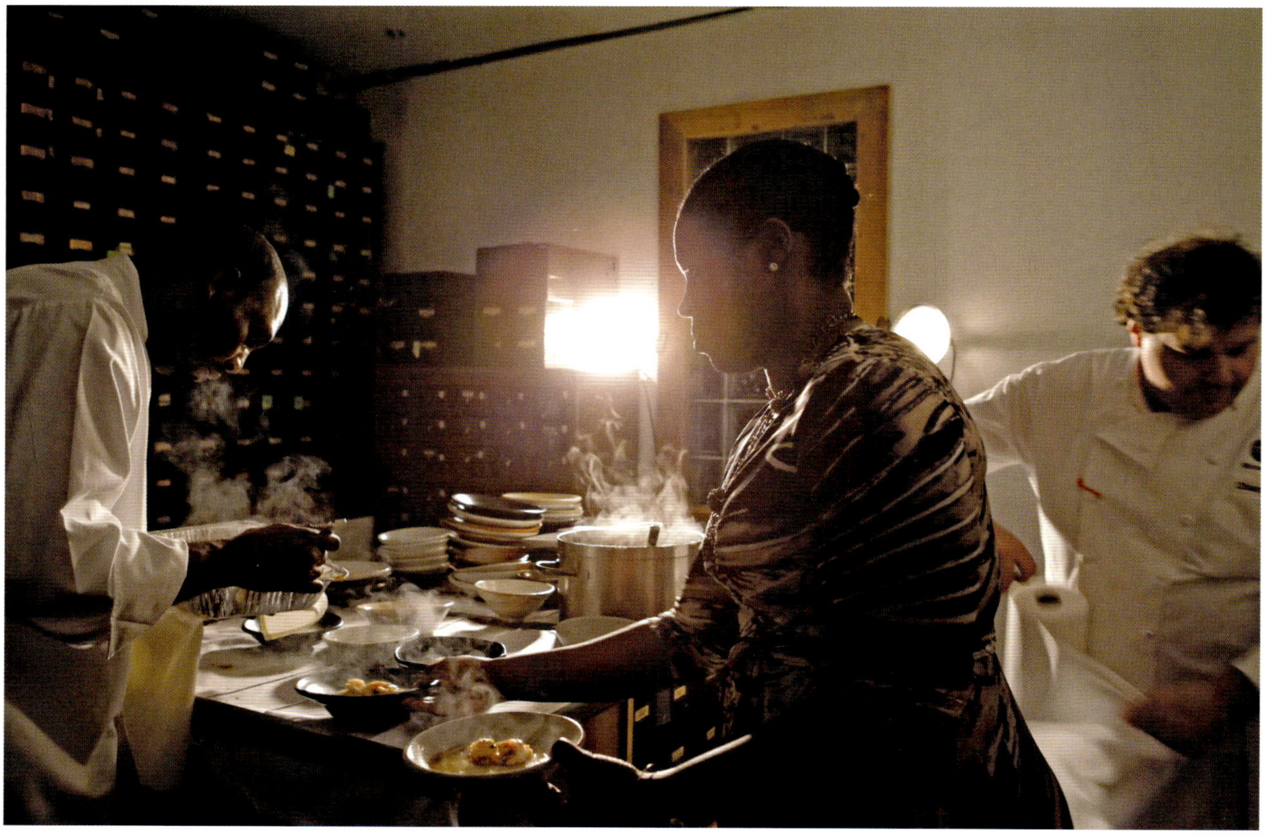

Erick Williams (left), Marlease Bushnell (center), and Michael Kornick (right) prepare and serve a *Soul Pavilion* dinner at Dorchester Projects, March 11, 2012

In some ways we're borrowing those ritual moments from tea ceremony. We're borrowing those moments from dinners at my house on Sundays, where if someone was visiting and was a really good singer, my mom might say, "Hey Tawana, you should get out there and sing a song." We'll have those moments that are both spontaneous and thoughtful, allowing people a more intimate, more vulnerable space.

SMART: Can you talk about the role performance plays in your practice?

TG: Performance for me has been a really wonderful mechanism of driving the point. There are ways in which the meal or an object says a lot about a thing. But because acts of performance have been so directly associated with acts of belief and ritual, performance has become a big part of my life. I developed a small ensemble called the Black Monks of Mississippi. The Black Monks will perform for the opening of *Feast* and we'll also be in residence during the *Feast* dinners to have these special moments where the sharing that happens is really thoughtful sharing, really resonant music. It dovetails or complements the amazing food that we're going to eat. Food and song, song and work, those things have always gone together for me. So I'm excited that more and more of the time, more and more of my artistic practice allows me to unify all of those things.

SMART: How would you describe the role of the meal in your practice?

TG: There have been moments in my practice when the meal seemed necessary. I use the meal as a vehicle for other things, not unlike my relationship with ceramic production and in some ways, art production. These projects that include the meal allow other things to take

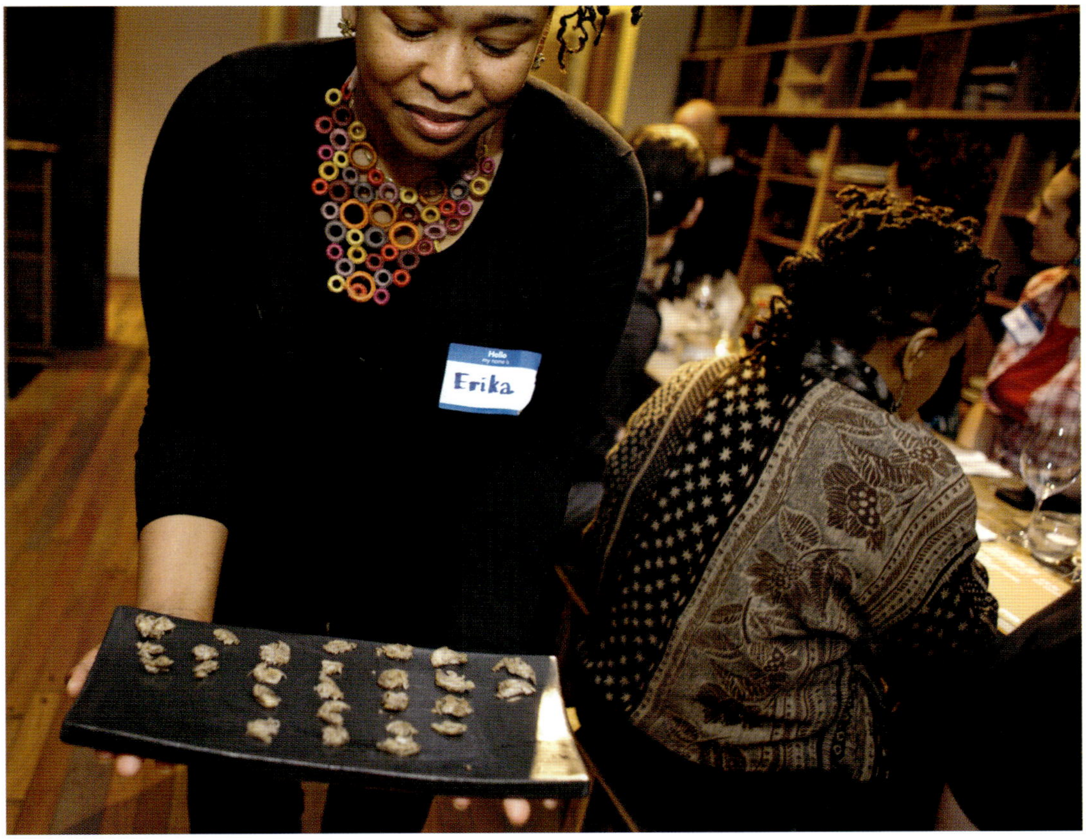

Erika Dudley serves "the black sacrament" (chitlins) at a *Soul Pavilion* dinner, Dorchester Projects, March 11, 2012

place. With the Yamaguchi Institute, for a project I did at the Hyde Park Art Center in Chicago, my intention was to explore ritual, cultural plurality, and the issue of space-based race politics. While clay and the meal were both necessary actions in the work, they allowed a platform for more complex moments of engagements. Now with the *Soul Manufacturing Corporation* and *Soul Pavilion*, I am more interested in cottage industry, and local forms of cultural production and economic regeneration in poor black communities. The food should be good and healthy nonetheless, but they are in service to some other schemes of mine.

SMART: What is the *Soul Food Starter Kit*?

TG: One of the things that I wanted to do in this exhibition was make sure that while I was doing all of this stuff on my block, there are also ways that some of the stuff from the block went back to the museum as much as the museum was also going to be here. I also wanted to objectify the idea of the soul food ritual. To do that I've developed this *Soul Food Starter Kit*—part fancy bento box, part big country pantry, and also just an opportunity to reflect on the history of food in contemporary practice. The *Soul Food Starter Kit*, let's say it's a meal for twelve. It would have everything you would need to have the perfect soul food meal wherever you are if you can move this 300- or 400-pound thing or if it sits at the Smart Museum as a home, or if it's in someone else's home. It allows us then to ask harder questions about the relationship between objects and ritual, between acts of generosity and the history of that generosity via food. I'm really excited about it. The *Starter Kits* also give us a chance to allow people to ask questions about their own cultural values and cultural utensils and ways of eating and ways of making meaning.

The work that I'm involved in has a lot of moving parts. It's great when there's an opportunity for an exhibition or a museum opportunity or an entrepreneurial opportunity to unite lots of the things that seem disparate. So my interest in space making and place making, alongside my history with ceramics, alongside my desire to reinvest in neighborhoods—those things fit really nicely together with *Feast*. I hope that the total work that I've been engaged in makes a lot of sense to the people who will come to the block and I hope that it makes sense to the people who live on the block. And maybe it's fun and new relationships are born.

SMART: Do questions about hospitality figure into your process or thinking?

TG: Absolutely. My mom taught me to be nice to people. I want the people who I work with to be kind of generous to people, even if we don't have lots to offer. I am always learning new ways of showing care. Hospitality is laced through it all. It's the action part of love and caring.

SMART: Can you say more about your collaboration with the potters, Haruka Komatsu, Yoko Matsumoto, and Kouichi Ohara?

TG: For *Feast*, I wanted to go back to the place where my love of ceramic production increased: Tokoname, Japan. Tokoname and its International Workshop of Ceramic Artists and Teachers was a special program that my teacher Ingrid Lilligren turned me on to. It's a place that really advanced my love for the material and Japanese culture. I wanted Japan to play a role in the creation of my ceremonial soul food wares. Who better to help think about ceremony than Japanese potters! I went to pitch the idea and three potters decided to take me up on my offer to stay on the South Side of Chicago with me and make pots for two months. These pots would become the permanent collection of works for the *Soul Pavilion*, and, folks would only be able to experience the works by having dinner with me and my neighbors. In many ways, *Feast* gave me permission to engage the world, not only around the conversation of food and utility, but also around hospitality, cultural exchange, and in some ways, renewal. I love when projects help you think bigger ideas and rethink ways of making and doing.

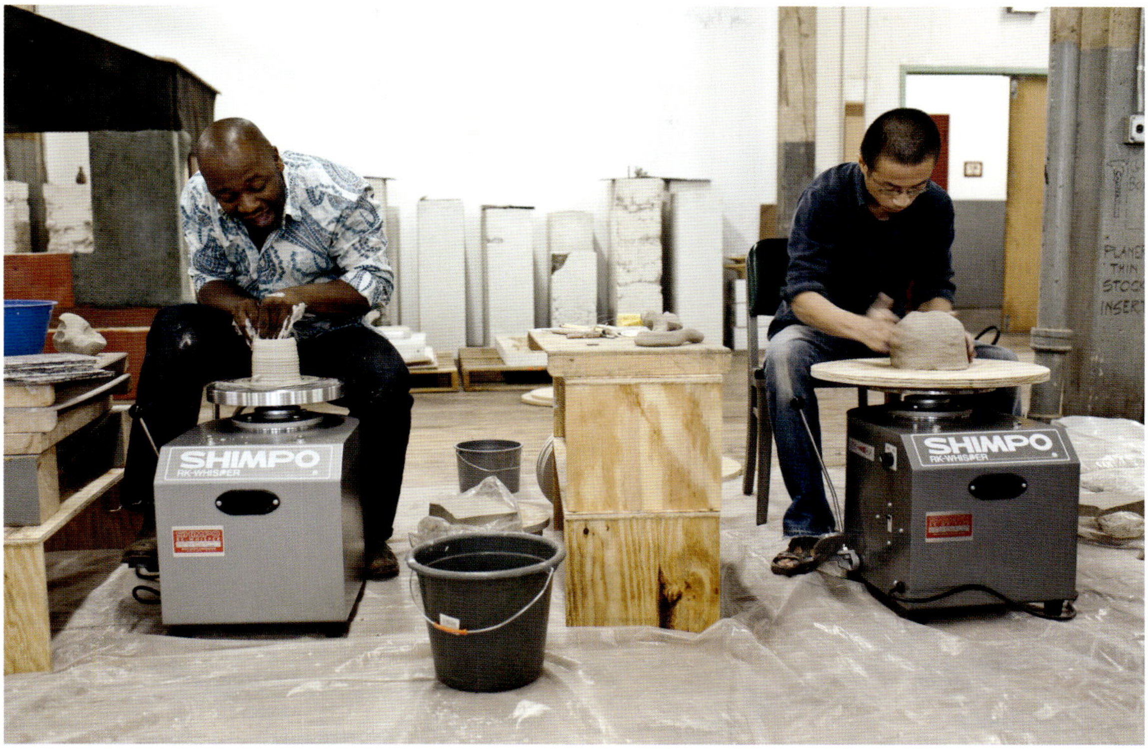

Gates (left) collaborated with Japanese potter Kouichi Ohara (right) to design and produce ceramics for *Soul Pavilion*

SMART: What does it mean to you to be included in a show called *Feast: Radical Hospitality in Contemporary Art*?

TG: It's exciting that soul food—my mom's simple recipes, and her life of making—might be important to others and the legacy of her generosity and the great ideas and recipes of others will continue to live a little while longer.

It also starts to marry things that were outside of my contemporary art practice, and that seemed for a long time incompatible. It gives me the opportunity to give thought to how soul food gets to live in the contemporary, and how so much of my practice, which is about a kind of radical hospitality (or fits nicely alongside that), also opens up whole new communities who are marginalized to the contemporary art world. So more of my world is made available or put in concert with my love of contemporary art practices. More of my friends have more reason to get to know each other because we're all directly involved in this act of sharing.

I also think that this becomes a timely moment to reflect on the role of non-object-based art and give light to practices that have always valued people and the opportunity for circumstance to make cool things happen. I feel really honored to be a part of it.

SMART: What do you hope people take away from your work?

TG: Cultural production (ritual making) and place making are a lot alike. Both require groups of people to decide over time that a set of ideas or a place are important. When ceremony is added to everyday things, they become more special. I am very excited to have a chance to reflect on the foods of black people in an expansive way. I hope people will leave also feeling as if ritual practices and more open forms of conviviality are important. There's a possibility that closed circles might open a bit and that things in Chicago could be a bit more mixed. I want people to take away an appetite for others.

Dorchester Projects Ritual Evening #044, May 10, 2011: Sermon 1

by Jacqueline Terrassa

> A pause, a rose, something on paper.
> —Lyn Hejinian, *My Life*[1]

We come for different reasons, and we may or may not tell ourselves what those reasons are. Ask yourself: Why did you come? We may not know. "I come to 6916 South Dorchester because . . ." "You came to this gathering to . . ." Our reasons may not be important and this question may not matter. The more significant question may be instead: What can I bring? Or: What is it that I offer?

The latter question—"What is it that I offer?"—is not about how we might be productive or even useful this evening. Instead, it is about being *generous without outcome*. And maybe this is why we come—maybe this is why I came to be part of an occasion without a predetermined end. We come to allow the evening to take us where it might, and in this way, we open ourselves up to a powerful process. Perhaps it's not unlike going to church or temple (though here I will speak for myself and what going to church has meant for me). At a place like church we are granted an *occasion to gather*—a time, a place, a setting, a ritual to join in—and in that structure we find permission to engage and to let go. Both.

Here, tonight, we're not striving to be better people. Maybe we just came for a really good meal. In fact, our host wants to be just that—a great host. He's not placing higher moral demands on us, though he *does ask something of us.* What he is asking of us is not to feel better from others by being here, or to grant him legitimacy by virtue of what each of us represents to each other. Instead, he is asking us to partake in *a ritual of generosity*.

What do *we* bring? What can *we* offer?

Our host offers us a space of ritual. In moments like this one—whether a dinner, an installation, a fire hose encased, or a redevelopment project—he offers us a specific structure. By this I mean a set of materials and social conditions that produce a beauty without definition.

A question often is asked of our host: Is it art? At first, the question was asked because he called himself a potter. Then it was asked because he sang with a group called The Black Monks of Mississippi: Is that art? And are they really monks? And he was also an art administrator and a teaching artist. He started orchestrating dinners and events. More questions: Is it art or entertainment? Art or audience development for museums? Art or super-special catering? Art or performance? When the community and workforce development activities began in earnest, the question became whether

RITUAL EVENING #045
SUNDAY, FEBRUARY 19 2012 6:30 PM
DORCHESTER PROJECTS // 6916 SOUTH DORCHESTER

:15	GREETING
:10	SMALL BITES (HORS D'OEUVRES)
:15	BLACK SACRAMENT
:07	SERMON 1
:05	BLACK EYED PEA FRITTERS // SOUTHERN RED BELL PUREE
:10	SOUL PAVILION
:15	FRIED OKRA // LEROY'S REMOULADE // POACHED MISSISSIPPI SHRIMP // CREOLE MAYO // SMOKED GULF CATFISH // PICKLED BANANA PEPPERS // WILD WATERCRESS // YELLOW MUSTARD SEED // LEMON
:07	SERMON 2
:15	COLLARDS AND SMOKED TURKEY // TURNIP TOPS AND BOTTOMS WITH FATBACK // HOE CAKES
:20	MADEA'S POT ROAST // BRAISED POTATOES // CARROTS AND POT LIQUOR
:05	TOAST
:15	RED VELVET CAKE
:05	GOODBYES

SOUL PAVILION

Menu from a *Soul Pavilion* dinner, February 19, 2012

the objects were candy for the art world. Once again, is it what *we* call art? Visibility is power. Power elicits suspicion. *What* we call it is irrelevant. What it's *about* is more complex, both more and less important. What matters most is the *intention* behind it and the *trust* that we are willing to place in that intention. *Trust is the one thing our host asks of us.*

"Back and backward, why, wide and wider. Such that art is inseparable from the search for reality," poet Lyn Heijinian observes.[2]

I offer you a moment to pause and dwell.

Jacqueline Terrassa is Managing Museum Educator for Gallery and Studio Programs at the Metropolitan Museum of Art, New York.

Terrassa delivered this text as a speech—a "sermon"—at one of a series of ritual evenings that Gates hosted during 2011 while preparing for *Feast*.

---

[1] Lyn Hejinian, *My Life* (Los Angeles: Green Integer, 2002).

[2] Ibid.

InCUBATE

WHILE STUDYING ARTS administration at the School of the Art Institute of Chicago, Roman Petruniak, Abigail Satinsky, and the late Ben Schaafsma decided to create a collaborative framework through which to experiment with flexible, sustainable, and ethical approaches to arts administration and arts funding. The result was InCUBATE: "Institute for Community Understanding Between Art and The Everyday." Bryce Dwyer and Matthew Joynt joined the group later. For a time, the InCUBATE project included a storefront space that housed an informal artists' residency, an archive, exhibitions, and public programs; the group currently organizes projects in a variety of ad hoc situations and spaces. All of their activities are linked by a research-based ethos that they describe as a "slow build,"[1] grounded by their commitment to developing and revising ideas in real time, and in conversation with others.

From 2007 to 2009, the group hosted *Sunday Soup* in their Chicago storefront space as a means to raise funds for creative projects: guests would contribute a modest sum for a meal, eat together, and review and vote on short proposals made by individuals or collaboratives seeking support. The democratically selected project proposal would receive the dinner funds. This microgrant program simultaneously created small funding streams, offered a countermodel to standard funding mechanisms, and helped to build a wider network of awareness and potential support for all of the projects presented for consideration. Soup became the primary medium for this project for both pragmatic and sensory reasons; as InCUBATE explains, "Soup is the center of the meal because it is nourishing, economical, and easy to prepare in large batches." InCUBATE's original *Sunday Soup* idea has since spread rapidly. With their support, the model has been adapted by other groups around the world who have embraced it as a direct, inventive, and pleasurable way to sustain creative work and friendships during the economic downturn. The most public manifestation of this phenomenon to date is *The International Day of Soup*: InCUBATE and other groups orchestrated more than one hundred soup-based community microgrant events that were held around the world on October 1, 2011, as part of Creative Time's *Living as Form* exhibition.

Sunday Soup was included in *Feast* as a project that sits on the edge of the exhibition's parameters. InCUBATE is not an artists' group, and *Sunday Soup* was not conceived as an art project—but it seemed crucial to include it in the exhibition as a local meal-based arts initiative that has had such a strong resonance, and as one that reinforces the potential of hospitality as a creative and administrative practice. This posed a challenge of representation, and InCUBATE considers the modest installation they made for the Chicago presentation of *Feast* as a productively failed attempt to give *Sunday Soup* meaningful form within the museum space. Inspired in part by the installation's inadequacy as a representation of their practice, and in part by their own interest in reworking some aspects of the Chicago *Sunday Soup*, InCUBATE launched a new iteration in May 2012 and plan to continue Chicago *Sunday Soup* as a regular collaboration with the Chicago-based nonprofit Roots and Culture and artist/chef Eric May. And as *Feast* travels, their participation in the exhibition will expand to include collaborations with each venue and other local groups to host a *Sunday Soup*, which will in turn be represented within a reworked version of their gallery installation. In this way, live components remain at the foreground of the project.

---

[1] "InCUBATE 2nd Year Report: The Slow Build—March 2009," September 24, 2012, http://incubate-chicago.org/about/.

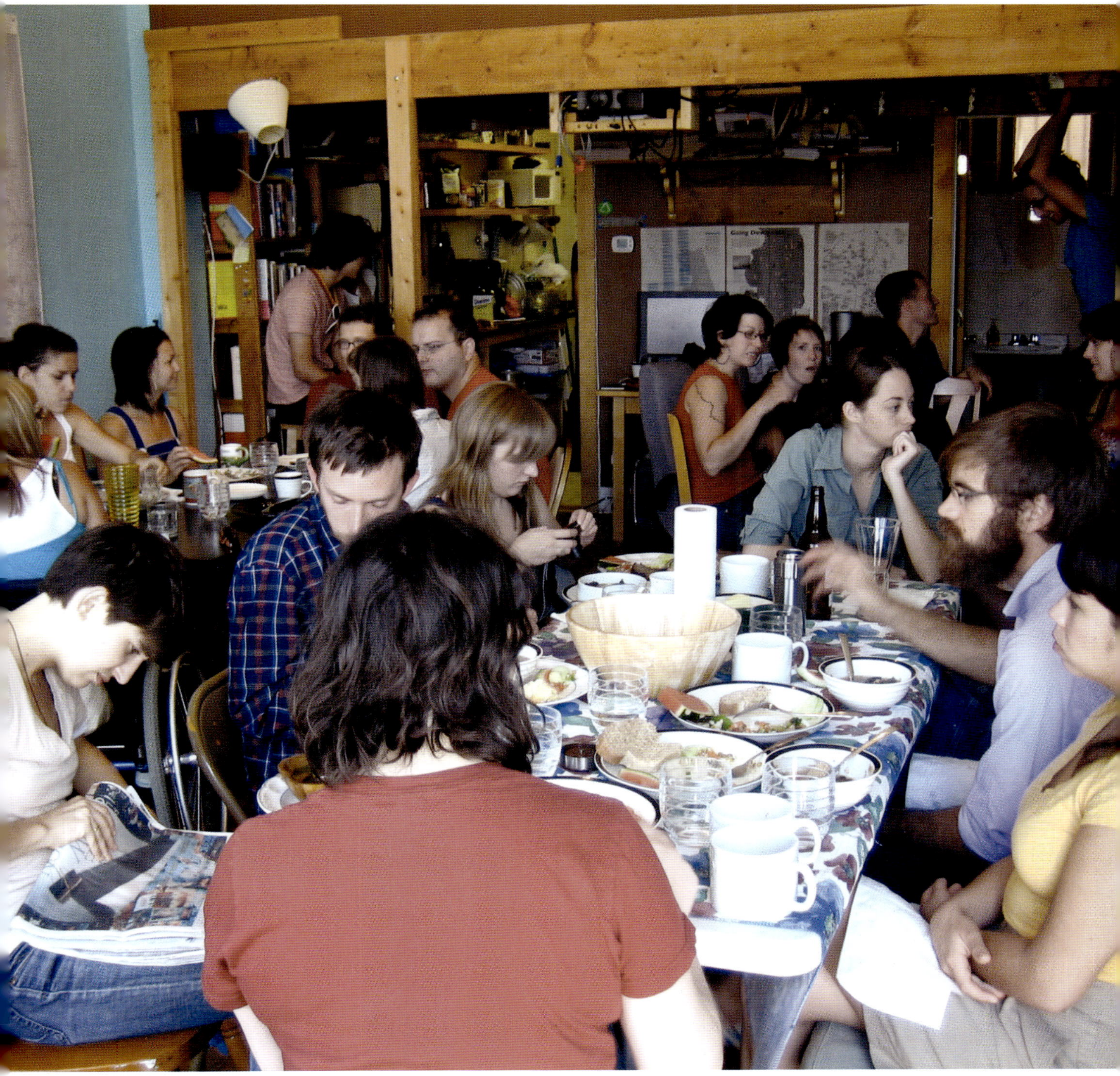

A *Sunday Soup* at InCUBATE's former Chicago space, 2009

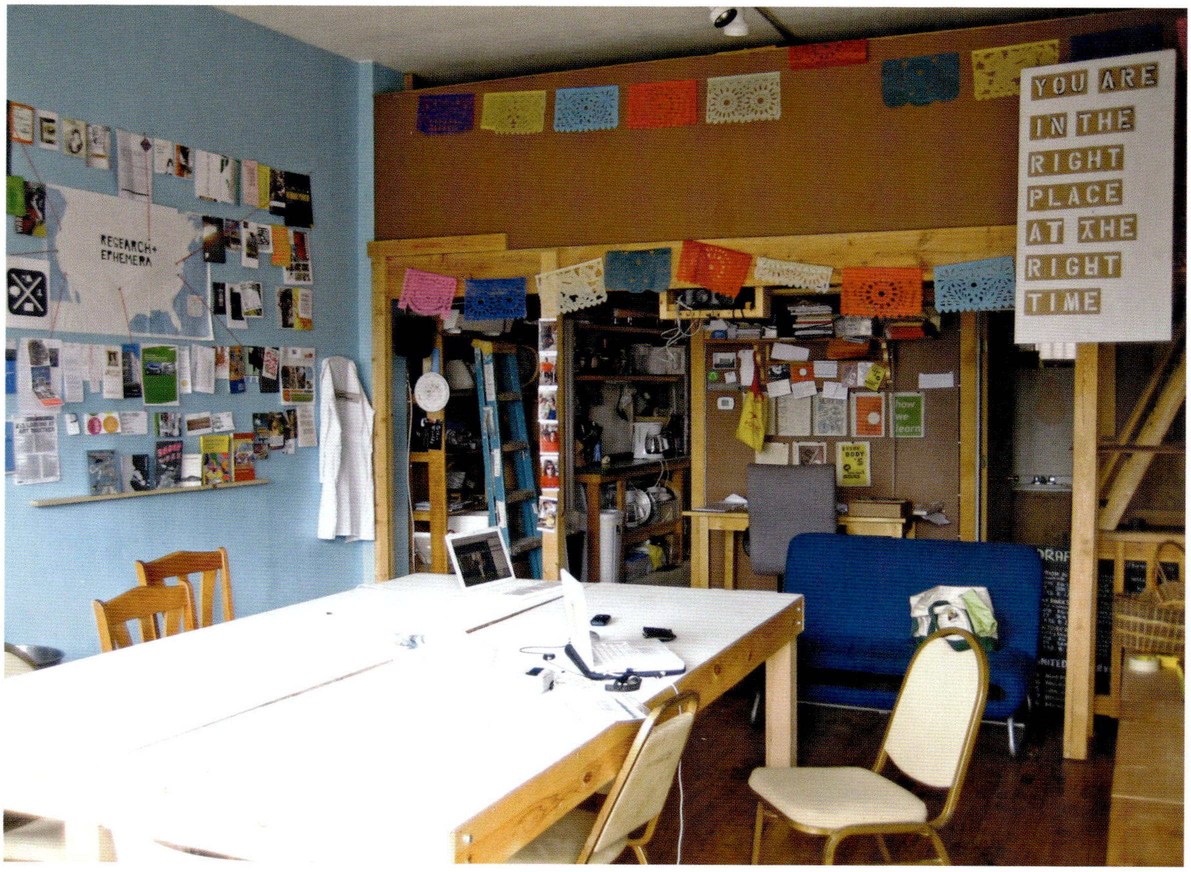

ABOVE: Many *Sunday Soup* gatherings were held in a multipurpose room at InCUBATE's former Chicago space, pictured here

OPPOSITE: *Sunday Soup*, 2007–ongoing, installation view, Smart Museum of Art, 2012

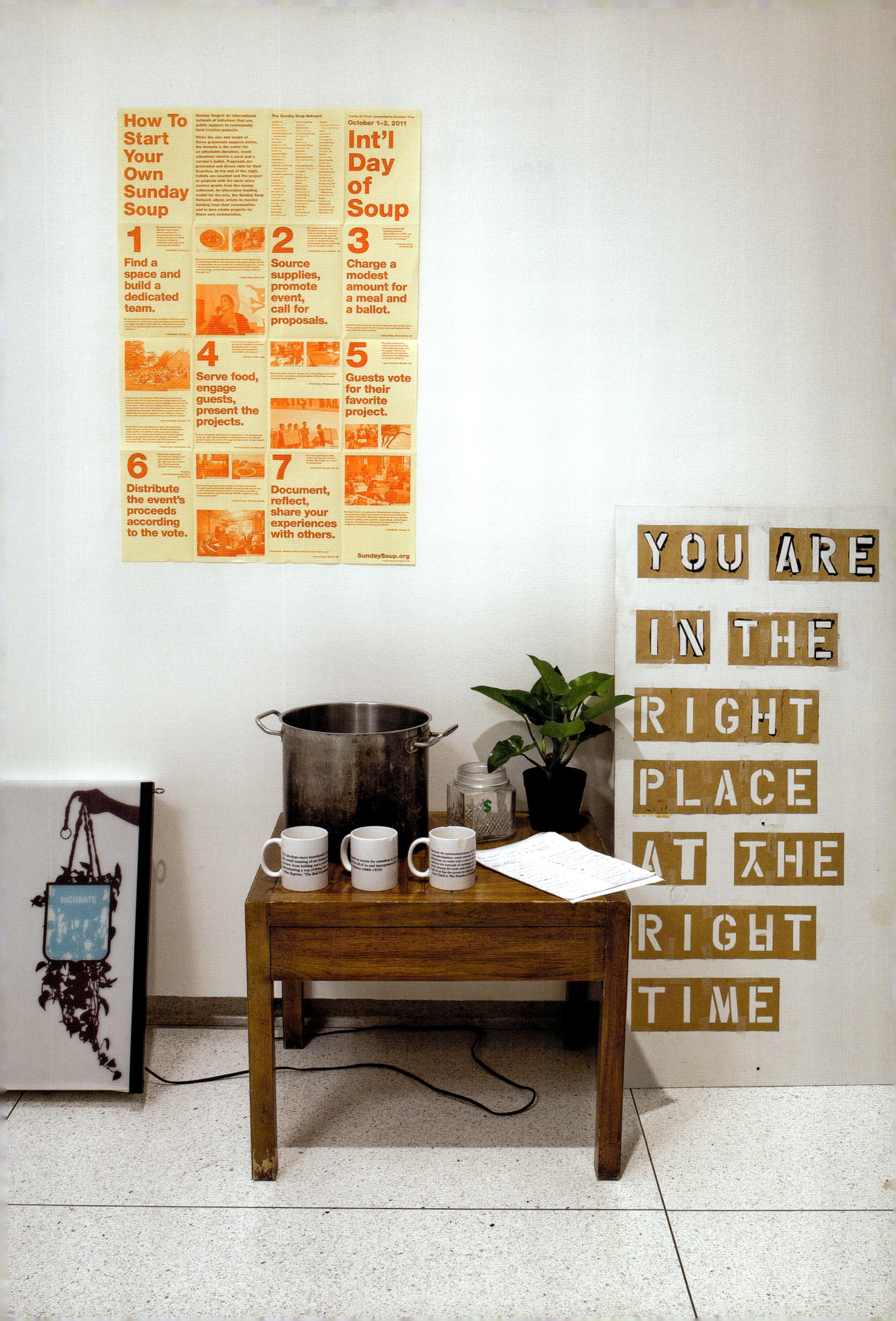
How To Start Your Own Sunday Soup
October 1–2, 2011
Int'l Day of Soup
1
Find a space and build a dedicated team.
2
Source supplies, promote event, call for proposals.
3
Charge a modest amount for a meal and a ballot.
4
Serve food, engage guests, present the projects.
5
Guests vote for their favorite project.
6
Distribute the event's proceeds according to the vote.
7
Document, reflect, share your experiences with others.
SundaySoup.org
YOU ARE
IN THE
RIGHT
PLACE
AT THE
RIGHT
TIME
INCUBATE

Sunday Soup

by Abigail Satinsky

WHEN I WAS LITTLE, my Christian friends would take me with them to church after Saturday night sleepovers, and I was alternately baffled by a religious tradition that seemed wholly alien to me and jealous of a community that seemed so involved in each others' lives. I grew up in an atheist Jewish family with a healthy dose of skepticism toward organized religion and its attendant institutions, but was secretly a little envious of belonging to a group with a shared belief system. Years later when I got to art school, I think I was still looking for my church. That's probably fairly common; after all, a lot of people enter the art world seeking that place where they belong rather than because they expect to make a living through art. This is one of the things that makes the art world such a funny place. It's hypercompetitive, filled with talented people competing for a limited number of opportunities, and financial success lies elusively somewhere between strategic networking and dumb luck. It's also full of people pursuing art out of love and working to build communities of mutual support. Most people want to have it both ways: they want to make a living and have their work not be about the money. I'm sympathetic. In fact, I have a messianic zeal to achieve this.

This desire lay behind the co-founding of InCUBATE in the winter of 2006 with Roman Petruniak, Ben Schaafsma (who passed away in the fall of 2008), and later Bryce Dwyer and Matthew Joynt. While studying to become curators, historians, and art administrators, we were inspired by the political and socially engaged art practices occurring locally in Chicago: groups and spaces like Temporary Services, Haha, Midwest Radical Cultural Corridor, Feel Tank, Stockyard Institute, Experimental Station, Mess Hall, and AREA Chicago. This lead to discussions about the negotiations and compromises we would encounter as professional administrators working in nonprofit and for-profit art spaces, which would perhaps put us at odds with these practices. We wondered how we could collaborate with artists and each other in a different, more experimental way. So we established our clubhouse: we rented a storefront space, created programs, and began to build a community of collaborators to question what kind of art world we wanted to operate in.

It seemed like a natural process and a typical Chicago approach: start an apartment space (Roman lived there for the first year), declare your intentions publicly, and figure it out as you go along. Our focus was on the economies that support art spaces. More specifically, we wondered if we didn't want to build a nonprofit with its logic of long-term growth and fiscal governance by a board of directors, where would the money come from? Even if we had wanted to go that route, we recognized that governmental support for the arts is minimal at best and private support is dictated by the priorities of granting foundations. We started with the idea that the way one goes about acquiring the necessary resources to sustain an art practice can be just as creative an endeavor as the utilization of those resources, and we proceeded from there.

We did a lot of projects to address those concerns, including organizing exhibitions and lectures about alternative economies, developing a residency program that helped fund our space, and researching historical and contemporary examples of artist-run support networks. Our inquiries were equally about assessing actual financial structures and working together to understand what kind of organizers we wanted to be. That meant that this practice couldn't just be a theoretical pursuit; it had to extend into practical projects that could be implemented in the world. We had no magic reserve of money, though we were in the privileged space of graduate school and had given up full-time jobs while in school, so the primary task at hand was to figure out how to fund our developing vision. By deciding not to become a traditional 501C3, we had limited grant and funding opportunities, so our working methodology became to think up creative, simple solutions to address the challenges with which were faced. We imagined that other groups probably faced similar problems, so we decided that if our solutions proved useful, we would

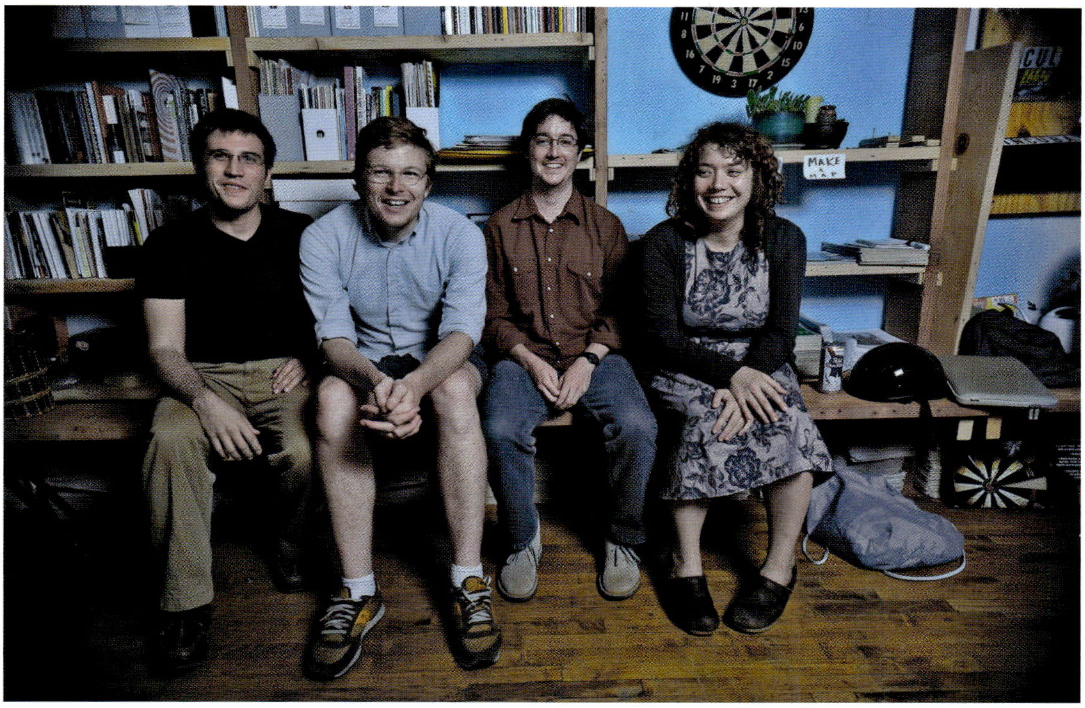

InCUBATE team Roman Petruniak, Matthew Joynt, Bryce Dwyer, and Abigail Satinsky, c. 2008

make them public; if not, they would be reexamined or thrown out all together. So we decided to start our own grant, *Sunday Soup*.

Sunday Soup, which initially ran from 2007 to 2010, was a monthly meal that generated money for a creative project fund to which anyone could apply. In particular, we hoped to fund projects that were locally focused, radically minded, and fell outside the realm of "art" proper. Patrons of *Sunday Soup* paid $10 for brunch and a presentation by a local artist or organizer (who most of the time also cooked the soup) and got one vote on which proposal received the proceeds from the meal. Our space's physical size controlled the size of the grant. We could seat around thirty-five to forty people, which therefore limited the grant to about $200 after costs. Our goal was to demystify the process of arts funding by making it direct, transparent, and democratic. It was important to us that everyone who came to our space—whether they were an artist or not—felt that they had a voice and a stake in supporting local culture. We did this by recognizing that the money had to come from somewhere and so we provided a service that we enjoyed creating and thought people would feel comfortable paying for. We asked artists to present their grant proposals in accessible language and to be clear about their goals. The people who came to our meal knew that the project they liked the most may not be the one that got the money, but that they could feel good about supporting whatever project got the prize in the end. It was obvious to both grantees and patrons that the process was a labor of love from beginning to end, creating an expectation that the winner would use the grant wisely. We funded projects such as Anne Elizabeth Moore's *New Girl Law*, a letter-pressed, hand-bound book created in conjunction with the thirty-two

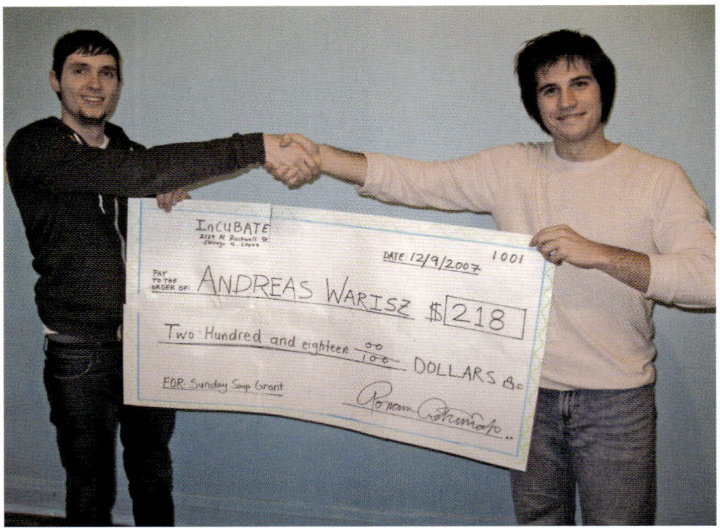

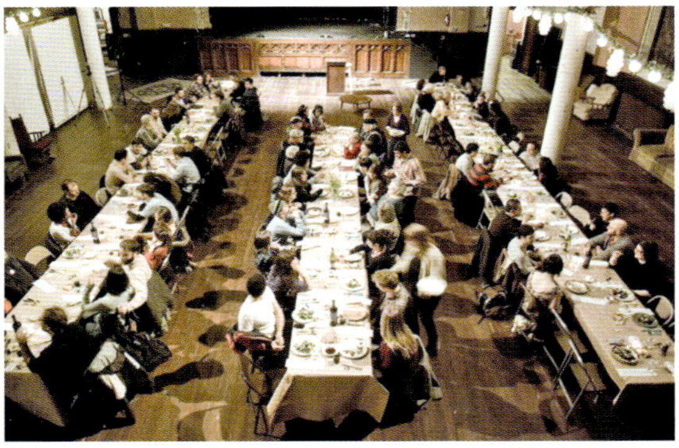

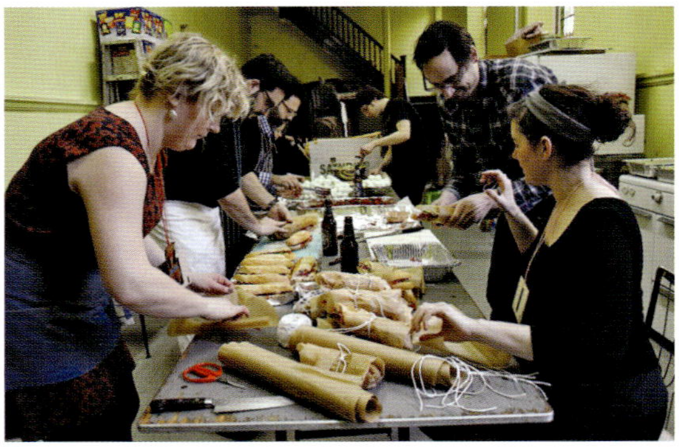

CLOCKWISE FROM TOP: Andreas Warisz is awarded a *Sunday Soup* microgrant, Chicago, 2007
Preparing for Brooklyn FEAST, 2010
STEW Baltimore, 2009

young Cambodian women leaders in Phnom Penh; Marc Moscato's research project "Brains Brilliancy Bohemia: Art and Politics in Jazz-age Chicago," which became a book and exhibition at Mess Hall; and bought a new office printer for AREA Chicago, a local magazine on art and activism in Chicago.

Sunday Soup worked because it was manageable in scale and built upon a group of people having face-to-face encounters across a table. We were admittedly not experts in either fundraising or in cooking. And what we were proposing was not an entirely new idea; we drew inspiration from spaghetti dinners and school bake sales as well as artist projects like Carol Gooden and Gordon Matta-Clark's FOOD, Josh Greene's *Service-Works*, Steve Lambert's *Co-Op Bar*, Joseph del Pesco and Scott Oliver's exhibition project the *Collective Foundation*, and efforts of the Present Group in Oakland, California. It was a public experiment; we were directly dependent on a gradually accumulating group of people who wanted to be involved with us in collectively pooling resources, sharing histories on what's already been done, and imagining the conditions for an ethical and critical art world that would support its constituents.

Sunday Soup has grown into an international network, with food-based microgranting initiatives in more than forty cities across the United States and Europe. Organizers have taken on the model and made it work for their own contexts and audiences. This network grew spontaneously and without any direct oversight from us. It happened after we installed temporary *Sunday Soup* cafés in various exhibitions or through artists who participated in our residency program, or just people who were interested in the same issues and heard about soup somehow. We weren't interested in franchising the model but we were very excited to see this basic formula adapted and put into action where it seemed relevant. For instance, organizers from FEAST in New York City have raised more than $15,000 since

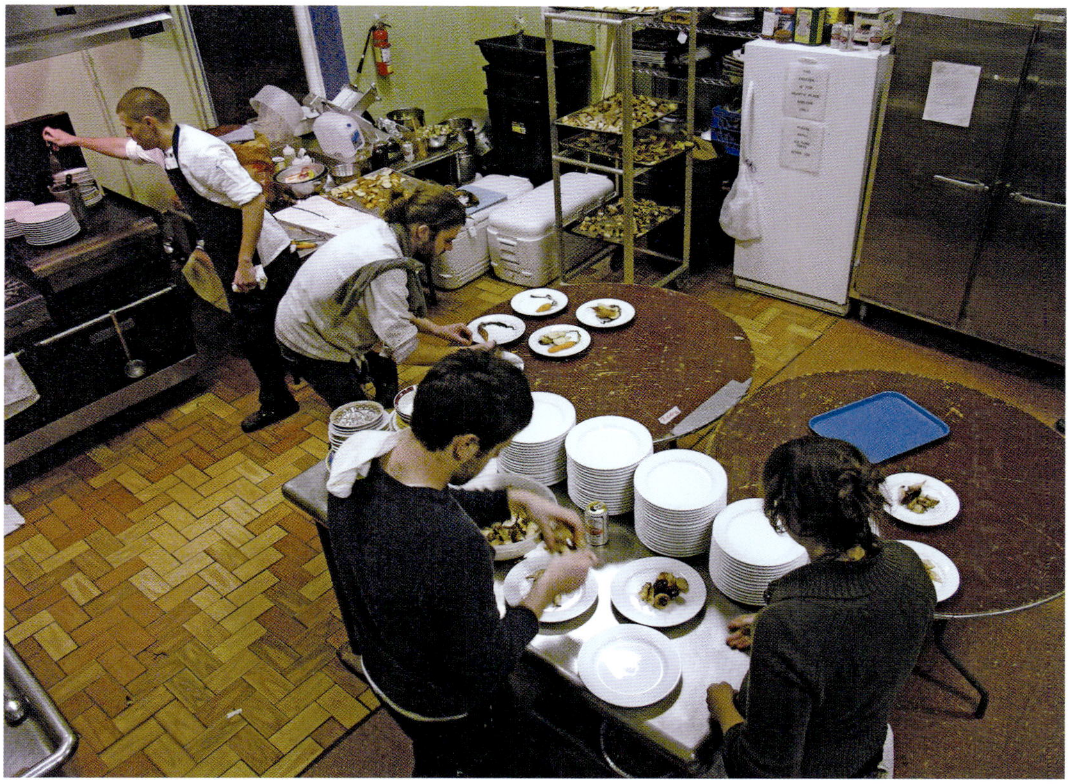

STEW Baltimore, 2009

2009. Run by a vibrant community of organizers and followers, they have been successful in starting FEASTs across the country. Milan's Granaio operates in a radically different funding climate, where contemporary art competes for state support with antiquities and there are very few forums for dialogue outside of the contemporary art institutions that are funded directly by private individuals. Milan's Granaio has spawned initiatives in Bologna and Venice. There has been a one-off Soup organized in Chisinau, Moldova, and ongoing programs in Kiev, Ukraine, and Newcastle upon Tyne, UK. At the time of writing, there are more than seventy-five projects happening in places such as Flagstaff, AZ; Los Angeles, CA; Washington, DC; Wilmington, DE; Dubuque and Iowa City, IA; Carbondale, IL; Boston and Northhampton, MA; Baltimore, MD; Ann Arbor, Detroit, Grand Rapids, Roseville, and Traverse City, MI; Minneapolis, MN; St. Louis and Kansas City, MO; Greensboro, NC; Rochester, NH; Syracuse, NY; Portland, OR; Philadelphia, Phoenixville, and Pittsburgh, PA; Providence, RI; Brattleboro, VT; Seattle, WA; Milwaukee, WI; Huntington, WV; and Toronto, Canada. There are at least three in operation in Detroit. FEAST in Hartford, CT, was initiated by Luis Cotto at the Center Without Walls initiative (he was at the time also on the City Council). Recently, we have tried to list all of the projects on one website, sundaysoup.org, and sometimes, when participants are going to be in central locations for an art conference or gathering, we meet as a group to compare notes and discuss issues. There isn't much organizing structure to the network and everyone operates autonomously; it's a friendly association and network for sharing resources. In October 2011, organizers from FEAST Brooklyn, FEAST Mass, Philly Stake, and *Sunday Soup* Chicago came together to host a communal dinner at

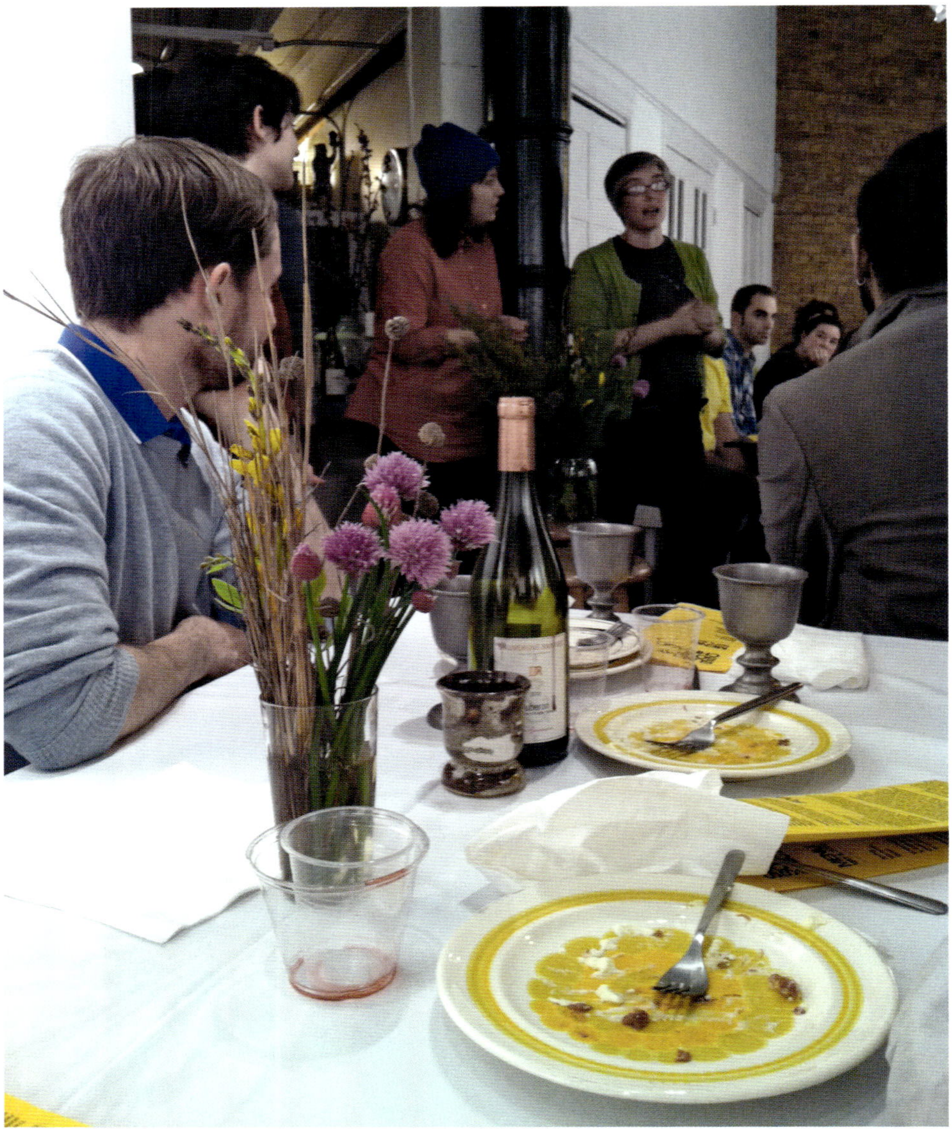

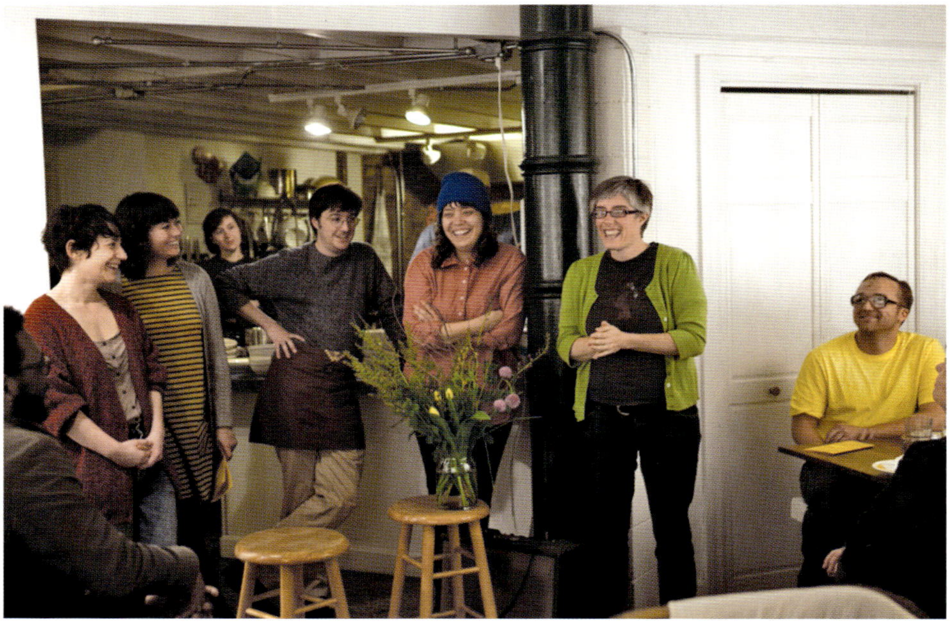

Sunday Soup relaunches at Roots & Culture, Chicago, May 6, 2012.
The evening's microgrant was awarded to Sarah Ross (in green sweater) for the Prison-Neighborhood Art Project.

Creative Time's *Living as Form* exhibition to raise money for a new microgranting project. Diners chose to fund the proposal from Townhouse Gallery in Cairo, Egypt.

I am amazed that the project has grown as it has. For the first year that we hosted *Sunday Soups*, barely anyone came. Five to six friends would come weekly between 1 and 4 pm to sit around a table with us and it was mostly the same people every time. God bless those people—though we hoped our endeavor would actually be relevant to those we didn't already know. Acquaintances would often say, "Oh great project, I'll come next week," and then never show up. I bring this up not as a side note to what then became a successful project. Rather, I think it raises a fundamental question about what motivates people to actually participate in a community art project that doesn't yet have a community.

One problem was that we weren't being especially good hosts. We expected people to come simply because it was a smart idea, but it was just that—an idea floating as a potential thing. It needed to be grounded in clear communication and in satisfying experience. We fixed the basics: we offered a better meal at a more conventional brunch time with the menu and presentation advertised beforehand with a distinct start and end time, so people didn't feel like they were walking into someone's apartment. We welcomed participants at the door and let them know where they could sit and how they could vote. We also programmed speakers who would draw a more diverse crowd. It seems obvious now and perhaps a little too mundane to explain, but conceptually it was about rethinking our own assumptions about the community we wanted to serve. We had to make gatherings relevant to other people: people who didn't usually show up to art events needed to feel welcomed and artists applying for the grant had to feel like their work was being taken seriously by an engaged group of voters. At the same time, people simply wanting to have a good Sunday brunch had to leave feeling satisfied.

There were multiple expectations to manage and things always become more complicated in practice. On a level I don't think we are that comfortable with, the project has a "pull yourself up by your bootstraps" mentality, in which artists become defeatist about receiving arts funding and so take the onus on themselves to create their own streams of income. We also started before the age of Kickstarter, so crowdsourced funding hadn't become as ubiquitous as it now, which raises its own discussion of how artists have to market their own projects in an overly crowded field. Our goal was to get into the messy side of these questions and not to critique arts philanthropy from afar without ever engaging its terms and assumptions or participating in its processes. The same goes for advocating on the level of governmental policy, since it was in these occasions that we honed our arguments as to why art does indeed matter in the larger culture. *Sunday Soup* provides the infrastructure in which to imagine collectively an alternative with a spirit of radical inclusiveness, where we seek out the opinions and voices of those who are usually marginalized when it comes to the issue of cultural funding. *Sunday Soup* was essentially a challenge to us to take a more active role in this process, debating why certain projects deserve financial support, and dreaming up other options. And while doing that work, we were also able to give artists money to produce their projects.

The convivial, family style meal is just one way to animate this situation—but an important one. Our questions needed to be asked in supportive environments, where social relationships build over time, and trust is one of the organizing principles. This applied to the participants as well as to InCUBATE as organizers. I can't say that we were always very good at it, but we attempted to take care of each other. Cooking and washing dishes together on Sunday afternoons was part of that. And there was also a lot of arguing and frustration with each other, along with reconciliation. When Ben Schaafsma, who originally came up with the idea of *Sunday Soup*, died in a car accident in 2008, I looked to the project for some kind of comfort. Ben was not the kind of person that you remember with a fuzzy glow, but rather through the way he worked and the ideas he was determined to launch into the world. It was through my relationship with him that I came to believe that the arts could actually enact transformational social change. He challenged me, and I trusted him. He had integrity and he expected a lot from the people he worked with. I miss him. Gathering in the space for the first *Sunday Soup* after he died—which included borscht made by artist Kelly Kaczynski and a lecture by art historian Lori Waxman about how the Surrealists, and Situationist International and Fluxus artists used walking as an aesthetic device for revolutionizing everyday life—was obviously sad and confusing for me but it was comforting to know that there was an occasion that kept his spirit present and a project that would continue to bring us together.

Two years after Ben died, I visited Baltimore's STEW, a joint initiative spearheaded by the Baltimore Development Cooperative and Red Emma's Bookstore Coffeehouse. Their meal is a locally sourced, five-course meal served to more than one hundred people, and their grant is geared toward funding social justice initiatives, with a voting system in which no applicant leaves empty-handed. The night I was there, the Better Waverly Community Arts Center, the House of Ruth Maryland's Advocate Through Art Program, and the United Workers made presentations and received funds. It was an overwhelming experience. The organizers had actively worked to build an inclusive and diverse community of participants, the meal was beautiful, and everyone seemed happy. That night I was there simply to pay my $10 and hang out, I was welcomed as a customer, and grateful to be able to give money to those projects. I knew that I could walk away from *Sunday Soup* after that night and be satisfied that it had happened at all. I knew Ben would have been happy to see STEW happen. I felt connected to a community of people that I did not have to know personally nor was it important that they knew Ben. As the project continues to grow, I try to be realistic about its scope. *Sunday Soup* is entirely dependent on the volunteer labor of the organizers who must have their own jobs to keep these micro-initiatives afloat. For InCUBATE, over time the experiment turned into an unpaid full-time job. While we felt a responsibility for the project, we decided to take a break from it in 2010. We took time to reassess why the project was important for us individually and to consider how it could fit into our personal lives going forward. That kind of self-care is at the center of this process. Building a healthy community-oriented project meant giving the organizers permission to take a break—and it also meant giving ourselves permission to return to the project. As we watched the network grow and pursued other projects, we realized we missed getting together for *Sunday Soup*, so in May 2012, we restarted the project as a quarterly gathering at Roots & Culture, an artist space in Chicago; we organize this new iteration of *Sunday Soup* with chef and artist Eric May, Elizabeth Chodos, Sara Knox Hunter, and others.

Often people participate in the project without knowing about InCUBATE or the larger network, which to us, is really a marker of its success. What's exciting is that people continue to organize projects like *Sunday Soup* because they feel a groundswell of energy driving it forward in which they are interrogating their own conditions as we tried to do. As a model, it is contingent upon a community invested in its own well-being, and as long as it's relevant to that community, it will persist.

I know that *Sunday Soup* does not embody systematic infrastructural change. It is not the perfectly formed replacement model for cultural funding, but rather a forum for discussion about how we were going to build our careers, work together cooperatively, and be happy doing so. It's neither an individual or group's discrete art project nor a business that anyone owns. Rather it is a technology, the making, modification and usage of tools to test out ideas of participatory democracy in the support of local culture, which thousands of people have participated in. I don't love all the iterations of the soup project equally nor am I the authority of best microfunding practices. But I now have the benefit of an international network of people I can reach out to for advice, people who I believe in some way are fellow travelers. Through *Sunday Soup*, I found the closest thing I was going to get to that place of belonging that I romanticized as a child, a site of shared belief that can be challenged and made real within the context of a community, that is about learning as you go along, together.

Abigail Satinsky is program director at threewalls, Chicago, and a founding member of InCUBATE.

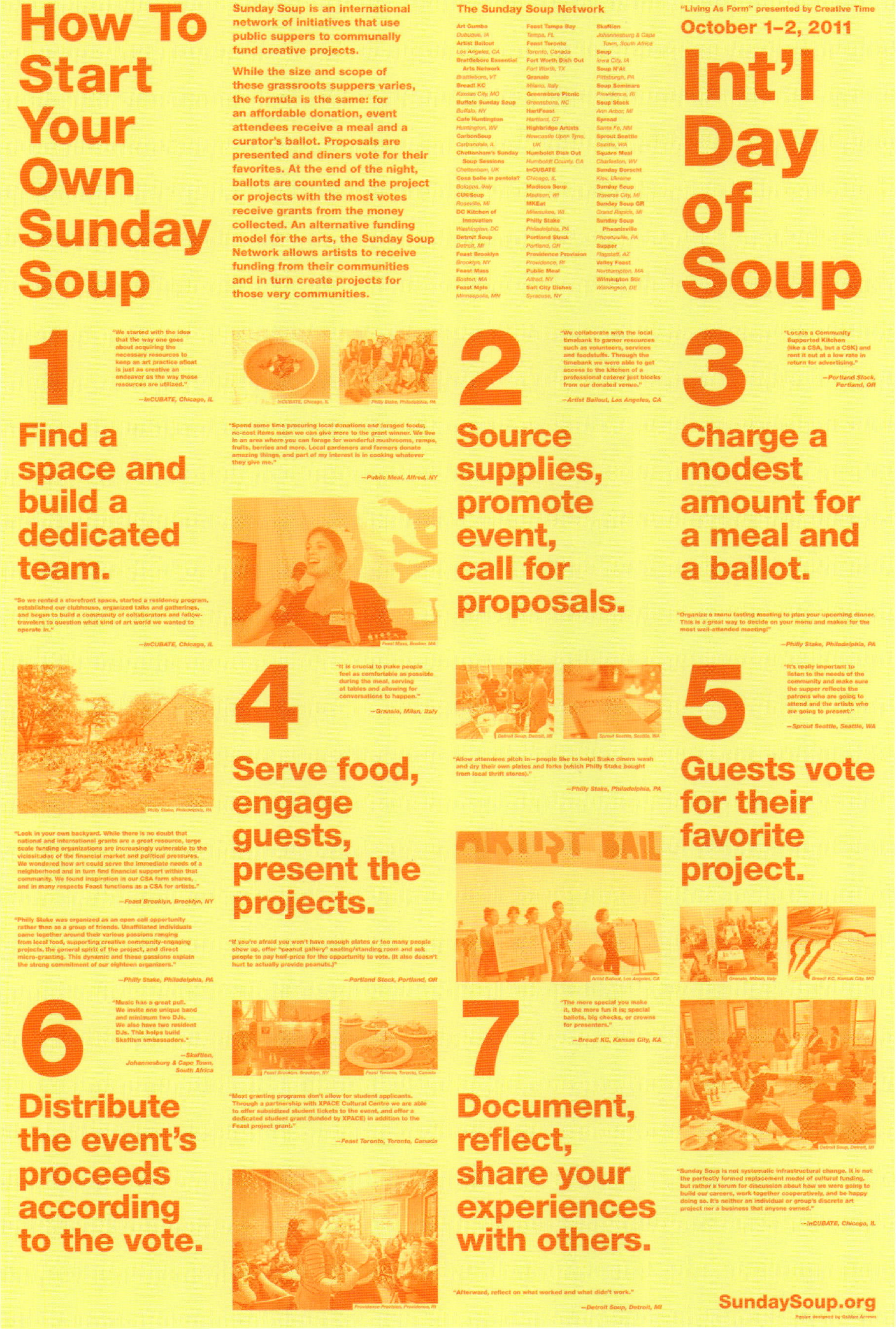

Poster for the International Day of Soup, October 1–2, 2011, presented by Creative Time as part of *Living as Form*

Mella Jaarsma

A LEADING FIGURE within Indonesian art communities, Mella Jaarsma has helped build catalytic cultural institutions: in 1988, she and her husband Nindityo Adipurnomo founded the Cemeti Art House—a key site of creative production, display, and international dialogue within Indonesia—and she also helped launch a related project, the Indonesian Visual Art Archive. Food and meals have figured in many projects at Cemeti and also feature prominently in Jaarsma's own work. Notably, she has used meals in projects like *Hi Inlander* (1998–99) and *The Feeder* (2003), both part of a larger series of works in which Jaarsma used contemporary performance art, traditional practices, and current ethnic and political tensions within Indonesian society as points of departure for elaborate costumes made of materials such as goat leather, fish skins, frog legs, and chicken feet.

Feast features several of Jaarsma's works that use meals to address cooperation and cross-cultural respect. She began to explore these topics in the aftermath of the repressive former president Suharto's resignation in 1998—a time of instability that included violent riots against Indonesians of ethnically Chinese heritage. *Feast* includes video documentation of a work that grew directly from these riots: *Pribumi Pribumi* (1998). In this performance, Jaarsma and other Western friends set up simple cooking stations along a Yogyakarta street and served Chinese food to passersby as a means to spark face-to-face dialogue about ethnic conflict. *Pribumi Pribumi* offers a culturally and politically specific counterpoint to the more open-ended *I Eat You Eat Me* (2001–12) also featured in the exhibition. In this performance, Jaarsma invites participants to partner up—each selecting food for the other, donning a lightweight span of metal held between leather yokes, and then feeding one another. When worn, the sculpture temporarily binds the participants, creating an intimate, mutually supported table surface for this shared meal. For *Feast*, Jaarsma created a new iteration of this piece for six participants. She used one for a performance in Yogyakarta timed to coincide with the opening of *Feast*, while a copy of the original sculpture was used by a group of University of Chicago students at an event organized by the Smart's Student Advisory Committee, and was then shown as a static object within the gallery. One participant, James Levinsohn, reflected on his shared meal: "In enacting Mella Jaarsma's piece, I experienced feeding another person and being fed by another person for the first time in my adult life . . . [throughout the meal] one constant remained—the way the ritual of feeding and being fed articulates power relations . . . In Jaarsma's piece, our proximity to those we have power toward makes us generous; one wishes this was the case more often outside of art."[1] To further bring the work to life in Chicago, a copy of the original two-person version of *I Eat You Eat Me* was available in the Smart Museum's café for visitors to use to feed each other in their own meal-performances.

---

[1] James Levinsohn, accessed September 24, 2012, https://blogs.uchicago.edu/feast/2012/02/i_eat_you_eat_me.html.

OPPOSITE: *I Eat You Eat Me*, 2001–12, performance with six University of Chicago students at the Smart Museum of Art, January 19, 2012

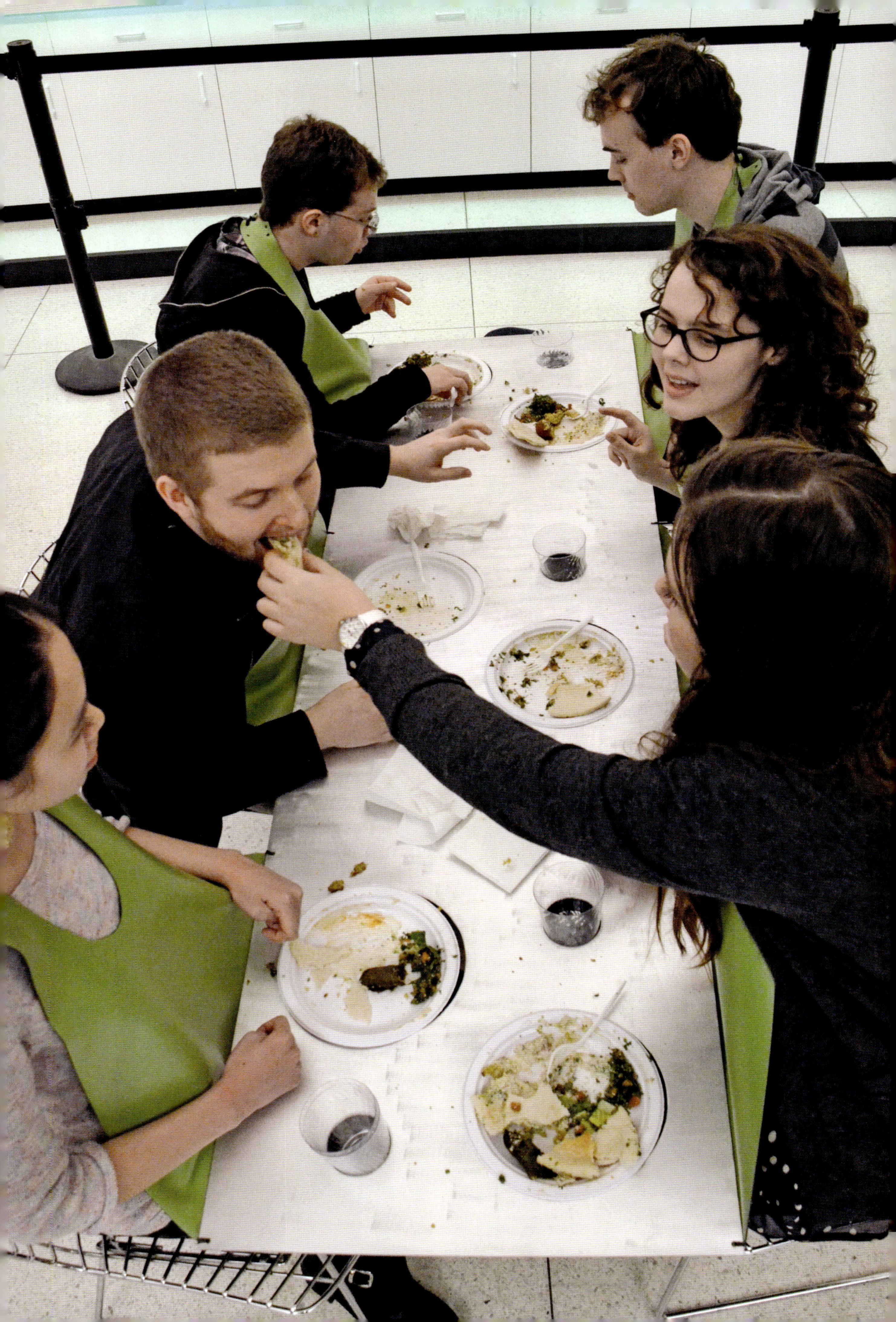

Interview

SMART: Can you describe your path as an artist and sources of inspiration for your work, either in or beyond the context of art?

MELLA JAARSMA: I have been living and working as an artist in Java, Indonesia, since 1984. By choosing to live within a totally different culture, after having grown up in the Netherlands, I became more aware of the values and norms of my own cultural background. This process made me conscious of differences between cultures and also taught me how to identify these differences. What we consider to be reality comes to us by means of contrasts in experiences. Multiple and different dimensions have entered my art and artmaking processes since I became part of this hybrid society in Indonesia. What interests me most about Indonesian contemporary art is the great variety of developments and movements that interact with social and cultural circumstances. I am intrigued by the awareness of the function of an artist to use their position to provoke a dialogue within this society. Indonesian culture has a strong traditional background, a rather new capitalistic consumerism, and complex political tensions.

My work focuses on an awareness of these experiences—ideas about our own existence in a certain place in a particular world. My existence in the hybrid feudal society in Java, where I have to deal with stereotyped roles of a foreigner as postcolonialist and explorer, and where I communicate through art, is what still fascinates me. My work is also about positioning "the native" and "the ethnic" and the acknowledgment that these categories could be reversed, depending on their surroundings.

SMART: Tell us about *Pribumi Pribumi* and how it fits into your broader practice.

MJ: Everyone who confronts my work is coming at it from different backgrounds and cultures, dealing with highly personal sets of taboos and therefore experiencing the work in different ways. I want my work to relate to these specific audiences, to deal with some of their taboos and interpretations. This takes great sensitivity, and therefore I try to find ways to open up dialogue, rather than work in a more confrontational way. I am not looking for symbols to make a meaningful artwork but I am searching for a phenomenological reality, like idioms, with visuals that speak for themselves.

During the political and racial riots in Indonesia in 1998, in the heat of ending the power of the Suharto regime, it didn't make sense to stay working in a studio while the students were so brave to demonstrate and risk their lives. I decided to do a performance on the street after the stories appeared with what happened to the ethnic Chinese during the riots. Chinese are the black sheep of Indonesian society and in times of chaos like the riots in 1998, anger was directed at this ethnic minority. The position of the Chinese in Indonesian society has its roots in the colonial era; the Chinese were the middlemen between the Dutch and the native Indonesians. They were the traders and got access to better education.

During the riots in 1998, Chinese-owned shops were set on fire, and killings and rapes took place in Jakarta and Surakarta. In Yogyakarta, the city where I live, Chinese started to protect their shops from burning and demolition by putting signs on their closed doors that said: "Native shop owner," or "Native Muslim shop owner." I was shocked to see this racial outburst, and one and a half month after Suharto resigned, I decided to do a performance on the street.

I looked for a way to communicate and open up a dialogue about what happened with the Chinese, and I decided to work with food. I used frog legs, because Chinese eat frog legs, and Muslim consider this delicacy to be unclean (*haram*), thus revealing different cultural perceptions. I created the performance *Pribumi Pribumi* in which I invited friends—all foreigners who live in Yogyakarta—to fry frog legs along the street and serve the food to the public. I used the position of my "Western" friends as we are also a minority but admired—a position I used to trigger questions from the public.

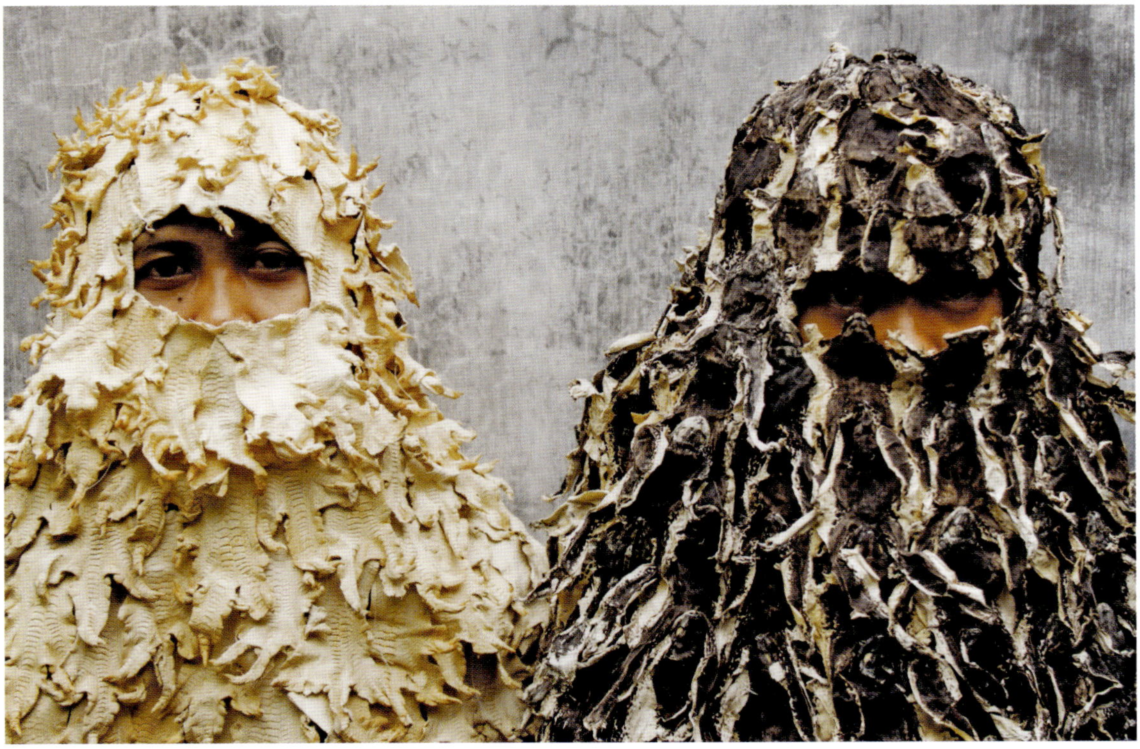

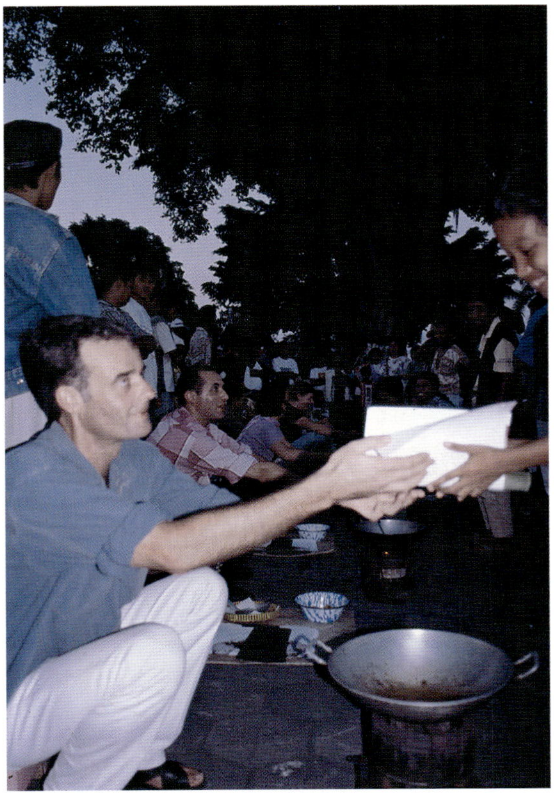

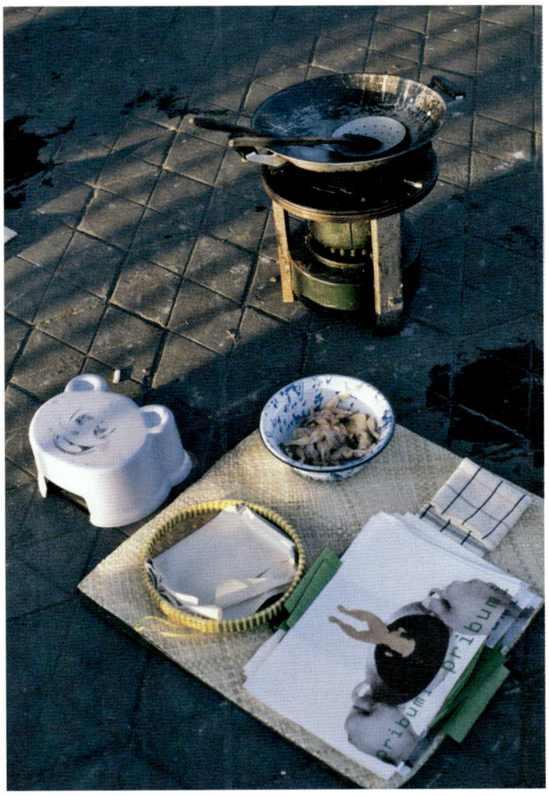

TOP: *Hi Inlander*, frog legs, chicken feet, fish, and kangaroo leather, 1998–99

BOTTOM ROW: Stills from *Pribumi Pribumi*, 1998, performance in Yogyakarta

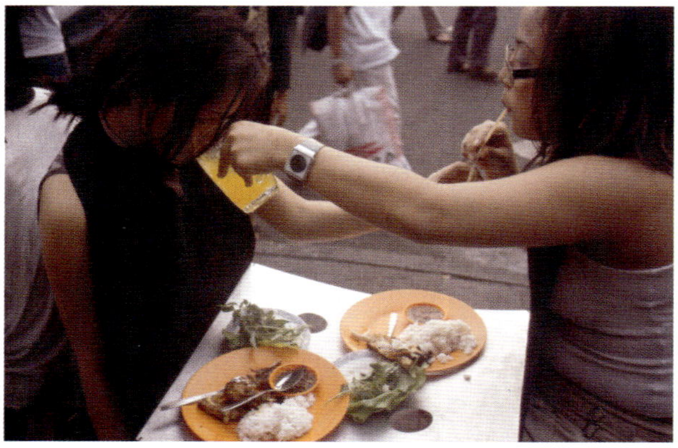

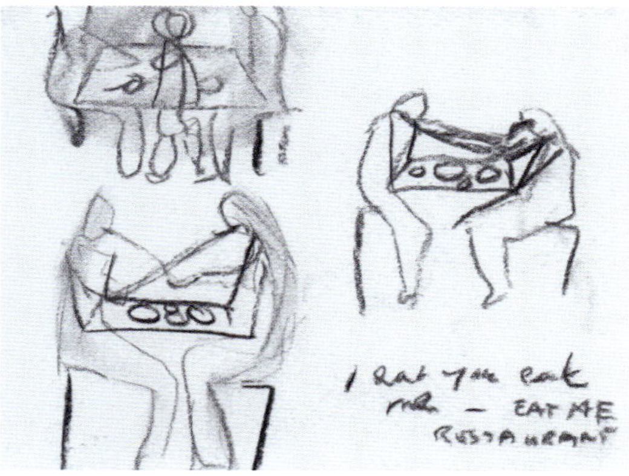

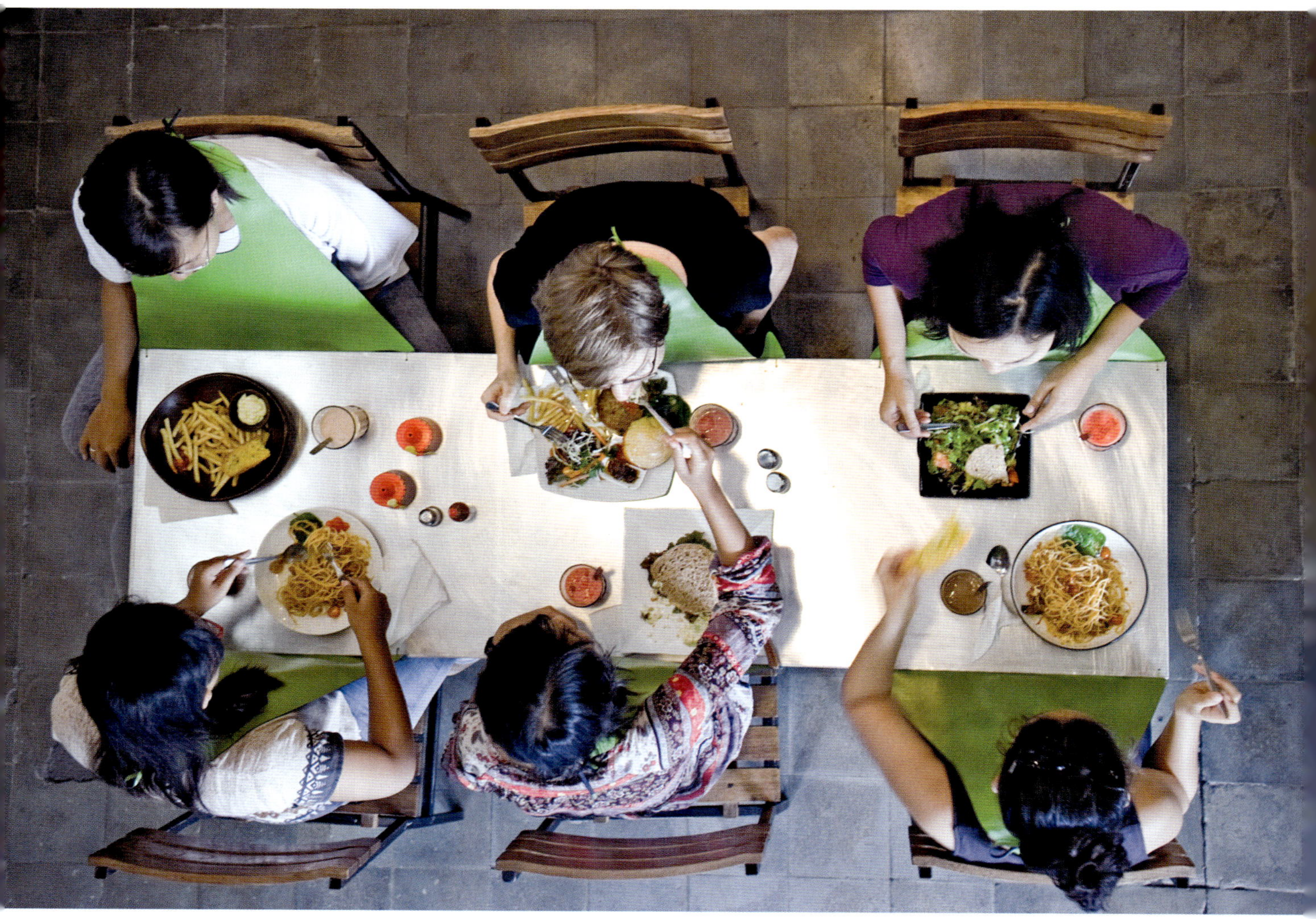

CLOCKWISE FROM TOP LEFT: *I Eat You Eat Me*, performance at Blok M, Jakarta, 2004

Sketch for *I Eat You Eat Me*, 2001

I Eat You Eat Me, performance at ViaVia Café, Yogyakarta, 2012

SMART: What does *pribumi* mean?

MJ: *Pribumi* means "native." It's also translated to mean "the first created from the earth," which is why I connected it to the frog legs, because the frog is also the animal that goes from the sea to the land. That's also why Muslims are not allowed to eat it; they see it as unclean since the animals go between the sea and the land.

SMART: What about the related series *The Warrior, The Healer, The Feeder*?

MJ: In this work, three models wear cloaks made out of different materials, representing the inevitable connections across killing, healing, and feeding. *The Warrior* is made out of used military outfits that were worn by sixteen Indonesian soldiers; the uniforms are mixed with seaweed to create a new warrior cloak. The lowest part with the seaweed hangs into a pan and is boiled into a soup that feeds the audience. The two other costumes are made out of natural medicines (*The Healer*) and squid (*The Feeder*), which are also boiled into soups to heal and feed the audience. I made this work in 2003, when the United States went to Iraq and at the same time that the Indonesian militaries went to Aceh, the northern province of Indonesia, "to settle" the independence movement there.

SMART: What about *I Eat You Eat Me*?

MJ: *I Eat You Eat Me* is an interesting way to find out about human character. I usually explain the concept of the work to two people who walk into a restaurant or food court: the eating performance is about having an intimate dinner, which I describe as "going into the skin of the other" in which a hanging table connects the two people. By creating this situation with the performance and the hanging tables, I ask them to think about the other, the taste of the other. You also have to order the food for the other (without talking about it first), and then when the food arrives, you feed the other. It's very intimate. You have to open your mouth for the other and the other has to feed you with the rhythm of your eating.

SMART: When did this project begin?

MJ: It started in 2001. I first I made it for an exhibition in Thailand. The curator got the idea to do it at a certain restaurant in Bangkok called Eat Me. It was a fancy restaurant so we had four of these hanging tables in between their tables, and when people arrived at the restaurant I asked them if they would be willing to join the performance. Some wanted to do it and some didn't so it was interesting to have that mixture. I also made a deal with the cook so that when people joined the performance they would get a free dinner. We had special menus offering six different types of food they could choose from.

SMART: How did people respond to the performance?

MJ: People were quite excited actually; they thought it was a great idea. Some people found it difficult to really think about what the other would like, although they had known each other for a long time. It's very hard not to start from your own taste. Some people just order ice cream because they want ice cream themselves. But they're not allowed to discuss the order. You have to try and imagine what the other wants to eat.

You also have to balance. The bib is hanging from your neck and is attached to the table and then to the neck of the other. So it's all about balance as well, you cannot be very aggressive. You have to sit quite still; as a result some people found it difficult to be relaxed. I hoped people would try to look more closely into the other and also to think less about themselves.

SMART: Tell us about the new version of the piece that you are making for *Feast*.

MJ: For *Feast*, it's an experiment to make the table for six people. As a university museum there are many young people, and I hope that by being in groups of six the students will feel connected and want to exchange not only food but also ideas and discussion. Simultaneous with the exhibition in Chicago, I want to do a performance in Yogyakarta, to see how it works. I'm going to stage the six-person performance in the same restaurant I did the other performance three years ago. It's a place where many people gather. There are students but also travelers, musicians, artists; everybody comes there. I won't determine who will participate ahead of time. I think it's interesting to see who comes to the restaurant and ask if they are willing to participate.

SMART: How would you describe the role of the meal in your practice?

MJ: I use food mainly as an idiom in which to communicate: through a confrontation with local food traditions, cultural differences can truly be experienced. In particular, meat consumption often creates reactions, from unfamiliar snacks like frog legs or caterpillars to more extreme examples such as cannibalism. Exchanging ideas about food and eating behaviors can open up a space for understanding personal, racial, religious, and ethnic differences.

Food is always very important not only in starting a dialogue but also in creating a feeling of comfort. Indonesia is one of the biggest Muslim countries in the world and most people don't drink alcohol. So food is very important. If you go somewhere there's always food on the table and people who want to invite you to eat. You have to eat a lot because it's an honor to the ones who invited you. It's not very polite to refuse food. It's connected with the hospitality of people here.

SMART: Could you say more about how hospitality figures into your process or thinking?

MJ: When I create a work, I often start thinking from the perspective of the audience. How can I create a situation of maximum connection? I often think about how to create a situation in which the public is participating in the work, or at least is open to new ideas. That's more important to me than being provocative, which may create a distance. It also has to do with the situation in Indonesia. Living here is very much about harmony. It's not as much about finding the truth; it's much more about learning how to balance. People are not very confrontational.

Hospitality involving food can be a starting point for the public or for a certain community to participate or be connected to my work, depending on the aim of my project. The setting in a gallery space or at any other venue like a restaurant is also important, again, depending on the idea/concept.

For example, for the *Asia Pacific Triennale 3* in 1999 at the Queensland Art Gallery in Brisbane, Australia, I exhibited four leather cloaks from frog legs, chicken feet, kangaroo skins, and fish skins. The different animal skin cloaks were worn during the opening by people from different ethnic origins and with different skin colors—a Sri Lankan, indigenous Australian, Japanese, and white Australian. I also designed three kitchen tables and offered the meat of these four animals with a variety of spices to be cooked by the international public. I set up this happening with the idea that preparing food and eating together opens up understanding of each other's cultures and stimulates communication.

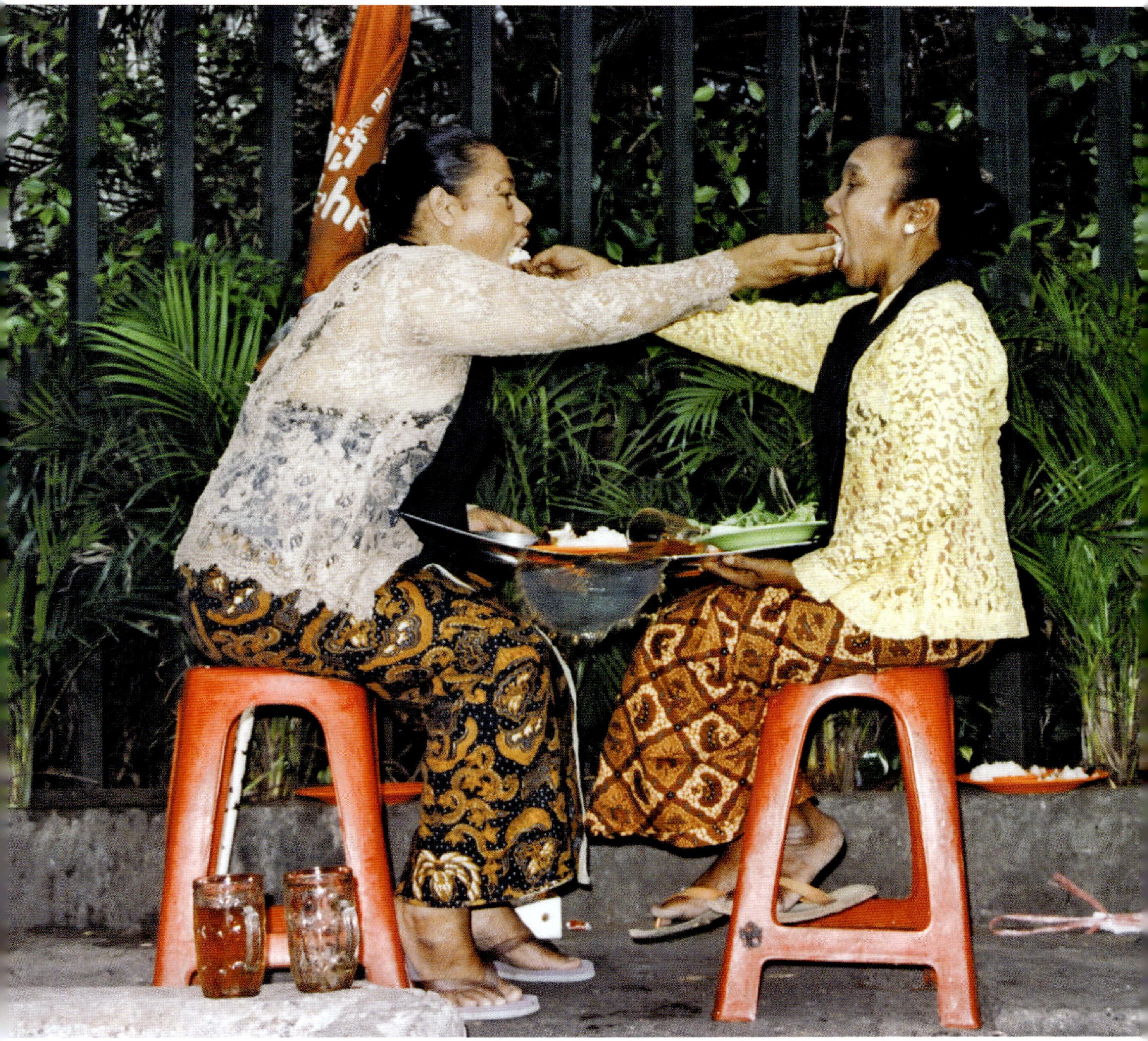

I Eat You Eat Me, 2001–12, performance in Jakarta, Indonesia, 2004

Lee Mingwei

AS A GRADUATE STUDENT, artist Lee Mingwei put up posters around Yale University asking people interested in "sharing foods and introspective conversation" to contact him. Responses poured in and Lee hosted a series of one-on-one dinners with strangers. This simple action—based on Lee's sense of hospitality, desire for connection, and spirit of adventure—evolved into *The Dining Project* (1997–present), which has since been staged at museums around the world. Generally guests are chosen by lottery, Lee prepares the meal himself, and he and each guest dine in the museum after hours within an elegant installation that cross-references minimal sculpture of the 1960s with Asian domestic architecture. For *Feast,* five guests dined with Lee in the Smart's galleries, with additional guests joining as the project traveled. For those visitors who encounter the work during open gallery hours—sans meal or diners—video documentation from prior meals animates the installation with close-cropped images of hands, food, and utensils, along with a murmur of conversation.

The Dining Project bridges personal and institutional forms of hospitality. Lee is a guest in each institution that presents *The Dining Project*. He is simultaneously the host of each meal, responsible for helping his guests feel welcome even within the cool spaces of museums—places that generally inspire behavior and etiquette quite different from that which occurs within the intimate private space of a home (or even an artist's studio). Drawing inspiration in part from his Buddhist background as well as family traditions of providing meals for strangers, Lee takes this responsibility of tending to his guests' needs seriously—inquiring after dietary requirements, shopping for and preparing the food himself, and gently reminding guests that they'll be dining without shoes . . . so they might want to bring a nice pair of socks. This attentiveness is crucial to all of Lee's projects. *The Dining Project* catapulted his career, leading to a series of projects in which Lee created works based on one-on-one interactions with strangers—sleeping next to each other, taking a walking tour around a city—as well as others that offer more open-ended opportunities for participation without the artist's direct presence. Considerations of what it means to be hospitable, how we come to trust one another, and how we try (and often fail) to satisfy our desire for intimacy in both private and public spaces have remained central to his practice.

OPPOSITE: Lee and guest Dory Fox share a meal at the Smart Museum of Art, February 13, 2012

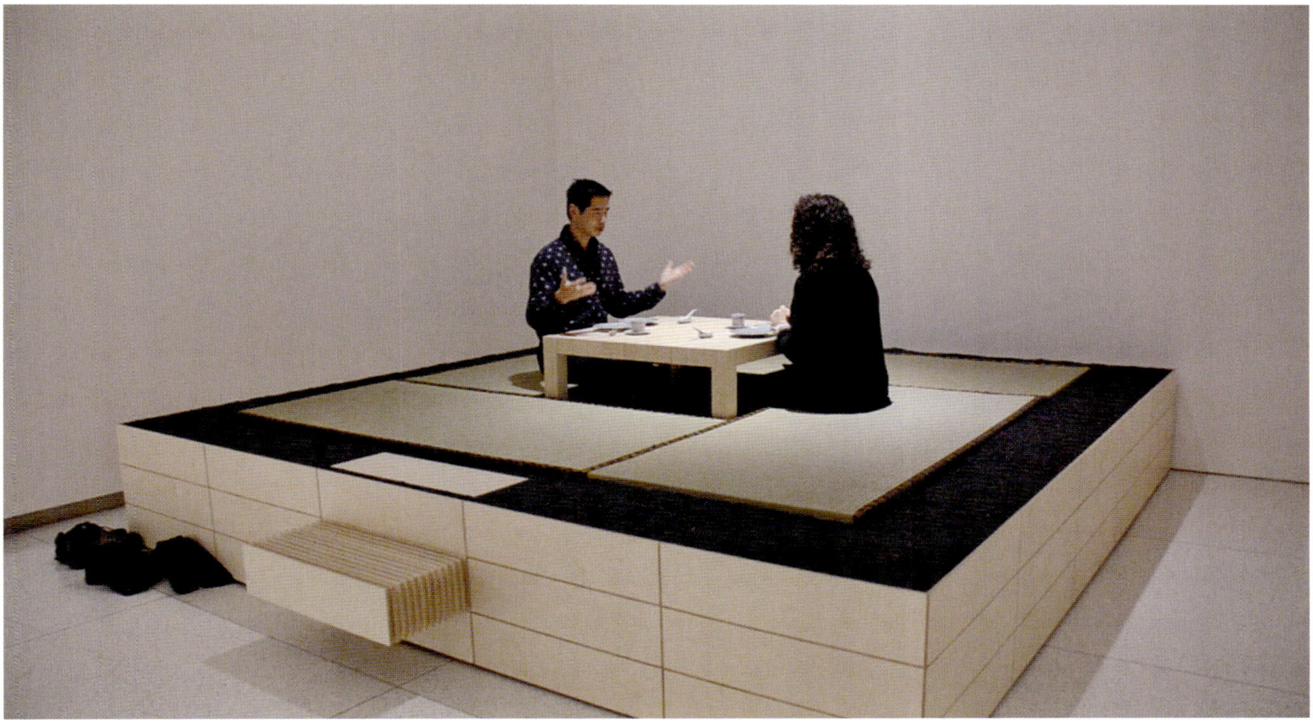

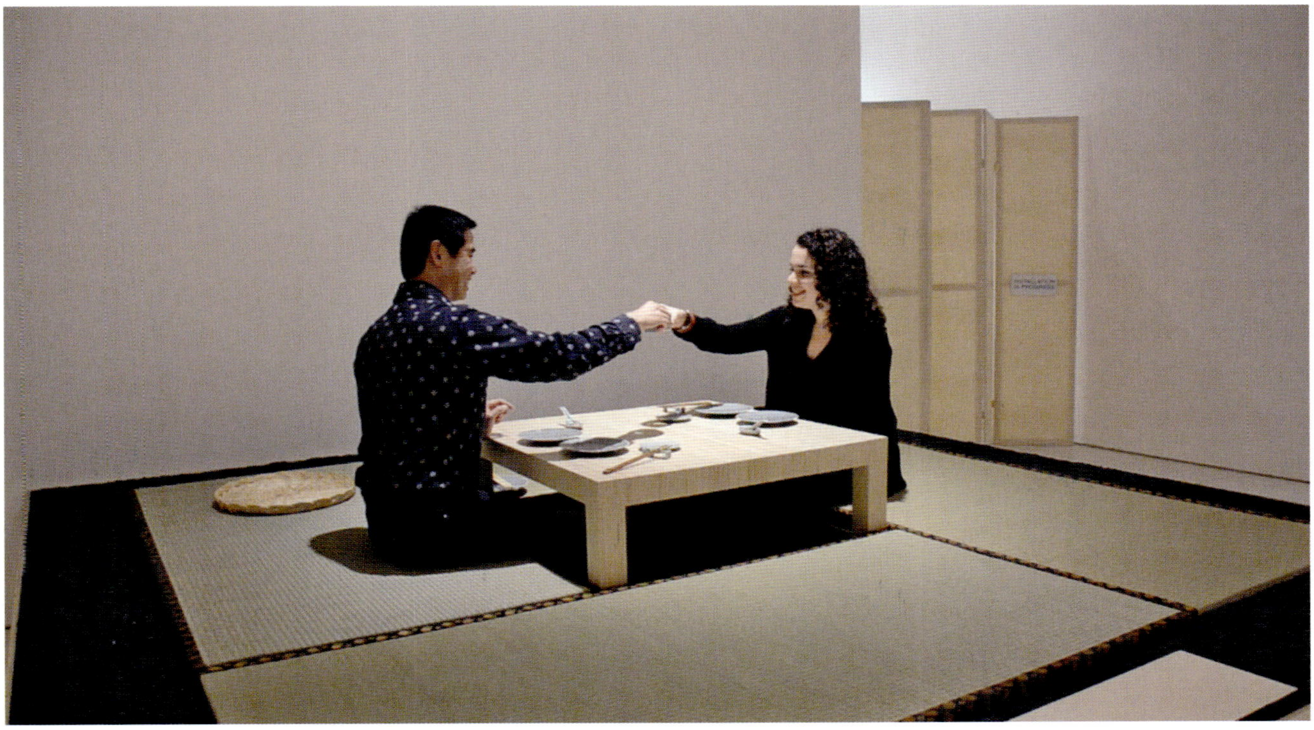

Interview

SMART: Can you describe your path as an artist and sources of inspiration for your work, either in or beyond the context of art?

LEE MINGWEI: The influence of my practice came from multiple sources. I'm Taiwanese, which has a lot of Japanese influences—Taiwan was occupied by Japan for fifty years—and also Chinese influences. That gave me an aesthetic sense that is quite minimal and clean-cut. But I'm very conscious of not using visual icons where people would say, "Oh, he's from a Chinese-speaking country," like a dragon or something like that.

I didn't have any inkling when I was growing up that one day I would become an artist. I was too busy fighting off my parents' wish that I become a medical doctor, just like my grandma, dad, uncles, aunties, and cousins. When I came to the United States, I was studying biology and architecture. As a biology student at University of Washington, I focused a lot on psychology—the human relationship part of it—without anticipating that I was actually going to use it in my later career as an artist. But my interest in human relationships was already quite clear at that time.

I also studied textiles and architecture at California College of Arts, and sculpture for my MFA at Yale. Studying architecture gives me a better sense of how physically my project can relate to the people when they come and walk around it and touch it or see it. Those practices become very handy when I do my projects. The conceptual part of my art is highly influenced by Chan Buddhists but also by Western theories of conceptual practice and also Fluxus and Joseph Beuys. Since I went to California College of the Arts in California, I studied with Suzanne Lacy and read a lot Allan Kaprow's work. Consequently, my work has a little bit of a Bay Area aesthetic, which I'm very proud of. A lot of these things come and go and become a part of my project.

Rirkrit Tiravanija was also an inspiration. When I was doing *The Dining Project*, one of my professors, John Newman said, "Do you know this artist, Rirkrit, who did this project at Gavin Brown's gallery?" At that time, he did the curry project. And I had no idea, so he said, "Let's invite him to teach." Rirkrit was there for a whole semester. We had a great conversation. I don't know if he remembers this. Both projects use food as intimacy and sharing, but they're completely different in terms of the essence of the work. His work is seemingly very extroverted, because the food is there and anybody can come and enjoy. But for him, it's an introverted project because he's not there anymore. He disappeared from the scene. In contrast, my project is seemingly very introverted because nobody sees the experience and it's only one person at a time after the museum closes. But personally it's very extroverted because I'm right there with the person who's dining. We had a wonderful and quite enlightening conversation because a lot of people later on would compare this project to the curry project that he did. I was so happy that we had that conversation because he really helped me understand my own work.

SMART: Tell us about *The Dining Project*—its impetus, intention, and production—and how it fits into your broader practice.

LM: When I arrived at New Haven in 1995 for graduate school, I felt quite isolated. My instinct is to go out and talk to people. So I put posters around campus, asking anyone who was interested in "introspective conversation and food sharing" to contact me. When I went back to my apartment that evening, I had about forty-five messages on my machine inquiring about the dinner. For the whole year at the graduate program, almost every other day, I invited one of these people to come to my studio. Before they arrived, I called to ask, "What is your dietary preference? Do you have an restriction or allergies?" And then I'd go to Chinatown to get the fresh ingredients and prepare the meal for them before they came. When they came, around 7:30 pm, the food would already be prepared and on the table, so all we did was enjoy the food, the company, and the conversation, and that was it. There was no recording of any sort for that first evolution of the project at Yale.

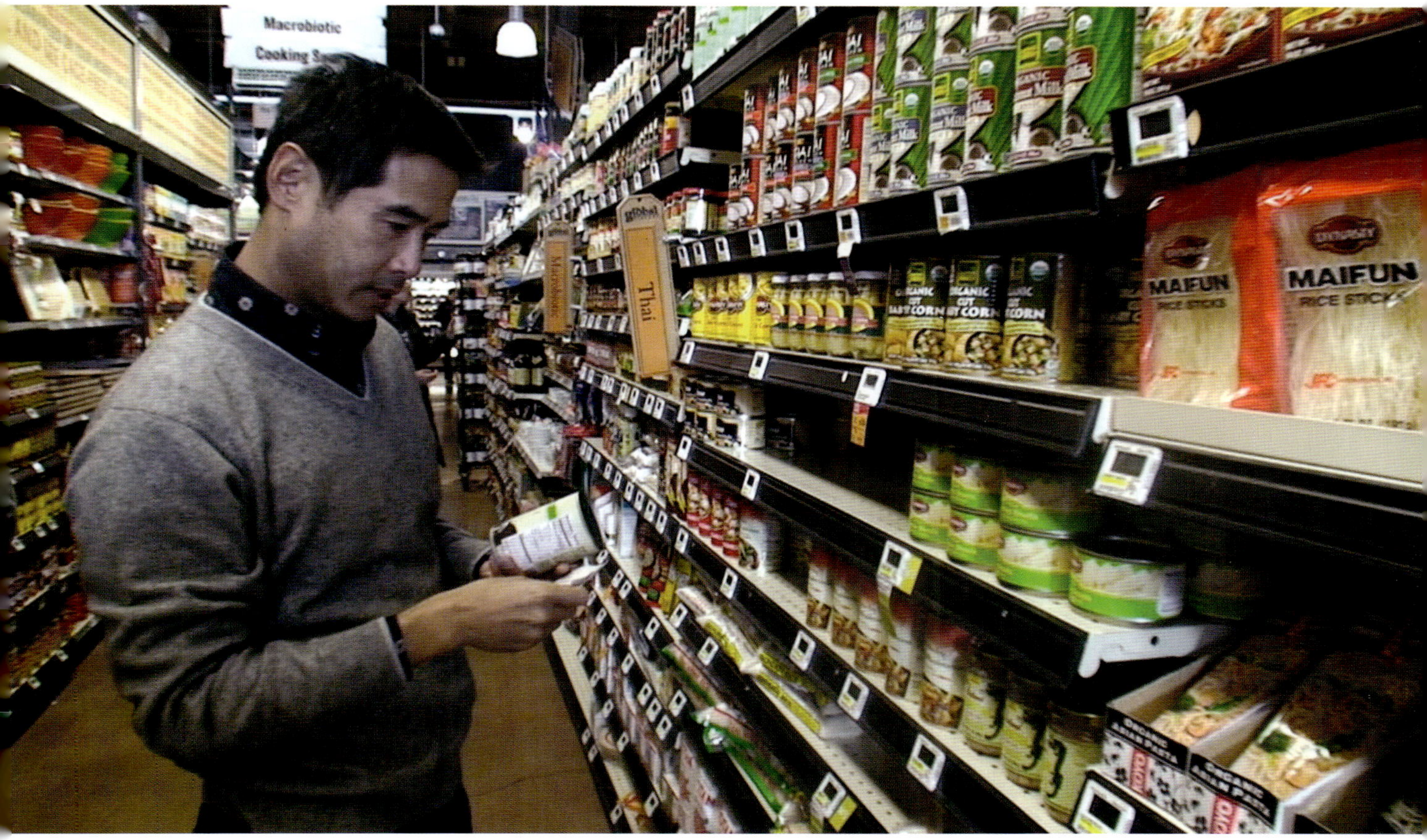

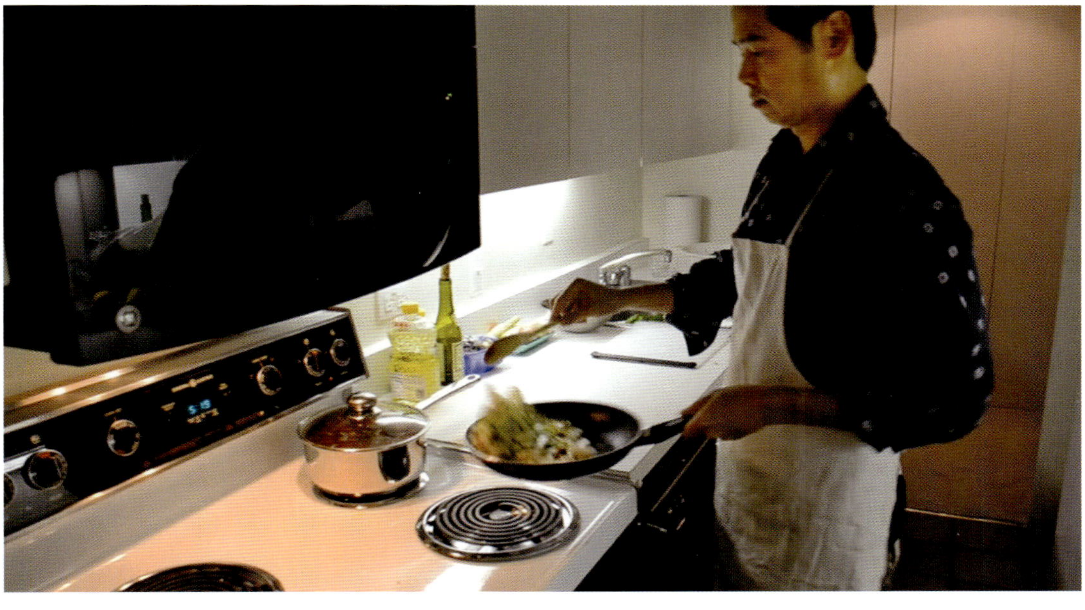

TOP: Lee shopping for ingredients for *The Dining Project*, February 12, 2012

BOTTOM: Lee preparing a dinner in Chicago, February 13, 2012

For the second stage of *The Dining Project*, I was invited to do a solo project at Lombard-Freid Projects in 1997 right after I graduated from school. We picked the diners through lottery. We had a little lottery card that asked people to write their name and phone number on it. So I'd pick the person and call them up. One of the people who came to dine with me was Eugenie Tsai who was then the curator at the Whitney Museum. She came to the dinner and I think she enjoyed it. The third evolution of that project was a year later at the Whitney Museum (in a solo show that also included *The Letter Writing Project*). The process was very similar. We also had the lottery cards there. The person would come at 7 pm because the museum closes at 6:30 and we would spend an hour or two or three to enjoy the meal that I had prepared.

SMART: What do people talk about at your dinners?

LM: The ranges of things people talk about are so great. At the Whitney Museum, I had sixty dinners because the show was about three and a half months long. They ranged from just a very simple, courteous conversation to one person who came and we were talking, talking, and talking and suddenly she said, "You know, I just came from my lawyer's place and I just signed the divorce contract with my husband." And she started crying. So there were so many of these very private moments that came because of this project and because of the self-selection of the people. Not everybody would go to the Whitney Museum, not everybody will put their name in the lottery, so I'm guaranteed to have a beautiful evening with these strangers.

SMART: Do you use any rituals or performative elements?

LM: I think the ritual for me when a person comes is to be as genuine as I can. There is no sort of physical ritual because I think that makes the other person feel like I know exactly what I'm doing, but they don't really know, and it's my territory. I don't want them to feel

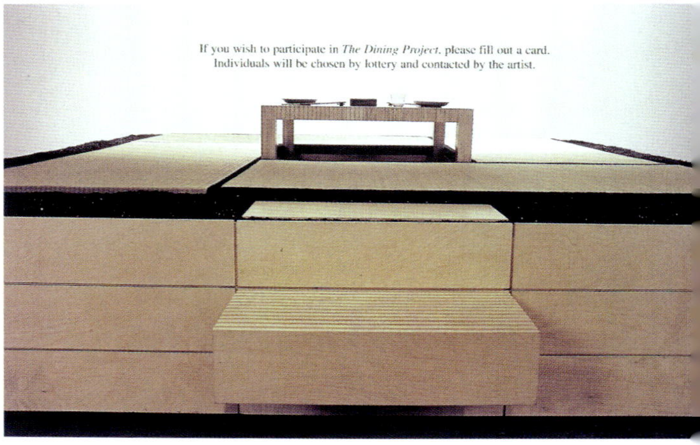

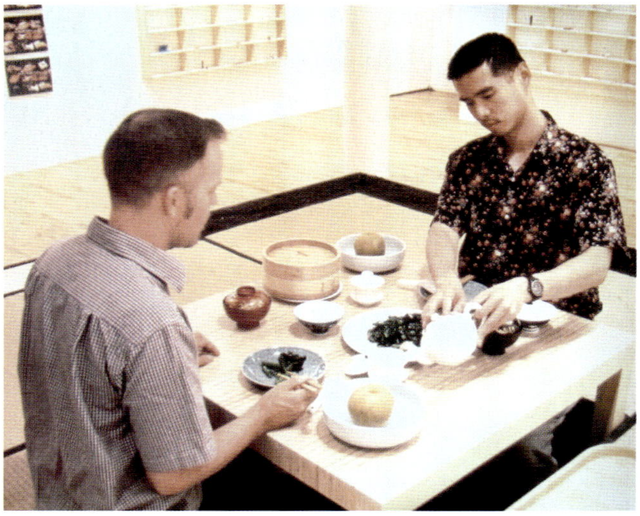

TOP: *The Dining Project*, Whitney Museum of American Art, 1998

BOTTOM: *The Dining Project*, Lombard-Freid Fine Arts (now Lombard-Freid Projects), New York, 1997

that, so it depends on the very first five seconds, whether we are going to hug or just shake hands. Any of these things could be possible.

SMART: How did you document the dinners?

LM: At Lombard-Freid, I only recorded the conversation, but the recording itself was kind of muted. Although you don't see us dining, you hear a murmur of some sort or conversation between two people. Later I videotaped the process, having the camera at the level of the table so that you only see the bowls, the chopsticks, the hands, the food going. You don't really see who's dining with me. You also hear the conversation so during the day I used this video and projected it onto the back wall of the platform so that you can see an idea of what happened at this particular place the night before or two nights before.

For the Smart Museum, I'm only recording the first dinner, which will then become the video shown during the rest of *Feast* in Chicago and as it tours. It is meant to provoke imagination when people come and see the work.

SMART: Is the experience of the dinner different when it's not recorded?

LM: The diners' experiences change quite a bit when they realize they are not being recorded, which is what I prefer. I believe that when documentation is going on—not only in this project, but in all my other performance projects—the psychology and emotions change quite a bit. It's almost like the state of an electron: when you look at the state, you change it from positive to negative just because you're looking at. So, ideally I don't want any recording. That solves the problem.

Growing up in Taiwan, I spent six summers in a Chan Buddhist monastery. I remember vividly that my teacher asked me to come and spend an hour with him. But when I went into his room he had an apple in his hand. He said, "I would like you to describe to me what this thing is for the next sixty minutes." And I thought, "Oh, that's really

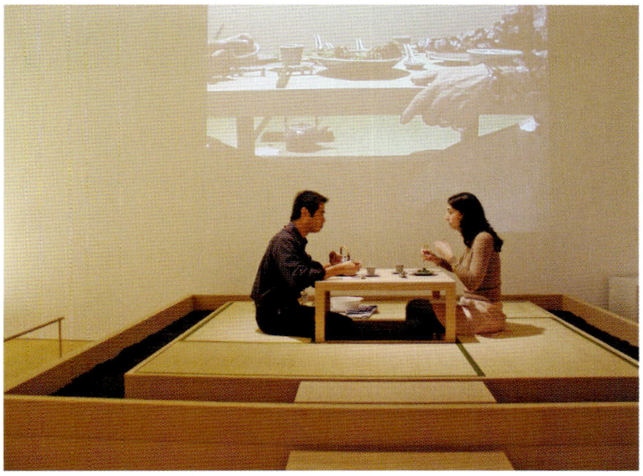

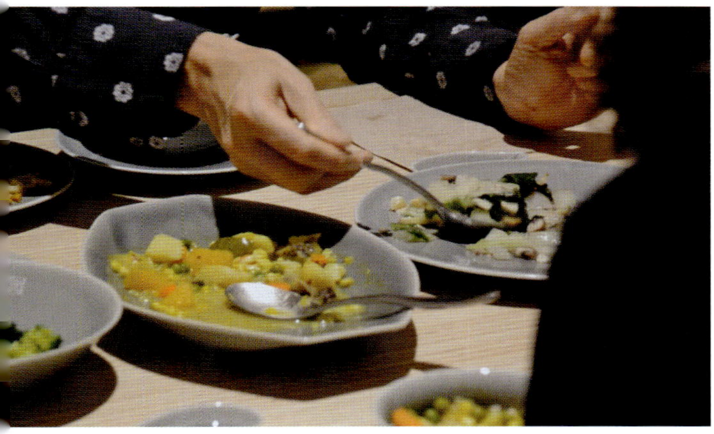

TOP: *The Dining Project*, Mori Art Museum, Tokyo, 2005

BOTTOM: *The Dining Project*, Smart Museum of Art, February 13, 2012

easy." I started going back in my memory for documentation of what "apple" was, or is, from the past twelve years (I was twelve years old). I said, "Well, apple is red, and it tastes good, and it smells good, it's a fruit, and blah blah blah," but after about thirty seconds I ran out of descriptions, or any of these things that were documented in my mind of what "apple" was supposed to be, so I was sitting there for the next fifty-eight-and-a-half minutes, just sweating, and didn't know what to do. At the end of sixty minutes, he then handed me the apple and then said, "Have a taste of it." I bit into it and I realized that was really what an apple is. It's nothing that came close to what I'd described. So that is a way of teaching or experiencing that documentation is really a very poor way of sharing with people what the actual thing is.

SMART: How did you develop the design for the sculptural installation portion of *The Dining Project*?

LM: The platform is very simple: 12 x 12 square feet, with four tatamis on top. Along the rim, there are a lot of black beans. It's visual, but also the idea of the bean: it's a food staple, but also it's a seed, it's the beginning of something, of a life, of a conversation, of a relationship. So is rice. I use the tatami because it's a form that I'm familiar with, from when I was growing up in Taiwan and also it has a beautiful aroma of the rice straw, which sets me into a very comfortable situation.

SMART: How would you describe the role of the meal in your practice?

LM: In *The Dining Project*, I use food as a medium for trust and intimacy between two strangers. Back in Taiwan, we are taught to share food with people—even strangers—that are in the immediate proximity. Therefore, this project connects to my very personal sense of hospitality in quite a few ways. I remember at home even today, when I go back to Taipei to see my parents, they often have extra pairs of chopsticks around because you never know if the next-door neighbor, or their kids, or friends, or anybody will come by. My grandmother was a doctor back in Taipei. When she retired, every morning she would wake up early in the morning, around 4 am, and she would prepare rice porridge for about twenty or thirty people, and at 6 am, she would bring out the pot and just stand in front of the house and whoever came, she would just give them a bowl of rice porridge. And often these are homeless people and beggars, or even just transient workers who were coming to the city to work. That idea of sharing is ingrained in my personality. Even today, my biggest pleasure is to cook a very simple meal for two friends or four friends during the weekend, and just talk about anything or everything we want, and use food as a medium for a sharing of hospitality and friendship.

SMART: Please say more about how hospitality and guest/host relationships play out in your projects.

LM: There are several categories in my practice. One is the one-on-one interactive component. Another one are these situations I set up for people. In the latter, the rule of the game is clearly expressed, so people do not need me to be there to experience the project. One-on-one projects, for example, *The Dining Project, The Sleeping Project, The Tourist Project*, or *The Mending Project*, are a way for me to be connected with the community who experiences my work. However, it's extremely draining emotionally and physically. After I did one of those one-on-one projects, psychologically I would go the other direction: I would create a project that is just insulation, which is so that I completely disappear from the scene. It's a way for me to protect myself, my own sanity. And I feel extremely honored when people can come and interact with me. However, people ask me,

"Does it have to be Lee Mingwei to be sitting there to mend the clothes, or to cook a meal with someone, or to sleep with a stranger?" I say, "No, it doesn't have to be Lee Mingwei. It's not because you're sleeping with Lee Mingwei, so it's art." As long as you and this person are strangers, that is the bare minimum—the most basic and the most important part of this project.

SMART: So you can envision a situation when one could enact *The Dining Project* without your presence.

LM: Definitely. I have already done it once at this place called Copia, north of San Francisco. Because I couldn't be there physically throughout the show, I did five meals myself, but in between I set up a situation. On one wall there was a lottery box, and on top of it, it says "provider." And on the other wall there is a lottery box, which says "receiver." The provider would be the one who cooks the meal and the receiver would be the one who comes to enjoy the meal. That actually worked out quite beautifully. It was a little bit hectic because each person is so different, and therefore it's a challenging task to maintain this project properly. But it's really quite an experience.

SMART: Could you talk about the experiences you try to create for the two different kinds of public for your work: the person who eats the food and then people who come to the museums?

LM: Yes, there are two different kinds of participants in my work. One is much more immediate: the chosen participant who comes because of the lottery. The second one is so much more distant: the ones who came and saw the documentation. They might think, "Oh, I wasn't even invited for the party." But there's a chance you might be invited by putting your name in.

The project would be similar even if I just set up a table at Grand Central Station and invited people to come and eat with me. I think the only small difference is, when it's placed in an institution such as a museum people go in there and start questioning: "Is this art? Could this be art?" That's what I want people to do with my work: to have a different idea of what art could be. And that's the beauty of putting this type of work in the museum.

SMART: Still, you create a very particular setting for the meal which is also an installation, so there's something more to it than just setting up a table.

LM: Yes. My architectural training definitely comes in when I create these works. For me, they have to be tactilely and also visually pleasant because I really could not imagine myself eating on an office table. The conversation would be so different. We are very sensitive beings. Imagine if you are in a very relaxed, very comfortable, very soothing dining situation, and the food hopefully is okay, the conversation will be so different than if you are at MacDonald's and on a plastic table. I'm not saying which one is better or worse, just that the conversation is so different, and I prefer the pristine situation.

SMART: What do you hope people take away from your work?

LM: I would like them to realize that they could be the person who is generous to other people through simple gestures like preparing a meal for someone.

Laura Letinsky

SINCE THE LATE 1990s, Laura Letinsky has been transforming domestic detritus into photographs that imbue the still life—one of the classic genres of Western art—with fresh formal possibilities and contemporary emotional resonance. In these pictures, Letinsky arranges evocative fragments left over from meals into precisely composed photographs that express the tensions latent within the domestic feast: its dark edges as well as its sensual and convivial pleasures. This approach grew out of her first major body of work, *Venus Inferred* (1989–96). Intimacy and distance commingle within that series of sensual yet subtly uneasy portraits of couples at home. Shifting to still life allowed Letinsky to more obliquely probe tender topics like the complexities of domestic experience, desire's inevitable slide into loss, and the drive to consume, while further extending her interest in the slippage between sensation and its photographic representation. Her images capitalize on the genre's history as well as its current glossy prevalence in lifestyle blogs and magazines.

Letinsky's still lifes have evolved considerably over time, as is evident in the works included in *Feast*. In early images, for instance *Untitled #12* from the series *Hardly More Than Ever,* (1999–2000), seemingly casual arrangements hint at narrative possibilities. Here, the intimately paired coffee cups might be read as markers of sweet domesticity if not for their marginalized and cropped placement: the picture centers instead on arcs of crumbs and spent petals that outline now-absent objects. *Untitled #6*, from the series *Rome* (2009), from nearly a decade later, depicts the aftermath of another kind of meal—a dinner and photograph commissioned by an Italian collector. This image includes elements we might associate with feasting—rich foods, sumptuous materials, luxury, and excess—but again, the mood is less convivial than melancholic. Letinsky depicts a scattering of upended glasses, precariously stacked plates, and leftover bits, all skirting a deep darkness just beyond the table's edge. She amplified this prickly mood by creating a vertiginous pictorial space in which dishes seem almost to slide out of the photograph.

Feast also includes a new image created for the exhibition. Letinksy had initially considered bringing her interests in the processes of hosting and cooking more strongly forward—perhaps by opening a temporary restaurant or holding a series of salons—but eventually decided to hew more tightly to her core interest in domestic aesthetics as they intersect with the ubiquity of photographic representation. Thus, in tandem with *Feast*'s opening in Chicago, Letinsky hosted the exhibiting artists for a luncheon at her home, preparing most of the dishes and serving them on a mix of old china and elegantly rustic porcelain that she also made herself. She photographed the remains and singled out a few fragments—candy, a slice of onion—to cut from her own photographs and rearrange into a new tableau that combines these fragments, magazine cutouts, and actual objects within an open white space. She describes this new way of working as "three dimensional collage." Like the meal, Letinsky made this photograph through a series of careful, private choices and gestures that selectively reveal elements of "the real" experience in order to make a new, sensual thing that exists both for her own pleasure and for the pleasure and consumption of others.[1]

---

[1] A professor at the University of Chicago, Letinsky also taught a new course in conjunction with *Feast*, "Food for Thought," co-created and co-taught with Stephanie Smith in 2011; Letinsky taught it again in 2012.

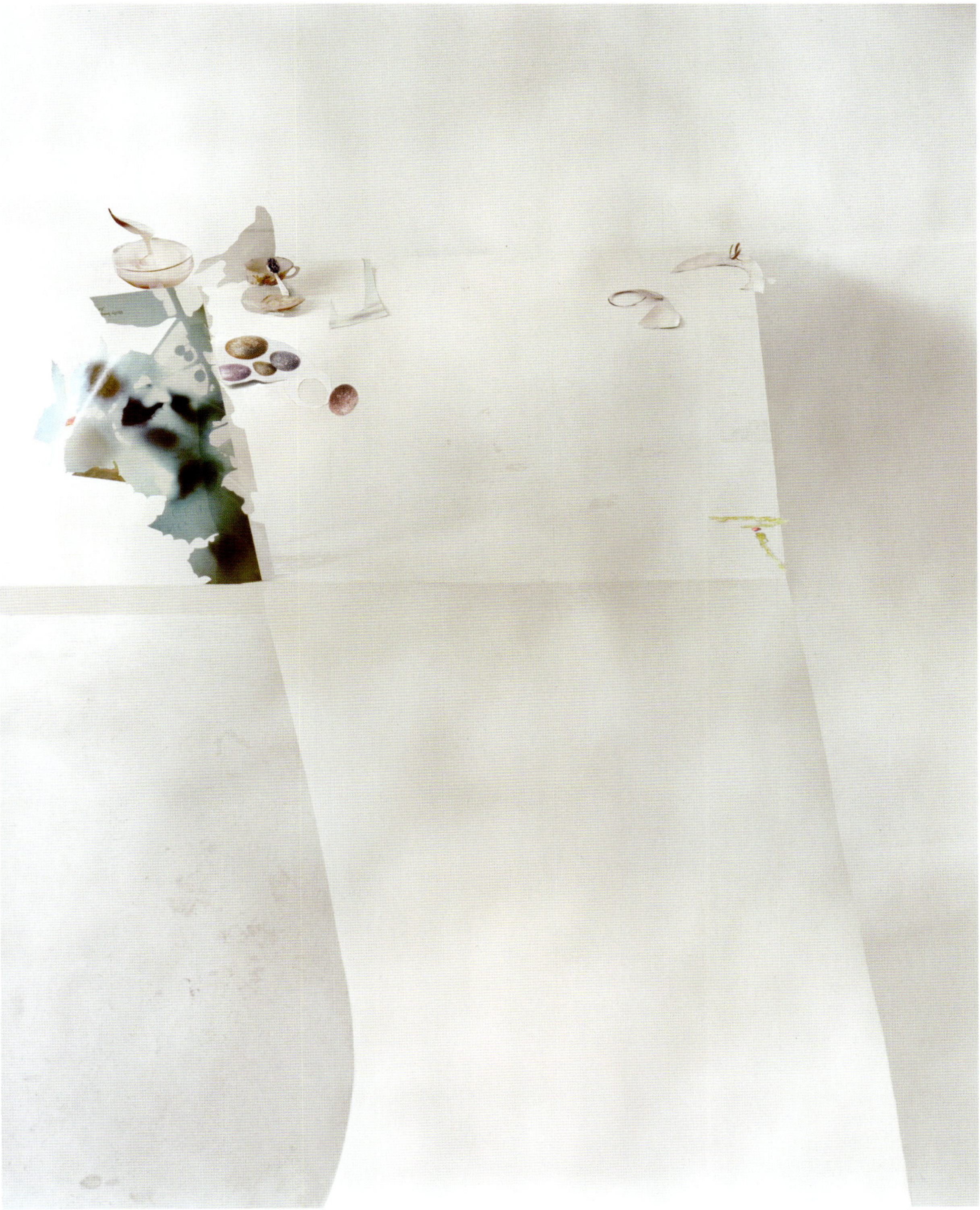

Untitled #37, from the series *Ill Form and Void Full*, 2012

Interview

SMART: Can you describe your trajectory as an artist?

LAURA LETINSKY: I'm not really sure what it entailed and certainly it only makes any kind of sense in hindsight. I always drew and painted and made art and wanted to be an artist and so wanted to go to art school. Since I was worried about financial stability and self-reliance, I started out in interior design, then switched to architecture once I realized that it was where the real decisions got made (reinforcing stereotypical ideas about gender to be sure), and then finally switched to art school. I realized that there was nothing to be lost, or gained, in this pursuit—that is, I wanted to be an artist and realized that I'd find a way to support myself and this activity, come hell or high water.

SMART: What are some relevant sources of inspiration for your work: either in or beyond the context of art?

LL: Painting has long been my "go to" source as it has powerfully shaped—visually and ideologically—what we expect and demand of photography. The language employed by painters is reiterated, albeit with technological and thus conceptual shifts, through contemporary media. The painters Caravaggio and Giorgio Morandi and the photographer E. J. Bellocq are artists I return to, as well as more recent artists including Daniel Gordon, Jessica Stockholder, and Richard Tuttle. Less and less I refer to visual artists' work as more and more I turn to literature by, to name a few: Anne Carson, Lydia Davis, Gertrude Stein, David Foster Wallace, and Diane Williams, as well as loud music in my studio by Bjork, Nick Cave, Arvo Pärt, and Sparklehorse.

SMART: What drew you to photography?

LL: When I began in art school, I wanted to paint but I was too enamored of the material of paint, of color. I was completely inarticulate with the medium and at the time, didn't know how to make sense of it. Photography enforced a restraint, a distancing because of the process, the delayed gratification that allowed me to engage in its communicable possibilities. The sense of transformation, of magic even though I knew how it worked, was just amazing.

I quickly realized through art history that two-dimensional form has a historical, narrative, and political trajectory. Or perhaps, many. That is, painting influenced ideas about photographs, determining what constitutes a good photograph, its form, narrative, and so on. I have drawn from this history to interrogate its valuations and ideology, trying to understand why certain ideas have become prevalent and naturalized. Painting, to me, doesn't operate on the level of trust and mistrust that photography parlays, as it doesn't claim a truth. Sure, it is associated with a kind of valuation but there isn't the same issue of what exists in the picture being tantamount to some notion of reality the way that there will always be with photography, even when it's pure abstraction. The sense of indexicality, of light touching the photographic surface—that direct sense/sensation is something ideologically wed to photographs. Painting is a different kind of fiction, a different seduction strategy and thus its apprehension is also a different beast.

SMART: Tell us about the earlier photographs exhibited in *Feast*—their compositional strategies, and their relationship to the emotional register of intimate domestic space.

LL: When I began the still life work it was a turning away from an earlier series (*Venus Inferred*) in which I photographed couples as an investigation of love, romance, and sexuality as perpetuated and mediated by photography. I had grown increasingly frustrated with the limitations of photography, and of love, or the body's ability to communicate. I was curious about the way environment—both the domestic space and the photographic space—set up a more complex and convoluted set of expectations and provocations.

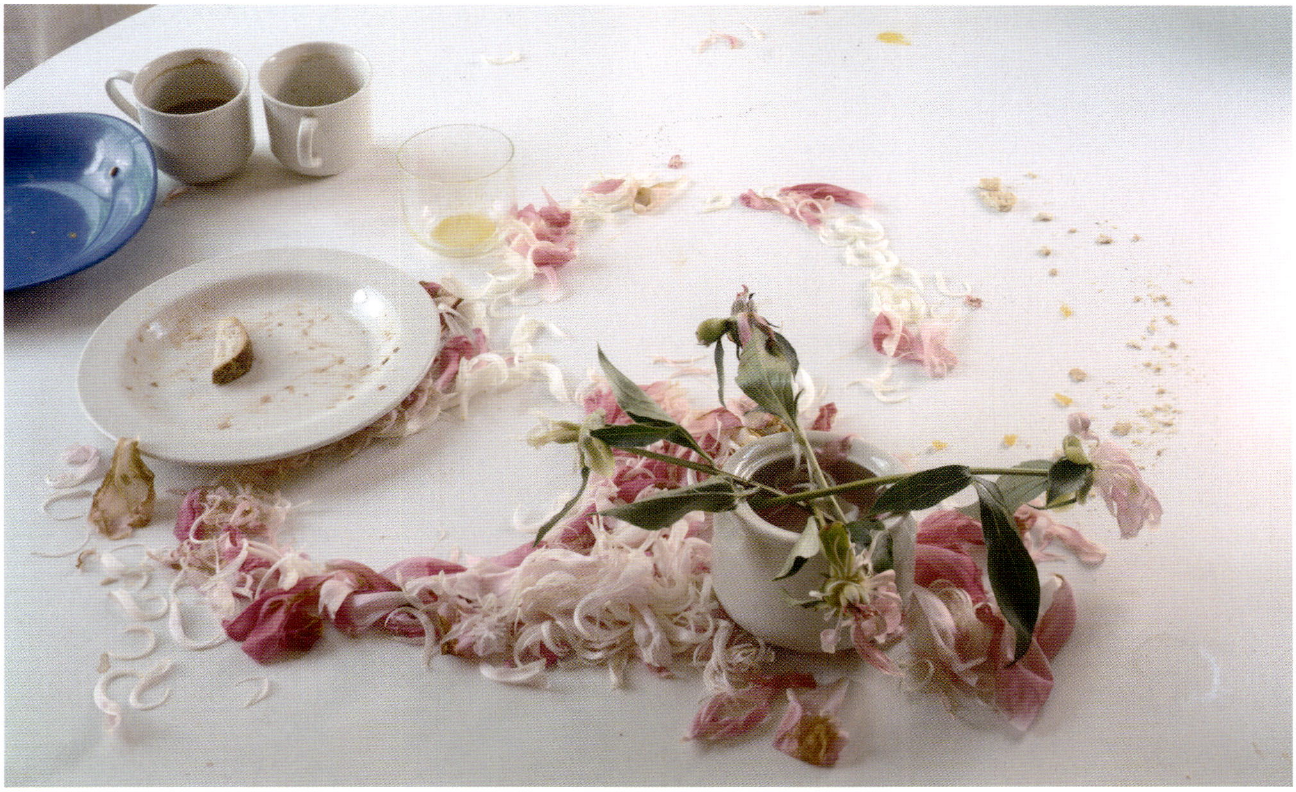

Untitled #22, from the series *Hardly More Than Ever* (formerly, *Morning and Melancholia*), 1999–2000

I had long been interested in the still life and the way this seemingly narrow scene spoke so much about the society that produced these images, that is, the way this arena of the home speaks to wider ideological and political ideas about intimacy, love, want, sustenance, repulsion, and so on. Not only what is pictured but how this site is pictured is critical to the ideas put forth. For example, the seventeenth-century northern European painters used this genre to set forth their ideas and ideals about the world and their aspirations through realistic, widely reproduced images that demanded photography's "invention." Today, photographic media is domineering in its description of "home," setting up expectations, desires, a pedagogy of what home should be and to which we should aspire. Of course I'm aware of the chicken-versus-the-egg issue in that we produce these images for popular consumption in an endless and ultimately unsatisfying cycle that necessitates more-more-more. More stuff, more pictures of stuff. In tackling this genre of still life I want my viewers to have the sensation of being off balance just as they think they know what they are looking at, in order to make them aware of the act of looking, of picturing, and to connect that to issues related to love, need, and want.

I've often used white space as akin to the white space of the wall upon which the images are hung. But a few years ago I began photographing in really low light and became interested in the tension of trying to see, both from too much light and not enough. I used these aspects to overload or veil in order to complicate the act of perception and of sight. I'm interested in that work of narrating the scene, of composing a visual trajectory through which the viewer moves and in which the viewer gets lost just when they least expect it because after all, it's the home, such a known entity, yet so consciously constructed, so much a projection of want, expectation, need, remorse, nostalgia, and so on.

SMART: Your photograph for *Feast* is part of a new approach to the still life. Could you describe the way you're working now?

LL: I began this recent work after a year's hiatus from making pictures. A number of factors conspired to contribute to a long-held mistrust of art, photography. Not to be melodramatic, but it was a moment of mistrust of everything. After a year or so of reading, writing, looking, and thinking, I was ready to make a big shift in my practice. Looking at the work that really engaged me, I knew my practice had to change so as to participate in a dialogue with which I was smitten, and so I began these (for lack of a better word) collages that I then photograph and present as singular images. The concerns in which I have always been mired persist. There's still a negotiation between the intimate or the small, and the social or the large. While everyone has a notion of "home," its construction remains firmly within our unconscious, its "Venus-on-the-half-shell" status a tender notion. And, like all that is "underneath," there's a lot of individual and collective energy involved in making it all seem natural but it's really such an all-consuming construction and conceptualization.

SMART: The idea of the leftover comes up a lot in your work. In the new work, where does the collage material come from? Is this gathering process akin to that of your prior still life photographs?

LL: The recent work builds on ongoing concerns but I hope I'm more articulate about them by using materials that already exist as images in order to make other images.
For me, the difference is that almost all the pictures are about desire and wanting, whereas the detritus in my earlier series had been cast off, destined as no-longer-picture-worthy. In the magazines and advertisements and pictures—mine and others'—from which I cull the source material, the thing pictured and/or the fact that it is pictured makes it picture-worthy: a thing of worth. Wanted. These images, in conjunction with various three-dimensional and scanned images and the constructions in which I picture them, contest the relationship between real and pictured, wanted and had, future and past.

I do think about making pictures as a parallel activity to cooking, to putting together tastes and sensations such that a fuller experience is possible—trying to awake consumers to the act of consumption as well as to what is being consumed.

SMART: Could you say more about the connection between making pictures and making meals?

LL: I understand the genre of still life as irreducibly about the social sphere in which it was produced, in which these images of home confirm, challenge, define, and contest our ideas, and ideals of this space which is both solitary and social. In terms of this show, I am excited to have this aspect of my work acknowledged as it has always been the subtext for my work. Just as still life has been a somewhat debased genre, associated with the small and the feminine, and therefore unworthy of serious attention, there now seems more general understanding of how this idea, this place, is nestled into larger, more all-encompassing political, social, and theoretical ideologies. As I see my home life feeding (ah, the bad puns abound!) into my work, and visa versa, hosting dinner parties has become more and more a part of my practice. Whether to call it art or life is indeed the question.

In terms of menu, as with my art, I begin with general sensations and ideas that I wish to

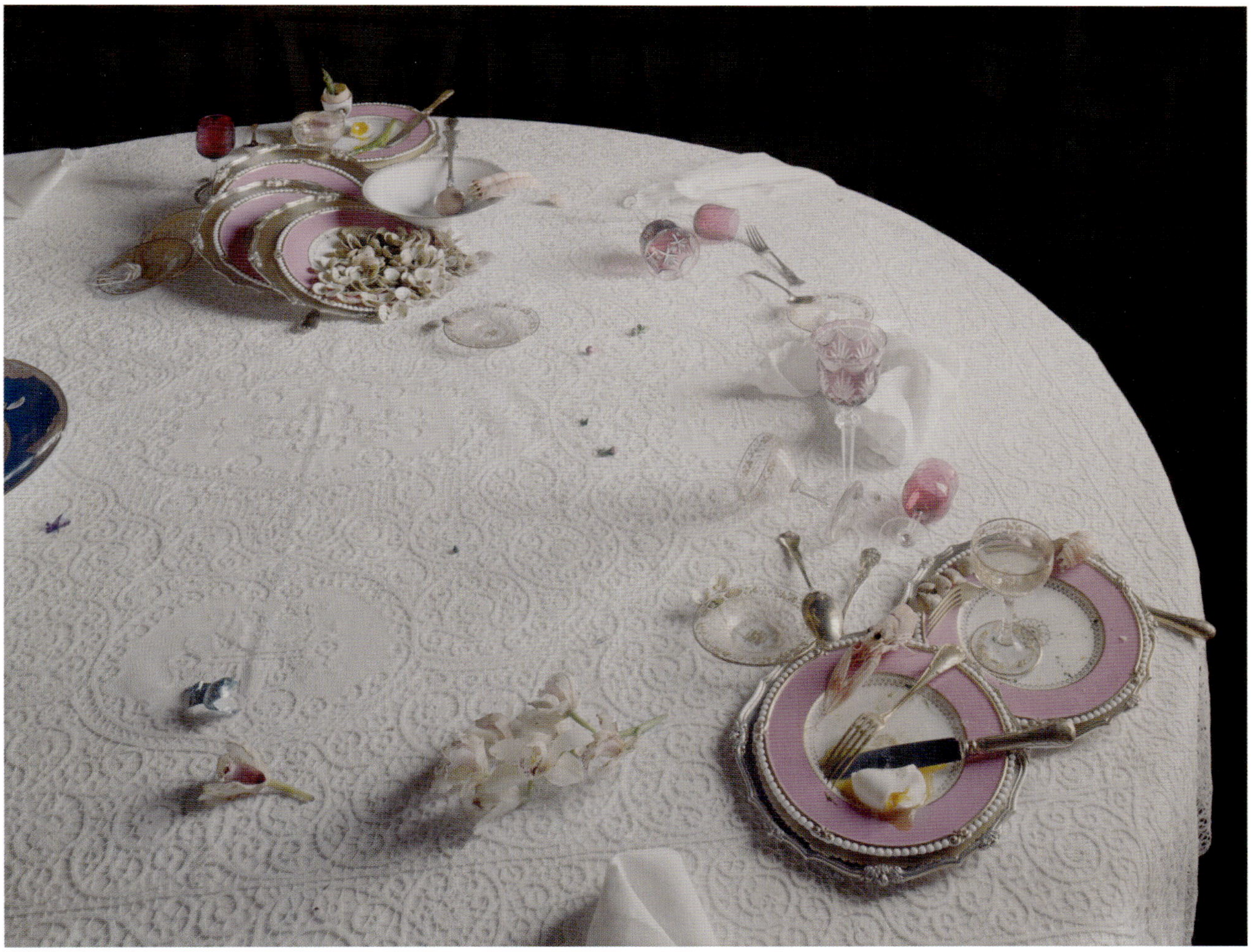

Untitled #6, from the series *Rome*, 2009

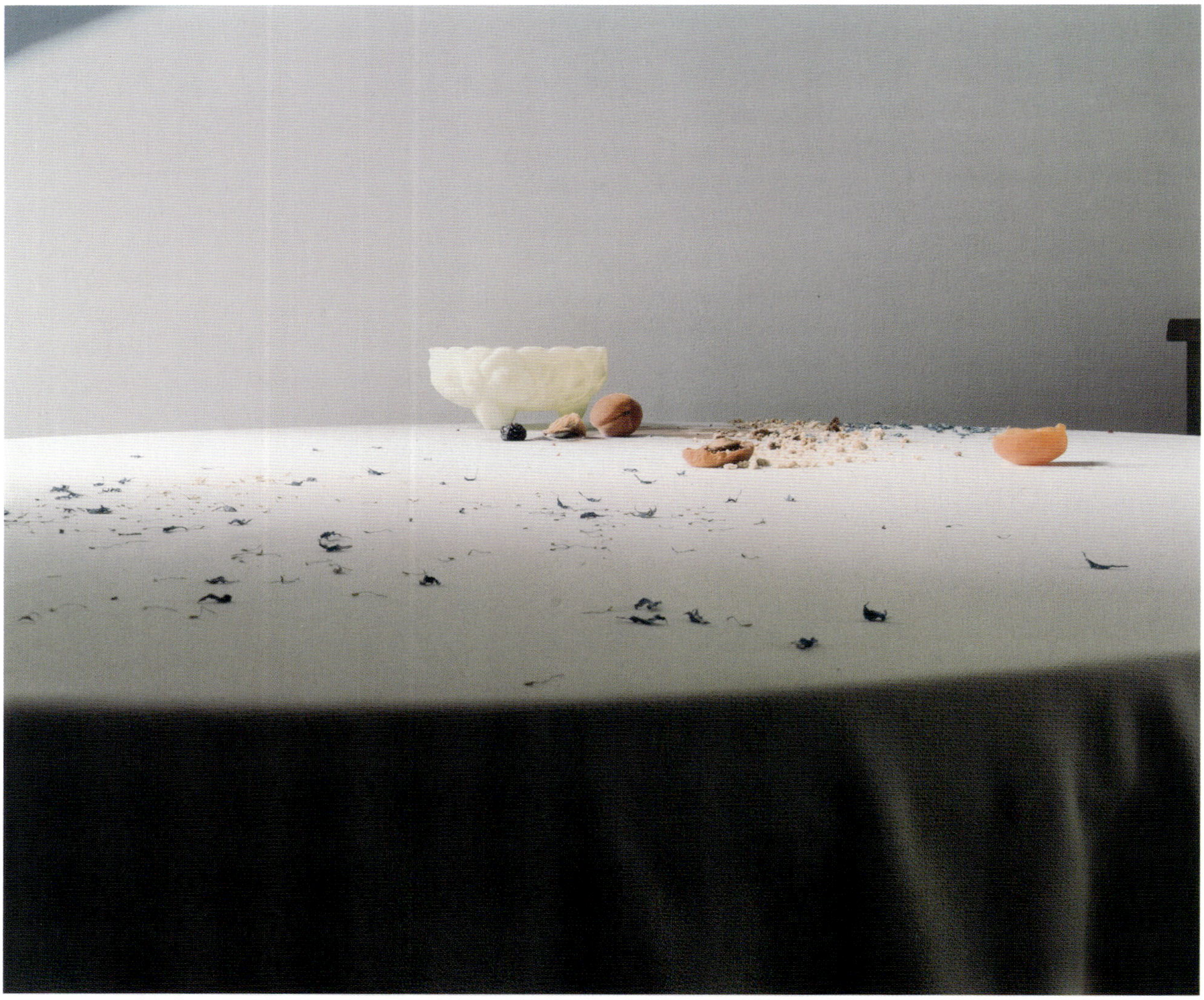

Untitled #80, from the series *Hardly More Than Ever*
(formerly, *Morning and Melancholia*), 2003

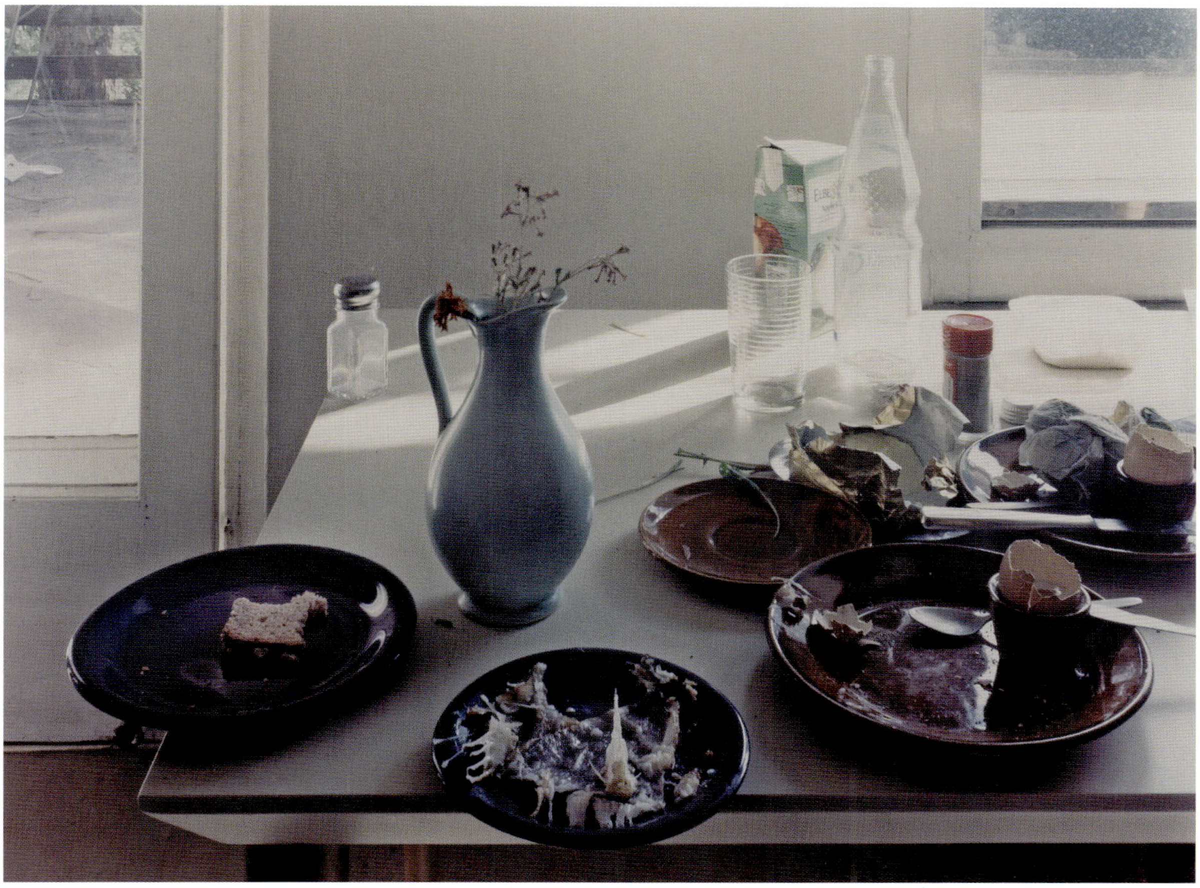

Untitled #12, from the series *Hardly More Than Ever*
(formerly, *Morning and Melancholia*), 1997

explicate, and then as the cooking or photographing commences, there's some degree of intuition, and compromise, trying to make a material behave in a certain manner, and acceptance of what is available. It's a process of translation of what I think I want and what is possible.

SMART: How did these issues factor into your decision to host a luncheon for participating artists in *Feast,* and to use that meal as the basis for a new photograph?

LL: Over the past few years I've been increasingly territorial about assuming hosting for departmental functions, relishing the opportunity to bring friends and others together to imbibe, eat, talk, and be together. I like setting up a pleasurable relaxed eating event as the ground for talk, friendship, and aesthetic apprehension. I do not mean this "apprehension" in the negative sense, but rather the uptake of aesthetic experience, which I guess does involve some anxiety, always, and maybe this is part of the pleasure? So, yes, I wanted to invite the artists over for lunch so as to set up this possibility. It is an extension of common social, familial, and communal events, but as I've already said, the attention to form and content abuts our ideas and definitions of art, particularly as my approach to hosting and cooking is attitudinally similar to that of making my photographs.

SMART: How would you describe the role of hospitality in your practice? Do questions about hospitality figure into your process or thinking?

LL: Hospitality matters to any artist who exhibits their work in that there's always the question of reception. Within modernism there's some idea that's been perpetuated about making art for art's sake and not playing to a patron/marketplace—as if we could separate ourselves from the world we inhabit. Prior to the last 150 or so years, artists had patrons and were thought of more as craftspersons, filling a niche, often quite literally. Now art is supposed to be free from such demands and instead artists produce work that they hope engages their audience.

I understand the art that I make as part of a discussion with other artists, thinkers, lookers, and in this way I guess there's always some wish to be a good hostess, although this requires a degree of criticality so as to challenge, provoke, seduce, and not quite satiate one's audience. Maybe like excellent meals, certain aspects remain prominent in memory and thought, perhaps fomenting further engagement—although that's a question.

SMART: What do you hope people take away from your work?

LL: The intentions of the artist and what one's looker/reader actually experiences can be quite different. That said, for me the work is about an exchange, a set of ambivalences that circulate around the intimate sphere as perpetuated through mass media. It's about wanting, getting, and wanting more; infatuation and its dissolution; trying to make the best of what I have; the relativity of any one perspective which the camera describes; the tremendous effort of making "love," home, beauty when it's not working and the ease and seeming naturalness when it is.

Feast artists and other guests at a lunch prepared and hosted by Letinsky at her home, February 16, 2012

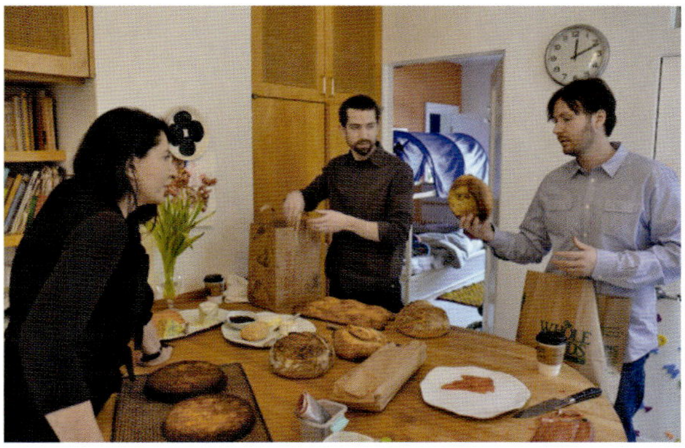

Left to right: Marina Abramović and architects/bread bakers Mason Pritchett and Casimir Kujawa

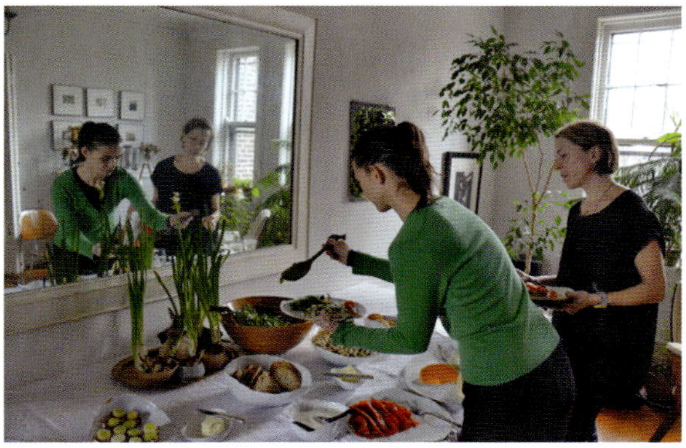

Ana Prvacki (left) and Letinsky (right)

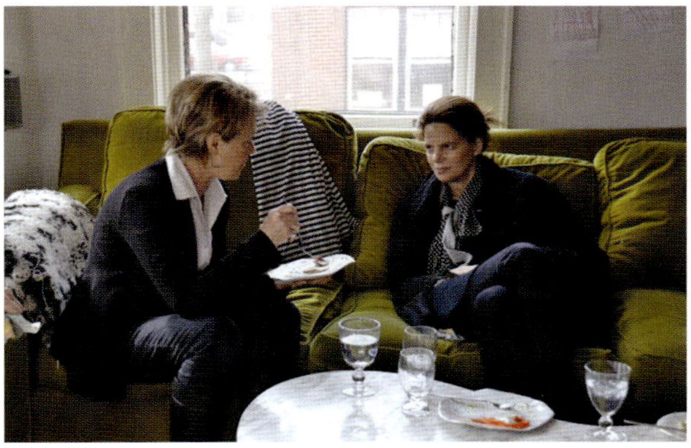

Suzanne Lacy (left) and Mary Ellen Carroll (right)

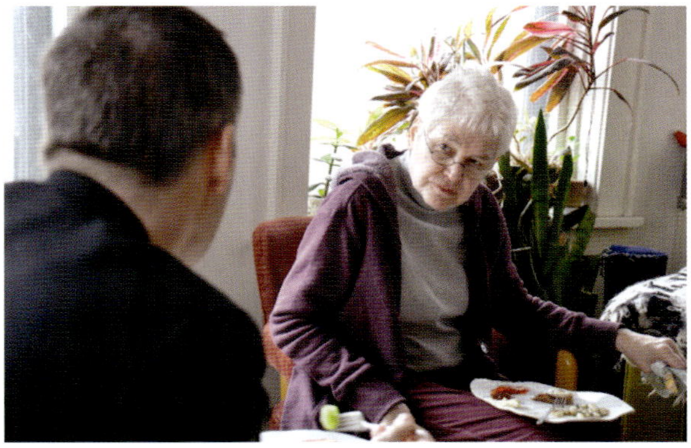

Architect Simon Dance (left) and Alison Knowles (right)

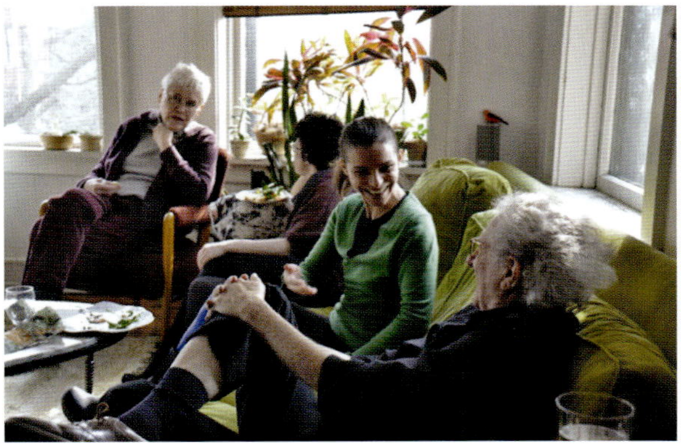

Left to right: Alison Knowles, Stephanie Smith, Ana Prvacki, and Tom Marioni

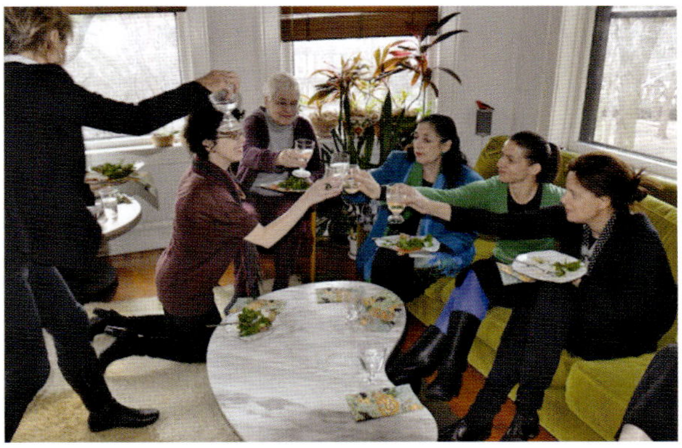

Left to right: Suzanne Lacy, Stephanie Smith, Alison Knowles, Bonnie Sherk, Ana Prvacki, and Mary Ellen Carroll

Mildred's Lane

MILDRED'S LANE IS AN ONGOING collaboration and experimental research- and event-based practice, created by the artists Mark Dion and J. Morgan Puett in 1998. In his individual practice, Dion explores questions of how we come to know and represent the natural world within the spaces of culture; his art draws heavily on ecology, archaeology, and old-fashioned modes of museum display (the diorama, for instance). Much of Puett's work, meanwhile, addresses the histories, production processes, economies, and radical potential of fashion and other artisanal and domestic crafts. The artists' interests and aesthetic strategies overlap across these topics, due in part to their shared love of nineteenth-century and rural aesthetics, and the related activities of teaching and hosting. These common interests infuse their ongoing work as Mildred's Lane.

Mildred's Lane is a place, a project, and a proposition. The place is ninety-six acres of rolling land in rural Pennsylvania that Dion and Puett bought in 1997 along with a few other friends. The place was, at first, their home. Both Dion and Puett are personally and professionally attuned to the subtleties of the natural world and to the careful design of domestic experience. Mildred's Lane offered a space away from urban life and the peripatetic demands of international art careers. It became a place where friends, colleagues, and neighbors could gather for beautiful meals and artful programs, including public lectures, performances, and massive bonfire parties. As a project, Mildred's Lane now extends those informal interactions through a more formal set of activities. Its work focuses on an experimental summer school/summer camp in which small groups of students, artists, curators, and writers gather for three-week sessions in which they collectively pursue art or research projects, while also sharing in the process of preparing meals and tending to the site. The proposition of Mildred's Lane is that this everyday work of thinking, talking, cleaning, cooking, and eating together should be grounded in an "ethics of comportment" that might allow us to "collectively create new modes of being in the world" if practiced with focus, intention, curiosity, and joy.

For *Feast,* Puett created an elaborate wall installation that distills the visual aesthetic of Mildred's Lane and documents some of the playful approaches to meals at the site. Various objects form a vaguely humanoid arrangement. The heart—or perhaps the belly—of the piece is a small refrigerator, one of a series of small-scale sculptures that Puett calls "refrigerator hooshes." At Mildred's Lane, every space is treated with aesthetic care, and Puett habitually arranges contents of her refrigerator into refined displays of foodstuffs, antique vessels, and old linen—a process that she terms "hooshing." Here, a small refrigerator offers a sculptural analogue for that domestic practice. It both contains and is surrounded by precisely arranged images, materials, tools, and artifacts, many of which relate to the production, collection, and consumption of food. A slideshow of Mildred's Lane imagery runs on a monitor inside, and it is draped with marked-up linen from one of Puett's "algorithmic dinners." This particular dinner was based on a game of Puett's invention: a "Scrabble Scramble" in which participants recombine the letters of their names to generate lists of ingredients and dishes, plan everything out on linen cloths like those shown here, and then work together to prepare the meal. In these dinners—as with every activity at Mildred's Lane—Dion, Puett, and their many friends and collaborators share the roles of host and guest: the artists foster the overall mood and sensibility but also ask that their guests taken on responsibility for the sensory, aesthetic, intellectual, and emotional tenor of the meal—a perfect embodiment of the collectively generated hospitality that underlies all of Mildred Lane's activities.

OPPOSITE: *Town & Country 2010 Sessions: Social Saturday* dinner setting for Fritz Haeg, at Mildred's Lane

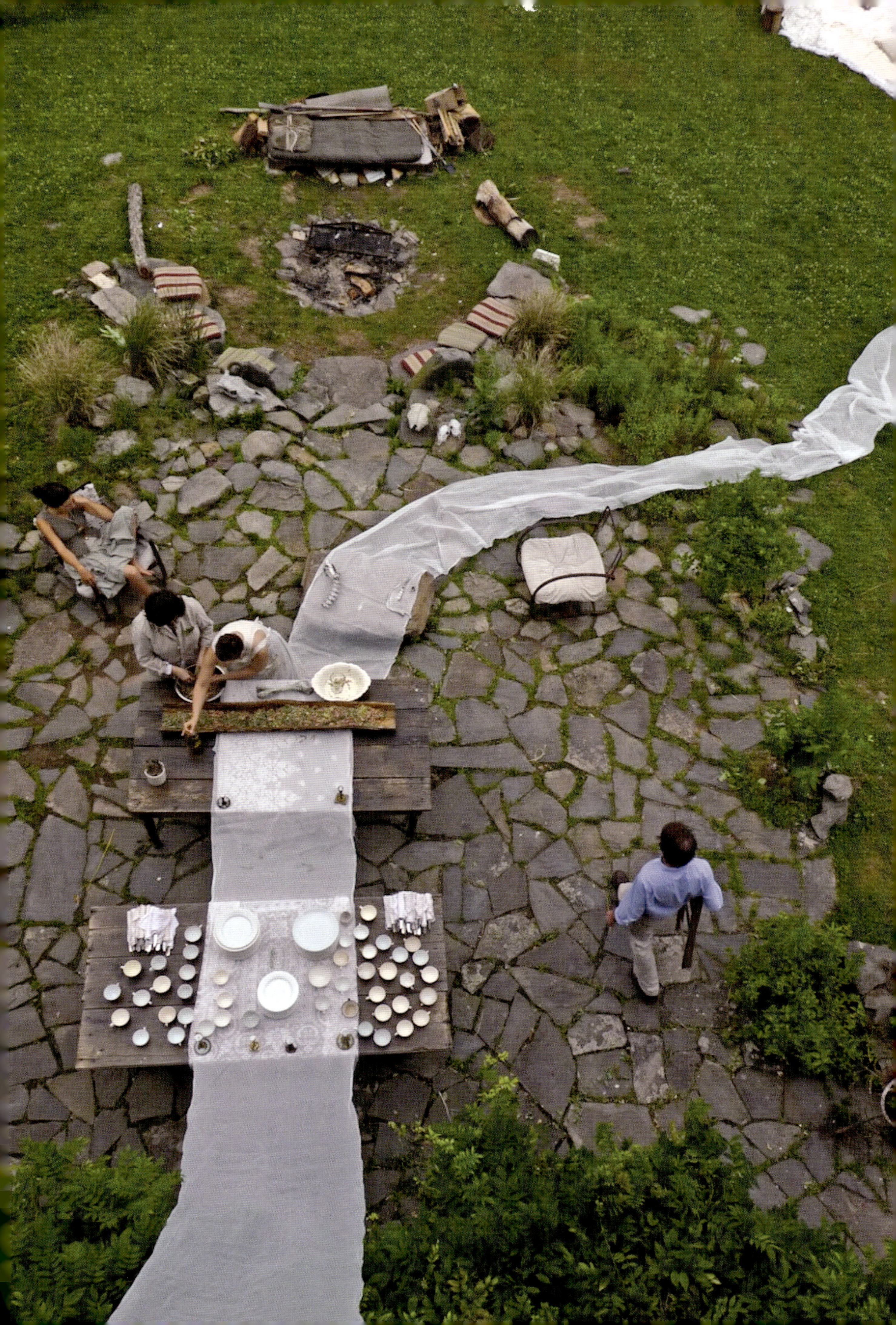

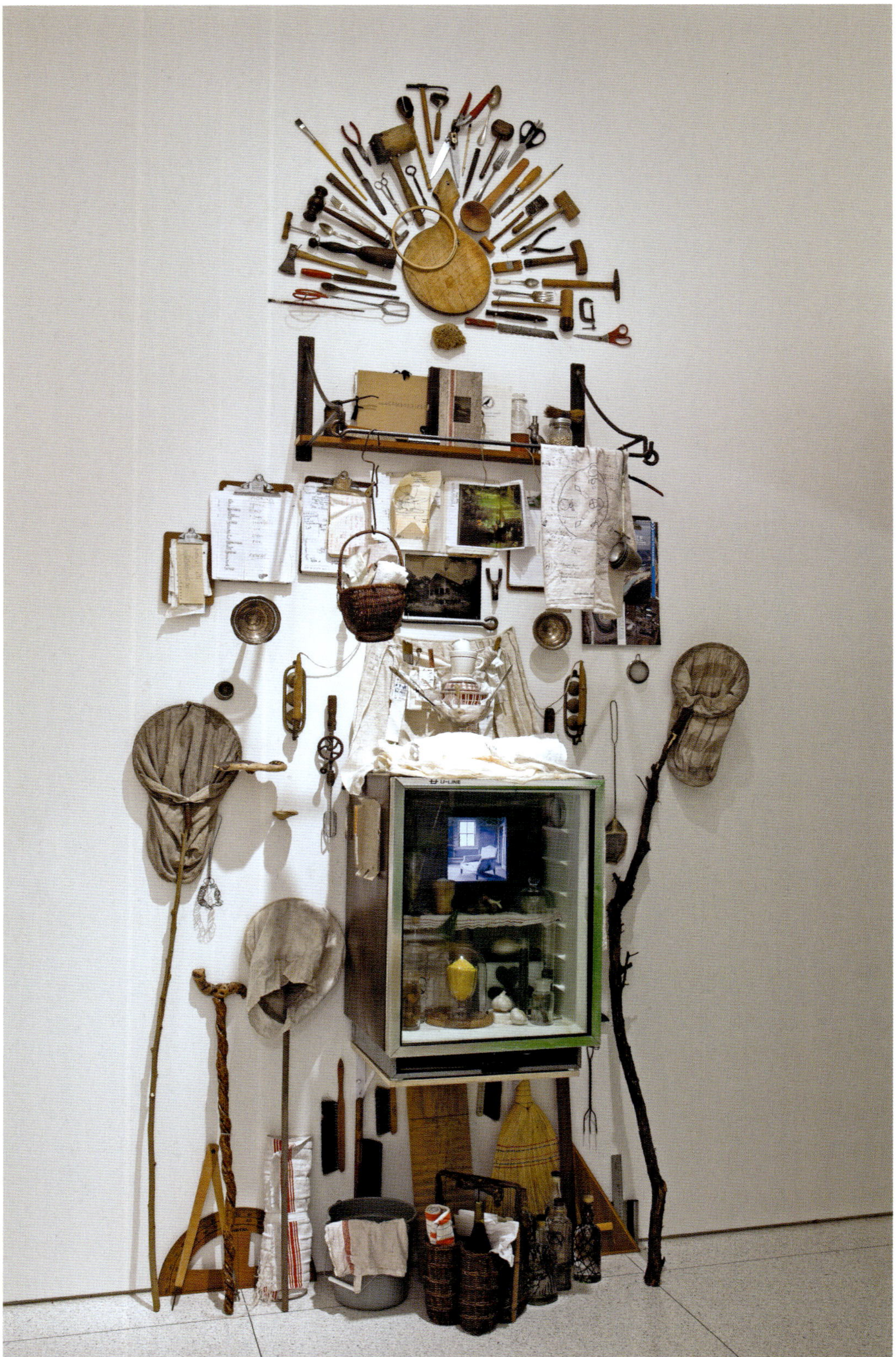

ABOVE AND OPPOSITE: *A Mildred's Lane Algorithmic Dinner and Refrigerator Hoosh*, installation view, Smart Museum of Art, 2012

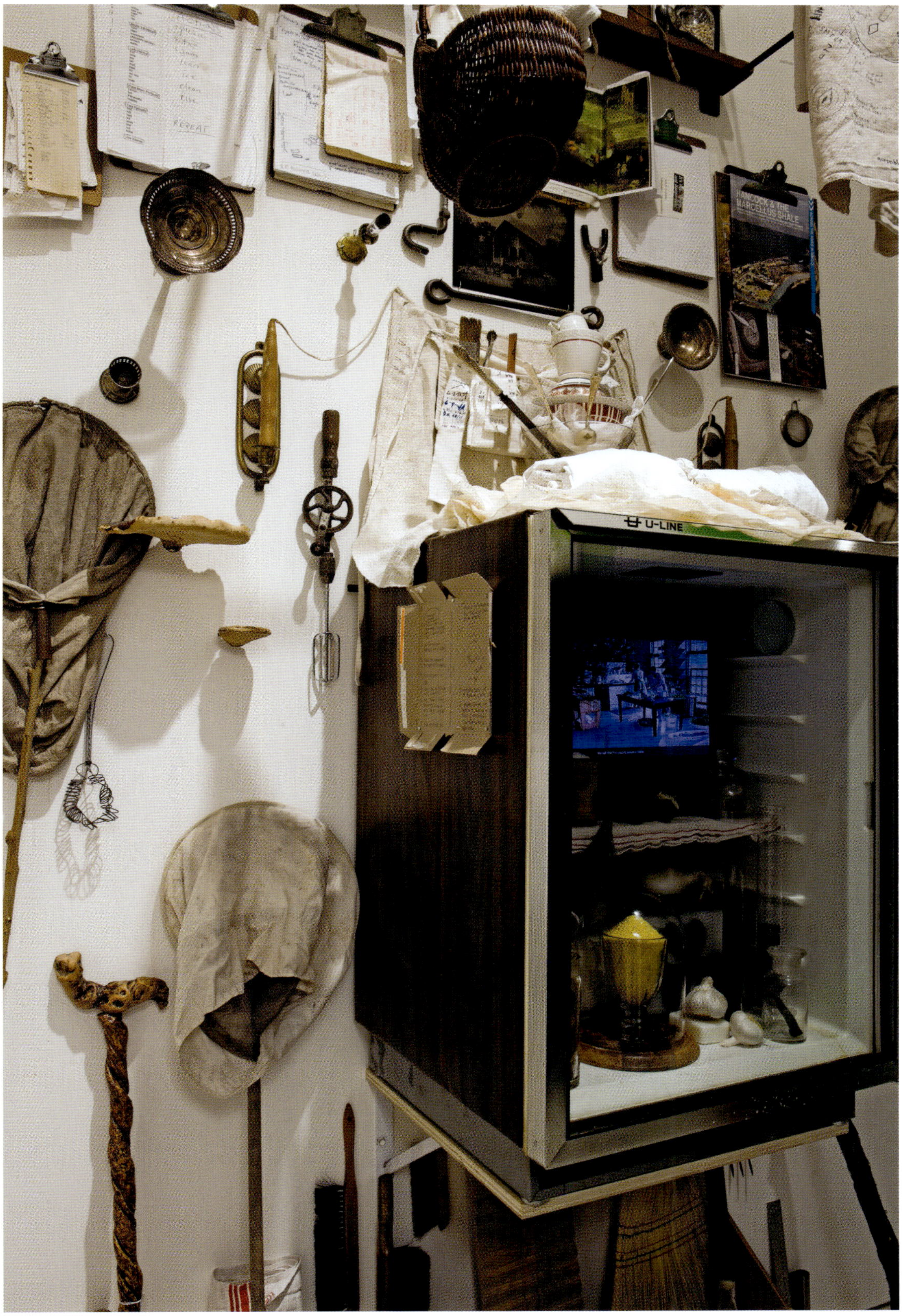
HANCOCK & THE
MARCELLUS SHALE
U-LINE
REPEAT

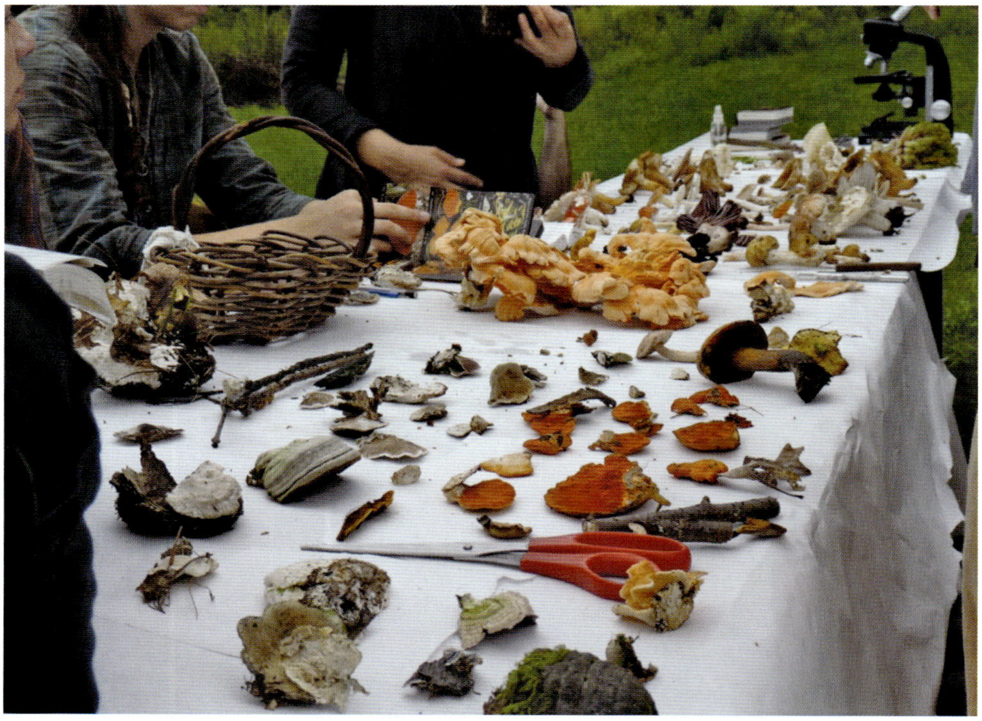

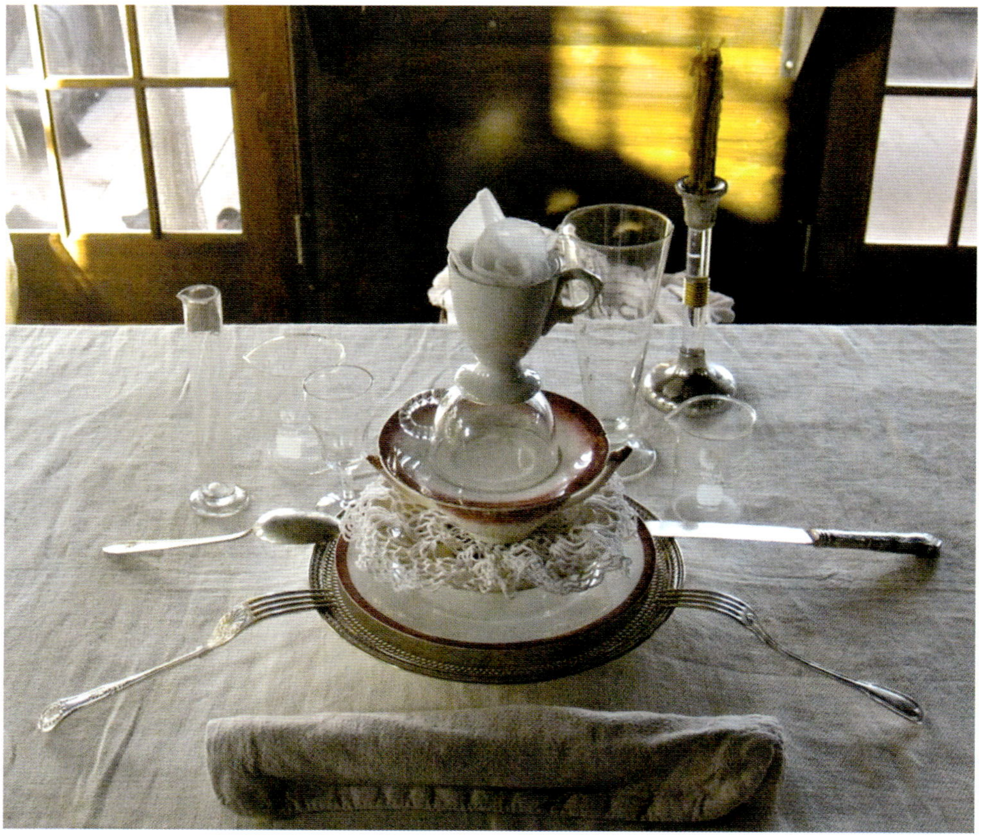

TOP: *Drift 2011 Sessions: Mushroom Hunt,* with Brian Holmes, Athena Kokoronis, Sarah Lewison, Claire Pentecost, and others, at Mildred's Lane

BOTTOM: *Teacup Dining:* standard formal dining setting at Mildred's Lane

From J. Morgan Puett—Mildred's Lane and The Mildred Complex(ity)

517 Plank Road, Beach Lake, PA 18405
P.O. Box 454, Narrowsburg Mews, Narrowsburg, NY 12764

January 5, 2012

> I am interested in new modes of being in the world—this evokes a social and political entanglement that incorporates questions about: (1) our relations to the environment; (2) systems of labor; (3) forms of dwelling; (4) inventive domesticating; and (5) clothing apparatuses—all of which comprise an ethics of comportment. This is embodied in The Mildred's Lane Project and The Mildred Complex(ity), which encompasses a working-living-researching-making strategy and is co-evolving a rigorous engagement with every aspect of life. . . . Being is a practice.
>
> —*J. Morgan Puett for Mildred's Lane*

Dear Stephanie,

Thank you for this invitation to be a part of your project, *Feast: Radical Hospitality in Contemporary Art.* Your list of participants, blog, and project descriptions are all powerfully compelling, we are proud to be involved and feel strongly aligned with your thinking. I will be representing *Mildred's Lane* in accepting your invitation to participate, and I will respond to your questions all at once here, and not in the same order so as to entangle them further. Mark is overwhelmed with work but may chime in. I am culling from our history, archive, projects, and website, but all too briefly. Let me start by telling you more about our unusual art project (place and practice), recent developments, and how we configure food, conviviality, and generosity into the event. One does not exist without the other and it is of course all about people. The friends that visit us year in and year out all generously contribute, co-curate, and inspire us—there are no servants here—we work together and food is the lively intersection.

Mildred's Lane is a rustic ninety-six acre site deep in the Pennsylvania woods, a mile from Narrowsburg, New York. It is an ongoing collaboration between myself (J. Morgan Puett), Mark Dion, our son Grey Rabbit Puett, friends, and colleagues. It is a domestic as well as a pedagogical experiment in developing ways of living-working-researching-discoursing, to foster social engagement in every aspect of life.

The project evolved slowly without us realizing it over the years that our art careers merge here—*Mildred's Lane*—with countless contributions, involvements, and collaborations from our greater community. Each summer for more than twelve years now, *Mildred's Lane Projects (MLP)* has offered a nontraditional educational residency program. The entire site is a shared studio and home project, where the Artist/Practitioner, the Student (fellows), and the Institution have collapsed roles. *MLP* fellows and visiting artists from all over the world gather here to share expanding notions of new and emergent art practices that situate themselves at the nexus of science, environmental activism, and transhistorical, and transdisciplinary practices. The entire site has become a living museum, or rather, a new contemporary art complex(ity)! These ideas are steadfast and heartfelt manifestations best formed in the eventful dinners.

Food and dining are at the core of these exchanges and are constantly emerging collaborations. After all, food is a collective event. These food projects have been most memorable for our participants and guests. We often make meals using an algorithmic process of collaboration that forces the participants to allow for dinner surprises. The algorithm is a set of steps or instructions to create new problems, while at the same time, making a democratic arrangement of events rather than a singularly authored or predetermined outcome. Quite simply, algorithms allow for an emergent, energetic, and socially engaged event. By creating a playful game inventing algorithms, a guest may quietly emerge as a dish, or may have indirectly informed a particular arrangement, or as we say, *hoosh*. Hooshing is another stylistic aspect of the event and is encompassed in the core philosophy of *Mildred's Lane—Workstyles*. *Workstyles* is a term for any practitioner's autobiographical and experiential working-thinking process (active systems-thinking) through a highly stylized and conceptual arrangement or hooshing of the everyday environment of things.

The place itself inspired all this, along with the remarkable woman farmer, Mildred Steffens (1902–1987), who grew up and lived her entire life at the site during the twentieth century, much of the time alone. We call her old 1830s homestead the *Mildred's Lane Historical Society and Museum*, and it is a preservation project, one of dozens of site-sensitive projects, experiments, discreet landscape interventions, and public events smattered across a portion of this wild and magical acreage. *Mildred's Lane*, the land, is a future preserve becoming.

Among many projects, *Retail 21st Century (R21c.)* has been a research-based, emergent collective and think tank convening at *Mildred's Lane* for that past four years. *R21c.* topics include: contemporary, post-recession economics strategies, changing art world dynamics, and new roles for the creative practitioner. We have been exploring new spaces of cultural production and social practice, which importantly include the creative and inventive domestic environment (clothing-fooding-dwelling). Quite experimentally, *R21c.* participants are concerned with the future of exchange. After last year's *R21c.* meeting, it was collectively decided that *Mildred's Lane* would establish an off-site space for a broader public discourse on exchange, thus coevolved *The Mildred Complex(ity)*.

Now, *Mildred's Lane* has come out of the woods and onto Main Street, U.S.A., in the form of a series of public collaborations with the Upper Delaware River Valley community. *Mildred's Lane and The Mildred Complex(ity)* is now a studio, office, and storefront in the *Narrowsburg Mews*, in Narrowsburg. This making-thinking-researching environment is the site and beginning of many collaborative projects proposed by *Mildred's Lane* and International Artists including: J. Morgan

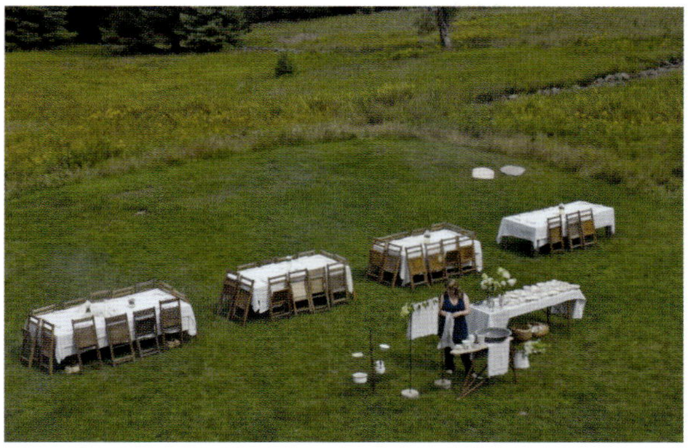

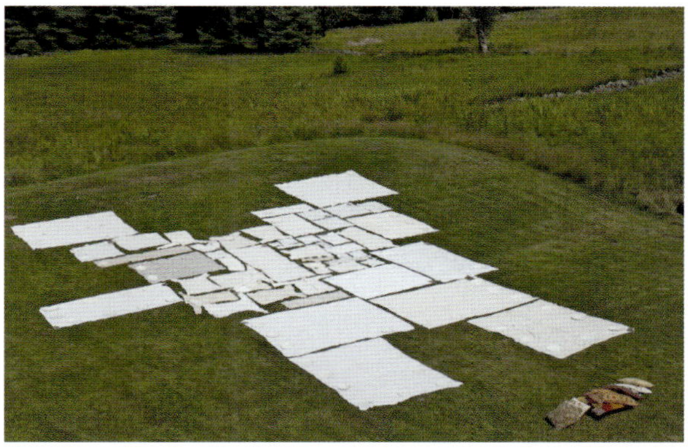

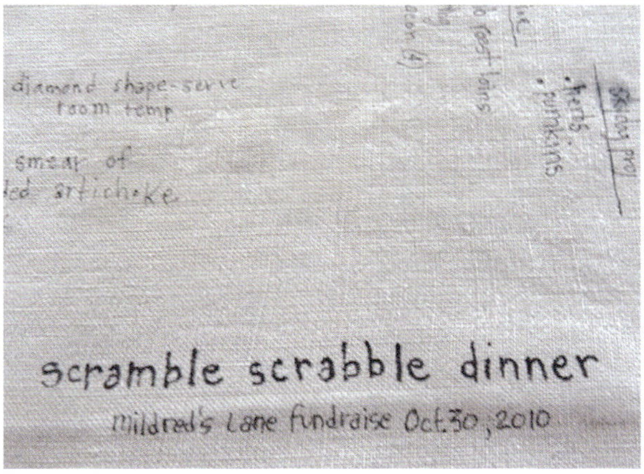

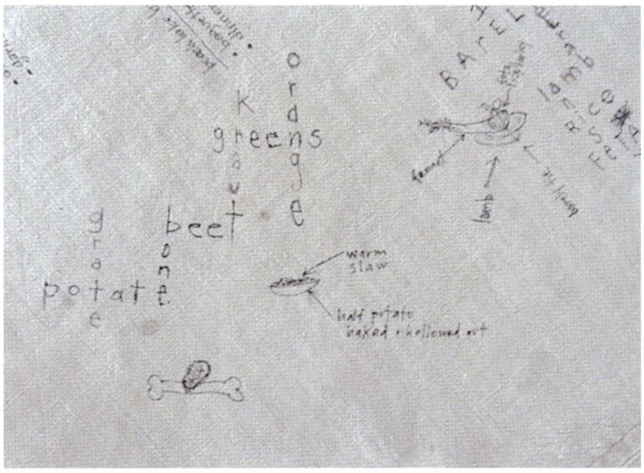

CLOCKWISE FROM TOP LEFT: *Retail 21c. 2009 Sessions: Social Saturday* dinner setting for Allison Smith, at Mildred's Lane

Retail 21c. 2009 Sessions: Barbie's Bruegal Picnic, Social Saturday dinner setting for Barbara DeVries, at Mildred's Lane

Scramble Scrabble 2010, algorithmic dinner game cloth for fundraiser at Mildred's Lane, 2010

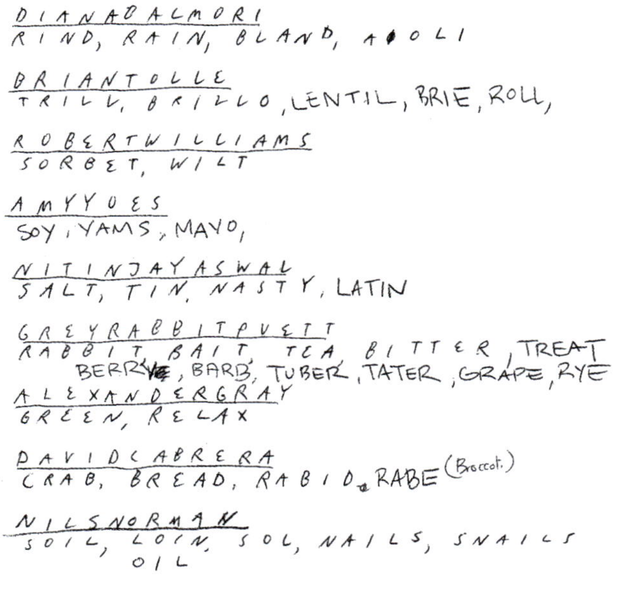

From an *Algorithmic Dinner* at Mildred's Lane

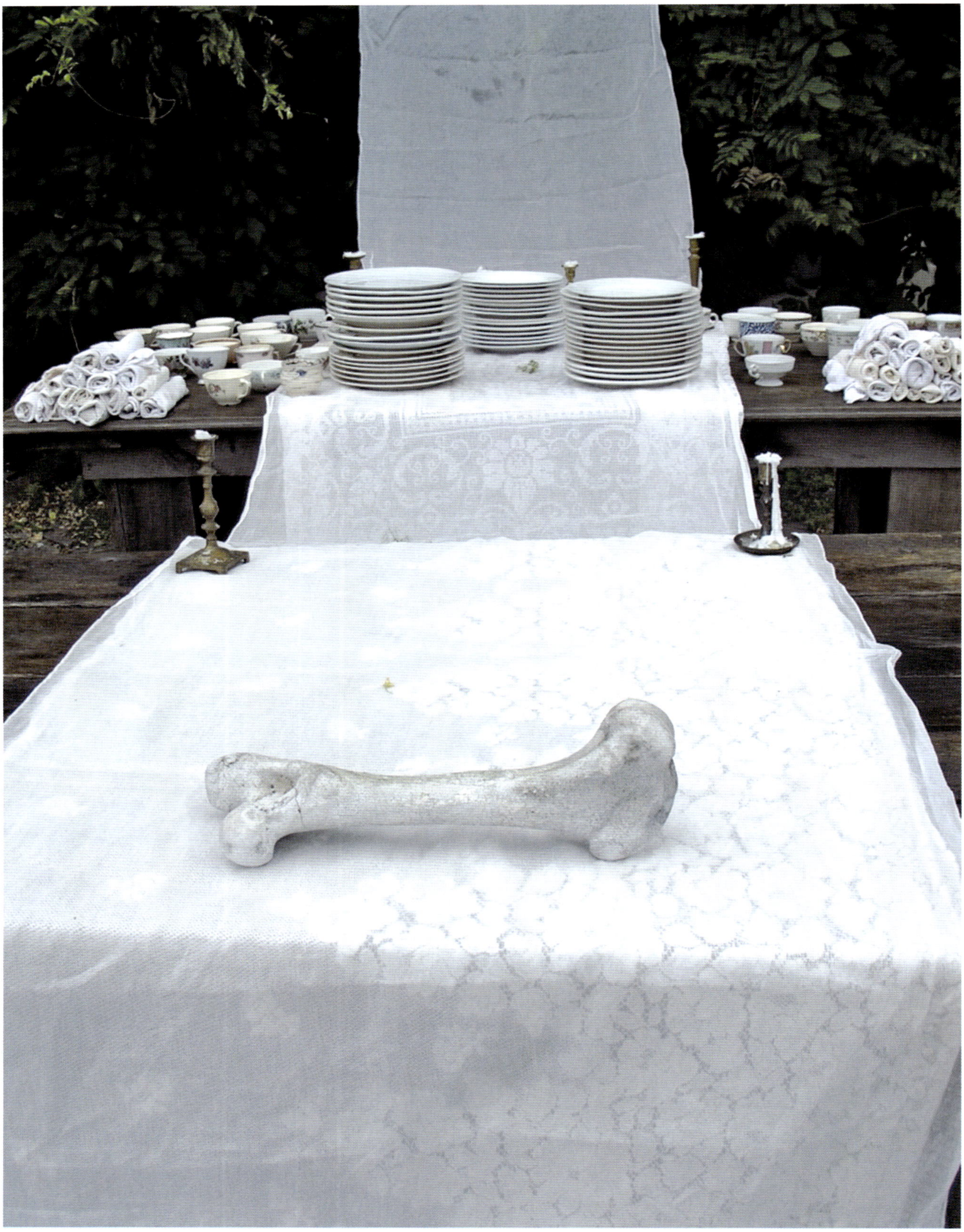

Town & Country 2010 Sessions: Social Saturday dinner setting for Fritz Haeg, at Mildred's Lane

Puett, Allison Smith, Claire Pentecost, Hope Ginsburg, Rebecca Purcell, Jeffrey Jenkins, Christine Hill, Mark Dion, Amy Yoes, Dead Skin Press, and many more to be announced.

The aims of these projects, having "Town and Country" presence and potency, concern the dynamics of people and production in the spirit of exchange. Projects proposed by *R21c.* and *MLP* artists may manifest in storefront projects, installations, performances, meals, and more; always *with* the community involved, and in particular geography to food and a renewed sociality charged with environmental activism.

An "ethics of comportment" offers us a way to navigate everyday experience. The term *comportment* is conceptualized here as belonging to or affecting a whole community, or commons; and, in consideration of our behavior as a constant negotiation with the environment—things and space, human and nonhuman. Rethinking our involvement with our everyday habits—fooding, shopping, making, cleaning, gaming, sleeping, reading, thinking, and doing—we attempt to make each gesture a sensitive and sustainable one. This attitude demands attention to what and who is before you, and after you, making way for the next gesture and requires generosity at all times. Such work stylings have no beginning and no end—they are the eventful actions that make up our lives, offering freedom and possibilities for new types of exchange as shared experiences.

A list of a few notable *Mildred's Lane* involvements and shared experiences:
Paul Bartow • Petra Lange-Berndt • Bob Braine • David Brooks • Nina Burleigh • D. Graham Burnett • Francis Cape • Jorge Colombo • Brian Conley • Courtney Dailey • Moyra Davey • Barbara DeVries • Mark Dion • Jeff Dolven • Robert Fitterman • Harrell Fletcher • Erik Freeland • Hope Ginsburg • Alastair Gordon • John Haskell • Fritz Haeg • Kimberley Hart • Pablo Helguera • Christine Hill • Brian Holmes • Jeffrey Jenkins • Natalie Jeremijenko • Leon Johnson • Jamie Keesling • Richard Klein • Athena Kokoronis • Steven Kurtz • Judith Leemann • Josiah McElheny • Monique Milleson • Sina Najafi • Nils Norman • Michael Oatman • Megan O'Connell • Nick Olson • Claire Pentecost • Liza Phillips • James Prosek • J. Morgan Puett • William Purcell • Grey Rabbit Puett • Rebecca Purcell • Jennifer Delos Reyes • Bret Schneider • Colleen Sheehy • Jason Simon • SkyDog Projects • Sal Randolph • Allison Smith • Lucia Sommer • Mark Thomann • Nato Thompson • Brian Tolle • J. Walker Tufts • Robert Williams • Bryan Wilson • Caroline Woolard • Lacey Wozny • Amy Yoes

There is more information and an archive of past programs, lectures, Social Saturdays, projects, dinners, events, retreats, and comportment workshops; please see our website www.mildredslane.com.

Warmly yours,
J. Morgan Puett
Ambassador of Entanglement

Julio Cesar Morales

MUCH OF JULIO CESAR MORALES'S ART considers the border between Mexico and the United States. He has explored historical shifts in this boundary, the surveillance and enforcement required to police it, and its perforation by informal economies. He often gives such abstract ideas concrete form by using real events as starting points for stories that unfold through a range of media—drawing, installation, performance, sculpture, video. For example, *Undocumented Interventions* (2006–present) includes delicate watercolors based on failed attempts to smuggle Mexicans into the United States—imagine line drawings of impassive children just visible within grinning piñatas—while the sculptural models and somber-hued drawings of *Narquitectos* (2009–present) depict actual tunnels and secret passages hidden within buildings that are sites of the cross-border drug trade. In all of these projects, he draws on his own background: Morales describes himself as bicultural and grew up in both Tijuana and San Diego. Now, he bases his practice in San Francisco where he also works as a curator, and where he founded the artist-run space Queen's Nails Annex/Projects (2003–present).

Morales has explored these contested territories in several projects developed in collaboration with chef Max La Rivière-Hedrick. *Feast* includes one of these works, *Interrupted Passage*, a project that considers the meal as a site of political negotiation and cultural exchange. It takes inspiration from a feast hosted in 1846 by the genteel rancher and general Mariano Guadalupe Vallejo—a turning point during a turbulent period for the region that ended with Mexico's loss of California. When taken prisoner by American soldiers, Vallejo—who was sympathetic to US rule of California—invited his captors into his home for a meal, choosing to negotiate rather than to fight. (His captors—less genteel—immediately went on to launch the short-lived but infamous Bear Flag Revolt.) With the general presiding over the feast in an impossibly complex role as both host and hostage, California began its passage away from Mexican rule. To open reconsideration of the contemporary relevance of the general's hospitable tactics, Morales and Rivière-Hedrick have served meals inspired by Vallejo's feast at a series of performances. Morales also collaborated with filmmaker Daniel Gorrell to create the two-channel video shown in *Feast*. They staged and filmed the meal at Vallejo's home, using costumed actors. The video builds tension through an impressionistic montage of lushly filmed close-ups—a hand knocking on a rose-hued door, impassive soldiers sitting in the parlor, cleavers rending vegetables, utensils in motion, the general's proud visage. We never hear dialogue, just a mildly ominous soundtrack that mixes ambient noise with electronic music, reinforcing both the artifice of the video and potential contemporaneity of the original occasion—a meal that signals the complex hybridity of America's past as well as its present.

OPPOSITE: Still from *Interrupted Passage*, 2008

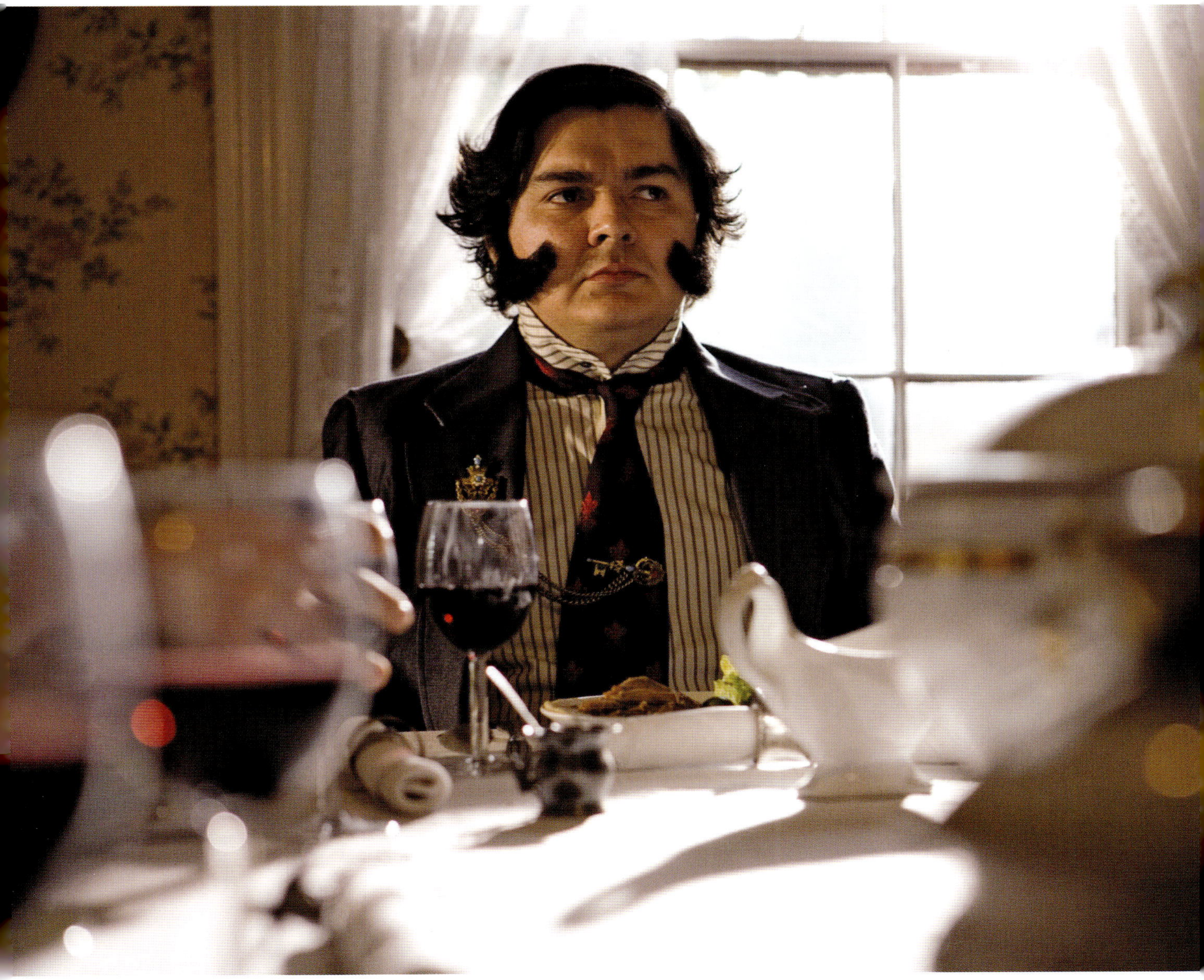

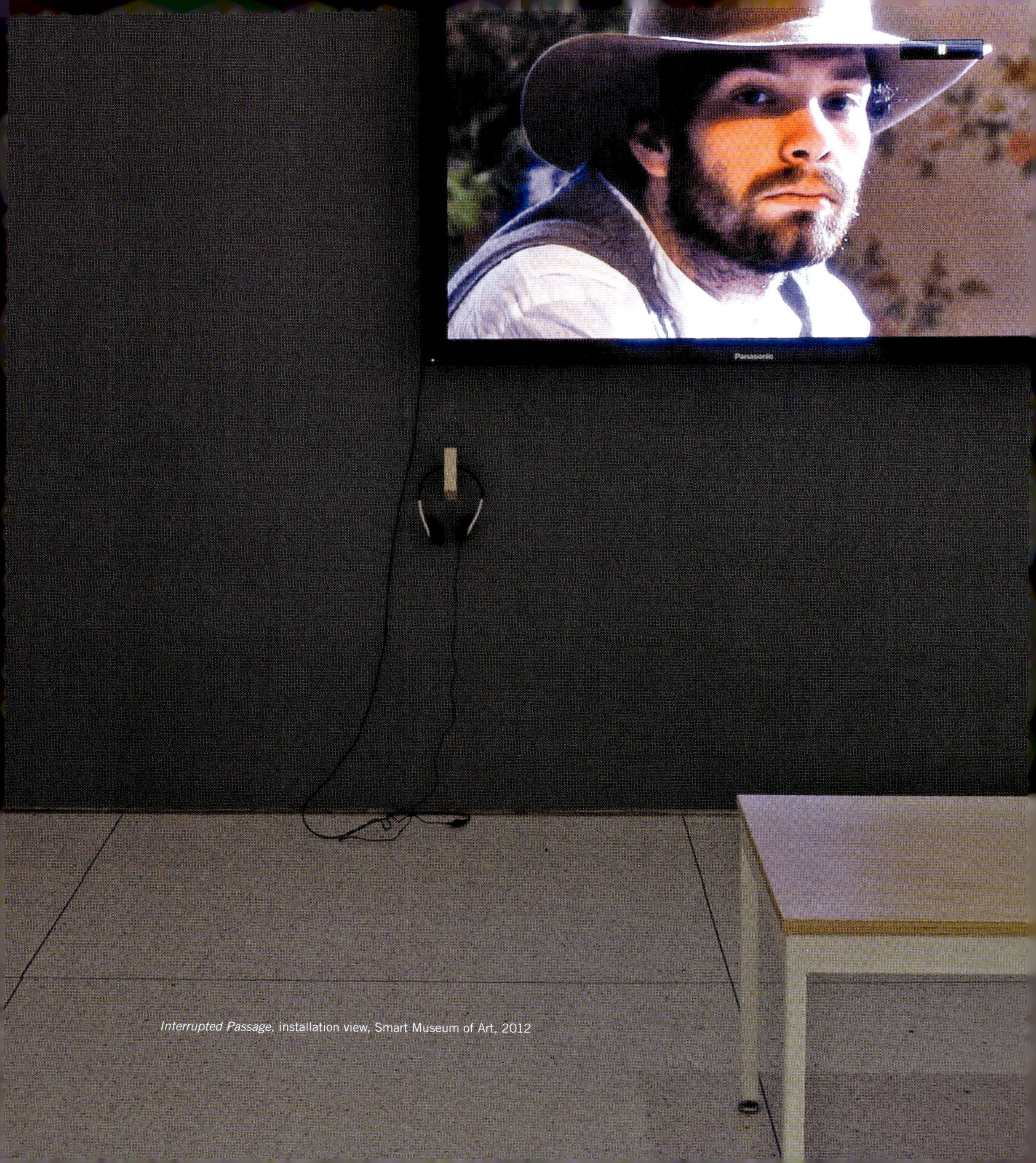

Interrupted Passage, installation view, Smart Museum of Art, 2012

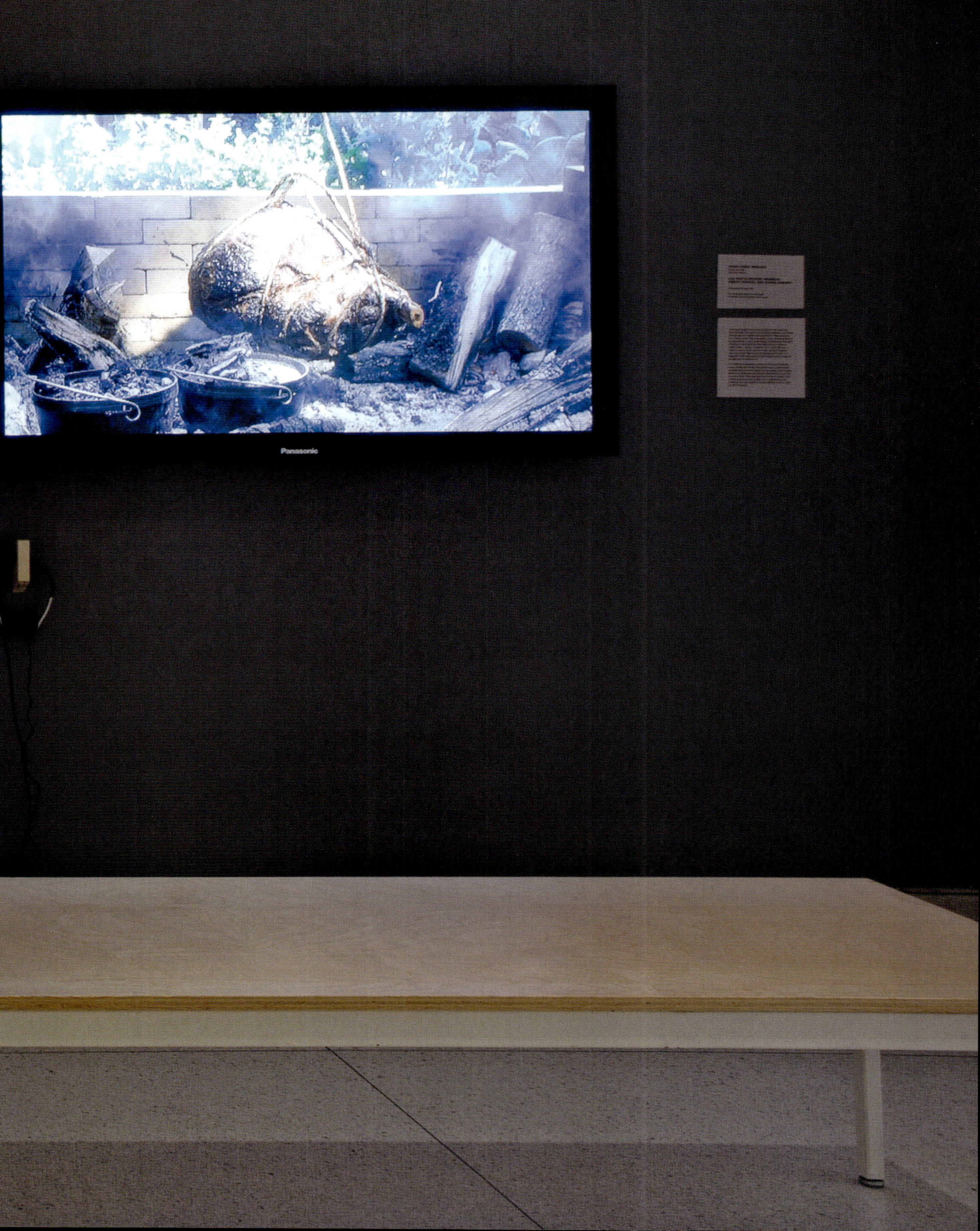
Panasonic

Interview

SMART: Can you describe your path as an artist and sources of inspiration for your work, either in or beyond the context of art?

JULIO CESAR MORALES: My path begins with being an immigrant to the United States from Mexico. When I first came to this country, I literally moved one block—from a neighborhood in Tijuana that is one of the northernmost points of Mexico to the tiny city of San Ysidro, the border town in San Diego, California. The experience of growing up on both sides of the border allowed me to develop a unique understanding of identity in relation to site and how one adapts to performance out of necessity—whether performing for the US border patrol to prove citizenship, or on the Mexican side to promote "authenticity." I take inspiration from the complex myths and histories about this area—from fiction (like the television show *Weeds*, which reinforces the stereotype of border towns as "sin cities"), to complex truths about the interdependent relationship between Mexico and the United States around tourism, immigration, drug trafficking—all of which is especially vivid in the contested state of California.

For years my family did not understand what I did, since I was the only one to go to college. Then when I was asked to develop a solo exhibition at the San Diego Museum of Contemporary Art, they came in along with about 1,500 people and said, "Okay, we get it. All this time we did not realize that your art was about us."

SMART: Tell us about *Interrupted Passage*—its impetus, intention, and production—and its relation to your broader practice.

JCM: *Interrupted Passage* is inspired by the last eight hours that California was still part of Mexico—when General Vallejo negotiated the future of California through a feast for his captors. I attempted to illustrate a forgotten passage of time by bringing together three very distant interpretations of that event from three perspectives: the American, Mexican, and official California histories.

Vallejo was famous for his bloodless rule. He foresaw that California was inevitably going to be taken by the United States, and he determined to keep that transition as bloodless as possible. When the US militia arrived to arrest him, Vallejo welcomed them into his own house and offered them black tea and then moved to homemade brandy. Over beverages, he proposed that if they arrested him he would not resist, but they must eat and drink first. His negotiation through generosity, libation, and food has been a critical inspiration for me and my food collaborator Max La Rivière-Hedrick. At all of our meal-performance projects, we usually begin with a welcoming drink for guests that says, "This is a different kind of hospitality."

SMART: Please say more about Vallejo's meal and *Interrupted Passage*.

JCM: The whole project really started with the dinner/feast that Vallejo made for his captors, which began with that tea and brandy, and worked its way to wine, salad and finally a whole steer that had been slaughtered and prepared for the meal. Max and I did extensive research in regards to what ingredients were available in the mid-1800s and also were advised by a California food anthropologist. For all the recipes we only used ingredients from that era that were "native" to California. Since what they ate is not completely known, we gathered our information and hints from various sources and came up with four variations of the dinner. We then, in turn, created a two-channel video piece based on a reenactment of Vallejo's meal as well as a series of performances in which we cooked for up to three hundred people per session.

As part of these performances, I learned from Max how to prepare these dishes—and added a couple of interesting ingredients, since we approximated and took liberty in regards to unknown ingredients. We were not interested in the authentic or accurate history but more in the conceptual idea of utilizing food as a conduit, translator, mediator, and negotiator. But still, we attempted to get as close to the actual meal as possible in order to see how the Americans became enamored with Vallejo and

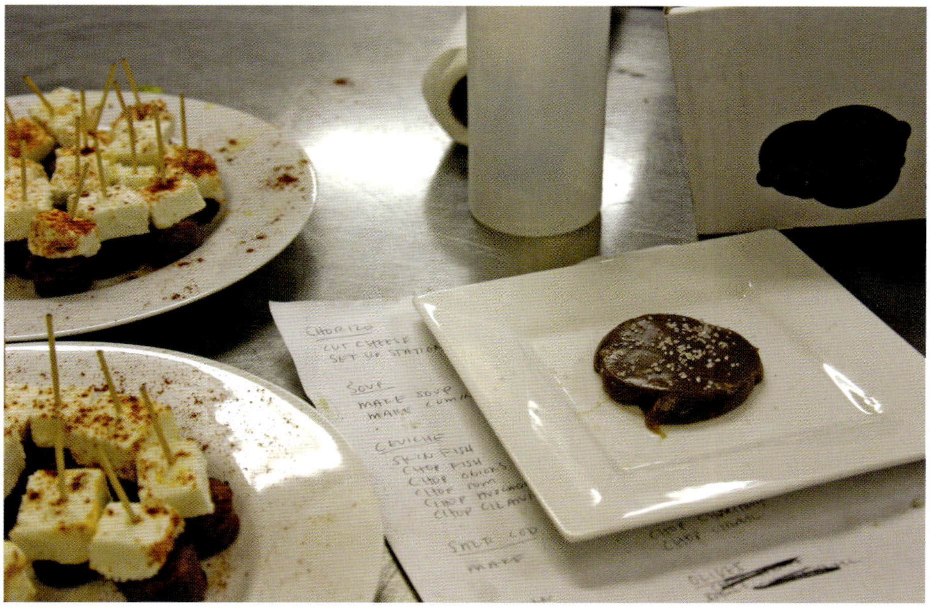

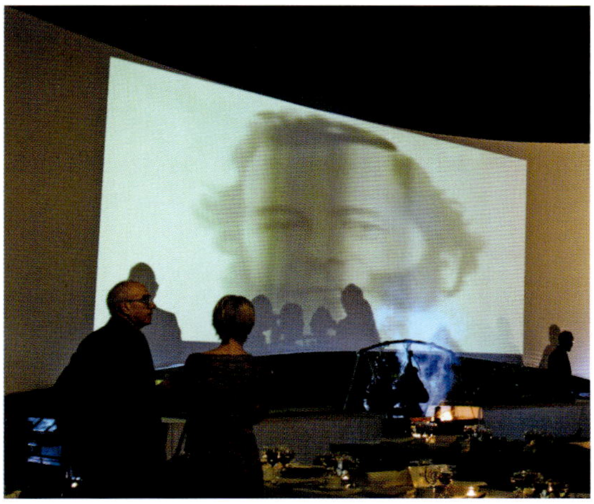

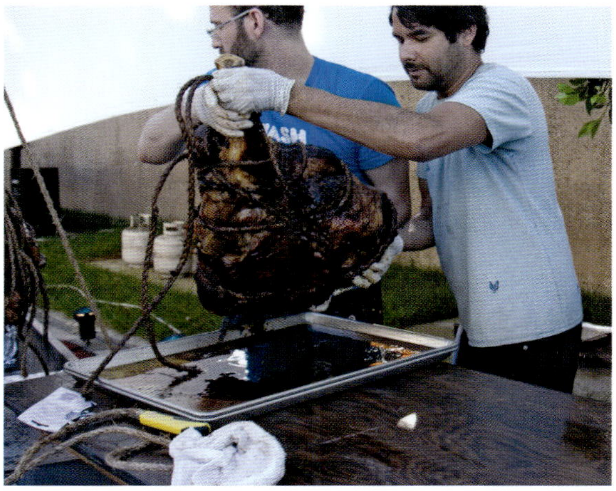

TOP AND BOTTOM LEFT: *Interrupted Passage* meal, served at the Orange County Museum of Art as part of the California Biennial, 2008
BOTTOM RIGHT: Max La Rivière-Hedrick (left) and Morales (right) preparing for the *Interrupted Passage* meal, 2008

his sophistication as a military leader and as a cultured man.

SMART: Why did you decide to create the video *Interrupted Passage* in addition to the meal-based performances?

JCM: The food-based performances were first to come as a project. Only later did we think of the food performances as a way to fundraise for shooting the video project. The video project is another form of residue and an alternative form of documentation.

The sensorial aspect to food almost seems impossible to translate to video. Max previously worked as a food stylist, but here the challenge was not to translate the taste of food but rather the experience of eating. Max prepared the meal in the video and was meant both to look good on video but also to taste

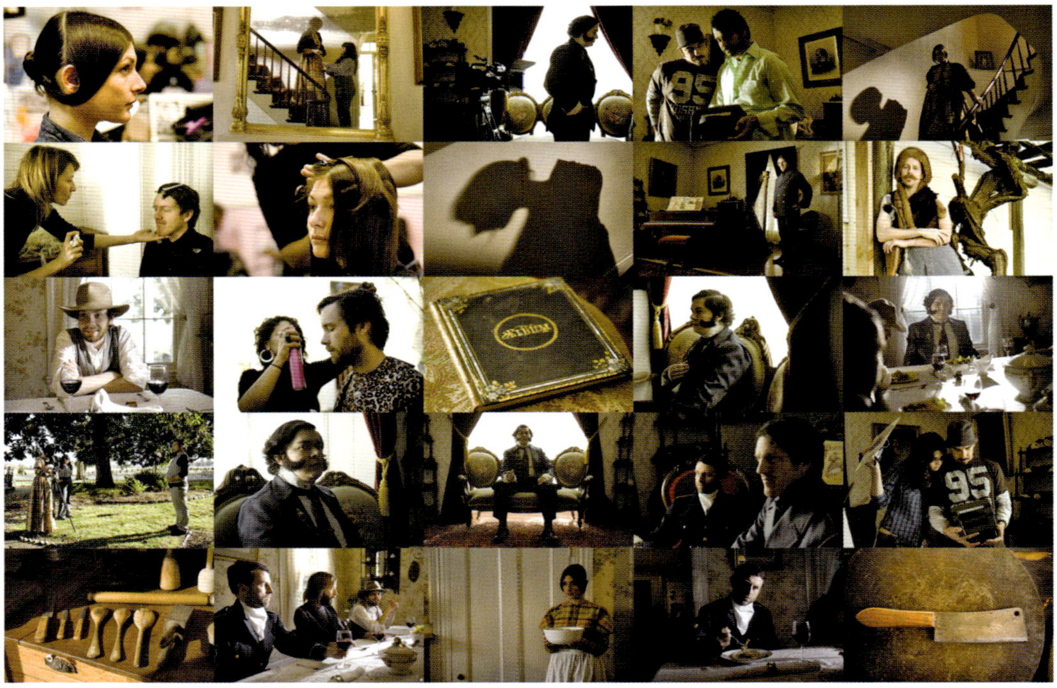

Images from the production of *Interrupted Passage*, 2008

good. One of the actors was a vegan at the time, and as he ate the meat he began to gag which is actually captured with the video. That added something of the authenticity of the experience that the Texas Militia might have encountered: the awkwardness of the meal prepared by Vallejo's chef, which must have been a collision of exotic textures and incomprehensible refined tastes.

SMART: Could you talk about the film's aesthetic strategies—for instance its narrative structure, tone, editing tactics, and use of sound?

JCM: The narrative is taken from Vallejo's biography and his recounting of how events unfolded that day in 1846. We literally followed how the day began and ended from his Chinese chef's slaughter of a steer to Vallejo being taken to jail later that evening and into Sacramento. The strategy for the video was to translate the Vallejo story through sound and movement only—no dialogue. The sound was the key to the editing process as it was a music piece created by the musician Murcof, one of the founders of the Nortec Collective, electronic musicians from Tijuana who mixed Norteñio music with electronic music—a perfect hybrid of music from the late 1800s and house music. The tone and usage of bass sounds served as a cue to edit the video as well as its classical music overtones. The composition for the video is the same music for both channels of video, but one is played forward as the other channel plays the music track backwards, so essentially they both begin and end at the same time. As for the direction for the actors—who are all artists—my only instruction was to come to the video shoot hungover and to not to sleep very much.

SMART: Tell us more about your collaboration with Max La Rivière-Hedrick. How did you start working together?

JCM: Max and I met in school at the San Francisco Art Institute and upon graduation he stopped making art and went into the kitchen and went on to become a chef. He worked in some of the best restaurants in San Francisco, so I approached him about the *Interrupted Passage* project and he just slowly became a collaborator. To this day we are developing performance-food projects.

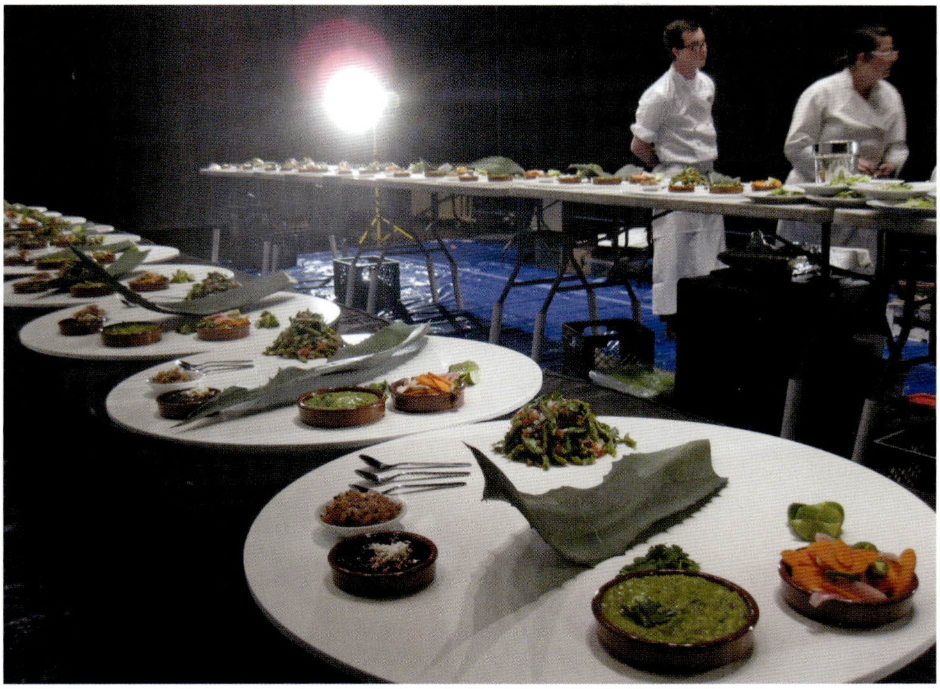

From *A Sors* meal performance at the Masonic Lodge, Regency Center, San Francisco, 2011

SMART: Please tell us more about these performances with Max. How do you establish the mood and the mise-en-scène? And how do the performances enact your larger concern with food as a conduit, versus simply recreating historic meals?

JCM: In our most recent project *A Sors*, we began the performance with a drink called a *Cordoba*, which was a beautiful cocktail made with Mezcal from Pierde Almas with Ethiopian coffee honey, bitter almond tincture, orange flower mist, and star anise. We walked through the crowd with smoking cinnamon sticks, spraying orange flower water. We played a custom-made soundscape, just for that stage of the evening. The goal was to saturate the senses, to reset the mind, the time, and mood. This predisposition sets the foundation for the rest of the performance.

Recreating a historical meal is impossible. We believe that good food is honest and can hide nothing. Food always tells a story; every small choice made in the preparation is revealed. We flat out acknowledge that even though we work with historians and food anthropologists, our projects by nature are new and modern combinations. We treat this idea as a foundation, and then we layer. We distill the story and ideas, and then intensify and focus. We challenge and teach. We use every aspect available to us—sound, smell, touch, timing, and storytelling. With food, it's a balancing act between not enough and too much. In general, food is a minefield with preferences, preconceptions, allergies, poor past experiences. In addition, dinner is considered a time of comfort and relaxation, not challenge. Often we hide the challenge and try to make it an experience, something fun or something guests can tell others about.

We are currently building a project on the artist Remedios Varo, called *La Alquimia de los Sueños*, to be performed in January 2012. We are basing a course on her recipe for erotic dreams, made up of many inedible things. The course will be served as a brick (one of the ingredients), that you must break open with a hammer, revealing another layer of chicken feathers (another ingredient), and then another layer of an egg and so on until you reach the edible center: her recipe in a Russian doll form. While messy and noisy, surprise, and wonder will hopefully disguise the challenge.

motiroti

INCORPORATED IN 1996 as a vehicle to produce the artistic ideas of Keith Khan, Ali Zaidi, and their collaborators, motiroti is an internationally acclaimed nonprofit arts organization that uses an interdisciplinary approach to challenge perceptions of culture, identity, and interconnectivity on a global scale. Indian by birth, Pakistani by migration, and British by chance, artistic director Ali Zaidi draws upon this cultural displacement to pursue creative explorations of commonality and difference through art. As the executive director of motiroti, Tim Jones has put the values of innovation, participation, and cultural democracy at the heart of his work as an arts producer and community activist.

Because of its collaborative nature and inherent activism, motiroti was awarded the 2011–12 Critical Encounters Artists in Residence at Columbia College Chicago. The residency, which focused on Rights, Radicals, and Revolutions, offered an opportunity to emphasize process over product and to merge civic engagement with aesthetic practice in the arts and media. Mindful of existing precedents for activist pedagogy in contemporary art practices, motiroti aims to make visible the commonalities, differences, and interdependence of communities, and to enable lasting social connections—rather than one that appears to be revolutionary, or utilizes shock value to disrupt oppressive systems—while leaving actual communities with little vision or support.

For *Feast*, motiroti invited museum visitors to contribute to an ongoing creative community-building project called *Potluck: Chicago*, which lifts its name from the collective meal to which everyone brings a dish. Using this metaphor, motiroti partnered with various local institutions, including Theaster Gates's *Dorchester Projects* and En Las Tablas Performing Arts Center, to gather a diverse body of participants interested in expanding their understanding of arts activism. *Potluck: Chicago* was launched in fall 2011 through a series of shared meals, skill workshops, and discussions about strategies for reimagining the social life of the city. As documented in the piece, the participants in the Potluck engaged in the initial stages of creative place making: imagining, evaluating, and becoming increasingly aware of the dynamic power of sociability. Deferring result and finalization, the participants engaged in exemplary enactments, taking risks, and pushing their own levels of comfort. From passing out plate invitations to a meal with strangers to fashioning sock puppet avatars for children, *Potluck: Chicago* looked to the social inequities that mark our neighborhoods and relationships with one another.

Through the portraits, reflective texts, and sites mapped within the installation, the commonalities and differences between each of us become visible points of conversation. Visitors to the exhibition contributed to the discourse by writing their responses to a series of questions on Post-it notes, which, in turn, filled the gaps between our initial actions. Beginning with the personal, visitors were asked to share their ideal comfort foods. From nan to kimchi to mac-n-cheese, the piece overflowed with the mutual belief that food not only provides sustenance, it also abates the anxiety of the unfamiliar and opens us to new experiences. Sated, yet curious, we can begin to extend ourselves to each other and consider what small acts could improve our communities. Culled into a composite portrait that moved beyond the first impression, the responses revealed our reciprocal need to be safe, recognized, fed, and educated. The final question looked to the future, asking visitors to communicate their biggest concerns for Chicago as a whole. Layers upon layers of Post-its affirmed mutual commitments to fighting segregation, homophobia, and violence. As a whole, this aggregate of data confirms the relevancy of local interactions and daily conversations through which participants can generate more equitable and relational methods of negotiating the diversity our body politic. As the visual evidence of a multitiered and ongoing project, *Potluck: Chicago* demonstrates the myriad of ways that we can come to the table and share ourselves with others.

Amy M. Mooney, Associate Professor of Art History, and the 2011–12 Critical Encounters Fellow at Columbia College Chicago wrote this text. She worked with motiroti, along with many others, to conceive, direct, and host every aspect of *Potluck: Chicago*.

OPPOSITE: *Potluck: Chicago,* 2012, plate, Smart Museum of Art, February 15, 2012

FOLLOWING PAGE: Installation view, Smart Museum of Art, 2012

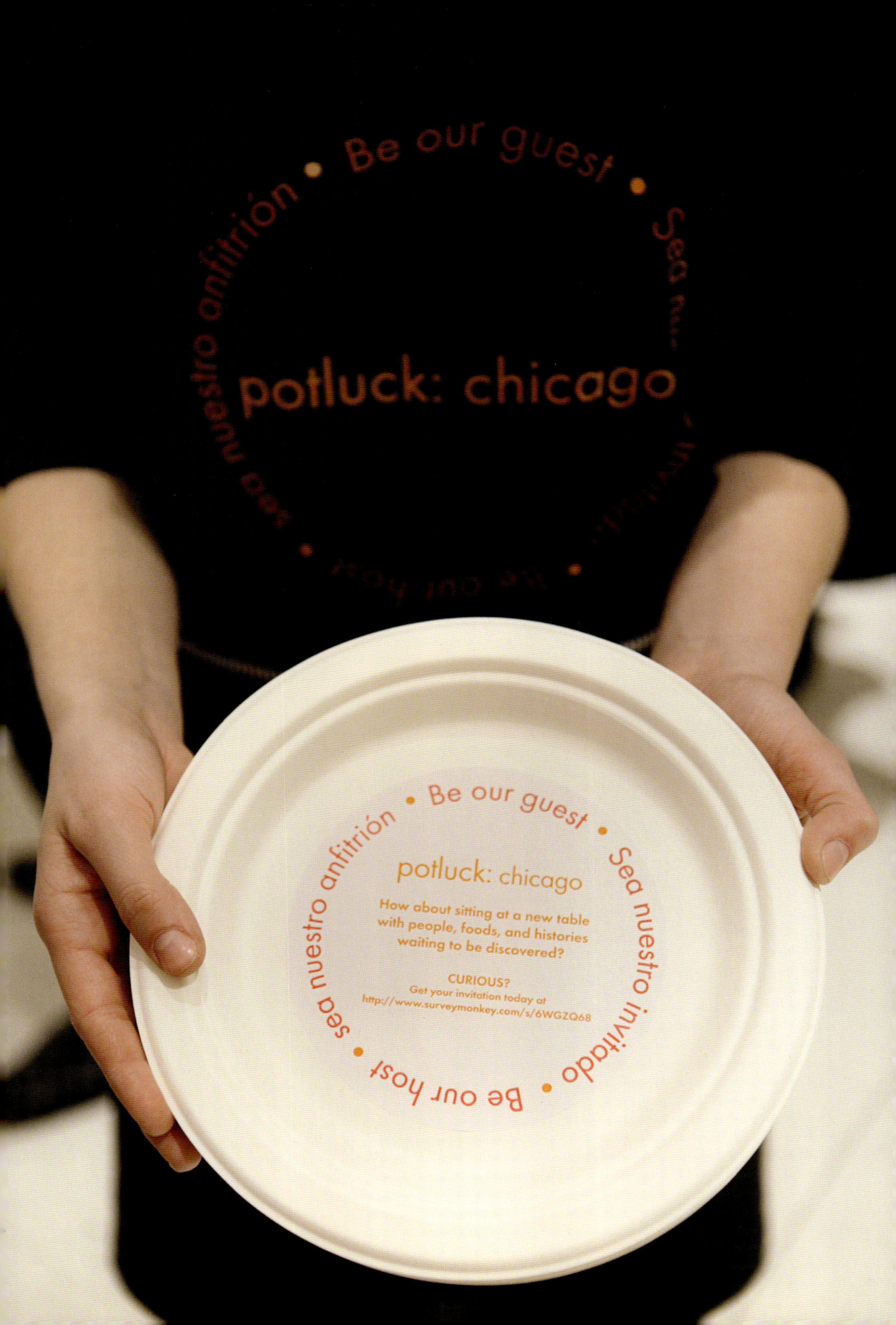
Be our guest
sea nuestro anfitrión
potluck: chicago
Be our guest
Sea nuestro invitado
Be our host
sea nuestro anfitrión
potluck: chicago
How about sitting at a new table with people, foods, and histories waiting to be discovered?
CURIOUS?
Get your invitation today at
http://www.surveymonkey.com/s/6WGZQ68

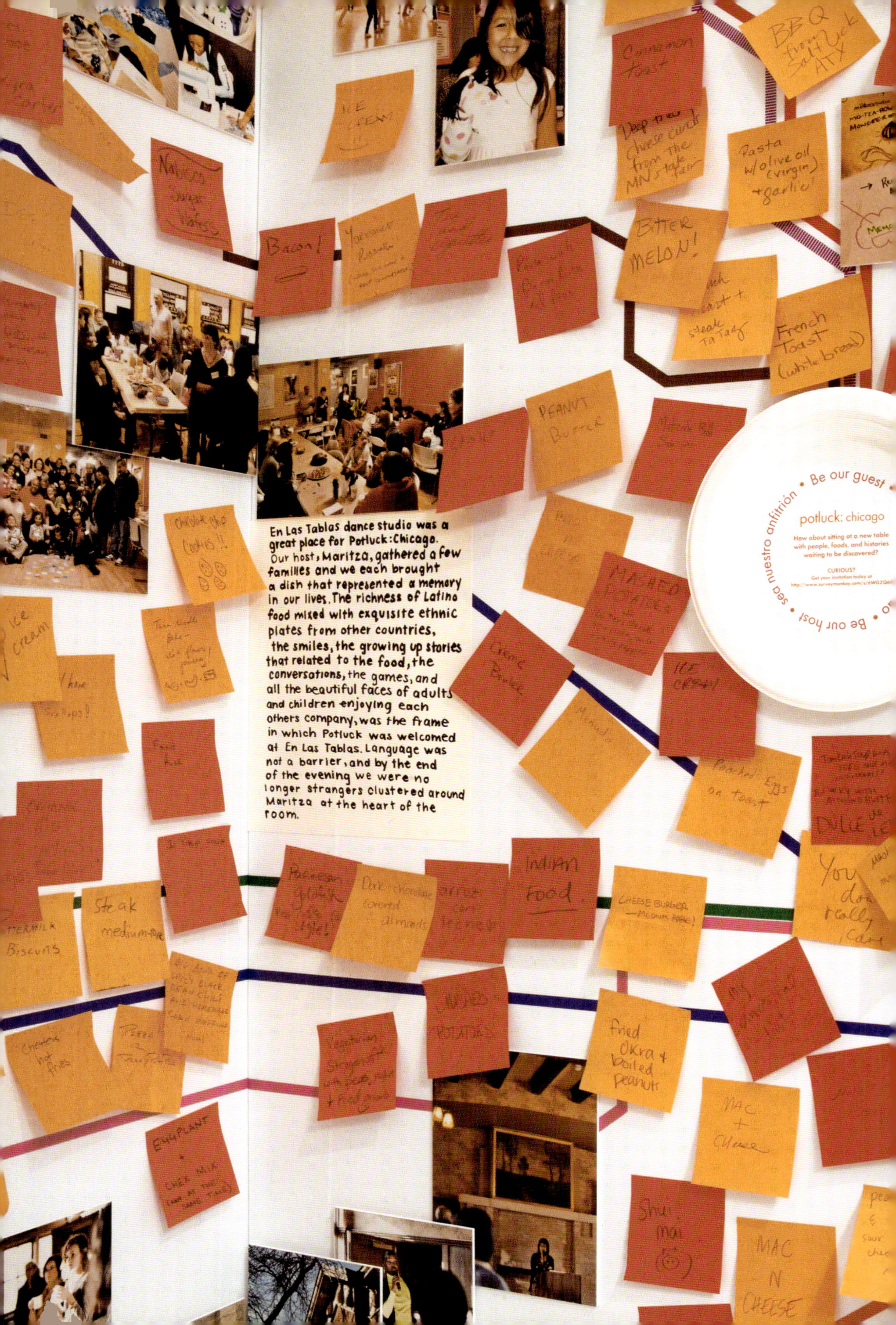
En Las Tablas dance studio was a great place for Potluck: Chicago. Our host, Maritza, gathered a few families and we each brought a dish that represented a memory in our lives. The richness of Latino food mixed with exquisite ethnic plates from other countries, the smiles, the growing up stories that related to the food, the conversations, the games, and all the beautiful faces of adults and children enjoying each others company, was the frame in which Potluck was welcomed at En Las Tablas. Language was not a barrier, and by the end of the evening we were no longer strangers clustered around Maritza at the heart of the room.
Be our guest
potluck: chicago
How about sitting at a new table with people, foods, and histories waiting to be discovered?
CURIOUS?
Be our host
sea nuestro anfitrión
Cinnamon toast
Pasta w/olive oil (virgin) + garlic!
Bacon!
BITTER MELON!
French Toast (white bread)
PEANUT BUTTER
ICE CREAM
Indian food.
Steak medium-rare
CHEESE BURGER — MEDIUM RARE!
fried Okra & boiled peanuts
MAC + Cheese
MAC N CHEESE
Poached Eggs on toast
EGGPLANT + CHEX MIX
Shui mai

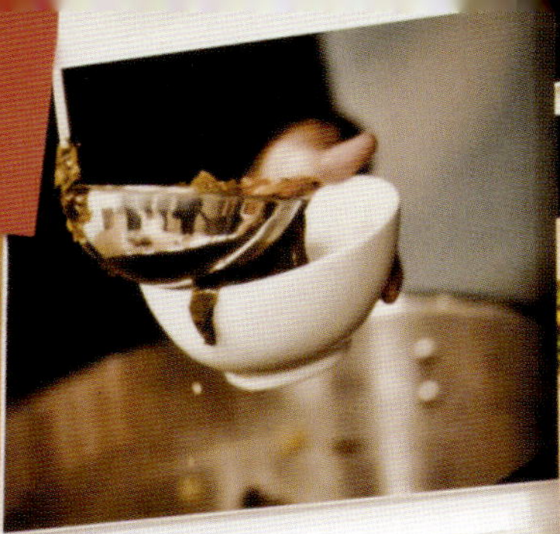

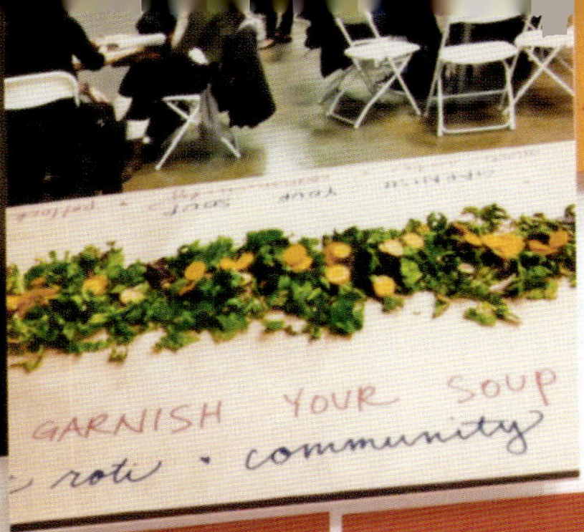

The Stone Soup Launch at Colu
College's Conaway Center brou
our project to a broader audier
Following the metaphor of Stone
soup, everyone contributed something: words, drawings, or actual
soup ingredients. All these aspects
combined to create a common
experience of wholeness, from
what was initially not shared.
From our conversations it was
clear we all wanted to participat
in a better future for our
city. Everyone left the evenin
feeling fulfilled, both with
food and food for thought.

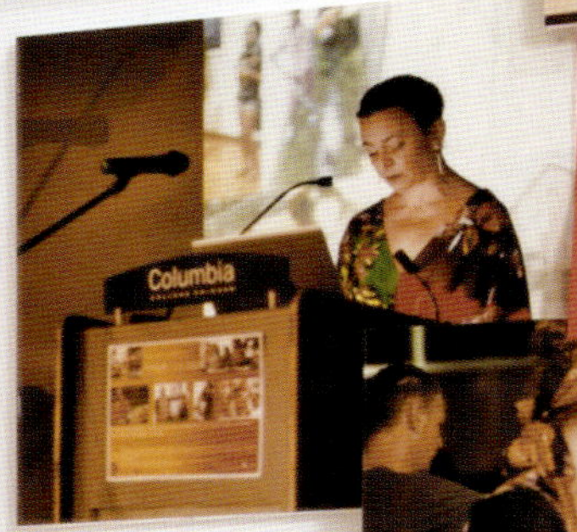

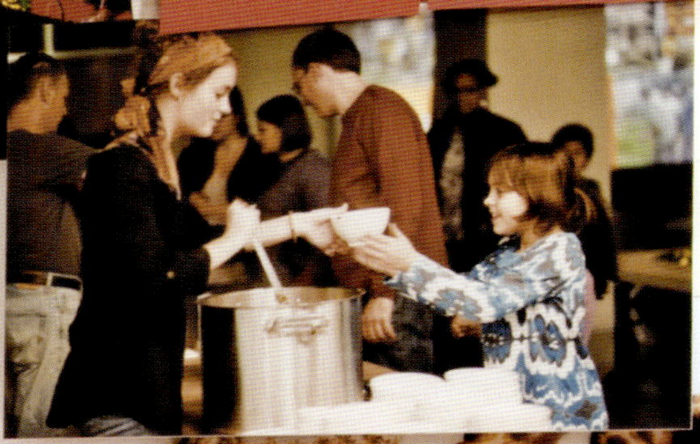

Oatmeal + xtras! yum!

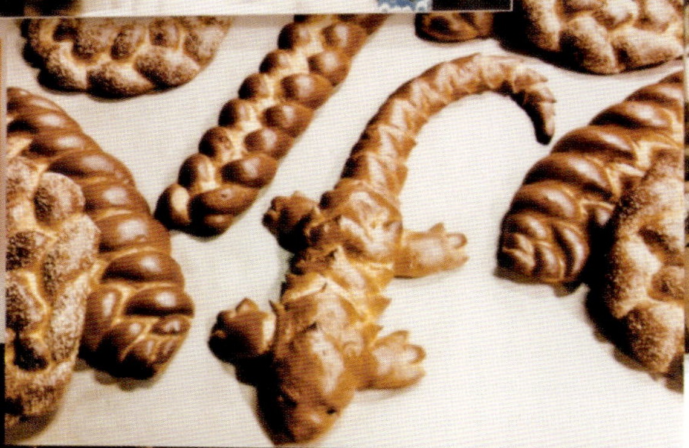

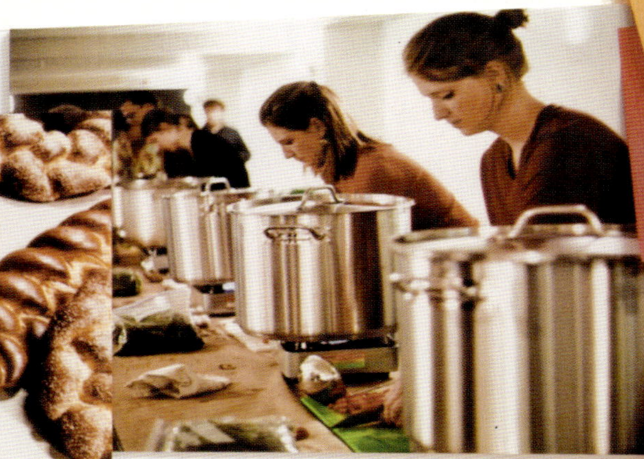

MY FAVORITE TREAT'S A CHEESELESS PIZZA

borsht

MEAT LOAF w/ gravy

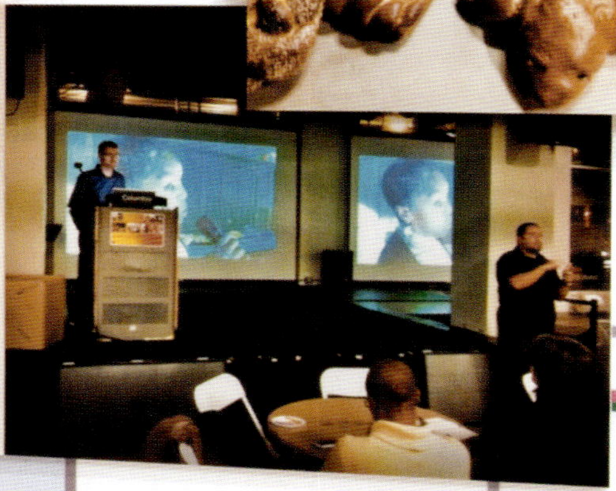

Grilled Cheese

chawanmushi Japanese egg custard

Pomme Frites

Oatmeal

eggies.

Everyone could feel th
creative energy at D
on our final day of workshops. Theaster
took us on a tour of the neighborhoo
and soon-to-be black cinema
house. On our walk, he talked
about revitalizing the block and
difficulties that came with
acquiring spaces. He only mentioned
the work it takes, never the
impossibilities. We later listened
to 3 storytellers; Mr. Bill, Mr. Gates
(Theaster's dad), and Ms. Jolly.
They each shared their histories,
all beginning with migration
from the south. Quoting Ms. Jolly,
"Passion is a funny thing... you
never know what you're going to
do." Making individual
committ

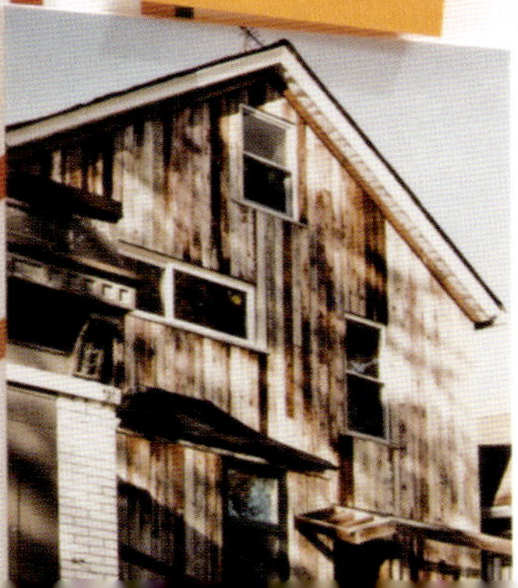

Interview

SMART: Can you describe your paths as artists and sources of inspiration for your work with motiroti, either in or beyond the context of art?

ALI ZAIDI: I chose to formally train as an artist because in 1986 I thought it was the only route to develop my talent of drawing and painting. I felt drawn to a language widely understood (design) rather than a cryptic language (fine arts). Like many graphic design graduates in Pakistan then, the advertising world was the usual outlet. A bevy of award-winning campaigns for consumer products only made me question the validity of the power and the misuse of it in making people believe that their lives were incomplete without the promises we made. I collaborated closely with a writer/journalist/copywriter in developing an antinarcotics campaign, which allowed me to subvert the representation of the commonly held belief as to who the drug users were. It was hugely gratifying in that it really brought home where the social problems were. Back then, in 1986, unbeknown to myself, I had put "process based" into the vocabulary of my practice by making work that relied on research and contribution from many. "Let a thousand flowers bloom" is a sensibility very dear to me. My personal practice, as well as motiroti's direction as a company, plays with notions of "difference" to sift commonality.

TIM JONES: I don't describe myself as an artist. In the United Kingdom, I'd be called a producer, which means I work to connect artists' work to audiences, find the money, and make sure the production values are outstanding. And I keep hunting for the sweet spots where great, progressive creative ideas meet meaningful resource, thereby helping nudge culture forward in positive ways. I've worked across most art forms with a consistent interest in community activism, cultural democracy, and interactive art of all kinds. Working in Chicago has been a real buzz—using the *Potluck* to connect into the great work and thinking going on at places like *Dorchester Projects* and the Jane Addams Hull-House Museum. And to find out about Artplace, which is working to use art to support local communities through an approach I'd like to see established in the UK. I've been part of motiroti for just over a year, though I've known of, and been blown away by, the company's work for over a decade.

Ali squirms when I say this, but in all honesty I feel privileged to be able to play a part in the company's history.

SMART: Tell us about *Potluck*—its impetus, intention, and production—and how the project fits into your broader practice.

TJ: *Potluck* is a new project for motiroti. It's come together over the past year, during which time Ali and I have been working closely together as artist and producer respectively. We've cheekily taken the name given to a shared meal to which everyone contributes a dish, and applied to a whole project, which has food sharing at the core, as well as elements of training and peer support for social artmakers. There's exploration of cities and formation of open networks too.

For motiroti right now, I understand *Potluck* to exist where three areas overlap. First: Ali's own artistic practice (particularly the use of food as a medium to enable new connections and collaborations). Second: the conversations motiroti has with those working in the "creative place making" business, or one of the sectors that interlock with it. Those exchanges center around how those of us in the world's increasing number of "plural cities" can do more than be grudgingly tolerant of, and actually be respectful of, those around us from different cultural heritages. There's a whole host of reasons why that's being understood as more than an obligation—it's an advantage, personally and collectively.

And third: recognizing that these are challenging times for the sustainability of small-scale arts organizations. If motiroti is to sustain, it needs to connect beyond the arts. We need to create projects that make sense locally, but which are also modular, and can be remounted or delivered in a range of locations and customized accordingly. That design-led thinking impacts on the day-to-day as well as the big picture of *Potluck*.

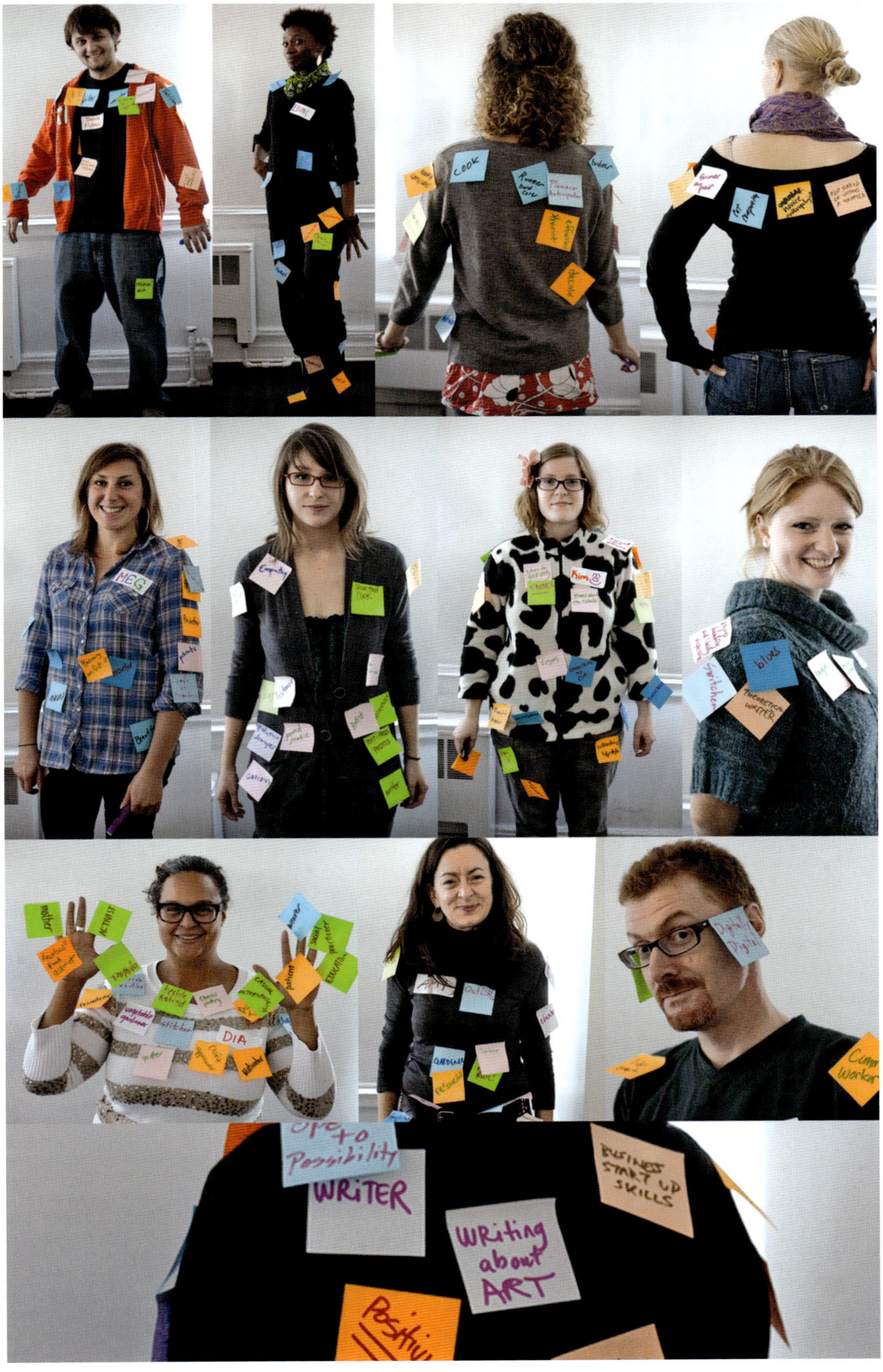

Potluck: Chicago participants map and model their contributions to the project

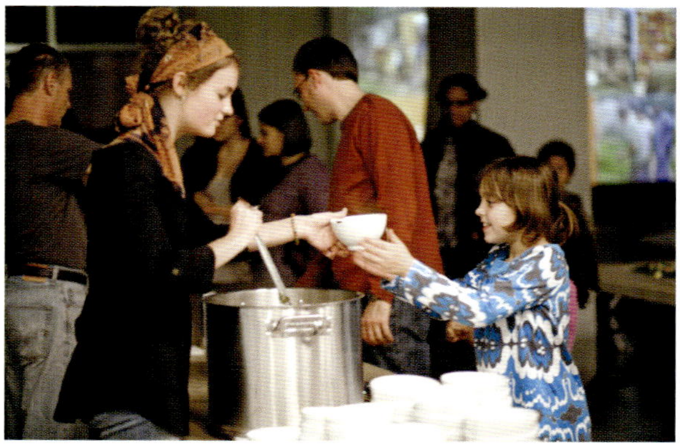

"Stone Soup" a *Potluck: Chicago* meal, Columbia College, 2012

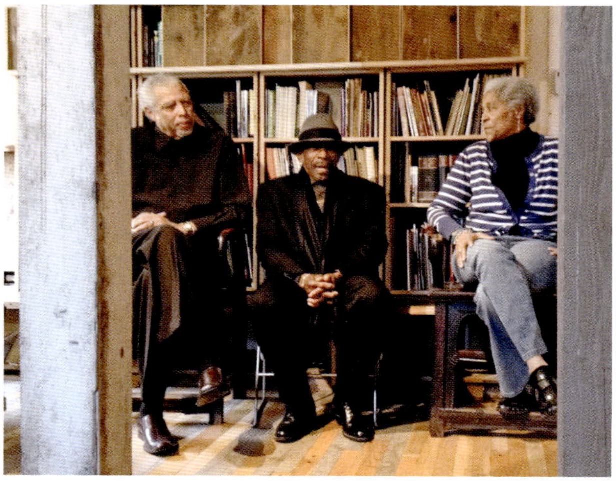

Potluck: Chicago at Dorchester Projects with neighbors Mr. Bill and Ms. Jolly, as well as Theaster Gates, Sr. (center), 2012

AZ: I have always admired the exchanges of tastes, knowledge, intimacies, and stories afforded by the breaking of bread. And given the nonhierarchical nature of a potluck, all people coming to the feast bring a contribution—however small or large, it is their gift. At gatherings where value is given to all, it makes it possible in theory to have safe spaces, where people can be at their best, contributing collectively to whatever the potluck's aims are agreed to be. We arrived at the idea of *The Potluck* as an expanded project through a deep-seated desire that values collaboration, acknowledging that ecosystem diversity is an asset and not a challenge. This practice stems from my personal inquiry that refutes superficial understanding of cultures, values personal stories over simplified generalizations, and tries to subvert in the re-telling.

TJ: I'd add that the general traits and aesthetics common to virtually all of motiroti's projects are in the mix. It aims to be graspable by anyone, at some level. It's hugely warm and positive, building bridges rather than taking sides. There's a recognition that there is no neutral or objective state but an infinity of subjective states, and we should enjoy these. It feels good, while allowing for people to engage with more complex critical, activist or political ideas to a degree they can determine themselves. Importantly, it's creating a context where people can sit down together who wouldn't otherwise.

SMART: How would you describe the role of the meal in your work?

AZ: We all eat. We have to eat and in order to do so, we rely, invent, and re-invent ways in which we are able to do so. To eat is the most basic and common act. Yet migration, displacement, discomfort, belonging, culture, nationhood, traditions, religion, language, etc., have all been developed reciprocally by that basic need. A collective meal indicates a watering hole-like convergence for me.

SMART: Do questions about hospitality figure into your process or thinking?

AZ: Growing to understand my difference and migration gave me a deeper appreciation of what *welcome* means. How to create spaces where welcome, and hospitality—and the behaviors in relation—can be foregrounded, played with, reflected upon. I'm also a couchsurfer, and through that I finds ways to make the dynamics of hosting and being a guest of strangers a frequent part of my lived experience. Tim and I were inspired by the curatorial text of an exhibition called *Faites Commes Chez Vous* at Raw Material Studios in Senegal recently:

> The notion of hospitality forcedly embodies the concept of the other or the foreigner, for the word requires a framework in which to layout the outsider or the guest. Borrowed from the

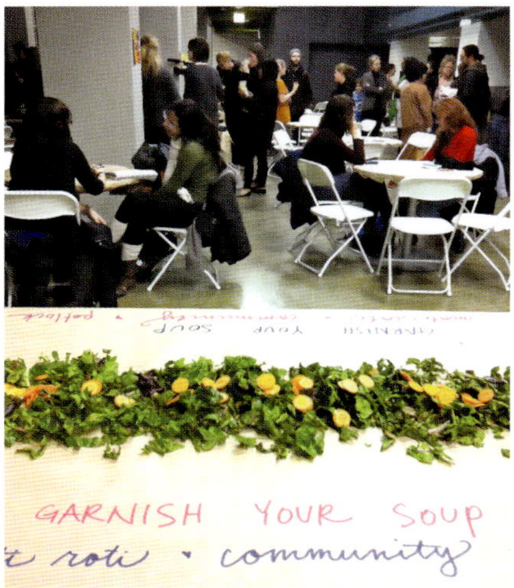

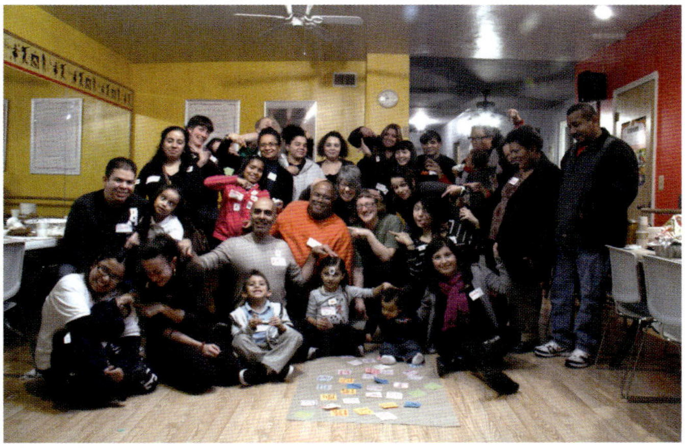

Potluck: Chicago at En Las Tablas Performing Arts Center, 2012

philosophy of Jacques Derrida, "Faites comme chez vous" is in itself a self-limiting invitation which means: please feel at home, but remember that this is not true, this is not your home and you are expected to respect my rules. In his thinking and writing on hospitality Derrida also distinguished between a guest and a parasite arguing that hospitality, reception or the welcome offered have to be submitted to a basic jurisdiction. Not all new arrivals are received as guests if they don't have the benefit of the right to hospitality or the right to asylum. The contemporary world is characterized by the constant movement and displacement of people, as well as by the increased unwillingness of countries to welcome migrants.[1]

TJ: So this interest starts with Ali and how he lives, keys into wider awarenesses and displacements, and through motiroti we seek to make creative projects and practices from it. At a simple level we run food sharing workshops around live performances that we tour; we have other ideas in development, small-scale to large, which create opportunities for diverse communities to guest and host each other within a motiroti-produced art event.

SMART: Can you describe a favorite story about your work?

AZ: *The Seed The Root* was a series of installations, performances and guided walks, inspired to shed old skins and engage with ideas of people like and unlike ourselves. Presented in 1995 in east London's Brick Lane, one of the installations was sited at Clifton restaurant, noted for its authentic Indian cuisine.

This was a collaboration with restaurant owner Shams Ud Din, whom I persuaded to prepare a menu of food as cooked by his mother and wife. More than 90 percent of "Indian" restaurants in London at the time were owned and run by Bangladeshis. In wanting to redress the representation and positioning of authenticity, Shams was photographed holding a huge platter of Bangladeshi vegetables flanked by his mother and wife. Free recipe postcards were sent out with takeaway meals and placed at the counter alongside a photographic intervention within the décor—kitsch painting of seductive India beauties in scantily dressed clothes adorned the walls. As a midway point in the guided walks, audiences ate the off-menu food specially prepared by Shams's family. It was a hoot! Within weeks Shams got so many letters requesting the same dishes to be part of the menu, he felt ready to drop the "authentic India" from his tag line. Within a year of being part of *The Seed The Root*, he used the words Bangladeshi cuisine and started an irreversible trend. Brick Lane today is "the" street to experience Bangladeshi food.

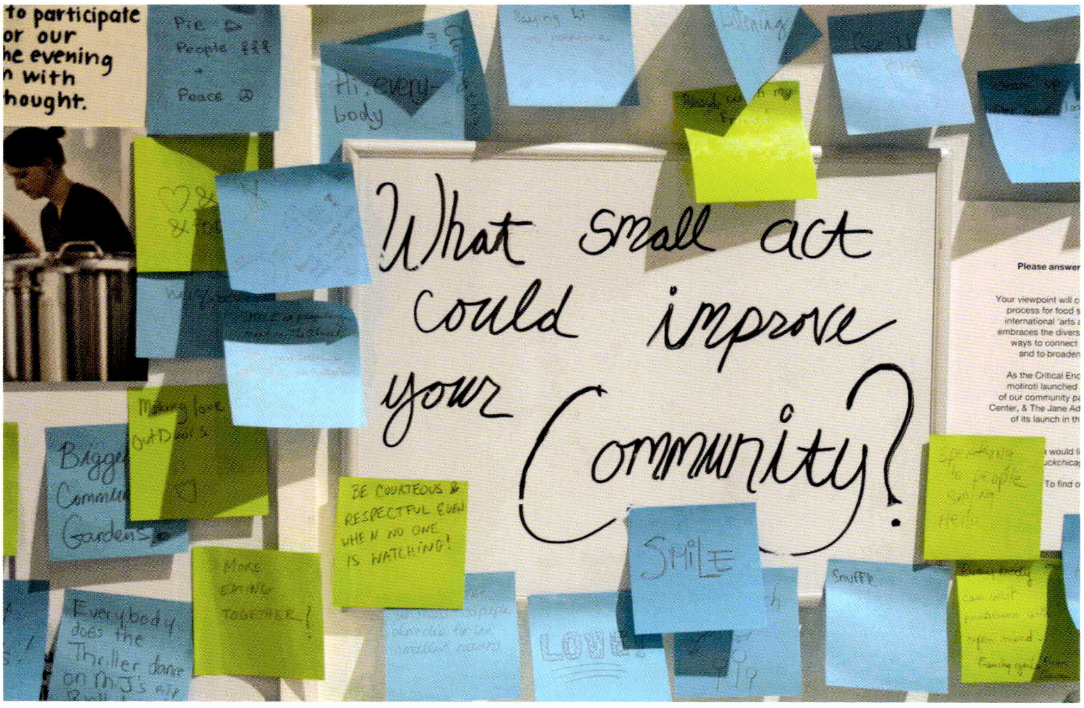

Potluck: Chicago, installation view, Smart Museum of Art, 2012. Visitors respond to motiroti's prompt: "What small act could improve your community?"

TJ: I was facilitating a conversation about the online components of *Potluck: Chicago* in November 2011, when I asked how our younger collaborators felt about the web in general. After self-deprecation, I found that even the least digitally-equipped twenty-somethings are all engaged. They're all blogging. The generation reaching adulthood now are so equipped, they don't know how much they know. And yet they're still young at an emotional level, and that's powerful, because young people don't know that some things are supposed to be impossible. That's a really exciting combination. It gives me hope for the future and makes me think about what part I can play in giving radical responsibility to emerging generations. Partly because the odds are so stacked against them in other ways, and partly because I think older generations are fast running out of ideas. And I think we can all sense that.

SMART: What does it mean to you to be included in a show called *Feast: Radical Hospitality in Contemporary Art*?

TJ: It's great, obviously. I'm a complete Suzanne Lacy fan, so it's an honor to be in some way in the same frame. We feel we've only just helped *The Potluck* get started in Chicago so it's also a bit daunting, as we're only in the process of understanding our process, as it were. It's a great endorsement and we're really encouraged that it will increase the project's profile and hopefully further opportunities. So far, *The Potluck* has been about illuminating liminal or overlooked spaces—socially, politically, geographically—in the city. So we're keen to ensure our presence in *Feast* can be understood to be as much about making visitors mindful of what's beyond the Museum's walls—a complex city of cultural pluralities which is very aware of, and sensitive about, a level of cultural/racial division that plays out geographically in ways that seem really stark from the point of view of this Londoner.

SMART: What do you hope people take away from your work?

TJ: *Potluck* isn't a takeaway. It's an exchange. Two-way transactions. I'd flip the question and ask what I hope people contribute, or let go of, when they engage in *Potluck*. I hope people can let their social guard down, and stay in the process long enough to strike up rapport with someone different from them,

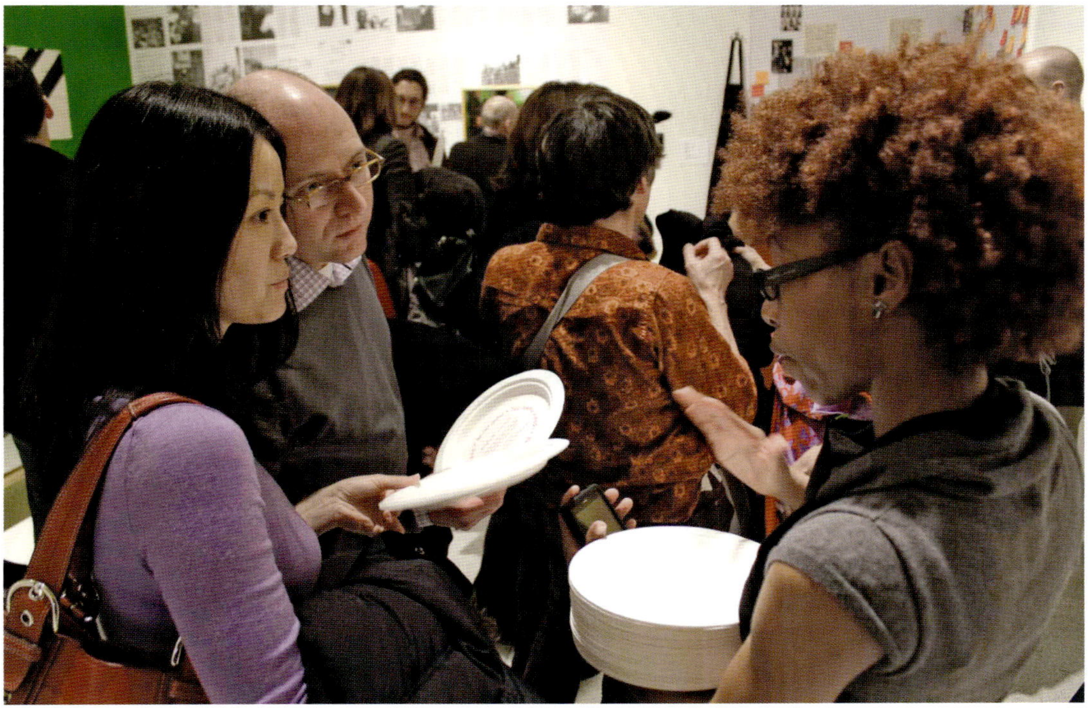

Potluck: Chicago participant La Keisha Leek invites *Feast* visitors to share a meal, Smart Museum of Art, February 15, 2012

and feel a sense that, particularly with food sharing providing a context, it isn't difficult to begin to relate to people who could become friends. During our process in Chicago we've discussed comfort zones a lot. I'd like each participant to feel they had given something to someone else through a small expansion of their comfort zone.

AZ: I have always admired and aspire to a "good handshake," which lies in the simple principle of mutuality. The complexity by which one hand holds, embraces, and exchanges the warmth with the other defines the "good." If the pressure is uneven it becomes a power game and *Potluck* is not playing power games, it is about sharing and sharing is joy. *Potluck: Chicago* was launched within a stone soup gathering. All those who attended knew they had to bring something to it. The story of the stone soup exists across cultures, and concerns a group of migrants who, after denied hospitality in a city, manage to get citizens to create an amazing soup beginning with nothing, simply by asking people to make very small contributions—a vegetable here, a spice there, and so on.

TJ: We feel it's a resonant story for these uncertain, austere times: connecting existing, latent resources already within a city or community, finding rewarding ways to create from crowd-sourced content.

AZ: And so to our event in Chicago: some brought carrots, some herbs from their window-box gardens, some brought salt, some ideas, some conversations, some brought their difference to alter the space. There was active participation and a spirit to share. It's difficult to create a thank-you list for encounters of this nature, and equally empowering in that each person inhabiting the space could call it their own! It was an event that lasted but a few hours. Some of the connections we hope would be followed through because of the principles of mutuality. Generosity of sharing is what one hopes would be taken away!

---

[1] Press release for *Faite Comme Chez Vous* (May 25–June 22, 2011) at Raw Material Company—Center for Art, Knowledge, and Society, Dakar, Senegal; curated by Charlotte Bagger Brandt and Koyo Kouoh, accessed July 25, 2012, http://rawmc.org/press/.

The National Bitter Melon Council

THE NATIONAL BITTER MELON COUNCIL (NBMC) is a collaborative group founded by Hiroko Kikuchi, Jeremy Chi-Ming Liu, and Andi Sutton in Boston in 2004. Their work centers on the bitter melon: a vegetable grown and consumed in tropical climates in Asia, East Africa, and Latin America but less common within the United States outside of Asian cuisines. The council uses this intensely flavored food to promote the paradoxical notion that bitterness can create community—without homogenizing difference or smoothing over the rough edges of experience.

To promote bitter melon for these purposes, the artists use the structure of an agricultural council. The use of serious "promotional council" language is key to their materials and projects, throughout which they maintain a strong NBMC visual identity, including the consistent use of a specific shade of bright green. The group organizes events, ranging from games to personality tests to intricate public interventions that promote the melon's growth and consumption and its representation as a culinary, nutritional, and creative medium. They even have a mascot: at some events, Council members wear a full-body Bitter Melon costume. The most comprehensive manifestation of The National Bitter Melon Council's work to date is the multipart publication, *Better Living through Bitter Melon: A Manual*. Combining elements of farmer's almanacs, Fluxus kits, cookbooks, art catalogues, and instruction manuals, this artists' book is intended to inspire new NBMC projects and seed future chapters of The National Bitter Melon Council. During *Feast*, The NBMC made Chicago one stop on their ongoing seeding tour, conducting a public event at the local gallery threewalls on May 7, 2012. They invited attendees to share in a Bitter Melon meal and discuss personal as well as citywide bitternesses, modeling the food's power as a conversation and community-building tool.

In *Feast,* The NBMC was represented by an installation combining elements from several interrelated projects; the space was branded and bounded by a wall painted NBMC green. In addition to a display of the many component parts of *Better Living through Bitter Melon*—which visitors were invited to handle with special gloves—the display documented two meal-based projects through two sets of framed napkins and place mats. Initially designed as accessories for a banquet that the artists staged in Boston in 2006, the napkin and place mat were used in a more intimate forum for *Feast*. The artists gave the following instructions to Sarah Mendelsohn, then a Smart Museum intern:

> Set the table for a dinner for two using the NBMC Place Mat and Napkin. Prepare a series of dishes using bitter melon that make use of every object in the place setting. Invite someone you don't know very well to eat with you. Eat and talk together.

Mendelsohn held this meal at her Chicago apartment in December 2012. The place mats and napkins were shown in the gallery framed: one set in its clean, dormant state, and one marked with use. This staining completed the work both by making the white-on-white embroidered text on the napkin more visible, and as a stand-in for the meal. Mendelsohn later reflected:

> There is something unusually awkward about being *asked* to express bitterness . . . Though the recipes and impetus for the meal were not my own, as cook, host, and diplomat to someone else's practice, I felt responsible for my guest, and for my hosts.[1]

[1] Blog entry, accessed September 24, 2012, https://blogs.uchicago.edu/feast/2011/12/a_bitter_melon_meal.html.

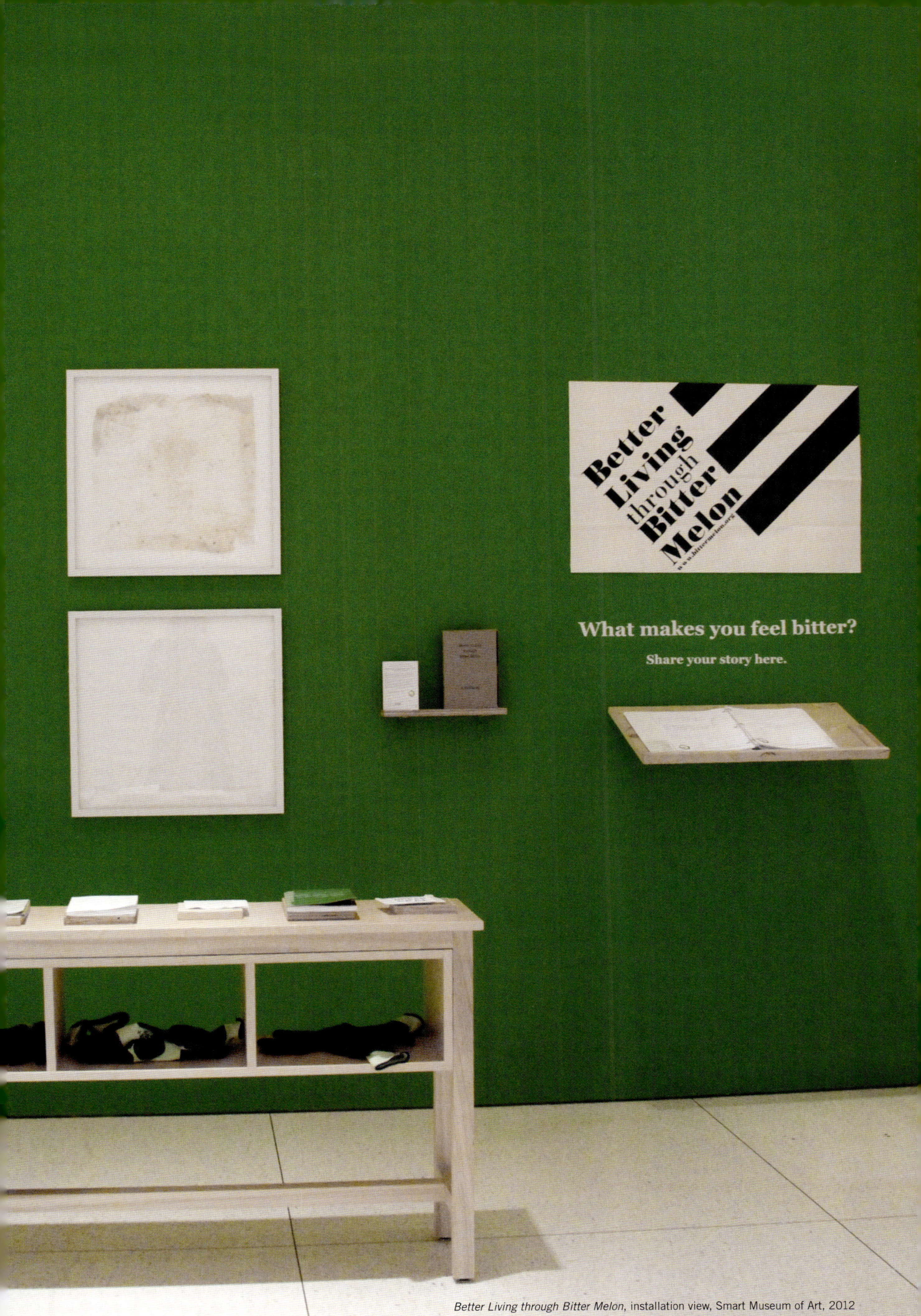

Better Living through Bitter Melon, installation view, Smart Museum of Art, 2012

Interview

SMART: Can you describe your paths as artists and sources of inspiration for your work, either in or beyond the context of art?

THE NATIONAL BITTER MELON COUNCIL: One thing is certain—we make the work that we do together, because we are who we are individually. Of course our thinking and individual and collective process draw inspiration from beyond our various specialties (and our individual personalities also have something to do with it too), but it's the different vocabularies that we bring to the table that create the shared articulation of what The National Bitter Melon Council is and what it could be.

Name: Jeremy Liu
Gender: Male
Ethnicity: Asian, Chinese American
Birthplace: New York City, NY
Mother tongue: English
Education: Bachelors of Science-Biology, Bachelors of Science-Environmental Studies, Tufts University
Research interests: Information and communication technology for community development; urban planning; real estate development; sustainable development; food justice; design thinking
Hobbies: None
Profession: Executive director of a neighborhood and community economic development not-for-profit social enterprise in Oakland, CA
Bitterness level: 2 out of 3

Name: Hiroko Kikuchi
Gender: Female
Ethnicity: Asian, Japanese
Birthplace: Tokyo, Japan
Mother tongue: Japanese
Education: Masters of fine arts—performance art and interdisciplinary practice
Research interests: Bitter Melon, community design, social and creative determinant of health, leadership development
Hobbies: People watching, cooking, and eating
Profession: Artist and co-principal of a firm to collaboratively develop projects, experiments, and methodologies that improve upon and introduce new ways of doing community and people development and planning.
Bitterness level: 2.999

Name: Andi Sutton
Gender: Female
Ethnicity: White, Midwestern American
Birthplace: Minneapolis, MN
Mother tongue: English
Education: Bachelors of arts, women's studies; bachelors of fine arts, performance art and video art, Tufts University and the School of the Museum of Fine Arts, Boston
Research interests: Bitter Melon, feminist theory and pedagogy, facilitative leadership, performance art methodology, sustainability (environmental, social, and relational), gender equality and social justice
Hobbies: Gardening, cooking, communication and laughter
Profession: Artist and program manager of a university graduate program in women's and gender studies
Bitterness level: 2.5

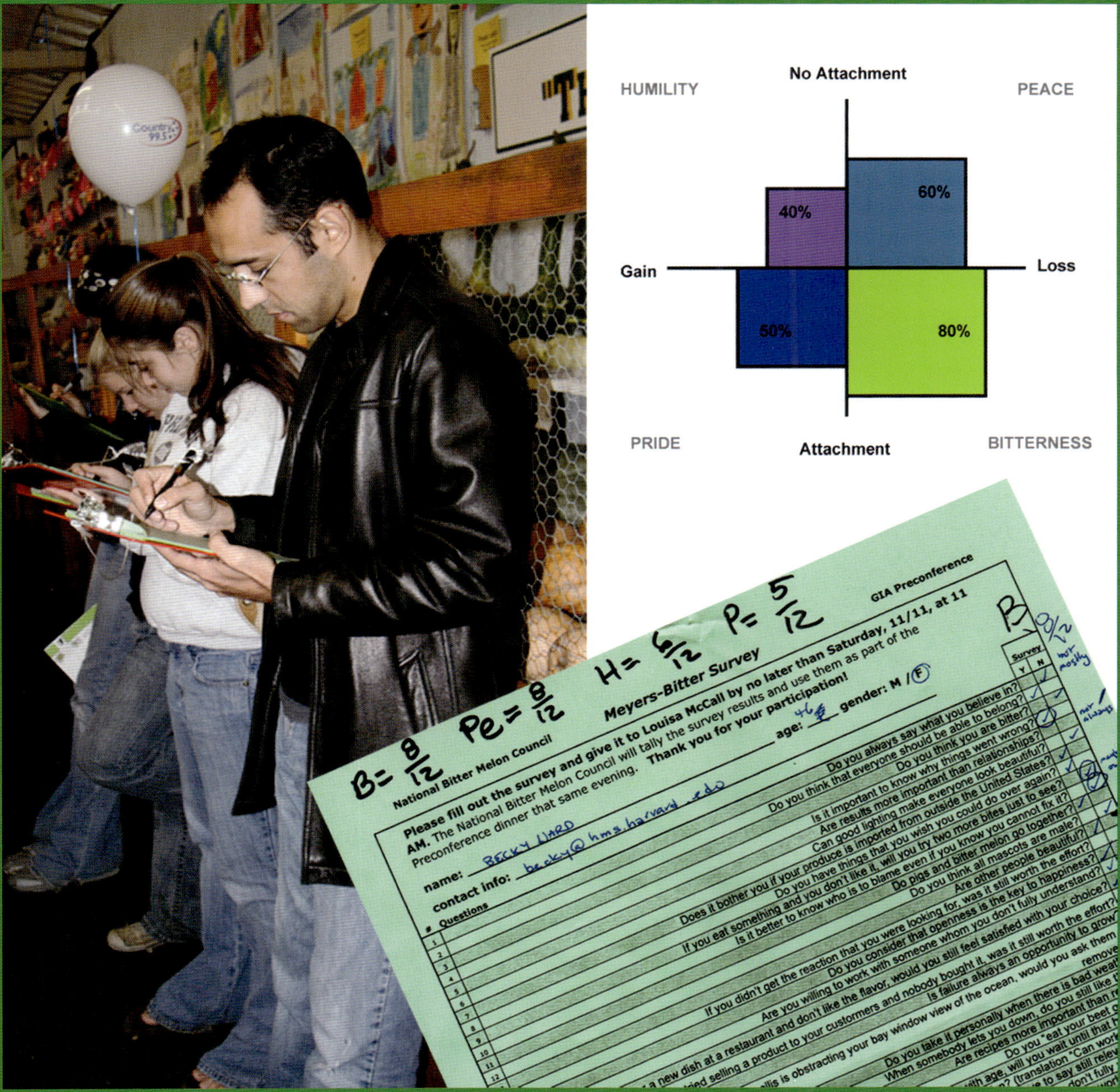

The Meyers-Bitter Survey as taken at the Topsfield Fair in Topsfield, Massachusetts, 2007

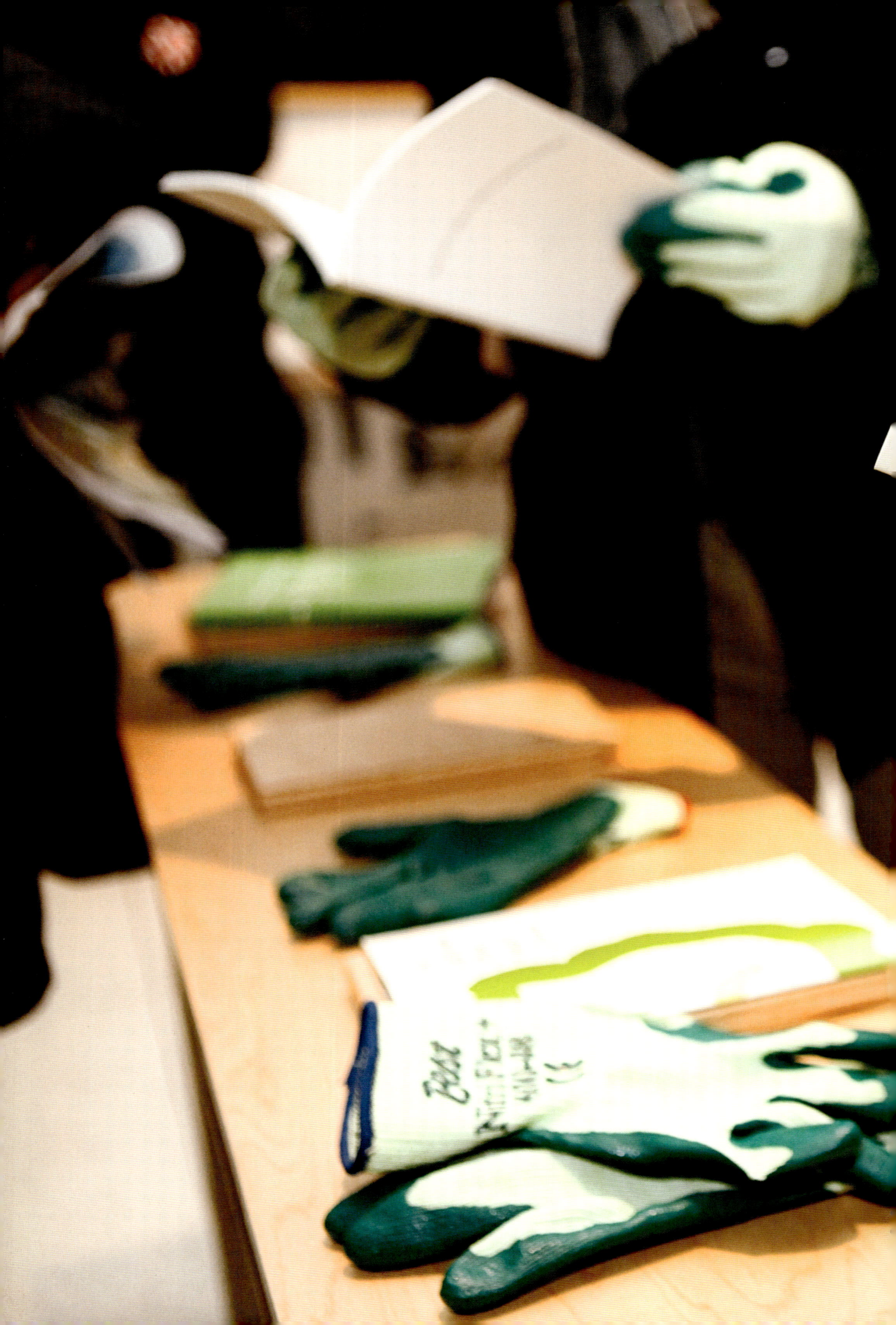

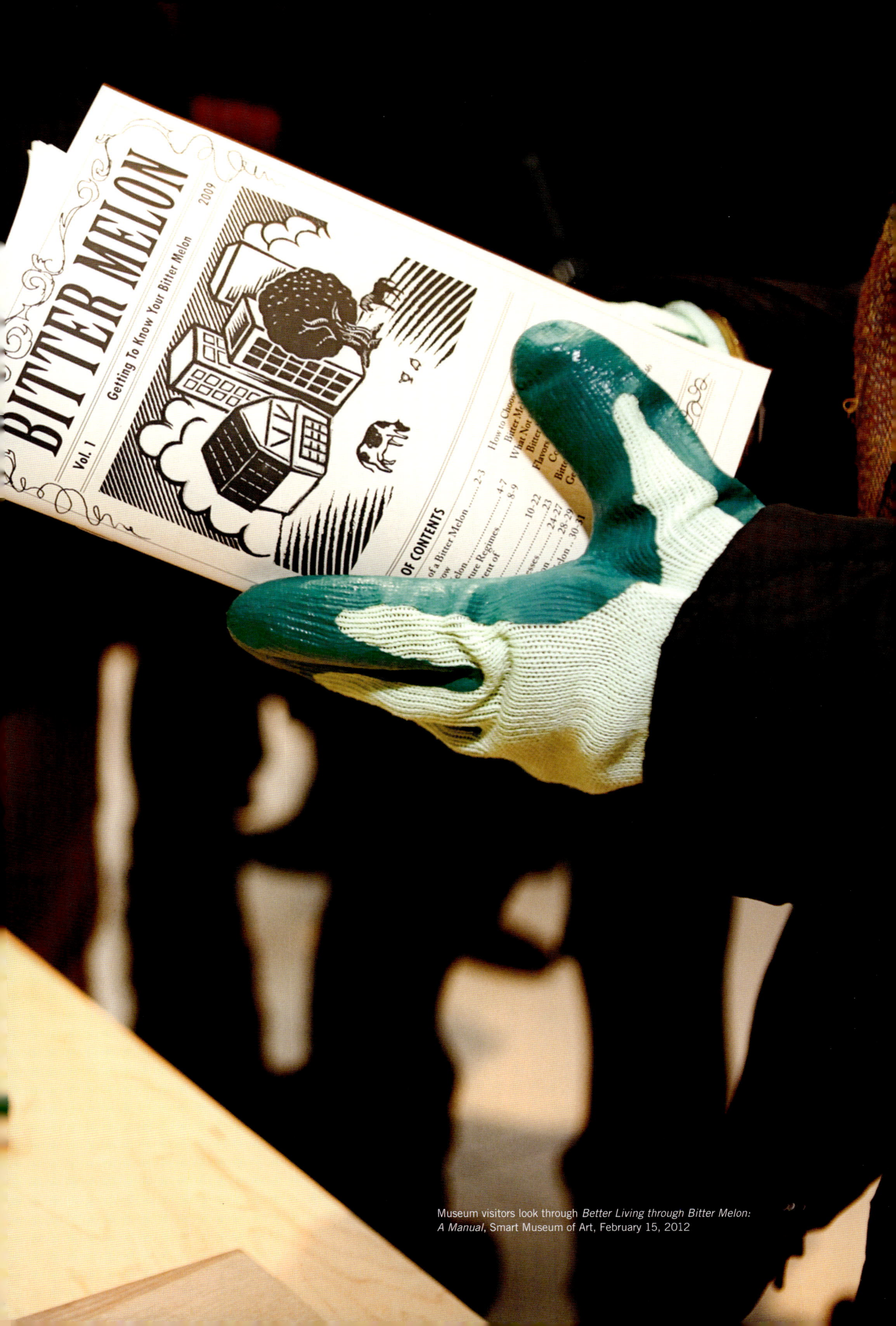

Museum visitors look through *Better Living through Bitter Melon: A Manual*, Smart Museum of Art, February 15, 2012

To articulate the sources of inspiration for us, we include the four C's: Community, Commodity, Cultivation, Creativity, which are the principle values that guide our work.

Community: The National Bitter Melon Council is a community; it builds community; it is a product of community. We vacillate between feeling a sense of loss and a sense of pride in community—forgotten, found, and created. There is a particular kind of community that The National Bitter Melon Council seeks to foster—one that is knit together and consists of equal parts yarn and adjoining absences and vacancies. We seek difference and use, adopt, and adapt it to create common experience and community. Indeed, we believe a sense of foreignness or otherness can create a community. From a phylogenetic perspective, bitter compounds in plants evolved as a defense against consumption by animals; in fact, *homo sapiens* is the only mammal to have developed an appreciation of bitterness, e.g. coffee, tea, and chocolate. Therefore, the appreciation of bitterness, the cultivation of a palette for bitterness across cultural-historical and ontogenetic timelines is the very thing that defines us as humans.

Commodity: The National Bitter Melon Council promotes the commercial, retail, culinary, health, nutritional, dialogic, Fluxus, and social use of *Momordica charantia* (Bitter Melon). It is a commodity of great value, but of questionable taste. Its value is deeply embedded in the process of coming to terms with it, its shape and off-putting morphology, as well as its bitter taste. The National Bitter Melon Council also trades in the commodity of meaning (or semiotics). The Council itself is the manufacture of new semiotic currency through the mining of existing social structure models and embedded community value. Our corporate mission is to expand the capacity of social structures to have new, reclaimed, unanticipated, surprising, and serendipitous semiotic value. In this way the Council claims and creates meaning where once none existed or was perceivable. Can we trade, exchange, or barter the semiotics of Bitter Melon? We can try; you can help.

Cultivation: Growing Bitter Melon is an adventure. Growing Bitter Melon means risking the stares, whispers, and frowns. "Ugly" and "bitter" are ostracized in favor of "pretty" and "sweet." The National Bitter Melon Council is an advocacy organization that seeks to eliminate these discriminations of aesthetic judgment. One strategy is to teach you to grow the biggest, best, and most bitter Bitter Melon, in a triumph of superlatives over subjective preferences. The other is to bring Bitter Melon to the people by widely disseminating the best practices for growing Bitter Melon regardless of one's location. Our Cultivation Goal is for Bitter Melon to be cultivated on every continent, in every country, and by all people. Cultivation is a metaphor for care. Bitter Melon is a symbol of the beauty, power, and potential of even the most bitter moment, experience, substance, and situation.

Creativity: Creativity, like diversity, explodes on the margins and in the interface between ideas, places, people, perspectives, and possibilities. The National Bitter Melon Council thrives by intentionally forcing the round peg into the square hole, or, in our case, the Bitter Melon into the vegetable promotion board. The Council relies upon its members, audience and participants as the collective actors of ideas that constitute our projects and initiatives. In our view, the act of cultivating is creative; the act of community building is creative; the act of commoditizing is creative; and the act of council is creative.

SMART: Please summarize the history of The National Bitter Melon Council.

NBMC: It all started in 2004 in the Berkeley Street Community Garden in the South End neighborhood of Boston, where—due to the numbers of Asian immigrant gardeners—the greatest concentration of Bitter Melon per capita grows. A group of artists, activists, and community members were involved in a year-long, site-specific research and performance project that considered the cultural, social, and spatial divisions in the garden, in the surrounding neighborhood of the South End, and in the local arts center (the Boston Center for the Arts). And so, with Bitter Melon in the garden and bitterness in the neighborhood's history, Bitter Melon became an ideal medium and muse for sparking conversation about bitterness in all forms: the promotion of bitterness as a tool for

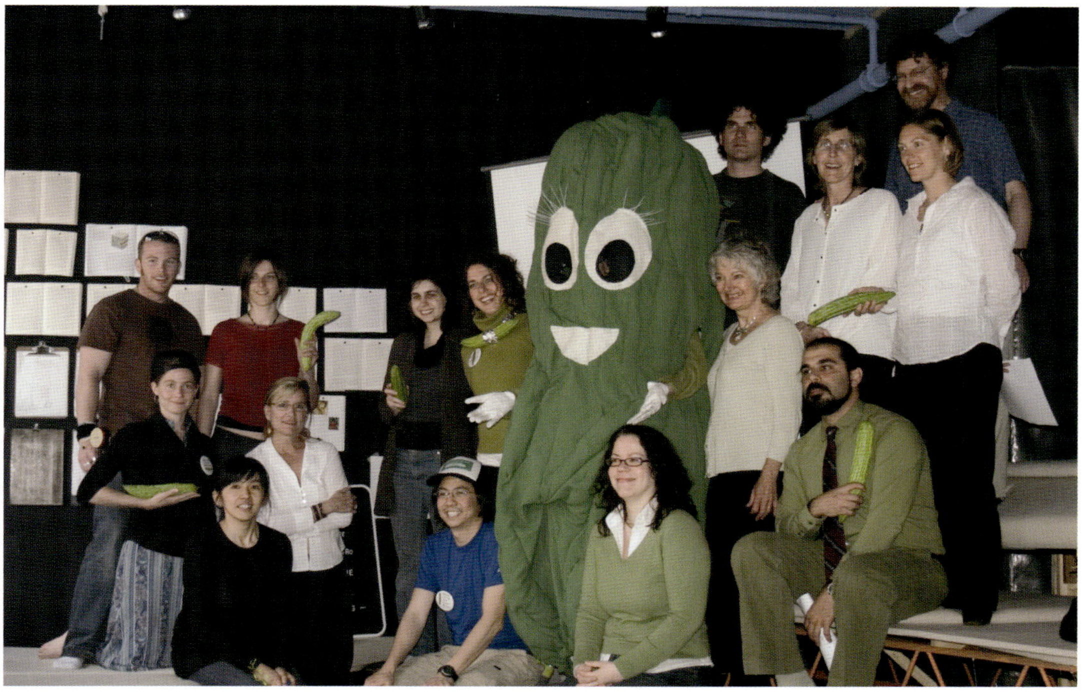

The National Bitter Melon Council Annual Meeting, held on Goya (Bitter Melon) Appreciation Day, Boston, 2007

community building; for connection; for the examination of difference and foreignness; and the deeper understanding of flavor and American-ness.

A gallery show brought to you by The National Bitter Melon Council in a neighborhood known for its food and its bitterness? A promotional council for a hyper-locally grown food product that is widely unknown to the residents and eating establishments in the neighborhood? Why not? And when this activity worked, so our work began.

Since that time, we have been making Bitter Melon–focused projects and sparking bitterness-focused conversation in art and non-art contexts. We've appeared in a vegetable exhibit competition at the oldest Agriculture Fair in the United States; at Community Supported Agriculture (CSA) farms; on panels at national conferences in gastronomy; on bitterness-inducing abandoned city lots; in seed-breeding and urban homeopathy experiments at West Coast museums; and are waiting to show up at (or in) your neighborhood, refrigerator, or kitchen table.

SMART: Tell us about the manual—its impetus, intention, and production—and how it fits into your broader practice.

NBMC: We first had the idea to create *Better Living through Bitter Melon: A Manual* (hereafter referred to as "the Manual") in 2008—several years before its final production. We were just developing a strategy that we're calling "performance documentation," i.e., a documentation practice for participatory, interventionist, conceptual, performance-based work that describes the work's past while realizing it in the present and creating it in the future. This strategy for documenting performance-based work allows the documentation to remain as active as a work itself—in fact, it allows the work to be created anew each time it is experienced. So, to document our work in the form of charts and graphs on PowerPoint presentations, an emotions-based survey, and an experiential kit with food and project recipes is to remain consistent with our persona, our site and context-specific practice, and our "Better Living through Bitter Melon" belief.

The action-based strategy of the Manual (at once performance documentation, a project, and a seed) had to do with our interest and need to grow the capacity of The National Bitter Melon Council. We had members around the world, but still the primary work was created and implemented by our core Executive Committee: Hiroko Kikuchi, Jeremy Liu, and Andi Sutton (with, from 2008 to early 2011, the additional collaboration of NBMC volunteer-at-large and illustrator Misa Saburi). We knew that while we were instrumentalizing Bitter Melon as a community development strategy, we were not the only ones who could put these projects into action. These works could be created and re-created as site- and context-specific events by anyone as long as there was a penchant for bitterness, a curiosity about community, and a bit of Bitter Melon to go around.

We looked to three things that inspire all of our work: Fluxus, food, and franchises. And what do each of these have in common? Recipes! And what is a manual, if not a recipe book in "how to" form? So, combining the recipe-format inspiration and performance documentation practice, we developed the Manual. Combining elements suggestive of Fluxus kits, farmer's almanacs, artist catalogues, and recipe books, we sought to create the feeling, the image, and the entity of The National Bitter Melon Council as an idea, a performance, and an organization, in portable, actionable form. The vision is that once someone uses *Better Living through Bitter Melon: A Manual*, the concrete sense of Better Living and Bitter Melon will serve as inspiration to use these methodologies in her/his home community, applied to the issues that are critical there. Thus, the Manual as a seed, as a franchising framework, and as an opportunity to build your own chapter of The National Bitter Melon Council.

SMART: How would you describe the role of the meal in your practice?

NBMC: Everyone can have an opinion about

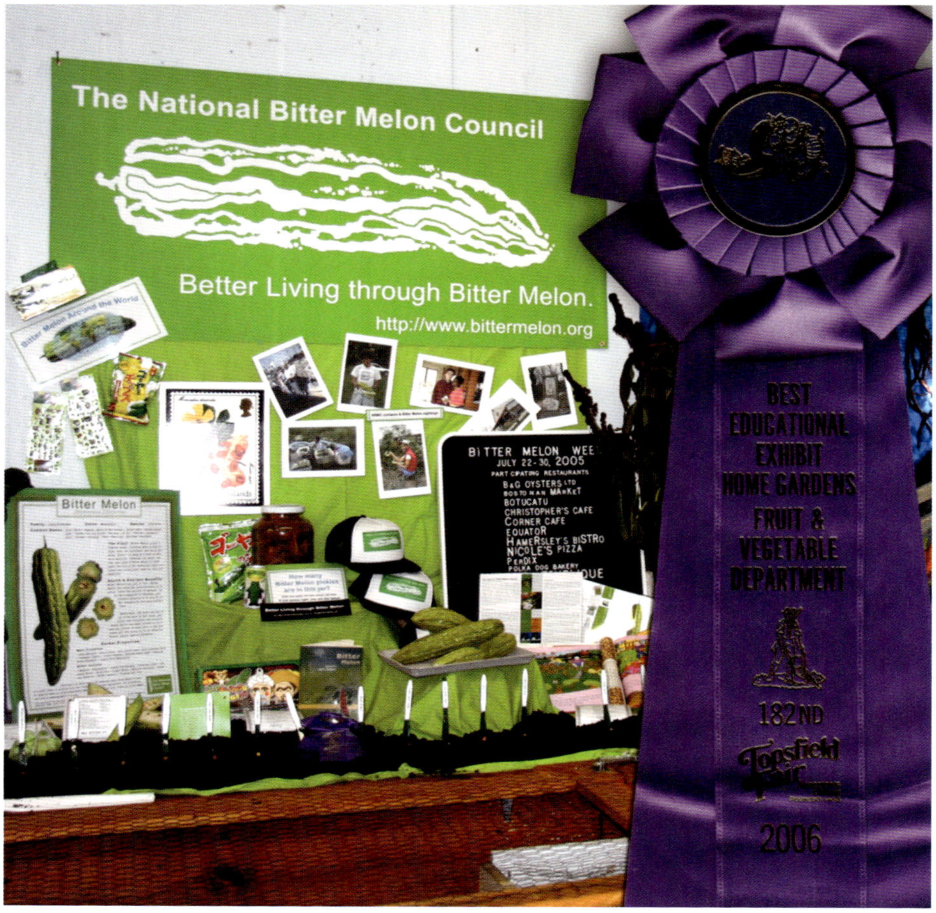

The National Bitter Melon Council took first prize for Best Educational Exhibit at the Topsfield Fair, Massachusetts, 2006

food, but not everyone feels like they can have an opinion about art. This is why we find food such a generative strategy for creating events that bring people of a wide variety of backgrounds, interests, and differences together. Food creates an opening through which others can experience newness, difference, uncertainty, and experimentation—because to experience food, you have to taste; to taste, you have to participate; and to participate, you have to act. For us this progression has led to a philosophy: *Bitter Melonism*. When we go from our attention to food to the use of the meal in our work *Bitter Melonism* is at play, so to explain the role of the meal is to explain *Bitter Melonism* itself.

The key tenet to *Bitter Melonism* is not just eating more Bitter Melon (though that can help). It is unity—unity through bitterness; unity through foreignness. Bitter Melon is largely unknown in much of mainstream American cuisine and in the cuisine of many industrialized countries in the West. But this very foreignness is what makes the vegetable a potent and enticing tool to build community. The commonness of its foreignness—particularly the intensity and demands of its bitter flavor—builds a foundation through which people can come together across other differences of color, culture, language, class, and more. Coming in contact with Bitter Melon for the first time, people always find a reaction, a gesture, an expression, and a few words to say about it. "It's ugly." "It's beautiful." "It's terrible (hand me a trash can!)." "It's . . . bitter." Sharing in this experience of extremes creates an atmosphere of curiosity and openness, and we use the structure of the meal (among other familiar food-based rituals and cultural frameworks) as the spark.

Building community through and because of the foreignness of a bitter flavor and the humanness of a bitter emotion is its very premise. It demonstrates that all things are equal—equally the same and equally different, all valid, all welcome, and all as fleeting as the lingering bitterness after a bite of Bitter Melon. It is a politics that combats the contemporary culture of fear. It is grounded in the faith that if one can bravely try a new and potentially off-putting taste, one might repeat that brave first step again, with Bitter Melon, with another unfamiliar flavor, with an unfamiliar experience, person, impulse, or opinion. Starting with the palate, *Bitter Melonism* seeds the understanding that expectation is not fact, that surprise is always possible, and that rich, freeing, savory possibility lies in exploration of the unknown. One Bitter Melon at a time.

The napkin and place mat were produced in 2006 for a commissioned piece, *Bitter Melon [A]side/Bitter Melon [In]side*, for the Grantmakers in the Arts (GIA) organization: a dinner performance for a preconference event for the GIA annual conference. The meal involved a collaboration with a local catering company, Cosmos Catering—a group that had never cooked with Bitter Melon before. We asked them to cook a nine-course meal that included Bitter Melon in every dish, but that did not taste at all like Bitter Melon. We wanted to consider how all of the participants—conference attendees, Provincetown Art Association and GIA staff, and we, the commissioned artists—were each [a]side and [in]side each other.

We designed the gallery space as a white-on-white dining arena, with matching flatware, tablecloths, etc. Continuing to play with the hidden and the visible, we created white napkins with the NBMC's artist statement silkscreened in white on top. We printed white place mats with a green silhouette of a Bitter Melon slice, the green hidden by the place settings. The text on the napkin was hard to read without wiping food from your face and hands and staining the background to make the words show up. And for the place mats, dinner participants did not see that they were anything but white sheets of paper until after the last plate was cleared, so they, too, ended up with food residue and stains. As a concluding action, we asked the diners to sign their place mats alongside signatures of The NBMC. With both, what began as an identical series of objects ended as individual collaborative art pieces, carrying the echo of each person's eating experience in the form of dropped pieces of food and residue from her/his utensils.

The napkin and the place mat are—in their unused state—proposals for collaboration. So when we were asked by Stephanie to include both pieces in the show it was important for us

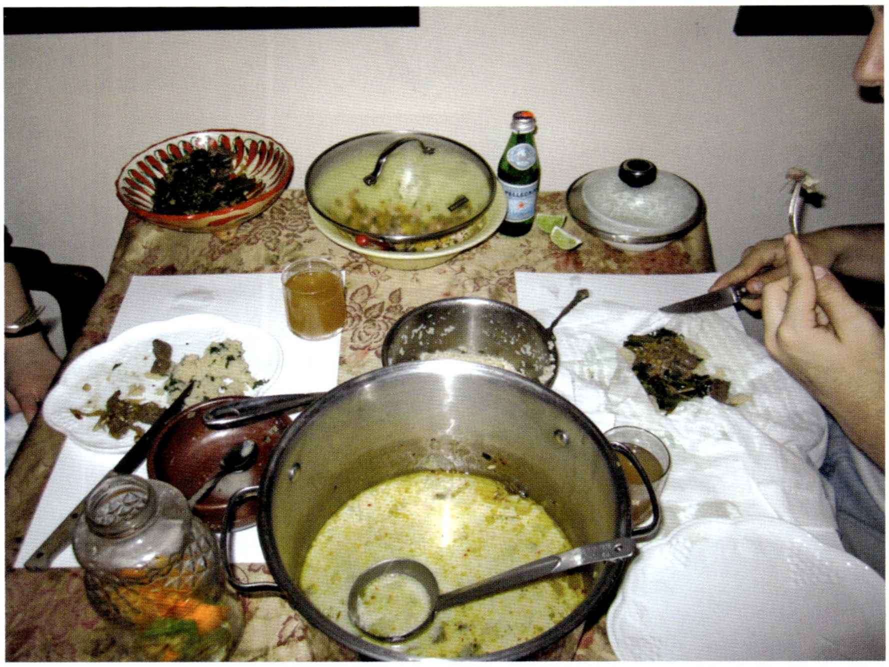

Smart Museum Intern Sarah Mendelsohn and guest Michael Bridges share a meal made from recipes in The National Bitter Melon Council's manual, 2012

that we include the used and unused versions. We wanted to co-create a new napkin and place mat within the context of *Feast*, so we asked if someone at the Smart Museum would partake in a performance to bring the napkin and place mat alive.

On December 5, 2011, Smart Museum intern Sarah Mendelsohn produced the piece. She prepared five different Bitter Melon dishes and shared them with a guest, using the napkins and place mats in her place settings. In Sarah's words:

> Having decided to prepare the bitter melons in a few different ways, and uncertain of the results, I became invested in the cooking process. Serving my guest, Michael Bridges, I was surprised by my feelings of apprehension. Was I feeling bitter? Do feelings of bitterness always figure into the roles of hosting and receiving, or of participating in someone else's project? . . . Over the course of this meal, and my conversation with Michael, my feelings of apprehension were subsumed by a sense of joint enterprise. Both aware that we were performing for each other, the dinner became a meditation on the nature of participation. Through our use, both guided by Andi's instructions and independent of them, the bitter melon dishes and NBMC-branded tableware became objects of enjoyment, disgust, abjection, humor, and absurdity.

We were excited by the range of dishes, the range of thoughts, and the range of bitternesses that the two of them shared. But, most of all, it was impressive to see how emphatically the napkins and place mats had been used. With the wrinkles and the tears, it was hard to see what part of each one had not been in contact with some part of the meal. With so much of the dinner document soaked in to the napkin and place mat, it was almost 'as if they had returned to us an instruction piece of their own: *try to recreate this bitterness-based meal.*

SMART: How would you describe the role of hospitality in your practice?

NBMC: Hospitality is a slippery word, and its slipperiness meant that coming to an answer to this question involved quite a bit of digging and debate. Because for us what's important

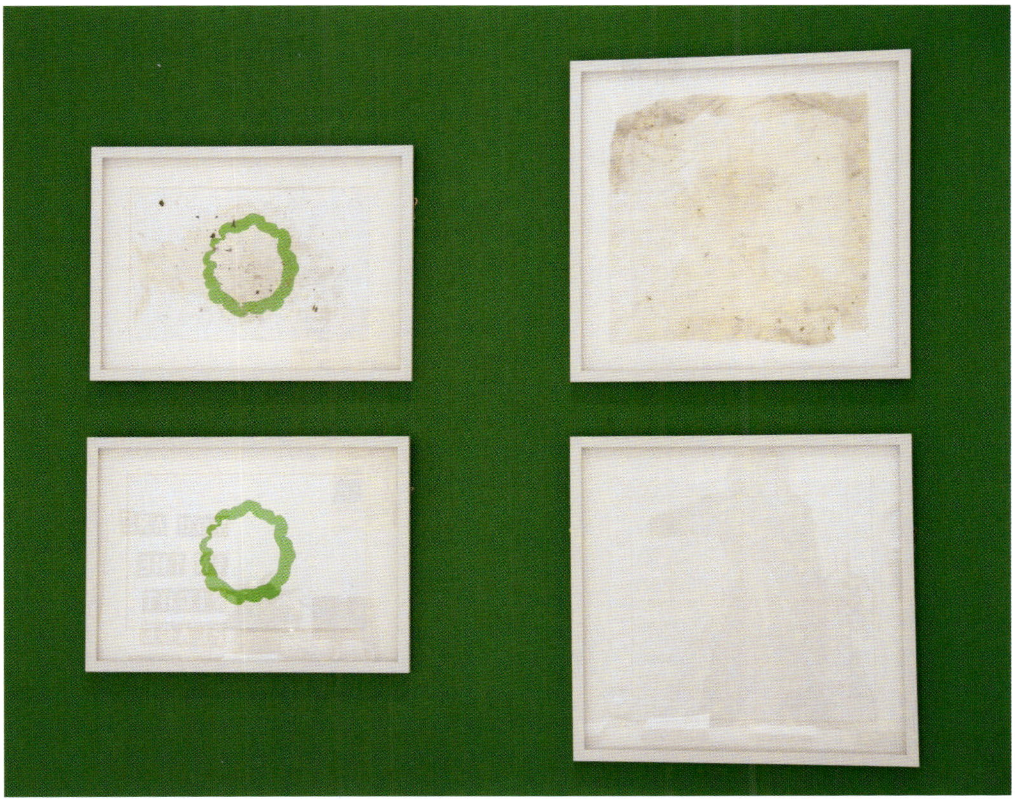

The napkin and place mat used during Mendelsohn's dinner, paired with their clean counterparts, installation view, Smart Museum of Art, 2012

and relevant is the word in adjective form: *hospitable*. Though the difference is subtle, in its difference is the complexity we seek in our work.

Our definition of hospitable—or hospitableness—is cultural resonance. Hospitableness is using cultural resonance to form an entry point, an environment, or a relationship. And these entry points come about in our design choices, in our persona, in the language we use to talk about what we do, and more. However, we feel that hospitableness is only relevant for us when it comes in concert with *inhospitableness*. When the cultural referent of the vegetable promotion board meets the ugly, intensely bitter, "foreign" Bitter Melon, hospitableness meets the inhospitable. And the productive rupture—curiosity, discovery, wonder, confusion—happens only with the meeting of the two. For when our work is solely hospitable, when there is no surprise or subversion (inhospitableness), we become *merely* a vegetable promotion board instead of *especially* a vegetable promotion board.

And yet, while hospitality is our mechanism of cultural resonance, it is also our display of sincerity. And perhaps that, too, puts the Radical in our Hospitality. Yes, we actually like Bitter Melon. Yes, we believe that bitterness is healthy for the body, the emotional self, and for community. Yes, we believe that The National Bitter Melon Council—as a project, a persona, a collective, and a functioning promotional council—is intriguing, productive, and resonant.
Yes, we believe in people and the possibility of connection through and because of the foreignness of Bitter Melon and bitterness. We have a celebratory, loving, un-ironic (call it "countercynical") relationship to the social structures that we incorporate and intervene into in our practice. And we believe that love, celebration, and critique can coexist. It's actually wonder, we think, that allows each of these to work together—wonder in experimentation, wonder in belief, and wonder in participation.

Ana Prvacki

ANA PRVACKI'S ART OFTEN REVEALS latent absurdities, social tensions, and unexpected moments of beauty lurking within barely conscious everyday experiences. She possesses a finely tuned awareness of subtle social and cultural codes—perhaps a natural byproduct of her international upbringing in Europe and Asia. This sensibility informs her art, as does extensive research. Her current work on hospitality and etiquette follows from her consultations with experts, as well as close and wide-ranging reading. But Prvacki's art wears this research lightly, usually taking the form of performances and videos marked by a gently surreal tone and dry comic sensibility. In the mid-2000s, for example, she created *ananatural*, a faux line of wellness products and activities that she advertised through catalogues of ideas and brief infomercial-style videos. Another recurrent strategy has been the transposition of familiar activities into "improper" settings. In her *Wandering Band* (2009–10), for instance, solo musicians stroll through museum collections and in public while practicing basic scales over and over—a usually private act and one of the less-beautiful (albeit necessary) parts of a creative process. In all of these projects, Prvacki takes a humane view of the awkward and even grotesque byproducts of our attempts to create beauty, to achieve well-being, and to belong.

For *Feast*, Prvacki extended these interests through a new iteration of her ongoing project *The Greeting Committee* (2011–ongoing). This work considers the complex dynamics of hospitality, particularly gestures of welcome offered to a guest crossing the threshold of a home or institution. One element of the project centers on the Serbian practice of offering guests a taste of a sweet fruit preserve called *slatko*. For *Feast*, Prvacki shared that custom with a wider and presumably largely non-Serbian public: several times each week, specially trained students and members of the Smart Museum's senior staff stood near the Smart's entrance to offer visitors a spoonful of strawberry *slatko* as they arrived at the museum.

This simple, even playful act opened up a set of problematics about the relationships between guest and host, especially as they move across cultures and contexts. Within the Serbian context, *slatko* is simultaneously generous and self-serving: meant both to sweeten the visit and to sweeten the tongue after one leaves, a reminder not to gossip and thus to respect and protect the host. Prvacki also tells a story about her Romanian mother's first encounter with *slatko* on her first visit to her Serbian father's home. Not knowing the ritual, she reacted to the mysterious offer by eating many spoonfuls of the jam (rather than the expected single bite), to the horror of her future in-laws. *The Greeting Committee* asks us to reflect on such tensions. A gesture of welcome can be just that—something that makes one feel welcome, respected, and at home—but it can also unsettle the guest: when it relies on unfamiliar or discomfiting cultural codes, or when displaced to an unexpected context. In gently calling attention to the complex roles of host and guest, *The Greeting Committee* ceremonially welcomed visitors to the museum and recruited them as active participants in the shared experience of *Feast*.

OPPOSITE: *The Greeting Committee*, perfomed by the artist, Smart Museum of Art, February 15, 2012

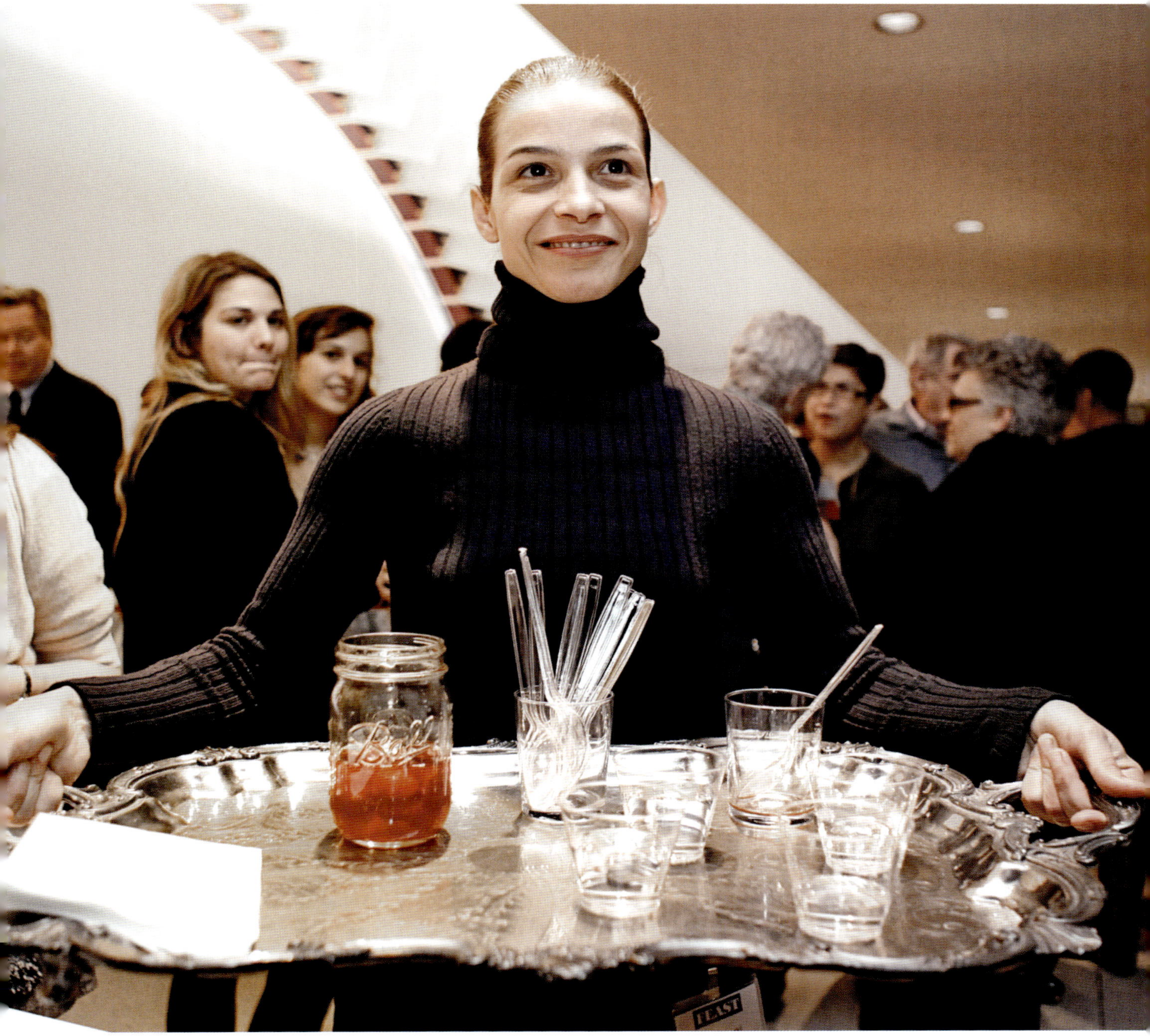
FEAST

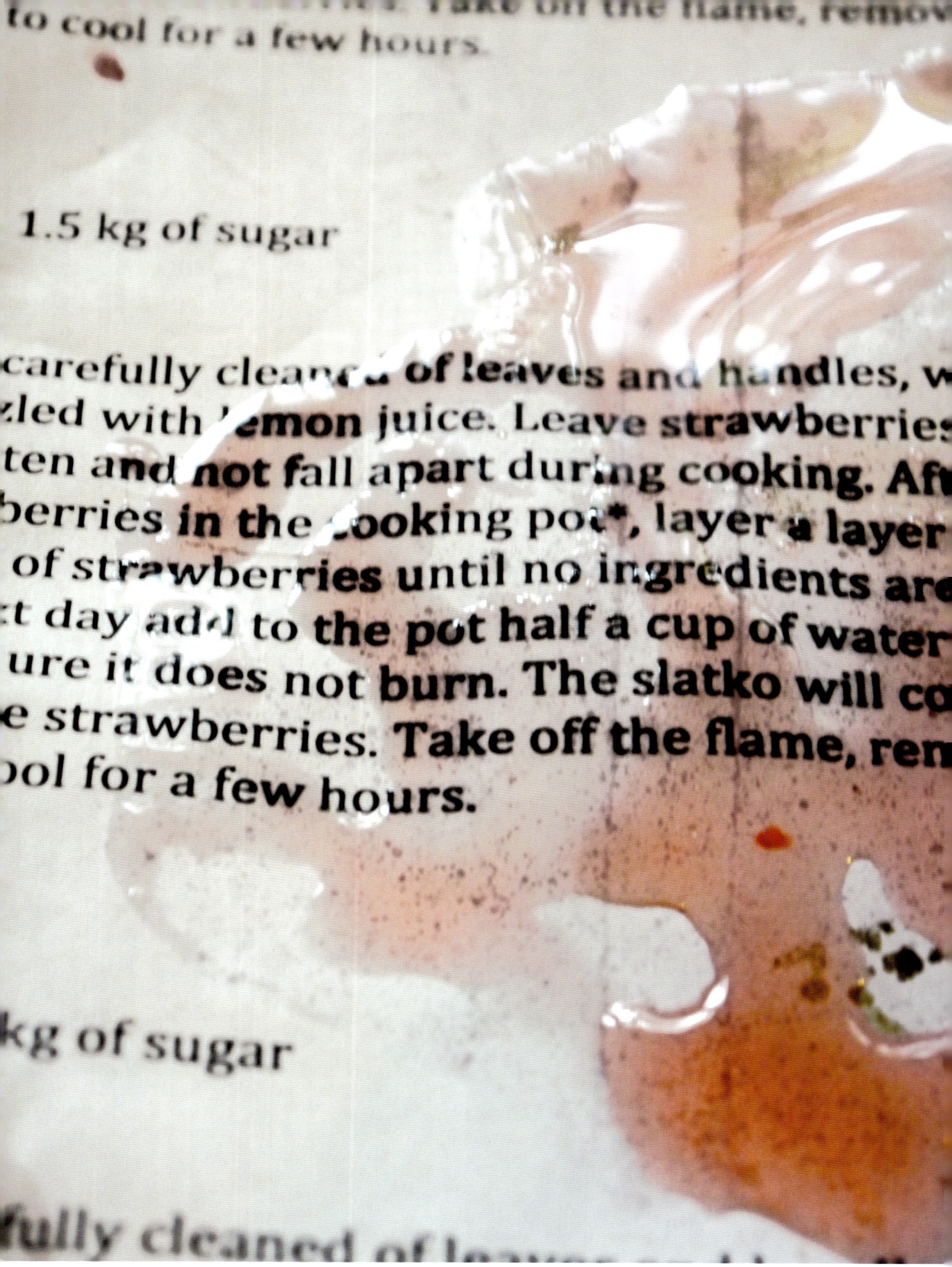

Prvacki's *slatko* recipe

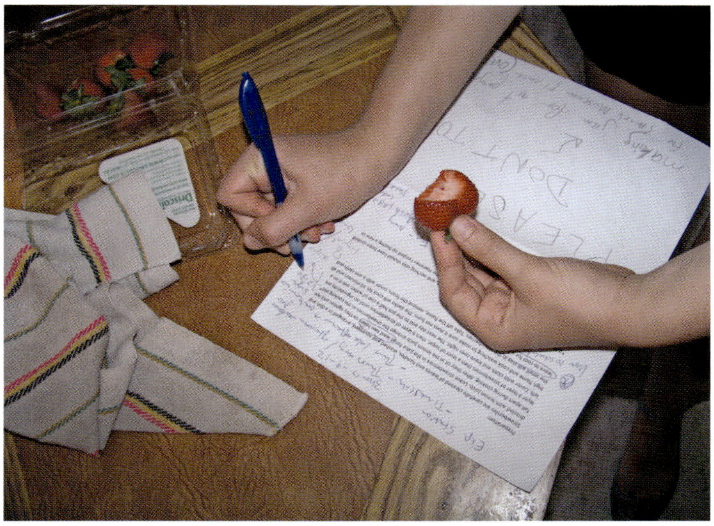

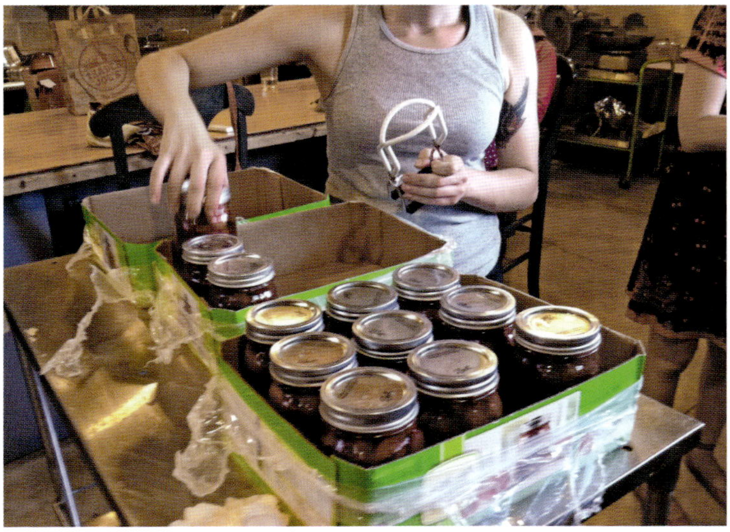

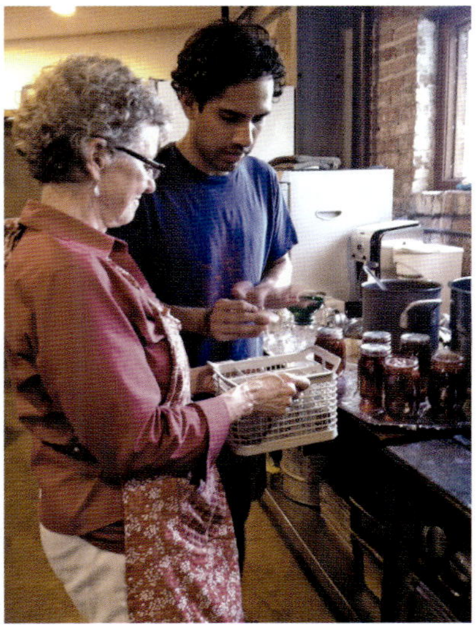

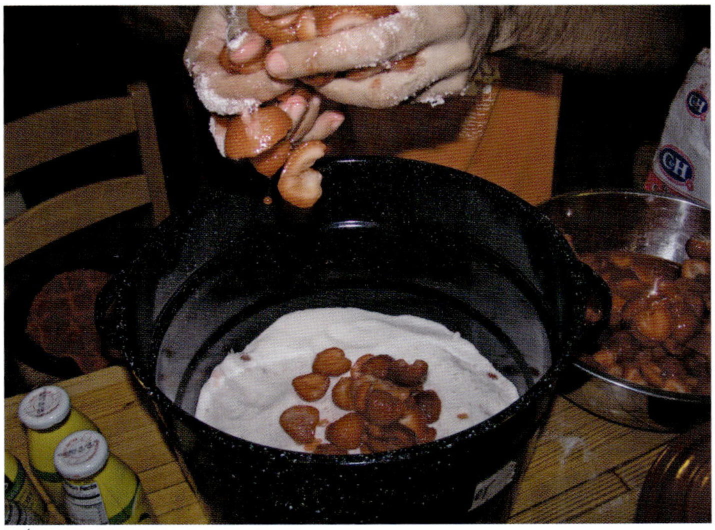

Smart Museum interns and Deborah Fortel (mother of curator Stephanie Smith) preparing *slatko*, Experimental Station, Chicago, 2011

Interview

SMART: Can you describe your history as an artist and sources of inspiration for your work?

ANA PRVACKI: Having moved and migrated most of my life—between Yugoslavia and Romania, Singapore, West Europe, and now living in Los Angeles—I have a great fascination with routine and daily practices and I have always been interested in how to make transitions (physical, emotional, spiritual) smoother, how to cohabitate more successfully, and how to centralize and integrate.

Some of my sources of inspiration are my grandmother's equanimity, Jacques Derrida's *Of Hospitality*, Martha Stewart with her *Everyday Living*, Borat with his cultural learnings, Amma hugging over 30 million people, the Singapore Kindness movement, Kwame Anthony Appiah's *Cosmopolitanism*, Emily Post's *Etiquette*, P. M. Forni's Civility project, and Hilary Clinton's gloved handshake. They have all played a role.

SMART: Could you say a little more about your interest in daily practices, your international upbringing, and how they shape your art?

AP: Practice is defined as "the actual application or use of an idea, belief, or method as opposed to theories about such application or use." I am interested in how we exercise and apply our morals and ethics in the everyday. I have been thinking a lot about my grandfather who was a theologian and a practicing Greco-Catholic priest during the Communist era. He also studied Sanskrit and comparative religions, and was part of a Marxist reading group, and a poet. All of those things were part of his personal intellectual and spiritual practice, which he exercised in spite of the harsh restrictions imposed by the Communist system.

Also, having studied music and theater, I was brought up with the routines of daily practice, and both of my parents are traditionally trained, very skilled visual artists. I very quickly became conscious of the subversive potential of such practices. So there is necessity for routine but also for constant innovation that would alleviate the boredom that arises with repetitive actions.

SMART: Please describe your ongoing project *The Greeting Committee*—its overall scope as well as its specific manifestation for *Feast*. Please also describe how the various iterations of the project have informed its development.

AP: *The Greeting Committee* aims to stimulate us to practice civility and congeniality. The first campaign took place at the Hammer Museum in Los Angeles. I worked with a team of etiquette instructors over a period of four days. We addressed and greeted each visitor that entered the museum while discussing and performing etiquette basics such as opening doors, introductions, body language, hand

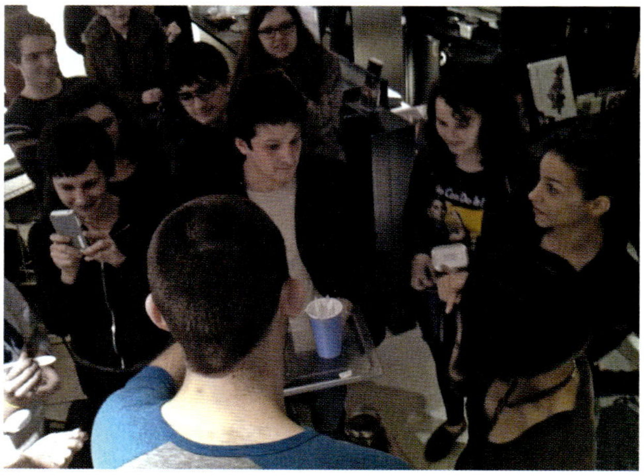

Prvacki (far right) and Smart student staff sample *slatko* as part of a training session on hospitality, Smart Museum of Art, February 2012

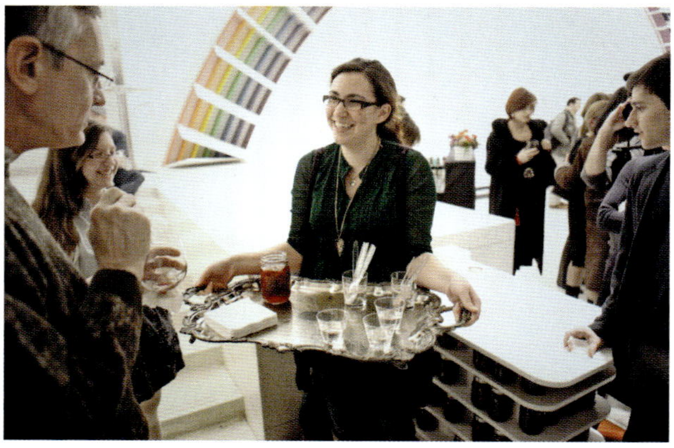

The Greeting Committee, Smart Museum of Art, February 15, 2012

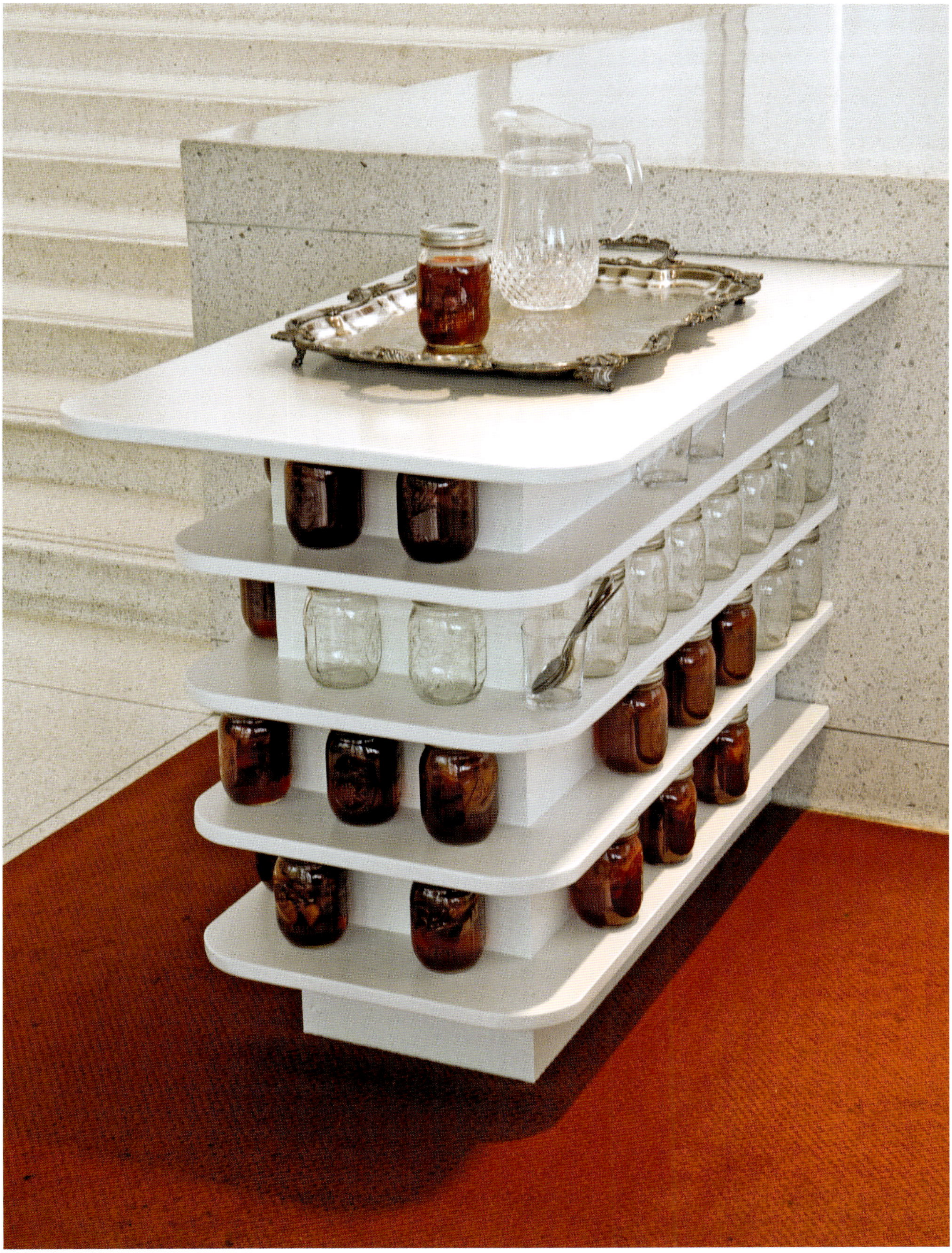

The Greeting Committee, installation view, Smart Museum of Art, 2012

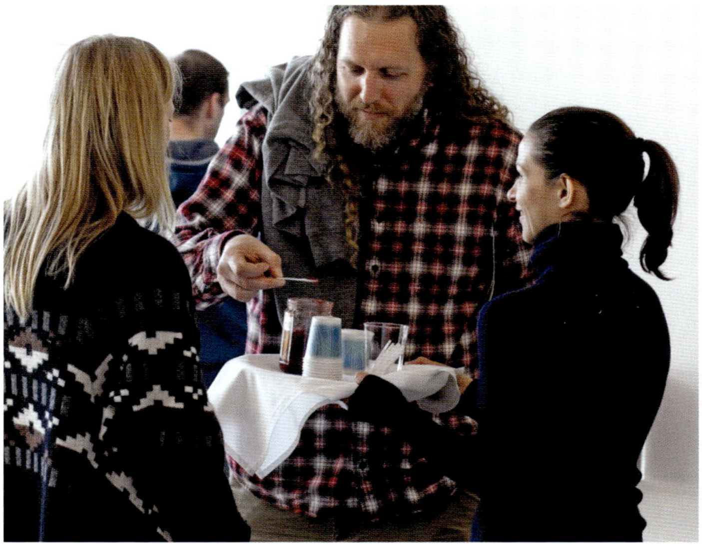

The Greeting Committee, Hammer Museum, Los Angeles, 2011

shake, and consuming party food (in this case, *slatko*). Of all the gestures, the feedback we got from the visitors shows that offering *slatko* was the one that made them feel most comfortable and involved.

For *Feast,* the main focus will be the distribution and sharing of *slatko*. In Serbian tradition, the offering of *slatko* is the first interaction and first impression one makes as a guest/host. But rather than just replicate the traditional social performance of serving *slatko*, for *Feast* I would like to introduce a kind of transparency to the exchange and make the purpose of the gesture more explicit. I am really interested in how it is meant to function to prevent gossip/criticism, and in what happens if the guest/visitor is informed that a taste of *slatko* is meant to make them like the visit and the exhibition better and not speak badly of it. So rather than reenacting the tradition, we zoom in on this detail and make it explicit.

SMART: Could you say more about the different people involved in the project, and how their participation connects to questions of hospitality as practiced within institutions and within homes?

AP: The *slatko* that will be offered to the visitors during *Feast* has been made by Smart Museum staff, students, friends, and the curator's mother, from a recipe given by the artist's mother. This is a very important element, especially in the discussion of home versus institutional hospitality. The fact that the *slatko* was produced by the host/mother is something that will be shared with the visitors. The institution should feel a certain pride in the *slatko* it offers.

SMART: How does the *slatko* project for *Feast* figure into your broader practice?

AP: All of my projects to some extent deal with social interaction and practice. They are interventions into daily life that are meant to transform the viewer's perception and experience of daily life and routine, providing solutions to our common problems, worries, and fears. In Serbian tradition, the offering of *slatko* is the first interaction and first impression one has as a guest/host. It addresses our social skills and tests our ability to engage with hopes to sweeten, befriend, disarm, and soothe.

SMART: You're focusing on the sweet sides of *slatko*, but you're also interested in issues of control, manipulation, and misunderstanding. Could you speak about how you address those darker sides of hospitality—along with a sincere interest in warmth/welcome?

AP: *Slatko* is always too sweet, that in itself is a kind of provocation. Like being too sweet, or too nice, it disturbs and makes people

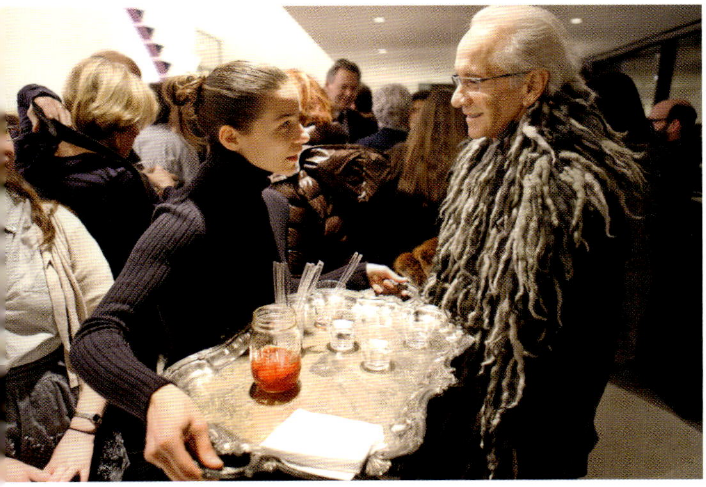

The Greeting Committee, Smart Museum of Art, February 15, 2012

uncomfortable. A spoon of *slatko* paralyzes you for a moment, almost numbs your taste buds and then you are invited to enter and in a sense "behave." We also want to sweeten the tongue of the visitor to assure they will not speak badly, preventing gossip/criticism. *Slatko* is anti-confrontational; *slatko* is anti-critical inquiry! Insisting on imposing congeniality is a very specific kind of aggression: What happens if we demand respect and hospitality without judgment and criticism?

SMART: The project is also playful and a bit humorous. Could you say a bit about the role of play and humor in your work?

AP: Humor is one of the ways to deal with tension and awkwardness; it is efficient even against injustice. Monty Python's deadliest joke comes to mind and I wonder if *slatko* could be used in warfare. As a theater student I was exposed to a lot of Commedia dell'arte and absurd theater, Ionesco has been a great influence on my work. I am still interested in the comedic potential of the inappropriate, and hospitality and etiquette offer a lot of opportunity for a faux pas!

SMART: How would you describe the role of the meal/hospitality in your practice? Do questions about hospitality figure into your process or thinking?

AP: I have been interested in the practices and techniques of the service industry for a long time and there is certainly a connection between service and hospitality, both on a corporate and private level. In a very cosmopolitan sense I am interested in how we serve and host our fellow citizens of the universe, at home and/or in institutions; our whole life we alternate between being guests and hosts.

Slatko at home is a historical tradition, when it is in a museum it becomes representational and self-conscious, the viewer is encourage to interpret the practice. This might include a process of critical enquiry and its relationship to other similar cultural practices.

SMART: What does it mean to you to be included in a show called *Feast: Radical Hospitality in Contemporary Art*?

AP: It is a very timely show. I also find it interesting that hospitality has become a somewhat controversial subject and etiquette and manners are often considered frivolous, yet today's political and social situation shows that we do not fully practice respect for other living beings or the planet. One of the etiquette instructors I have been collaborating with, Vertuhi Keshishyan, told me once, "You can't have two sets of manners, two social codes—one for those you admire and want to impress, another for those whom you consider unimportant." I think most of us fail to have this kind of equanimity in our daily life, and I think that is the biggest controversy of all. (Bertolt Brecht's play *The Good Person of Szechwan* is a great example of this.)

SMART: What do you hope people take away from your work?

AP: Traditionally *slatko* is meant to "sweeten the visit" and is offered with the hopes of a pleasant and congenial visit. It is also said to "sweeten the tongue" preventing gossip and misunderstanding. I literally hope visitors enjoy their visit, say nice things about the show, and leave with a contagious sense of hospitality.

Sudsiri Pui-Ock

OVER THE PAST DECADE, cross-cultural exchange and the desire to connect—to nature, to other people, and to one's own inner life—have been central subjects within Sudsiri Pui-Ock's art. These preoccupations have been shaped by extensive time working abroad: although now based in her home city of Chiang Mai, Thailand, Pui-Ock spent much of the mid-2000s at artist residencies in Israel, Japan, and the Netherlands. In several projects during this period, she exploited the cross-cultural references inherent in food. In the installation *The Door is Open* (2005), for example, she assembled slices of bread into flower-like shapes. Scattered across the gallery's concrete floor like lilies floating in a pond, these objects playfully intermingled associations—a stereotypically Asian landscape, traditional Thai methods of elaborately carving and assembling food, cheap Western foodstuffs, and the sculptural vocabulary of global installation art. Along with installation, Pui-Ock works in performance and video: she often creates spare, meditative performances for the camera.

Food-based installation and performance-based video come together in Pui-Ock's project *The Dinner* (2004). Pui-Ock created this work while at the Rijksakademie, a two-year international artist-in-residence program in Amsterdam. It grew in part from her habit of making her studio the site of casual meals for new colleagues, and in part from her fascination with the mass-produced Delft-style ceramics she found for sale throughout Amsterdam. Many of these trinkets are produced in Asian factories (including some near her home in Chiang Mai) and then shipped to Europe to be sold as "authentic" Dutch souvenirs. Inspired by these objects, she created a set of eight place settings that use the traditional blue-and-white style to depict stories of her own movement between Asia and the Netherlands. In a performance, she set out the dishes for eight on a long low table and served an elaborate meal to herself, eating alone and moving between place settings. This performance now exists as an installation of the table and place setting, and a typically spare, quiet video. This video—the only part of the project presented in *Feast*—consists of one unvarying shot: of the low table, the bare studio, and a wide doorway as the artist moves in and out of the frame to set the table and eat her solitary feast.

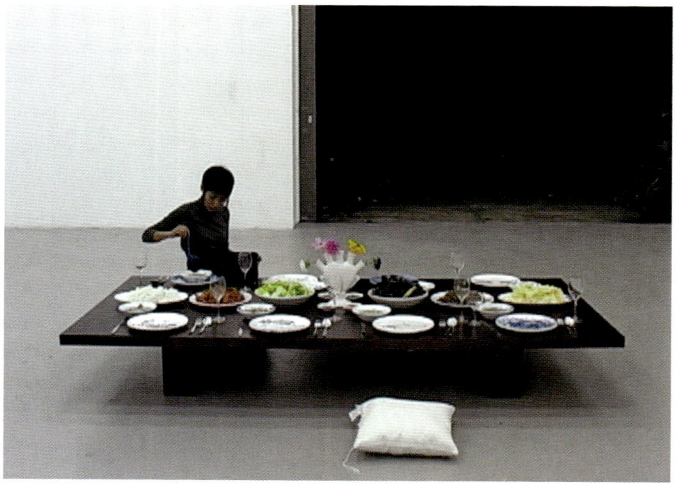

ABOVE: Still from *The Dinner*, 2005

OPPOSITE: *The Dinner*, installation view, Rijksakademie van Beeldende Kunsten, Amsterdam, September 20, 2005

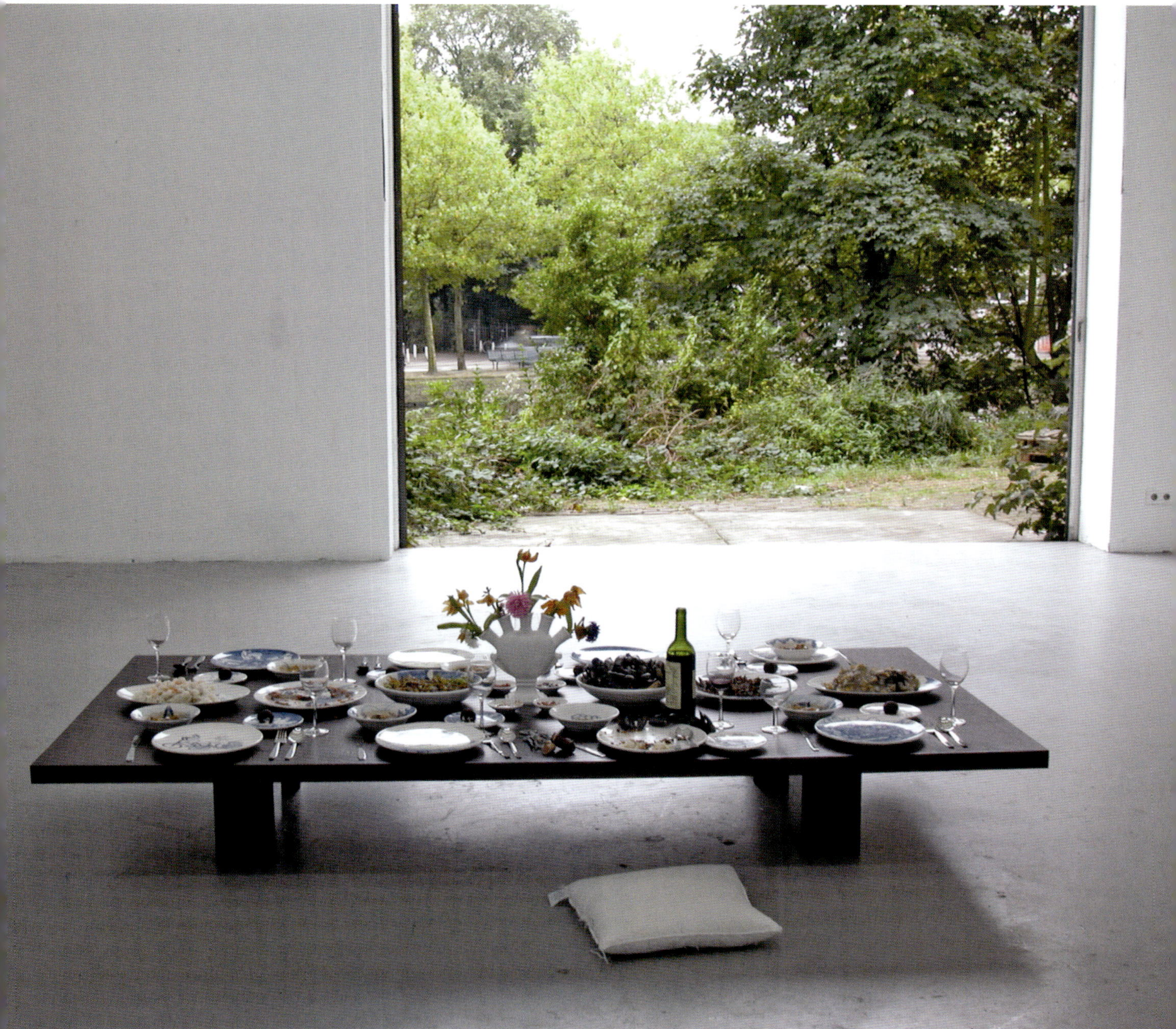

Interview

SMART: Can you describe your path as an artist?

SUDSIRI PUI-OCK: My artwork is part of my life. I'm just living my life. The conflicts, questions, struggles, and philosophy that living brings me become my art. I use any technique that best supports each idea. Technique-wise I'm very experimental. Concept-wise, I'm interested in the existence of the self and the meaning of life.

Topics I use in my work are related to my life at each time. For instance, in the performance *Step Forward* (2001), I took a walk between home and studio every day on the same route: life is all about circles of repetitions. In the installation *Fitting* (2003), a collection of my skirts and drawings of those skirts showed how each skirt I found in secondhand markets over many years began to fit to my self and my attitude. Fixing, changing, adjusting, keeping are all qualities we need to be with our clothes, as well as relations of our self to friends, family, or entire world we live in. Or in *The Street of Two Birds* (2006), I made a rubbing of a manhole cover in the middle of a busy road in Japan. Being a stranger is the situation when you perceive something different from others, when you act in ways that others don't expect and you get an unexpected reaction.

Some of the projects consider the relationship between humans and nature. For the video *Farmer* (2009), I observed a farmer working on his land. Life is a continuation of repetition and connection with nature. For the *Pumpkin Project* (2011) I carved real pumpkins. It's about impermanence: all things are subject to change. Carved pumpkins are man-made beauty. We are not satisfied with what already is there but make it even more beautiful, thereby triggering even faster decay.

SMART: Tell us about *The Dinner*—its impetus,

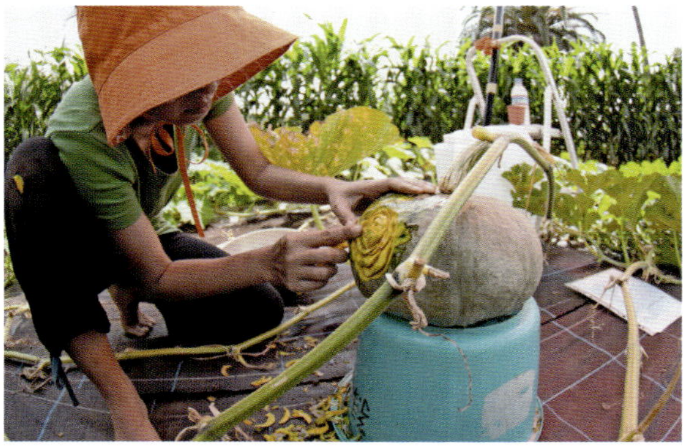

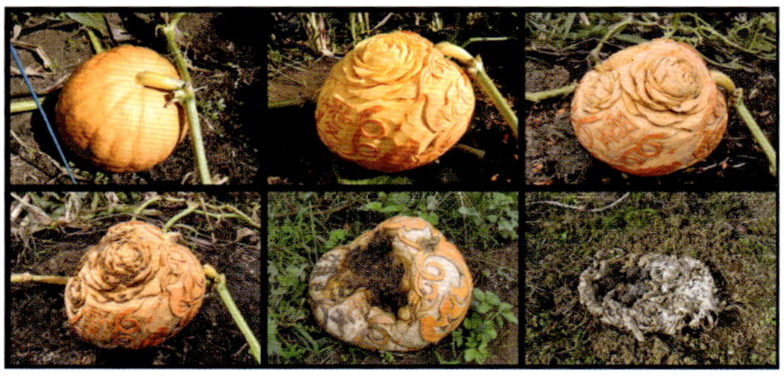

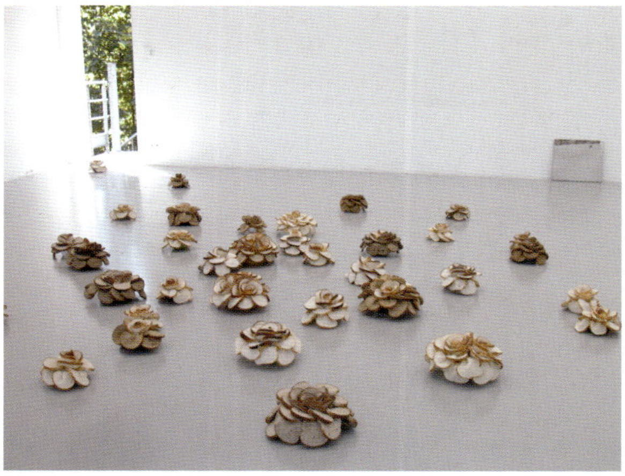

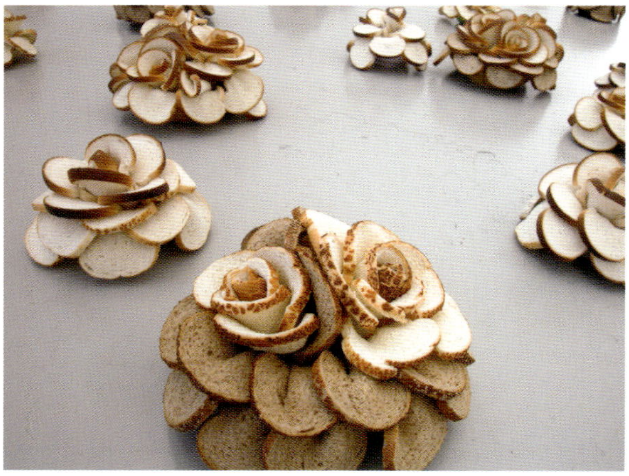

TOP ROW: *Pumpkin Project*, Yokohama Triennale, Japan, 2011

BOTTOM ROW: *The Door Is Open*, installation view, Rijksakademie van Beeldende Kunsten, Amsterdam, 2005

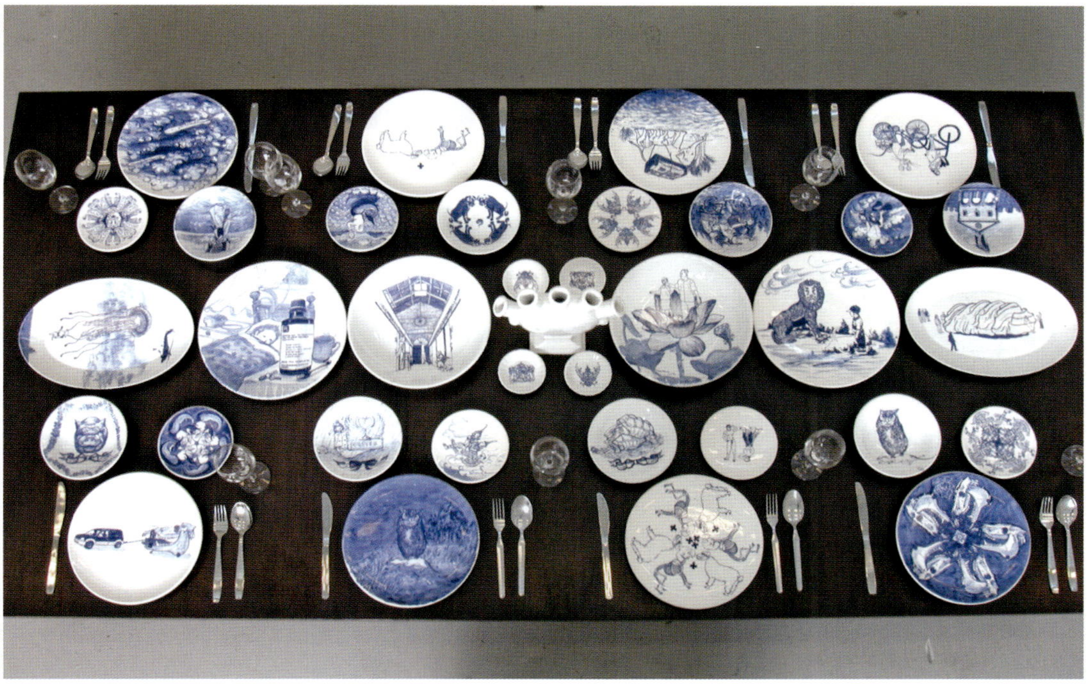

The Dinner, installation view, Rijksakademie van Beeldende Kunsten, Amsterdam, September 30, 2005

intention, and production—and how it fits into your broader practice.

SPO: *The Dinner* consists of several parts. During two years of living in Holland, I made ceramic plates based on drawings, then made an installation and video of myself serving dinner for eight people on those plates and eating alone. This conveys that we are all alone within: you can be surrounded by many people or your loved ones, but you are the only one who can see your mind and deal with it.

The plates are made in the ceramic tradition of *Delfts Blauw* (Delftware). The Dutch take pride in it, and it is part of their national art heritage. During the seventeenth century—a time when few countries traveled across the world for trading—ceramics using this technique were imported to Holland from China.

Later, the passion for these ceramic wares drove the Dutch to produce their own versions in the small city of Delft, where the cost was less. In the beginning the drawings of blue on white were still similar to Chinese designs and patterns, but later were adapted to European designs. At present, *Delfts Blauw* from Delft is a luxury souvenir from Holland. Ironically, the inexpensive Delftware-style souvenirs like those with the drawing of a little Dutch boy and girl kissing each other are made in China and Lampang, near my home town in Thailand. I remember that I used to see little ceramic windmills and Dutch boys and girls kissing in every ceramic shop in Chiang Mai. I even got some of them when I was a child. As they didn't pass quality control for export they were very cheap, maybe not more than 5 Thai baht. I am interested in these mixings across Asian and European culture, so I used that style to make ceramic plates with drawings that were inspired by my real-life experience as a Thai visitor in the Netherlands. They show stories of things or people that existed, or that I wished for or imagined were there, during the two years that I was in Holland.

SMART: Please say more about the performance of *The Dinner*, and your choice to make the video of yourself eating that meal alone in your studio—but at a table beautifully set for eight guests.

SPO: "Eating alone is boring" is the phrase we often hear. It is true when we are far away from home. That's why we have to cook and eat

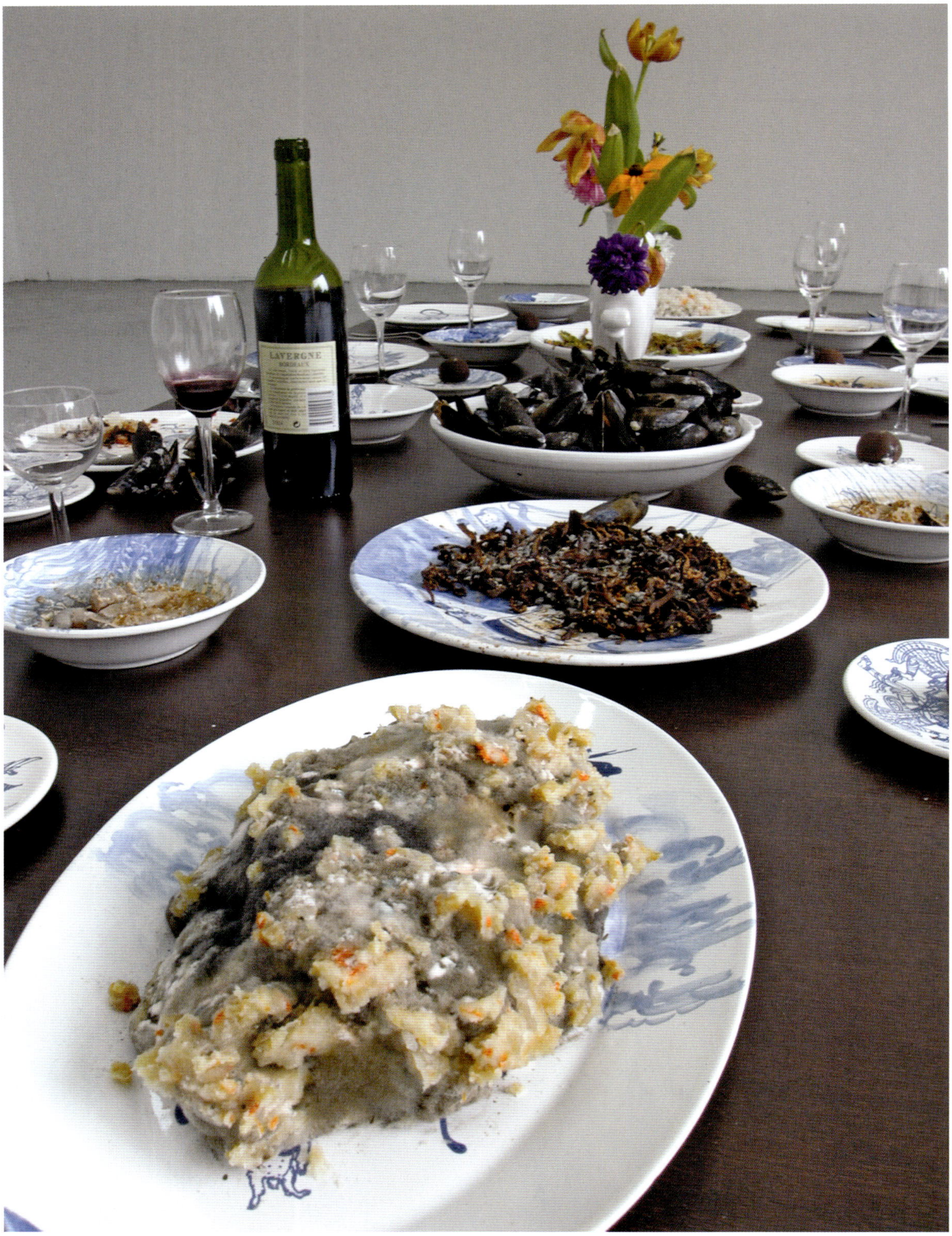

ABOVE AND OPPOSITE: *The Dinner*, installation views, Rijksakademie van Beeldende Kunsten, Amsterdam, September 30, 2005

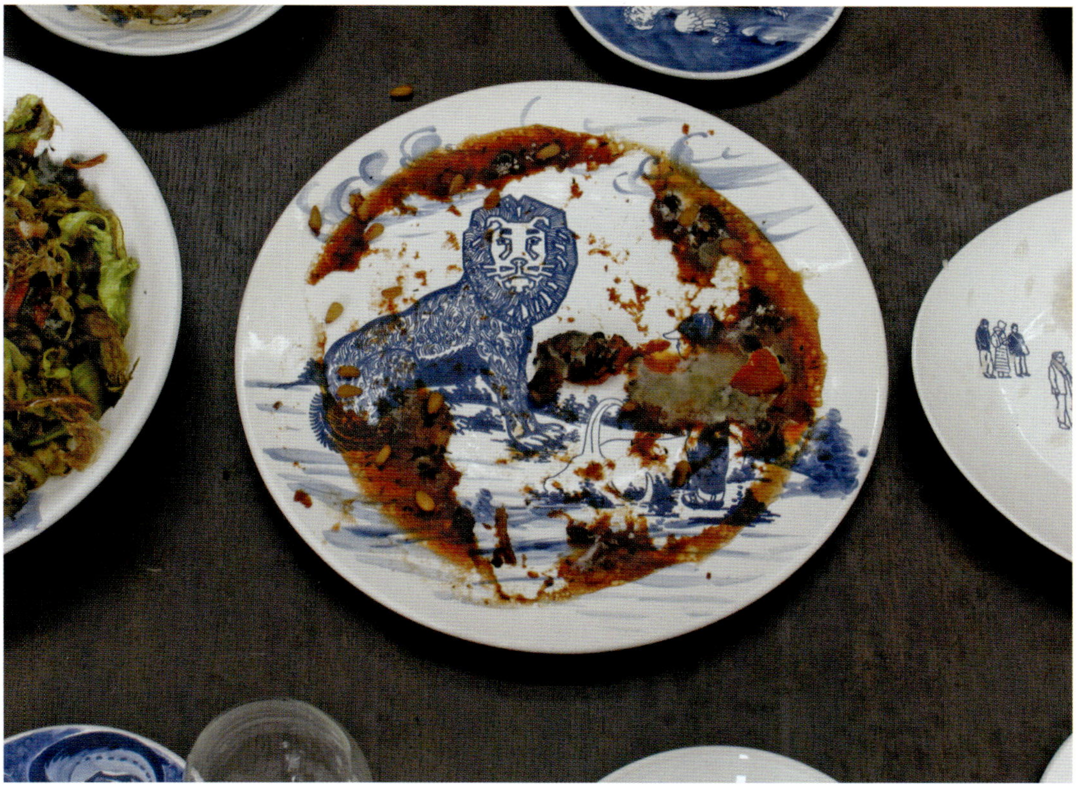

together. During my stay in Holland, I cooked often and hardly ate alone. I got to know new friends as well as a variety of foods served on the table. Dinner was the time of happiness.

However, the loneliness still existed in the back of my mind. The realization that "only we really understand our mind" is like the time when we have to eat alone.

SMART: It sounds as if you're addressing different ways of being alone—a kind of loneliness that can come with travel and immigration and displacement, as well as a more metaphysical or spiritual kind of loneliness. Could you say a little more about those ideas in relation to *The Dinner*?

SPO: There are two different kinds. You can be alone without feeling lonely or you can be around people or try to have people around you as much as possible but still feel so lonely inside.

SMART: Your videos are often very quiet and slow-paced. That is true of *The Dinner*. Not much happens—you set the table, you eat. But in part because you're so focused and calm, it seems as if you're asking the viewer to slow down as well, to pay attention to details of the performance and perhaps also to their own inner experience. Is that part of your intention with this piece?

SPO: I really like that point of view. For my part, my video has no story. We are used to looking for a story; we are easily drawn into other people's stories. My video invites people to slow down—there is not much story to follow. People might feel irritated that nothing happens in the video. Then after a while, when they accept it, they will taste the slow, simple, ordinary atmosphere around a small woman eating alone. One time I saw half the audience walk in and watch the video for fifteen seconds and leave the room, while the other half stayed till the end . . . well . . . the video doesn't have an ending actually.

SMART: How would you describe the role of the meal/hospitality in your practice?

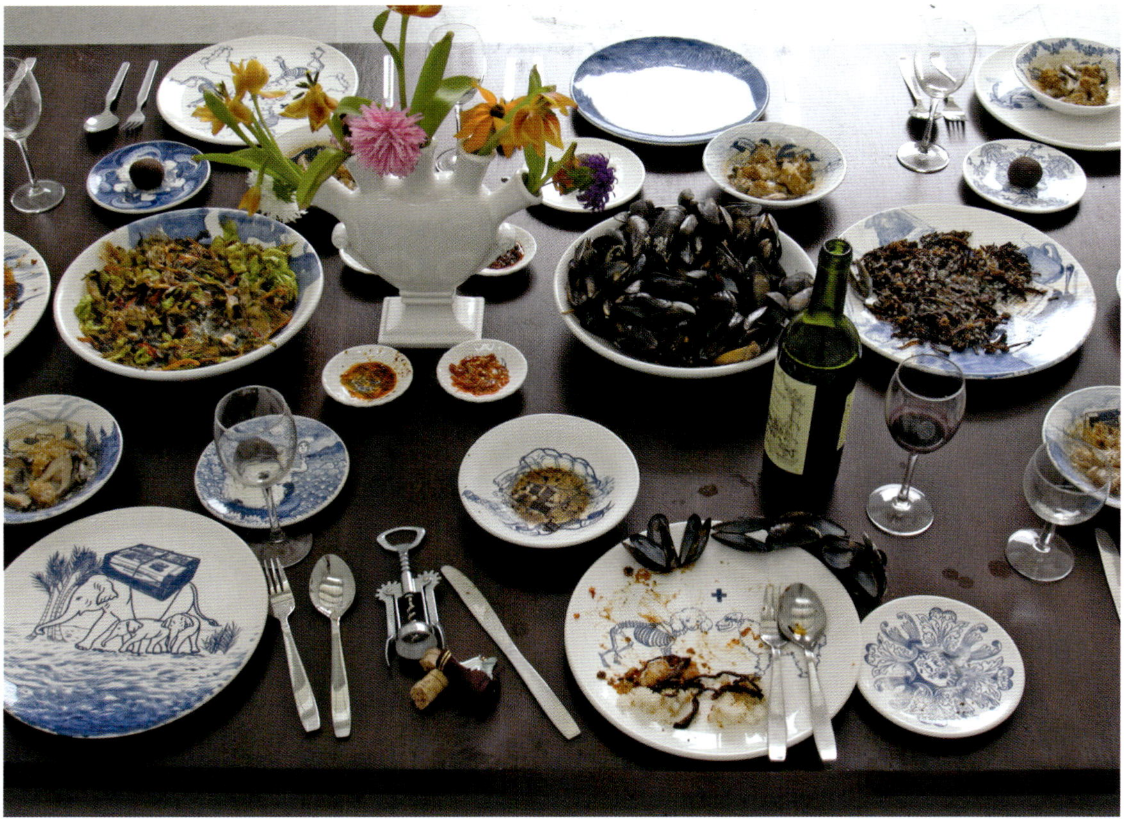

The Dinner, installation view, Rijksakademie van Beeldende Kunsten, Amsterdam, September 30, 2005

SPO: Eating is a basic need of all life. Most humans eat three times a day. I spend approximately two hours each meal, which is six hours in the kitchen and at the table, equal to one third of waking hours of the day (eighteen hours awake, six hours asleep). What we do during the other twelve hours of waking? In one way or another we're looking for food! So, we're basically busy with feeding our body all our life.

I found that in Asia we have a culture of food sharing more than in the West. When you meet someone, you go to eat together. Food is enjoying and sharing. This even shows up in the way we serve food: in a plate for everyone to share. Everyone takes food from the main dishes on the table to their plate as they want. In the West, they usually serve food to each person. I find that very private and limited.

When I was in Amsterdam, I often invited friends to eat with me. I hardly had dinners alone. They were quite surprised that I kept offering food for free. I was surprised by their surprise as well.

In Thailand, no one dies of hunger. Only those living in concrete big cities have a chance to die of hunger, because we have good earth and good weather all year long. You put a seed in the ground and it grows. You always find things to eat in your land: bamboo shoots, leaves, roots, flowers, etc. But in Europe, it's cold most of the time. If you don't plant and plan to stock your food, you might die of hunger during the seasons that nothing grows. This is my conclusion why people in Asia (especially Thailand) give food as part of their hospitality culture.

SMART: Describe a favorite story about your work.

SPO: In many of my works made in Holland, I used a mouse as a symbol of myself. The story began when I first moved into a shared apartment that had so many mice and cockroaches. We went to the office of the housing company to report the pest situation. They said: "We don't have mice in Holland. And if your house has cockroaches, their eggs must have came in your suitcase from Thailand."

Let's imagine this: In a house—any house in the world, from a luxury apartment in New York to a small apartment in Amsterdam—there are, of course, humans and mice! If there are humans, there are mice too, even if no one wants to accept them in their house. But every house has mice, as long as the history of human kind (unwritten history anyway). Without being accepted by humans, the mice have always done very well in close connection with humans. That's how I felt in Holland: A mouse in a Dutch house. Other Western immigrants are friendly welcomed into the human house like pets. Someone Dutch may find my comments offensive. But this situation of cohabitation among humans and mice happens everywhere in the world—I can see that in Thailand as well, but here different people are put in those roles.

SMART: Now that you have moved back home to Thailand, have the themes of cross-cultural exchange, guests, hosts, and home that seem so important to *The Dinner* remained important to your art?

SPO: No, as I stated before, my work is very much connected to my life at each moment, but cross-cultural exchange is not my focus at the moment.

SMART: Have you been influenced by the Chiang Mai Social Installation projects that Rirkrit Tiravanija, Navin Rawanchaikul, and others produced during the 1990s? Your work seems generally very intimate and inward-focused as opposed to those large social, public projects. And are there other artists —in Thailand or the west, past or present—whose work you find particularly inspiring?

SPO: It is difficult to say whether I was influenced by them. I was a student at the time they were already world-famous. I was curious about what they were doing, but I chose a very different approach. I began with the smallest social unit as opposed to them starting out on a large scale. There is little tangible work of art for those artists, but rather an experience that can be shared by many. You could compare it to politicians. The first thing they do is to get people to believe in them. For me, one human is part of the society, so the story of one human makes the picture of the nation. The effort to change the large social order will not succeed if it can't touch that one heart. So I start out from the other end.

I'm inspired so much by the work and life of Araya Rasdjamroensook, who was my advisor during my five years of undergraduate art school. Also Bill Viola, whose videos I was drawn into. I was once sitting in the last row of a lecture he gave at the Mori Art Museum, Tokyo, on the occasion of his retrospective show. For hours he talked about many things including those hard stretches between the creative times, days, months, years. I had tears in my eyes and trembled. It was overwhelming for me. I walked to him after the talk but didn't dare to say anything or shake his hand with my sweaty shaky hand but just gave him a pale smile.

When I'm down, I always think of this.

SMART: What do you hope people take away from your work?

SPO: They take what they can get. That's how art works. Artists create art from a certain inspiration but once it's done it's up to what the audience can perceive. Perception is very much according to each person's background. It is like a Rorschach test: what they see/take away tells more about them than the work.

Michael Rakowitz

THROUGH PUBLIC PROJECTS as well as multidisciplinary gallery presentations, Michael Rakowitz asks nuanced questions and relays moving, often surprising tales about politically charged topics like homelessness and war. His first major project was the *paraSITE* series (1997–ongoing) of portable, inflatable shelters designed with homeless individuals. This aesthetically rich and ethically grounded mode of collaboration recurs throughout his subsequent work, in tandem with an archaeological, research-driven mode of unearthing, assembling, and reframing resonant stories, relationships, and artifacts.

After the United States invaded Iraq in 2003, Rakowitz began to bring his family history and culinary heritage as an American of Iraqi-Jewish descent into projects that explore far-reaching effects of the Iraq conflict. *Enemy Kitchen* (2003–ongoing) began as a series of workshops in which Rakowitz taught small groups to make his family's Iraqi recipes. In *Return* (2004–ongoing), Rakowitz reopened his grandfather's New York-based import-export business, Davisons & Co., in part to bring the first post-embargo shipment of Iraqi-grown dates into the US. In both projects, Rakowitz activated the sensual materiality and metaphoric potential of these specific foods and the circumstances in which they are (or are not) produced and consumed.

As a central commission for *Feast*, Rakowitz adapted the *Enemy Kitchen* concept in a new mobile sculpture and participatory project, *Enemy Kitchen (Food Truck)* (2012). Rakowitz assembled a team including chefs Milad and Maikl Shaer—owners of Milo's Pita Place, a Chicago restaurant that serves Iraqi cuisine under the neutral label "middle eastern"—along with sous-chefs and servers from Iraq Veterans Against the War and the Iraqi Mutual Aid Society (an immigrants' group). They served specialties like *kubba mosul* (meat pie) out of a retrofitted food truck: a mobile sculpture that provides the hub of this participatory project. The truck served more than one thousand patrons in diverse neighborhoods around Chicago during *Feast*'s run, inspiring both verbal attacks and warm discussion between members of the public and the veterans and immigrants who collaboratively produced and served these meals.[1] A highly visible and symbolically charged object, the truck was painted Davisons & Co. green, emblazoned with the Enemy Kitchen logo, adorned with a flag that merged Iraq's colors with the pattern of the City of Chicago's flag to create a new hybrid for the Iraqi community of Chicago, and fitted with a dispenser for rosewater (used in Middle Eastern hospitality traditions). Dishes were served on paper replicas of Saddam Hussein's china, asserting Rakowitz's interests in cultural history and global political mythology: what does it mean to eat off of throwaway replicas of Hussein's china, and how are we as diners implicated? Rakowitz has now turned the truck over to the Shaer brothers, who hope to continue *Enemy Kitchen (Food Truck)* as an ongoing business venture that will further extend Rakowitz's initial vision.

The project touched the museum space lightly, in two forms. *Enemies and Kitchens* (2012), an ethnographic-style display of artifacts and texts, charted the history of Rakowitz's Iraqi food-based projects. This presentation questions the formal conventions through which we receive cultural information, and evokes our distance from events like the Iraq conflict that abstractly shape our lives. As a final touch, an Enemy Kitchen-branded rosewater dispenser placed near the museum's exit allowed visitors to spritz their hands and hair with scent, as a concrete embodiment of complicated, cross-cultural hospitality.

Sarah Mendelsohn contributed to this text.

---

[1] The truck initially skated just under the radar of Chicago's notoriously tough food truck regulations by giving food away rather than selling it. By the close of the exhibition, Rakowitz and the Shaer brothers had navigated the complex bureaucratic channels required to license the truck as a fully fledged business—a bureaucratic process most likely familiar to any immigrant seeking official status, recognition, and welcome.

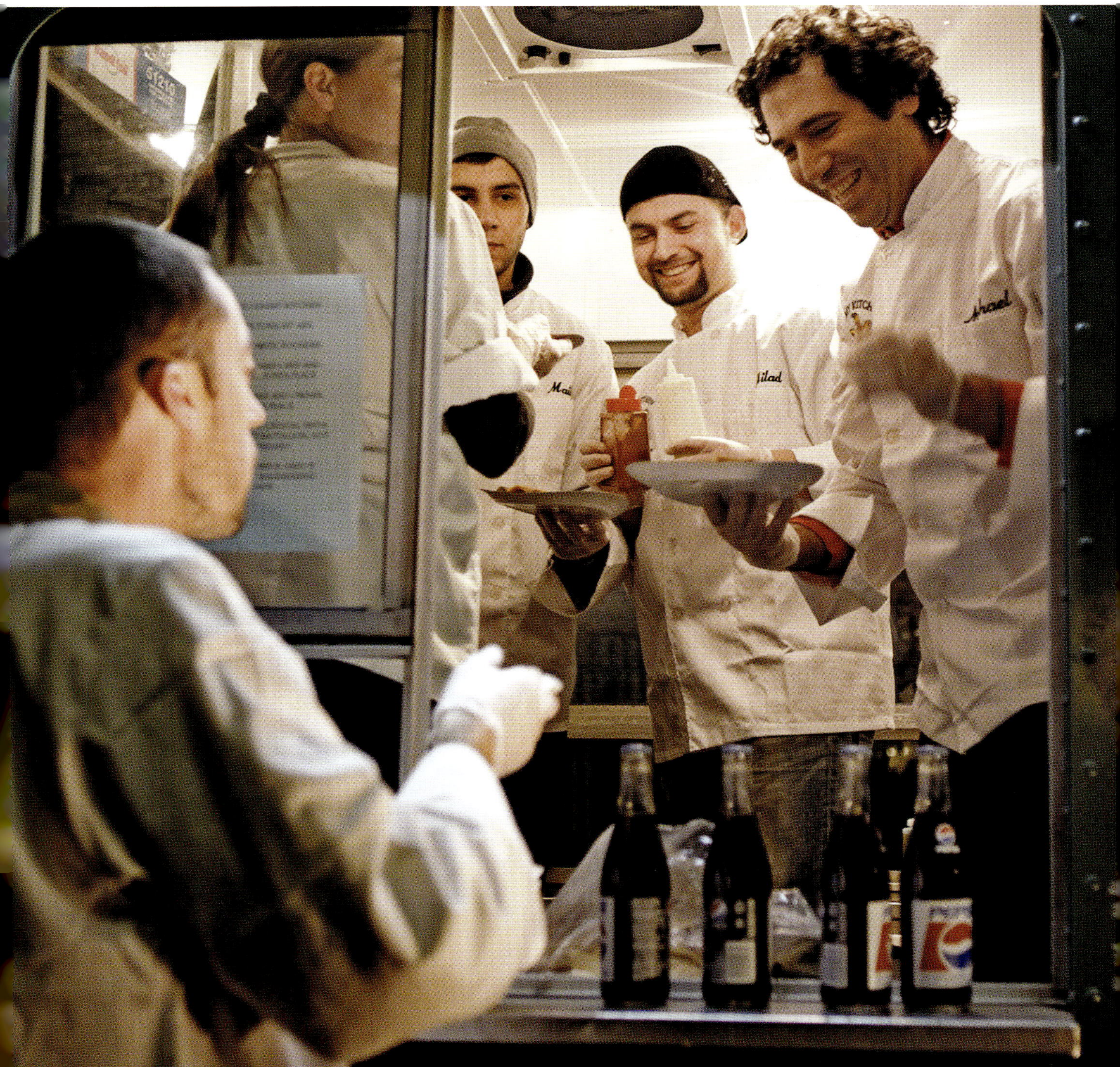

Enemy Kitchen (Food Truck) at the Smart Museum of Art, February 15, 2012

Interview

SMART: Can you describe your path as an artist and sources of inspiration for your work, either in or beyond the context of art?

MICHAEL RAKOWITZ: My parents recognized my abilities as a draughtsman early on and encouraged me to become an artist. Each year, we took trips to different cities around the world. These were never leisure vacations, but rather intensive and engaged visits to museums, galleries, cathedrals, and archaeological sites. It was visits to places like Teotihuacan outside of Mexico City and Uxmal in the Yucatan where I was introduced to the intersection of sculpture, urban planning, and the choreography of belief and ritual. And, something was truly at stake in those places that wasn't present in the paintings and sculptures I'd seen in museums, as many of the sculptural platforms I was drawn to served as stages for human sacrifice. Naturally, I was very inspired.

In August of 1990, three weeks after Iraq invaded Kuwait, my parents took us to Israel for my younger brother Robert's Bar Mitzvah. We were astonished by Israel. My mother actually had bad memories of the place from when she was younger and her Baghdadi Jewish parents took the family there for her sister Olivia's wedding in 1966. My mother recalled the barbed wire running through Jerusalem separating Israel from Jordan, and as she climbed a wall and got too close to the boundary, a Jordanian border guard aimed his rifle at her. Only twenty years earlier, she had been exiled from neighboring Iraq as a one-year-old, along with the rest of her family.

I ended up loving Jerusalem when I witnessed my mother, unafraid by the warnings issued to American tourists to avoid this part of the city, walking through the Muslim Quarter. Stopping and speaking with shopkeepers in Arabic, they all were intrigued by her dialect and accent—Jewish Ghetto-Iraqi-Arabic. She was having a blast, and it suddenly felt like home. The aroma of *kofta* (balls of ground meat) and kebab being barbecued smelled like my mother's cooking. I suddenly felt connected to my family's history in a way I hadn't before.

My parents took us to the YMCA building in West Jerusalem, which boasts an observation tower allowing visitors to look as far east as Jordan on a clear day. I looked at the sand dunes in the distance and thought, "enemy sand." I was looking into a seemingly endless desert, and somewhere along the way, there was a border demarcating two nation states. This was 1990, four years before Israel signed a treaty with Jordan, and the news of the moment was that King Hussein was going to keep Jordan neutral in any potential conflict with Iraq. Looking further into the distance, I wondered how wide Jordan was, and if there was any chance that the dunes I was looking at could be Iraqi.

When I was sixteen years old, the dean of my high school, Peter DeFilippo saw my work in the annual art show and said I had the drawings of a sculptor and asked me to pursue a stone carving apprenticeship in his studio. And so I began to carve stone, which was magical. I became addicted. In fact, it remains to this day the material and process that I enjoy the most, only I haven't enlisted it since, as it never made sense as a material choice for subsequent projects in art school and beyond.[1]

Having learned this new technique, my professional life as an artist began. I applied to art schools against the backdrop of the first Persian Gulf War, and enrolled with the blessing and support of my parents, who encouraged me to pursue graphic design—an early 1990s way of ensuring one could make money as an artist. My training as a designer fostered a real consideration of audience and sender/receiver relationships. It also bolstered my appreciation of a kind of poetic pragmatism. When I transitioned into the sculpture program during my sophomore year at Purchase College, I trained with a minimalist, but found that I was unimpressed with the final destination of artworks in the student gallery.

Instead, I began interfacing with architecture, placing work in the mortar between bricks of the studio building where I studied, in the baffles of the fluorescent lighting strips that lined the hallways. Allan Wexler taught a course as a Visiting Artist and changed my life. Allan's work was very much inspired by his traditional Jewish upbringing, where one's first architectural experience happens with the building of the sukkah, a temporary shelter

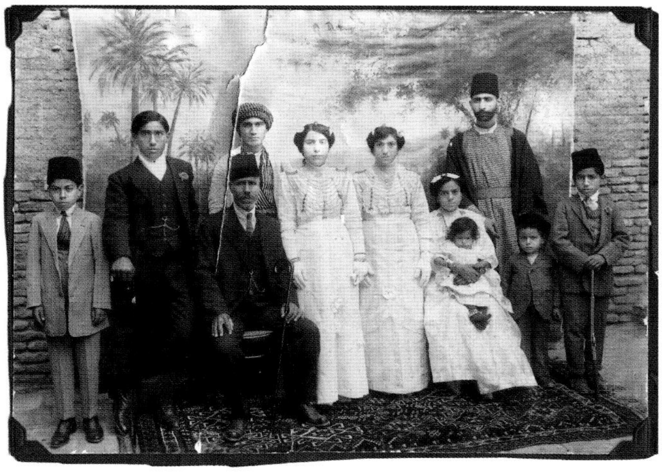

Nissim Isaac David, Rakowitz's grandfather, with his family, c. 1920

where families eat, sleep and pray during the holiday of Sukkot, a kind of harvest holiday that apparently inspired Thanksgiving. Allan's embracing of these traditional cultural experiences resonated deeply with me, and would ultimately inspire my later projects and my practice in general. Through my architectural interventions, I ultimately became interested in architecture. By Allan's recommendation, I ended up reaching out to James Wines, co-founder of Sculpture In The Environment (SITE), and working for SITE for about eighteen months, as an archivist. This experience exposed me to some incredible concepts, including the unbuilt works and unrealized projects of many architects. These were the most inspiring plans, often made impossible only because city governments would never allow the freedoms such projects proposed, or because the ideas were too transgressive politically.

During the two years I attended the graduate program in Public Art at MIT, I studied with artists Krzysztof Wodiczko and Dennis Adams. Like them, I also wanted to make apparitions appear, and to make the unbuilt or impossible projects one might relegate to the archive actually happen, even if it was to happen on a small scale. Such a strategy might accommodate new realities and might achieve a model of the culture many of us demand or yearn for. And so this is the tactic I came to employ, all the while allowing for my own familial and cultural history to come through in a manner that was not simply autobiographical.

SMART: Can you summarize the history of *Enemy Kitchen*?

MR: Since college, I have learned how to cook different Iraqi dishes from my mother. I always enjoyed learning from her and she would always say, "You know, there are no Iraqi restaurants in New York." This was true at the time, but in March 2007, an Iraqi restaurant named La Kabbr opened up in Hell's Kitchen. Perhaps it is a result of the geographic distance of Iraq to the US, or the tiny amount of Iraqi refugees the American government has actually allowed into this country, but there is a lack of cultural visibility of anything Iraqi in this country besides oil and war. This kind of visibility can serve as a vehicle for alternative discourse. For example, shortly after September 11, 2001, I was in the East Village in New York City. On St. Mark's Place, there was a long line of people, stretching down the block. It turned out they were all waiting to get in to Khyber Pass, an Afghani restaurant, to support the owners and staff and to eat there as a gesture of peace. There were incidents here and there of taxi drivers, mosques and Middle Eastern businesses being targeted and even boycotted. I thought this gesture was beautiful and it was based around the collective consumption of a specific kind of food. Three years later, this gesture inspired *Enemy Kitchen*, an ongoing project where I work with my mother and compile Baghdadi recipes and teach them to different public audiences.

The project was first presented by More Art in 2006. I cooked with a group of middle school and high school students who live in Chelsea and participate in after-school and summer programs at the Hudson Guild Community Center. Some had relatives in the US Army stationed in Iraq. Preparing and then consuming the food, opened up another context in which the word "Iraq" could be discussed—in this case, through food, and culinary history—as representative of culture and not as a stream of green-tinted images shown on CNN of a war-torn place.

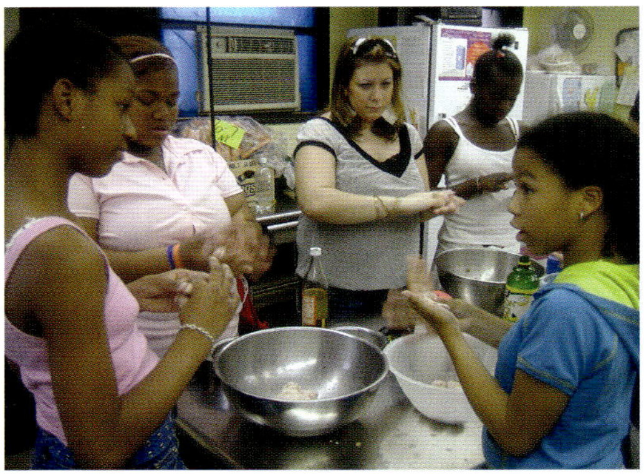

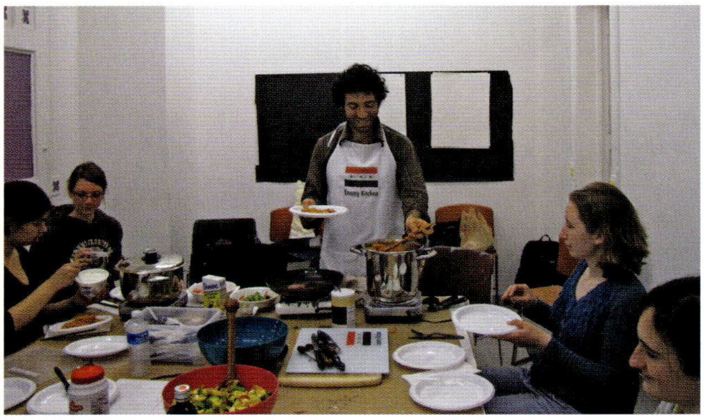

TOP: Rakowitz conducts an *Enemy Kitchen* workshop, 2004

BOTTOM: Rakowitz and students in Stephanie Smith and Laura Letinsky's course "Food for Thought," University of Chicago, spring 2011

Since its initial iteration in 2006, *Enemy Kitchen* has been performed at several art institutions, and while the gathering was always pleasant and meaningful, it lacked the friction that was made possible by the fearlessness of the teenagers in that first group. When the entire room more or less feels the same thing, things become too comfortable and the project became more about reassurance and reinforcement, which I suppose is not useless, but it wasn't what I was interested in pushing.

I performed an *Enemy Kitchen* barbecue at the National Vietnam Veterans Museum in Chicago on Memorial Day, 2009. Together with members of Iraq Veterans Against the War and Vietnam Veterans Against the War, we grilled Iraqi *kofta* instead of traditional frankfurters and hamburgers. Vets from two different generations discussed the experiences and traumas of combat, with one conversation tackling the topic of who deserved to be hanged first, Kissinger or Rumsfeld. I thought in this case the project set against the backdrop of this somber day was quite moving, and did not need any of the more pedagogical layers that usually feature in the discussion that occurs while the meal is being made.

SMART: Tell us about the *Enemy Kitchen* food truck you're creating for *Feast*—its impetus, intention, and production—and how it fits into your broader practice.

MR: The food truck is an extension of the project that I'd always intended, which was the evolution of *Enemy Kitchen* into a permanent restaurant and community hub for Chicago's Iraqi expat community, one of the oldest and largest in the United States. It turned out that while there were not any Iraqi restaurants in New York City, save for La Kabbr, there were a number of them in Chicago. Although most prefer to advertise themselves as Mediterranean or simply Middle Eastern, their menus reveal dishes that are unmistakably Iraqi: *masgouf*, potato chops, *kubba* soup, etc.

In making the project mobile, it allows all different communities in Chicago and the suburbs to have access to Iraqi cuisine and to experience the work. Mobility is an important feature in many of my public projects, where new topographies of the city emerge. For example, when I introduced *paraSITE* in Boston and Cambridge, the homeless inhabitants of the shelters began remapping their city according to which buildings had heating vents that could serve as adequate hosts for these inflatable structures.

Since Milo's is on Chicago's North Side, *Enemy Kitchen* gives them an opportunity to increase the exposure of their restaurant, but also allows the project to address different demographics. Chicago's South Side has seen an enormous number of its young men and women go off to fight in Iraq, and from what I know most soldiers based in Iraq were usually eating from the commissaries on the bases, which featured KFC, Burger King, etc. So, it was possible to be stationed in Iraq for years and to never eat an Iraqi meal. Perhaps the truck will be able to provide these veterans with their first taste of Iraqi food.

And in thinking about this, it inspired me to add a layer to the recipe of the project. I thought that it would be interesting to have the staff assisting in the preparation of the food and its serving to be hired from Chicago's large community of US veterans who fought in the Iraq War. In this way, it inverts the power dynamic of the invasion and occupation, and puts the American soldier in the position of taking orders and instructions from the Iraqi chef, but it also creates a situation for the customer where the people who are in front of them and serving their food can in some way represent the two sides of the conflict, at least in cultural terms. And, it is in these casual business settings where conversations may happen. One thing that attracted me to being the shopkeeper in *Return* was that the proprietor of a business often functions as a raconteur or storyteller within a community. Thus, I could tell the story of the circuitous route of the dates I imported from Baghdad to Brooklyn in a matter-of-fact way, one that was not theatrical or contrived. A customer buying food from the truck might ask a question about Iraq that would elicit different answers from each member of the staff, and perhaps spark discussions, debates, arguments, etc. For me, this is a way of enabling an experience many Americans have never had by creating an opportunity for them to interact

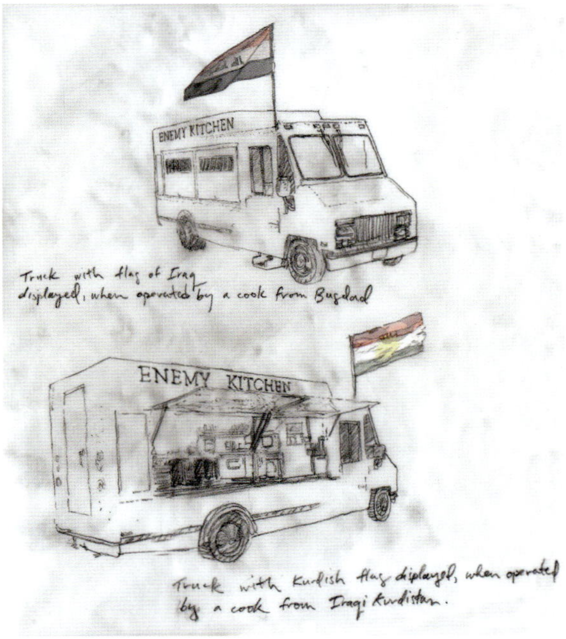

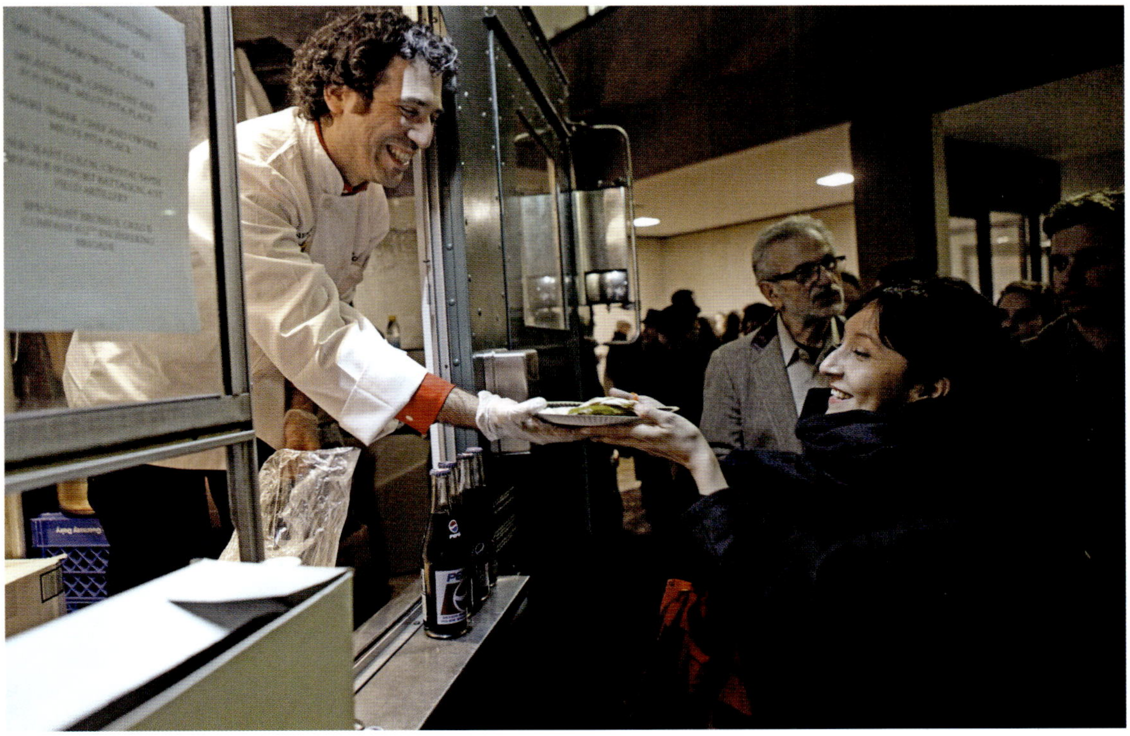

TOP: Sketch for *Enemy Kitchen (Food Truck)*, 2012

BOTTOM: *Enemy Kitchen (Food Truck)* at the Smart Museum of Art, February 15, 2012

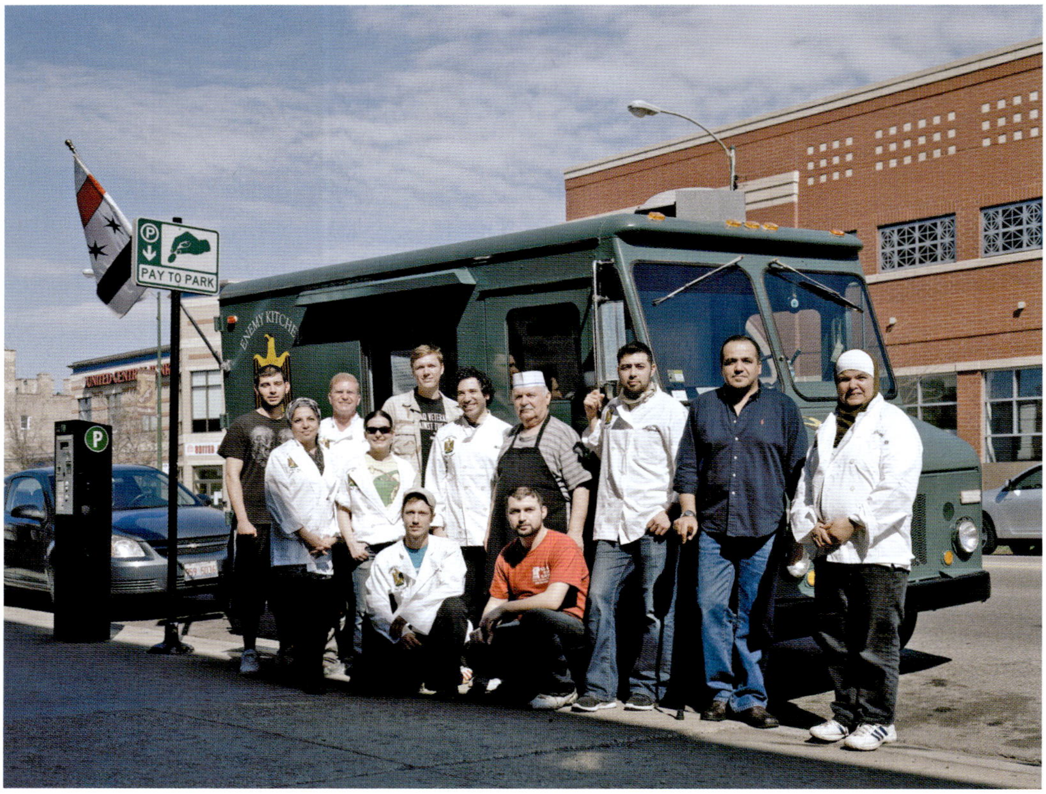

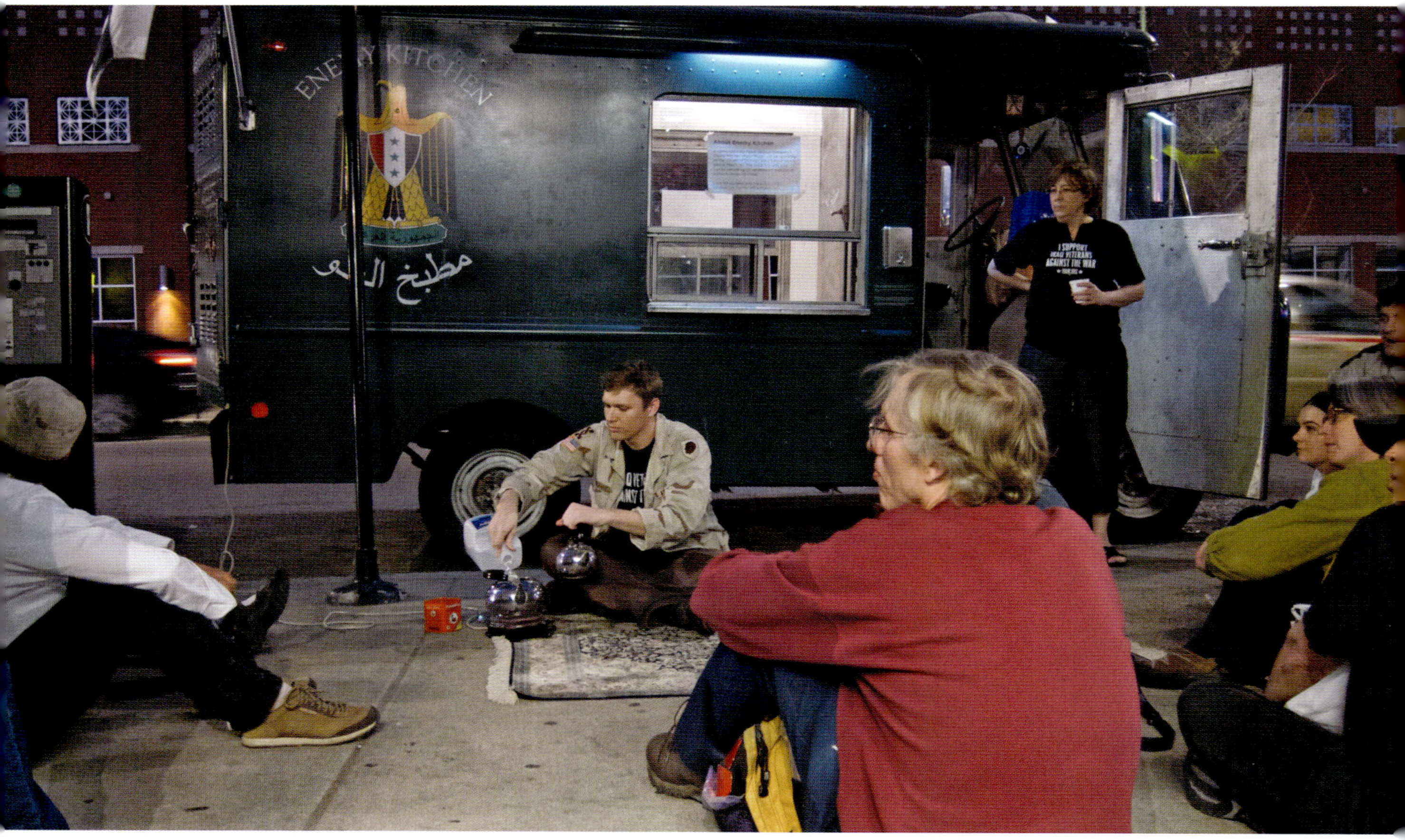

TOP: *Enemy Kitchen (Food Truck)* project team, Chicago, 2012

BOTTOM: Iraq Veterans Against the War member Aaron Hughes performs *TEA* outside Milo's Pita Place to mark the anniversary of the US invasion of Iraq, March 19, 2012

with an Iraqi and a US soldier, thereby disabling the distance that made it so easy for the war to be conducted. And hopefully, this experience and these stories will follow the customer home, not only through memory, but through the senses that can conjure memory.

In Iraq, when a guest leaves a house where they've just had a meal, the host will pour several small drops of rose water onto the top of the guest's head so the fragrant aroma follows them home and lingers, reminding them of the pleasant meal and evening. When diners finish their meals at the truck, they are invited to spray their hands with rosewater from an elegant dispenser and to run their hands through their hair.

When we were planning the food truck, I really liked the suggestion Stephanie made about setting up a Twitter account to tell people the truck's location, where it is going, and to even have them track it. She made the connection between the truck and the mobile units that were rumored to be making chemical weapons, driving around in the Iraq desert, as was falsely claimed during Colin Powell's speech to the United Nations in February 2003. That's another layer that I like very much.

SMART: Tell us about the plates you will use to serve the food from the truck.

MR: The truck will serve the food on paper plates that feature the same design as the porcelain hospitality plates looted from Saddam Hussein's palaces following the "Shock and Awe" campaign of the US Invasion. Iraqis entered these symbols of the government's power, and began taking many of the household items, including flatware and silverware. Many Iraqis have since used these plates in their own homes as their daily dishware, which I think is a very interesting dispersal of power, a kind of roleplay.

I had already been working with Saddam's plates when I was invited by Creative Time last year to collaborate with a restaurant called Park Avenue. I told the chef, Kevin Lasko, "Look, I just want to have Iraqi date syrup clearly listed somewhere on the menu—not as Product of Lebanon, the Netherlands or any other third party, as is normally the case due to Homeland Security restrictions. I want to fearlessly say where this ingredient comes from." The practice today in a lot of restaurants is to make the customer feel comfortable by listing the provenance of their food: the farm where the vegetables were harvested, where the cattle was raised, etc. But in this case, telling the diner the date syrup comes from Iraq could also create discomfort simultaneously. Kevin agreed, and proposed a chop of venison served atop the date syrup. We added some tahini, like in the traditional Iraqi desert debes wa'rashi. The American deer hunt meets the Iraqi date harvest. Then I said, "Well, here's my real intervention in all of this. I want the dish to be

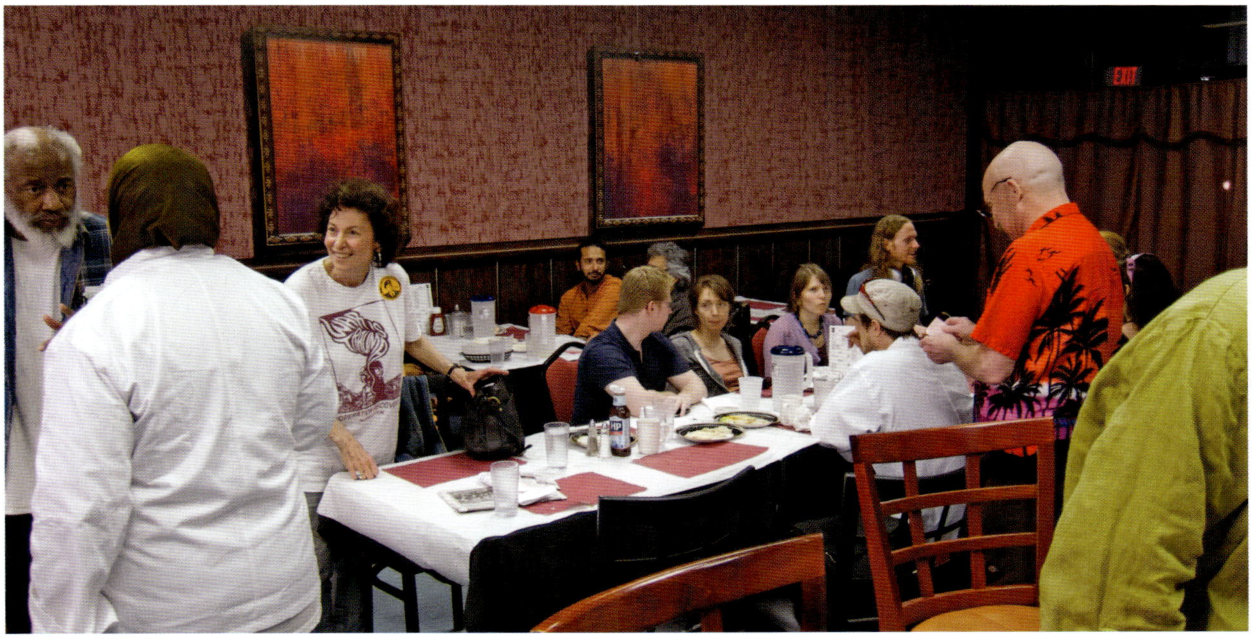

Friends and collaborators gather at Milo's Pita Place to mark the anniversary of the US invasion of Iraq, March 18, 2012

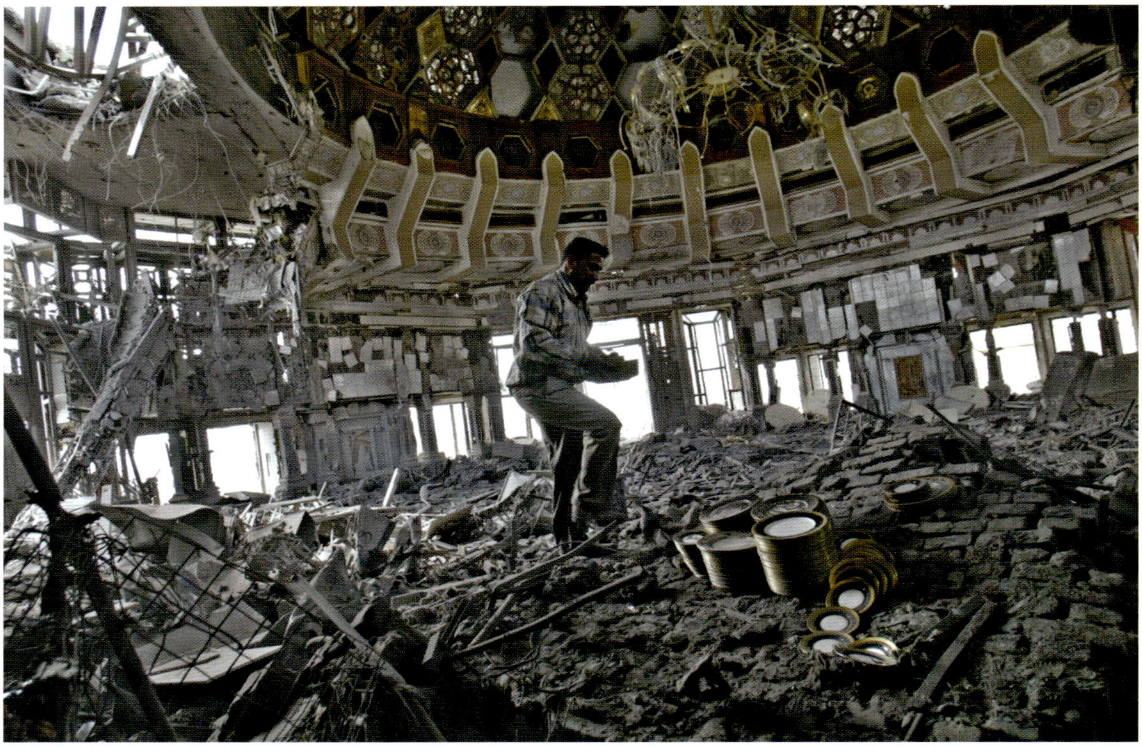

ABOVE: One of Saddam Hussein's residences in the aftermath of the US invasion

OPPOSITE: *Spoils*, detail of dish served on Hussein's china at Park Avenue Autumn (produced by Creative Time), 2011

served on plates that were looted from Saddam Hussein's palaces in 2003."

I figured one of the ways to really heighten the experience was to have something that would triangulate the diner's tongue; the sweetness of the date syrup; and the bitterness of this surface that it's served upon. The resulting tension was something I welcomed at a dinner table in this kind of posh restaurant. The dish then becomes as much about refusal as about consumption. The possibility that one would see this delicious dish but wouldn't be able to eat it because of the provenance of the plate that it's served on—I found this really, really strange and very beautiful at the same time, and very real. It puts the diner into a position where they have to make a decision and perform their ethics.

The coda to that story about the plates was that two days before that project was supposed to end, on Thanksgiving 2011, I was forwarded a cease and desist letter that had been received by the restaurant, telling them to stop using the plates. This had come from a mysterious source, we didn't know who had issued the cease and desist. We knew that it came from a law firm, but it wasn't clear who had issued it. We saw that the State Department was copied on all the correspondence, but it could have just been an angry citizen who decided that they didn't like what we were doing. I became interested now in who was it that issued the cease and desist, and it turned out that the State Department was in touch with Creative Time the week after Thanksgiving and basically it said that the Iraqi government had asked for the project to conclude and for the plates to then be taken into possession by the State Department. I thought this was the perfect ending to the project.

I envisioned a kind of *Raiders of the Lost Ark* scenario where the plates were going to be taken to some warehouse and sit in a crate. Then, in the beginning of December, I was visiting my family in New York and I was copied on an e-mail in which the State Department stated they wanted to get the plates as soon as possible, they wanted to take them into custody. At this point the language of the whole thing had gone from "cease and desist" to "demanding the surrender of the Iraqi plates belonging to Saddam Hussein." It was kind of hysterical that the Americans wanted even the inanimate objects to surrender.

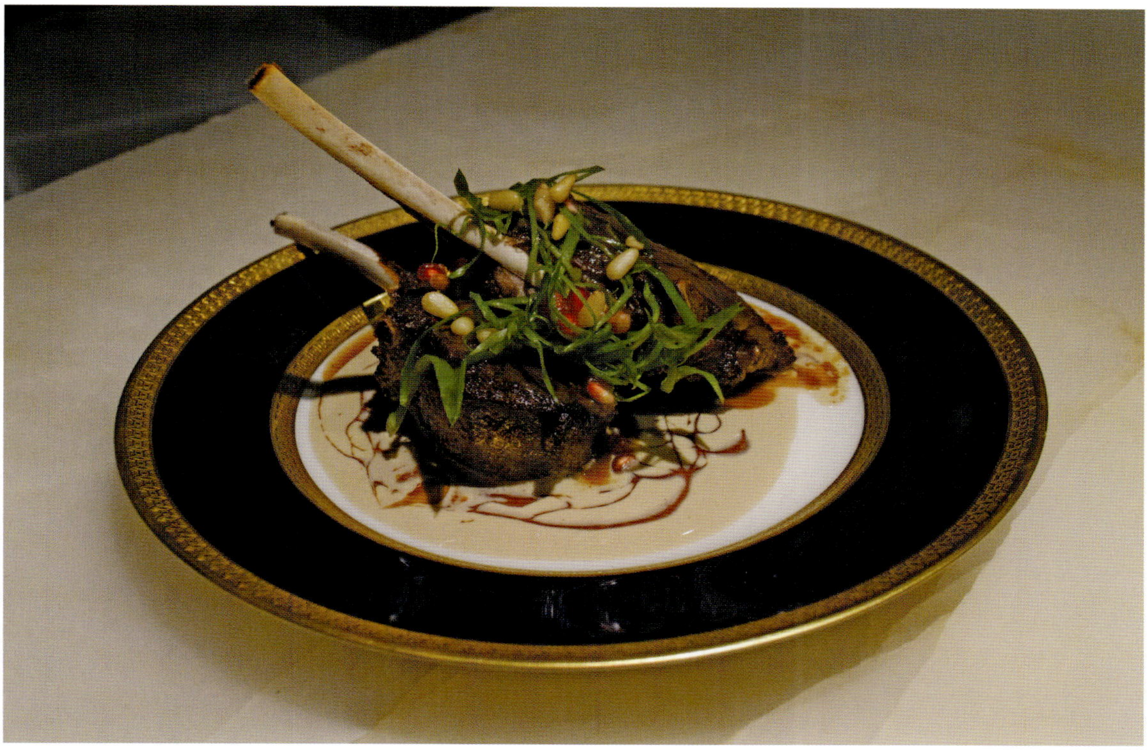

The following day I went to Creative Time's offices and two US Marshals came to take the plates. At that point I'm delivering a mini lecture as they're asking me about the different plates: "This belonged to King Faisal and it was found in Saddam's palaces, oh and this one was the hospitality plate, or these were made for him specially by Bernardaud Porcelain in Limoges, France." They're telling me this is one of the weirdest things they've had to do as US Marshals, but they're also typical New York City detectives. When I asked them where the plates were going afterwards, they said they were going right up to 79th Street, to the Iraqi Mission to the UN, which was basically the Iraqi Embassy. I said, "Really? I thought this was going to stay in the State Department's custody for a while." They said, "No, we can tell you that this order came directly from Washington." Prime Minister Nouri al-Maliki was in town the previous day to meet with Obama and apparently this was on their agenda and the Iraqi Prime Minister wanted the plates on his private plane heading back to Iraq, and so I asked if we could go with them, and they said, "You can't ride with us," and so we ended up tailing them in a taxi with a video camera on hand, and I went to the Iraqi Embassy. I called my mother and I said, "You know, I'm actually on Iraqi soil." When you're in a country's embassy, you're technically on the soil of that country. So I was the first member of our family to go back to Iraq at that point since 1946.[2]

SMART: How would you describe the role of the meal/hospitality in your practice?

MR: For me, the meal can be considered a production of consumable objects that allows for a conversation. The conversation might be produced in the preparation of the meal among collaborators in the kitchen, and it might be produced around the table. It is therefore not surprising to me that artists invested in situational or, (shudder) relational practices keep returning to the meal or gastronomy as a way to produce the kind of conversations or relationships that socially engaged work often seeks to produce.

However, in my own practice, the meal came very much out of a sense of urgency to create a cultural visibility of a place that had been reduced in the media as being a battlefield and nothing more. I had some personal

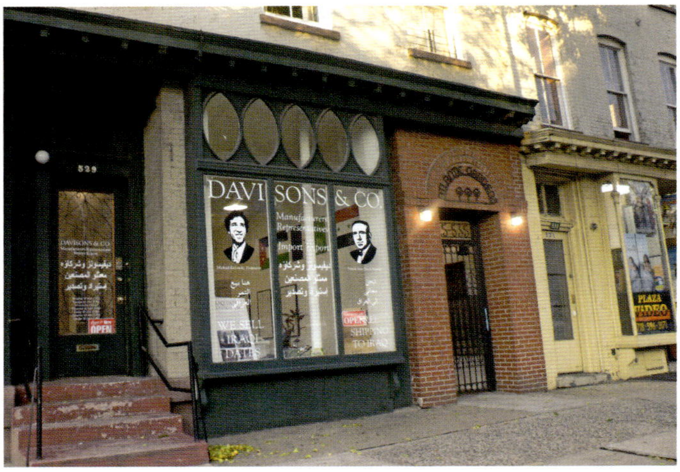

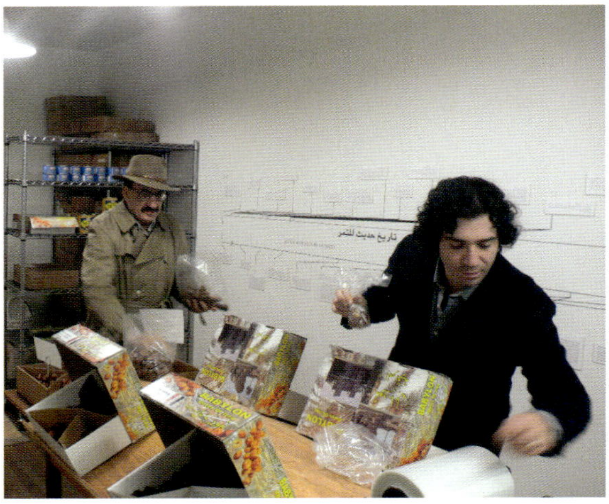

Exterior (left) and interior (right) views of Rakowitz's *Return* project (produced by Creative Time), Brooklyn, 2006

experience, growing up around my mother's and grandmother's food and thought this might be a way of setting up an experience for a participant to have some tangible connection with Iraq that was cultural, personal, and would invade their own bodies.

In terms of hospitality, I should probably state for clarification that I am a teacher. I am in the business of disseminating information even if it leads to confusion, of responding to work even if it creates friction. But in this role of teaching, there is always a desire I feel to communicate and to be understood. I find that it helps to create an atmosphere of trust and even mutuality.

However, I think this probably goes back even a bit further. Growing up in a Middle Eastern family, hospitality is taken seriously. The provision of food or shelter to guests and strangers was elementary. I guess all my work is very much in keeping with those traditions. And, I come back to something Stephanie once wrote in her essay about my gallery-based projects, specifically about being "the good guide," explaining the traces of an object's history, its provenance, and its place in a larger narrative, as seen through some of my drawings. I like the way that gets put, but I'm also willing to throw that into a little bit of crisis and say: I'll be the good guide about really horrible information and create potentially disturbing yet pleasant interactions. I'll be the person who can accommodate the impossible situation. So, if Iraqi dates can't come into the States because it's way too expensive, I'll take that art grant and put it all towards this ridiculous import, and then I'll be able to explain why it's art: because it's impossible right now in this world. But I'm very willing to explain that and to bring people along for that ride. So in that sense I think that when you're a public artist, in my case and with the mentors that I've had along the way, the exciting thing has always been about communication. That's where I see hospitality playing a major role in my work, and not just in the operation of a food truck.

SMART: Describe a favorite story about your work.

MR: My most gratifying moment in the first version of *Enemy Kitchen* was when, after eight

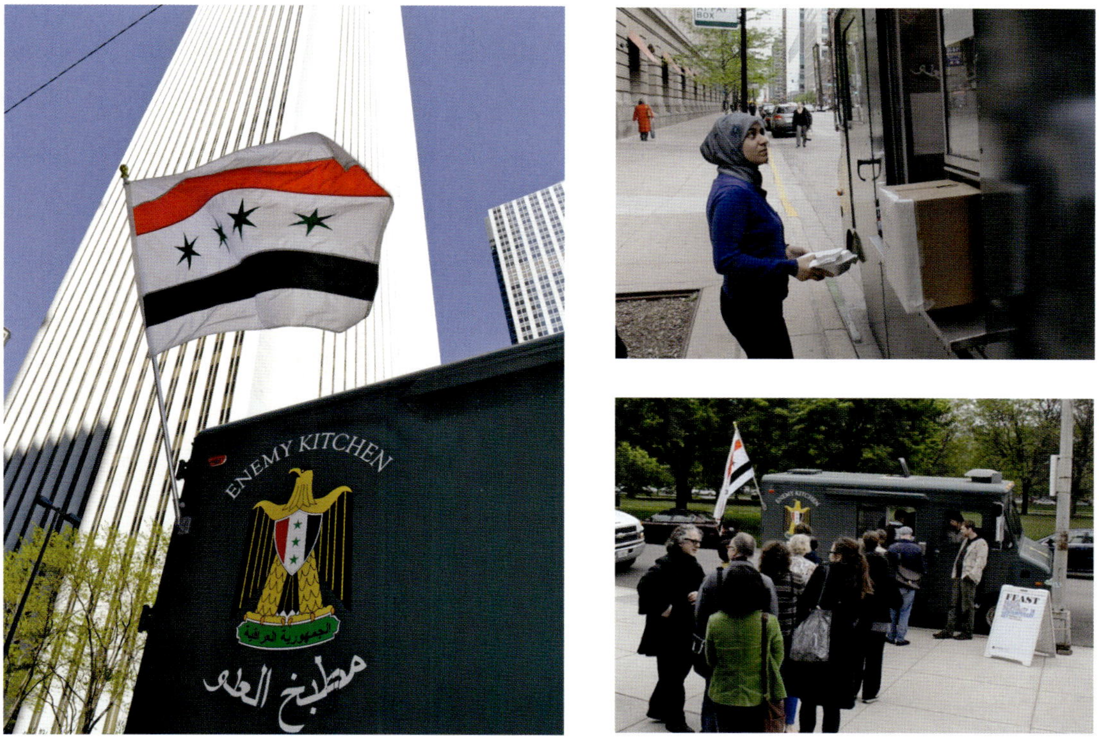

Enemy Kitchen (Food Truck) at sites around Chicago, 2012

weekly sessions learning how to cook Iraqi food, the students at the Hudson Guild Community Center proposed to teach me something about their families' recipes since they now knew so much about mine. Most of them were of African American and Latino heritage. One of the students, Hyasheem, asked, "Do Iraqis make Southern fried chicken?" I answered that no, to my knowledge there was nothing like it in Iraqi cuisine. "Well, then let's invent it," he said. It was awesome! He taught me how to do a shake-n-bake batter, and we used all the spices and herbs they'd learned about: cumin, sumac, a little turmeric, etc. And so Iraqi fried chicken was born.

SMART: What do you hope people take away from your work?

MR: An order of *masgouf, debes wa'rashi* for dessert, and a spritz of rose water to remember the meal.

---

[1] Since the time of this interview, Rakowitz has found a new occasion to use stone in his work: *What Dust Will Rise?* (2012), presented at dOCUMENTA (13) in Kassel. Displayed alongside remains of books damaged by fire during the bombings of the Fridericianum in 1941, for this presentation Rakowitz, in collaboration with stone carvers from Afganistan and Italy, and using stones from Bamiyan, re-created a number of the lost volumes of the Fridericianum.

[2] Rakowitz added: "The door keeps opening and closing and people are bringing in documents to fax and stamp and everything, and the handover was made official. This was basically a repatriation ceremony between the United States Marshals and the ambassadorial staff. Then they invited us in and the plates were out on the ambassador's table, and they thanked us for our cooperation, and I asked them what the next step was, and they said they're going to go on display for the Iraqi people. It became clear that what they were going to reopen with Saddam's palaces as museums for the Iraqi public, to show them how their former leader lived."

Ayman Ramadan

AYMAN RAMADAN DRAWS INSPIRATION from everyday urban experience. Many of his projects have stemmed from close observation of working-class street life in bustling, cosmopolitan Cairo—his home since moving from a nearby village as a young man. In his early work, Ramadan translated such observations into quasi-figurative sculpture and strongly narrative installations like *Baladi Bus* (2004), which combines video footage of Cairo with a metal sculpture depicting citizens in transit through daily urban routines. He hoped that these projects would be legible not only to an art audience but also to the workers who have been both his subjects and collaborators. Since 2008, Ramadan has studied abroad; he left Cairo for a fellowship at the Rijksakademie in Amsterdam shortly before the Arab Spring uprisings began, and while urban experience and Cairo itself remain a strong and recurring source of inspiration, Ramadan's more recent work addresses a broader range of subject matter and encompass a wider range of media—photography and found-object sculpture as well as video installation.

Several of Ramadan's projects have centered on the consumption of food and drink, as in a series of "tea and ink" workshops or *Koshary min Zamman* (2008). In the latter, *koshary* becomes a vehicle through which to consider the ongoing failures of international diplomacy. A traditional Egyptian dish, *koshary* combines lentils, chickpeas, pasta, rice, and tomatoes into a quick, filling meal that is available from small shops and street vendors throughout Egypt—a comfort food as well as a cheap staple. Ramadan's piece evokes Cairo's *koshary* shops through a display of specially designed take-away containers for Ramadan's own fictional brand of *koshary*, complete with digitally altered photographs depicting world leaders apparently eating his dish. (Ramadan sometimes makes and serves the dish to gallery visitors as well.) In this project, cheap, heavy food becomes a metaphor for the sedating influence of current political rhetoric about peace in the Middle East, which only provides temporary satiation.

Feast includes *Iftar* (2004), the first project in which Ramadan used the meal as a vehicle to explore charged topics of class, politics, and religion. At the time, the artist was working at the Townhouse Gallery, an international contemporary art space in Cairo. He invited thirteen laborers from nearby streets to recreate an *iftar*—the evening meal that breaks the daily fasts observed by Muslims during the holy month of Ramadan. Many Egyptians share this meal at home with friends and family, but communal tables are also set up in the streets to ensure that, at least during this sacred season, even the destitute or displaced can break their religious fast, often with meals of *koshary*. Ramadan staged his *iftar* at a long table, referring to those communal tables, and arranged the workers along one side to recall the composition of Leonardo da Vinci's *The Last Supper* (1495–98). The connection to a masterwork of Western painting is further enhanced by the rich dark hues of videographer Deborah Stokes's filming. Ramadan's choice to make a group of poor urban laborers visible as the subjects of his artwork was inspired in part by his desire to call attention both to Islamic traditions of hospitality and to their inadequacy in the face of persistent class divisions in Egypt. *Iftar* exists in two forms—as a stand-alone video, as shown in *Feast*—and as a video accompanied by an installation of figurative metal sculpture placed along a rough wooden table. In either version, it offers a poetic and pointed account of hospitable care for others.

OPPOSITE: Still from *Iftar*, 2004

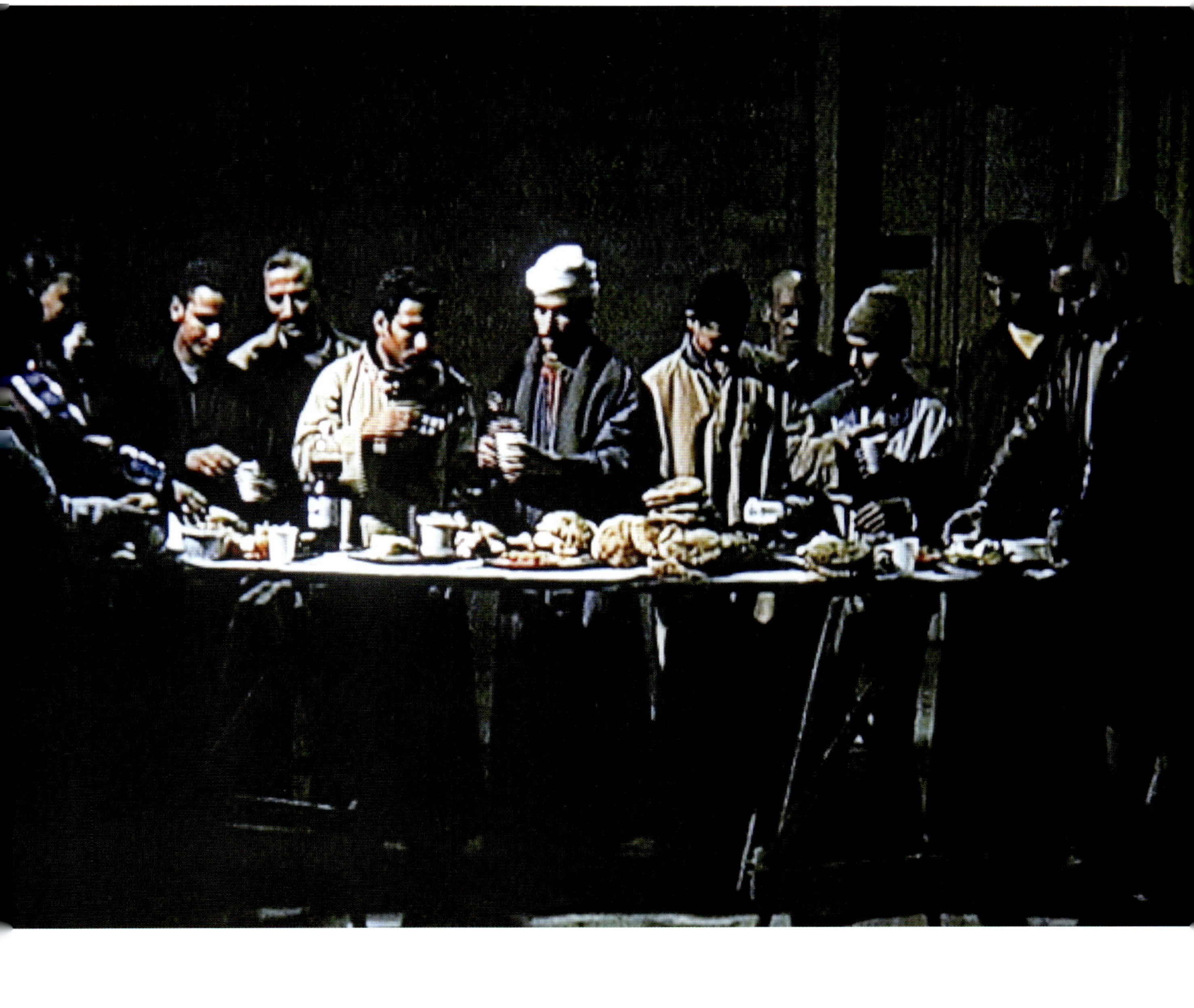

Interview

SMART: Can you describe your path as an artist and sources of inspiration for your work, either in or beyond the context of art?

RAMADAN: My work is inherently site-specific and always deeply socially engaged. Through minimalist metal sculpture, video, and photography (often combined in one installation), I attempt to create immersive environments that provoke the viewer to consider issues relating to labor, the anonymity of the individual in the urban landscape, and frustrations stemming from local political realities. I draw on a wide range of influences, from pop culture to global politics to Islamic traditions, in my explorations of contemporary Middle Eastern experience.

SMART: Tell us about *Iftar*—its impetus, intention, and production—and how it fits into your broader practice.

AR: All my life I have been tied to the street and the people who work in the street. Whether in the village or Cairo, life is hard for the average person. No one is interested in them, their lives, or their problems. In Egypt it is considered offensive or a bad thing to take pictures of the ordinary people and the lives they are forced to live, as the government feels it gives a bad impression of the country. I never understood this. If the government is ashamed of the way people are forced to live, then it should change it, not hide it.

During Ramadan, in almost every street in the country, people stop working and break their fast together at tables like the one in the video. Most of the tables are charity tables and like the one in *Iftar*. They provide not just a meal but also a sense of belonging. Anyone can join the table and is welcome and equal to the others. It is the true spirit of Islam. When I saw a copy of the Da Vinci's *Last Supper*, I thought it was a Muslim *iftar*. When the Christian significance was explained to me, I was sure the meaning was the same. Why was the rest of the world celebrating a simple supper shared by a group of simple men while in Egypt, that meal was taking place every day and was a source of shame? By trying to film this *iftar* in a way that drew from Da Vinci's painting I thought that people would recognize the dignity that is involved in those meals.

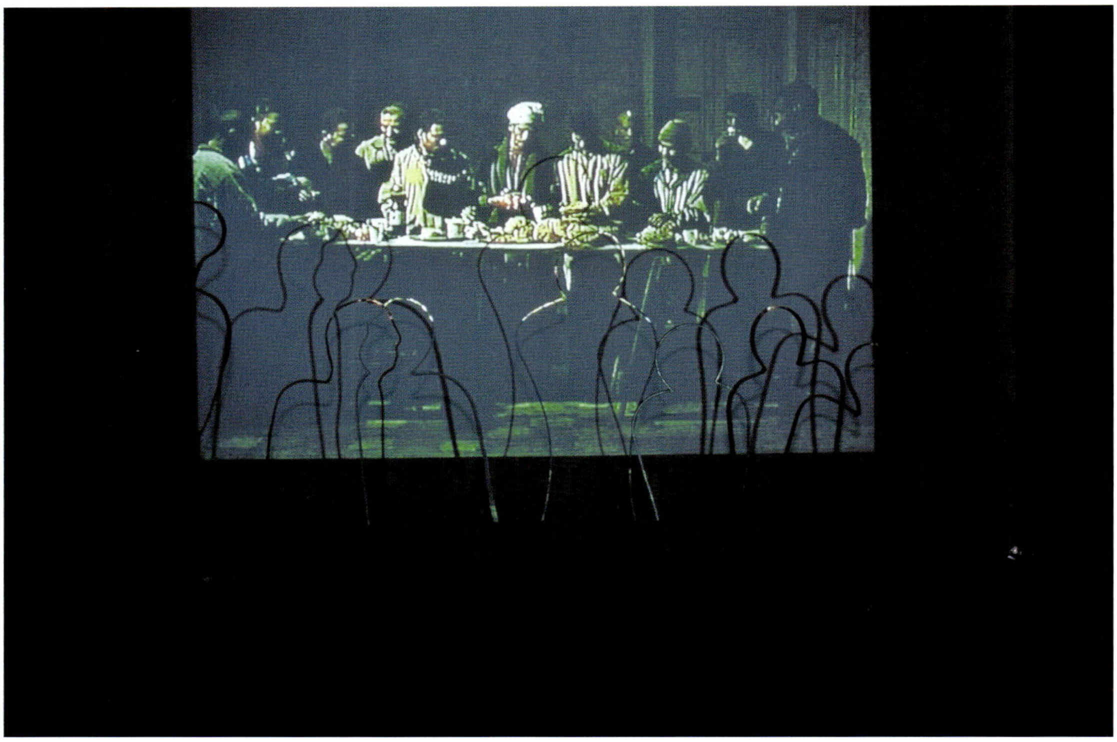

ABOVE AND OPPOSITE: *Iftar*, installation views with metal sculptures, Townhouse Gallery, Cairo, 2004

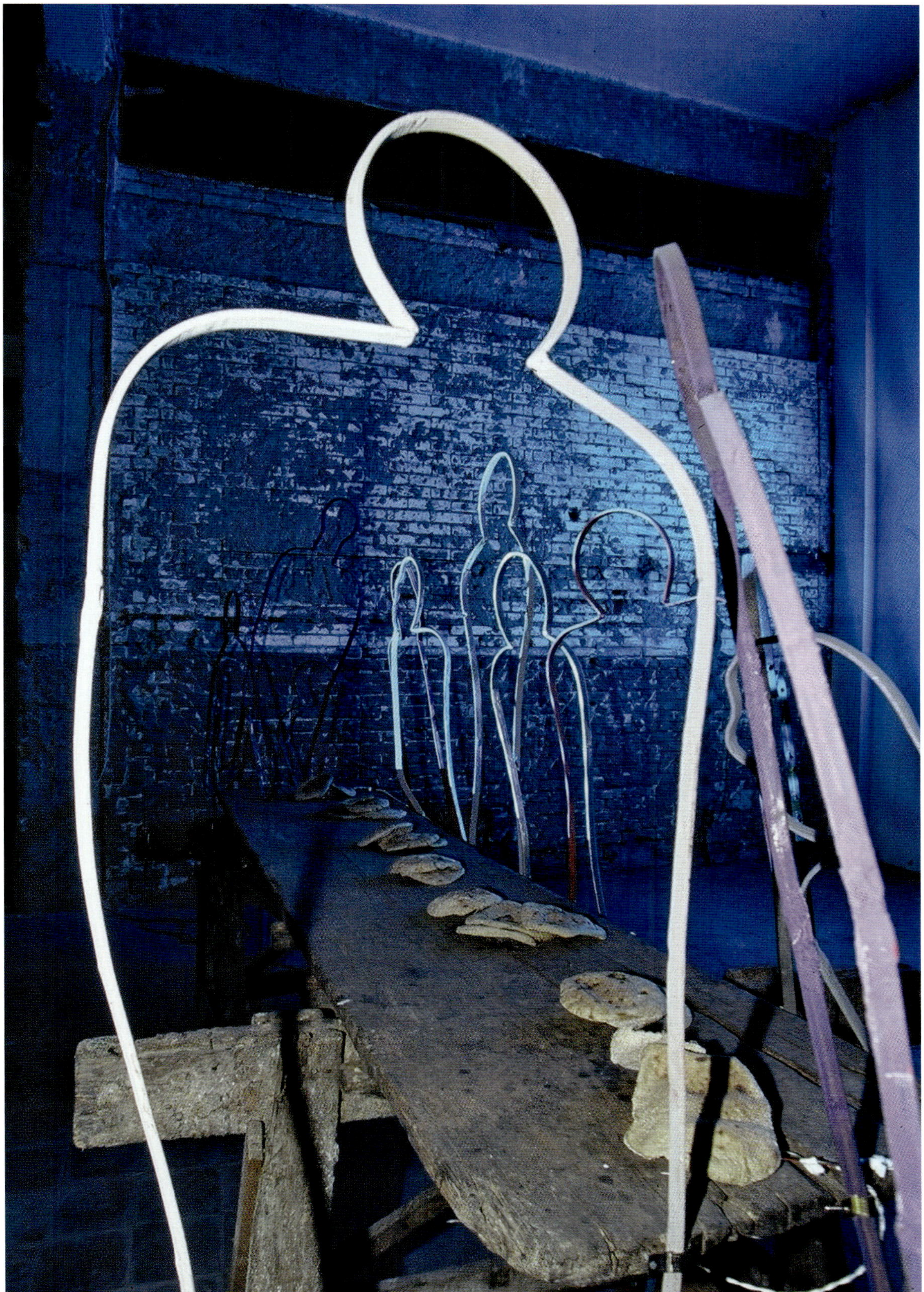

Iftar shows the role of the meal in the daily life of the people in the street and how they get together at the end of the day to break their fast together. It shows how everyone feels like a family and shares the meal together with other people who don't know them. It might be the first time they meet, but they still share the meal together like family.

SMART: That recognition of visual continuity between Da Vinci's *Last Supper* and Muslim *iftar* is very powerful. Have you looked to other examples from Western art history to inform your own work?

AR: No. *Iftar* was more about the relationship between Muslims and Christians in Egypt. Many Christians have photographs of *The Last Supper* in their home or books. Da Vinci's painting and the *iftar* of Ramadan look the same; all that's different is the people but they are doing the same thing. Hundreds and hundreds of years go by but we are all eating together in the same table.

SMART: Do other Egyptian customs of meals or hospitality evoke the same kind of dignity that you describe in the *iftar* meals?

AR: *Iftar* is not just about the charity of the food but is about everything that happens in this month of Ramadan. When Egyptians eat together at one table, they forgive each other for what happened before that month and can be friends again. Or they might be fighting in the daytime because it is hot and they're fasting with no water and no food, but when the time of *iftar* comes they forget all that happened in the day and start talking again. I've been in the street of downtown Cairo, talking to the people and watching what happens during the day, then coming to eat the *iftar* at the same table we used in the video. It makes me feel this work more.

SMART: Do questions about hospitality figure into your process or thinking?

AR: Yes. In the Middle East, hospitality is very important. You have to do your part for your guest. At the same time, your guest has to finish the food you give to him in order to show that he likes you. In Egypt we have a saying that if you love someone, you eat his food and this will make him happy. Food connects people. But this is not only true here. Anywhere in the world, when you go to a new

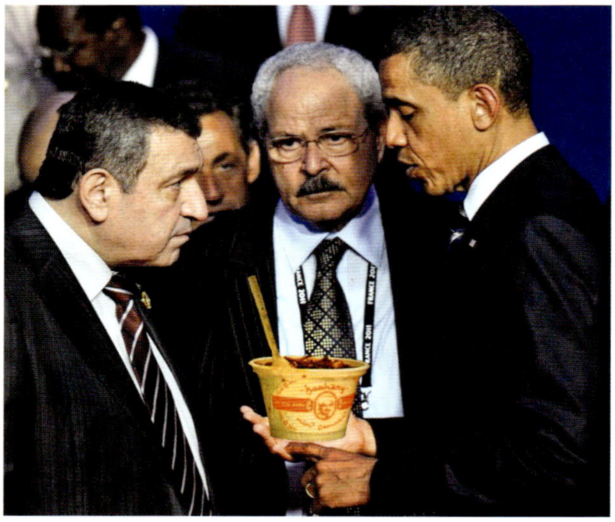

ABOVE, RIGHT AND OPPOSITE: Digital photographs from *Koshary* series, 2011

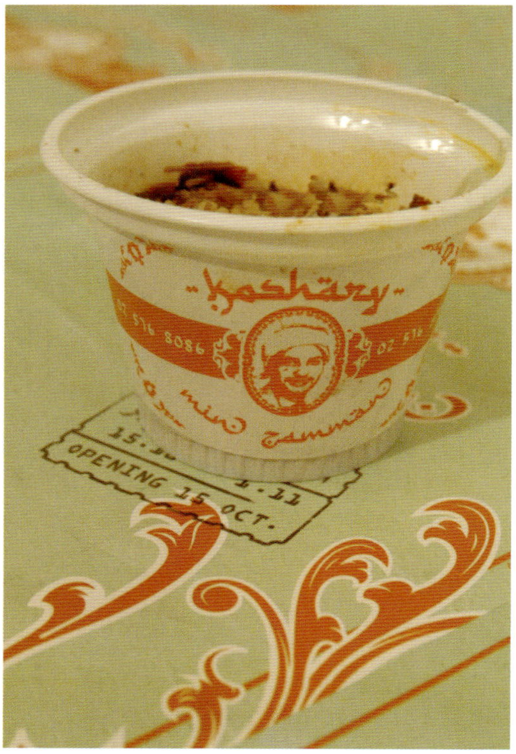

place or party and you don't know anyone, you might see yourself not talking and no one is talking to you, but then the food comes and everyone shares the same thing and starts to talk to each other. They get to know each other around the table.

SMART: Describe a favorite story about your work.

AR: When *Iftar* was shown in Cairo, the press condemned it as defamation of the country and wanted the gallery closed. For me it was interesting that they were never aware of the religious connection but concentrated on the fact that my work was depicting poor people eating with their hands.

SMART: What was the outcome of the press condemnation? Did the gallery keep your work on view? Did the press stories lead to any larger discussion about *iftar*, class, religion, or hospitality in Cairo at that time?

AR: Yes, the gallery had to close the show and take the work down because the police asked the director of the gallery to sign a paper saying he can't show this work in Egypt any more. The idea of seeing people come together eating and talk about life did not make them happy because an *iftar* in the month of Ramadan is the only time people can come together and share their ideas and talk together in free way.

SMART: What does it mean to you to be included in a show called *Feast: Radical Hospitality in Contemporary Art*?

AR: It gives me an opportunity to show the hospitality of my culture in a different way.

SMART: What do you hope people take away from your work?

AR: That we are all the same. We all must forgive each other and get together at one table. Muslim, Christian, white, black: we are all the same.

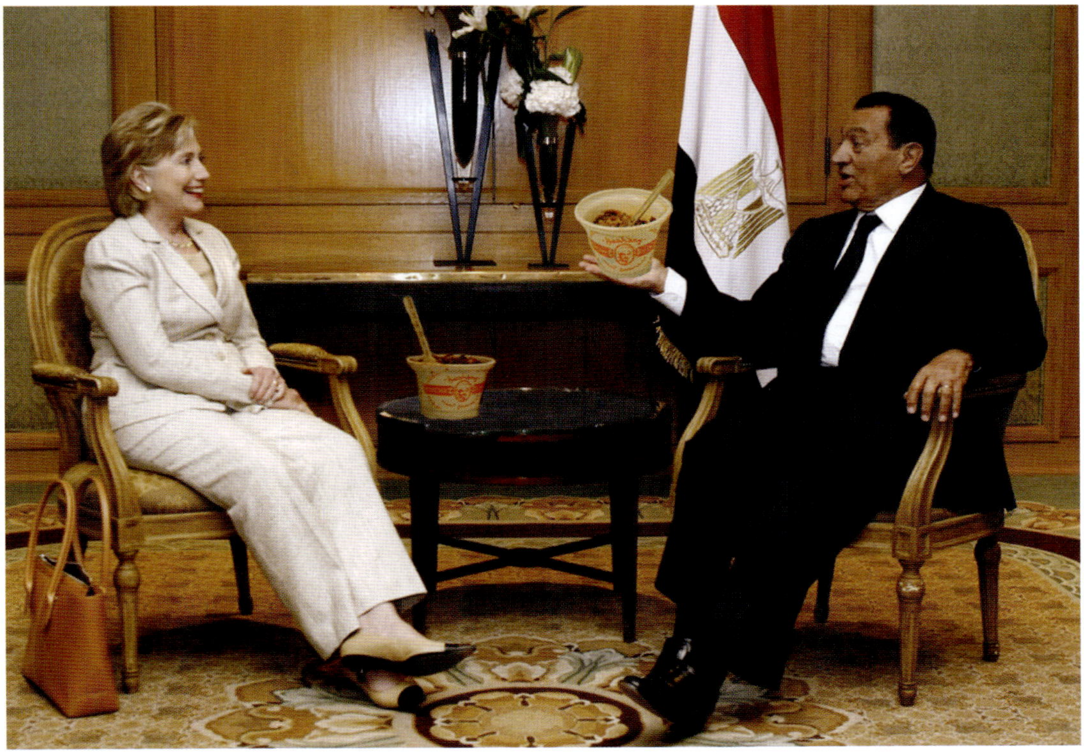

Red76

RED76 IS A COLLABORATIVE ENTITY and research practice that formed in Portland, Oregon, in 2000. Many of their projects are conceived as series that entail collaborative participation and build over time within a set framework—the format of a dinner party, the pages of a zine. These projects reflect an activist interest in art's capacity to contribute to social change: although clear-eyed in their understandings of art's limits, Red76 asks project participants to engage in reflection and critique, with the hope of reinvigorating the potential that together we might build more robust and creative forms of democracy, community, and public space. Their methods tend to be informal and seriously playful and their projects occur in spaces ranging from domestic dining rooms to bars to laundromats to museums. Many of Red76's projects are initiated by Sam Gould, who led the projects included in *Feast*; regular collaborators including Laura Baldwin, Gabriel Mindel-Saloman, Zefrey Throwell, Dan S. Wang, and Mike Wolf.

Feast included documentation of the group's *Revolutionary Table* project and launched a new work, *Occupy Yr. Home*. The former is a Bush-era project in which Red76 organized small, informal meals around the country to encourage conversation about democracy, citizenship, and the power of collective speech. Red76 sees the table as another kind of medium to foster and disseminate spirited debate. For this project, the table's function as medium and site for the creation of what the artists call "horizontal social space" was supported in real time by a highly localized radio broadcast via a short-distance radio transmitter: in advance of each dinner the host invited their neighbors to listen in. After the fact, the discussion was further spread via documentation in Red76's website and its newsprint zine, the *Journal of Radical Shimming* (JRS). Within the museum, photocopies of one issue of JRS formed a wallpaper backdrop behind a series of photographs: the images provided a sense of mood, people, and spaces, while the journal itself fleshed those images out through text.

Occupy Yr. Home builds on this notion of table as medium, while further dispersing this project of building publics by hosting dinners. Inspired in part by the Occupy Wall Street protests that emerged globally during 2011, Red76 decided to organize a series of gatherings that would continue the spirit of those public conversations indoors, within homes and around dining tables. They started the project in winter as most of the protest camps had been dispersed (by choice, by force, or by weather) and as Occupy slipped out of the news cycle. Red76 sought another means to foster thoughtful, radical speech and action. Their project asked: "In what ways might we consider our life at home as the most elemental and productive space to contemplate our political consciousness and the relationships that form out of that consciousness, from the table and out into the streets?" They created a free handout—an offset broadsheet—to inspire participation: in addition to the curated meals that they have held already in Baltimore, Brooklyn, Chicago, Kansas City, Kosovo, and the others that will continue as *Feast* travels, Red76 invites members of the public to host their own dinners and share the results via the *Occupy Yr. Home* website.

OPPOSITE: *Revolutionary Table*, installation view, Smart Museum of Art, 2012

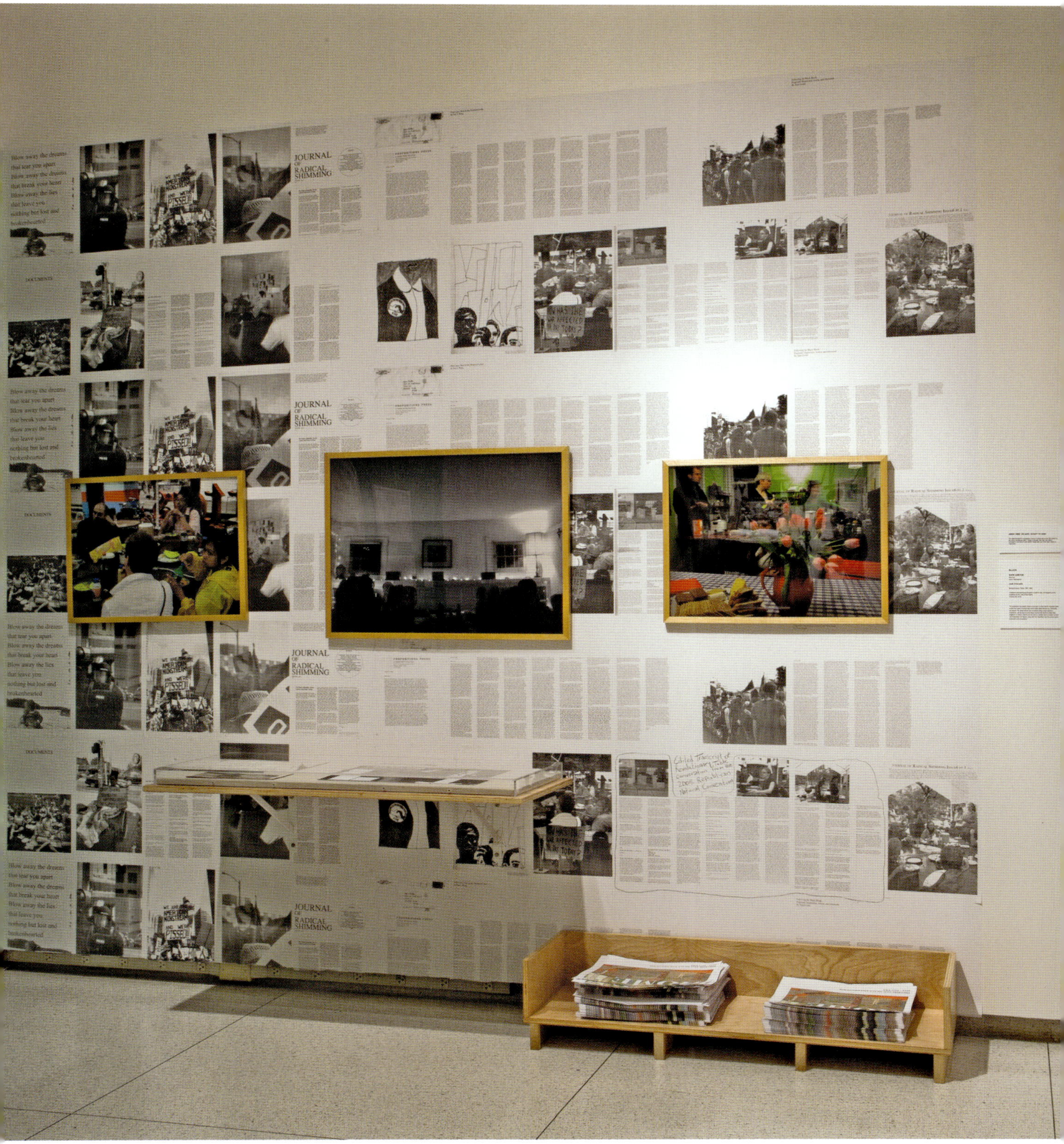
Blow away the dreams
that tear you apart
Blow away the dreams
that break your heart
Blow away the lies
that leave you
nothing but lost and
brokenhearted
DOCUMENTS
JOURNAL
OF
RADICAL
SHIMMING
WE ARE AMERICANS
AND WE'RE PISSED!

Interview

SMART: Please tell us a bit more about Red76. It's essentially a framework for projects that you conceive and then develop in collaboration with others, correct? What inspired that structure, and the name *Red76*?

SAM GOULD, ON BEHALF OF RED76: Well, for starters the name *Red76* came about from Jef and I sitting around after we decided we were going to "start something." We'd only really ever started bands before, so that was the framework we were used to. We threw around a bunch of names and Red76 was the one that stuck. It's seemed the most loaded and simultaneously ambiguous.

And yes, essentially the way Red76 works is that I'll have some idea that has been stuck inside my head for some time and I will begin to discuss it with others with whom I often collaborate. Other times these ideas develop in conversation with people I may not have worked with much before, if at all, but the idea strikes a way to develop a relationship. More often than not though, the way projects materialize is the former—a continued conversation with collaborators that get realized and fleshed out through the creation of public projects in many different forms. The structure for the work developed over time. Red76 began as a way to develop a parallel platform for displaying art and gathering artists together to make their own venue. In time it became more about making work than displaying it, though some of that has stuck to a large degree. I think from the get-go the notion of "association" has played a huge role in the work. The modes in which we work though come about very similarly to the content of the projects, really they are hand in hand. The modes, or context in which the work becomes visible, are as much the content as the actual content.

SMART: Please tell us about the history and impetus of *Revolutionary Table*.

RED76: In late January 2007, Red76 began a project called *Revolutionary Spirit*. It was a discursive and disjointed venture, whose aim was to amass a great many actions and discussions across the country with the desire to form a public around the question "What does revolution mean to America today?" The project lasted two years and served as the sole output of the group in that time period. All of the work during this time had that question at

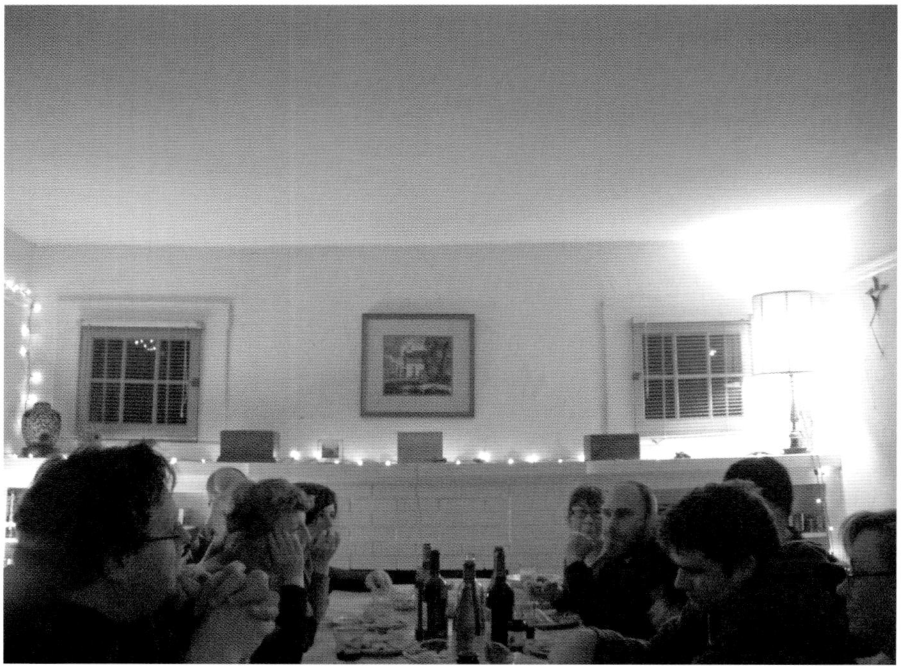

Revolutionary Table, 2008 Republican National Convention, St. Paul, Minnesota

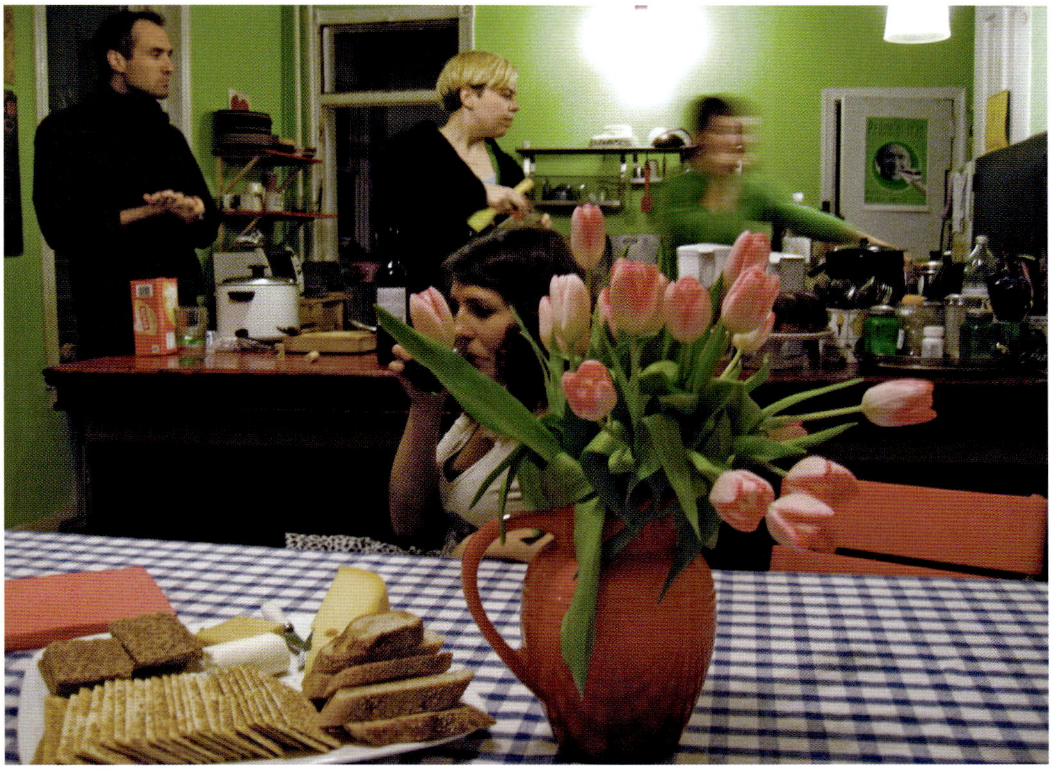

Revolutionary Table dinner, Philadelphia, February, 2007

its core in some form or another. The project was a direct response to the political climate of the final years of the Bush era. While in retrospect it could be argued that we're in worse shape now than ever before, those times seemed to radiate an urgency that the group felt inclined to inhabit.

Revolutionary Table was one of the projects for *Revolutionary Spirit*. Activating sites across the country, *Revolutionary Table* asked friends of Red76 to plan dinners at their home wherein friends and strangers alike would meet at their kitchen table and discuss an issue that the host felt had a local and political urgency to it. The set-up was simple. We would ask a person to host a meal. That person would invite a few friends and ask those friends to invite another person along. An intimate dinner would be arranged. Everyone would bring along a bottle of something. A meal would be set and a discussion would be held, informally, like almost any other meal you might share in your home. The only differences in this case were that the conversation was directed, and the talk around the table was recorded and broadcast via a radio transmitter around the neighborhood. Prior to each dinner, guests would be asked to write an invitation to their neighbors to listen in, making available the broadcast frequency and maybe a cell phone number in case anyone wanted to call in. Before dinner was served, guests—often with cocktails in hand—would traverse the neighborhood distributing these handwritten invitations to listen in.

A table is a form of media as coherent as a newspaper or a website—they just vary in their range of dissemination. For many of our projects, the table acts as a form of media that fosters intimate dialogue. So, in this sense, *Occupy Yr. Home* is not so different from *Revolutionary Table* apart from the context in which it is activated and the associations we're interested in activating. But context and association adjust everything. *Revolutionary Table* was shaped by the political climate of the

2000s; we wanted to consider the contemporary relevance of the sociopolitical lineage of the United States as a country founded on revolutionary thought and ideology.

SMART: Please say more about *Occupy Yr. Home,* your new project for *Feast.*

RED76: I see *Occupy Yr. Home* as continuing those themes, but breaking them down to their elemental forms of agency. It's an argument for an internalization of Occupation mentality: a call to start at the table and move outward.

In cities across the United States, for the run of *Feast,* as well as continuing onward as it tours over the next few years, we will be organizing small, intimate dinners across the country, asking people to bring friends to their table and consider how they might most effectively occupy their own home. We're asking them to think about larger questions of good living, civic participation, and social justice—in all their anarchic messiness—on a day-to-day level, starting in their home. We're not talking about buying organic, or driving less, or attaching solar panels on the roof, though choices like that are certainly part of it. The questions that were most powerful about the sited occupations across the country during fall 2011 revolved around how we're willing to live our lives—our whole lives, not just particular points along the way—in terms of specific demands and end goals. That's at the heart of the conversations we're interested in having. It's about each of us playing a role in the reformation of the consciousness of our country. In practical terms, these meals will happen over a series of years. While we will initiate, document, and respond to some of the meals, anyone can host their own *Occupy Yr. Home* meal. We'll do what we can to make space to promote those conversations online and in print.

SMART: How would you describe the role of the meal in your work?

RED76: The meal plays as vital a role as any other form of media. The meal acts as a space of recognition, in that everyone is at the table. You don't need to agree with one another, you don't need to see eye to eye, but you do all need to agree to be there together. In this way of thinking about eating together at the table

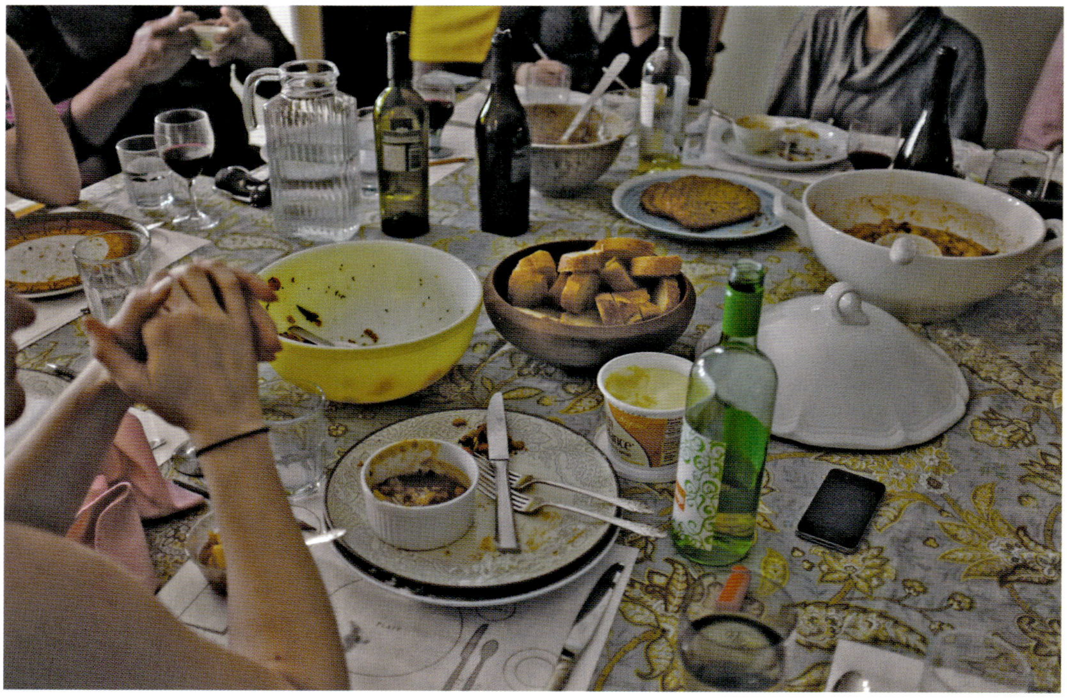

LEFT: *Occupy Yr. Home* dinner, Chicago, 2012

OPPOSITE: *Occupy Yr. Home* dinner, Kosovo, 2012

I'm especially interested in *Occupy Yr. Home* in parallel with the occupations that took place around the country this fall. They acted as spaces of convergence for any number of individuals and groups to address how this country needed to move into the future. These people didn't need to agree with one another, and many didn't. That was a critique for some but a major selling point for me: no demands needed to be met because with such a disparate array of grievances, the occupations turned into horizontal spaces that addressed core elements of where this country has gone wrong, rather than soap boxes for specific political agendas and a furtherance of electoral politics as we have seen it over the last thirty years since the rise of Reagan-era fiscal conservatism, hand in hand with religious and social fundamentalism.

SMART: Do questions about hospitality figure into your process or thinking?

RED76: Absolutely, though possibly not in the way that it might normally be considered. I think about hospitality in this way of working very similarly to the way I think about generosity, in that it needs to be flattened and made transparent. The core goal for me in engaging in this line of practice is to create spaces and actions that others might consider and possibly take on in their own way, which encourage horizontality, honest listening, and personal responsibility. So, in this sense, it is not about being "good," but about being mindful and owning up to your own actions and desires as well as genuinely considering and encouraging others to do the same. Hospitality is a tool like any other in this regard. It's a way to consider people within the space of action, a way to understand the parameters of the area in which we'll play out these considerations.

SMART: Describe a favorite story about your work.

RED76: It's hard to see, sometimes, how this work alters the world around us. I see it as a cumulative strategy, wherein makers of all sorts are engaging similar ideas to help alter a sociopolitical landscape that they view as unjust and unethical. That's the long and short of it for me, the most elemental way for me to view my practice. With that said, it's really nice sometimes to see the work you do

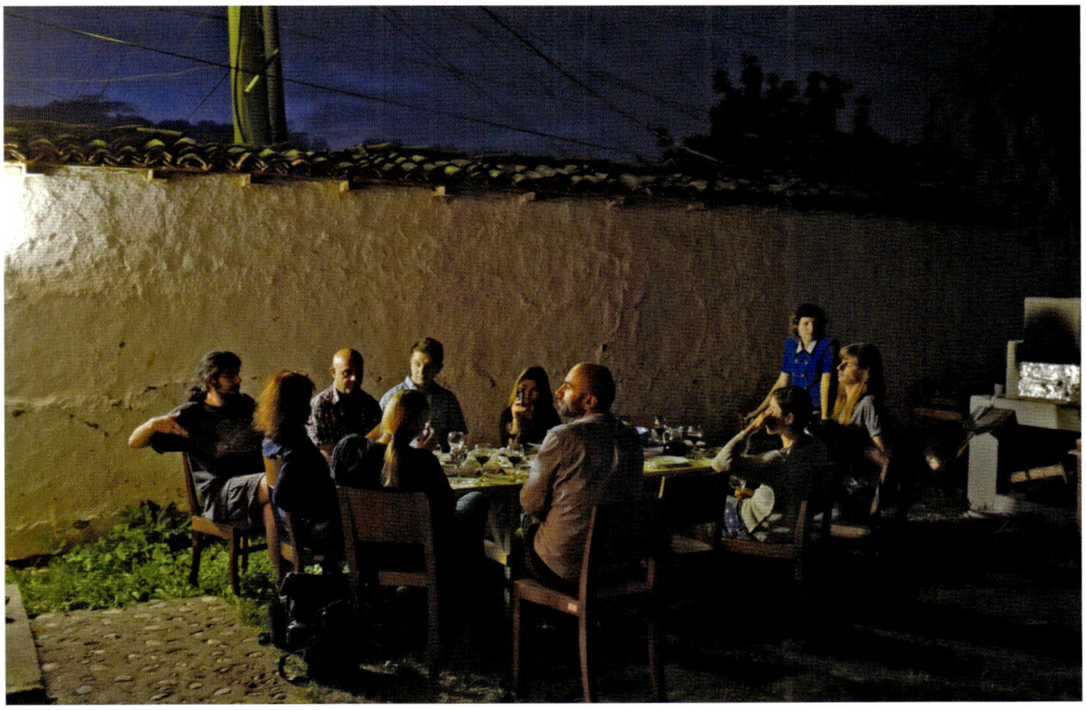

actually start to do just that, to engage first-hand in that cause and effect.

One instance of this for me was when Red76 and Iraq Veterans Against the War were collaborating on a project together called *Befriend a Recruiter*, an anti-recruitment campaigned aimed at tying up the time of military recruiters and making their jobs more difficult through friendly conversation and subterfuge. This was during *Revolutionary Spirit*, sometime around 2008. Around this time I was out having a beer with some friends after playing our weekly game of basketball and I received a call from a number in Tennessee. I had no idea who it was, but I seem to have a compulsion about answering calls from unknown numbers. The call was from an eighteen-year-old kid who was going to be graduating from high school in a matter of days. I had set up a toll-free number for the project for people to call to learn more about the initiative and had redirected the service earlier for some reason to call my number directly. So, at that moment, any call to *Befriend a Recruiter* went straight to my cell phone. This kid was extremely pissed at what we were doing. He didn't like the fact that he saw us doing something completely "anti-American," especially in light of the fact that, as he saw it he was taking the initiative as a young man to go and defend his country and its "freedoms." This easily could have turned into a shouting match, but I recognized that the caller wasn't just angry but confused. He didn't simply not like what Red76 and IVAW were up to—from his experience up until that point he truly could not understand why we would even do it. It seemed completely alien to him. We wound up staying on the phone for over an hour, and I discussed with him that while I disagreed with his reasoning for joining the army, and worried about his future safety, the reason that we were engaging in this project was very much in line with why he felt the need to join the Army. In the end, we agreed that we each had the right to be Americans in the best way we saw fit to our ideals and desires regarding what we thought the country stood for, or at least should stand for.

It was an incredible turn. This was a phone call that could have been a name-calling shouting match, and instead it turned into a space of recognition, a moment wherein we each realized that we had to accept one another, if not agree with how we were attempting to arrive at a space that we both recognized was vital for the continuation of the country. I walked away from that phone call reinvested in why I do all of this work that, at times, can seem like the excavation of a mountain with nothing but a teaspoon.

SMART: What does it mean to you to be included in a show called *Feast: Radical Hospitality in Contemporary Art*?

RED76: It means that this accumulation of practice that I spoke of actually means something, and that the last fifteen years of people explicitly working in this manner for a desired, if not murky, outcome is slowly beginning to become visible in a way that it has not up till now. It will be interesting to see what begins to take shape over the next fifteen years.

SMART: What do you hope people take away from your work?

RED76: A feeling of agency and a realization that if they want to get anything done they are going to have to do it for themselves.

OPPOSITE: *Revolutionary Table*, installation view, Smart Museum of Art, 2012

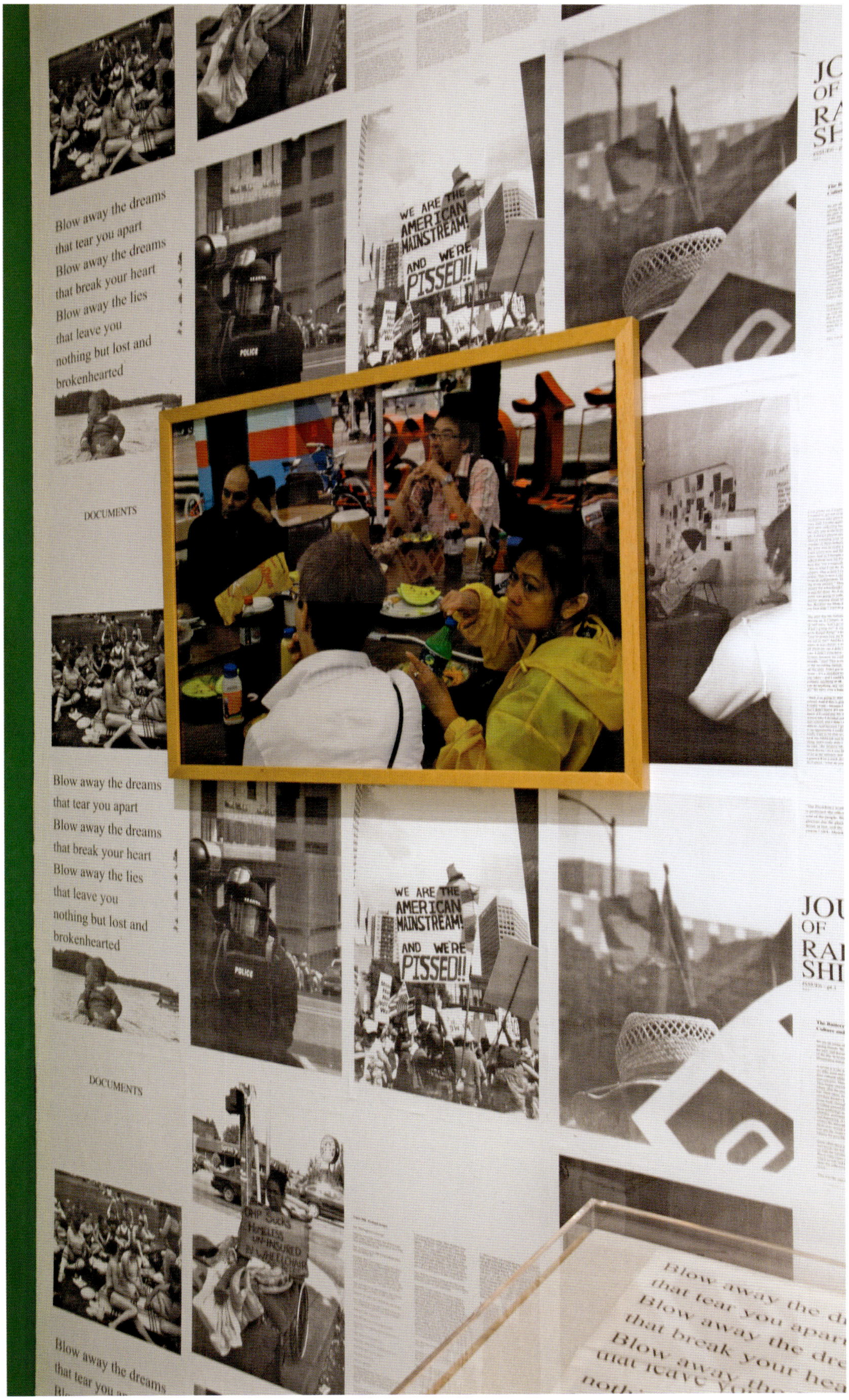
Blow away the dreams
that tear you apart
Blow away the dreams
that break your heart
Blow away the lies
that leave you
nothing but lost and
brokenhearted
DOCUMENTS
WE ARE THE AMERICAN MAINSTREAM! AND WE'RE PISSED!!
POLICE

Excerpts from

Occupy Yr. Home (2012–2015: A Disbributed Meal)

by Red76

It's winter of 2011 and the Occupations have gone fallow. But like any healthy plant its roots are strong and ready for an awakening. Regardless, winters are harsh, and sometimes it's murder to yearn for the arrival of spring, when life and energy will break through the hard ground beneath our treading footsteps. So here in late December we began to reconsider our understanding of what it means to Occupy and where the power lies. What's so special about a commons? Certainly the convergence of many with the purpose of addressing their grievances and a desire to rally around their divergent ideals is something to agitate for, but all crowds disperse. We are nomadic, and in the end, we are alone within ourselves. Our strength lies in our actions, our voice, emanating from a singular core of desire and purpose, and the accumulative residue of those actions and those voices. What can we do to aerate this landscape and let the light bleed into it? Maybe we've got it all in reverse? Maybe we should sit down and consider where we're interested in this starting for ourselves?

Our most potent terrain, the landscape which generates almost all that we see in the world, is also often our most private. So let's begin by occupying our own homes, starting at the kitchen table, out of the bedroom, the living room, into the yard, and into the streets. We don't just mean consumption— what we buy and how we use it. While consuming less, shopping locally, saving energy through any number of measures is important (and needed) it remains, as an ethics lived in the day-to-day, part of a larger system which is killing us. Negation only serves as a means towards co-option. Nothing is ever really taken away, it's just replaced. Rather than replacing the broken elements of an external system that does not have our best interests at heart, let's consider means in which we can begin to exercise the muscles of a new system, generated within, energetically radiating outwards: from ourselves, throughout our homes, becoming visible within the spaces between us, fracturing the windows of our personas.

It's with these considerations that we have begun to organize a series of gatherings at tables across the country. It's at these tables that we will discuss where to begin, how to reconsider where we reside within the discourse of the moment. Where does the action begin? How does the energy circulate? What sorts of agreements should we arrive at for ourselves and with one another to help expand our landscape? We've been having these conversations with ourselves. We want to have more of them, and we invite you to do the same.

Occupy Yr. Home gathers friends at kitchen tables to discuss these ideas over food and drink, meals prepared like any other, mild celebrations of our daily communing. They are not spectacle, ready to burn. They are energetically plain. Friends and strangers alike activate these tables with their ideas and desires, which are then documented in a variety of forms to be disseminated online, in print, and through the continued conversations of those who encounter the problems and possibilities generated across these occupied landscapes of affection. As each table is set, each meal is prepared and eaten together, we hope that the accumulation of these conversations will serve as a discursive terrain, a space for anyone to inhabit and consider how they wish to occupy their own home.

This excerpt was previously published in Red76, "Occupy Yr. Home. (2012–2015: A Distributed Meal)," accessed July 30, 2012, www.red76.com/occupyyrhome.html.

David Robbins

DAVID ROBBINS HAS CENTERED much of his creative practice around three broad topics: the figure of the artist, the nature of comedy, and the overlap between "high" art and "popular" entertainment. All three merged in a key early work, *Talent* (1986). Based in New York at the time, Robbins hired a photography portrait studio to make glossy black-and-white head shots of eighteen visual artists, including Jeff Koons, Cindy Sherman, and Robbins himself. By depicting these serious artists in the same commercial style used to market performers, Robbins skewered the notion of artistic profile, presenting his peers and himself as eager to please and available for hire. Robbins has continued to explore these themes in a variety of formats and media, most recently in his book *Concrete Comedy: An Alternative History of Twentieth-Century Comedy* (2011). Robbins coined the phrase "concrete comedy," to define a physical, object- and discrete gesture-based comedic sensibility within art and culture over the past century—a sensibility Robbins advocates.

"Are you a Socialist or a Socialite?" With its wry, ambiguous blend of pleasure and power, this question is at the heart of another major project: the *Ice Cream Social*. It began in 1993, when Robbins commissioned another artist to make an abstract painting based on the pink-and-brown-dots-on-a-white-ground motif used by the Baskin-Robbins ice cream chain as part of the brand's visual grammar. (The artist has no relation to the store's namesake, but uses this chance connection to the chain and its particular brand of capitalist pop-culture Americana as a generative mechanism for his work.) He exhibited the resulting painting in a Baskin-Robbins store in New York for one night and invited a group of friends to the unveiling; the success of the opening party inspired him to delve further into the themes, visual language, and social import of the American tradition of the ice cream social, thereby updating and reinventing a ritual previously identified with small town life. Robbins has since hosted ice cream socials in museums and galleries around the world. Visually, the events always maintain the restricted Baskin-Robbins palette, and details such as cake decorations evoke a sweetly surreal alternate universe: pink-brown-and-white American flags, bar codes made of icing, and a confectionery transposition of a standard Baskin-Robbins "31 flavors" décor item—a round "clock cake" displaying 31 at every hour. (Robbins always begins his *Ice Cream Socials* with an invocation whose first line, "Where the clock strikes 31 . . .", transports us to a realm outside daily life.)

Robbins has extended the scope of his *Ice Cream Social* brand through interrelated spin-offs, including a novella about the realization of an alternate *Ice Cream Social* via a fictionalized alter-ego, Mark Baskin. He created a TV show as well, as a pilot for the Sundance Channel—a variety show/dance party/collaborative performance, which Robbins describes as "a Warhol Factory party crossed with The Mickey Mouse Club." The show featured irresistible elements such as a house band, The Ingredients, who sing about "The Mainstream:" "Try and stop it, flowing through you." Through such works, Robbins has purposefully cross-promoted the *Ice Cream Social* as a multimedia product that mirrors the ways that other entertainment products move through contemporary society. Playing with the elastic formality of branding in both art and entertainment, Robbins transforms *Ice Cream Social* into a vehicle delivering pleasure and meta-critique; mixing the projection of fun with both self-awareness of contrivance and pleasure, through objects and events imbued with a culturally specific sense of innocent fun, community, and nostalgia for an earlier phase of American society.

For *Feast*, Robbins created a new iteration of the installation grammar he has evolved for use in this project: a refrigerator covered with photos of past socials and topped with hand-made ceramic ice cream bowls, a monitor playing the Sundance pilot, and a copy of the novella—all backed by a pink-brown-white painted super-graphic design, incorporating campaign bunting and cartoony drips. On the closing day of the exhibition, hundreds joined an *Ice Cream Social* that featured special cakes designed by Robbins. The presentation of these objects offered yet one more example of the elasticity of the *Ice Cream Social*, which, the artist notes, morphs "the *Ice Cream Social* 'brand' so as to explore opportunities in multiple contexts without sacrificing consistency of message and meaning."

Sarah Mendelsohn contributed to this text.

OPPOSITE: *Ice Cream Social*, 1993–2008, installation view, Smart Museum of Art, 2012

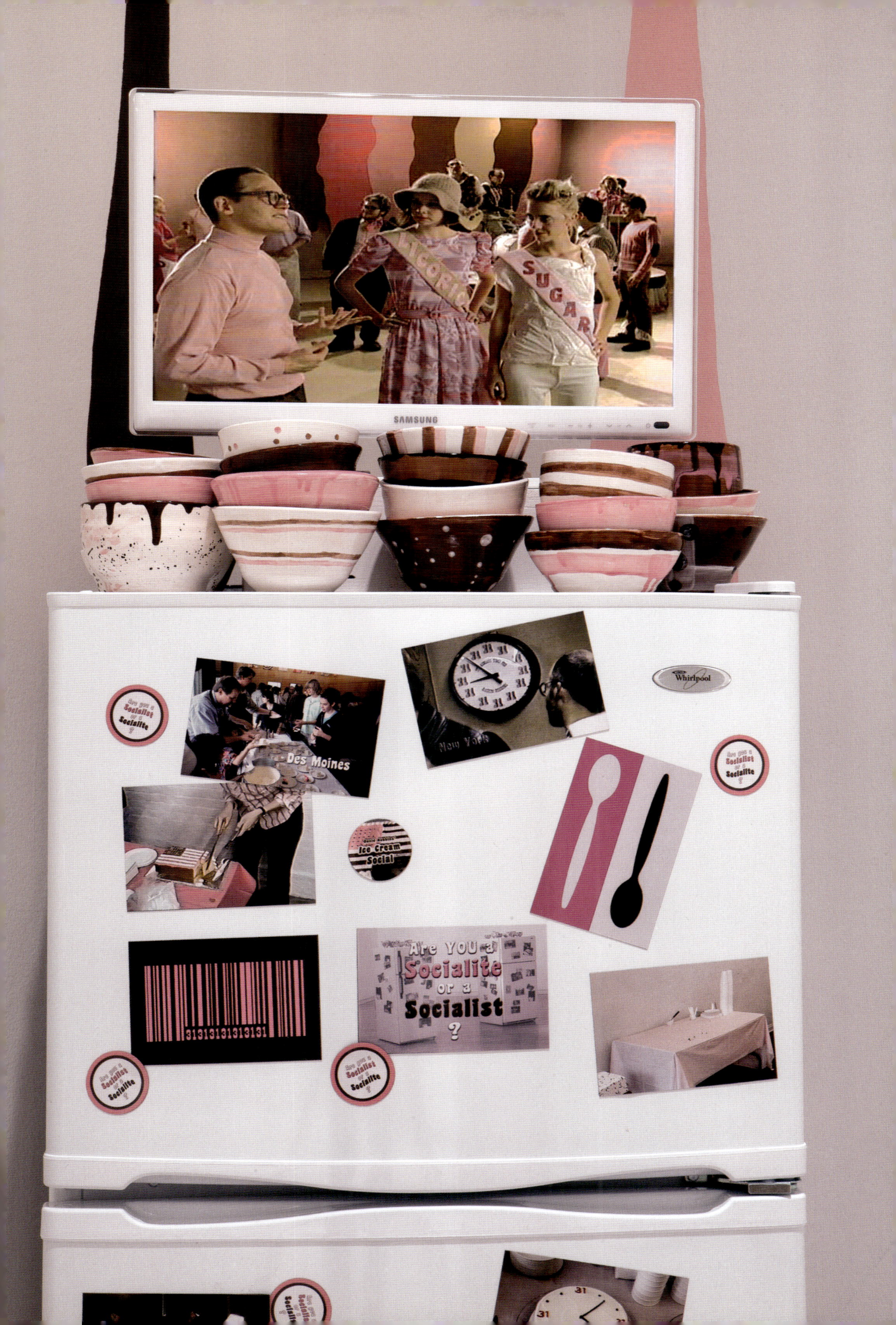
SAMSUNG
SUGAR
Des Moines
New York
Whirlpool
Ice Cream Social
Are YOU a Socialite or a Socialist ?

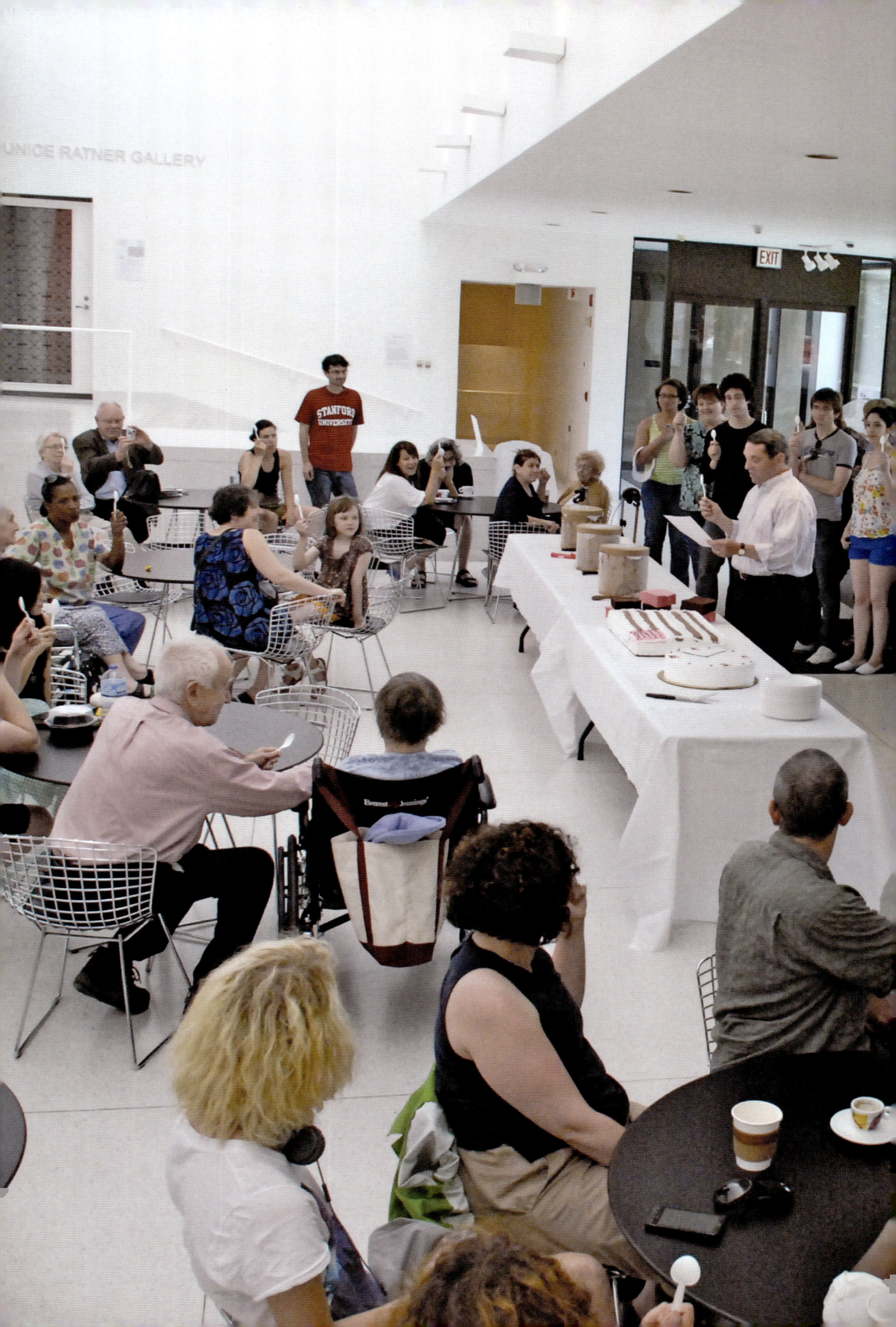
UNICE RATNER GALLERY
EXIT
STANFORD UNIVERSITY

Hundreds attended the *Ice Cream Social* that marked the end of the exhibition. Standing in for the artist, the Smart Museum's director Anthony Hirschel began the event with Robbins's standard invocation:

Where the clock strikes 31
Players conspiring in the enjoyment of enjoyment
Unfurl the pink and brown of the Insupportable
Against animal virtue's blooded tribe
To savor the Ice Cream Social
Cold, licking sweet, always melting,
And empty of all save their pleasure in it,
Sticky enough.

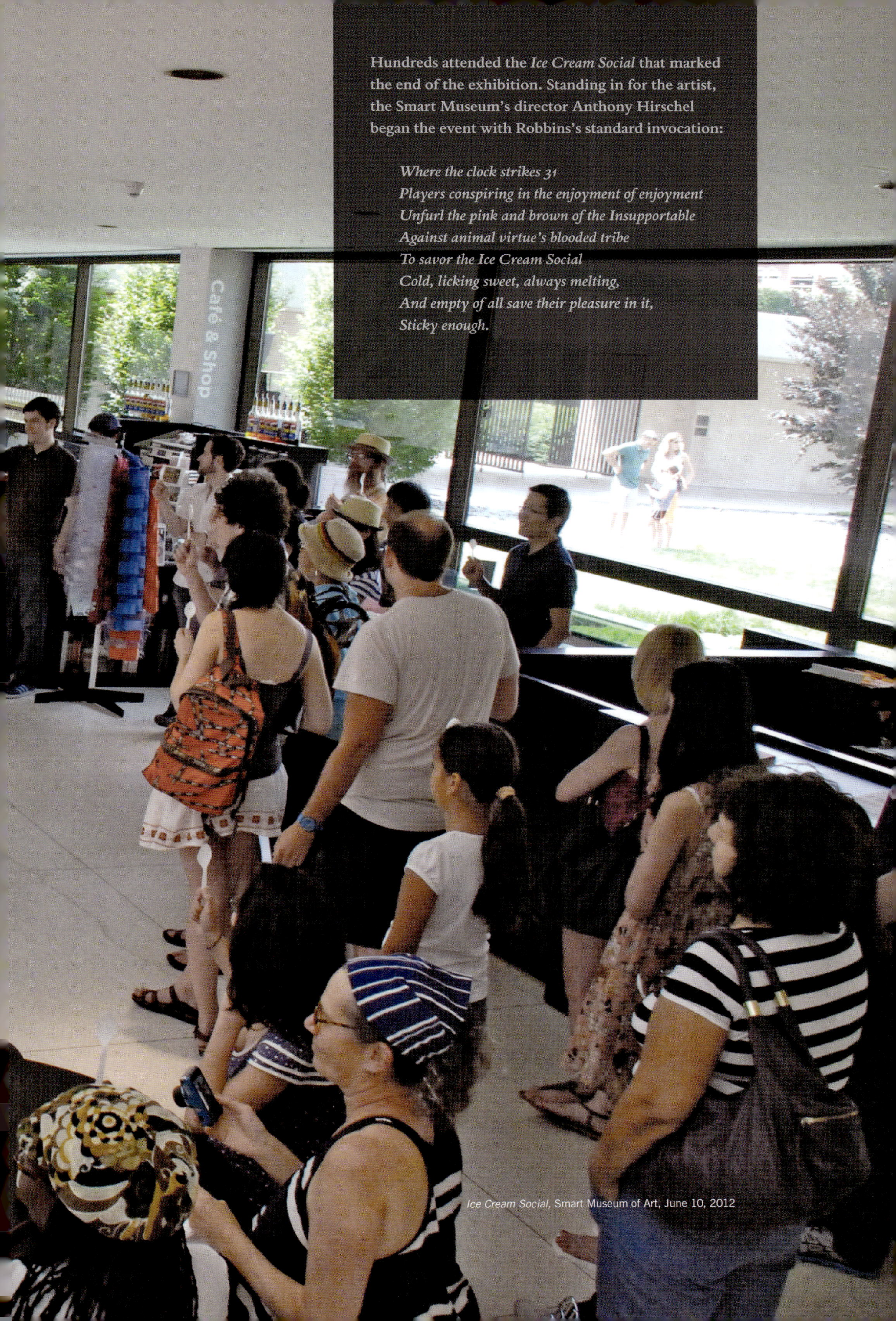

Ice Cream Social, Smart Museum of Art, June 10, 2012

Excerpts from

Notes on the Ice Cream Social

by David Robbins

Relational Aesthetics and Morphing Forms

While I arrived at the *Ice Cream Social* concept intuitively and independently, through my work in comedy, and only learned the term "relational aesthetics" within the past year or two, it is certainly true that the *Ice Cream Social* is about bringing people together on a platform of artifice sympathetic to the formation of new social rituals. My ice cream socials establish self-conscious, temporary communities. What is this community? For what purpose has it been formed? Though I'm interested in these questions, to my mind the ICS is equally a platform for bringing together forms of expression—formats, media, contexts. Paintings and digital prints, live events, a novella, a TV pilot, a movie script—a formal "morphing," with a concomitant leveling of formal hierarchies, has been a crucial aspect of the project's own narrative. As it has evolved, the ICS has reconciled media and communication contexts with heretofore competing, often conflicting cultural agendas. The story of the ICS is in part the story of its movement from a culturally marginal presentational form to mainstream presentational forms—from a painting to television and movies.

Parasitism and Politics

How does someone with an art mind-set go about working directly in mass media? With relation to the source inspiration, what is the degree of parasitism? In other words, is it possible for a self-described artist to make, say, genuine television and not video art *about* television? As far as aesthetic matters go, at this point in the Social's development, these are the questions that intrigue, motivate, and keep me on track.

I'm not interested to introduce things—materials, subject matter, concepts—into the art context. That seems to me to have been the work of modernism, and a habit of imagination left over from modernism. Instead, with the ICS I'm interested in pushing certain ambitions for the culture and certain attitudes heretofore associated with the art context in the direction of the mainstream. I'm interested to work as an artist in mainstream forms, from a position of respect for mainstream forms. My ambition isn't to get video art shown on a television program or channel. My ambition is to make television shows for popular consumption. What might such shows be like?

Until recently, the gap between "art" and mainstream media was quite large. Only the networks and movie studios possessed the necessary technology. Some of the resentment and "critique" that artists have aimed at mainstream media is attributable, I believe, to their frustration at having been "frozen out" of using powerful, modern communication technology. Today, though, the artist who wants to work in mass media forms needn't adopt that negative stance. The technology gap is closing, and an artist can now create with the same equipment that many filmmakers and television makers use. While it's true that mass media distribution systems still favor status quo entertainment product, as imaginations that have been trained in other traditions increasingly produce in mainstream formats those distribution systems will gradually feel the pressure, and eventually discover the commercial advantage of opening up. It's only a matter of time.

These excerpts were previously presented as *Notes on Ice Cream Social*, from *ICE CREAM SOCIAL: David Robbins, 1993–2004*, Miller Gallery at Carnegie Mellon University, Pittsburgh, Pennsylvania (January 14–March 13, 2005).

Excerpts from
Ice Cream Social
by David Robbins

Where the Clock Strikes 31

The ridiculous is as delicate as spun sugar. Staging it before the world's indifference demands from the manufacturer discipline and rigor, plus a seriousness of purpose, which can itself reach the level of the absurd.

Although Mark's painting was to be a simple abstraction, and not particularly ambitious visually—a dot here, a dot there, what could be difficult?—its execution in fact turned out to be complicated.

Specifically, there was a content problem to solve. A big one. For when the pink and brown dots were removed from the context of the Baskin-Robbins décor, they became just that: dots, dumb, blank and empty. *Only* silly. *Only* vacant. Whatever other content had been in them was suddenly out like a light.

Certain aspects of the painting's production were predetermined. The colors had to match those of the company's logo. The scale of the painting had to be small enough to fit on a wall likely crowded with cardboard posters promoting sundaes, shakes, and ice cream cakes. In fact, in regard to the painting's appearance there was only one truly complex thing to be decided: the arrangement of the dots on the canvas.

Over this, though, Mark agonized. Why should any composition of dots be arranged one way and not another? There was, finally, no reason, so long as the dots' organization was based upon taste. In pursuit of a more objective method of composition he used his Lapdog computer to randomly generate a series of dot patterns. All the dots were the same size, just as they were in the Baskin-Robbins logo. When the patterns were printed out, gray ink on white paper, some were nearly handsome, some nearly poignant, others almost funny.

None, however, answered a more fundamental question: Did he really wish the dots to represent pure chance? After all, as an organizing principle, chance was as flabby and arbitrary as personal taste. Finding neither subjectivity nor happenstance wholly satisfactory, Mark simply took a vacation from the problem, and stashed the printouts in a desk file.

Several months later, when enough life had passed to make him a slightly different person, he revived the painting project. During this second go-round he patiently re-examined each page. Eventually he selected the two strongest candidates. While pulling the pages from the messy pile, he happened to pass the two in front of his desk lamp. Strong backlighting rendered both translucent, like pages of illuminated manuscript, and enabled him to read their patterns as one. Instantly he recognized that the pair in combination offered the solution. Not only was the visual design a strong, balanced composition but the method of its origination cut impersonal, computer-generated chance with a measure of humble human accident. Each "system" of chance rested in composure against the other. Their partnership was perfect.

Partnership figured in the physical production of the painting, as well, since Mark wanted it to be carried out by another's hand. The Baskin-Robbins corporation sought, through the décor and the designation "parlor," to suggest the intimacy of a modest partnership, and he wanted to wire that same confusion—of the personal and the impersonal—into the painting's own imagination.

Finding a young painter in need of money is among the world's easier tasks. By putting out word among the staff at some of the local art supply shops Mark obtained the names of several struggling talents. After interviewing them he decided to hire a painter who employed the airbrush technique in her own work. Although not a skill required for the simple pink, brown, and white painting, Mark thought it fitting to employ someone who'd already made a commitment to the dispassionate commercial surface.

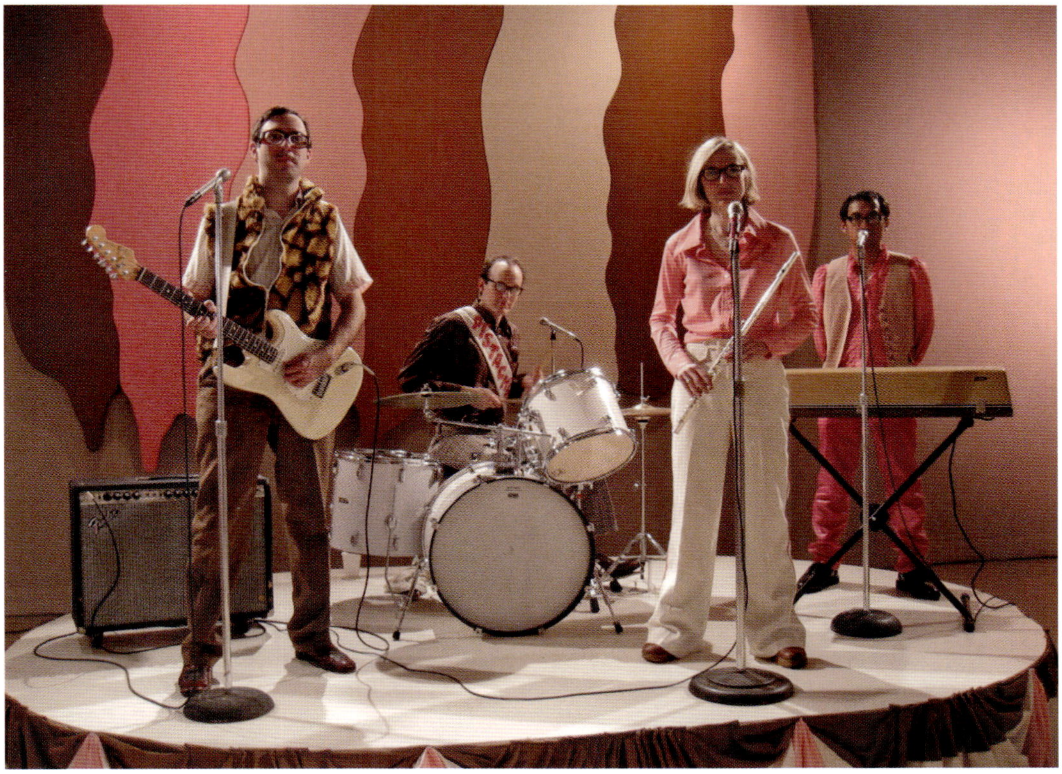

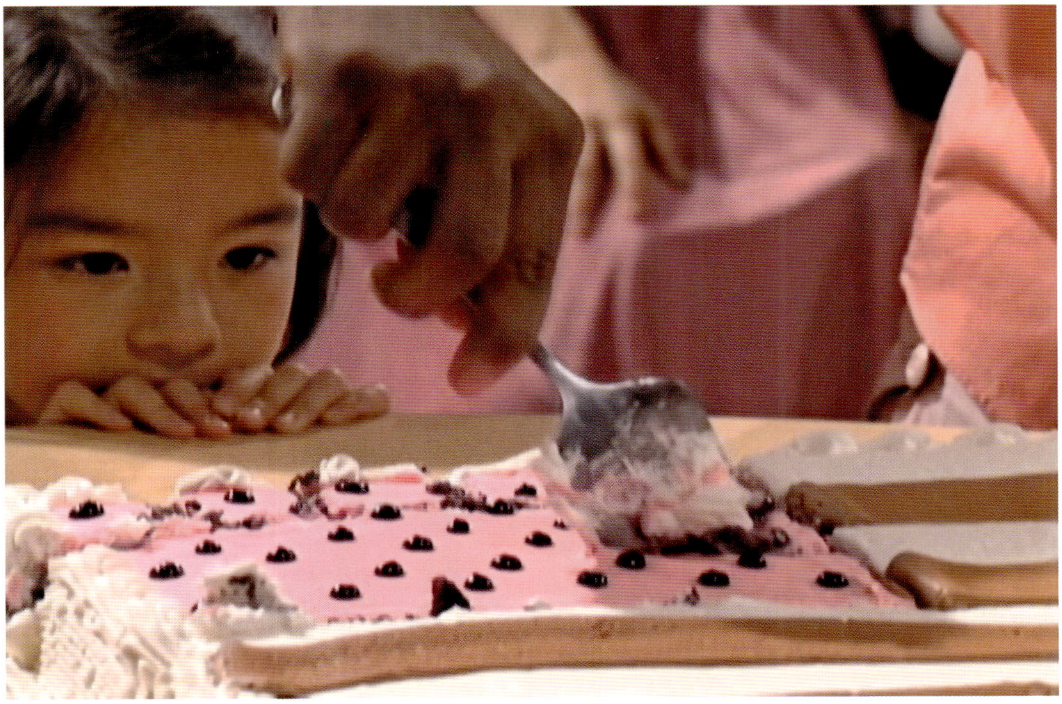

Stills from *The Ice Cream Social*, Sundance Channel TV pilot, 2003

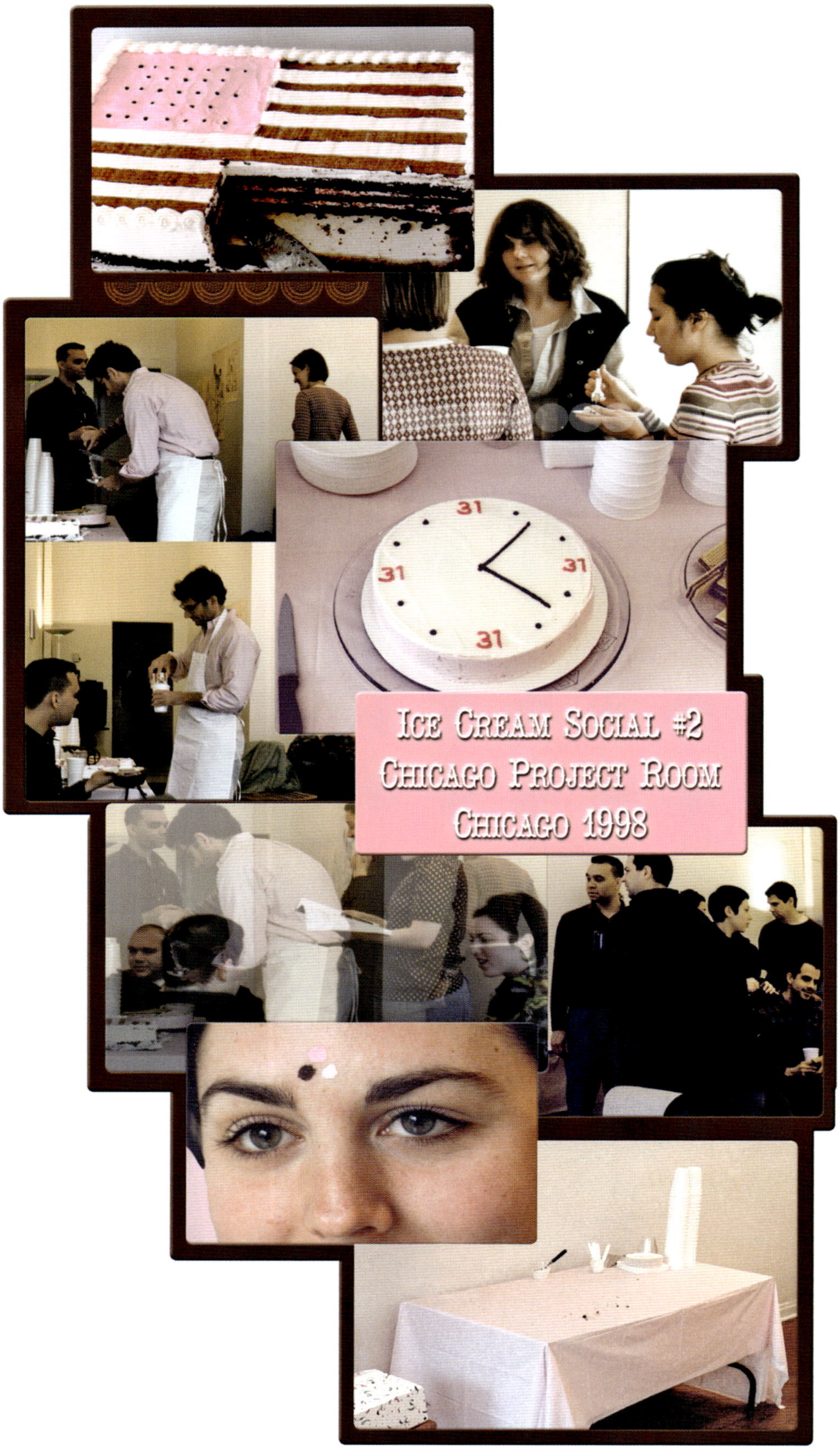

Documentation from *Ice Cream Social #2*,
Chicago Project Room, 1998

After Molly the painter had agreed to his terms he handed over the clipped-together design, established the dimensions and color choices, and paid her half her fee in advance in order to depersonalize the meeting. He was management, she labor. This was business.

Two weeks later, on the first snowfall of winter, when Mark came to collect the painting he was immensely pleased with the result. Flat pastel pink and brown dots floated in a calm white field. Painted in matte, uninflected acrylic, the painting looked matter-of-fact, blank but alert, an intelligence awaiting programming.

The painting completed, the next chore dropped into the chute: finding a suitable Baskin-Robbins in which to hang the thing. The room had to be large enough to accommodate perhaps two dozen people comfortably, and it had to feature enough undecorated wall space to afford an uncluttered view of the painting. Mark tramped through the snow to examine possibilities in the Laketown, Perrin Park, and Winslet neighborhoods, but only one parlor, on the corner of Dunlap and 23rd, between an Entertainment Recycling Center and a Sunset Liquor'n'Video outlet, met both conditions. Although far from beautiful, the space was clean and in good condition.

The manager was a friendly middle-aged Cantonese named John Chin. Mr. Chin was tall, and as he listened patiently to the stranger he gazed down at him with placid brown eyes which had taken in stronger challenges. Mark made no attempt to disguise or misrepresent what he was doing, but instead told the proprietor exactly what he hoped to accomplish by installing a painting based on the Baskin-Robbins dots. To his surprise, Mr. Chin agreed immediately. "There should be more of this kind of innocent fun," said the older man. As Mr. Chin did not want regular customers to be scared away by the sight of some kind of private event, and Mark did not want guests to have to pay for ice cream, the two agreed to a fee of fifty dollars for the short period of time that the painting would be hung. Together they settled on a date for the event.

The crucial arrangements made, Mark turned his attention to promotion. He designed an announcement using the same P. T. Barnum font favored by the Baskin-Robbins company, and photocopied it onto vivid pink paper.

> YOU are invited to an
> ICE CREAM SOCIAL
> January 3
> 8:30 pm
> Baskin-Robbins at 23rd and Dunlap
> FREE ICE CREAM!

It wasn't until he'd started stapling the small posters upon telephone poles and bulletin boards that he became aware of the absurdity of inviting total strangers to join him for ice cream in the dead of winter. He wondered whether anyone at all would bother to show up. But when Trace Weaver, emerging from a taxi on her way to a production meeting at a recording studio, spotted the pink announcement, an audience of at least one was guaranteed. Trace adored ice cream, and everything good was even better when free.

On the evening of the Ice Cream Social, Mark dressed in the understated costume he'd set aside; pink oxford-cloth button-down shirt, white jeans, brown shoes. He arrived at the Baskin-Robbins early in order to hang the painting. The parlor glowed cold white in the night.

"Nice painting," said Mr. Chin after the object had been unwrapped. "You make that?"

"I caused it to exist. Yes."

Mr. Chin helped him with the hanging. To avoid making any permanent marks in the wall Mark had brought two strips of Velcro. That did the trick.

The arrival of the first guests transformed Mark into a host. "How are you this evening? C'mon in. I'm Mark. Please be sure to have some ice cream. My treat. Just go up to the counter and ask Mr. Chin or his assistant Ling. Uh huh, any flavor you like, that's right. Hi. Thanks for coming. Notice the painting? Yup. Ice cream's free." Strangers wandered in, singly and in pairs. White people and

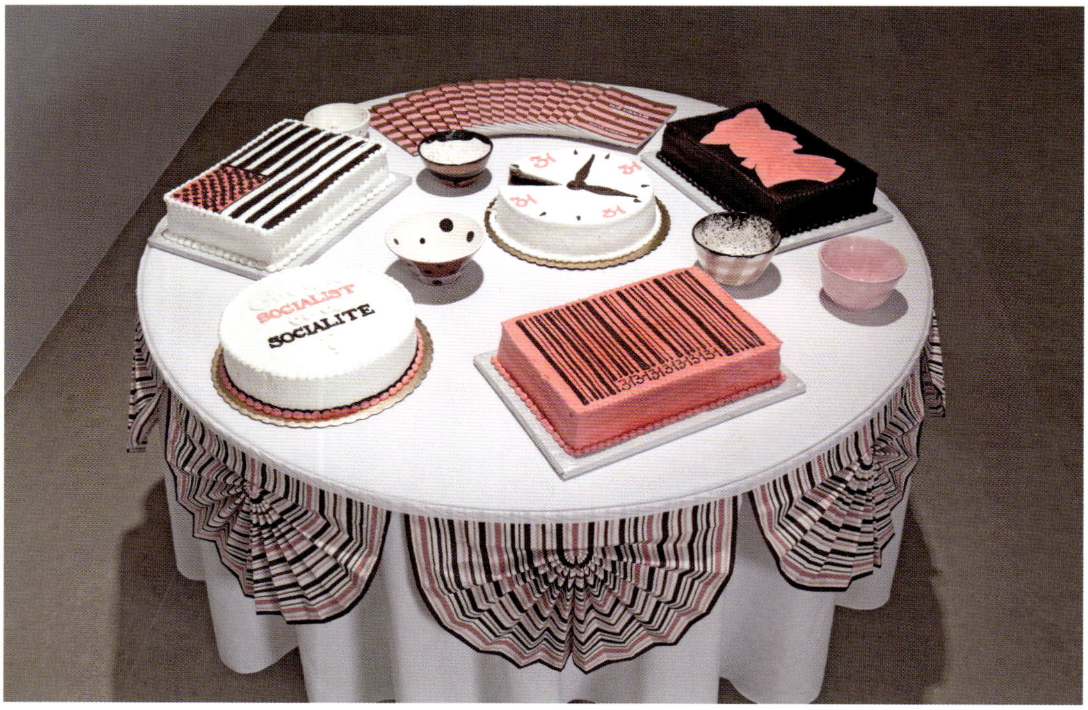

Ice Cream Social, installation view, Greene Naftali Gallery, New York,
March 2–April 2, 2011

black. Latino and Asian. Children with their parents. People dressed in parkas and tweed topcoats, denim jackets and leather bombers. Some people carried cameras, video or still . . .

The tiny space soon became crowded. Bodies circulated. Mark buzzed about the room, flush with the confidence of the inventor. He encouraged any reticent party to enjoy some ice cream. No small number of guests needed encouragement.

"Is this the event?" asked a tall young woman whose short white hair and black glasses communicated "art school."

"Possibly you are the event," replied Mark in all sincerity.

"To be honest with you I can't quite locate *where* the event is," noted a middle-aged fellow attired in a gray business suit. He wore rubbers on his shoes, and wire-rim glasses.

"Oh?"

"Nope. Keeps shifting. Between your guests, the ice cream, the space, and the painting, it refuses to settle down."

"Plus there's my name." Mark told the fellow his name.

"Interesting," said the gray man, nodding. "Interesting."

An unlovely man in his thirties joined their conversation. He wore a plaid flannel shirt and jeans. "So what do you want us to be doing?"

"Doing?"

"Yeah. I can't figure out what's expected of me here," replied the man. "I don't get it."

"Nothing is expected of you," Mark assured him. "The Ice Cream Social is just a reason to gather. You've gathered. Relax and enjoy it."

The plaid man persisted. "I know what to do at an art opening," said he, "and I know what to do at an ice cream parlor but I don't know what to do with a combination of the two."

Mark offered only a smile.

Occasionally, customers wandered into the store on their own, to purchase a cone or a pint.

"What is this, the ice cream convention?" laughed a young black woman sassily, on her way out the door, cone in hand.

Through it all, the painting acquired memory. Whatever additional meaning might come to be heaped on it in the future, the meaning of the painting could never be entirely separated from this event. Mark was thrilled to learn that it was possible to program art.

After allowing a few minutes more to pass, he judged the room ready and made his way behind the counter, where an obviously amused Mr. Chin shook his hand before receding to the sidelines. Mark stood for a moment looking across the counter at the eager faces expectantly gazing back at him. A roomful of strangers, united by a single experience. The hum of voices in the room quieted, and he addressed his guests.

"I've written a poem to commemorate the event." With all eyes on him, he nervously plunged ahead:

Where the clock strikes 31
Players conspiring in the enjoyment of enjoyment
Unfurl the pink and brown of the insupportable
Against animal virtue's blooded tribes
To savor the Ice Cream Social
Cold, licking-sweet, always melting and,
Empty of all save their pleasure in it, sticky enough.

Unaccustomed to having a love poem addressed to them, the crowd was a mosaic of baffled faces . . .

He looked over the heads of the audience at the painting which, having taken on certain of the conditions of a mirror, now seemed to reflect the entire room.

"Thank you for coming tonight and being a part of our temporary community," said Mark. "Hope you take a good memory along with you; I know the painting will!"

With that, the Ice Cream Social began to melt away. Some of the bolder guests came forward, cones blobby and dripping, to thank their host.

"That was very entertaining," said a woman who introduced herself as Trace Weaver, extending a business card.

Mark took the card. The Quid Pro Quo Company. Famed Quidco! And the woman was smiling at him!

"It was like TV without the TV," commented another woman with long sleek auburn bangs cut at an acute angle.

"Brilliant! I'll have to remember that!" said Mark.

"Yes," agreed Trace Weaver of Quidco, nodding. "That *is* a good one."

"Definitely postmedia," commented a pale bookish looking fellow.

Mark wrinkled his nose. "Too severe, don't you think? Suggests rupture. Let's stress continuum. 'Après-media' perhaps?"

Everyone agreed that was much better.

This excerpt has been previously published in David Robbins, *The Ice Cream Social* (Zurich: JRP: Ringier, 2004), 31–45.

Rirkrit Tiravanija

SINCE THE BEGINNING of his practice, Rirkrit Tiravanija has invited the public into situations in which unexpected offerings of food and hospitality serve as tools to shift perception and spark engagement. Born in Argentina, Tiravanija studied art in Chicago and New York in the late 1980s and was strongly influenced by then-dominant conceptual practices and institutional critique. His work bears perhaps equally strong traces of the social practices, Buddhist traditions, and cuisine of his native Thailand. The center of gravity in Tiravanija's work lies in creating ephemeral situations that involve interaction with the public, and in the 1990s he was one of several artists championed by curator and critic Nicholas Bourriaud as exemplars of what Bourriaud termed "relational aesthetics"—an influential but much-debated label. Currently based between New York and Chiang Mai, Tiravanija is also known as a co-founder with fellow artist Kamin Lerdchaiprasert of The Land, a collaborative project in Chiang Mai, Thailand, which offers a longer-term site for explorations of hospitality, food, and art: it mixes traditional agricultural practices with sculptural/architectural interventions and serves as an occasional informal retreat and pedagogical space for creative practitioners and students.

Tiravanija first began to use Thai food with the project *untitled (1989)* for a group exhibition curated by the artist Robert Longo, *Outside the Clock: Beyond Good and Elvis*. Tiravanija prepared a dish of curry and left the spicy dish simmering on one pedestal; another held cans and boxes and leftover ingredients from its making so that the piece became a kind of three-dimensional, multisensorial still life. Tiravanija later made many projects in which he not only made curry but actually served it to the public, most notably *untitled 1992 (free)* in which he moved the staff's working areas into the front of the gallery, cooked curry for the public in the back rooms, and left the remains as an installation. Variations on the project have since become one of his signature gestures, recurring in many subsequent works. His early projects used food as a means to unsettle usual modes of interaction within commercial and institutional art spaces by creating an unexpected sensory and social experience. They also tapped into issues of exoticism raised by the choice to serve simple Thai food—then still a relatively unfamiliar cuisine in America—and by artist's status as a cosmopolitan immigrant.

Feast signaled Tiravanija's foundational importance to the current wave of interest in meal- and conviviality-based practices by presenting materials from the first project in which he prepared and served food for the public. Shortly after that first curry project in 1989, Tiravanija was invited to create a project in the project space at Paula Allen Gallery in New York by the gallery's new director, Randy Alexander. Alexander gave Tiravanija free rein, resulting in *untitled 1990 (pad thai)*, a "situational event and installation" in which the artist prepared and served this classic Thai dish and left the remains on view for several weeks as an installation. After closing the installation, many individual elements were then sold as sculptures, including one object presented in *Feast*: a wok whose interior still bears gritty traces of Tiravanija's cooking. The piece comes with the box in which it was purchased; it is stored in the box when not on view, and then presented on the box itself in gently elevating gesture that recalls many art historical ghosts, from Marcel Duchamp's readymades to Andy Warhol's Brillo boxes. The wok was presented in *Feast* along with copies of the press release and installation views from that first installation. The Chicago presentation also included *For documentation only, active photograph*, an exquisite wall piece that Tiravanija made in 1990 for Alexander—a gift from the artist who had just hosted the public, to the curator who had hosted his art.

OPPOSITE: *untitled 1990 (pad thai)*, installation view, Paula Allen Gallery, New York, 1990

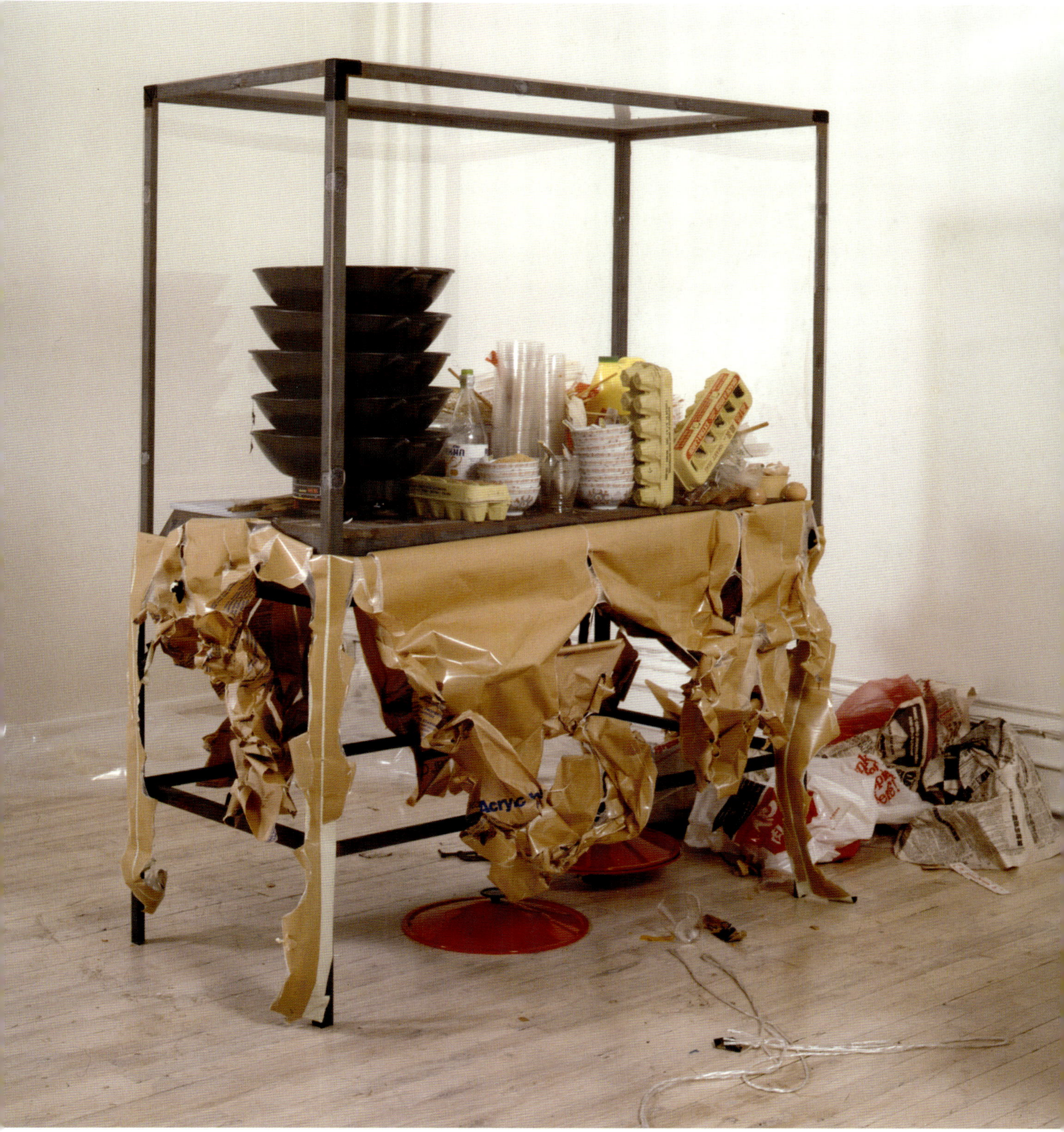

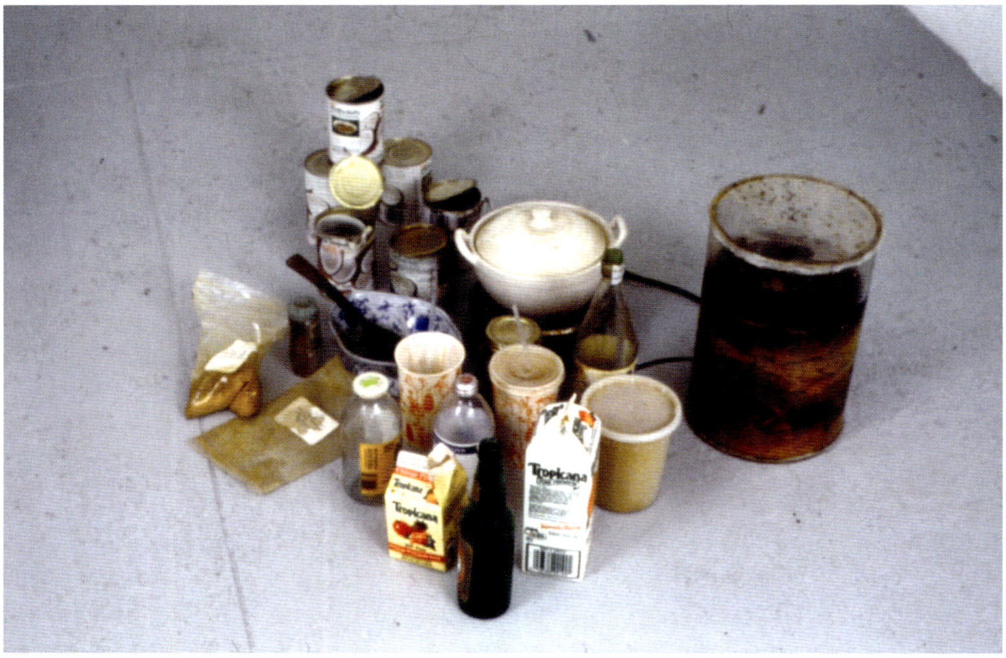

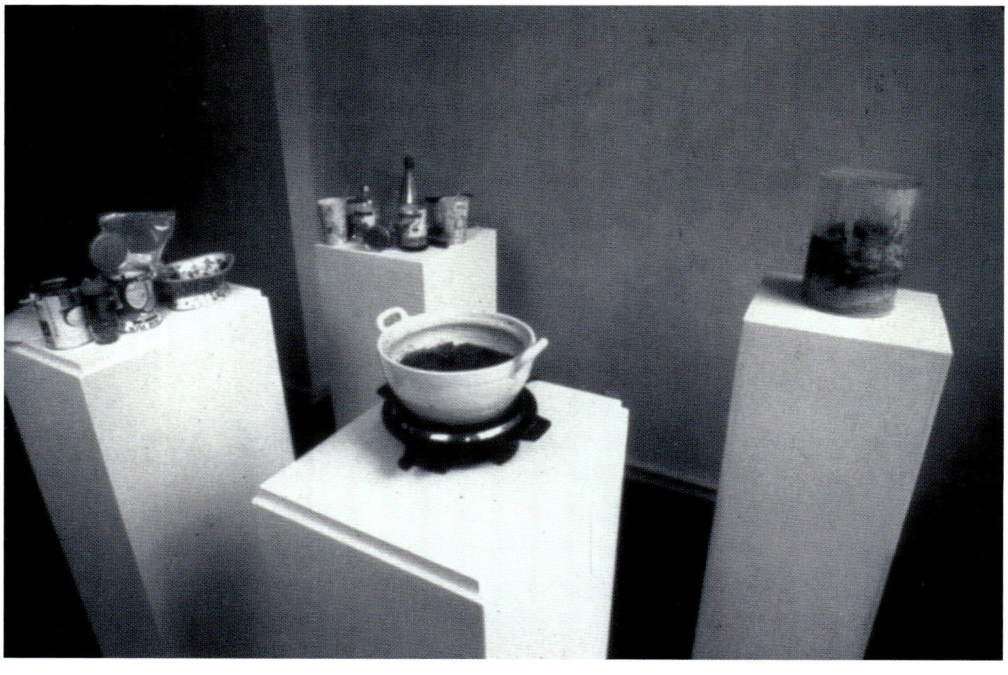

TOP AND BOTTOM: *untitled ()*, installation views, Scott Hanson Gallery, New York, 1989

OPPOSITE: *untitled 1990 (pad thai)* press release for Paula Allen Gallery, New York, 1990

Paula Allen Gallery

560 Broadway
New York, N.Y. 10012
(212) 334-9710

FOR IMMEDIATE RELEASE
INFORMATION: Randy Alexander
212-334-9710

"PAD THAI" A PROJECT BY RIRKRIT TIRAVANIJA

DATES: February 14- March 3, 1990

OPENING: February 17, 6 - 8 pm

HOURS: Tuesday - Saturday, 10am - 6pm

The Paula Allen Gallery will present "Pad Thai," a situational event and installation conceived by Rirkrit Tiravanija. "Pad Thai" will open February 17 from 6-8pm when the artist will prepare and serve the following recipe for Pad Thai:

> Heat the oil on a wok and fry the garlic until golden. Quickly add the shrimp and stir-fry until heated through. Add the sugar, fish sauce and ketchup and stir until dissolved. Add beaten eggs, letting them set slightly, then stir to scramble. Add the noodles and toss and stir for about 2 minutes. Reserving about 4 tablespoons of the bean sprouts, add the remainder to the wok. Stir over heat until the bean sprouts are barely cooked. Turn the Pad Thai onto a platter, placing the reserved, raw bean sprouts on one side.
>
> Presentation: Sprinkle the noodles with the garnish ingredients in the following order: Shrimp powder, peanuts, chili flakes, green onions, coriander leaves. Ring the platter with the lime slices and serve.

The remains of the opening will continue as an installation in the project room through March 3rd.

"Pad Thai" is conceived as an event that addresses the perception and notion of cultural reception, and its transformation from object to idea.

Rirkrit Tiravanija came from Thailand ten years ago to North America. He attended various arts schools and has been recently included in an exhibition at the Scott Hanson Gallery, "Outside the Clock: Beyond Good and Elvis", curated by Robert Longo. This is his first solo exhibition.

# # # # #

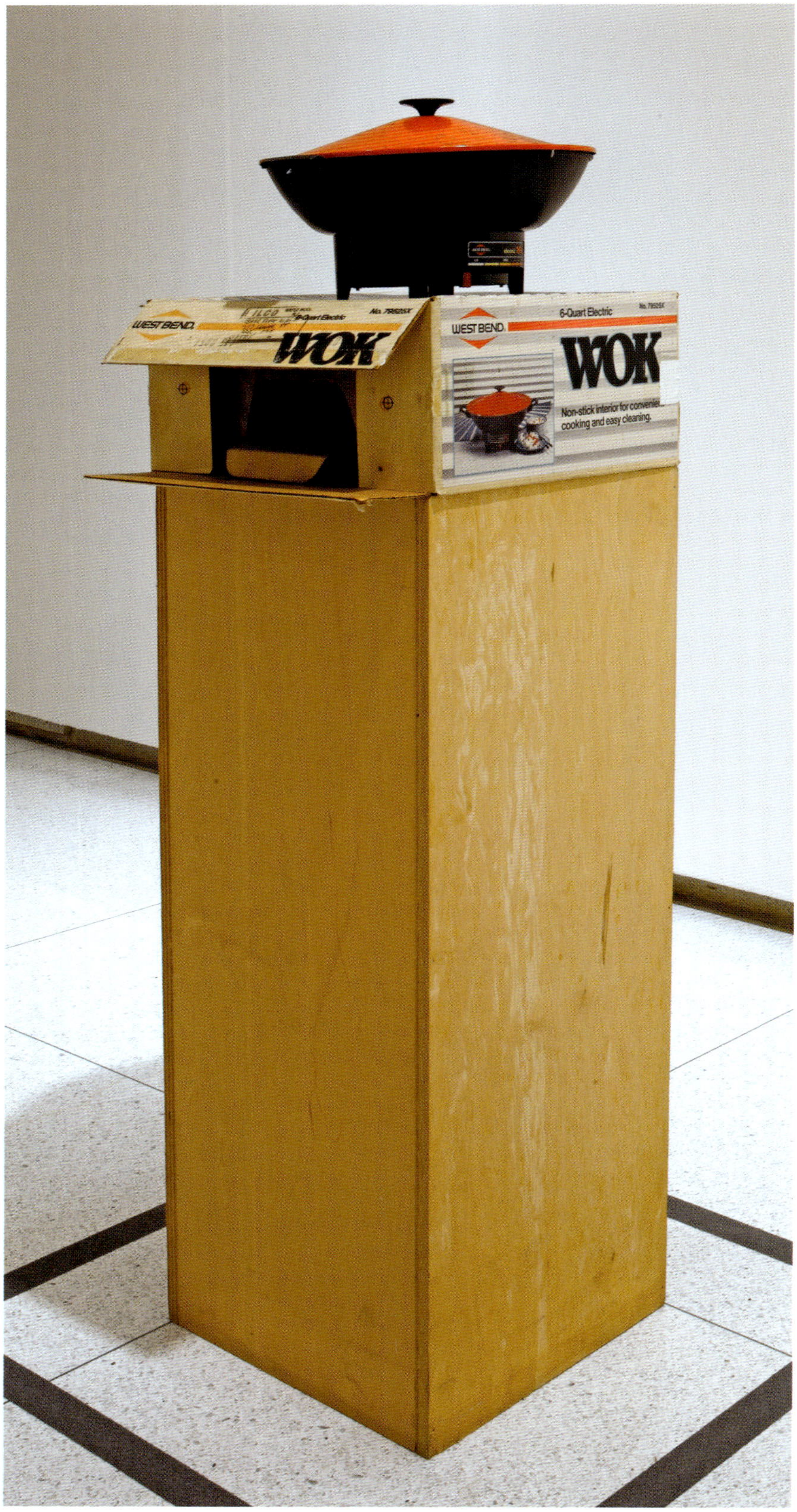

ABOVE: *untitled 1990 (wok)*, installation view, Smart Museum of Art, 2012

OPPOSITE: *For documentation only, active photograph*, 1990, installation view, Smart Museum of Art, 2012

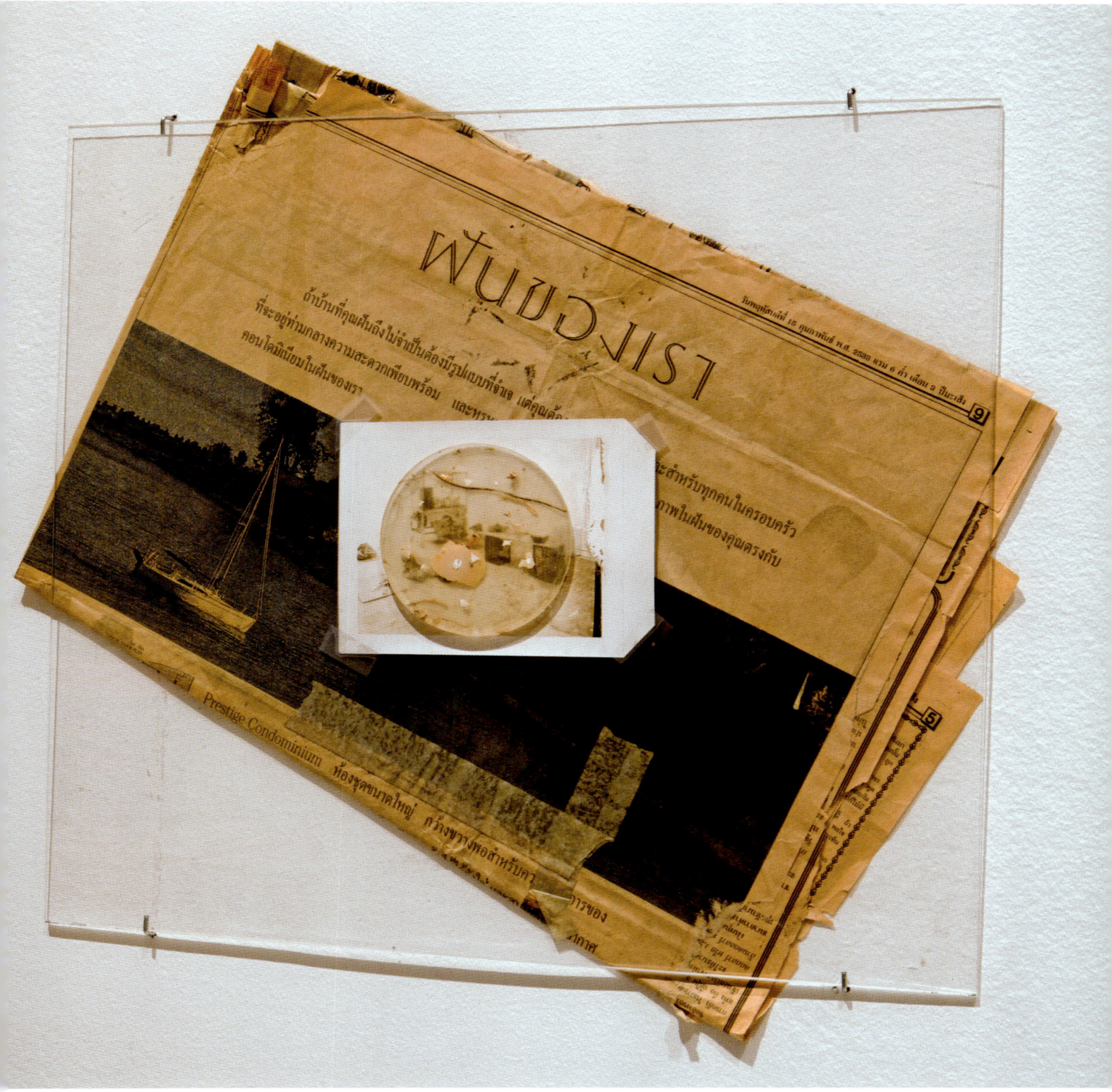
ฝันของเรา
Prestige Condominium

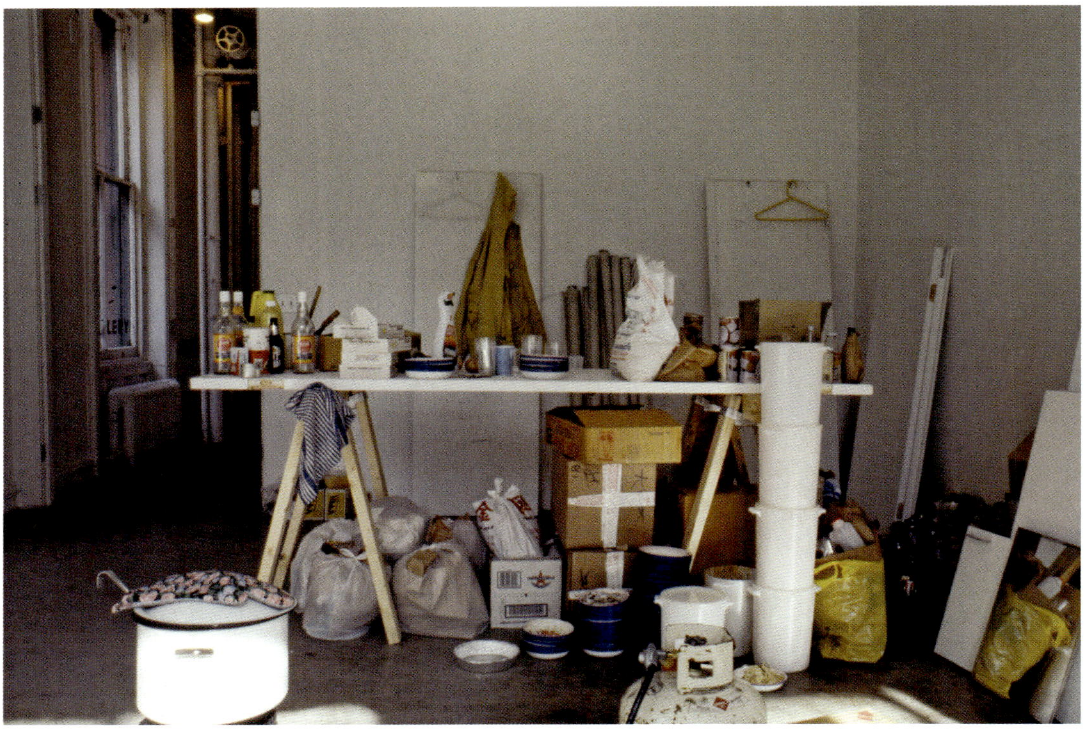

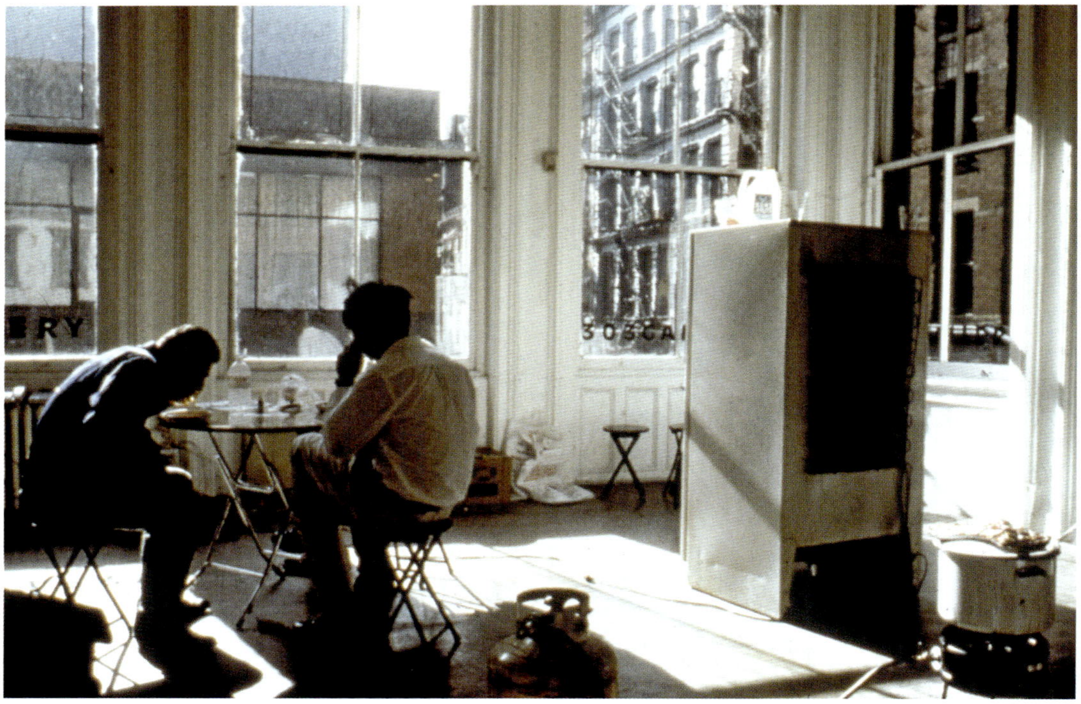

ABOVE AND OPPOSITE: *untitled 1992 (free)*, installation views, 303 Gallery, New York, 1992

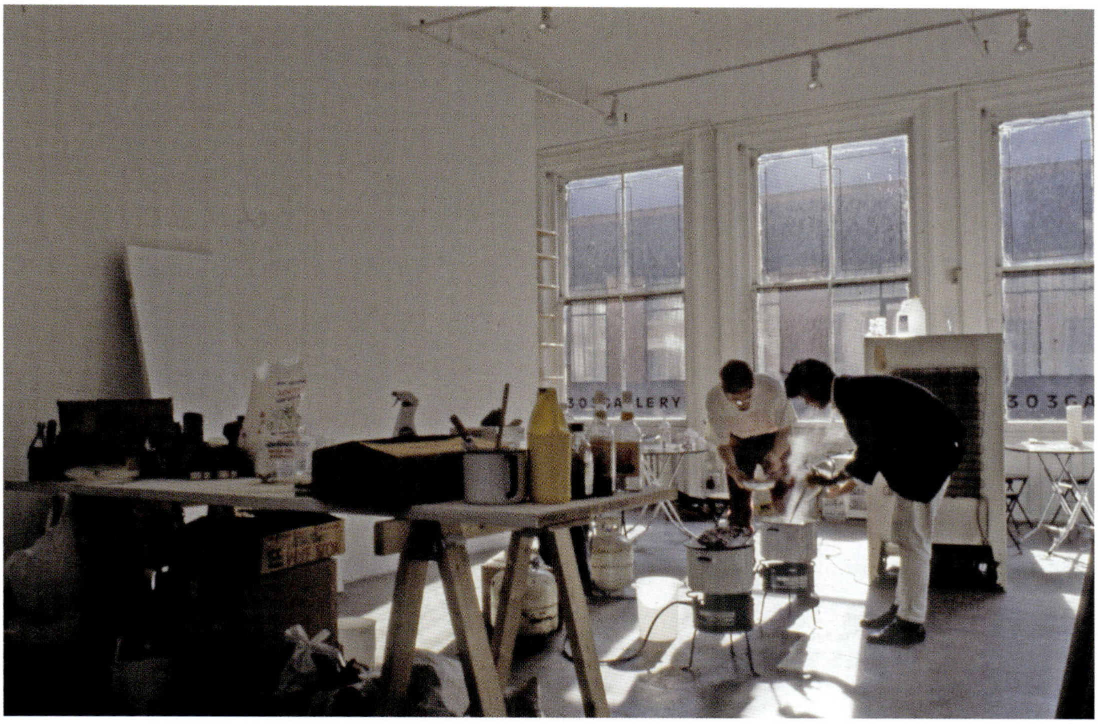

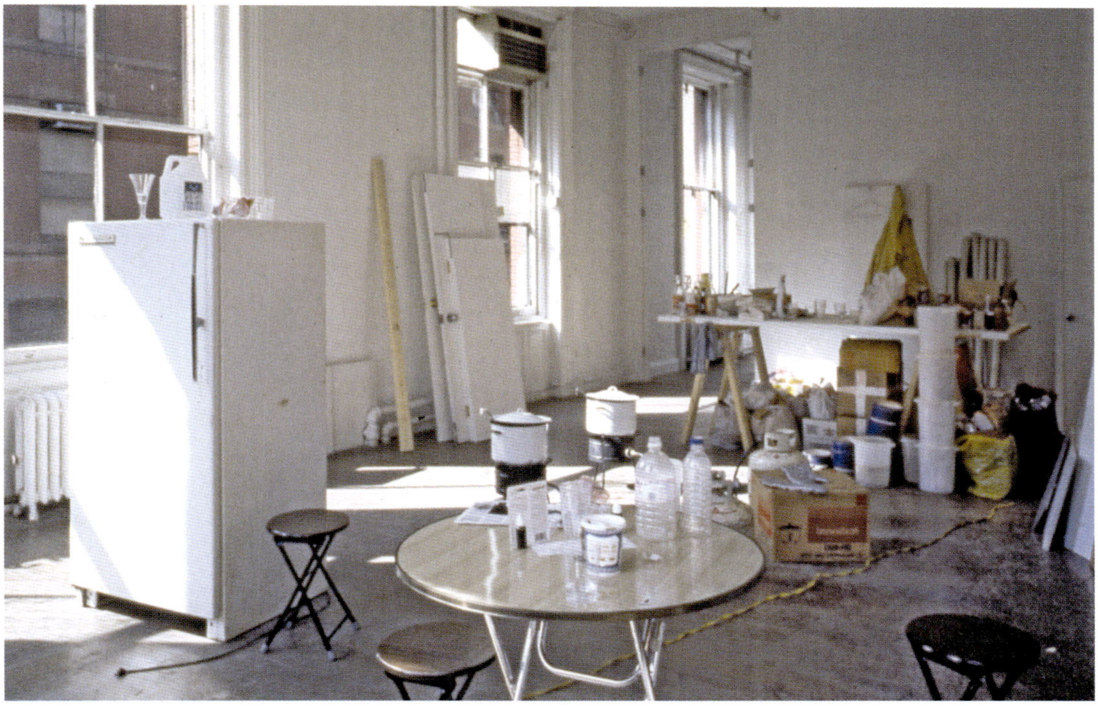

In the following text, used as the script for an audioguide to accompany his retrospective at the Museum Boijmans Van Beuningen (2004), Tiravanija presents a discussion of his work in the third person . . . The museum did not show any of his past works, just empty spaces that related to the original venues.

The Docent turns away from the window and leads the group into the partitioned room to the left of the space . . . it is the replicated approximation of a space which is the project room of the Paul Allen Gallery . . . the Docent lines everyone up against the wall as if there was an installation in the middle of the room and proceeds to talk . . .

Docent: The relative success of *pad thai* from 1990 and the perplexed confusion following his first one man exhibition *untitled blind*, put Tiravanija on the radar of the New York art world where one exhibition can make or break an artist overnight. We now move forward to the year 1992 and Tiravanija's second solo exhibition in New York, with the work *untitled in parenthesis free.* Once again, the reintroduction of food as the key element in the approach of the work is central. In tandem with this element, Tiravanija makes references to the core ideas of conceptual art that question the idealism behind the relevance of authorship and authenticity. There are two parts to the exhibition: we enter to find an exhibition space that is full to the brim with an eclectic mix of objects. The overall view is that of the overpacked storage space of a gallery. It is full of artworks in frames (many are photographs since gallery 303 concentrated very strongly on photography), some paintings and parts and pieces of sculptures. When you enter from the elevator you can see a painted black cartwheel belonging to a Karen Kilimnik installation. Behind this is a curiously tall woodchip crate standing upright framing a column but not quite reaching the ceiling; there are drawers for drawings, cardboard boxes full of unknown contents and some boxes with tennis shoes and a toothbrush—all have been dragged out from all corners of the gallery and put on display as if to make an exhibition of the entire contents of the gallery.

There is an aisle running around and through the room and we can make our way through the storage and behind the pile of art, etc. Once we make our way to the back of the gallery we are surprised to discover the desk of the gallery owner, and her assistants sitting there amongst the pile. They are working as if it was just another day. Here the intimacy of the gallery has been exposed: walls, cupboards, storage racks of art and even the toilet were stripped bare without doors to hinder the view of all possible corners of the rooms in the gallery.

We can smell the scent of a steaming pot of jasmine rice, with its very distinct combination of water and the perfume of jasmine. It's enough to make one curious with hunger, and as we make our way through the space we come to the room at the end of the hallway, well lit, with windows, at the corner of the building. Sunlight pours in from an October afternoon, and already we feel the compression of the gallery lifted from our shoulders. There are people sitting around

round tables and on stools, they are talking, reading the guide for galleries, weighing their next move. The 303 Gallery is at the corner of Spring and Greene Streets in SoHo, New York formerly the main art district of the city.

There is a mess of doors leaning against the walls in this room: doors presumably of the gallery. They are unhinged and stacked. To the right as we enter is a makeshift table made from sawhorses, and yet another door from the space. A couple of people seem to be busying themselves with the preparation of some vegetables—the chopping and cutting; opening gallon cans of bamboo shoots. In the middle of the room there are two pots cooking on camping rings. One seems to have been prepared already, the other is on its way. People are helping themselves to the rice from a cooker large enough to feed the whole Island of Manhattan. Right next to the low gas cookers is an old used refrigerator, white, with hints of age around the edges. As one sits down for the bowl (white enamel with blue rims) of food, one begins to realize that this is a distinctively different experience from others we have had in an art gallery or with art. There are also many milky white cylindrical buckets which seem to be sloshing with waste food, all that is left over. In the refrigerator there are Thai long beans, Thai roundish green eggplants, as well as the mini pea eggplants, looking rather green, with a strong bitterness to their taste. Bitter and stronger. And some packets of green curry.

The exhibition came at an economically depressed moment in New York that provided fertile grounds to establish it as the cornerstone of Tiravanija's practice. We don't use the word *practice* lightly—it's as if the artist were a doctor administering the viewer with a dose of opiate to cure all maladies.

Tiravanija described the work at this time as comparable to reaching out, removing Marcel Duchamp's *Urinal* from its pedestal, reinstalling it back on the wall, and then, in an act of return to its original use, pissing into it.

Interest in the identity of the artistic has now been fully recovered to the point that the work simply is the artist or simply by the artist. Yet there is a prevalent sensibility to his endeavor, one of which: (a) resists artifice; (b) resists the time and space continuum that has been imposed on the ontological structure of artmaking; (c) resists unnecessary staging of a reality which does not exist. [*The ghost has been shifting around now . . . we can hear him going on and on about works which do not necessarily correlate to what the Docent has been speaking about . . .*]

This text was previously presented as part of the exhibition *Rirkrit Tiravanija: A Retrospective*, Rotterdam, Museum Boijmans van Beuningen, 2004.

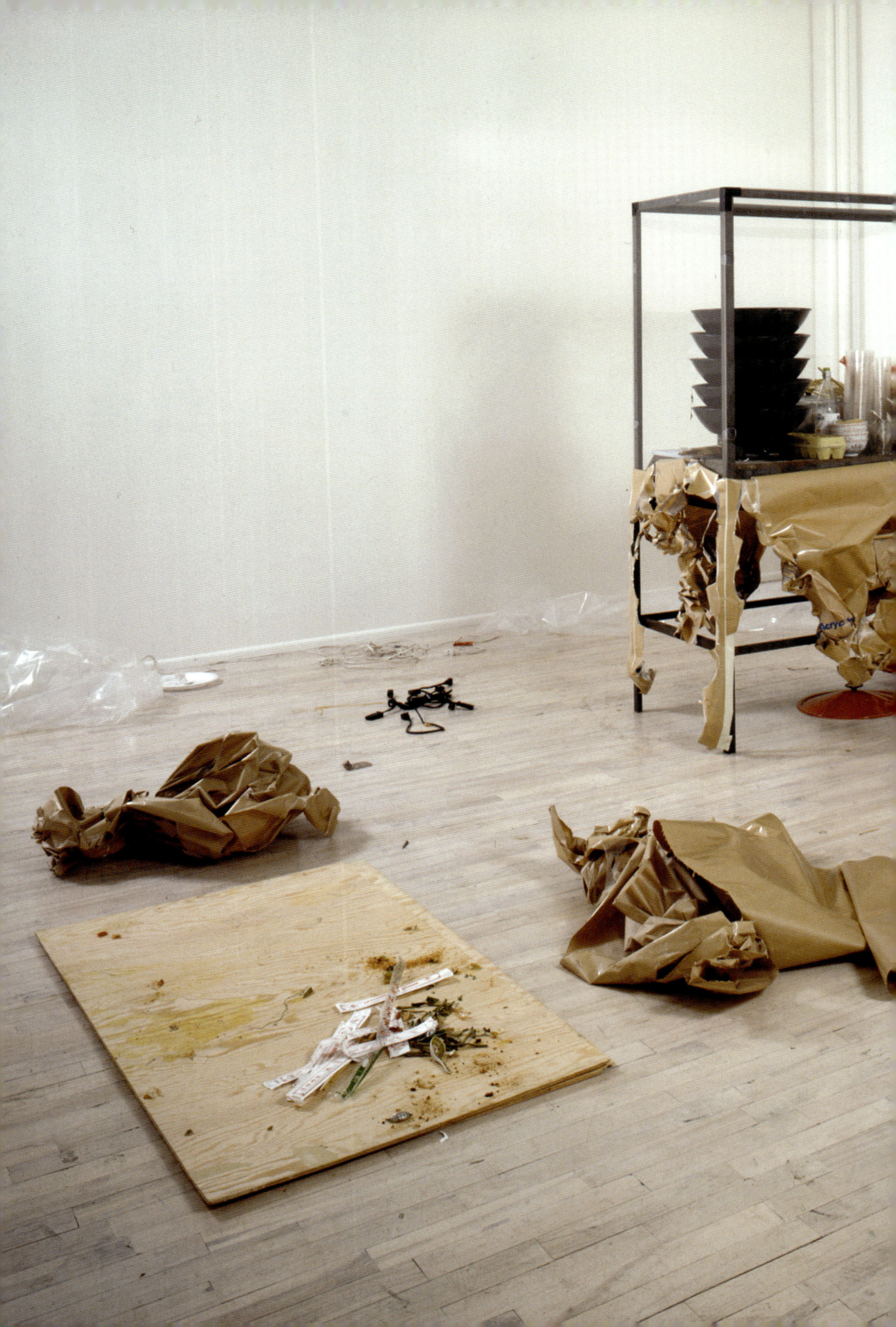

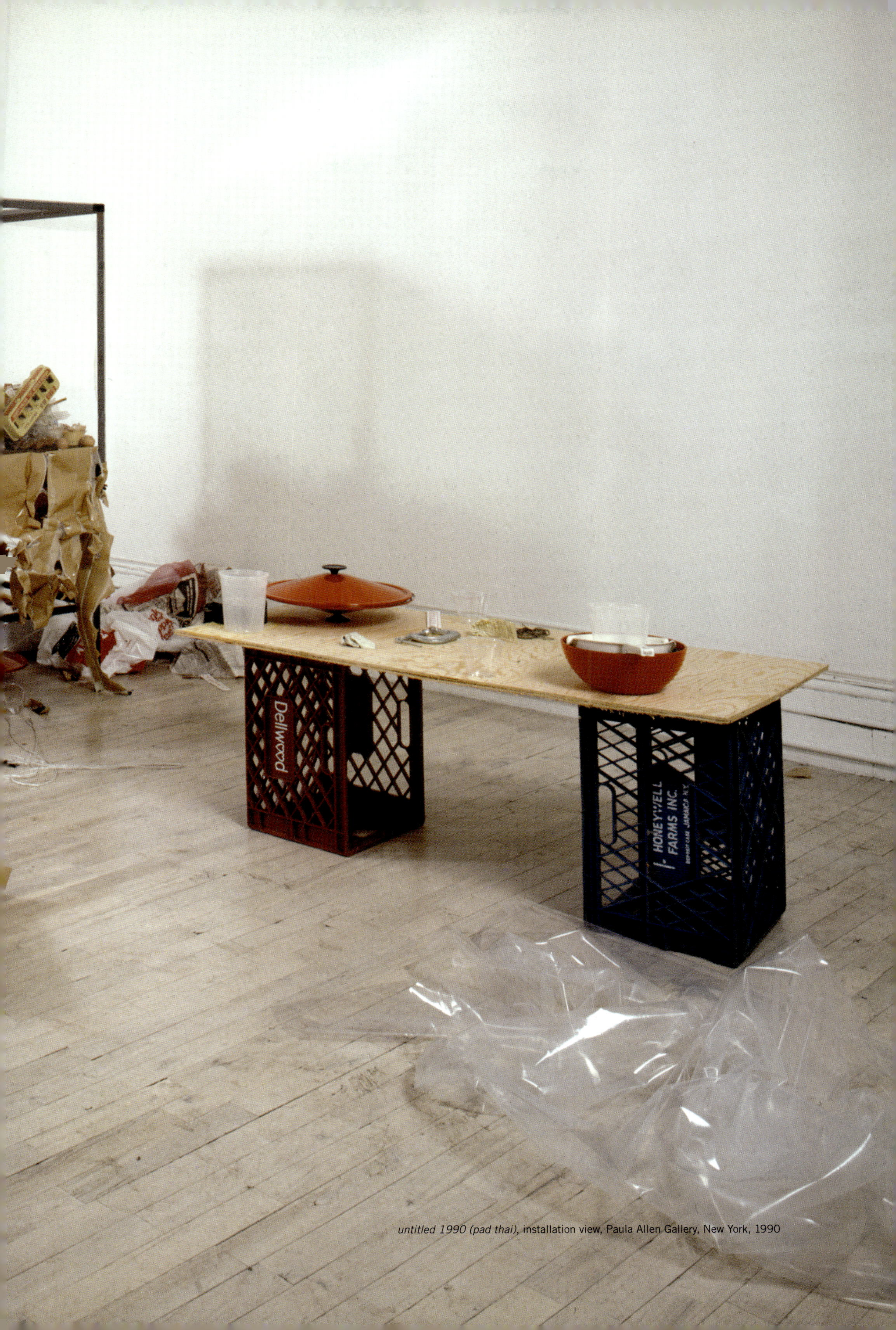

untitled 1990 (pad thai), installation view, Paula Allen Gallery, New York, 1990

ESSAYS

The texts that follow move from ancient dining halls to imagined encounters in bars with Franz Kafka to the open-air kitchens of rural Thailand. Contributed by writers whose practices span art history and criticism, philosophy, and archaeology, these texts elaborate and extend the exhibition's themes—particularly its considerations of hospitality, and of feasting across time and place.

Toast
Anthony Huberman

I'd like to take this opportunity to ask you to join me in toasting and in thanking the artists. All the artists. To any artist who is in this room right now, or to any artist who is not in this room right now: thank you. I realize this seems like a rather common thing to say, but I think it actually isn't common enough. For me, the theme of hospitality evokes the idea that we usually tend to think of the curator as being the artist's host. The curator invites the artist to the institution, and the artist makes an exhibition as a guest of that institution. I'd like to use this toast to suggest that it's actually the other way around. Curators are always the guests of the artists we choose to work with. We knock on their doors and ask whether they would be open to having us spend some time in their studio, a place they so carefully constructed over the course of many years. This is the place of their ideas, their questions, their images, their objects, their convictions, their speculations. As a curator, I am always a guest in this place. It is the artist's territory, the artist's house, and I hope to be able to spend some time there. This doesn't mean that there is no room for my voice to be heard in this place. Like any houseguest at any dinner party, I won't sit quietly at the table without saying a word. That would be rude. I have my own opinions and impressions about subjects that might come up, and I will share them with my host. We all know that a dinner party is only any good when there are active and vivid exchanges between those sharing a meal. And since as a curator, I have knocked on the door of this particular artist for specific reasons, I will have plenty of things to say. And like at any dinner party, those contributions might lead to a lively conversation, or they might not. My host might find my opinions or impressions to be really engaging or might find them to be really boring. In the end, my goal is for an artist to be able to then decide whether or not they want to open their home to me and have me spend more time there. That decision is obviously always theirs to make. The artists I have worked with are the ones who opened their door to me, heard my opinions and impressions, and thought I would be a guest they would enjoy having around for a while. What ultimately comes out of our time spent together, which might be a museum exhibition or a catalogue essay or an event or whatever else, is a curator's chance to represent the experience of having been the artist's guest, a chance to contribute an insight or a perspective that is respectful but hopefully also productive and generative, and sometimes even provocative. It's a chance for a curator to say thank you. In a way, it's a chance to raise a glass, tell some revealing stories, and give an artist a toast. Too many people think of exhibitions as explanation machines, but maybe we could think of an exhibition as a toast, as a way to thank artists, not dissect them. So once again, to all the artists: thank you for your hospitality. Cheers.

Anthony Huberman is Director of The Artist's Institute and Distinguished Lecturer at Hunter College, New York.

A Heavenly Supper: Three Dead White Men and Some Artists in Search of an Explanation

Charles Esche

IMAGINE AN OAK-PANELLED DINING ROOM—the kind you might find in a Viennese aristocrat's home. Around the long, highly polished dining table are three thoughtful but entertaining dead, white men: Franz Kafka, Georges Bataille, and Jacques Derrida. While they eat, they tell each other stories, loudly enough so that everyone else in the room can overhear them. Slowly these other occupants—artists or people like myself who are connected to art—take the remaining seats at the table as their tales unfold.

A Stranger in a European Landscape

The first story begins in the immortal head of Franz Kafka. He takes us to a small settlement in the Bohemian hills. The year is 1922. A slight man sits on the bed in a hotel room. He asks for an explanation. The landlady responds: "You are not from the Castle, you are not from the village, you are not anything. Or rather, unfortunately, you are something, a stranger, a man who is not wanted and is in everybody's way, a man who is always causing trouble . . . a man whose intentions are unknown, a man who has seduced dear little Frieda and who, unfortunately, we must allow to marry her."[1]

Now if Kafka were to look at the world today, he might imagine our dubious hero K walking into a café in Brussels in the center of old, tired western Europe. It's winter. K frowns, takes off his hat and scarf, and approaches the bar. He speaks French with a foreign accent: "I am not from the European Union, I am not from this city, but I have a question." "Of course," replies the barmaid, "you and your question are welcome. We are open and ready to serve you." The intervening ninety years have made quite a difference it seems. In place of brutal sincerity (for that is what we hear from the Czech landlady), we get distant Brussels hospitality, according to which the customer is always right—at least as long as he pays. Our contemporary K is therefore unlikely to be confronted with the infinitely subdivided world of Brussels' politics and language rights in this bar. Nor will he meet his servant girl and future lover, for relationships today are forged through different media. In all events, K will not connect to his fellow drinkers, nor will they touch him emotionally or physically. Instead, he will be smiled at, addressed politely, and left in his isolation. He will be dealt with efficiently and courteously in ways that could never be described as inhospitable, even if they hide a trace of hostility. He will learn much about Brussels history in its museums and a little about its citizens and culture at a distance. It is the way of contemporary travel and it mostly produces modest contentment in the professional tourist. Above all, he will remain a stranger in a way that does not cause trouble or reveal his motivations. In other words, our K has been neutralized and become simply a number to add to visitor statistics. In this, he has made life easier for himself and less stressful for his hosts. Yet he might also have lost something in the process, something we might call "relational" but which I'd rather describe as "social," however roughly that society might treat him. That loss also possibly explains why you are here looking at *Feast* or reading this text in the first place.

Excess

"I will begin with a basic fact: The living organism . . . ordinarily receives more energy than is necessary for maintaining life; the excess energy (wealth) can be used for the growth of a system (e.g. an organism); if the system can no longer grow, or if the excess cannot be completely absorbed in its growth, it must necessarily be lost without profit; it must be spent, willingly or not, gloriously or catastrophically."[2]

Georges Bataille's basic facts are drawn together in his proposal for studying what he calls "the general economy." Picture him seated at our table, laying out a system of analysis that places human production and consumption into the much wider field of society, culture, psychology, war, the biosphere, and the universe. It is a concept whose time seems to have arrived. In the face of the credit crunch, the Euro meltdown and the debt debacle, we may need to think again about what we need to do with our wealth and how we can best squander the profits that we cannot absorb. Reinvesting them in ever more fanciful duplication schemes simply suspends the problem and lands us where we are today—a situation where many citizens of the West seem unwilling to raise questions about the forms of valuation and validation that our post-anticommunist societies have determined.[3] Bataille questions: "Do we spend our excess gloriously enough?" If I'm honest, I'm not very impressed by the way our financial masters have distributed their excess over the last twenty years, but I'd have to admit that they spent a great deal of it on art. Even now, with economies in crisis, the auction houses are exceeding their own expectations and the masters are probably slightly surprised at their ongoing capacity to indulge themselves. We may hope it is temporary, but at this moment of crisis, our leaders seem far more concerned with reconstructing the old system than with thinking its values anew.

Our narrator understands that art was always one of the prime destinations of choice for the excess that needs to be squandered. From popes and sultans to dictators and the super-rich, every great work of art has had the support of political powers—whether individual or collective—and every artist has needed an entrepreneur of some kind to make his or her life liveable. Yet today, in the era of the creative economy, the wires and lines of separation have become tangled and capital market makers pride themselves on their artistry while artworks become sensible investments. Even though the theory of general economy explains that art and business are inevitably linked through the general circulation of energy, Bataille would never want to reduce one to a copy of the other. Examples from the past already show that there were more intense and glorious ways to squander wealth than we currently seem to have the capacity to pursue, even while the rich are richer than they ever were. While art may be a legitimate part of the general economy, it is not produced to add more excess but the absolute opposite. Art should squander and burn it, in ways that are fantastical, celebratory, and hopefully nonviolent. Art is then one of the few means of production that can drain off what might otherwise be used for more pernicious or vainglorious purposes. At the time when there is hardly any room beyond a constantly circulating market for proposals, products, things, and ideas in general, then that squandering must take on other forms than the traditional media of fine art. That's why we might be interested in the kind of exchanges or participations that come together around the galleries at *Feast*. Here are artists not only clinging to the tail of the exuberant economic monster, but feeding its mind and heart in ways it can't quite digest comfortably.

It is Possible to Become Impossible

Jacques Derrida begins: "For there to be hospitality there must be a door. But if there is a door, there is no longer hospitality . . . As soon as there is a door and windows it means that someone has a key to them and consequently controls the conditions of hospitality. There must be a threshold . . . It is (therefore) necessary to be the impossible. If there is hospitality the impossible must be done."[4]

We may imagine that Derrida would prefer to analyze the semantic origins of every word we have been using thus far—*stranger*, *excess*, and *hospitality*, among others—before making a statement of any kind. His colleagues, however, force him to comment. Already in the construction of a new word, *hostipitality*, he reveals the beautiful paradox at the essence of hospitality and its intimate connection to hostility. Hospitality requires a host who has power over a guest, but this control is the opposite of hospitality and contains within it an aggression against the visitor. He also brings us a new metaphor, that of the door, and suggests that it is the location where hospitality might be judged to take place in the world. The door is a line built for the purpose of making an entrance—a place to secure as much as to welcome. The way out of the paradox is to become an unexpected visitor, an intruder who is not repulsed but accepted unconditionally. Such an act would, of course, demand that the potential host becomes a non-host and occupies the same position as the guest, at which point, hospitality performs the impossible or self-destructs. Conceptually it is fascinating, but what happens if it is put into action? To construct real hospitality in three dimensions is to behave wilfully, as though it is possible to become impossible.

I would like to suggest, even for a moment, that this impossibility is one of the capacities to which art can lay claim. While the demands on art from populism, financial rectitude, and cynical inspection sometimes seem to render it impotent in the face of the pragmatist-realists, this impossibility seems to me worthy of the ancient traditions of art and its more recent avant-garde heritage. While Derrida opens the door to "impossibilism," he doesn't follow through, so let us again imagine the table when, at the end of his story, the three dead men are joined by artists and others who are invested in making a (limited) reality out of his theories. Let's say even more directly that many of them are gathered for *Feast* itself. What is needed in the exhibition is an artistic act that escapes its moorings as object or materialized emotion and enters into a fragile relationship with those others who choose to enter into the work and thus refuse to be only guests. Both are running the same risk—the likelihood of failure. This move is certainly not the easiest for an artist to make, but perhaps it is the most necessary in a condition where values need to be reassessed. If we can generalize at all about the artists whose work is included in *Feast*, they all do more than observe social phenomena, as a painter or filmmaker might. Rather, they try to confront conditions and change things through small gestures and weak signals for how it might be otherwise. They offer a hand or a tool and wait to see what will happen. Then they watch, learn, and try again. Many of their projects are long-lasting and require as much a commitment of time as conviction. They fight against producing circulated goods while demanding that some of the excess comes their way. Their agency is at stake; the capacity to act in whatever way is possible in any given circumstance. Sometimes they find they have none. That's why it might often fail in the pragmatic sense, while succeeding as impossibility in the face of the possible.

For our final scene, let's imagine our three dead white men having gathered their artist friends around them, who in turn have gathered the subjects of this impossible hospitality. All now share an idea that the trinity of the stranger, the master of excess, and the non-host are core identities that any radical feasting must negotiate. They see the problems on earth. It is a world where the rich estrange themselves from the rest. A world of ultra-intense, just-in-time circulation of products, where hospitality is rationed at the door and strangers only get the time of day if they can pay for it. In these circumstances, it is a gift to allow other ideas to articulate themselves, even in unlikely quarters. After all, this feast might be just about to begin.

Charles Esche is Director of the Van Abbemuseum, Eindhoven, Netherlands, and co-founder and co-editor of *Afterall* Journal and Afterall Books.

---

[1] Franz Kafka, *The Castle (Der Schloß)*, trans. Anthea Bell (Oxford, UK: Oxford University Press, 1992 [1926]).

[2] Georges Bataille, *The Accursed Share* (*La Part Maudite*), vol. 1 (1967), trans. Robert Hurley (New York: Zone Books, 1991).

[3] I was tempted to write *postcapitalist*, but it still seems too apocalyptic. At least I think there's a consensus that we live in a world where the menace of communism no longer determines political and cultural policy, nor the actions of corporate business. Given how fundamentally communism shaped the West since 1945, it feels right to declare our times to be, at the least, post-anti-communist and hope to be understood.

[4] Extracts from Jacques Derrida, "Hostipitality," *Angelaki Journal of the Theoretical Humanities* 3, no. 5 (1999).

Exotic Hospitality in the Land of Tolerance

Irina Aristarkhova

Prologue

ONE OF MY RELATIVES (let's call him Ivan) was sent to the war in Chechnya during his military service. His unit was abducted and there was a suspicion they were "sold" by one of their own men. They were beaten up and split into smaller groups. The Chechen abductors "sold" him, or probably, passed him as a "gift" to an old couple living in a remote village. Ivan did various manual jobs and was treated well. One day, while working in the field, he decided to leave. He was not sure where to go, so Ivan just walked toward the mountains. He encountered a Chechen man. The man was happy to meet a Russian soldier as he hoped to sell him, or so he said. Ivan did not care as he was tired and just wanted to rest and to eat. While having a meal in the Chechen man's house, they chatted (after all, Russian was the lingua franca in the former USSR). They discovered that each had a younger sister. After feeding Ivan, his host-owner brought him to a visible footpath and said: "Just follow this road all the way, it leads to Dagestan, out of here." And they parted. Ivan was walking for a long time, and then he saw an old man on a donkey crossing the road. It was Dagestan. The Dagestani man asked him: "Where would you like me to take you?" Ivan replied: "To a police post." There he was immediately put on a train with other Russians who were discharged and coming back home. He made a friend on the train and brought him to his house near Moscow for a meal, before his friend left for Siberia. Ivan is now married and has a child.

Europe and Hospitality

Immanuel Kant, who is usually credited with the elaboration of the modern Western conception of ethics and morality, judged nations according to their hospitality: the way they treated strangers in their lands. In his "Anthropology from a Pragmatic Point of View" (a lecture from the 1770s, published posthumously) Kant formulated his opinion on "The Character of the Nations."[1] From this text it becomes clear that he was rare among philosophers in the European tradition in considering hospitality worth thinking about (albeit in a limited manner compared to his development of other concepts), and even worth using to judge national character. Elsewhere Kant clearly criticized Europeans' inability to treat guests with hospitality, and their abuse of the hospitality of others in colonized lands.[2] However, what is more important for us here is that Kant positioned hospitality as a universal criterion for judging national character, though his own view of hospitality remained, problematically, the "true" measurement.

According to Kant, the Germans comprise the most hospitable nation (it is not clear whether this means the most hospitable in Europe or in the world), defined by the way they relate to strangers, and they have—as a result of that?—the best national character: "The Germans are more hospitable to strangers than any other nation . . . "[3] The national character of the French is also defined by their relation to foreigners. Unlike the Germans, whose main national trait is "good character," Kant states that France is a "courteous nation" especially to strangers, and they are also "curious" about others—something that becomes a crucial point in Derrida's analysis of hospitality: the desire for the other and his or her difference. For Kant, this curiosity comes from the "femininity" of the French nobility, who partake in a so-called ladylike way of speaking and behaving: "the language of ladies has become the language shared by all high society. It cannot be disputed at all that an inclination of such a nature must also have influence on the ready willingness in rendering services, helpful benevolence, and the gradual development of human kindness according to principles."[4] Derrida went even further to claim that hospitality is feminine par excellence, as I discuss critically elsewhere.[5] To simplify somewhat the words of Kant, we conclude that the French are kind to foreigners because they use "ladies' language," which makes them, supposedly, want to serve and please. This connection between hospitality and women is lost when one considers the matters of peace and war in Kant and further in Derrida.

With regard to the English people, Kant applies a notion also rare in Western philosophy: he judges national character through kindness. The English, according to Kant, are not only inhospitable to strangers, but even to their own people as a result of a fundamental lack of kindness compared to the French people:

> The English people has a character . . . that is more directly contrasted to that of the French people than to any other, because it renounces all kindness to others and even to people of their own; while kindness has been the most prominent social quality of the French. The English merely claim respect for themselves, so that, by the way, everybody can live according to his own will. For his own countrymen the Englishman establishes great benevolent institutions unheard of among all other peoples. But the foreigner who has been driven to England's shores by fate, and has fallen into dire need, will be left to die on the dunghill because he is not an Englishman, that is, not a human being.[6]

It is possible to argue that Kant's views of national characteristics are rather marginal to his overall corpus of works, especially as they were based on secondary sources and friends' opinions (after all, Kant never traveled). However, Kant himself did not seem to consider these notes marginal: this was almost the last text he prepared for publication before his death. It shows that the elderly Kant did not consider this lecture from the 1770s ungrounded and unimportant: on the contrary, he revisited it at the end of his life. Therefore, we might state with at least some certainty that Kant indeed prioritized the ethics of host-guest relations. This European philosopher who is often heralded as the original reference point for European thought on hospitality, considered national character through a focus on nation's treatment of strangers, foreigners, and their own people.

What is hospitality, then, as defined by Kant? He did not provide a detailed account. His treatment of hospitality was mostly abstract and sketchy. He did not specify whether it entails bodily behavior, the hosting of a guest in one's home, giving shelter, food, or special treatment compared to that normally given to family members. Kant did not elaborate a particular scenario of hospitality: what kind of situation may occur and how one should act. To put it simply, the question is whether it is enough to open the door and provide a glass of water to a thirsty stranger who asked for it—or does hospitality entail a smile, a welcoming to one's home, and an offer before a request is made or even conceived?

Here is the primary Kantian definition, an often-cited passage taken from the text *To Perpetual Peace*: "Hospitality signifies the claim of a stranger entering foreign territory to be treated by its owner without hostility."[7] Both Levinas and Derrida take this definition further, and position hospitality as a much more radical notion, which includes not only treatment of the Other without hostility, but also a gesture of welcome, such as a smile, in addition to providing him or her with a refuge in the time of need. Derrida cites the European tradition of "cities of refuge," and relates it to modern France.[8] Levinas discusses it in terms of Jewish history in times of persecution, war, and exile. Both of them go back to the primary texts of the Talmud, the Koran, and the Bible as the sources for foundational stories of hospitality.[9]

Founding Stories of Hospitality

At the end of one of his texts on hospitality, Derrida recites two "founding scene[s] of Abrahamesque hospitality," one from Genesis, and another one from Judges 19: 23–30. In the second story, the master of the house went out to people who wanted to "penetrate" his pilgrim-guest, and told them:

> "No, my brothers; I implore you, do not commit this crime. This man has become my guest; do not commit such an infamy. Here is my daughter; she is a virgin; I will give her to you. Possess her, do what you please with her, but do not commit such an infamy against this man."
>
> The men would not listen to him. So the Levite took his concubine and brought her out to them. They had intercourse with her and outraged her all night till morning; when dawn was breaking they let her go.
>
> At daybreak the girl came and fell on the threshold of her husband's host, and she stayed there till it was full day. In the morning her husband got up and opened the door of the house . . . (He) picked up his knife, took hold of his concubine, and limb by limb cut her into twelve pieces; then he sent her all through the land of Israel. He instructed his messengers as follows, "This is what you are to say to all the Israelites, 'Has any man seen such a thing from the day Israelites came out of the land of Egypt, until this very day? Ponder on this, discuss it; then give your verdict.'" And all who saw it declared, "Never such a thing been done or been seen since the Israelites came out of the land of Egypt."[10]

At the very end Derrida asks: "Are we the heirs to this tradition of hospitality? Up to what point? Where should we place the invariant, if it is one, across this logic and these narratives? They testify without end in our memory."[11]

Here we come across a situation of refusal of hospitality: the host protected his guest at the expense of "his" woman. She served the role of a substitute or a sacrifice—a subject that Derrida writes about extensively in analyzing hospitality. In that sense, this is not unconditional hospitality—what is asked for is not really provided. What is given out is a substitute. To give out a concubine, a wife, or a daughter is to refuse unconditional hospitality, to be a bad host, ultimately. Or is it? It was refused to those who wanted to harm the guest, thus, jeopardizing the law of hospitality. This situation is not at all abstract for Levinas and Derrida, who both refer it to the Holocaust. European hosts of various nations had the choice of either extending their hospitality to their Others, Jews, communists, Gypsies, homosexuals, and so on—and probably risking their own lives—or abandoning hospitality, leading to the assured suffering and probable death of their guests. Derrida recollects how France disowned its Jewish citizens of Algeria by taking their citizenship away during World War II.[12] This was done voluntarily, without Germany asking for it. The relation between host and guest is still one of the most politicized and complicated relationships, today in particular for immigrant "guests.'"[13]

In order to look at more stories that consider the whole range of unconditional hospitality, we turn to an example from a non-Abrahamic culture. In her excellent book *Sacrificed Wife/Sacrificer's Wife: Women, Ritual and Hospitality in Ancient India* (1995), Stephanie Jamison carefully traces one particular detail of the complex role that hospitality plays in Indian tradition, specifically Vedic texts.[14] It is directly related to "cultures of hospitality." According to Jamison, hospitality is one of the central themes of Sanskrit culture, elaborated and developed: "Hospitality, the appropriate behavior between host and guest, is a theme that infuses Sanskrit literature and as cultural behavior remains crucial to the present day. The duties of a host are set forth quite extensively in the official dharma and grhya manuals, and this codification of hostly behavior can be traced back to earlier texts . . . It is also a constantly recurring motif in literary texts in Sanskrit and other Indic languages."[15]

In one of the founding texts, the first man, Manu, is asked by two guests to give away his wife in order to perform a (hospitality) ritual. When he is ready to give her away to be sacrificed, the god Indra appears and tells him to perform the ritual with his two guests instead (as a punishment for demanding his wife, presumably). After Manu hesitates to kill his two guests, Indra replies: "A lord of guests [host] is master of his guests."[16] Thus Manu's wife is set free. Another version of this story sees the wife actually killed. Jamison explains: "Manu surrenders his possessions and his wife to strangers because of his obligations to hospitality and to the exchange relations on which hospitality depends. The source of the stranger's power and their loss of power is the same: the ambiguous and dangerous qualities intrinsic to the roles of both host and guest. This story expresses succinctly the real anxieties of hospitality that must have accompanied the inherited and dharmically enjoined host-guest relation."[17]

Thus, the anxieties of hospitality, as Jamison calls them, are constitutive to the relations between host and guest. It is played out every time guests enter the house, or another "hospitality situation" occurs. Here, woman, just as in the Biblical story, embodies the symbolic nature of hospitality, and her role, though central, is based on her sacrifice. The importance of offering food at any cost, as a matter constitutive of "pure hospitality" as a center of community, is presented with utmost clarity and enacted in various scenarios. Another example tells us a fable of a fowler who captures a pigeon. Her pigeon husband is devastated, but she insists that her husband welcomes the fowler and asks him the question that sets hospitality in motion: "What can I do for you?" Though this sounds to us today ironically more appropriate for a situation within a "hospitality industry," this question is an embodiment of hospitality. It signifies the vulnerability of the guest and the responsibility of the host, and vice versa. In the fable, the pigeon-husband then attempts to supply the fowler's needs. He first makes a fire as a protection from the cold, and when the fowler asks for food, the pigeon must make the humiliating admission that he has none. After some thought and preparation, he ceremonially enters the fire himself, to make of himself the cooked food he needs to offer the fowler. "Hospitality can hardly exact any higher price than self-immolation."[18]

The question is, how far should one go to practice hospitality, and what price should hospitality exact? This fable elaborates on the scenario of Derrida's unconditional hospitality graphically: the price is anything. Anything should be provided for a guest, otherwise it is not pure hospitality; hospitality demands everything. This is the point of anxiety: the question "What can I do for you?" can be read as "I would do anything for you, my guest." Though it is a test of faith too, it is presented primarily as a test of hospitality as ethics of everyday life and relation with others. Another story comes directly to the point of what unconditional hospitality entails, without compromise or substitute:

> A Brahman comes to Sibi in search of food and orders Sibi to prepare, cook, and serve his son Brhadgarbha as his meal. He agrees and sets about doing it, while the Brahman occupies the preparation time by burning down Sibi's house and its outbuildings. When Sibi finally catches up with him, Sibi merely says: "Your food is ready, sir." But the Brahman refuses it and orders Sibi to eat instead—in other words to eat his own son, whom he has already cooked for the Brahman's meal. Even then Sibi begins to comply, but the Brahman finally relents, snatches his hand away, and restores the son to life. Again it is Sibi's lack of anger and willingness to obey that impress and please the Brahman.[19]

One can never be sure who the guest is. These various details elaborate what pure hospitality means, and what limitations one needs to be aware of. Again it is important to stress that in both traditions, Abrahamic as well as Vedic, women usually play the role of mediator, and rarely appear as receivers of hospitality. It is as though the traditions would crumble if women stopped playing these roles.

Hospitality is born out of constraint and not as a result of abundance and excess. Therefore, hospitality should be found independent of one's means, whether financial, in terms of property, or otherwise. Pure hospitality means to put oneself at risk, to put oneself in a difficult situation—to the point of absurdity, from a "reasonable" point of view. Otherwise it should be normal—to help, welcome, support, give. The position of the guest is precarious, too. One should avoid asking for too much, one tries not to inconvenience one's host. But the guest should also allow the host to be hospitable, to enable his or her hospitality. Certainly, hospitality is not only a matter of individual decision, it is a matter of community and relations within community.

Tolerance and Hospitality

We might notice now that the Kantian definition of hospitality radically differs from the stories detailed above, both Vedic and Abrahamic. For Kant, universal hospitality is a matter of not being hostile to one's guest, provided the guest follows the rules of "good behavior." The guest can hope then to receive a "right of temporary visitation" (what today is known to us as a visa?). Derrida, though beginning with the Kantian definition, is also dissatisfied with it, especially in its application to the two main others of contemporary European culture: the Jew and the immigrant. The turn to hospitality is presented as a result of the urgent need to respond to what is happening in Europe, as revealed in the expression "Fortress Europe." Tolerance is seen as no longer sufficient, or even as hypocritical. The relation between the two concepts, "tolerance" and "hospitality," is not a simple matter of philosophical or political preference. Both have a history and both are part of a particular cultural concern. It would be prudent to assume, then, that if European culture is dissatisfied with the concept and practice of "tolerance," it is because it has a long tradition of it, and relation to it. It is dissatisfied with its own tradition of treating others with tolerance. Discussions on assimilation and on the extent to which immigrant "guests" should follow "host" country's customs seem to be an extension of the European culture of tolerance and its measure. The question is, what should the guest do to be well tolerated and, possibly, accepted as one of "us." Since it has been practiced and elaborated within legal and political discourses, tolerance has become a culturally recognized concept. Explaining why tolerance is not a sufficient concept for Derrida, Giovanna Borradori argues:

> Derrida's treatment of hospitality comes straight from Kant. Hospitality is a more compassionate, and ultimately effective, alternative to tolerance. Tolerance is, according to Derrida, a paternalistic concept irremediably tainted by religious, and specifically Christian, implications developed in the Europe of the 1500s. For him, tolerance is a less neutral moral and political concept than it makes itself out to be. Also, he is bothered by the lack of authentic openness to the other that tolerance entails; the phrase "threshold of tolerance," which was used in France to indicate the limit beyond which it was no longer decent to ask a national community to welcome any more foreigners and immigrants, reveals this problematic implication.[20]

Indeed, Derrida saw in hospitality a deconstructive potential. It is tolerance, however, and not hospitality, which is institutionalized in European societies. Hospitality is a much more unusual concept in Europe. A question we are likely to hear is, "How much longer can we tolerate this situation with immigrants?"; the issue of the limits of tolerance is being used in political campaigns across Europe.

It is problematic to appropriate hospitality as "one's own" on the basis of its universality. That is why I would disagree profoundly with Derrida when he says that "[not] only is there a culture of hospitality, but there is no culture that is not also a culture of hospitality. All cultures compete in this regard and present themselves more hospitable than the others. Hospitality—this is culture itself."[21] The phrase "every culture is a culture of hospitality" can be also read as an appropriation of hospitality, through the implication that my culture is a culture of hospitality. This seems problematic particularly in relation to those cultures that have championed tolerance and the institution of visa.

To summarize: When we appropriate a concept of hospitality as ours, when we assume European hospitality just because "every culture is a culture of hospitality," we violate important historical, philosophical, and cultural differences. After examining examples from the Vedic tradition, it becomes clearer that hospitality, until recently, has been an underdeveloped concept in European thought, a marginal concern. Those scenarios are far from the Kantian idea of temporary visitation. They can help us further inform the scenarios of "unconditional hospitality" offered by Derrida. The Abrahamic, the Vedic, and the recent European definitions of hospitality, however, include women within host-guest relations mostly as mediators, or silent providers of familial, domestically based hospitality and the feeling of "being at home with oneself." Finally, European tradition developed a discourse of tolerance, which subsequently spread to other Western countries and is most commonly expressed in the idea of tolerating the differences of guests and immigrants through some unifying basis. This basis usually takes the form of the "European values" of democracy, fraternity, freedom, equality, and—tolerance. I have tried to argue here that one cannot simply replace tolerance with hospitality, because the former has a much richer meaning both socially and institutionally within Europe. The history of tolerance needs to be examined more carefully while we move toward desiring hospitality—to make sure that one does not collapse into the other, just as it is problematic to conflate cultures of hospitality with cultures of tolerance.

Epilogue

No need for stories, poems and myths that might shock European readers by their "exotic hospitality" of eating sons, cooking oneself, or being hospitable to one's murderers. Ivan was at war, and he went to kill people—this is why soldiers are sent to war. Two people saved his life, by offering him food, shelter, and direction, though they could well have used their host status in the opposite way. Ivan is alive today because of unconditional hospitality. "Chechens are people. Dagestanis are people. We are bastards." That is all Ivan has to say today "on the character of the nations."

Irina Aristarkhova is Associate Professor of Art & Design, History of Art, and Women's Studies at the University of Michigan.

This essay is a revised version of a text originally published in *Manifesta Coffee Break—Refugee—Hospitality—Occupation: Visual Art and Contemporary Curatorial Work in a Changing Europe*, ed. Paul Domela (Liverpool: Liverpool Biennial of Contemporary Art, 2005), 65–74.

[1] Immanel Kant, *Anthropology from a Pragmatic Point of View*, trans. Mary J. Gregor (The Hague: Nijhoff, 1974).

[2] Kant, *Pragmatic Point of View*; and Immanuel Kant, *To Perpetual Peace: A Philosophical Sketch*, trans. Ted Humphrey (Indianapolis: Hackett Publishing Company, 2003 [1795]), www.mtholyoke.edu/acad/intrel/kant/kant1.htm.

[3] Kant, *Pragmatic Point of View*, 233–34. According to a European Union report, Germany has taken the highest number of immigrants per capita in the last two decades, compared to other EU nations, with the United Kingdom coming second. Source: European Social Statistics: Migration. European Commission (Luxemburg: Office for the Official Publications of European Communities, 2002).

[4] Kant, *Pragmatic Point of View*, 228.

[5] Irina Aristarkhova, "Hospitality and the Maternal," in *Hypatia: A Journal of Feminist Philosophy* 27, no. 1 (2010/2012), accessed December 14, 2011, http://onlinelibrary.wiley.com/doi/10.1111/j.1527-2001.2010.01147.x/abstract. Irina Aristarkhova, *Hospitality of the Matrix: Philosophy, Biomedicine, and Culture* (New York: Columbia University Press, 2012).

[6] Kant, *Pragmatic Point of View*, 230.

[7] Kant, *Perpetual Peace: A Philosophical Essay*, trans. Mary Campbell Smith (New York and London: Garland Publishing, 1972), 137.

[8] Jacques Derrida, *Adieu To Emmanuel Levinas*, trans. Pascale-Anne Brault and Michael Naas (Stanford, CA: Stanford University Press, 1999); Jacques Derrida, *Acts of Religion*, ed. Gil Anidjar (New York and London: Routledge, 2002); Jacques Derrida and Anne Dufourmantelle, *Of Hospitality: Anne Dufourmantelle Invites Jacques Derrida to Respond*, trans. Rachel Bowlby (Stanford, CA: Stanford University Press, 2000); and Jacques Derrida, *On Cosmopolitanism and Forgiveness* (New York and London: Routledge, 2001).

[9] Emmanuel Levinas, *Totality and Infinity: An Essay on Exteriority*, trans. Alphonso Lingis (The Hague: Nijhoff, 2002 [1961]).

[10] Judges, quoted in Derrida and Dufourmantelle, *Of Hospitality*, 153–54.

[11] Ibid., 154.

[12] See Ibid., 143, and Derrida, *Adieu To Emmanuel Levinas*.

[13] For an excellent book on this topic, see Mireille Rosello, *Postcolonial Hospitality: The Immigrant as Guest* (Stanford, CA: Stanford University Press, 2001).

[14] Stephanie Jamison, *Sacrificed Wife/Sacrificer's Wife: Women, Ritual and Hospitality in Ancient India* (Oxford, UK: Oxford University Press, 1995). Jamison uses various terms, such as *Vedic tradition, Aryan society, Sanskrit texts*, and refers to their members as "our Indo-European ancient ancestors." I use the Jamison's text here because it also allows me to provide a gender sensitive reading of Vedic definition of hospitality. Since this article was published in 2005, more comparisons between European and Indian notions of hospitality have appeared, for example: Silby K. George "Hospitality as Openness to the Other: Levinas, Derrida, and the Indian Hospitality Ethos" *Journal of Human Values* 15, no. 1 (2009): 29–47.

[15] Jamison, *Sacrificed Wife/Sacrificer's Wife*, 157.

[16] Ibid., 22–23.

[17] Ibid., 25.

[18] Ibid., 163.

[19] Ibid., 169.

[20] Nader Vossoughian "Conversation with Giovanna Borradori: Derrida, Habermas, and Philosophy in a Time of Terror" (2003), *Interview*, January 20, 2004; accessed February 10, 2005, http://www.agglutinations.com/archives/000033.html.

[21] Derrida, *Acts of Religion*, 360–61.

The Anti-Angelic Host: Reading the Politics of Hosting Culture Through the Writing of Virginia Woolf

Jan Verwoert

TIMING MATTERS! The way in which power is divided and affirmed depends on the ability to act on cue when performing one's part in the social game. The dinner party, banquet, and ball are classic occasions for this game to be played. But since, in the age of "hire and fire," life at work is a permanent talent contest, the pressure to perform and charm is on, perpetually. Recognition is awarded on the grounds of who can deliver a good show of potential on cue, when required. The temporal logic governing the economy of recognition is therefore that of the theatrical event—dramatic build-up, crisis, triumph, or defeat—is what a fast-paced, competitive culture thrives on, as it produces its real-life (soap) operas in everyday social scenarios.

What is obscured by the enhanced theatricality of contemporary "high performance" culture, however, is an altogether different horizon of social temporality: the way time flows offstage when social relations are forged, fostered, and maintained over long periods of time to allow for social services to be provided, cultural events to be planned, and audiences to be built. This is the labor of constant care. It needs to be invested to maintain the social stage on which competitive performers can then make their appearance. The irony is: work that must be done to host an event is highly uneventful. The temporal horizon of sustained social communication, preparation, administration, and maintenance is that of long durations. Many small acts (e-mails, phone calls, etc.) eventually add up to something. But in themselves they are too many, too unspectacular, and too extended over time to be convertible into the theatrical logic of instantaneous onstage delivery. The award ceremony organizer is hardly ever the prize winner.

This is why a painful contradiction has developed in contemporary society: Providing social services and producing cultural events is a growth industry. Still, we lack the concepts to recognize the value of this form of labor as such. The heightened theatricality of "high performance" work culture, on the contrary, is rather geared toward rendering the value of long-term, offstage labor invisible, as it restores power to the age-old role model of the charismatic performer who knows how to play it fast. The contradiction between the invisible labor of hosting and the power of onstage performance, however, has long been present in our culture. In many ways, it seems, we may have technologically upgraded our lifestyles but emotionally never fully outgrown certain traditional value terms and role models.

A wide array of socio-psychological tools of analysis are by now at our disposal to dissect how power relations are negotiated and imbalances reified in the arena of human affairs. And these tools are crucial! Beyond analysis, however, the challenge is to touch on those residual intuitions that determine how we feel we should play our part in the social game. For even if we know that certain things are wrong, that doesn't mean we wouldn't still viscerally experience—and intuitively act in accordance with—certain expectations or feelings of entitlement that remain present in the social fabric (and hence make us subject ourselves to particular demands, acquire and develop some skills and sensitivities rather than others).

Art and literature do arguably have the capacity to tap into, and hence enable us to work through, the emotions that shape our experience on a precognitive level. One stunningly acute articulation of the social intuitions driving the interplay between a dedicated host and a cast of cultural performers takes place in Virginia Woolf's novel, *To the Lighthouse*. The relevance of her writing is undiminished—if not increased—because she bears witness to a historical threshold moment in which modern role models for highly individualized cultural performances are not just becoming available but coexisting and clashing with more traditional models of organizing the social. If we admit that we have skirted along this threshold rather than ever fully crossing it, Woolf's writing indeed gives us an invaluable chance to grasp, on a deeply intuitive level, how the sensitivities of those who host the social relate to the assumptions of those who perform in it. Phenomenologically that means: She permits us to sense how social time is made to flow, who makes it flow, who goes with that flow, and profits from it—and thereby hopefully enables us to exorcise some of the demons and recognize some of the potentials that linger within the horizon of hosting (and) cultural performance.

The Invisible Labor of the Host

In *To The Lighthouse,* Virginia Woolf lays out a scenario of exemplary hospitality: A family of ten, the Ramsays, spends the annual summer vacation with guests in their country house on the Scottish coast. An aged scientist, a zealous young university lecturer, a faded poet (and opium addict), a couple about to be engaged, and the central female character, a young painter named Lily Briscoe, have what appears to be a wonderful time with the family. The flow of conversation is pleasant and easy on long walks and during dinners. People come together to talk, yet equally happily retreat again to pursue their own activities and read, write, paint, or play in the house or garden. There is a perfectly relaxed, organic rhythm to the manner in which the expanded family convenes and disbands, reassembles, and scatters again. Clocks seem to have stopped ticking. The pace at which days pass into nights indeed seems set only by the pulse of communal life, by the manner in which the heart of the expanded family beats as it contracts and expands again. The temporal experience the novel imparts is thus one of sheer social time, freed from the constraints imposed by the temporal economies of work and commerce. The place that allows time to flow in this manner is the house and garden at the coast, yes, but these in turn are sited in a world opened up by Woolf's words. In this sense, the space in which social time flows freely is her language, spaced and paced in a manner that is uniquely hers: stunningly steady and succinct, synched to the frequency at which a highly alert mind perceives the colors and contours of the environment: in a crisp, clear flow of impressions. In this sense, the scenario of exemplary hospitality is a situation in the world as well as an occurrence in a particular writer's language.

Yet, while Woolf tends to the cast of her characters with her words like a most attentive host would, the manner in which she portrays the act of hosting in the story is far from ambivalent. For it is very much through the eyes of Lily Briscoe, a young modern woman with artistic ambitions, that she describes the function of the host as wedded to the traditional role of the lady of the house, which the older woman, Mrs. Ramsay, has performed for her entire life. Their relationship is complicated by the fact that Lily Briscoe cannot hope to fully bridge the gap that her modern position creates between her and Mrs. Ramsay. From the latter's traditional point of view, finding a man to marry is a priority and she deems the desire for artistic accomplishments instead as inappropriate for a woman. As a result, sympathy and support in regard to her pursuits is something the younger of the two knows she cannot receive from the older. Still, Lily seeks to be close to the lady of the house in order to fully comprehend the secret of her hosting skills and honor the constant invisible labor through which she renders the inspired conviviality possible. She recognizes that this intuitive knowledge lies in the secrets of a special savoir faire, "which if one could spell them out, would teach one everything, but they would never be offered openly, never made public."[1] Between the lines, it becomes ever more clear that the very impression that social life finds its own organic rhythm all by itself is deceptive. This is because there is a force behind the process in which things come to seem that way: The lady of house, mother and host, has perfected the art of invisible social engineering. She is the heart producing the even pulse of conviviality. She senses and preempts possible disturbances, seats people around the dinner table in just the right pairings, and, with her imperceptible touch, erases any blemish and comforts any ego that might have been bruised by the hard words of an unthinking speaker. Remaining invisible—like the divine hand of providence—is the triumph of her art, the proof of her perfection as an accomplished host.

Woolf's portrayal of the art of hosting is hence equally an act of paying respect and a betrayal. For, by rendering the host visible, Woolf undoes the host's own understanding of her role by making her an actor walking the stage rather than silently choreographing the social scene from the sidelines. So, despite the fact that Woolf hosts her host in a language that portrays her in the most movingly honorable way, there is next to no intimacy to the relationship between the two women (Lily and Mrs. Ramsay). This is largely because, while the host is in touch with everyone in the expanded family and touches up every mark of discomfort, she remains emotionally untouchable herself. Close to everyone and always on hand when needed, Mrs. Ramsay is infinitely distant and out of reach, alone in her world of ceaseless care. At the end of a long day spent creating the social, Woolf describes how she retreats, literally spent, into the splendid isolation of her self-less mind:

> He went. Immediately, Mrs. Ramsay seemed to fold herself together, one petal closed in another, and the whole fabric fell in exhaustion upon itself, so that she had only strength enough to move her finger, in exquisite abandonment to exhaustion, across the page of Grimm's fairy story, while there throbbed through her, like the pulse in a spring which has expanded to its full width and now gently ceases to beat, the rapture of successful creation.[2]

Yet, as she is the force animating the social, her being is immanent to the social fabric and therefore cannot be extracted from that fabric in the form of one distinct persona. Her contours are blurry because she exists in all there is, socially. To talk to her, one who would have to talk to the society she creates as a whole. Which one can't. She is absent from her creation by virtue of being present in each and every of its aspects. It's a paradox of theological proportions! Which Woolf chooses to emphasize by means of a sudden plot twist: The host, caring for others, never for herself, hence neither acknowledging nor sharing the knowledge of her decaying health, dies from one day to the next, leaving the world that only she could animate in ruins.

Performing Affect, Consuming the Social, Killing the Angel

Woolf portrays the painful irony of the situation in a manner full of understanding, though it borders on social caricature performed with subtle black humor. The official head of the family, Mr. Ramsay, as husband of the host, is a distinguished thinker and writer. He is not a bad man. Yet still, he is so entrapped in his own sense of entitlement that, despite his education and intelligence, he is largely oblivious to the labor of his wife's considerable efforts to build and sustain his daily reality. Stumbling through the ruins of this reality after her death, he falls back on the only language of feelings that his literary and philosophical education have provided: the idiom of the romantic quest, the words of yearning and lament. He takes his children out on a boat trip in the sea to the lighthouse that they have been looking at from their garden. Out on the waves, in the boat with what is left of his family, the drama of the occasion prompts him to express his desperation at the loss of his wife: a theatrical display of grand emotion, well staged against the sublime backdrop of the solitary tower out at sea:

> Sitting in the boat, he bowed, he crouched himself, acting instantly his part —the part of the desolate man, widowed, bereft; and so called up before him in hosts people sympathizing with him; staged for himself as he sat in the boat, a little drama; which required of him decreptitude and exhaustion

> and sorrow (he raised his hands and looked at the thinness of them, to confirm his dream) and then there was given him in abundance women's sympathy, and he imagined how they would soothe him and sympathize with him, and so getting in his dream some reflection of the exquisite pleasure women's sympathy was to him, he sighed and said gently and mournfully,
>
> *But I beneath a rougher sea,*
> *Was whelmed in deeper gulfs than he,*
>
> so that the mournful words were heard quite clearly by them all.[3]

It's not that his emotions are not somehow also heartfelt. Still they are mobilized with the aim to produce an effect on a public and thus remain inseparable from the theatrical techniques intuitively rehearsed to generate that effect. The inherent theatricality of his emotion evinces the gap that separates his mental world from the universe that Mrs. Ramsay created and sustained. His moment of emotional release is (unconsciously, yet carefully staged as) momentary, instant, eventful, and climatic; dramatically visible. Her emotional labor, on the contrary has been invisible, lifelong, constant, with no release other than death. His intuitive feeling for dramatic timing, momentary built-up and climatic effect couldn't be more different from her sustained sensitivity for the long-durational processes of creating social time. What happens on his stage fails to touch on the emotions she invested by creating this stage. Very sadly so. But while Woolf portrays the head of the family as a self-important, over-educated fool, she equally makes it clear that he merely does what a man in his position, at this time, would have felt and done. He represents what society entitles him to be, a position that his wife, in fact, also considered her vocation to enable and support. He is partially, if not largely, her creation, too.

And, after all, he is a writer. Which brings a different irony into play. For Woolf is a writer, too. And her alter ego in the novel, the young woman painter, is as ambitious as he is in his quest for the grand and sublime. So in many ways, ironically, her speaking position is as removed from that of the lady of the house she honors, as it is close to the man she mocks. His role is utterly defined and limited by the laws of his patriarchal privileges. Still, he lives the life of the mind that the young female protagonist also pursues. So much of what she says about him, *mutatis mutandis*, could also, in one way or another, at some point in her future career, apply to her. One thing they share, for instance, is a sense of ambition (and its discontents). She is at the beginning of her career and still troubled by doubts about how and whether to embark on it. He is already well established, but similarly tormented by doubts. For even though his works are known, he believes he hasn't yet received the recognition he deserves. For years now, he has been writing on his putative magnum opus, the definite articulation of his thought system to outmatch his opponents and set the record straight. Even if she doesn't subscribe to that particular brand of megalomania, the female protagonist nevertheless admits to searching for accomplishments in her art and judges herself severely on these grounds.

Finally, both effectively consume the sociability that is generated for them by the lady of the house. Arguably, she does so consciously, while he simply takes for granted that the household is maintained and the entertainment of guests arranged for him. Instead of showing his appreciation, the head of the family instead much more frequently uses the social environment created for him as a welcome backdrop against which to stage the singularity of his putative genius (e.g. by pointing out the intellectual shortcomings of his guests to his wife, by secretly lamenting her limited capacity to comprehend the flights of his intellect, and by harboring the feeling that he would have written better books had he not compromised his philosophical pursuits by committing himself to the prosaic reality of married life . . .). Still, consciously or unthinkingly, as producers of art and thinking, both characters effectively remain consumers of the social life, space, and time that their host creates for them. What makes the difference is, the manner in which Woolf manifests her debt, as a writer and artist to the host, by dedicating *To the Lighthouse* to the description of her art, and hosting the host in her language.

But there is a catch. For while she uses her art to honor the host, Woolf equally keeps pointing to the tensions that, for her, persist between her commitment to artistic pursuits and the moral embrace of the social responsibilities wedded to the traditional role of the female host. In a most pronouncedly aggressive manner, she in fact speaks out against the constraints of the traditional role in her essay "Professions for Women" (originally delivered as a speech to the London National Society for Women's Service on January 21, 1931). Here, she asserts that the only way to liberate her practice and write freely was to actively renounce the expectations placed on her as a woman and reject the role of the lady of the house she had previously portrayed in the guise of Mrs. Ramsay:

> In those days—the last of Queen Victoria—every house had its Angel. And when I came to write I encountered her with the very first words. The shadow of her wings fell on my page; I heard the rustling of her skirts in the room . . . I turned upon her and caught her by the throat. I did my best to kill her. My excuse, if I were to be had up in a court of law, would be that I acted in self-defence. Had I not killed her she would have killed me. She would have plucked the heart out of my writing. For, as I found, directly I put pen to paper, you cannot review even a novel without having a mind of your own, without expressing what you think to be the truth about human relations, morality, sex. And all these questions, according to the Angel of the House, cannot be dealt with freely and openly by women; they must charm, they must conciliate, they must—to put it bluntly—tell lies if they are to succeed. Thus, whenever I felt the shadow of her wing or the radiance of her halo upon my page, I took up the inkpot and flung it at her. She died hard. Her fictitious nature was of great assistance to her. It is far harder to kill a phantom than a reality. She was always creeping back when I thought I had despatched her. Though I flatter myself that I killed her in the end, the struggle was severe; it took much time that had better have been spent upon learning Greek grammar; in roaming the world in search of adventures. But it was a real experience; it was an experience that was found to befall all women writers at the time. Killing the Angel in the House was part of the occupation of a woman writer.[4]

So there is a strong ambiguity to the position that Woolf takes vis-à-vis the savoir faire of hosting associated with the traditional role of the lady of the house. On the one hand, she shows the utmost appreciation for the deep understanding of human affairs and power to create social life by hosting the host as the pivotal figure of her novel. On the other hand, she pronouncedly speaks out against the tacit moral imperative to "charm" and "conciliate" that forced the traditional practitioners of the art of hosting to curb their powers in relation to public appearance. How are we today to think through this tension at the heart of her thoughts?

Contemporary Lines of Flight: Angels with Inkpots? Or Anti-Angelic Hosts?

As Woolf herself writes, the spirit of the Angel of the House is a revenant from another era. Still, its invisible spectral presence perpetually grows stronger in the field of social services and cultural production today: The more demand to turn culture into a spectacle increases, the more the labor of cultural workers organizing those spectacles in hours and hours of communicative work becomes invisible. The labor behind the scenes is effaced by the high visibility of the result it produces. While some aspects of the traditional gender roles have changed and overt patriarchal structures are in the process of being dismantled in many places, certain specters still return frequently to rear their ugly heads. The strong focus on the performative aspects of work in Post-Fordist working environments has effectively made working culture more theatrical. The manner in which the value of work is in many fields today determined in the form of so-called "performance evaluations" effectively privileges those who know how to put on a good show in the opportune moments. It massively disadvantages those whose labor cannot be rendered visible in the mode of instant impressive delivery required when the eyes of evaluators are on you.

Since one central aspect of hosting (cultural events, artists, audiences) involves the careful maintenance and cultivation of social relations, its temporal horizon is that of long durations, and its medium are many small communicative acts (phone calls, e-mails, conversations) through which, as Woolf puts it, "the thing is made that endures:"[5] i.e., the social tie is tied and the trust is generated on the basis of which collaborations in culture lead to the production of events. None of this can effectively be rendered visible as such, when evidence of professional credentials are expected to be produced on the spot by deans, donors, board members, shareholders, media representatives, etc., during an official or unofficial performance review. To speak about the kind and amount of mundane work—the daily correspondences and financial housekeeping—that actually has to be done to prepare an event is hardly going to sound eventful enough to create the kind of buzz needed to sell yourself as a promising managerial talent or inspired leader. In the cultural field, moreover, the unofficial reviews often enough happen during dinner parties or festive events, so the ability to impressively perform and confirm one's potentials when drunk further reinforces traditional patterns and privileges. Created and expanded over centuries, the patriarchal culture offers a vast repertoire of roles to play, things to say, and gestures that may be performed by a man who needs to charmingly assert his authority in an inebriated state (and "ham things up" without losing face). This repertoire seems intuitively accessible to men; its successful use reinforced by by the relentless depiction and repetition of such gestures by male characters within popular media; there is little risk of misunderstandings. The repertoire available for women is still limited by the relative short history of their access to public power positions.

A service-oriented labor culture acknowledges social communication as a form of work. Consequently, the work of the mediators and communicators, which, in the days of Woolf and up until fairly recently, would have been understood as a secondary form of productivity has today been acknowledged as a primary force in the production of culture. In the arts, the appreciation of conceptual work that consists of small communicative acts or takes on the form of long-term projects testifies to this development, as does the acceptance of the curator as a peer to the artist in terms of creative potentials and cultural credits. In parts of the cultural sphere attuned to these developments, a lot of the poses for dramatically staging the presumptive singularity of male genius that Woolf targeted, have therefore been rendered (partially) unusable. This shift is one important factor for the change in the cultural field brought about by the work of women artists and organizers. Still, the forces of resistance against these changes continue to be strong. Very much so, because the pressure to perform that has risen parallel to the changes in the working culture in turn strengthens the dominance of conventional patterns and power structures in cultural institutions as well as on the art market and in popular media where grand gestures and fast timing matter more than ever. CEOs, museum directors, and stand-up comedians, for instance, today still tend to be predominantly male. And not a few rely on invisible task forces of angels to run their house from its office while they front the operation and take credit for it in public. This situation is as unacceptable now as it always was.

This is not the end of the story. To host the hosts of culture in a culture and language attentive to the invisible sides of the art of hosting continues to be a crucial challenge. And here Woolf remains exemplary in her manner of attuning her language to an awareness of the long-term processes in which this labor is realized, without forcing them to prove their worth in theatrical gestures that would only deny their own modalities of constituting cultural values. Still, Woolf hurls the ink pot at the angel. Is she right to do so? Would it, from a contemporary perspective, not be more just to tell the story of angels armed with ink pots: of hosts who know the secrets of the invisible art of hosting as well as the techniques of commanding the laws of representation? On one hand, this question is rhetorical. And the answer is, "Of course." On the other hand, however, Woolf's insistence on breaking the tradition—and resistance against simply accommodating the knowledge inherent to the traditional role of the lady of the house in her modern understanding of feminist cultural agency—needs to be taken seriously. For what she attacks here is not simply a convention but very much also a morality. She seeks to exorcise the moral sense of duty to be blamed for the intuitive internalization of unjustified social demands. If we attempt to think about this symbolic act together with her dedication to hosting the host in her language, then the challenged to be faced is: What concepts and criteria can we mobilize to embrace the labor of hosting as a primary form of cultural production without taking recourse to morality? What would an adequately anti-angelic language be that debunks a conventional repertoire of self-sacrificial altruism and instead acknowledges that hosting could be as amoral a joy and practice as writing?

Jan Verwoert is a Berlin-based writer and critic. He teaches within the Piet Zwart Institute, Rotterdam, the de Appel curatorial program, the Netherlands, and the Ha'Midrasha School of Art, Tel Aviv.

---

[1] Virginia Woolf, *To the Lighthouse* (San Diego, New York, London: Harcourt, 1981 [1927]), 51.

[2] Ibid., 38.

[3] Ibid., 166.

[4] Virginia Woolf, "Professions for Women" in *Women and Writing*, ed. Michèle Barrett (San Diego, New York, London: Harcourt, 1942), 57–63, 59f. I thank Melinda Braathen for sharing this essay with me.

[5] Woolf, *To the Lighthouse*, 105.

Feasts and Philosophers: Continuity and Change in Theories of Taste

Carolyn Korsmeyer

DOUBTLESS ALL BUT THE MOST ascetic philosophers have feasted from time to time. Eating, drinking, and the sense of taste, however, have rarely entered into their theories except by way of caution: Beware the indulgence of the body and its tempting pleasures! The distinction between the satisfaction of physical appetite and the contemplative transports of aesthetic enjoyment has been promoted more or less continuously since the advent of modern theories of the arts. In 1762, one of the leaders of the burgeoning field of aesthetics confidently wrote: "The fine arts are designed to give pleasure to the eye and ear, disregarding the inferior senses."[1] This commonplace sentiment from Henry Home, Lord Kames summed up the assumption that objects of smell, touch, and taste fall outside the scope of art, an idea that was firmly grounded in theories of beauty, aesthetic value, and the proper nature of appreciation. One can only imagine how Lord Kames and his friends might wonder at the varieties of sensuous and reflective experiences offered by *Feast: Radical Hospitality in Contemporary Art*, though I like to think that at least one of them, the iconoclast David Hume, would have been both baffled and delighted.

The distinction between aesthetic and gustatory taste—as well as the presumption of the superiority of the former over the latter—represents a view of sense experience expressed in philosophical writings as early as Plato, though it became a central point of aesthetic theory only in the European Enlightenment. The idea is not universal. In the traditions of China, Japan, and India, for example, the severance of aesthetic and gustatory tastes was evidently never as assiduous as it became with the rise of the notion of fine art or *beaux arts* in Europe.[2] In the Euro-American tradition, however, the separation of two varieties of taste became especially pronounced in the eighteenth century, at the same time that the concept of "fine" art became detached from a larger and more heterogeneous category that also included decorative and applied arts.[3]

This was but one of a number of mutually implicative, conceptual changes that have long influenced perspectives on the sense of taste. Of special importance is the fact that the development of modern aesthetic theory arose in the wake of a philosophical shift that identified beauty as a brand of pleasure rather than an objective quality. As a consequence, the distinction between the satisfactions of appetite and the more contemplative pleasures of the aesthetic kind seemed especially necessary. The grounds for this attitude are not hard to understand, for even if beauty is a type of pleasure, this pinnacle of value is not reducible to simple animal satisfactions. Eating, drinking, and sex represent the animal part of our nature in many cultural traditions, for they are activities that we share with other living creatures. But the creation of arts and the development of sciences are strictly human accomplishments. It stands to reason, therefore, that the bodily pleasures delivered by taste, smell, and touch must be of a different kind from the contemplative satisfactions of art. In the philosophic shorthand often employed, aesthetic taste is "disinterested," meaning that no personal desire or appetite need be satisfied to arouse pleasure; in contrast, bodily pleasures remain "interested."[4]

Whether taste can operate "aesthetically" and whether food and drink should be counted among the "arts" pose two different questions, although they tend to arise together in discussion. In addition to the brief against the pleasures of a bodily sense is the fact that the objects of taste—food and drink—are perishable. The table produces only temporary achievements, quickly consumed, in comparison to the museum and gallery where artworks can hang for centuries, or to the concert hall, where masterworks can be performed repeatedly. Moreover, in appreciating food, one causes it to disappear, whereas generations may stand before more enduring products such as buildings, paintings, and sculptures; and music—at least scored music—can be heard over and over across time.[5] Finally, there is an intractable, practical consideration that often dominates the value ascribed to things we eat. We can live without art, but food has instrumental value that has little to do with its aesthetic merits, since nutrition is needed to sustain a living organism. Such, anyhow, is the standard brief against the aesthetic and the artistic standing of food and drink.

From the vantage of the twenty-first century, the assumption that actual eating does not represent an exercise of taste in the aesthetic sense might appear to be merely a relic of older sensibilities. This would be an overly simple conclusion, however, since questions about the nature of beauty and the foundations for artistic value remain dauntingly complex. Nevertheless, today traditional divisions between the "higher" and "lower" senses are converging in both art practice and aesthetic theory, which necessitates a reconsideration of the role of taste in culture and in aesthetic communities. Of course, this is not the first time that food has been advanced as an art form or medium. The potential alliance between aesthetic and gustatory taste has waxed and waned over the last two centuries, and the relations between "art" and "feast" have been addressed from at least three highly dissimilar sensibilities, which for short I shall label "Gourmet Delight," "Challenge," and "Invitation."

The first, the "gourmet" approach, is probably most familiar, for fine, appreciative dining and the delights it occasions seem, on the face of it, to be the most likely counterparts to enjoyment of fine art. From time to time, such an idea has gained philosophical traction. In the century after the major European theories about beauty and art appeared, another set of writers sought to include well-prepared meals within the domain of art. Writers on food and taste such as Jean-Anthelme Brillat-Savarin and Grimod de la Reynière in France, and William Kitchener, Launcelot Sturgeon, and Thomas Walker in Britain wrote encomia to fine cuisine and gustatory sensibility, promoting gastronomy as an art equal to the fine arts of painting and music.[6] As Denise Gigante observes, "The Enlightenment obsession with the concept of taste was the motivation behind the first forms of gastronomical writing in French and English. The so-called Man of Taste was a 'rational epicure,' no mere unthinking eater or glutton driven by physical compulsion."[7] Attempting to satisfy the reigning standard of disinterested attention, enthusiastic gastronomers narrowed the gap between aesthetic and gustatory taste by recommending that appetite be appeased before reaching the table. The starving person eats to live, not to savor quality. This person does not appreciate good food any more than someone dashing into a building to escape the rain appreciates its architecture. The sensibilities cultivated by the gastronomic writers rose above the need for nutrition and bodily fuel. They focused on the means to develop a discerning palate that savors the subtleties of flavor, that notices balance among dishes, sequence of service, and—not to neglect the other senses—that appreciates the visual grace of surroundings and the conversation of amiable company.

How successful was the gastronomic quest for entry into the world of fine art? Though the attempt to blend the two sorts of taste was inventive, philosophical theory was reluctant to embrace the gastronomic argument, largely, I believe, because so much was at stake with the identification of beauty with pleasure.[8] What is more, while the gourmet perspective is still promoted today, and along very similar lines, such a brief for food as art and the tongue as an organ of aesthetic discernment quickly reaches limits. Those limits are contained within the chief criterion for excellence in cuisine: namely, that it taste good. This may seem an odd critique, for who would praise bad-tasting food? The aim of fine eating is that food be delicious, just as the aim of fine art is—or may seem to be—that it be beautiful. Pursuing that parallel, the appreciative eater is a connoisseur whose palate can discern a spectrum of subtleties, just as the art expert can judge excellence in sculpture and painting. The comparison is apt to some degree, but it is only partially successful.

Artists themselves will be the first to point out that art has never been constrained by beauty, at least by beauty of the easily pleasant sort. That is the territory of "mere" decoration (though one could make a stronger case for decoration as well). But the worlds of art are filled with difficult content, including pain, sorrow, suffering, and cruelty—all reminders of the tragedies that fortune can dispense. Sometimes art with such difficult content is also beautiful, but often it is not. The harrowing and the horrid can be as aesthetically powerful as the beautiful. But this recognition poses a difficult question to the gastronomer: What can the dining table produce that bears the equivalent weight of the most profound works of art? The palate does not tolerate equivalent values. Certainly, nutritious eating does not demand foods that are delicious, and there are items eaten for symbolic reasons that are not particularly tasty, such as the bitter herbs of the Passover Seder. Even symbolic tastes, however, must not poison. Creative cooks and teasers of the senses, including the inventions of molecular gastronomers, can surprise and provoke, and such shocks to the senses dramatically arouse intellectual as well as sensuous engagement with what we eat. But if foods cause actual suffering they simply lose their clientele. Unlike the objects of the eye and the ear, objects of taste, smell, and touch can sicken, poison, and kill.

Does the gourmet approach represent the limit of what food can do? Is taste essentially an exercise of a sense that delivers some pleasures and affords conviviality, but remains relatively free from profound meaning or content? Not at all, for the act of tasting is fully as complex in its own way as is the exercise of other senses, though if we stick with the gourmet approach those possibilities are not as obvious because gustatory enjoyment is so near at hand. As noted earlier, unlike other artistic materials, foodstuffs decay rapidly and pretty soon disappear altogether. While at first the instability of medium seems to widen the distance between food and art, the very properties of foodstuffs that seem to undercut its usefulness as a medium for art at the same time provide a wealth of meaning that artists exploit. The things we eat and drink are transient. They decay and rot, they spoil and mold, and in the end they disgust. Because food is fresh, appealing, and edible for only a short time, eating lends itself to a sort of natural symbolism that includes signs of corporeality, decay, and mortality—aspects of life that one might prefer not to think about. Artistic exploration of the fragility of food and drink arouses affective responses that are the reverse of the satisfaction of appetite. An opposite of the *delicious* is the *disgusting*, and there is plenty of art that deliberately and intensely sets out to disgust, including food-based works that *challenge* sensibilities.

In traditional figurative painting, the symbolic use of food to disturb the viewer's sense of comfort and complacency has a venerable history. Still life painting provides a wealth of reminders of mortality, where foods are depicted in various stages of decay, infested with flies, and visited by scavenging vermin. Such paintings deliver a moral message and bear didactic labels such as *Vanitas* and *Memento mori*. (*Vanity of vanities, all is vanity. Remember, you will die.*)[9] Not pleasant thoughts, even though the paintings conveying these truisms may be deft, admirably skillful, and even beautiful. In these traditions, of course, we are referring to *depicted* foods, and though they picture items that will decay, the canvas and paint of their own substance are far more durable. We are still within the territory of representation, and if gustatory taste is aroused, it is only through imagination. (Disgust, since it can be triggered by vision as well as taste and smell, may be aroused quite directly by the depiction of decay and rot.[10]) But what about more direct artistic stimulation—rather than simulation—of the bodily senses? Here we engage the uses of foodstuffs as the medium of artworks.

It is only recently that artists in the fine art traditions have employed actual food substances as a medium for gallery installations and performances. The literal presentation of unstable organic materials—not only foods but also bodily products such as urine and blood—has been employed in the last several decades to challenge sensibilities on a brutally visceral level and extend the limits of appreciation. When deliberately crafted to these ends, food becomes a medium that is not consumed; rather, such uses of foodstuffs occur—indeed can only occur—in the art world.[11] Food's presence in this sort of art is more than untraditional; it is daring, difficult, confrontational, sometimes obnoxious, always thought-provoking.

Some of these works are striking for their unexpected employment of materials, such as Janine Antoni's sculptures from chocolate and lard, hewn in part with her own teeth. Others exploit the decay inevitable with their materials of choice, such as Jana Sterbak's *Meat Dress* and *Meat Chair* (1987). Visitors to these exhibits witnessed the gradual drying and putrefaction of the substances, eventually available only in photographs and written records. Damian Hirst's animal fragments are preserved in vitrines, though the flies and maggots feasting on *Let's Eat Out Today* (1990–91) present a more unstable sight. To such examples we can add others that employ products of the human body, such as Marc Quinn's *Self* (1991), a self-portrait bust made from his own frozen blood, and Andreas Serrano's controversial *Piss Christ* (1987).[12] The kinship among all these works includes the uses of materials that are not only unconventional but that foreground corporeality and its vulnerability to decay and putrefaction by means of the very substances that undergo such lowly transmogrifications. Objects of taste and smell are not just represented; they are present.

The context for works such as these weaves together several threads, including a particularly violent rejection of the Anglo-European fine art tradition with its values of beauty and aesthetic refinement, a movement that has been going on for more than a century. The immediate impact of many such works includes disgust, but it is a disgust deliberately evoked and, on the part of a receptive audience, appreciatively received. In extreme cases, appreciation is just this side of vomiting.

Unpleasant it may be, but there is an important general insight that is gained by the artistic uses of food to disgust, for the strong emotive response discloses meaning in especially dramatic ways.[13] All emotions possess meaning. Sorrow signals loss, for example; embarrassment indicates publically witnessed clumsiness; fear alerts us to danger. Disgust conveys meanings that include aspects of death and mortality, and occasionally it carries a weird kind of eroticism. Disgust is by no means the only response that imparts meanings to the foods we eat—or that we cannot countenance eating. But it vividly demonstrates the fact that foods, along with the sensations they arouse, possess cognitive as well as sensuous significance, including the deep existential meanings that surround mortality.

On a more quotidian level, the things we eat and drink daily also have meanings, though they are so routine and familiar that they are often overlooked. And here is where the "Invitation" aspect of food and art enters the picture. Hospitality, the signature concept of *Feast*, is perhaps the oldest and most basic significance that shared food and drink enacts. Certain cultures explicitly recognize the bond that offering and accepting food forges, as with the "guest friend" of ancient Greece or the tradition among the Bedouin, which holds that one who shares bread and salt falls under the host's protection. Even without formally recognized relationships, the practice of offering food and drink to visitors, including strangers, exists in many cultures. Offering food may appear a routine and relatively trivial gesture, for when practices become everyday matters, their cognitive significance sinks into habit. Consider, however, what we presume when we accept food and drink from others: that it is palatable and good, indicated when the host eats the same things. That we are at least momentarily among equals. Sharing food and drink presumes above all else a moment of trust, and the act of eating can itself forge bonds of obligation and alliance. Unlike the gourmet convergence of aesthetic and gustatory taste, hospitality does not aim at fancy food and refined connoisseurship, though of course it does not rule them out. But some of the most generous acts are the simplest, represented famously in the ancient tale of Baucus and Philamon—an impoverished couple who shared their meager stores of food with gods—a classic story of generosity and hospitality.

Of significance to *Feast* is its geographic reach. Artists from across the globe, among them Rirkrit Tiravanija and Lee Mingwei, have pioneered the gestures of invitation and hospitality that the exhibit promotes. Certain works, such as Michael Rakowitz's *Enemy Kitchen* (2004–ongoing), explicitly reference the division of cultures and raise the hope that becoming accustomed to alien flavors might be a small route to healing those divisions. Not everyone who visits the Smart Museum of Art will be able to share the food on offer, though all can observe and reflect upon the gestures of hospitality. Observer status is familiar within art institutions, where looking rather than participation is the norm in the subject-object relationship between audience and artwork. But at least some of the visitors to *Feast* will become, for a moment, components in the art. For those who do not, is this like looking in the window where a party is in progress? Works such as these are too new, I believe, to be confident about the relationships in play, although the term "relational aesthetics" has been coined to capture the interaction between artist-host and audience-guest.[14]

It is thought-provoking to compare these art gestures with the much more ordinary phenomenon of "ethnic" restaurants. Immigrants from anywhere to anywhere else often establish restaurants that offer their home cuisine to citizens of their new residence—along with adjustments that accommodate local availability of ingredients, thereby enacting shifts in the ethnic cuisine itself. (Once in Poland I was struck by the amount of cabbage served in a Mexican restaurant in place of what was—for me—more familiar lettuce.) Sampling ethnic cuisine is sometimes regarded as a dubious brand of culinary tourism, which of course it can be. But eating the cuisine of others is also a way to establish bonds and even friendships.[15]

Feast: Radical Hospitality in Contemporary Art includes pieces in which this sort of invitation is central: shared eating as artistic hospitality. These works are not only exhibits, they are activities often with larger social purposes, as with the community feasts that Suzanne Lacy staged in the 1970s when such works took on a particular political coloration. Inasmuch as they bypass conventional art institutions, many artists seek to reduce the gap between the so-called high culture of museums and galleries and ordinary life. Changes and challenges to the hierarchies of the art world extend into and permeate social relations in general.

In many ways the artist-orchestrated meal is like an act of hospitality of the sort that takes place in the home, but the venue of the art museum gives rise to artistic properties that would be absent if we were simply eating at a restaurant or at a friend's home. That is, the foods presented in the exhibit do not escape the roles of art. Grabbing a bite at a hot dog stand is just a quick and unreflective gobble. Accepting a morsel from an artist-stranger is certainly an act of trust, but it is also an action where that trust becomes part of the quality of the work, and it may also be an unwitting performance, perhaps a ritual. Offering a cup of coffee to a guest is a hospitable act; offering a bite of food as part of an exhibit is a vivid comment upon hospitality, upending the presumptions about categories of strangers and friends. As such, it demands reflection and interpretation—of the gesture and its intent, of the privacy of the sensation and the public nature of the act. A dirty dish in the kitchen sink is just a dirty dish. In the gallery it may be an object of whimsy, wit, or even threat.[16] The dynamic and sometimes unpredictable nature of the artist-orchestrated meal produces interpretive possibilities that are hard to foresee with exactness.

While there are some radical discontinuities between the exhibits housed within *Feast* and past histories of the arts, there are also continuities and shared themes. This is charmingly evident in those pieces where eating has already occurred and has left behind its familiar residue. Daniel Spoerri's "snare pictures"—after-meal collations of used plates and flatware mounted as collages—are literal, preserved instances of the remnants of meals. Laura Letinsky's photographs of rumpled tables capture the moments when diners have departed. Both echo the famous whimsical "unswept floors" of ancient Rome, where discarded bones, food scraps, and scavenging mice make up the patterns on the mosaic underfoot, creating the impression that one walks amid debris. Instantiation, representation, and illusion join in reminding us that eating and hospitality—just like an exhibit—have an inescapable aftermath: Clean up.

Carolyn Korsmeyer is Professor in the Department of Philosophy at the University at Buffalo.

---

[1] Henry Home, Lord Kames, *The Elements of Criticism* (1762/1970) vol. I. (Hildesheim, NY: Georg Olms Verlag, 6–7.)

[2] This complex comparison can only be alluded to in this limited space. For some general insight into what counts as "art" in different cultures, see Richard Anderson, *Calliope's Sisters: A Comparative Study of Philosophies of Art* (Englewood Cliffs, NJ: Prentice-Hall, 1990); Yuriko Saito, *Everyday Aesthetics* (New York: Oxford University Press, 2007); and Larry Shiner, *The Invention of Art: A Cultural History* (Chicago: University of Chicago Press, 2001), introduction. See also Joanna Waley-Cohen, "The Quest for Perfect Balance: Taste and Gastronomy in Imperial China," in Paul Freedman, ed., *Food: The History of Taste* (Berkeley and Los Angeles: University of California Press, 2007), chapter 3.

[3] Shiner, *The Invention of Art,* Part II.

[4] Eventually this term became more or less standard. For an early and influential text, see Immanuel Kant, *Critique of Judgment* (1790), especially the "First Moment of Beauty" in the section labeled "The Analytic of the Beautiful." See *Critique of Judgment,* trans. Werner S. Pluhar (Indianapolis: Hackett Publishing, c. 1987).

[5] This is not to say that "experiences" of what is heard remain the same. On the complexities of music, see Peter Kivy, *Authenticities: Philosophical Reflections on Musical Performance* (Ithaca, NY: Cornell University Press, 1995).

[6] For a selection of such writings, see Denise Gigante, *Gusto: Essential Writings in Nineteenth-Century Gastronomy* (New York: Routledge, 2005). See also her *Taste: A Literary History* (New Haven: Yale University Press, 2005).

[7] Gigante, *Gusto*, "Introduction," xix.

[8] I have argued this case in "Tastes and Pleasures," Special issue of *Romantic Circles Praxis* (January 2007): "Romantic Gastronomy," ed. Denise Gigante, http://www.rc.umd.edu/praxis.

[9] Sylvie Malaguzzi surveys the various meanings of foodstuffs and themes of eating in *Food and Feasting in Art,* trans. Brian Phillips (Los Angeles: J. Paul Getty Museum, 2008).

[10] Carolyn Korsmeyer, *Savoring Disgust: The Foul and the Fair in Aesthetics* (New York: Oxford University Press, 2011), esp. chapters 1–2.

[11] This is not to say that one never eats rotten foods. In fact, quite a lot of food is prepared with the aids of molds and bacteria, sometimes teasing the limits of disgust. See Korsmeyer, *Savoring Disgust,* chapter 3.

[12] For commentary on some of these works and their place in philosophical theories of art, see Cynthia Freeland, *But Is It Art: An Introduction to Art Theory* (New York: Oxford University Press, 2001).

[13] Two general studies of disgust are William Ian Miller, *The Anatomy of Disgust* (Cambridge, MA: Harvard University Press, 1997); and Aurel Kolnai, *On Disgust*, ed. Barry Smith and Carolyn Korsmeyer (Chicago: Open Court, 2004).

[14] See Nicolas Bourriaud, *Relational Aesthetics* (Paris: Presses du Réel, 1998).

[15] Lisa Heldke, *Exotic Appetites: Ruminations of a Food Adventurer* (New York: Routledge, 2003).

[16] Arthur Danto has famously analyzed the difference between the properties of artworks and mere "real things" in *The Transfiguration of the Commonplace* (Cambridge, MA: Harvard University Press, 1981).

Feasts in the Middle East: History of the Long Term

Geoff Emberling

FEASTS AND BANQUETS as represented in art, historical documents, and material remains have always been interesting to scholars, but recent work—particularly the 2001 volume, *Feasts: Archaeological and Ethnographic Perspectives on Food, Politics, and Power,* edited by Michael Dietler and Brian Hayden—has focused analytical attention of archaeologists, at least, on the many ways in which feasts can be more than just a good time. Within a broad definition of "communal consumption of food and/or drink" in an unusual or ritual context, the volume's editors suggested some ways to identify feasts archaeologically—through remains of unusual food, vessels, facilities, and ritual objects—and showed how feasts could serve to develop political alliances, enhance prestige, and provide economic benefits to hosts and guests.[1] Feasting is both an ancient and a common human practice, one that is developed in distinctive cultural traditions and used in specific historical contexts. Feasts therefore are a window on fundamental negotiations in human societies.

Archaeology and Feasts Today

Archaeologists investigate past cultures, but we often work in modern cultural contexts quite different from our own. So we necessarily develop understandings of preparing, serving, and eating food and drink in new contexts that range from daily meals to the more highly formalized settings that could be called feasts or banquets. The otherness of these encounters puts archaeologists in the position of outsiders trying to understand practices and structures that are foreign to us. Artists commenting on feasting practices in our own culture travel the opposite direction, perhaps, marking the familiar as strange. Feasts can also inform our understanding of the ancient past.

Working in the Middle East, for instance, archaeologists inevitably encounter local cuisines and ways of eating. In more traditional contexts, these may include sitting or reclining on the floor, eating with fingers (right hand only), and an expectation that one doesn't talk much while eating. When you are a guest in a traditional village house, your hosts may not eat with you, but will serve food prepared by women of the household, who may not appear at all. The hosts may join in eating with their guests, or may wait until guests are finished and then eat from what is left on the plates. An extravagant feast may focus on a whole sheep, boiled and served with herbs on a mound of rice, with bread and perhaps salads and dips of various kinds. Some of these expectations would be quite different if you were served a meal in a large city like Damascus or Baghdad, where international travel and contact would make some of these differences less apparent. Such experiences expose an entire world of cultural differences that encompass the obligations of an Arab host, the separation of genders, and ideas about the time and place for sociability.

Such experiences are useful for an archaeologist thinking about how to interpret cultural practices from material remains. The size of dishes, for instance, might indicate the number of people expected to eat together. Middle Eastern feasts are not served on small individual plates with individual utensils, but are rather served on large plates and eaten communally: initiating an experience that brings guest and host together socially, while creating reciprocal obligations. Archaeologists might also infer power, wealth, and social status from the kinds of food served and also from the size and grandeur of the space in which guests are accommodated.

In living and working together with local people, archaeologists may also be pulled into local political conflicts—which can be a fraught but also illuminating experience. My archaeological research on the ancient Mesopotamian world has focused on the excavation of Tell Brak, a site that grew to become one of the world's first cities shortly after 4000 BCE. While working on that excavation, living in tents on the site itself next to a village, I became involved in a long-standing feud that culminated in two meals with a local sheikh—an experience that shows how feasting can reproduce power.

The feud began as a dispute between two families in the village who had both worked for the excavation. When the first directors of the site began work there in 1976, they made arrangements with the local landowning family, the Sultans, to provide housing, cook meals, and store the dig's equipment during the off-season. The arrangement did not work well, and the directors eventually hired a different family named Aswad, whose members had long ago been slaves: coffeemakers for local sheikhs of the great Shammar tribe. In modern times, this family had struggled, but over the years through regular work on the dig, the Aswads became prosperous and thus were perceived as a social threat by the Sultan family.

In 2000, the conflict reached alarming dimensions. One day as we were setting up camp, a pickup came racing up the dirt road, bearing a member of the Sultan family who told me that if any member of the Aswad family were employed at our site, the Sultans would beat or shoot them. He said the Aswads were slaves, lower than the soles of his shoes, and that the animals in his fields were better than the Aswads. Some unpaid loans and fistfights between the families had added to the long-standing tension. The dig could not function smoothly without the Aswads, yet the prospect of a shoot-out among the tents of our camp was not a welcome prospect. In an attempt to understand the problem and identify options, I consulted with local officials, and for a variety of political and practical reasons, all advised me that it would be best if the problem could be handled by tribal authority.

As it happened, the sheikh of the Jubbur tribe—the tribe to which the Sultan family belonged—had a country estate near the excavation site. He stopped by one day to talk and later invited the dig staff to lunch at his house in Hasake. Thus, our hope for a resolution of this village and tribal dispute came down to a formal meeting in which we were told to expect that food and drink would be served—that is, a feast, or as it happened, two quite different episodes of eating and drinking. Our Syrian friends and colleagues coached us extensively on how to behave, which added to our anxieties leading up to the meeting. One clear rule, for example, was not to accept food or drink from the sheikh before discussing our problems.

We drove to the sheikh's house in the local town of Hasake. I was nervous as I was led in to the sheikh's long audience hall, lined with pillows along the walls, and sat on the floor as he reclined in front of a coffee brazier. After some conversation in English and Arabic, he asked what he could do for us. I mentioned that we had some trouble with the Sultan family and he said he would take care of it, without asking for details. It was a great performance of sheikhly power and authority. Once we had finished this brief discussion, the sheikh's coffee maker served bitter Arabic coffee with cardamom, and talk turned to less political issues. The rest of the dig staff was then invited to a large meal outside the formal confines of the audience hall, on the patio. The meal consisted mainly of different kinds of grilled meats—the culinary symbol of wealth and status in rural Syria.

These two gatherings, with their specific settings and ritualized sequences of negotiating problems and solutions and then eating together, thus established a social and political relationship between the expedition and the sheikh. The meal set a process in motion that, while imperfect, eventually established a compromise between the two families and preserved peace at Tell Brak.

Feasting Across Millennia

While we were negotiating with the sheikh, as it happened, we were in the midst of excavating a building nearly 6,000 years old that had served as the feasting hall of a leader who may have played a very similar role within the community at Tell Brak. Tell Brak is a particularly important site for understanding why people first built cities. Excavations at the other well-known early Mesopotamian city, called Uruk and located in southern Iraq, focused on the monumental temple and palace area at the center of the site, leaving us with very few ideas of how anyone apart from kings and the elite might have lived. But of course early cities were not entirely controlled by kings, and the daily practices through which authority and identities of the rest of the population were established, maintained, and modified are scarcely known from Uruk. The recent finding that Tell Brak was a city by 3700 BCE gave us an opportunity to investigate those questions.

The feasting hall is a small house with a long enclosed courtyard.[2] The house itself is of the absolutely typical form; the courtyard is much rarer, and the archaeological remains within the house are unique in the detailed information they provide about how a structure of this type would have been used. Although rebuilt several times, the feasting hall consistently provided a focal point at one short end marked by a bench and niches that would have established a place where a host could sit or recline while elevated above guests. Facilities for cooking in the courtyard included unusually large domed brick ovens and a kind of ancient grill.

The material we excavated in this feasting hall offers many clues about how some kinds of feasts were conducted at Tell Brak. The ceramic assemblage, for instance, was dominated by individual serving plates that had been mass-produced, some with clear evidence of wheel-turning. The animal bones found in the building—which would have reflected food eaten there—were dominated by sheep and goats, as is usual at the site, but also included small game birds (still hunted in the area today), rabbits, and fox limb bones that were probably attached to pelts rather than being part of a meal; at least they are not a usual part of the animal bone assemblage.

The latest level of this structure had been burned, like much of the site, by invaders from southern Iraq. In the remains of the fire, we recovered a cluster of five maceheads—ovoid stones pierced by a hole for a handle. These are traditionally taken as symbols of political authority in Mesopotamia, suggesting that political authority was being publicly marked in the same space that housed the feasts. Thus, in this building we have clear evidence of unusually large-scale food preparation and serving. The display of higher status—and, I would argue, political position—is suggested by the presence of a privileged location that is architecturally marked and raised above the level of the rest of the hall, as well as by the maceheads and fox pelts.

It is worth considering what kind of person would have hosted feasts in such a structure. An intriguing suggestion of the wealth he may have accumulated is provided by a hoard found in a small residence immediately to the east of the feasting hall and perhaps accessible via a doorway from it. The owner of this hall was not a city ruler or high temple official, most likely, but an intermediate level official, and I have argued elsewhere that it is most likely the head of a lineage or larger kin-based group—someone like a sheikh or an elder. Thus, we have for the first time evidence of the political and social practices that made up the daily lives of people in the cities. It is possible, in fact, that leaders at this level—in regular contact with their followers—were more responsible for building the early cities than the kings who otherwise took the credit.

There is surprisingly little direct evidence of feasts in ancient Mesopotamia during the following centuries, with the exception of banquet scenes of around 2500 BC, which are represented in art but have not been localized in excavation elite.[3] I therefore skip over a couple of millennia to the Neo-Assyrian empire when we see a similar practice. I will focus on the first of its capital cities—ancient Kalhu or modern Nimrud, where the earliest palace on the site was built under the supervision of King Ashurnasirpal II in the early ninth century BCE.

It has long been recognized that the architectural form of the throne rooms in Assyrian royal and provincial palaces alike is repeated at smaller scale throughout Assyrian architecture. The classic shape is a long, narrow room with a privileged seating position at one end, marked by a platform. Behind the seated position was a suite of rooms that could be used for storage, bathing, and food preparation. These spaces, including the throne rooms, were sites for the performance of political power, and at least some of them retain evidence that feasts were carried out there.

Excavations in the outer courtyard of the palace at Nimrud recovered high quality "palace ware" cups, storage jars that may have contained wine and oil, food preparation areas, and cuneiform tablets that document a range of administrative activities, all in reception suites.[4] These Assyrian reception suites suggest a relationship between the preparation and serving of food in a context of political and administrative activities that has striking similarities to those of much earlier Tell Brak, as well as to our meal with the sheikh—relationships of authority and submission would have been performed and reinforced by walks down a long room, approaching the figure of authority, and these relationships would be further reinforced by ritualized sharing of food and drink.

Of course, other kinds of feasts took place in Mesopotamia, the best documented being those of royal scale that involved thousands of participants, sometimes over multiple days. These feasts, which could commemorate royal deeds or mark religious festivals, had entirely different purposes than those described above, which likely focused on negotiation and maintenance of relationships within and around a city. They were redistributive, could serve diplomatic functions, and above all legitimized the position of the king. Ashurnasirpal himself recorded on a stele in his palace that he had inaugurated the city of Kalhu with a feast to which he invited almost seventy thousand guests.

These snapshots of the long history of feasting in ancient Mesopotamia and the more modern Middle East propose that there may be elements of continuity over the long term. Leaders served feasts in particular architectural contexts to focus attention on themselves and their social position while putting themselves in a position to exercise authority, establish and maintain alliances, and resolve disputes. This story could be extended into earlier times, when some scholars have suggested that large structures in earlier towns were used for feasting. And more work would need to be done to document feasting in the many centuries not covered in this overview. Yet the possibility that the exercise of political authority in particular contexts has been an important feature of Middle Eastern societies over thousands of years suggests the potency of the feast.

Geoff Emberling is Visiting Scholar at the Kelsey Museum of Archaeology at the University of Michigan.

---

[1] See Michael Dietler and Brian Hayden, eds. *Feasts: Archaeological and Ethnographic Perspectives on Food, Politics, and Power* (Washington, DC: Smithsonian Institution Press, 2001), 3.

[2] Geoff Emberling and H. McDonald, "Excavations at Tell Brak 2000: Preliminary Report" *Iraq* 63 (2000), 21–54.

[3] See Denise Schmandt-Besserat, "Feasting in the Ancient Near East," in Dietler and Hayden, 391–403; and Susan Pollock, "Feasts, Funerals, and Fast Food in Early Mesopotamian States," in *The Archeology and Politics of Food and Feasting in Early States and Empires*, ed. Tamara Bray (New York: Kluwer Academic Press, 2003), 17–38.

[4] Joan and David Oates, *Nimrud: An Assyrian Imperial City Revealed* (London: British School of Archaeology in Iraq, 2001).

Hoong khao blachot maa
David Teh

> *Hoong khao blachot maa; bping plaa blachot maew*
> You steam rice to tease a dog; you grill fish to tease a cat.
> —Thai proverb

I.

IN KEEPING WITH a well-established expat rule of thumb—that the less you pay for a meal, the better it will be—it's hard to spend more than a dollar or two at my favorite restaurant in the Kingdom of Thailand. The kitchen of Pa Noo (Auntie Rat) is a humble, open-plan timber affair, sitting in her front yard by a winding country lane on the edge of Dansai. All Pa Noo does is cook, day in, day out. If no customers show up, the stuff is eaten by family or neighbors, or thrown out. If you're bringing a few people, you can call ahead to warn her. But the traffic is slow up here. The province's name, Loei, means "beyond." Laos is a stone's throw to the north; the rest of the horizon takes in the dry, rugged hills of Isaan—Thailand's northeast—hemmed by the broad arc of the Mekong.

Too big to be a village yet too small to be a city, Dansai and its fertile hinterland are nestled among the steep ridges of the Petchabun Range, cool enough for tangy citrus, a myriad of mushrooms, herbs, edible ferns, and other vegetables you've never seen before. Everything's organic at Pa Noo's, but you wouldn't know it until you see and taste her food. Homestyle *Isaan*, she calls it. There's no hyperbole here, no menu, no branding at all, not even a sign. Nor are there any secrets—she'll tell you, if you're interested, how she makes her vegetable preserve from the leaves of a small tree that stands nearby, and how much of it will perfect the dressing on a colorful garden salad. Pretty much everything she serves is either homegrown, wild, swapped, or bought from other townsfolk. One travels to the furthest corner of the realm for a meal bursting with undoctored flavors, with minimum value-added, 100 percent free of semiotics.

A famed wandering monk, passing by here perhaps a century ago, advised us to be wary of labels (*saññа*):

> *Saññas* grab hold of things outside and pull them in to fool the mind, making it think in confusion and go out searching, wandering astray. . . . The mind goes wrong because it trusts its *saññas*, attached to its likes, leaving this plane of being, going to that, wandering till it's dizzy, forgetting itself, completely obscure to itself . . . *Saññas* say "good" and grasp at "bad" and force [the heart] to fasten on loving and hating . . .[1]

We would be naïve to think that the so-called linguistic turn was a matter only for Western theorists and philosophers. Its effects are all around us, since the banalization of semiotics has accompanied an even more momentous semiotization of the banal. Even our daily bread has become semiotically saturated, a contentious, politicized terrain. Of course, as links in a globalized system of production, we have good reason to be circumspect; but it's to our eyes not our taste buds that we entrust this judgment. Grazing the supermarket aisles, we are interested not in how something will *taste*, but in where it comes from and how; in its chemical composition; its carbon footprint; whether it's biodynamic, GM-free, free-range, fair-trade, sustainably farmed, responsibly packaged. What we eat may not have changed much, but what we *consume*—how it is valued, and what it means—are questions that lead far beyond our immediate "plane of being."

II.

The present exhibition makes visible a formal genealogy, locating the alimentary turns in a certain trajectory of vanguard art. Its roots lie close to the iconoclastic source of twentieth-century modernism. It resurfaced in the 1960s and 1970s, amid conceptual and performance strategies now recognized as core ingredients of our "contemporary." And it finally blossomed in the 1990s, in the social or "relational" vogue with which art history's lens is increasingly tinted. Certain currents may be found throughout: the determined expansion of art's material resources; celebration of the quotidian versus the formal hauteur of elitist aesthetics; humor, conviviality, and unabashed utopianism; and immediacy, renewed through participatory and other real-time encounters. Yet the discontinuities are perhaps more telling, for art history's trestle tables would straddle a whole century of conflict and change: between the first and second courses, a profound lapse of western society's faith in *techne* and its corollary, the ideological schism opened by modernity's appalling new destructive power, and between the second and third, the collapse of that ideological polarity and *techne* redeemed by a prodigious new communicational power.

It may be hard to see past the irony of tracing the origins of our conviviality to the celebrants of destruction, of war as "the world's only hygiene." Indeed, we might wish to go back a step further in the long courtship between art and everyday life, to what Roger Shattuck dubbed "the Banquet Years," that is, Paris of the Belle Époque, when a certain hospitality still formed the background, rather than the "orchestrated" exception, to the flow of artistic life—its medium rather than its content. There, we find a culture of exhibitionism perhaps not so different from our own. Paris was a stage, Shattuck writes, "where the excitement of performance gave every deed the double significance of private gesture and public action."[2] This dialectical tension that so energized the dinner tables of the avant-garde has only multiplied since, though as the spectacle took the excitement into our homes and made it the banal norm, artists were at pains to suppress it. (Think of a deadpan Martha Rosler in *Semiotics of the Kitchen*, 1975.) To stay afloat in the rising tide of communication, art has had to reckon with the reigning *ambivalence* of these media that connect us but also keep us separate. And it is in the course of this reckoning that the artist-made meal becomes most visible.

Thinking semiotically, the Futurists perhaps inaugurate a process in which food is detached from the realm of material needs and is overcoded, made to signify in a new way. *What one eats* became an expression of a new mode of being—the engineering of a modern, individual subjectivity. But since the 1960s, when the Green Revolution promised to make scarcity a thing of the past, food's symbolic register has submerged in a mundane abundance. *How one eats*—the social frame of a newly politicized everyday—became more important than the menu (as in Rosler's kitchen videos). The frames of institutionalized modern art were not spared, as artists shifted the emphasis to *where and with whom one eats* (Spoerri, Marioni, or Matta-Clark; and the feminist meals of the 1970s). In these examples, we also notice an attempt to revive food's symbolic currency in the name of an unmediated and unreified sociality held to be endangered in both art and technological society at large. But ironically, with this return to the immediacy of communion, *food becomes medium*. And if the urgency of this gesture strikes such a chord today, so has a familiar tension resurfaced, one to which today's vanguard—and their critics—are keenly attuned: that to expand art's communicative amplitude (by *publicizing*), it seems necessary also to personalize the experience of art (by *privatizing*).

III.

Thus far in our typology, a meal's context has mattered more than its content. Only the Futurists married culinary innovation to artistic innovation. Since the time of the Futurists, artists have tended to be less than fastidious about what is served, preferring openness and the unforeseeable to the *telos* of a more ingenuous modernism. To insist that the cuisine be good—let alone inventive—could be seen as *mauvais goût*, contrary to the spirit of the thing. But if our relational aesthetes seem more akin to the 1970s group, it is perhaps only because responsibility for culinary innovation and adventure has already been democratized, foisted upon all of us in the globalization of food supply and the attendant spectacle of cosmopolitan consumption. It is no accident that transnational agribusiness and the celebrity chef are creatures of the same age. At the same time, the diet of the postmodern city indexes the shifting position of a newly material "culture" in the postindustrial economy.[3] The artist-made meal thus flirts with a double reification, a double sublimation, for it is *doubly cultural*: at once a sacrament dispensed by the artist-priest, and a privileged repository of cultural essence (or of a hybridity essentialized as "global"). Artistic valorizations of the culinary are best taken with a grain of salt.

Food is, of course, not the only culture to have been globalized in this period. The familiar intellectual arc we retrace here, from Europe to America, was followed by a conspicuous dilation as contemporary art—by the 1990s, a mode of production and circulation with unabashedly global pretensions—undertook a self-conscious de-centering. In its global enfranchisement some see the undoing of a Euro-American cultural hegemony; while for others, it simply recolonizes culturally what had earlier been colonized physically. Either way, we are so thoroughly implicated in this process that we may scarcely hope to view it with the innocence of a tourist.

Food's recent resurgence in contemporary art coincides closely with Southeast Asia's emergence on this global stage. Food is a natural concern for this region's contemporary artists—as subject if not as raw material—given its prevalence in official and popular projections of nation, its valence as an everyday marker of identity, difference, and fusion in these diverse and highly syncretic cultures. It is hardly incidental that several artists associated with the region (though none is unproblematically "native" to it) appear in *Feast*. Such figures may be pivotal for understanding the migrations of form at issue here. But while they appear to bridge two cultures, and two traditions of modern art, we should not cross that bridge without first addressing a more pressing question: What could our typology of the artist-made meal possibly mean in this part of the world, which shares few, if any, of its art historical precedents, and where the sharing of food and its meanings might still be hitched to very different cultural moorings?

For those who would traffic in cultural signage, context can be a double-edged sword—too specific, it risks exoticism; too vague, it flirts with misappropriation. This may explain the reluctance of some artists to provide it. And is it not, after all, the sacred potential of the shared meal to transcend our cultural differences? But the critic enjoys no such latitude, and Thailand—conspicuous source of both globalized art and globalized food—seems a fitting place for a cautionary case study.

IV.

In September 2010, debate erupted in Bangkok around an Australian restaurateur, David Thompson, who professed to be reviving a Thai culinary tradition that he described as "decaying." Thompson had made himself a ripe target by winning a Michelin star—a first for Thai cuisine—for his London restaurant, *nahm*, and then by opening a branch in downtown Bangkok. He is not the only *farang* chef to have caused such a stir, but touting his new venture in the *New York Times*, his comments came at a moment of acute national insecurity, just months after scores of red-shirt protestors were slain in a brutal military crackdown in Bangkok's streets, Thailand's worst political violence since the 1970s.[4] A slew of Op-Ed pieces followed what one local foodie called a "slap in the face" for the Thai people, underscoring their sensitivity.[5] Thompson does know a thing or two about Thai cooking—he authored several books on the subject and has studied and practiced it more assiduously than most of his competitors. And he is right that most of what's eaten in Bangkok these days is much further removed from the soil of tradition than people would like to think. But at 1500 Baht per head—enough to feed fifty people street-side—his menus derive from aristocratic sources and the "authenticity" he seeks has little to do with any typical or all-encompassing Thai-ness.

Yet what's striking about the brouhaha over Thompson's remarks is how, for self-styled liberals (notably, *haut bourgeois* newspaper columnists), it became a pretext for recuperating the heterogeneity at the core of "tradition" for reinvestment in *the national*. A *farang* with local knowledge served as a convenient proxy for a vague recognition of difference and the need for "reconciliation"—a timely reminder that Thai chauvinism, for all its essentialist appeals, was constituted precisely, and by necessity, in the absorption of otherness. Nor was it any longer just a diversity captured and distilled into a mythic unity (the universal solvent of Thai nationalism in the last century) but also a diversity rendered *as such*, the ingredients of a no-less mythical plurality.[6]

Methods may have changed, but the appropriation of provincial and neighboring cultures by central Siamese power continues a much longer process that began with living bodies and their material surplus: labor and food. Indeed, all the classical states of mainland Southeast Asia came about through one device: the concentration of labor power *from elsewhere* for the purposes of cultivation.[7] Their glory closely indexed the available surplus of this one grain. They were, as James Scott writes in his "anarchist history" of the region, "in every case a polyglot population," the culture of each a "work in progress, a kind of contingent vector sum of the various peoples and cultures who chose to identify with it or who were incorporated by force." Since their absorption was a strategic necessity, assimilation was relatively easy, and identity was largely a matter of performance, rather than birth or blood—a principle no less axiomatic after centuries of colonial and postcolonial ethnologizing.[8]

The symbolic currency of rice is thus deep-rooted, and very much intact—a single crop held to secure individual sustenance, political continuity, and everything in between. Indeed, images of agricultural abundance have been the sine qua non of Siamese kingship for more than a thousand years. Etched deep in the culture, these impressions remain prevalent in the national imaginary, despite the fact that Thailand's economy is no longer, at its base, agrarian. (And this *décalage* between culture and economy both reflects and compounds the country's present political unraveling.[9]) Alimentary excess is still—despite the preponderance of the market economy—more or less a fact of everyday life for most people, and perhaps has less aristocratic associations than elsewhere. The giving of food alms to processions of monks is symbolic of wider notions of giving (*dana'a*) in Theravada Buddhism. Not only is it the province of both rich and poor, but it is in Theravadin tradition quite literally a quotidian practice. While it has receded from daily life with urbanization and the waning esteem of the clergy, it is nonetheless still an unexceptional sight, especially in the provinces. Nor are monks the only beneficiaries. Food offerings are just as often made to ghosts, ancestors, and animals, according to a layered matrix of beliefs—Brahmanic, Chinese, animist—still widely maintained despite suppression by the Theravada orthodoxy.

Against this background, it's little wonder that the *denial* of food has also taken on a supercharged symbolic potency. The protests that overturned a military government in 1992, for example, were led by a retired general, Chamlong Srimuang, whose grass roots constituency lay in an ascetic Buddhist sect. Members of the Santi Asoke movement preach anticonsumerism, sustainable agriculture, and strict moral rigor, and eat one vegetarian meal a day (a forbearance that, in mouth-watering Thailand, cannot but inspire some sort of respect). Their moralism was pivotal in the vaguely democratizing shift of the early 1990s, but it was Chamlong's political trump card—a hunger strike, widely televised and very nearly terminal—that brought the nation to a standstill and forced the political crisis to a head.[10]

V.

There is ample reason, then, for the close identification between Thailand and its cuisine. Food is a common obsession, and the vital lubricant of almost every form of social interaction. A typical Thai greeting, translated literally, means "Have you eaten yet?" (*gin khao yang?*) Thailand's 70 million inhabitants are not, by Western standards, particularly well-off, but they are pretty well fed. Abroad, meanwhile, Thai restaurants are a ubiquitous feature of the global cityscape (even if we're as likely to find a Lao or a Chinese behind the wok); and it is widely agreed that Thai food—even the approximation that sometimes passes for it—is delicious.

Clichés perhaps, but they are all true. Yet, however fitting, the stereotype is less interesting than what it elides: the heterogeneity at the heart of Thai nationhood and cuisine, which reflects closely the success with which the dominant culture has over many centuries appropriated a wide array of ethnic others. Thais are not blind to the diversity, yet it is naturalized, which is to say neutralized, a thousand times a day with the mere utterance of a national shibboleth. For the notion of Thai-ness (*kwampenthai*)—at best a kaleidoscopic amalgam of other cultures, at worst, a fascist myth—is in any case a most powerful solvent. Hence, the peculiar irony that what is most adulterated is often embraced as national essence, by the faultless logic that as Thai-ness is itself hybrid, the otherness it absorbs can thus be "very Thai." This paradox reveals itself most sharply when the word *Thai* is attached to food.

Som tum is a salad of julienned green papaya, pounded in a *krok* (a deep ceramic mortar) with fresh chilli, lime, garlic, fish sauce, and small plum tomatoes. It can be found on any street in the kingdom, though everybody knows it belongs to the country's impoverished northeast (Isaan, which is ethnically Lao, not Siamese). It is typically seasoned with fermented fish juice (*pla ra*) and a little salted freshwater crab, which isn't really eaten, but whose smashed carapace will leach its briny contents into the dish. In Bangkok, though, these latter ingredients are often substituted with roasted peanuts, dried shrimp, and lashings of sugar. Now, as with all Thai cooking, there is room for adaptation, but *som tum* should always be cheap, healthy, spicy and a little smelly; if it's not, one has cause for suspicion. Ironically, it is the sweeter, *farang*-friendly version that is known as *som tum thai*, though it is universally agreed that the more savory, smellier, spicier version is the real thing. It is telling that the national moniker designates the urban variant (cosmopolitanized, dumbed-down for foreign consumption) and that it does so without any appeal to authenticity.

It bears remembering here that the adjective *Thai* does not connote some immemorial past, but is obscurely welded to the modern—it has only named the nation since the 1930s when the absolute monarchy of Siam became the constitutional monarchy called Thailand. For the militarist leaders of the time, the name-change was in fact a deliberate *departure* from tradition, reframing the nation as international and modern. The well-known dish *pad thai* (which made a celebrated appearance in international contemporary art in 1990) emerged during this pivotal period. Like most "Thai heritage," it was in fact largely a modern concoction, exemplary not for its rootedness in Siam's past, but on the contrary for its obvious debts to a process of immigrant mutation, and its later investment by modern chauvinism. The basic format (stir-fried rice noodles) is found throughout Southeast Asia and is more or less Chinese, though it is said to have arrived with Vietnamese settlers in Ayutthaya, the cosmopolitan seat of Siamese power until 1767. As served in today's capital, it is flavored with tamarind paste, shrimp, pickled cabbage, rice vinegar, sugar, fried tofu, and egg, and garnished with Chinese chives, bean sprouts, and a wedge of lime. The customer is then expected to add dried chilli, crushed peanuts, and more sugar, to taste.

In this case, the dish's national anointment came about not by convention but by fiat, when military strongman Field Marshal Plaek Phibulsongkram promoted noodle-making as part of a sweeping wartime campaign to economize on the domestic consumption of rice (then Thailand's chief export product). The new, modern *pad thai* conveniently doubled as a vehicle for nationalist fervor, taking a Chinese form and with an ironic twist, rebaptising it as "Thai." (Though any feel-good narrative of cultural hybridity quickly founders on the political shoals of a period in which Chinese newspapers were banned, Chinese schools were torched, and Chinese leaders were killed and exiled.)

No meal, however traditional, however extraordinary, transcends its time and place. And a curry cooked in Thailand is apt to have a very different resonance to the same curry cooked in a SoHo gallery. What it signifies—on both material and symbolic tables, and for the political animal that would sup from both—it signifies historically, yet this historical dimension is often the first thing to disappear when food is enjoined as a marker of identity.[11] Hence, perhaps, the imperative we can detect in recent Thai artist-made meals to restore food to its specific, sociohistorical coordinates.

VI.

Food is a constant feature of Thai contemporary art. Indeed, it appears often enough to warrant a whole taxonomy of the alimentary, which I will sketch here by way of a speculative conclusion. My intention is not to fix a durable set of art historical types, but rather, to show the breadth of approaches to this theme, and that its significance is much more than just thematic.

At the first, most basic, material level, food is a business sustaining art as a cottage industry. Most art galleries in Thailand—especially outside of Bangkok—also serve food and drinks, and many artists embrace, rather than resist, the association. Hence, comedian-*cum*-artist Udom Taepanich's ice-cream shop in Chiang Mai; and Angkrit Ajchariyasophon's gallery in his family's *gway jiab* restaurant (which he still runs) in Chiang Rai. Here we might also include the provisions made for exhibition openings, ranging from the Spartan to the lavish, as fundamental to sociality in art circles as anywhere. At a second level, we find *food and its exchange aestheticized*, often referencing codes of identity (gender, nationality, etc.) and practices of everyday life including art and faith. The breast desserts of Pinaree Sanpitak are exemplary here, as are the spices in some of Montien Boonma's installations. Whether it's eaten or not, this sort of work emphasizes the sensory experience of food, though not in an Epicurean sense (for the good Buddhist eats to live, and not the reverse). More typically, nourishment dons the habit of simplicity, modesty, and repetition.

Montien's recursive meditations on form, especially the fundamental symbolism of the rice-bowl in his drawings and installations, establish a third stratum in which food and its trappings are not just aestheticized but thematized, raised to the status of an ideological figure, which may be ecological, spiritual, ethnopolitical, philosophical, or all of the above. Thus, uncooked rice has wielded a blunt political symbolism in the performance art of Vasan Sitthiket and Mongkol Plienbangchang. A more multivalent figure is the rice *field*. In its best-known iterations—The Land Foundation near Chiang Mai, and Sakarin Krue-On's *Terraced Rice Fields* at Documenta XII—it has tapped a deep agrosymbolism at home, while being consumed as a kind of exotic minimalism abroad, laying out an ethical smorgasbord of anticapitalism, localism, communitarian idealism, collaboration and experiment, environmentalism, and "socially engaged" Buddhism. Both projects offer a metaphoric hinge between physical sustenance and the social dimensions of "sustainability." The topical global appeal is obvious, but in the Thai political landscape this is treacherous ground, claimed decisively by the palace since the financial meltdown of 1997–98.[12]

A fourth category sees food de-aestheticized, its quotidian function as social lubricant elevated and celebrated in its own right. Often a kind of culinary *bricolage* where the situation determines the menu and the qualities of the food recede, this mode is geared instead toward interaction and participation. At its best, it challenges art institutions to expend their resources in ways that cross the usual wires of investment and return, changing the rhythms of social intercourse that take place there. Here, our two typologies become closely intertwined, as exemplified by Rirkrit Tiravanija's cooking projects, or in the domestications of emerging installation artist, Arin Rungjang.

In the final category (to my mind, the most compelling), food serves as a vector for specific social histories. Ethnological awareness comes to the fore and the outcome is often documentary in spirit, if not in form. Hence, Sutthirat Supaparinya's video, *Taste of Noodles* (2006), traces a culinary type from Northern Thailand, locating parallel traditions across various national borders. Food is both an exemplary migratory form, carrier of cultural codes across space and time, and a testament to shared and mixed (*pre*-national) origins, a tacit critique of the modern state with its arbitrary borders and cultural streamlining. Sometimes the approach is more localized. In a recent project at the Jim Thompson Farm in Khorat, artist Worathep Akkaboothara collected living recipes from the surrounding villages, oral knowledge he then compiled and printed in an illustrated cooking diary.[13] Participatory "cooking battles" were staged at the farm, fuelled by a specially cultivated herb and vegetable patch, showing how this living heritage is peculiar to its community and environment.

But the most outstanding example of this geopolitical mode took in a far wider, deterritorialized field. Pratchaya Phinthong's *Donne plus que tu prends* (2010–11) took the form of a kind of working holiday with Isaan contract workers hired to pick wild berries in Swedish Lapland. This seasonal industry relies on the principle of *allemansrätten*, an ancient right of common access to uncultivated land. It's not agriculture, exactly, but a kind of *prospecting*, the mere collection of a natural bounty, yet unfeasible with First World labor. The freedom to roam, however, also exposes the visitors to the perils of competing claims on the land, including those of hunters and bears (also fond of berries).

Migrant labor is a well-worn theme in contemporary art. But rather than emphasize his compatriots' work conditions—precarious indeed, physically, economically, and legally—Pratchaya highlighted the *conditions of possibility* of this dangerous adventure, from its physical, calorific economy to the profit motive the rice farmer shares with the transnational capitalist (however unequal their profits). The artist chose not to trace the berries' inflating exchange value—wild foodstuffs increasingly seen as the ultimate luxury in *haute cuisine*[14]—for the primary commodities here are labor and time, including his own. He documented what he could, while participating full-time in a six-week harvest. Much of the documentation focuses on the workers' search for sustenance, incidental hunting and gathering that punctuates the working day with something akin to *play*—angling for unfamiliar fish, stalking pheasants with a slingshot, modern-day explorers improvising in a wholly foreign environment. In one sequence, they clamor around the gleaming innards of a freshly butchered moose, amused by the challenge of identifying edible bits, based on their analogous experience with buffalo.

In this project, the meal is a communion literalized, stripped of all symbolic and semiotic baggage. Returned to its reality principle, hunger, it recovers an immediacy it could never achieve in the artist-orchestrated séance. Food remains a focal point, but is neither medium nor metaphor. No longer thematized, it is *realized*, grounded in the all too mobile bodies that drive our celebrated migrations of culture.

For all its overdetermined symbolic status—as an avatar of "culture," as the exemplary currency of sharing, as article of ethnopolitical faith—food may still anchor us to our most immediate plane of being. But as its semiotic resources are exploited by global capital on one side, by conservative national interests on the other, artists enter this busy kitchen at their own risk. With Thailand's political order hungry for myths that might resolve its intractable contradictions, a kind of raw, culinary realism may be the only line of flight.

David Teh is Assistant Professor in the Department of English Language and Literature at the National University of Singapore.

---

[1] *Sañña* may connote concepts or allusions, or the process of ideation itself. Phra Ajaan Mun Bhuridatta Mahathera, "The Ballad of Liberation from the Khandhas" [c.1930], in *Access to Insight*, trans. Thanissaro Bhikkhu (Valley Center, CA: Metta Forest Monastery, 2010), http://www.accesstoinsight.org/lib/thai/mun/ballad.html.

[2] Roger Shattuck, *The Banquet Years: The Origins of the Avant-Garde in France: 1885 to World War I* (North Stratford, NH: Ayer Company Publishers, revised edition, 2000), 6.

[3] Far from escaping the ambient informationalization of values, food has been rendered by late capitalism as a knowledge product. See Paul Romer, "Economic Growth" in *The Concise Encyclopedia of Economics* (online), http://www.econlib.org/library/Enc/EconomicGrowth.html

[4] *Farang* is Thai for "Western" or "Westerner"; see: http://www.nytimes.com/2010/09/25/world/asia/25chef.html.

[5] Cf. the confused response to Rirkrit's cooking works. See, e.g., the discussion of Chettana Nakavajara's criticisms in Pandit Chanrochanakit, "Feeling Contemporary: The Politics and Aesthetics in Rirkrit Tiravanija's Art," in *Nothing: A Retrospective*, exhibition catalogue (Chiang Mai: Chiang Mai University Art Museum, 2005), 37.

[6] This shift is nowhere more apparent than in state museums. Whereas the older claim to Tai ethnic origins lingers in older institutions, newer ones such as the Museum of Siam (opened in 2008) have begun to celebrate premodern Siam's ethnic heterogeneity. See also Hong Lysa, "Twenty Years of 'Sinlapa Watthanatham': Cultural Politics in Thailand in the 1980s and 1990s," *Journal of Southeast Asian Studies* 31, no. 1 (March 2000): 26–47.

[7] James C. Scott, *The Art of Not Being Governed: An Anarchist History of Southeast Asia* (New Haven and London: Yale University Press, 2009), 80.

[8] Ibid.

[9] Historian Thongchai Winichakul has recently argued that the current impasse stems from a modern aristocracy unable to appreciate the transformation it has wrought on a no longer agrarian labor force. "Thailand's Crisis and the Rise of Asia" (public lecture, Asian Civilizations Museum, Singapore, June 7, 2011).

[10] See generally, Alan Klima, *The Funeral Casino: Meditation, Massacre and Exchange with the Dead in Thailand* (Princeton, NJ: Princeton University Press, 2002). By any international standard, the democratic credentials of Santi Asoke and its political vehicle, Chamlong's Palang Dhamma Party, were shaky at best. They later aligned closely with the "yellow-shirt" protests against Thaksin Shinawatra (himself one of Palang Dhamma's less than ascetic alumni), and hence with a reactionary monarchism.

[11] See Michael Taussig, "The Sun Gives Without Receiving," in *Walter Benjamin's Grave* (Chicago and London: University of Chicago Press, 2006), 69ff.

[12] On the dangers of this iconography, see David Teh, "The Perils of Utopia: Sakarin Krue-on's *Terraced Rice Fields Project*," *Aan* 2, no. 2 (October–December, 2009), (in Thai). Available in English at: www.readjournal.org/ann-english/david-teh -sakarin-krue-on%E2%80%99s-terraced-rice-fields-project/. To my knowledge, neither of the cited projects makes explicit reference to King Bhumipol's "sufficiency economy" policy. Artists may be mindful of the rich symbolism attached to rice, but tend to say little about its political dimensions. See e.g., Hans Ulrich Obrist, ed., *Hans Ulrich Obrist and Rirkrit Tiravanija: The Conversation Series*, vol. 20 (Cologne: Walther König, 2011), 92.

[13] Worathep Akkaboothara, *Plateau's Flavour: A Cooking Diary* (Bangkok: Jim Thompson Art Center, 2011). The farm is an agricultural theme park built by the Thai Silk Company in Nakorn Ratchasima province, a few hours' drive northeast of Bangkok.

[14] The project was exhibited at CAC Brétigny near Paris (2010) and at GaMEC Bergamo, Italy (2011), coinciding with the rise to the top of world restaurant rankings of Copenhagen's *noma*, its menu heavily reliant on seasonal foraging.

Checklist of the Exhibition

PROLOGUE AND ORIGINS

Felix Gonzalez-Torres
American, born in Cuba, 1957–1996

"Untitled" (Portrait of Ross in L.A.), 1991
Multicolored candies, individually wrapped in cellophane
Ideal weight 175 lbs
Installation dimensions variable
© Felix Gonzalez-Torres Foundation
Art Institute of Chicago, promised gift of Howard and Donna Stone

Laura Letinsky
American, born in Canada, 1962

Untitled #6, 2009
From the series *Rome*; Ed. 2/9
Chromogenic print
35 × 45 in. (88.9 × 114.3 cm)
Framed: 44 15/16 × 54 1/2 × 2 1/4 in.
(114.1 × 138.4 × 5.7 cm)
Smart Museum of Art, The University of Chicago; Purchase, the Paul and Miriam Kirkley Fund for Acquisitions, 2012.27

The Italian Futurists

Filippo Tomaso (F. T.) Marinetti
Italian, 1876–1944

Reproduction of "Manifesto della Cucina Futurista" (Manifesto of Futurist Cooking) as printed in *Gazzetta del Popolo* (Turin, December 28, 1930)
Chromogenic print (exhibition print)
17 3/8 × 23 7/8 × 1/4 in. (44.2 × 60.7 × 0.6 cm)
Courtesy the Getty Research Institute, Los Angeles (920092)

Documentation of the Taverna del Santopalato (Restaurant of the Holy Palate), c. 1931
Vintage gelatin silver print
5 3/16 × 7 1/16 in. (13.1 × 18 cm)
Framed: 15 1/8 × 19 1/8 in. (38.4 × 48.6 cm)
Photograph by unknown photo-reporter, Ottolenghi, Turin
Fondazione Echuarren-Salaris, Rome

Documentation of the Taverna del Santopalato (Restaurant of the Holy Palate), c. 1931
Vintage gelatin silver print
4 5/16 × 6 3/4 in. (11 × 17.2 cm)
Photographer unknown
Fondazione Echuarren-Salaris, Rome

Documentation of a Futurist banquet, c. 1931–32
Chromogenic prints (exhibition prints)
Four prints, each: 9 3/16 × 10 in. (23.3 × 25.4 cm)
Photographers unknown
Courtesy Beinecke Rare Book and Manuscript Library, Yale University

Nikolay Diulgheroff
Bulgarian, 1901–1982

Poster for the Taverna del Santopalato (Restaurant of the Holy Palate), c. 1932
Chromogenic print (exhibition print)
23 15/16 × 17 3/8 in. (60.8 × 44.1 cm)
Fondazione Echuarren-Salaris, Rome

Filippo Tomaso (F. T.) Marinetti
Italian, 1876–1944
and **Luigi Colombo Fillia**
Italian, 1904–1936

La cucina futurista
Milan: Sonzogno, 1932
Book
7 1/15 × 4 3/4 × 1 3/15 in. (18 x 12 × 3 cm)
Two copies: one lent by Charles Deering McCormick Library of Special Collections, Northwestern University Library, one lent by Detroit Institute of Art Research Library

The Futurist Cookbook
San Francisco: Bedford Arts, 1989
Book, translated by Suzanne Brill
9 5/8 × 7 3/8 × 5/8 in. (24.4 × 18.8 × 1.5 cm)

CONCEPTUAL AND PERFORMATIVE FEASTS

Marina Abramović
Serbian, b. 1946
and **Ulay**
German, b. 1943

Communist Body/Fascist Body, 1979/2012
Ed. 1/3
Mixed media installation including fabric, glass, metal, paper, plastic, utensils, wood, and 16mm film transferred to DVD (color, sound, 41:40 minutes)
Installation dimensions variable;
minimum 192 × 264 in. (487.7 × 670.6 cm)
Installation furniture fabricated by
Peter Superti
Courtesy the artists and Sean Kelly, New York

Alison Knowles
American, b. 1933

The Identical Lunch, 1967/2012
Tuna fish sandwich on plate, glass of buttermilk or a cup of soup, vitrine, stool, and cloth
Installation dimensions variable
Courtesy the artist

Journal of the Identical Lunch
San Francisco: Nova Broadcast Press, 1971
Artist's book
7⅞ × 5 × ⅛ in. (20 × 12.7 × 0.3 cm)
Collection of the artist

Identical Lunch, 1993
Silkscreen on canvas
Six panels, each: 16 × 16 in. (40.6 × 40.6 cm)
Collection Adam and Beth Lustbader,
Bannockburn, Illinois

Identical Lunch Symphony, 2012
Participatory artwork performed at the Logan Center for the Arts, University of Chicago, May 5, 2012
Commission, Smart Museum of Art
Courtesy the artist

Philip Corner
American, b. 1933
The Identical Lunch
San Francisco: Nova Broadcast, 1973
Artist's book
7 13/16 × 6 × 3/16 in. (19.8 × 15.2 × 0.5 cm)
Collection Alison Knowles

Suzanne Lacy
American, b. 1945

with Linda Pruess
American, b. 1953
International Dinner Party, 1979/2012
Mixed media installation recreating performance setting, including original map and facsimiles of telegrams and binders
Installation dimensions variable, approximately 96 × 192 × 24 in. (243.8 × 487.7 × 61 cm)
Courtesy the artist

with Linda Pruess
American, b. 1953
International Dinner Party, 1979/2012
Archival material
Installation dimensions variable
Courtesy the artist

with Laverne Dunn
American, b. 1950
River Meetings: Lives of Women in the Delta, 1981–82
Chromogenic prints (exhibition prints) and archival materials
Installation dimensions variable; four prints, each: approximately 30 × 20 in. (76.2 × 50.8 cm)
Photography by Phyllis Parun
Courtesy the artist

Tom Marioni
American, b. 1937

The Act of Drinking Beer with Friends Is the Highest Form of Art, 1970–ongoing
Participatory artwork performed at the Smart Museum of Art, February 15, March 1, April 5, May 3, and June 7, 2012; and installation including bar, chairs, free beer, refrigerator, table, vinyl lettering, and the three following works listed
Courtesy the artist

An Aid to Communication, 1999/2012
Bottles and wood
78 × 49 × 3½ in. (198.1 × 124.5 × 8.9 cm)
Courtesy the artist

Golden Rectangle Beer, 2004
Video (color, silent, 16:16 minutes) and audio track (variable length)
Courtesy the artist

Out of Body Free Hand Circle, 2012
Graphite on prepared wall
84 × 84 in. (213.4 × 213.4 cm)
Courtesy the artist

Gordon Matta-Clark

American, 1943–1978

with FOOD collaborators
Advertisements for FOOD in *Avalanche* Issue 3 (Fall 1971), Issue 4 (Spring 1972), and Issue 5 (Summer 1972)
Three magazines, each: 9¼ × 9¼ in. (23.5 × 23.5 cm)
For Chicago, Houston, and Santa Fe venues: Lent by Charles Deering McCormick Library of Special Collections, Northwestern University Library of Special Collections, Northwestern University
For other venues: Collection of Rhona Hoffman, Chicago

with Robert Frank
Swiss, b. 1924
A Day in the Life of Food, 1971–73
16mm film transferred to DVD (black-and-white, sound, 42:39 minutes)
Courtesy Electronic Arts Intermix (EAI), New York

FOOD, 1972/2006
Triptych; Ed. 1/30
Gelatin silver prints
Framed: 36⅝ × 20 × 1½ in. (93 × 50.8 × 3.8 cm)
Each print: 11 × 14 in. (27.9 × 35.6 cm)
Photography by Cosmos Andrew Sarchiapone
Courtesy the Estate of Gordon Matta-Clark and David Zwirner, New York

Allen Ruppersberg

American, b. 1944

Al's Café, 1969/2012
Chromogenic prints (exhibition prints)
10 prints, each framed: 8⅞ × 10⅞ in. (22.5 × 27.6 cm)
Photography of interior and meals by Gary Krueger
Photography of menu by Augusta Wood
Courtesy the artist

Bonnie Ora Sherk

American, b. 1945

Public Lunch, 1971/2012
16 mm film transferred to DVD (black-and-white, sound, 7:25 minutes) and chromogenic prints (exhibition prints)
One print: 30 × 40 in. (76.2 × 101.6 cm); four prints, each: 16 × 20 in. (40.6 × 50.8 cm)
Courtesy the artist

Short Order Cook, 1973–74/2012
Chromogenic prints (exhibition prints)
9 prints, each: 20 × 30 in. (50.8 × 76.2 cm)
Courtesy the artist

Barbara T. Smith

American, b. 1931

Ritual Meal, 1969
Vintage gelatin silver prints
Three prints, each: 8 × 10 in. (20.3 × 25.4 cm)
Framed, each: 15 1/16 × 19 1/16 in. (38.3 × 48.4 cm)
Courtesy the artist and the Box, Los Angeles, CA

Ritual Meal, 1969
16 mm film transferred to video (black-and-white and color, sound, 11:30 minutes)
Courtesy the artist and the Box, Los Angeles, CA

Daniel Spoerri

Swiss, born in Romania, 1930

29 Variations on a Meal, 1964
Allan Stone Gallery, New York, NY
Exhibition postcard
Ink on paper
6 × 6⅞ in. (15.2 × 17.5 cm)
Collection of Stephanie Snyder, Portland, OR

Daniel Spoerri's Room No. 631 at the Chelsea Hotel, 1965
Green Gallery at the Chelsea Hotel, New York, NY (March 3–15, 1965)
Folding exhibition mailer/brochure
Ink on paper
Open: 21 × 10½ in. (53.3 × 26.7 cm)
Essay by Allan Kaprow
Photographs by Peter Moore
Two copies, both collection of Stephanie Snyder, Portland, OR

The Mythological Travels of a Modern Sir John Mandeville, Being an Account of the Magic, Meatballs and Other Monkey Business Peculiar to the Sojourn of Daniel Spoerri Upon the Isle of Symi, Together With Divers Speculations Thereon
New York: Something Else Press, 1970
Book
8 1/8 × 5 5/8 × 1 3/16 in. (20.6 × 14.2 × 3 cm)
Translated by Emmett Williams
Collection of Stephanie Snyder, Portland, OR

Daniel Spoerri presents Eat Art, Robin Page, 49 Cones with Original Watercolours, 1970
Eat Art Gallery, Düsseldorf, Germany
(Opening: March 12, 1970)
Exhibition poster/announcement; ink on paper
17 × 12 in. (43.2 × 30.5 cm)
Framed: 18 1/16 × 13 1/8 in. (45.9 × 33.3 cm)
Collection of Stephanie Snyder, Portland, OR

Daniel Spoerri Presents Eat Art, Arman "Candy", 1970
Eat Art Gallery, Düsseldorf, Germany
(Opening: December 11, 1970)
Exhibition poster/announcement; ink on paper
17 × 12 in. (43.2 × 30.5 cm)
Framed: 17 15/16 × 13 in. (45.6 × 33 cm)
Collection of Stephanie Snyder, Portland, OR

*Daniel Spoerri presents Eat Art, *in memoriam friends*, 1971
Eat Art Gallery, Düsseldorf, Germany
(Opening: January 22, 1971)
Exhibition poster/announcement; ink on paper
17 × 12 in. (43.2 × 30.5 cm)
Framed: 18 3/16 × 13 1/8 in. (46.1 × 33.3 cm)
Collection of Stephanie Snyder, Portland, OR

Daniel Spoerri presents Eat Art, César, c. 1971–72
Eat Art Gallery, Düsseldorf, Germany
Exhibition poster/announcement; ink on paper
17 × 12 in. (43.2 × 30.5 cm)
Framed: 17 15/16 × 13 in. (45.6 × 33 cm)
Collection of Stephanie Snyder, Portland, OR

Tableau piège, 17. Juni 1972, 1972
Assemblage on wood, in case frame
27 7/8 × 27 7/8 × 16 in. (70.8 × 70.8 × 40.6 cm)
Smart Museum of Art, The University of Chicago; Purchase, the Paul and Miriam Kirkley Fund for Acquisitions, 2011.40

Fallenbild, 1973
Les Nouveaux Réalistes, Ars Viva Edition; Ed. 423/600
Lithograph in offset printed in colors and collage with 8 elements, mounted on cardboard support
Closed: 19 11/16 × 19 11/16 in. (50 × 50 cm)
Open: 6 × 27 × 27 in. (15.2 × 68.6 × 68.6 cm)
Smart Museum of Art, The University of Chicago; Purchase, the Paul and Miriam Kirkley Fund for Acquisitions, 2011.41.1

Eliane Ganz Gallery, EAT ART Dinner, September 28, 1975, 1975
San Francisco, California
Archival exhibition prints made from original photographs in the collection of the Anne Bremer Memorial Library, San Francisco Art Institute, San Francisco, CA
13 prints, each: 18 × 24 in. (45.7 × 61 cm)
Framed: 17 1/2 × 23 3/8 in. (44.5 × 59.4 cm)
Reed College Art Collection, gift of the Anne Bremer Memorial Library, San Francisco Art Institute

Zehn Suppenrezepte, 1984
Boxed portfolio of ten sheets; Ed. 75/75
Folding sheets and colophon housed in a linen-covered box
10 sheets, each 17 3/4 × 24 1/2 in. (45.1 × 62.23 cm)
Colophon page single sheet:
17 3/4 in. × 12 1/4 in. (45.1 × 31.1 cm)
Closed folio box dimensions: 18 × 14 × 1 1/2 in. (45.7 × 35.6 × 3.8 cm)
Recipes by Daniel Spoerri
Illustrations by Fritz Schwegler
Published by Francsco Conz, Verona
Reed College Art Collection, Portland, OR

SOCIAL AND CRITICAL FEASTS

Sonja Alhäuser
German, b. 1968

Flying Feast, 2012
Participatory artwork performed at the Smart Museum of Art, February 15, 2012; and mixed-media installation including margarine sculptures and the following work listed
Installation dimensions variable
Commission, Smart Museum of Art
Courtesy the artist

Flying Feast, 2012
Ink and gouache on paper with metal grommets
55¼ × 132 in. (140.3 × 335.3 cm)
Smart Museum of Art, The University of Chicago; Purchase, the Paul and Miriam Kirkley Fund for Acquisitions, 2012.31

Mary Ellen Carroll
American, b. 1961

Itinerant Gastronomy, 1996–ongoing
Mixed media installation including text installation, archival materials, artifacts, and chromogenic prints (exhibition prints)
Installation dimensions variable
Courtesy the artist

Open Outcry, 2012
Itinerant Gastronomy participatory artwork performed at Chicago Board of Trade, CME Group, January 23, 2012; and mixed-media installation including architectural models listed below, furniture, ephemera, and video (color, sound, 14:39 minutes)
Installation dimensions variable
Videography by Michael Isabell
Furniture design in collaboration with Simon Dance/Simon Dance Design
Commission, Smart Museum of Art
Courtesy the artist

with Simon Dance/Simon Dance Design
British (English)
Architectural Models for Open Outcry, 2012
Board, mat board, and plastic
Installation dimensions variable
Courtesy Simon Dance Design

Fallen Fruit
(Collaboration with David Burns, Matias Viegener, and Austin Young)
American, 2004–ongoing

Neighborhood Infusions, 2008–ongoing
Participatory artwork performed at the Logan Center for the Arts, University of Chicago, May 5, 2012, and installation including fruit-infused vodka
Installation dimensions variable
Vodka produced in collaboration with the Greenbar Collective, Los Angeles, CA
Courtesy the artists

Theaster Gates
American, b. 1974

Soul Food Starter Kit, 2012
Ceramics, graphite, metal, wood, and graphite on wood (manifesto)
Installation dimensions variable, approximately 60 × 36 × 24 in. (152.4 × 91.4 × 61 cm)
Smart Museum of Art, The University of Chicago; Purchase, the Paul and Miriam Kirkley Fund for Acquisitions, 2012.30

Soul Pavilion, 2012
Participatory artwork performed at Dorchester Projects, Chicago, February 19, March 11, April 15, and May 20, 2012
Ceramics produced with Kouichi Ohara
Meals produced with Erika Dudley, Michael Kornick, and Erick Williams
Performances by the Black Monks of Mississippi
Sermons by Irma Dixon, Orron Kenyatta, and others
Commission, Smart Museum of Art
Courtesy the artist and Kavi Gupta, Chicago

InCUBATE
American, 2006–ongoing

Sunday Soup, 2007–present
Mixed media installation with variable elements including the following works:
Robert Snowden's *You are in the right place at the right time*, 2008
Project Empathy's *InCUBATE Lightbox*
How to Start Your Own Sunday Soup designed by FEAST MASS with contributions from the International Sunday Soup Network
Installation dimensions variable
Courtesy the artists

Mella Jaarsma
Dutch, b. 1960

Pribumi Pribumi, 1998
Video (color, sound, 12:31 minutes)
Courtesy the artist

I Eat You Eat Me, 2001/2012
Participatory artwork and installation including wearable leather and metal sculpture (six-person version) and two-channel video (color, sound, 5:45 and 10:05 minutes)
Installation dimensions variable
Sculpture: 65 × 75 in. (165.1 × 190.5 cm)
Courtesy the artist

I Eat You Eat Me, 2001–ongoing
Participatory artwork and installation including wearable leather and metal sculpture (two-person version)
Installation dimensions variable
Courtesy the artist

Lee Mingwei
Taiwanese, b. 1964

The Dining Project, 1998–ongoing
Participatory artwork performed at the Smart Museum of Art, February 13, February 14, April 30, May 1, and May 2, 2012; and installation including black beans, ceramics, tatami mats, wood, and video (color, sound, 1:15:25 hours)
Installation approximately 144 × 144 × 144 in. (365.8 × 365.8 × 365.8 cm)
Courtesy the artist and Lombard-Freid Projects, New York

Laura Letinsky
American, born in Canada, 1962

Untitled #12, 1997
From the series *Hardly More Than Ever* (formerly, *Morning and Melancholia*); Ed. 3/15
Chromogenic print
Sheet: 20 × 24 in. (50.8 × 61 cm)
Framed: 25⅜ × 31⅜ × 2¼ in. (64.5 × 79.7 × 5.7 cm)
Smart Museum of Art, The University of Chicago; Purchase, gift of Carl Rungius, by exchange, 2001.40

Untitled #22, 1999–2000
From the series *Hardly More Than Ever* (formerly, *Morning and Melancholia*); Ed. 6/15
Chromogenic print
Sheet: 20 × 24 in. (50.8 × 61 cm)
Framed: 25⅜ × 31⅜ × 2¼ in. (64.5 × 79.7 × 5.7 cm)
Smart Museum of Art, The University of Chicago; Purchase, gift of Carl Rungius, by exchange, 2001.41

Untitled #80, 2003
From the series *Hardly More Than Ever*; Ed. 1/3 artist's proof impressions; Ed. of 15 with 3 artist's proof impressions
Chromogenic print archivally mounted to Sintra
Sheet: 29½ × 34⅜ in. (74.9 × 87.3 cm)
Framed: 30⅜ × 35⅜ × 1¾ in. (77.2 × 89.9 × 4.4 cm)
Smart Museum of Art, The University of Chicago; Anonymous Gift, 2006.6

Untitled #37, 2012
From the series *Ill Form and Void Full*; Ed. 1/9
Chromogenic print
Framed: 54 13/16 × 44 15/16 × 2¼ in. (139.2 × 114.1 × 5.7 cm)
Commission, Smart Museum of Art
Smart Museum of Art, The University of Chicago; Gift of the artist, 2012.22

Mildred's Lane
Collective based in Pennsylvania, 1998–ongoing
with **Mark Dion**
American, b. 1961
and J. Morgan Puett
American, b. 1957

A Mildred's Lane Algorithmic Dinner and Refrigerator Hoosh, 2012
Mixed media installation including digital media, fabric, glass, metal, organic material, paper, tools, utensils, water, wine cooler, and wood
Digital slideshow (color images with captions, 15:28 minutes)
Approximately 162 × 78 × 30 in. (411.5 × 198.1 × 76.2 cm)
Courtesy the artists

Julio César Morales
Mexican, b. 1966

with Max La Rivière-Hedrick
Interrupted Passage, 2008
Two-channel video installation (color, sound, 15:33 minutes)
Installation dimensions variable
Courtesy the artist and Frey Norris Contemporary and Modern, San Francisco

motiroti
Collective based in London, 1996–ongoing
with Ali Zaidi
Indian/Pakistani/British, b. 1969
and Tim Jones
British, b. 1969

Potluck: Chicago, 2012
Participatory artwork performed at various sites in Chicago, 2011–2012; and installation including apron, digital media, map, paper, and photographic documentation
Installation dimensions variable
Commissioned by Columbia College Chicago
Courtesy the artists

The National Bitter Melon Council
Collective based in Boston, 2004–ongoing

Better Living through Bitter Melon, 2012
Participatory artwork performed in Chicago, December 5, 2011; and installation including artist's books, comment book, two framed napkins (one used), two framed placemats (one used), gloves, paint, posters, and wood
Installation dimensions variable, approximately 120 × 180 × 60 in. (304.8 × 457.2 × 152.4 cm)
Courtesy the artists

Ana Prvacki
Serbian, b. 1976

The Greeting Committee, 2011–ongoing
Participatory artwork performed at the Smart Museum of Art, February 12–June 10, 2012; and installation including carpet, glass, homemade jam, metal, paper, and wood
Installation: approximately 36 × 60 × 84 in. (91.4 × 152.4 × 213.4 cm)
Courtesy the artist

Sudsiri Pui-Ock
Thai, b. 1976

The Dinner, 2005
Video (color, sound, 15:00 minutes)
Installation dimensions variable
Videography by Judit Kurtag
Courtesy the artist

Michael Rakowitz
American, b. 1973

Enemies and Kitchens, 2012
Mixed media installation including chromogenic prints (exhibition prints), drawing (colored pencil and graphite on paper), ephemera, fabric, paper, Plexiglas, wood, vinyl lettering, and video (color, sound, 9:54 minutes)
Installation dimensions variable, approximately 72 × 144 × 30 in. (182.9 × 365.8 × 76.2 cm)
Framed drawing: 19½ × 19½ in. (49.5 × 49.5 cm)
Courtesy the artist and Lombard-Freid Projects, New York

Enemy Kitchen (Food Truck), 2012
Participatory artwork performed at various sites in Chicago, February 12–June 10, 2012
Meals prepared and served in collaboration with Milad and Maikl Shaer, and members of the Iraqi Mutual Aid Society and Iraq Veterans Against the War (IVAM)
Tea performances by Aaron Hughes, IVAM
Commission, Smart Museum of Art
Courtesy the artist and Lombard-Freid Projects, New York

Enemy Kitchen (Rosewater), 2012
Glass, metal, and rosewater
8 3/16 × 4 7/8 × 2 11/16 in. (20.8 × 12.4 × 6.9 cm)
Courtesy the artist and Lombard-Freid Projects, New York

Ayman Ramadan
Egyptian, b. 1980

Iftar, 2004
Video (color, sound, 8:51 minutes)
Installation dimensions variable
Courtesy the artist

Red76
Collaborative artists, based in Minneapolis, MN, 2000–ongoing

Revolutionary Table, 2007–2008
Installation including chromogenic prints (exhibition prints), and printed matter
Installation dimensions variable, approximately 120 × 144 × 24 in. (304.8 × 365.8 × 61 cm)
Photo 1: framed: 20 1/2 × 27 1/8 in. (52.1 × 68.9 cm)
Photo 2: framed: 25 1/8 × 33 1/8 in. (63.8 × 84.1 cm)
Photo 3: framed: 20 5/8 × 17 1/8 in. (52.4 × 43.5 cm)
Courtesy the artists

Occupy Yr. Home, 2012–ongoing
Participatory project performed in Chicago, IL, February 2012; Brooklyn, NY, March 2012; Baltimore, MD, April 2012; Kansas City, MO, May 2012; Pristina, Kosovo, June 2012; and installation of wooden box and flyers
Installation dimensions variable
Box: 10 1/2 × 48 × 15 in. (26.7 × 121.9 × 38.1 cm)
Courtesy the artists

David Robbins
American, b. 1957

Ice Cream Social, 1993–2008
Participatory artwork performed at the Smart Museum of Art, June 10, 2012; and installation including artist's books, ceramics, chromogenic prints (exhibition prints), magnets, refrigerator, and video (color, sound, 8:38 minutes)
Installation dimensions variable
Courtesy the artist

Rirkrit Tiravanija
Thai, b. 1961

For documentation only, active photograph, 1990
From *Pad Thai*, February 17–March 3, 1990 at Paula Allan Gallery, New York, NY
Fading black-and-white polaroid photograph, cast resin, dirty Plexiglas, scrap, and newspaper
Dimensions variable, approximately 15 × 17 in. (38.1 × 43.2 cm)
Collection of Randy Alexander

untitled 1990 (pad thai), 1990
Exhibition press release and documentation photographs (exhibition prints)
Dimensions variable
Photography by Randy Alexander
Collection of Randy Alexander

untitled 1990 (wok), 1990
Wok, food remnants, box, and pedestal
Installation dimensions variable
Collection of Eileen and Michael Cohen

untitled 1992 (red, green, yellow curry), 1992
Ed. 4/10 plus 2 artist's proofs; (RT 033)
Aluminum cans, curry, and labels
Each: 3 × 3 × 1 in. (7.6 × 7.6 × 2.5 cm)
Published by Gavin Brown's enterprise
Courtesy the artist and Gavin Brown's enterprise, New York

Note: Some participatory artworks are only presented at the Smart Museum of Art; other artists and participatory artworks will be added by presenting venues as the exhibition travels.

Acknowledgments

Marina Abramović, *Communist Body/ Fascist Body*
Thanks to: Ulay, Sean Kelly and Sean Kelly Gallery, Jo Lewington, Danica Newell, Cecile Panzieri, Sidney Russell, and Peter Superti

Sonja Alhäuser, *Flying Feast*
Performers, Smart Museum of Art, University of Chicago: Eamon Boylan, Alexis Chaney, Emily Jusino, Naomi Itzkoff, Penelope Murav, Ivan Pyzow, Natalie Reinhart, Fred Schmidt-Arenales, Cassandra Troyan, and David Wind

Sculpting assistants, Smart Museum of Art, University of Chicago: Whitney Chi, Stef Etow, Dory Fox, Zoe Petticord, Theo Shure, and May Yeung

Additional thanks to: Clare Fentress, and Stephan and Wilhelmine Homann

Mary Ellen Carroll, *Open Outcry*
Project team and collaborators: Simon Dance/ Simon Dance Design, Ron Gilles, Michael Isabell, Laura Madera-Nadal, Seth McCormick, Philip Ording, and Lindsay Phillips

Lunch participants: Erika Allen, Jude Becker, Homaro Cantu, Dionna Griffin-Irons, John Pietrzak, Stephanie Smith, Candace Vogler, and Glen Wyle

Fallen Fruit, *Neighborhood Infusions*
Thanks to: Greenbar Collective

Theaster Gates, *Soul Pavilion*
Project team, collaborators, and The Black Monks of Mississippi: Yaw Agyeman, LeRoy Bach, Marlease Bushnell, Beninda Davenport, Matthew Dercole, Irma Dixon and family, Erika Dudley, David Frej, Nancy Frej, Yoko Fukuta, Marva Jolly, Haruka Kamatsu, Lisa Kornick, Michael Kornick, Khari Lemuel, Nancy Lerner, Kouichi Ohara, Sara Pooley, Erick Williams, Kate Hadley Williams, and Titus Wonsey

Additional thanks to: Art Institute of Chicago; Chicago Community Trust; Lill Street Art Center; MK Restaurant; Otherwise, Inc.; and Rebuild Foundation

InCUBATE, *Sunday Soup*
Thanks to: All the organizers in the *Sunday Soup* Network

Mella Jaarsma, *I Eat You Eat Me*
Performers, Yogykarta, Indonesia, January 16, 2012: Erryl Setiya Devivta, Fransisca Maria, Ingvild Sovang, Siat Sari Trikusumawardhani, Dina Usman, and Citra Ayu Wardani

Performers, Smart Museum of Art, University of Chicago, January 19, 2012: Stephanie Dering, Adam Dunlavy, Alicia French, Kristen Gindler, John Harness, James Levinsohn, Nicole Reyna, Jessica Ro, Isabel Wade, David Wind, and Hope Withrow

Additional thanks to: Chulalongkorn University Bangkok, Mie Cornoedus, Eat Me Restaurant, Bangkok, Apinan Poshyananda, Ruang Rupa, Jakarta, and ViaVia Travelers Café, Yogyakarta

Alison Knowles, *Identical Lunch Symphony*
Performers, Logan Center for the Arts, University of Chicago, May 5, 2012: Jeff Abell, Bruce Adams, Annie Feldmeier Adams, Sally Alatalo, Simon Anderson, Liliana Angulo, Juan Carlos Arias, Diego Arispe-Bazan, Emily Capper, Scarlet Ji Yeon Kim, Lilly Lerer, Janice Misurell-Mitchell, Alex Rauch, Ana Maria Reyes, Katja D. Rivera, Fred Schmidt-Arenales, Theo Shure, Lauren Silvers, Tina Tahir, and May Yeung

Additional thanks to: Philip Corner, Jan Herman

Suzanne Lacy, *International Dinner Party* and *River Meetings: Lives of Women in the Delta*
Project collaborators: Laverne Dunn and Linda Pruess

Additional thanks to: Judy Chicago and Mary Jane Jacob

Laura Letinsky, *Untitled #37* from the series *Ill Form and Void Full*
Artists' Lunch participants, February 16, 2012: Marina Abramović, Mary Ellen Carroll, Simon Dance, Alison Knowles, Casimir Kujawa, Suzanne Lacy, Jeremy Liu, Tom Marioni, Mason Pritchett, Ana Prvacki, J. Morgan Puett, Bonnie Ora Sherk, Stephanie Smith, and Andi Sutton

Sous chefs: Clare Fentress and Sarah Mendelsohn

Additional thanks to: Yancey Richardson, Walker Waugh and crew, Ada Letinsky, Aron Gent, the University of Chicago, Tony Wight, and Clyde and Louis

Lee Mingwei, *The Dining Project*
Dinner participants, Smart Museum of Art, University of Chicago: Dory Fox, Megan Larmer, Kim Mims, Dan Peterman, and Anne Yoder

Tom Marioni, *The Act of Drinking Beer with Friends Is the Highest Form of Art*
Bartenders, February 15, 2012: Diego Arispe-Bazan, Rudy Bernal, Sarah Mendelsohn, and Joseph Rynkiewicz

Bartenders, March 1, 2012: Madeleine Grynsztejn, and Anthony Hirschel

Bartenders, April 5, 2012: BBU: Epic, Illekt, and Jasson Perez & DJ Esquire

Bartenders, May 3, 2012: Young Chicago Authors: Britteney Connor, and J. W. Basilo

Bartenders, June 7, 2012: Neo-Futurists: Jessica Anne, Kurt Chiang, Trevor Dawkins, Phil Ridarelli, and Caitlin Stainken

motiroti, *Potluck: Chicago*
Project participants: Hannah Anderton, Katie Binhack, Nicolette Caldwell, Deirdre Colgan, Nidia Coy, Jessica Egan, David Flynn, Hannah Friedman, Kim Guare, Cassie Hamrick, Grant Penfield Haugen, Eboni Senai Hawkins, Tempest Hazel, Maria Hewett, Anni Holm, Lakeisha Leek, Zachary Michael, Chelsea Middendorf, Amy M. Mooney, Elizabeth Nungaray, Dia Penning, Meg Peterson, Brian Shaw, Helen Slade, Michael St. John, and Casey Winkleman

Partner organizations, Chicago: Columbia College Chicago (Kathleen Beste, Stephen Desantis, Lott Hill, Anne Marie Mitchell, Alexa Rittichier, Darren Wallace); Dorchester Projects (Mr. Bill, Marlease Bushnell, Theaster Gates, Mr. Gates Sr., Mejay Gula, Ms. Jolly); En Las Tablas (Maritza Nazario); Jane Addams Hull-House Museum (Tara Lane, Lisa Lee, Harish Patel, Heather Radke); Inspiration Kitchens (Avril Greenberg); and South Side Hub of Production (David Durstewitz, Laura Shaeffer)

Additional thanks to: Academic Affairs and Critical Encounters at Columbia College Chicago, Center for Innovation in Teaching Excellence, and The Ellen Stone Bellic Institute for the Study of Women and Gender in the Arts and Media

The National Bitter Melon Council, *Better Living Through Bitter Melon*
Thanks to: Misa Saburi, all collaborating chefs, farmers, activists, and other project participants

Ana Prvacki, *Greeting Committee*
Slatko servers, Smart Museum of Art, University of Chicago: Maggie Borowitz, Whitney Chi, Kristen Gindler, Faith Laken, Tracy Lee, Penelope Murav, Theo Rossi, Harmon Siegel, Becky Singerman, Isabel Wade, and David Wind

Additional thanks to: The artist's parents and Deborah Fortel (mother of curator Stephanie Smith)

Michael Rakowitz, *Enemy Kitchen (Food Tuck)*
Project team and collaborators: Azhar Abdulnabi, Sabah al Adlai, Greg Broseus, Crystal Colon, Aaron Hughes, Bana Khattan, Ash Khyrie, Ray Klemchuk, Ahlam Mahmood, Ghassan Nawfil, Maikl Shaer, Milad Shaer, Peter Skvara, Alejandro Villatoro, and Michael Younan

Red76
Project collaborators: Lauren Beck, Rachel Ellison, Nabiha Kahn and Cassandra Troyan (Chicago); Dylan Gautier and Kendra Sullivan (Brooklyn); Sean Starowitz (Kansas City); Baltimore Development Cooperative (Baltimore); and Stacion (Kosovo)

Bonnie Ora Sherk, *Public Lunch* and *Short Order Cook*
Thanks to: The San Francisco Zoo and Tony Smull

Barbara T. Smith, *Ritual Meal*
Thanks to: Stanley and Elyse Grinstein, Joseph Byrd, and Dick Kilgroe

Stephanie Snyder, *Hospitality as Witness in the Work of Daniel Spoerri*
Thanks to: Colleen Gotze

Lori Waxman, *The Banquet Years: FOOD, A SoHo Restaurant*
Thanks to: Carol McCoy (née Gooden), Tina Girouard, Bob Kushner, and Rob Storr

Stephanie Smith
Thanks to: the artists (first and always); their collaborators and all those they thank on the preceding pages; past and current Smart Museum senior staff, especially Rudy Bernal, Michael Christiano, Patrick Flanagan, Breck Furnas, Justin Glasson, Anthony Hirschel, Ray Klemchuk, C.J. Lind, Peg Liput, Jessica Moss, Kate Nardin, Joyce Norman, Sara Patrello, Sarah Polachek, Angela Steinmetz, and the Board of Governors; all the student staff and interns who helped along the way, including Chris Aque, Diego Arispe-Bazan, Emily Capper, Sarah Mendelsohn, Kim Mims, Marisa Nakasone, Tatiana Natzke, and Jenn Sichel; the book team (the authors; Lisa Meyerowitz, Sarah Mendelsohn, and Jason Pickleman); programming collaborators including Zachary Cahill, Leslie Danzig, Tara Lane, Lisa Lee, and Bill Michel; all of the venues who are hosting the show; all the project's supporters, especially the Emily Hall Tremaine Foundation for believing in *Feast* from the very beginning, and also the Andy Warhol Foundation for the Visual Arts, the Chicago Community Trust, Helen Zell, the Chauncey and Marion Deering McCormick Foundation, the Richard and Mary L. Gray Foundation, the University of Chicago's Arts Council, and Janis Kanter and Tom McCormick; and the friends, family, and colleagues who shared ideas and expertise and who challenged and supported me through every phase of the project.

REPRODUCTION CREDITS

All works of art copyright the artists, heirs, and assigns. Every effort has been made to contact rights holders for all reproductions. Additional rights please contact the Smart Museum of Art.

The following texts and excerpts appearing in this volume are reprinted by permission:

"The Futurist Manifesto of Cooking" (Filippo Tommaso Marinetti, included in *The Futurist Cookbook* trans. Suzanne Brill © 1989 Bedford Arts, San Francisco

"Communist Body/Fascist Body" Performance text © 1979 Marina Abramović

"Journal of the Identical Lunch" © 1971 Alison Knowles

Beer, Art and Philosophy: A Memoir © 2007 Tom Marioni

"The Banquet Years: FOOD, a SoHo Restaurant" © 2008 Lori Waxman and *Gastronomica*

"Interview with Allen Ruppersberg" © 2011 Allen Ruppersberg and Kadist Foundation, San Francisco

"Occupy Yr. Home *(2012–2015: A Distributed Meal)*" © 2012 Red76

"Notes on the Ice Cream Social" © 2005 David Robbins and Miller Gallery, Carnegie Mellon University, Pittsburgh

Ice Cream Social © 2004 David Robbins and JRP: Ringier, Zurich

"No Ghosts in the Wall" © 2004 Rirkrit Tiravanija and Museum Boijmans van Beuningen

"Toast" © 2012 Anthony Huberman

"Exotic Hospitality in the Land of Tolerance" © 2012 Irina Aristarkhova, adapted from an essay in *Manifesta Coffee Break—Refugee—Hospitality—Occupation: Visual Art and Contemporary Curatorial Work in a Changing Europe*, 2005

All images are courtesy the artists unless otherwise noted.

The following images have been reproduced in this volume with permissions:

© Marina Abramović Archives, Courtesy of Marina Abramović and Sean Kelly Gallery, New York: p. 52, 54–55, 59

© Marina Abramović Archives: p. 56–57

Photo by Cristian Alexa: p. 235

Courtesy Randy Alexander, New York: p. 335, 337, 339, 344–345

© 2012 Artists Rights Society (ARS), New York / ProLitteris, Zurich: p. 141

© 2012 Artists Rights Society (ARS), New York / ProLitteris, Zurich, courtesy of Reed College Art Collection, gift of the Anne Bremer Memorial Library, San Francisco Art Institute: p. 145

© 2012 Artists Rights Society (ARS), New York / ProLitteris, Zurich, Collection of Stephanie Snyder, Portland, OR: p. 147, 148, 150–151

© 2012 Artists Rights Society (ARS), New York / SIAE, Rome, courtesy Collection Fondazione Echaurren-Salaris, Rome: p. 33, 37

© Associated Press, photo David Guttenfelder: p. 302

© Beinecke Rare Book and Manuscript Library, Yale University: p. 33

Photo by Scott Berzofsky: p. 207

Photo by Aubrey Boonstra, courtesy of Chicago Humanities Festival: p. 60

Photo by Greg Broseus: p. 300

© Mary Ellen Carroll/MEC, design studios: p. 167, 174–175, 169, 171, 172–173, 176–177

© Mary Ellen Carroll/MEC, design studios and Simon Dance/Simon Dance Design: p. 170

Chicago Daily Tribune, December 11 © 1931 Chicago Tribune. All rights reserved. Used by permission and protected by the Copyright Laws of the United States. The printing, copying, redistribution, or retransmission of this Content without express written permission is prohibited: p. 40

Photos by Michael Christiano: p. 93 (bottom), 94 (top, bottom left), 98, 324–335

Photo by Mie Cornoedus: 216 (bottom)

Photos by Stef Etow: p. 163

© Fallen Fruit (David Burns, Matias Viegener, and Austin Young): p. 179, 180–181, 183, 184–185, 186

Photos by Fallen Fruit: p. 183 (top)

Photo by Carsten Gliese: p. 161 (left)

© The Getty Research Institute, Los Angeles (920092): p. 35

Photos by Lloyd DeGrane: p. 93 (top), 98, 190

Photos by Julio Duffo: p. 249, 254

Poster designed by Golden Arrows: p. 211

Photo courtesy Kavi Gupta Gallery, Chicago: p. 192

Photo by Joanne Hendricks, Cookbooks, New York: p. 169 (top)

Photo by Claire Haasl: p. 201

Courtesy of Hannah B Higgins: p. 43

Photo by George Hirose: p. 235 (top)

Photo by Peter Hoffman: p. 197

Photos by Mella Jaarsma: p. 215, 216 (top), 219

Photo by InCUBATE: p. 202

Photo by InCUBATE neighbor: p. 205

Photo by Stacee Kalmanovsky: p. 298 (bottom)

Photo by Kate Khatib: p. 206 (bottom left)

Photo by Christopher Kissock, courtesy of Creative Time, New York: p. 303

Photos by Gary Krueger: p. 119, 122, 123, 124, 125

Photo by Achim Kukulies: p. 161 (right)

Photo by Judit Kurtag: p. 286

Photo by Richard Landry, courtesy of Richard Landry: p. 101

Photos by Jeremy Lawson: p. 5, 85, 87, 94 (bottom right), 157, 160 (right), 162, 193, 257, 270–271, 279, 282 (right), 285, 295, 299 (bottom), 398–399

Photo by Elisa Leshowitz: p. 169 (bottom)

Photos by Leigh Loftus: p. 167, 174, 175

Photo by Chelsea Middendorf: p. 264

Photo by Amy M. Mooney: p. 264 (right)

Photos by Peter Moore: p. 150

Photo by Julio Cesar Morales: p. 253 (top)

Photos by Kristine Moss: p. 280, 281 (middle left, bottom)

Courtesy Green Naftali Gallery, New York: p. 332

Photo by Kramer O'Neill: p. 206 (bottom right)

Photo by Jesse Nichols: p. 255

Courtesy Gallery Wendi Norris, San Francisco: p. 249, 254, 250–251, 253, 255

© Sudsiri Pui-Ock: p. 286, 287, 288, 289, 290, 291, 292

Photos by Sara Pooley: p. 189, 191 (bottom), 194, 195

Photos by Phyllis Puran: p. 79

© Ayman Ramadan: p. 307, 308, 309, 310, 311

Photo by Natalie Reinhart: p. 276

Courtesy of Yancey Richardson Gallery, New York, and Valerie Carberry Gallery, Chicago: p. 235

© David Robbins: p. 323, 324–325, 329, 330, 332

Courtesy of Andrea Rosen Gallery, New York: p. 30–31

Photos by Steven Rosofsky: p. 71, 179, 186, 213, 221, 223, 235 (bottom), 305 (right)

© Andrew Cosmos Sarchiapone, photos by Andrew Cosmos Sarchiapone: p. 102, 103, 109, 110

Photo by Amber Seeley: p. 183 (bottom)

Photo by Abigail Satinsky: p. 206 (top)

Photo by Jenn Sichel: p. 281 (top)

© Barbara T. Smith, photos by William Ransom: p. 135, 137, 138 (top, bottom), 139

© Barbara T. Smith. Photo by Barbara T. Smith: p. 138 (middle)

Photos by Stephanie Smith: p. 164, 206 (top), 281 (middle right), 282 (left), 305 (left)

Photos by Michael St. John: p. 263 (right), 265

Photos by The National Bitter Melon Council: p. 269, 273, 274

Photo by Kristine Thompson: p. 253 (bottom)

© Rirkrit Tiravanija, courtesy of Gavin Brown's enterprise, New York: 336, 340, 341

Photos by Michael Tropea: p. 10–11, 22–23, 29, 51, 53, 68, 69, 76, 90–91, 141, 142–143, 158–159, 160 (left), 170, 176–177, 180–181, 190, 191 (top), 203, 229, 231, 233, 240, 241, 250–251, 258–259, 267, 277, 283, 307, 313, 319, 323, 338, 339

Photo by Tom Van Eynde: p. 234, 235

Photo by Junya Watari: p. 288 (top right)

Photo by Casey Winkleman: p. 262 (left)

Photo by Marianne Williams, courtesy of the Hammer Museum, Los Angeles: p. 284

Photos by Augusta Wood: p. 120, 121

Courtesy Yokohama Triennale 2011: p. 288 (top left)

Photos by Ali Zaidi: p. 261, 263 (left)

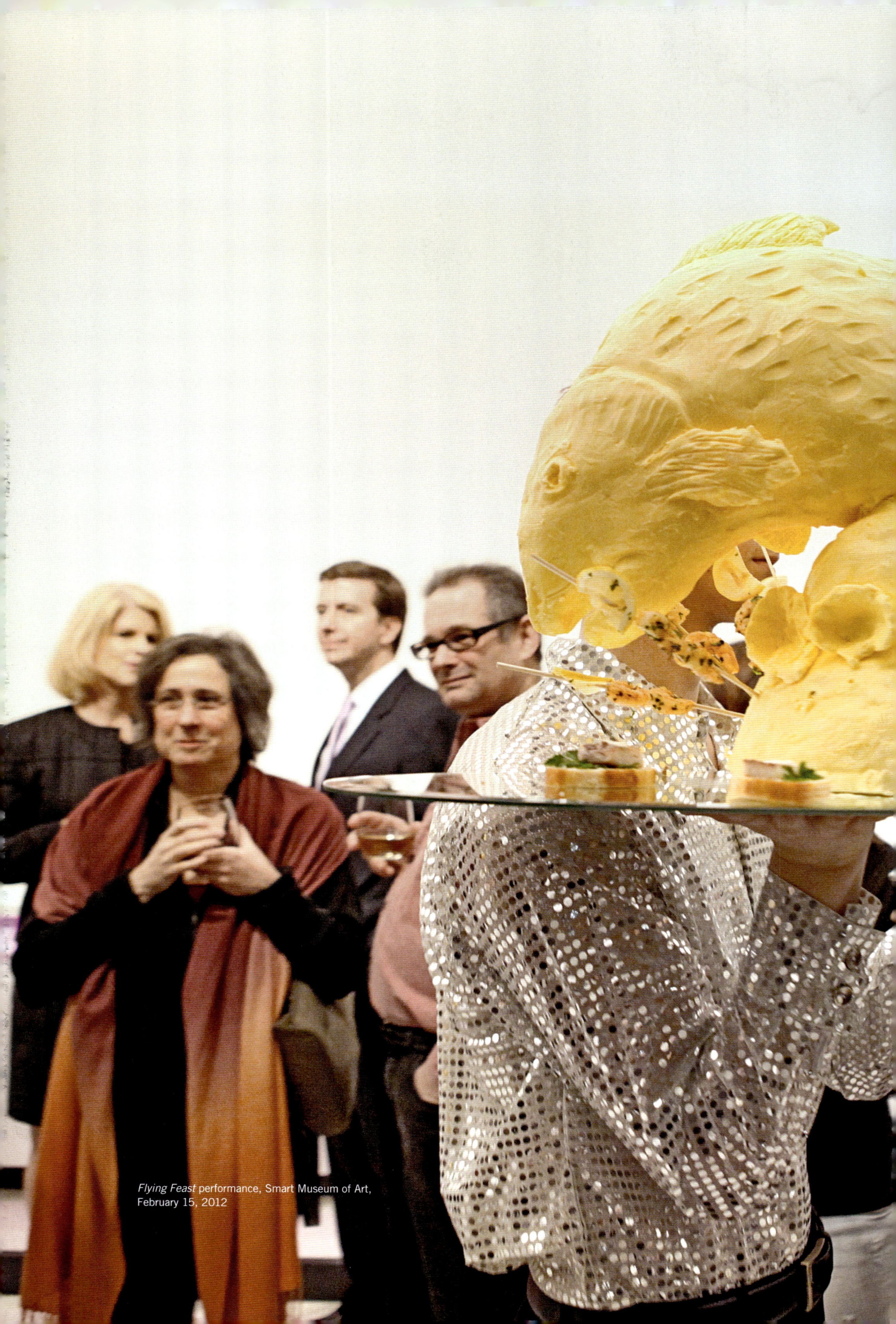

Flying Feast performance, Smart Museum of Art, February 15, 2012

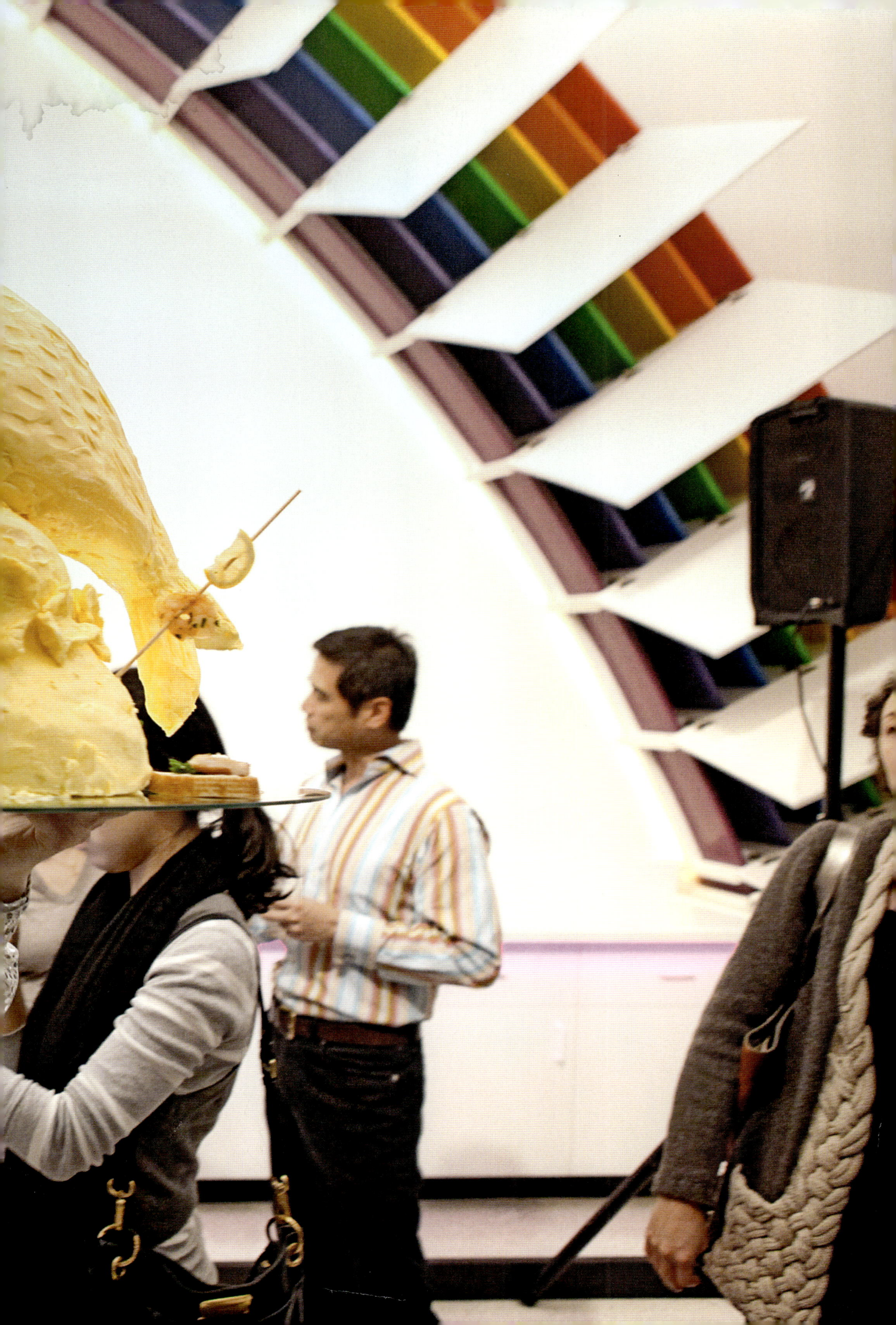

Thank You!